CISSP: Certified Information Systems Security Professional

The Official (ISC)²® CISSP® CBK® Reference

Sixth Edition

ARTHUR DEANE
AARON KRAUS

SYBEX®
A Wiley Brand

Library of Congress Control Number: 2021942306

Lead Authors

ARTHUR DEANE, CISSP, CCSP, is a senior director at Capital One Financial, where he leads information security activities in the Card division. Prior to Capital One, Arthur held security leadership roles at Google, Amazon, and PwC, in addition to several security engineering and consulting roles with the U.S. federal government.

Arthur is an adjunct professor at American University and a member of the Computer Science Advisory Board at Howard University. He holds a bachelor's degree in electrical engineering from Rochester Institute of Technology (RIT) and a master's degree in information security from the University of Maryland. Arthur is also the author of *CCSP for Dummies*.

AARON KRAUS, CISSP, CCSP, is an information security professional with more than 15 years of experience in security risk management, auditing, and teaching cybersecurity topics. He has worked in security and compliance leadership roles across industries including U.S. federal government civilian agencies, financial services, insurance, and technology startups.

Aaron is a course author, instructor, and cybersecurity curriculum dean at Learning Tree International, and he most recently taught the Official (ISC)² CISSP CBK Review Seminar. He is a co-author of *The Official (ISC)² Guide to the CCSP CBK, 3rd Edition*, and served as technical editor for numerous Wiley publications including *(ISC)² CCSP Certified Cloud Security Professional Official Study Guide, 2nd Edition*; *CCSP Official (ISC)² Practice Tests*; *The Official (ISC)² Guide to the CISSP CBK Reference, 5th Edition*; and *(ISC)² CISSP Certified Information Systems Security Professional Official Practice Tests, 2nd Edition*.

Technical Reviewer

MICHAEL S. WILLS, CAMS, CISSP, SSCP, is assistant professor of applied and innovative information technologies at the College of Business at Embry-Riddle Aeronautical University – Worldwide, where he continues his graduate and undergraduate teaching and research in cybersecurity and information assurance.

Mike has also been an advisor on science and technology policy to the UK's Joint Intelligence Committee, Ministry of Justice, and Defense Science and Technology Laboratories, helping them to evolve an operational and policy consensus relating topics from cryptography and virtual worlds, through the burgeoning surveillance society, to the proliferation of weapons of mass disruption (not just "destruction") and their effects on global, regional, national, and personal security. For a time, this had him sometimes known as the UK's nonresident expert on outer space law.

Mike has been supporting the work of (ISC)² by writing, editing, and updating books, study guides, and course materials for both their SSCP and CISSP programs. He wrote the *SSCP Official Study Guide, 2nd Edition* (Sybex, 2019), followed quickly by the *SSCP Official Common Book of Knowledge, 5th Edition*. He was lead author for the 2021 update of (ISC)²'s official CISSP and SSCP training materials. Mike has also contributed to several industry roundtables and white papers on digital identity and cyber fraud detection and prevention and has been a panelist and webinar presenter on these and related topics for ACAMS.

Contents at a Glance

Contents

Foreword

EARNING THE GLOBALLY RECOGNIZED CISSP® security certification is a proven way to build your career and demonstrate deep knowledge of cybersecurity concepts across a broad range of domains. Whether you are picking up this book to supplement your preparation to sit for the exam or are an existing CISSP using it as a desk reference, you'll find the *The Official (ISC)²® CISSP® CBK® Reference* to be the perfect primer on the security concepts covered in the eight domains of the CISSP CBK.

The CISSP is the most globally recognized certification in the information security market. It immediately signifies that the holder has the advanced cybersecurity skills and knowledge to design, engineer, implement, and manage information security programs and teams that protect against increasingly sophisticated attacks. It also conveys an adherence to best practices, policies, and procedures established by (ISC)² cybersecurity experts.

The recognized leader in the field of information security education and certification, (ISC)² promotes the development of information security professionals throughout the world. As a CISSP with all the benefits of (ISC)² membership, you are part of a global network of more than 161,000 certified professionals who are working to inspire a safe and secure cyber world.

Drawing from a comprehensive, up-to-date global body of knowledge, the *CISSP CBK* provides you with valuable insights on the skills, techniques, and best practices a security professional should be familiar with, including how different elements of the information technology ecosystem interact.

If you are an experienced CISSP, you will find this edition of the *CISSP CBK* an indispensable reference. If you are still gaining the experience and knowledge you need to join the ranks of CISSPs, the *CISSP CBK* is a deep dive that can be used to supplement your studies.

As the largest nonprofit membership body of certified information security professionals worldwide, (ISC)² recognizes the need to identify and validate not only information security competency, but also the ability to build, manage, and lead a security organization. Written by a team of subject matter experts, this comprehensive compendium covers all CISSP objectives and subobjectives in a structured format with common practices for each objective, a common lexicon and references to widely accepted computing standards and case studies.

The opportunity has never been greater for dedicated professionals to advance their careers and inspire a safe and secure cyber world. The *CISSP CBK* will be your constant companion in protecting your organization and will serve you for years to come.

Sincerely,

Clar Rosso
CEO, (ISC)²

Introduction

THE CERTIFIED INFORMATION SYSTEMS Security Professional (CISSP) certification identifies a professional who has demonstrated skills, knowledge, and abilities across a wide array of security practices and principles. The exam covers eight domains of practice, which are codified in the CISSP Common Body of Knowledge (CBK). The CBK presents topics that a CISSP can use in their daily role to identify and manage security risks to data and information systems and is built on a foundation comprising fundamental security concepts of confidentiality, integrity, availability, nonrepudiation, and authenticity (CIANA), as well as privacy and security (CIANA+PS). A variety of controls can be implemented for both data and systems, with the goal of either safeguarding or mitigating security risks to each of these foundational principles.

Global professionals take many paths into information security, and each candidate's experience must be combined with variations in practice and perspective across industries and regions due to the global reach of the certification. For most security practitioners, achieving CISSP requires study and learning new disciplines, and professionals are unlikely to work across all eight domains on a daily basis. The CISSP CBK is a baseline standard of security knowledge to help security practitioners deal with new and evolving risks, and this guide provides easy reference to aid practitioners in applying security topics and principles. This baseline must be connected with the reader's own experience and the unique operating environment of the reader's organization to be effective. The rapid pace of change in security also demands that practitioners continuously maintain their knowledge, so CISSP credential holders are also expected to maintain their knowledge via continuing education. Reference materials like this guide, along with other content sources such as industry conferences, webinars, and research are vital to maintaining this knowledge.

The domains presented in the CBK are progressive, starting with a foundation of basic security and risk management concepts in Chapter 1, "Security and Risk Management," as well as fundamental topics of identifying, valuing, and applying proper risk mitigations for asset security in Chapter 2, "Asset Security." Applying security to complex technology environments can be achieved by applying architecture and engineering concepts, which are presented in Chapter 3, "Security Architecture and Engineering."

Chapter 4, "Communication and Network Security," details both the critical risks to as well as the critical defensive role played by communications networks, and Chapter 5, "Identity and Access Management," covers the crucial practices of identifying users (both human and nonhuman) and controlling their access to systems, data, and other resources. Once a security program is designed, it is vital to gather information about and assess its effectiveness, which is covered in Chapter 6, "Security Assessment and Testing," and keep the entire affair running — also known as security operations or SecOps, which is covered in Chapter 7, "Security Operations." Finally, the vital role played by software is addressed in Chapter 8, "Software Development Security," which covers both principles of securely developing software as well as risks and threats to software and development environments. The following presents overviews for each of these chapters in a little more detail.

Security and Risk Management

The foundation of the CISSP CBK is the assessment and management of risk to data and the information systems that process it. The Security and Risk Management domain introduces the foundational CIANA+PS concepts needed to build a risk management program. Using these concepts, a security practitioner can build a program for governance, risk, and compliance (GRC), which allows the organization to design a system of governance needed to implement security controls. These controls should address the risks faced by the organization as well as any necessary legal and regulatory compliance obligations.

Risk management principles must be applied throughout an organization's operations, so topics of business continuity (BC), personnel security, and supply chain risk management are also introduced in this domain. Ensuring that operations can continue in the event of a disruption supports the goal of availability, while properly designed personnel security controls require training programs and well-documented policies and other security guidance.

One critical concept is presented in this domain: the (ISC)^2 code of professional ethics. All CISSP candidates must agree to be bound by the code as part of the certification process, and credential holders face penalties up to and including loss of their credentials for violating the code. Regardless of what area of security a practitioner is working in, the need to preserve the integrity of the profession by adhering to a code of ethics is critical to fostering trust in the security profession.

Asset Security

Assets are anything that an organization uses to generate value, including ideas, processes, information, and computing hardware. Classifying and categorizing assets allows organizations to prioritize limited security resources to achieve a proper balance of costs and benefits, and this domain introduces important concepts of asset valuation, classification and categorization, and asset handling to apply appropriate protection based on an asset's value. The value of an asset dictates the level of protection it requires, which is often expressed as a security baseline or compliance obligation that the asset owner must meet.

CISSP credential holders will spend a large amount of their time focused on data and information security concerns. The data lifecycle is introduced in this domain to provide distinct phases for determining data security requirements. Protection begins by defining roles and processes for handling data, and once the data is created, these processes must be followed. This includes managing data throughout creation, use, archival, and eventual destruction when no longer needed, and it focuses on data in three main states: in use, in transit, and at rest.

Handling sensitive data for many organizations will involve legal or regulatory obligations to protect specific data types, such as personally identifiable information (PII) or transactional data related to payment cards. Payment card data is regulated by the Payment Card Industry (PCI) Council, and PII often requires protections to comply with regional or local laws like the European Union General Data Protection Regulation (EU GDPR). Both compliance frameworks dictate specific protection obligations an organization must meet when collecting, handling, and using the regulated data.

Security Architecture and Engineering

The Security Architecture and Engineering domain covers topics relevant to implementing and managing security controls across a variety of systems. Secure design principles are introduced that are used to build a security program, such as secure defaults, zero trust, and privacy by design. Common security models are also covered in this domain, which provide an abstract way of viewing a system or environment and allow for identification of security requirements related to the CIANA+PS principles. Specific system types are discussed in detail to highlight the application of security controls in a variety of architectures, including client- and server-based systems, industrial control systems (ICSs), Internet of Things (IoT), and emerging system types like microservices and containerized applications.

This domain presents the foundational details of cryptography and introduces topics covering basic definitions of encryption, hashing, and various cryptographic methods, as well as attacks against cryptography known as cryptanalysis. Applications of cryptography are integrated throughout all domains where relevant, such as the use of encryption in secure network protocols, which is covered in Chapter 4. Physical architecture security — including fire suppression and detection, secure facility design, and environmental control — is also introduced in this domain.

Communication and Network Security

One major value of modern information systems lies in their ability to share and exchange data, so fundamentals of networking are presented in the Communication and Network Security domain along with details of implementing adequate security protections for these communications. This domain introduces common models used for network services, including the Open Systems Interconnection (OSI) and Transmission Control Protocol/Internet Protocol (TCP/IP) models. These layered abstractions provide a method for identifying specific security risks and control capabilities to safeguard data, and the domain presents fundamentals, risks, and countermeasures available at each level of the OSI and TCP/IP models.

Properly securing networks and communications requires strategic planning to ensure proper architectural choices are made and implemented. Concepts of secure network design — such as planning and segmentation, availability of hardware, and network access control (NAC) — are introduced in this domain. Common network types and their specific security risks are introduced as well, including software-defined networks (SDNs), voice networks, and remote access and collaboration technologies.

Identity and Access Management

Controlling access to assets is one of the fundamental goals of security and offers the ability to safeguard all five CIANA+PS security concepts. Properly identifying users and authenticating the access they request can preserve confidentiality and authenticity of information, while properly implemented controls reduce the risk of lost or corrupted data, thereby preserving availability and integrity. Logging the actions taken by identified users or accounts supports nonrepudiation by verifiably demonstrating which user or process performed took a particular action.

The Identity and Access Management (IAM) domain introduces important concepts related to identifying subjects and controlling their access to objects. Subjects can be users, processes, or other systems, and objects are typically systems or data that a subject is trying to access. IAM requirements are presented through four fundamental aspects, including identification, authentication, authorization, and accountability (IAAA). The domain also presents important concepts for managing identities and access, including federation and the use of third-party identity service providers.

Security Assessment and Testing

It is necessary to evaluate the effectiveness of security controls to determine if they are providing sufficient risk mitigation. Assessment, testing, and auditing are methods presented in this domain that allow a security practitioner to identify deficiencies in the security program and prioritize remedial activities.

Assessment and testing can be performed as an internal or external function; while both are appropriate for monitoring security program status, there are situations that require external evaluations. For instance, third-party audits are common in situations where an assessment must be conducted that is free of any conflict of interest. External audit reports, such as the Service Organization Control or SOC 2, can be useful for organizations to communicate details of their security practices to external parties like vendors or business partners. In this case, the auditor's independence from the audited organization provides additional assurance to consumers of the report.

Ethical penetration testing and related technical testing topics are presented in this domain, including test coverage and breach attack simulations. These types of tests can be conducted against a range of targets from individual information systems to entire organizations and are a valuable tool to identify deficiencies in security controls. The disclosure and handling of any findings from such testing is also discussed, including legal and ethical implications of information that might be discovered.

An ongoing assessment and testing program is also useful for establishing continuous monitoring and supporting compliance needs. Properly designed and implemented strategies for testing security controls, vulnerabilities, and attack simulations measure the effectiveness of the organization's existing control program. Any identified deficiencies must be addressed to ensure adequate risk management.

Security Operations

Security Operations (SecOps) is a companion to the other domains in the CBK, and this chapter deals with implementing, operating, and maintaining infrastructure needed to enable the organization's security program. Security practitioners must first perform a risk assessment and then design and operate security controls spanning technology, people, and process to mitigate those risks. SecOps is a key integration point between security teams and other parts of the organization such as Human Resources (HR) for key tasks like designing job rotations or segregation of duties, or a network engineering team that is responsible for implementing and maintaining firewalls and intrusion detection systems (IDSs).

Logical security aspects of SecOps include running and maintaining a security operations center (SOC), which is becoming an increasingly crucial part of a security program. The SOC centralizes information like threat intelligence, incident response, and security alerts, permitting information sharing, more efficient response, and oversight for the security program and functions. Planning for and exercising crucial business plans like business continuity and disaster recovery (BCDR) are also an important element of SecOps.

SecOps also encompasses important physical security concepts like facility design and environmental controls, which are often completely new concepts for security practitioners who have experience in cybersecurity or information technology (IT). However, the physical security of information systems and the data they contain is an important element of maintaining all aspects of security. In some cases, physical limitations like existing or shared buildings are drivers for additional logical controls to compensate for potential unauthorized physical access.

Software Development Security

Information systems rely on software, so proper security is essential for the tools and processes used to develop software. This includes both custom-built software as well as purchased system components that are integrated into information systems. Cloud computing is changing the paradigm of software development, so this domain also includes security requirements for computing resources that are consumed as a service like software as a service (SaaS), platform as a service (PaaS), and emerging architectures like containerization and microservices.

Software can be both a target for attackers and the attack vector. The increasingly complex software environment makes use of open-source software, prebuilt modules and libraries, and distributed applications to provide greater speed for developers and functionality for users. These business advantages, however, introduce risks like the potential for untrustworthy third-party code to be included in an application or attackers targeting remote access features.

Adequate security in the software development lifecycle (SDLC) requires a combined approach addressing people, process, and technology. This domain revisits the critical personnel security concept of training, with a specific focus on developer security training. Well-documented software development methodologies, guidelines, and procedures are essential process controls covered in the domain. Technology controls encompassing both the software development environment and software security testing are presented, as well as testing approaches for application security (AppSec) including static and dynamic testing.

Security and Risk Management

DOMAIN 1 OF THE CISSP Common Body of Knowledge (CBK) covers the foundational topics of building and managing a risk-based information security program. This domain covers a wide variety of concepts upon which the remainder of the CBK builds.

Before diving into the heart of security and risk management concepts, this chapter begins with coverage of professional ethics and how they apply in the field of information security. Understanding your responsibilities as a security professional is equally as important as knowing how to apply the security concepts. We then move on to topics related to understanding your organization's mission, strategy, goals, and business objectives, and evaluating how to properly satisfy your organization's business needs securely.

Understanding risk management, and how its concepts apply to information security, is one of the most important things you should take away from this chapter. We describe risk management concepts and explain how to apply them within your organization's security program. In addition, understanding relevant legal, regulatory, and compliance requirements is a critical component of every information security program. Domain 1 includes coverage of concepts such as cybercrimes and data breaches, import/export controls, and requirements for conducting various types of investigations.

This chapter introduces the human element of security and includes coverage of methods for educating your organization's employees on key security concepts. We cover the structure of a security awareness program and discuss how to evaluate the effectiveness of your education and training methods.

UNDERSTAND, ADHERE TO, AND PROMOTE PROFESSIONAL ETHICS

Understanding and following a strict code of ethics should be a top priority for any security professional. As a CISSP (or any information security professional who is certified by (ISC)^2), you are required to understand and fully commit to supporting the (ISC)^2 Code of Ethics. Any (ISC)^2 member who knowingly violates the (ISC)^2 Code of Ethics will be subject to peer review and potential penalties, which may include revocation of the member's (ISC)^2 certification(s).

(ISC)^2 Code of Professional Ethics

The (ISC)^2 Code of Ethics Preamble is as follows:

- The safety and welfare of society and the common good, duty to our principals, and to each other, requires that we adhere, and be seen to adhere, to the highest ethical standards of behavior.

- Therefore, strict adherence to this Code of Ethics is a condition of certification.

In short, the Code of Ethics Preamble states that it is required that every CISSP certified member not only follows the Code of Ethics but must be visibly seen as following the Code of Ethics. Even the perception of impropriety or ethical deviation may bring into question a member's standing. As such, CISSP certified members must serve as visible ethical leaders within their organizations and industry, at all times.

The (ISC)^2 Code of Ethics includes four canons that are intended to serve as high-level guidelines to augment, not replace, members' professional judgment. The (ISC)^2 Code of Ethics Canons are as follows:

- **Canon I:** Protect society, the common good, necessary public trust and confidence, and the infrastructure.

- **Canon II:** Act honorably, honestly, justly, responsibly, and legally.

- **Canon III:** Provide diligent and competent service to principals.
- **Canon IV:** Advance and protect the profession.

Adhering to and promoting the (ISC)² Code of Ethics not only includes being mindful of your own professional behaviors, but also being aware of your peers' behaviors. (ISC)² requires that any member who observes another member breaching the Code of Ethics follow the published ethics complaint procedure. Failure to do so may be considered breach of Canon IV. Additional information on the (ISC)² Code of Ethics and the ethics complaint procedures can be found at www.isc2.org/Ethics.

Organizational Code of Ethics

In addition to the (ISC)² Code of Ethics, as an information security professional, you must be aware of any code of ethics that you are required to uphold by your employer or industry. Similar to the (ISC)² Code of Ethics, these other organizational codes of ethics should not be considered replacements for sound judgment and moral behavior. As a CISSP, you are a leader within your organization. As such, you should lead by example in adhering to your organization's Code of Ethics.

✔ Ethics and the Internet

In January 1989, right around the dawn of the internet, the Internet Activities Board (IAB) released a memo titled "Ethics and the Internet" (RFC 1087) as a statement of policy concerning ethical use of the internet. Although the memo is ancient by technology standards, the principles within it are still relevant today; as a CISSP, you should understand and adhere to these principles.

RFC 1087 characterizes as unethical and unacceptable any activity that purposely

- "seeks to gain unauthorized access to the resources of the Internet"

- "disrupts the intended use of the Internet"

- "wastes resources (people, capacity, computer) through such actions

- "destroys the integrity of computer-based information

- "compromises the privacy of users"

Interestingly enough, this memo that debuted in the very early days of the internet — even before there was structured thought around information security — aligns directly with the CIA Triad and privacy principles that guide information security professionals in the 21st century.

Information security refers to the processes and methodologies involved in safeguarding information and underlying systems from inappropriate access, use, modification, or disturbance. This is most often described by three critical security concepts: confidentiality, integrity, and availability. Together, these three principles form the pillars of information security known as the *CIA Triad* (see Figure 1.1).

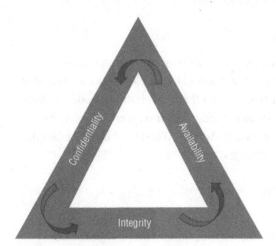

FIGURE 1.1 CIA Triad

Although different types of systems and data may prioritize one principle over the others, all three security concepts work together and depend on each other to successfully maintain information security. Confidentiality, integrity, and availability are the most critical characteristics that information security provides, and understanding each of these principles is a basic requirement for all information security professionals. As such, a common understanding of the meaning of each of the elements in the CIA Triad allows security professionals to communicate effectively.

Confidentiality

The first principle of the CIA Triad is confidentiality. *Confidentiality* is the concept of limiting access to data to authorized users and systems and restricting access from unauthorized parties. In other words, confidentiality guarantees that only intended people are able to access information and resources. In short, the goal of confidentiality is to prevent unauthorized access to data, as it pertains to viewing, copying, or moving the data. Organizations that fail to protect data confidentiality run the risk of violating contractual and regulatory obligations around data protection. In addition, companies with known breaches of confidentiality commonly experience reputational damage that benefits their competitors and potentially impacts their bottom line.

The concept of confidentiality is closely related to the security best practice of *least privilege*, which asserts that access to information should be granted only on a need-to-know basis. Under least privilege, users are only given enough access to do their jobs — no more and no less.

Privacy is a field that is closely related to security and is focused on the confidentiality of personal data specifically. Information that can be used to uniquely identify a person, such as names, birthdates, and Social Security numbers, are considered *personally iden-tifiable information* (PII), which is usually required by law to be kept highly confidential. Privacy requirements are introduced later in this chapter, in the section "Determine Compliance and Other Requirements."

Numerous malicious acts target data confidentiality, including phishing and other forms of social engineering, credential (e.g., password) theft, network sniffing, and others. In addition to malicious acts, confidentiality may be compromised by human error, oversight, or mere negligence. Such examples include failure to encrypt sensitive data, misrouted emails, or displaying sensitive information on your computer monitor while unauthorized viewers are in the vicinity.

Confidentiality is often the security concept that data owners care about the most, and there are many security controls available to assist with this. Encryption, multifactor authentication, and role-based access controls are a few measures that can help ensure data confidentiality. Extensive personnel training is a hugely important measure for reducing risk associated with human error and negligence. We address data confidenti-ality and discuss relevant controls throughout the remainder of this book.

Integrity

The second principle of the CIA Triad is integrity. *Integrity* is the concept of maintaining the accuracy, validity, and completeness of data and systems. It ensures that data is not manipulated by anyone other than an authorized party with an authorized purpose, and that any unauthorized manipulation is easily identifiable as such. The primary goal of integrity is to ensure that all data remains intact, correct, and reliable. Failure to properly protect data integrity can have a negative impact on business processes, including leading to personnel making improper decisions or potentially harmful actions, due to having incorrect information.

As with confidentiality, integrity may be compromised by malicious acts, human error, oversight, or negligence. Viruses, compromise of poorly written code, and inten-tional modification are examples of malicious threats that may violate integrity, and we discuss others throughout this book. In addition, integrity violations can occur when an administrator enters the wrong command in a database, when an administrator alters the wrong line in a configuration file, or when a user accidentally introduces malware into their system through a phishing email.

Data backups, software version control, strict access control, and cryptographic hashes are some measures that help ensure data integrity by preventing unauthorized modifications or by allowing tampered data to be restored to a known-good state. Similar to confidentiality, extensive security awareness training is a major factor in preventing non-malicious integrity violations.

Authenticity and nonrepudiation are two concepts that are closely related to integrity. *Authenticity* refers to ensuring that data is genuine and that all parties are who they say they are. *Nonrepudiation* is a legal principle that has a strong parallel in the information security world; this concept requires ensuring that no party is able to deny their actions (e.g., creating, modifying, or deleting data). Digital signatures are the most common mechanisms used to establish authenticity and nonrepudiation in information systems.

Availability

The third and final principle of the CIA Triad is availability. *Availability* is the concept focused on ensuring that authorized users can access data when they need it. In enterprise environments, the concept of availability entails providing assurance that legitimate parties have timely and uninterrupted access to the systems and data that they need to do their jobs. Threats against availability can interfere or even halt an organization's business operations. An extended disruption of critical systems and data may lead to reputational damage that results in loss of customers and revenue.

Related concepts that should be considered alongside availability include the following:

- *Accessibility* refers to the ability and ease of a user to use a resource or access data when needed. This involves removing barriers for authorized users to access these resources and data. For example, consider a file that's stored on your company's internal network drive. As long as the file is intact and the network drive is up and running, that file can be considered available. However, if someone were to move that file to a protected folder on the shared drive, you may lack the required permissions to access that file — the data is still available but is no longer accessible.

- *Usability* refers to the ability of a user to meet their needs with available data. If you have ever needed to edit a Google doc (or any other file) and noticed that you have been granted only read-only permissions, then that file was absolutely available but lacked sufficient usability.

- *Timeliness* refers to the time expectation for availability of information and resources and is the measure of the time between when information is expected and when it is available for use. Ensuring timeliness requires that data is available to authorized users within an acceptable period of time. For cloud services and other situations that involve a third party managing data, timeliness is a key factor that must be agreed upon and documented in service level agreements (SLAs).

There are many threats to data and system availability, and they may be either malicious or nonmalicious, either man-made or naturally occurring. Malicious availability threats include denial-of-service (DoS) attacks, object deletion, and ransomware attacks. While malicious compromise of availability tends to get all the buzz, there are various nonmalicious threats that can interfere with resource and data availability. Some common examples include hardware failures, software errors, and environmental threats such as power outages, floods, excessive heat, and so forth. When planning your information security program, it's essential that you thoroughly consider both human-based and naturally occurring threats and develop mitigations that address all threat vectors.

Mechanisms such as data backups, redundant storage, backup power supply, and web application firewalls (WAFs) can help prevent disruption of system and information availability. For systems that have a requirement for high availability and continuous uptime, cloud computing offers added redundancy and extra assurance of availability.

Limitations of the CIA Triad

The CIA Triad evolved out of theoretical work done in the mid-1960s. Precisely because of its simplicity, the rise of distributed systems and a vast number of new applications for new technology has caused researchers and security practitioners to extend the triad's coverage.

Guaranteeing the identities of parties involved in communications is essential to confidentiality. The CIA Triad does not directly address the issues of authenticity and nonrepudiation, but the point of nonrepudiation is that neither party can deny that they participated in the communication. This extension of the triad uniquely addresses aspects of confidentiality and integrity that were never considered in the early theoretical work.

The National Institute of Standards and Technology (NIST) Special Publication 800-33, "Underlying Technical Models for Information Technology Security," included the CIA Triad as three of its five security objectives, but added the concepts of accountability (that actions of an entity may be traced uniquely to that entity) and assurance (the basis for confidence that the security measures, both technical and operational, work as intended to protect the system and the information it processes). The NIST work remains influential as an effort to codify best-practice approaches to systems security.

Perhaps the most widely accepted extension to the CIA Triad was proposed by information security pioneer Donn B. Parker. In extending the triad, Parker incorporated three additional concepts into the model, arguing that these concepts were both atomic (could not be further broken down conceptually) and nonoverlapping. This framework has come to be known as the Parkerian Hexad. The Parkerian Hexad contains the following concepts:

- **Confidentiality:** The limits on who has access to information
- **Integrity:** Whether the information is in its intended state
- **Availability:** Whether the information can be accessed in a timely manner
- **Authenticity:** The proper attribution of the person who created the information
- **Utility:** The usefulness of the information
- **Possession or control:** The physical state where the information is maintained

Subsequent academic work produced dozens of other information security models, all aimed at the same fundamental issue — how to characterize information security risks.

In addition to security topics codified in the CIA Triad and related models, the concept of privacy has grown to be a core consideration of security professionals. *Privacy*, as defined in the (ISC)² glossary, is the right of human individuals to control the distribution of information about themselves. Privacy, though often managed outside of organizations' central security team, is closely related to the principle of confidentiality and must be a priority for every organization that handles employee or customer personal information. We discuss privacy in several sections throughout the rest of this book.

For the security professional, a solid understanding of the CIA Triad is essential when communicating about information security practice, but it's important to consider related topics not covered by the triad.

EVALUATE AND APPLY SECURITY GOVERNANCE PRINCIPLES

Security governance is the set of responsibilities, policies, and procedures related to defining, managing, and overseeing security practices at an organization. Security is often mistakenly considered to be an IT issue; in actuality, securing an organization's assets and data is a business issue and requires a high level of planning and oversight by people throughout the entire organization, not just the IT department. Because security is a wide-ranging business issue, security governance commonly overlaps with corporate governance and IT governance for an organization. As such, security governance is typically led by executive management at a company, usually including the board of directors. Applying security governance principles involves the following:

- Aligning the organization's security function to the company's business strategy, goals, mission, and objectives

- Defining and managing organizational processes that require security involvement or oversight (e.g., acquisitions, divestitures, and governance committees)

- Developing security roles and responsibilities throughout the organization

- Identifying one or more security control frameworks to align your organization with

- Conducting due diligence and due care activities on an ongoing basis

Alignment of the Security Function to Business Strategy, Goals, Mission, and Objectives

An effective security function must be in alignment with the company's business strategy, goals, mission, and business objectives. Each of these elements should be considered during the creation and management of the organization's information security program and policies.

Companies that fail to properly align their security program with their business strategy, goals, mission, and objectives often perceive security as a business blocker; these companies frequently experience information security as a hurdle that must be cleared to get things accomplished. On the contrary, an information security function that is tightly aligned with a company's strategy and mission can serve as a business enabler, where security is built into the fabric of the company and helps drive toward common goals and objectives. In other words, a company should achieve its mission thanks in part to security, not *despite* security.

A *mission statement* is a simple declaration that defines a company's function and purpose; a mission statement summarizes what the company is, what it does, and why the company exists to do those things. A mission statement should be used to drive all corporate activities, including the organization's allocation of time, finances, and effort.

A *business strategy* describes the actions that a company takes to achieve its goals and objectives. Whereas a mission statement describes *what* will be achieved, an organization's business strategy identifies exactly *how* the mission will be accomplished. A company's mission statement rarely changes, but an organization's strategy must be flexible enough to change as the business environment changes.

A *goal*, in business, is something that an organization expects to achieve or accomplish. Business goals help a company plan for success, and an organization's goals should contribute to its mission. Many companies use the SMART criteria to define their organizational goals. *SMART* is a mnemonic acronym that defines criteria for creating quality goals. A SMART goal must exhibit the following characteristics:

- **Specific:** State what you will do using real numbers and real deadlines.

- **Measurable:** Identify a way to evaluate progress and measure success (or failure). Use metrics or data targets to ensure that the goal is trackable.

- **Achievable or Attainable:** Establish challenging, but possible, goals that are within your scope.
- **Relevant:** Establish a goal that is pertinent to your overall mission and vision and aligned with your organization's values and strategy.
- **Time-bound:** State when you will get the goal done, using specific dates or timeframes.

An *objective* is a milestone or a specific step that contributes to an organization reaching its goals and achieving its mission. Objectives are used to define incremental steps toward achieving a broader goal. Much like SMART goals, organizations often use the SMART framework to define quality objectives. While many people incorrectly use the terms *goal* and *objective* interchangeably, you should understand that an objective is a short-term milestone that supports a longer-term goal.

When establishing your organization's security function, you should begin by defining a security strategy that aligns with your organization's overall business strategy and mission statement. You should develop a set of specific, measurable, achievable, relevant, and time-bound goals and objectives that will help you efficiently maintain the confidentiality, integrity, and availability of your company's systems and information without disrupting your organization's ability to achieve its business goals and objectives. Running an effective security program demands careful consideration of business needs and organizational strategy, in addition to legal and compliance requirements, and requires governance to manage the effectiveness of the security function within the overall organization.

Organizational Processes

People who consider information security a purely IT matter are more prone to focusing solely on the technologies that fit into a security program. As a CISSP, you should know that a mature information security program is more than a collection of firewalls, intrusion detection systems and intrusion prevention systems (IDSs/IPS), and other tools thrown together — a well-managed security program requires processes in place to provide oversight of activities by executive members of the organization. *Security governance* is the set of all organizational processes involved in defining and managing information security policies and procedures, including the oversight to ensure that those policies and procedures follow the direction of the organization's strategy and mission.

Governance Committees

A *governance committee* is a group of executives and leaders who regularly meet to set the direction of the company's security function and provide guidance to help the security function align with the company's overall mission and business strategy. Governance committees review ongoing and planned projects, operational metrics, and any other security matters that may concern the business as a whole. The primary objective of a governance committee is to provide oversight for the company's security function, while ensuring that the security function continues to meet the needs of the organization and its stakeholders.

There are many organizational processes that require a heavy dose of security governance. Mergers, acquisitions, and divestitures are major business events that come with a great deal of security risk that a company must manage.

Mergers and Acquisitions

A *merger* is the combining of two separate organizations that creates a new, joint organization. An *acquisition* is the takeover of one organization by another. While mergers and acquisitions (M&A) have different business approaches, they share many of the same security concerns and are often discussed together.

There are countless potential security risks when a company acquires another company or when two organizations decide to merge. For any merger or acquisition, it's imperative that organizations consider these risks and identify appropriate mitigations before pulling the trigger. Some M&A risk factors to consider include the following:

- **Absorbing the unknown:** When merging with or acquiring another organization, you are absorbing its entire IT infrastructure — good or bad. This means that you are acquiring systems that are likely managed differently from your own, and there may be significant differences in the security controls and processes in place. In addition, the acquired company may use homegrown or highly customized applications that will need to be securely integrated into your existing environment. Further, the acquired or absorbed company may use a different approach to threat modeling and vulnerability management (if they do these at all). Differences in security processes may result in operational challenges and inconsistent procedures during and after integration of the two businesses.

- **Creating new attack vectors:** By adding in new systems and platforms, you are potentially creating new routes for your company to be attacked. For example, if your organization uses Windows and macOS and you acquire a company that has a fleet of Linux systems, you now have a third operating system to manage and secure.

- **Impacting resources:** Mergers and acquisitions are challenging for everyone involved. Your IT teams may be stretched thin as they try to come up to speed on the newly acquired infrastructure while also keeping the existing systems running securely.

- **Disgruntled employees:** In addition to the burnout that employees may feel, corporate M&A can cause severe dissatisfaction in employees who were completely happy in their previously standalone company. Insider threat is commonly considered a top security concern, and acquiring disgruntled employees poses a severe threat to an organization.

A company's security function should play a key role during any M&A conversations and should help identify potential issues related to the target organization's security posture, operations, or policy. If the two organizations have greatly different security postures, it's usually best to reconsider the deal or, at the least, consider fixing key security gaps before connecting the two company's networks and systems. Considering the risks from the previous list, an acquiring company (or both companies in a merger) should perform the following activities prior to completing an M&A deal:

- Review the company's information security policies and procedures to determine how thorough they are. Take note of any missing security policies/procedures that may indicate a low level of security maturity.

- Review the company's data assets and determine any applicable regulatory or compliance requirements (e.g., PCI, HIPAA, GDPR, etc.). Take particular note of any regulations that may present new requirements for your organization.

- Review the organization's personnel security policies to identify potential issues or concerns. For example, your company may have compliance requirements to conduct a specific type of background check, and the target company may not be compliant.

- Identify any proprietary or custom applications managed by the company and request static and dynamic application security tests be run against them to demonstrate their security posture. (SAST and DAST are covered in Chapter 8, "Software Development and Security.")

- Request results from a recent penetration test (pentest) that includes network, operating system, application, and database testing. Any critical or high findings should have a plan for remediation or mitigation.

- Review the organization's use of third-party and open-source software to ensure that the software is safe and appropriately licensed.

The previous list is not intended to be comprehensive, but rather a starting point for things to consider prior to any mergers and acquisitions. Your security team needs to be an integral part of the M&A process from the initial talks through integration.

Divestitures

A *divestiture* is the act of selling off or disposing of a subset of business interests or assets. An organization may pursue a divestiture for a number of reasons: political, social, or strictly financial. Divestitures often occur when management decides that a certain part of the business no longer aligns with the company's business strategy or mission. Divestitures also frequently happen after a merger or acquisition, in cases where the merger or acquisition creates redundancies within the combined organization.

Information usually accompanies the physical assets and interests that a company divests, which presents a major concern for information security. The biggest security concern in a divestiture involves maintaining confidentiality as the company gets rid of assets that may contain sensitive or proprietary information. As a CISSP, you should ensure that your organization takes the following actions prior to completing a divestiture:

- Identify and categorize all assets that are involved in the divestiture; this includes hardware, software, and information assets. Creating a complete inventory of all impacted assets is a critical first step to ensuring a secure divestiture.

- Decouple impacted systems from your remaining infrastructure. Your company likely uses common human resources (HR), accounting, and technology systems (such as a virtual private network, email, etc.) to support the entire company. The assets being divested must be removed from this common infrastructure and spun out for the new organization to own and manage.

- Review all access permissions. You must identify who has access to the impacted assets and determine whether they need to maintain that access. People are sometimes part of a divestiture, and a subset of the employee base may leave with other divested assets. If that is the case in your divestiture, you must appropriately revoke unnecessary permissions while leaving required permissions intact.

- Consult your legal and compliance teams to ensure that you follow all required regulatory and compliance requirements around data retention, deletion, etc.

During a divestiture, both companies (i.e., the divesting and the divested company) must consider how the business transaction impacts their respective security program. Each company must ensure that their security controls, operations, policies and procedures, and governance structure continue to support the newly restructured companies. If the divested company was sold to another company (i.e., as part of an acquisition), then the purchasing company must update its security program to accommodate for its newly acquired assets. In cases where a divested company leads to the formation of a completely new entity, the new company must create an all-new security function (and the supporting policies, procedures, and governance structure) to appropriately manage information security.

Much like mergers and acquisitions, divestitures can present a number of security challenges for organizations. Similarly, the key to a successful divestiture is active involvement by your security team from the early planning phases all the way through completion of the divestiture.

Organizational Roles and Responsibilities

People who don't work in security often look at security professionals as the only employees responsible for keeping systems and information secure. Of course, as information security professionals, we know that it is really *everyone's* job to keep the organization's assets and information secure — that means from the chief executive officer (CEO) down to the most junior clerk in the mailroom, and everyone in between. As a CISSP, one of your jobs is to evangelize security throughout your company, while helping to define security roles and responsibilities throughout the organization.

Your organization should define security roles and responsibilities within your information security policy, and it should align with roles and responsibilities defined in other organizational policies. It's important that roles and responsibilities are defined for and understood by employees of every level and line of business, as well as third parties such as contractors and vendors.

Different companies have different roles, but the following designations are some of the most commonly seen information security roles:

- **Chief information security officer (CISO):** A *CISO* is the senior-level executive within an organization who is responsible for the overall management and supervision of the information security program. The CISO drives the organization's security strategy and vision and is ultimately responsible for the security of the company's systems and information. While corporate reporting structures vary by company size and industry, most CISOs now report to a company's chief information officer (CIO) or CEO.

- **Chief security officer (CSO):** A *CSO* is a senior-level executive within an organization who is generally responsible for all physical security and personnel security matters. Many organizations have merged CSO responsibilities into the CISO role, but you should be aware of the potential distinction between the two. To make matters even more confusing, some organizations refer to their overall security leader as a CSO (instead of CISO). You should lean on context anytime you see these titles used.

- **Security analyst:** A *security analyst* is someone with technical expertise in one or more security domains who executes the day-to-day security work. This may include things such as data analysis, firewall rule management, incident handling, and other operational activities.

- **Manager or program manager:** In security, a *manager* (or *program manager*) is someone who owns one or more processes related to information security. A security manager may be the owner for compliance, vulnerability management, or any other broad set of responsibilities that are executed by security analysts.

- **Director:** In security, a *director* is generally a manager of managers who is responsible for the overall strategic guidance of a group of security programs.

NOTE   While the role of CISO has traditionally reported to a company's CIO, that trend is changing. Organizations increasingly view information security as not only an IT issue but a business issue. As a result, many argue that CISOs should report directly to a company's CEO.

As previously mentioned, security is everyone's responsibility. Outside of the information security roles and responsibilities described in the previous list, every user within an organization plays an important role in keeping information secure. A *user* (or *end user*) includes any person who accesses or handles an organization's information systems or data. Users may include full-time and part-time employees, interns, contractors, consultants, vendors, partners, and so on. Some general user responsibilities include the following:

- Understand, agree to, and adhere to all information security policies, procedures, standards, and guidelines, as well as any relevant regulatory and compliance requirements. Users are also responsible for satisfying contractual obligations (such as nondisclosure agreements) that affect the confidentiality of the company's information and processes.

- Complete all required information security training and awareness activities by their required completion dates.

- Report any actual or suspected security violations or breaches to appropriate personnel in a timely manner.

Security Control Frameworks

Poor security management is one of the primary culprits for many organizations' security problems. Security management can be accomplished by adopting a top-down approach, bottom-up approach, or some combination of the two.

Historically, enterprises have utilized more of a *bottom-up approach* to security, in which the IT department takes security seriously and attempts to develop a security function for the company. With this approach, operations staff identify security needs and issues and push those findings up the chain to senior management to provide guidance and funding. This approach tends to result in a company taking reactive measures rather than instituting proactive policies, and often leads to underfunded security programs.

In a *top-down approach*, senior leadership starts by understanding the regulations and security threats faced by the organization, and initiates strategies, policies, and guidelines that are pushed down throughout the rest of the organization. With a top-down approach, information security is evangelized by the most senior executives at the company, which ensures that security is prioritized and in alignment with the company's overall business strategy. An effective top-down approach requires strong governance (as discussed earlier in this chapter) that starts with aligning with one or more security control frameworks.

A *security control* is a technical, operational, or management safeguard used to prevent, detect, minimize, or counteract security threats. (ISC)² defines a *security control framework* as "a notional construct outlining the organization's approach to security, including a list of specific security processes, procedures, and solutions used by the organization." Organizations often adopt a security control framework to assist with meeting legal and regulatory compliance obligations, while also helping to build a security program that maintains the confidentiality, integrity, and availability of the company's assets.

NOTE   Technical controls are system-based safeguards and countermeasures — things like firewalls, IDS/IPS, and data loss prevention (DLP). Operational controls are safeguards and countermeasures that are primarily implemented and executed by people (as opposed to systems); security guards are a common example. Management controls include policies, procedures, and other countermeasures that control (or manage) the information security risk. Management controls are sometimes referred to as *administrative controls*, but this should not be confused with activities associated with a system admin (sysadmin). The lines between the three categories can often blur (i.e., many controls fit into more than one of the categories), and many organizations have discontinued use of the terms to avoid confusion. You should be familiar with the concepts, should you come across the terminology in your organization.

Organizations often select security control frameworks based on their industry. For example, the Payment Card Industry (PCI) control framework is a global framework used by financial services organizations and companies that handle cardholder data. In the United States, the Health Insurance Portability and Accountability Act (HIPAA) offers a control framework for healthcare organizations and companies that handle protected health information (PHI). Aside from PCI and HIPAA (which are covered later in this chapter), ISO/IEC, NIST, and CIS provide some of the most frequently adopted security control frameworks used by organizations across multiple industries. While there are many other control frameworks available, you should be familiar with the following frameworks, at a minimum:

- ISO/IEC 27001
- ISO/IEC 27002
- NIST 800-53
- NIST Cybersecurity Framework
- CIS Critical Security Controls

NOTE   The HITRUST (originally known as the Health Information Trust Alliance) Common Security Framework (CSF) was originally developed to address the overlapping regulatory environment in which many healthcare providers operate. It has evolved over time to provide a comprehensive, prescriptive framework that can be used for organizations that exchange any type of sensitive and/or regulated data. Taking into account both risk-based and compliance-based considerations, the HITRUST provides an auditable framework for the evaluation of an organization's security environment.

NOTE   Control Objectives for Information Technologies (COBIT) is a framework developed by ISACA (previously known as the Information Systems Audit and Control Association) for overall information technology management and governance and is perhaps the most popular IT governance framework used in industry. While it is not a security-specific control framework, it does outline end-to-end IT governance objectives and processes that encompass many security requirements and concepts. Visit www.isaca.org if you want to learn more about the COBIT framework.

ISO/IEC 27001

ISO/IEC 27001 (sometimes referred to as just ISO 27001) is an information security standard published by the International Organization for Standardization (ISO) and the International Electrotechnical Commission (IEC). ISO 27001 is the most popular standard within the ISO/IEC 27000 family of standards and is focused on the creation and maintenance of an *information security management system* (ISMS), which ISO defines as "a systematic approach to managing sensitive company information so that it remains secure." In plain English, an ISMS is a set of people, processes, and technologies that manages the overall security of a company's systems and data. ISO/IEC 27001 describes the overall components of an ISMS, and this standard is the basis for many organization's security programs.

As of this writing, the most recent revision to ISO/IEC 27001 was in 2013, though its parent, ISO/IEC 27000, was revised in 2018. ISO 27001:2013 contains 114 controls across 14 domains, as follows:

- Information security policies
- Organization of information security
- Human resource security
- Asset management
- Access control
- Cryptography
- Physical and environmental security
- Operations security
- Communications security
- System acquisition, development, and maintenance
- Supplier relationships
- Information security incident management
- Information security aspects of business continuity management
- Compliance

ISO/IEC 27002

ISO/IEC 27002 (again, often referred to as just ISO 27002) is titled "Security Techniques — Code of practice for information security controls." This standard builds on ISO 27001 by providing guidelines for organizations to select, implement, and manage security controls based on their own security risk profile. In other words, ISO 27002 is a bit more prescriptive than ISO 27001, as it provides best-practice recommendations for organizations to build and maintain their ISMSs.

NIST 800-53

The National Institute of Standards and Technology is a nonregulatory agency of the U.S. Department of Commerce, whose mission is to promote innovation and industrial competitiveness by advancing standards and technologies. NIST publishes and manages a variety of special publications related to information security, cloud computing, and other technologies. NIST 800-53, "Security and Privacy Controls for Federal Information Systems and Organizations," is NIST's massive security control framework. Though NIST

800-53 was initially created to aid U.S. government agencies in managing their security programs, it is widely regarded as one of the most comprehensive baselines of security controls and is referenced across many industries around the globe. NIST 800-53 defines hundreds of security controls across the following 18 control families:

- Access control (AC)
- Awareness and training (AT)
- Audit and accountability (AU)
- Security assessment and authorization (CA)
- Configuration management (CM)
- Contingency planning (CP)
- Identification and authentication (IA)
- Incident response (IR)
- Maintenance (MA)
- Media protection (MP)
- Physical and environmental protection (PE)
- Planning (PL)
- Personnel security (PS)
- Risk assessment (RA)
- System and services acquisition (SA)
- System and communications protection (SC)
- System and information integrity (SI)
- Program management (PM)

NOTE   The latest revision of NIST 800-53, Rev. 5, was released in September 2020.

NIST Cybersecurity Framework

The NIST Cybersecurity Framework (CSF), first published in 2014, is a collection of standards, guidelines, and best practices to manage cybersecurity risk. As of this writing, NIST CSF v1.1 is the current version and was released in 2018. NIST CSF was initially developed with a focus on industries considered "critical infrastructure" — industries such as banking, energy, and communications. It has since become a go-to controls framework for companies of all sizes and across all business sectors.

The NIST CSF aligns with controls and best practices in NIST 800-53 and other control frameworks, but was designed to be a more flexible and understandable option for private-sector companies to adapt. The NIST Cybersecurity Framework consists of five core functions, each with multiple subdivisions NIST calls categories. (See Figure 1.2.)

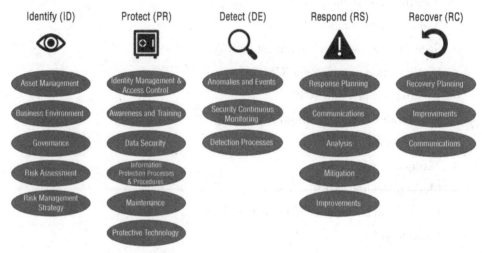

FIGURE 1.2 **NIST Cybersecurity Framework**

The five core functions within NIST CSF are intended to be performed simultaneously and continuously to form a culture of assessing and addressing cybersecurity risk. NIST defines the purpose of each of the five core functions as follows:

- **Identify (ID):** Develop an organizational understanding to manage cybersecurity risk to systems, people, assets, data, and capabilities.

- **Protect (PR):** Develop and implement appropriate safeguards to ensure delivery of critical services.

- **Detect (DE):** Develop and implement appropriate activities to identify the occurrence of a cybersecurity event.

- **Respond (RS):** Develop and implement appropriate activities to take action regarding a detected cybersecurity incident.

- **Recover (RC):** Develop and implement appropriate activities to maintain plans for resilience and restore any capabilities or services that were impaired due to a cybersecurity incident.

The five core functions are divided into 23 categories, and these categories are further divided into a total of 108 subcategories. Each subcategory describes a specific security control or desired outcome. Visit www.nist.gov/cyberframework for the complete list of subcategories and additional guidance on using the NIST Cybersecurity Framework.

CIS Critical Security Controls

The CIS Critical Security Controls (or CIS Controls) is a publication of 20 best-practice guidelines for information security. The publication was initially created by SANS Institute but was transferred to the Center for Internet Security (CIS) in 2015. Today, you may see these 20 critical controls labeled CIS CSC, CIS 20, Sans Top 20, or other variants.

CIS Controls v7.1 was released in April 2019, and identifies the basic, foundational, and organizational controls that CIS recommends mitigating the most common attacks against networks and systems. According to the Center for Internet Security, the 20 Critical Security Controls are as follows:

- **CIS Control 1:** Inventory and Control of Hardware Assets
- **CIS Control 2:** Inventory and Control of Software Assets
- **CIS Control 3:** Continuous Vulnerability Management
- **CIS Control 4:** Controlled Use of Administrative Privileges
- **CIS Control 5:** Secure Configuration for Hardware and Software on Mobile Devices, Laptops, Workstations, and Servers
- **CIS Control 6:** Maintenance, Monitoring, and Analysis of Audit Logs
- **CIS Control 7:** Email and Web Browser Protections
- **CIS Control 8:** Malware Defenses
- **CIS Control 9:** Limitation and Control of Network Ports, Protocols, and Services
- **CIS Control 10:** Data Recovery Capabilities
- **CIS Control 11:** Secure Configuration for Network Devices, such as Firewalls, Routers, and Switches
- **CIS Control 12:** Boundary Defense
- **CIS Control 13:** Data Protection
- **CIS Control 14:** Controlled Access Based on the Need to Know
- **CIS Control 15:** Wireless Access Control
- **CIS Control 16:** Account Monitoring and Control
- **CIS Control 17:** Implement a Security Awareness and Training Program
- **CIS Control 18:** Application Software Security
- **CIS Control 19:** Incident Response and Management
- **CIS Control 20:** Penetration Tests and Red Team Exercises

NOTE The controls and subcontrols within the CIS CSC break down into what are known as Implementation Groups. According to CIS, "Implementation Groups provide a simple and accessible way to help organizations of different classes focus their security resources, and still leverage the value of the CIS Controls program . . . ." In essence, these Implementation Groups help organizations prioritize controls and identify the subcontrols that are most reasonable for level of expertise and their risk profile. Visit www.cissecurity.org for more information on the CSC and their Implementation Groups.

Due Care and Due Diligence

Governance requires that the individuals setting the strategic direction and mission of the organization act on behalf of the stakeholders. The minimum standard for their governance action requires that they act with due care. *Due care* is a legal term used to describe the conduct that a reasonable person would exercise in a given situation. In business, due care is using reasonable care to protect the interests of your organization. More specifically, in regard to information security, due care relates to the conduct that a reasonable person would exercise to maintain the confidentiality, integrity, and availability of their organization's assets. This concept of "reasonable" can be a bit nebulous at first, but it is intended to protect a person or organization from accusations of negligence. In short, court decisions around the world have demonstrated that a person's actions can be assumed "reasonable" if a person of similar background and experience, confronted with the same situation would enact the same or similar actions. Examples of due care in security are activities like scanning and patching security vulnerabilities, enabling security logging, and writing restrictive firewall rules that enforce least privilege (discussed in Chapter 3, "Security Architecture and Engineering").

Due diligence is another legal concept that relates to continually ensuring that behavior maintains due care. In other words, due diligence is the ongoing execution and monitoring of due care. In relation to information security, due diligence relates to the ongoing actions that an organization and its personnel conduct to ensure organizational assets are reasonably protected. Examples of due diligence in security are activities like reviewing security log output for suspicious activity and conducting penetration tests to determine if firewall rules are sufficiently restrictive.

The concepts of due care and due diligence are incredibly important in the legal and finance world, but they must also be understood by information security professionals. Exercising due care and conducting due diligence are required to avoid claims of negligence in court. The CISSP CBK aims to establish the set of knowledge and activities required of a "reasonable" security leader.

DETERMINE COMPLIANCE AND OTHER REQUIREMENTS

(ISC)² defines *compliance* as adherence to a mandate; it includes the set of activities that an organization conducts to understand and satisfy all applicable laws, regulatory requirements, industry standards, and contractual agreements.

Legislative and Regulatory Requirements

Many compliance expectations come from statutory or regulatory requirements that apply broadly to all industries. Others are specific to certain industries or products. This ever-changing set of expectations requires a continuous review of organizational practices to ensure that information is protected in compliance with all applicable requirements.

NOTE   Because there are many compliance requirements that relate to information security, many people often confuse the two or assume that being compliant is the same as being secure. As a CISSP, you should understand that compliance requirements generally serve as a solid *baseline* for security, but being compliant with security regulations and standards is only the first step toward being secure.

The first challenge in identifying compliance requirements involves knowing which jurisdiction has the legal authority to set those requirements. *Jurisdiction* is a legal concept that establishes the official power to make legal decisions and judgments. It is not enough to know the relevant geography or political boundaries; jurisdiction may also be influenced by international treaties and agreements, the activity of your organization, or any number of other factors. Regardless of the example laws and regulations listed in this text, information security practitioners must be aware of the nuances of the jurisdictions in which they operate.

In most jurisdictions, laws are established to define what is permissible and what is not. In U.S. law, the word *law* refers to any rule that, if broken, subjects a party to criminal punishment or civil liability. Laws may be generally categorized into two parts: statutes and regulations. Statutes are written and adopted by the jurisdiction's legislative body (e.g., U.S. Congress), while regulations are more detailed rules on how the execution of a statute will be performed. Both statutes and regulations are legally enforceable, but regulations are subordinate to statutes.

There is a growing number of legislative and regulatory requirements in the United States and around the world, but there are two overarching U.S. laws that you should be familiar with:

- U.S. Computer Security Act of 1987
- U.S. Federal Information Security Management Act (FISMA) of 2002

U.S. Computer Security Act of 1987

The Computer Security Act was enacted by the U.S. Congress in 1987 with the objective of improving the security and privacy of sensitive information stored on U.S. federal government computers. The act contains provisions that require establishment of minimally acceptable security practices for federal government computer systems, as well as establishment of security policies for government agencies to meet those practices. As part of this act, security awareness training was established as a requirement for any federal government employee using government computer systems.

The Computer Security Act establishes that the National Institute for Standards and Technology, an agency within the U.S. Department of Commerce, is responsible for setting computer security standards for unclassified, nonmilitary government computer systems, while the National Security Agency (NSA) is responsible for setting security guidance for classified government and military systems and applications.

The Computer Security Act of 1987 was repealed by the Federal Information Security Management Act (FISMA) of 2002, which is discussed next.

U.S. Federal Information Security Management Act (FISMA) of 2002

The Federal Information Security Management Act, commonly referred to as FISMA (pronounced "fizz-muh"), is a U.S. law enacted in 2002 that greatly extends the Computer Security Act of 1987. FISMA acknowledges the importance of information security to the United States' economic and national security interests and requires that all U.S. federal government agencies and nongovernment organizations that provide information services to these agencies conduct risk-based security assessments that align with the NIST Risk Management Framework (RMF).

Industry Standards and Other Compliance Requirements

Aside from national, state, and local laws and regulations, your organization may be required to comply with certain regulations and standards based on your industry or the type of services you provide. The most prominent industry standards that you should be aware of include the following:

- U.S. Sarbanes–Oxley Act of 2002 (SOX)
- System and Organization Controls (SOC)
- Payment Card Industry Data Security Standard (PCI DSS)

U.S. Sarbanes–Oxley Act of 2002

Following several high-profile corporate and accounting scandals, the SOX was enacted in the United States to reestablish public trust in publicly traded companies and public accounting firms. SOX required companies to implement a wide range of controls intended to minimize conflicts of interest, provide investors with appropriate risk information, place civil and criminal penalties on executives for providing false financial disclosures, and provide protections for whistleblowers who report inappropriate actions to regulators.

Under SOX, the Public Company Accounting Oversight Board (PCAOB) was established as a nonprofit organization responsible for overseeing the implementation of SOX. PCAOB's "Auditing Standards" identify the role that information systems play in maintaining financial records and requires auditors to assess the use of IT as it relates to maintaining and preparing financial statements. As part of PCAOB standards, auditors should broadly consider information security risks that could have a material impact on a company's financial statements. Even though SOX is largely a financially focused law, the regulation has a real and growing impact on IT and information security.

System and Organization Controls

Often confused with SOX (discussed previously), SOC stands for System and Organization Controls and is an auditing framework that gives organizations the flexibility to be audited based on their own needs. There are three commonly used types of SOC audits and reports, aptly named SOC 1, SOC 2, and SOC 3. The three audit and report types align with standards outlined in Statement on Standards for Attestation Engagements

(SSAE) 18, which was published by the American Institute of Certified Public Accountants (AICPA) in 2017 (with amendments made via SSAE 20 in 2019).

- **SOC 1:** An audit and compliance report that focuses strictly on a company's financial statements and controls that can impact a customer's financial statements. A company that performs credit card processing is likely to require a SOC 1 audit and compliance report.

- **SOC 2:** An audit and compliance report that evaluates an organization based on AICPA's five "Trust Services principles": privacy, security, availability, processing integrity, and confidentiality. Many organizations undergo SOC 2 auditing and present a SOC 2 report to regulators and customers to demonstrate compliance with industry standard security controls.

- **SOC 3:** This is a "lite" version of a SOC 2 report and abstracts or removes all sensitive details. A SOC 3 report generally indicates whether an organization has demonstrated each of the five Trust Services principles without disclosing specifics (like exactly what they do or don't do). Companies make SOC 3 reports available to the public and restrict SOC 2 reports to trusted parties.

Payment Card Industry Data Security Standard

If your organization handles payment card information (i.e., credit or debit cards), you are likely required to demonstrate PCI DSS compliance. PCI DSS is a proprietary security standard established in 2004. PCI DSS establishes technical and operational requirements for merchants and service providers that accept or process cardholder data and/or sensitive authentication data, as well as for software developers and manufacturers of the applications and devices used in payment card transactions.

NOTE The Payment Card Industry Security Standards Council (PCI SSC) was formed in late 2006 with the goal of ongoing management of the PCI DSS. The PCI SSC is composed of MasterCard Worldwide, Visa International, American Express, Discover Financial Services, and Japan Credit Bureau. To learn more about the Council and the PCI DSS, visit www .pcisecuritystandards.org.

The PCI DSS includes more than 200 security controls organized into 12 requirements, further categorized into 6 goals that generally align with security best practices. Per the PCI SSC, the PCI DSS covers the following:

- Build and Maintain a Secure Network

  Requirement 1: Install and maintain a firewall configuration to protect cardholder data.

Requirement 2: Do not use vendor-supplied defaults for system passwords and other security parameters.

- Protect Cardholder Data

    Requirement 3: Protect stored cardholder data.
    Requirement 4: Encrypt transmission of cardholder data across open, public networks.

- Maintain a Vulnerability Management Program

    Requirement 5: Use and regularly update antivirus software or programs.
    Requirement 6: Develop and maintain secure systems and applications.

- Implement Strong Access Control Measures

    Requirement 7: Restrict access to cardholder data by business need to know.
    Requirement 8: Assign a unique ID to each person with computer access.
    Requirement 9: Restrict physical access to cardholder data.

- Regularly Monitor and Test Networks

    Requirement 10: Track and monitor all access to network resources and cardholder data.
    Requirement 11: Regularly test security systems and processes.

- Maintain an Information Security Policy

    Requirement 12: Maintain a policy that addresses information security for employees and contractors.

Although PCI DSS is not yet a legal requirement, it is often a contractual requirement, and a prime example of an industry standard that is used to mandate, enforce, and audit security standards for applicable organizations across almost all jurisdictions. Because it is not a legislation, PCI DSS is not governed by or enforced by any government body. Instead, compliance with PCI DSS is assessed and enforced by the payment card companies (e.g., Visa, Mastercard, American Express, etc.) mentioned earlier in this section. Failure to satisfy PCI DSS requirements can cost an organization its ability to receive and process such payment card transactions.

Privacy Requirements

Privacy entails limiting access to personal information to authorized parties for authorized uses; in essence, privacy is maintaining the confidentiality of personal information specifically (as opposed to all sensitive data, in general). As more and more of our personal data moves online, privacy has become one of the biggest security-related concerns for regulators, organizations, and users.

Personal information such as your name, address, and Social Security number is considered personally identifiable information, which must be kept confidential. PII is often subject to some combination of contractual and regulatory privacy requirements. While the source of the requirements may vary, the seriousness with which organizations should take these requirements does not change. As a CISSP, you must know what PII and other personal data your organization handles, and you must understand all legal, contractual, and regulatory requirements that govern the privacy of that data.

UNDERSTAND LEGAL AND REGULATORY ISSUES THAT PERTAIN TO INFORMATION SECURITY IN A HOLISTIC CONTEXT

As a CISSP, you must be aware of the legal and regulatory requirements that pertain to information security — both broadly and within your particular industry and/or geographic regions. Having a strong understanding of legal and regulatory issues involves being familiar with the security threats that face information systems as well as the national, state, and local regulations that govern your organization's handling of sensitive data and systems. For both the CISSP exam and the "real world," you must be familiar with the laws and regulations that govern handling of cybercrimes and data breaches, licensing and intellectual property handling, import/export controls, transborder data flow, and (of course) privacy.

NOTE Misdemeanor and felony are two legal terms that you'll see throughout this section; these two terms describe criminal acts of varying degrees. In U.S. law, a *misdemeanor* is any "lesser" criminal act that is punishable by less than 12 months in prison. Prison time is often (but, not always) substituted with fines, probation, or community service are often (not always) for misdemeanor charges. A *felony*, under U.S. law, is a more serious criminal offense that carries more serious penalties, including jail time over 12 months (and as high as one's lifetime). In other countries, such as France, Germany, and Switzerland, serious offenses (i.e., "felonies" in the United States) are described as crimes, while less serious offenses are called *misdemeanors* or *delicts*. Other countries, such as Brazil, use the term *contravention* to describe less serious offenses.

Cybercrimes and Data Breaches

A *cybercrime* is any criminal activity that directly involves computers or the internet. In a cybercrime, a computer may be the tool used to execute the criminal activity, or it may be the target of the criminal activity. There are three major categories of cybercrimes:

- **Crimes against people:** These crimes include cyberstalking, online harassment, identity theft, and credit card fraud.

- **Crimes against property:** Property in this case may include information stored within a computer, or the computer itself. These crimes include hacking, distribution of computer viruses, computer vandalism, intellectual property (IP) theft, and copyright infringement.

- **Crimes against government:** Any cybercrime committed against a government organization is considered an attack on that nation's sovereignty. This category of cybercrime may include hacking, theft of confidential information, or cyber terrorism. Hacktivism is another cybercrime that involves hackers seeking to make a political statement with their attacks. Hacktivists often target government entities but may also target other organizations with whom they disagree.

A *data breach* is a specific cybercrime where information is accessed or stolen by a cybercriminal without authorization. The target of a data breach is the information system and the data stored within it. Data breaches, and cybercrimes more broadly, may pose a threat to a person, a company, or an entire nation. As such, there are many laws that govern and regulate how cybercrimes are prevented, detected, and handled.

As a CISSP, you should be familiar with the following global cybercrime and information security laws and regulations:

- U.S. Computer Fraud and Abuse Act of 1986

- U.S. Electronic Communications Privacy Act (ECPA) of 1986

- U.S. Economic Espionage Act of 1996

- U.S. Child Pornography Prevention Act of 1996

- U.S. Identity Theft and Assumption Deterrence Act of 1998

- USA PATRIOT Act of 2001

- U.S. Homeland Security Act of 2002

- U.S. Controlling the Assault of Non-Solicited Pornography and Marketing (CAN-SPAM) Act of 2003

- U.S. Intelligence Reform and Terrorism Prevention Act of 2004

- The Council of Europe's Convention on Cybercrime of 2001

- The Computer Misuse Act 1990 (U.K.)

- Information Technology Act of 2000 (India)

- Cybercrime Act 2001 (Australia)

NOTE   Many of the regulations in this section have been around for decades. While most of them are still relevant as of this book's writing, the legal landscape is dynamic and changes every year.

U.S. Computer Fraud and Abuse Act of 1986, 18 U.S.C. § 1030

The U.S. Computer Fraud and Abuse Act of 1986 is the oldest and, yet, still possibly the most relevant cybercrime law currently in effect in the United States. The law has been revised over the years, and you should be familiar with both its original form and the revisions discussed in this section.

The Computer Fraud and Abuse Act (CFAA) is a cybercrime bill that was enacted in 1986 as an amendment to the Comprehensive Crime Control Act of 1984. The CFAA was created to clarify definitions of computer fraud and abuse and to extend existing law to include intangible property such as computer data. Although the CFAA now covers all computing devices, the original law was written to cover "federal interest computers" — a term that was changed to "protected computers" in a 1996 amendment to the act. Section 1030(e)(2) defines a protected computer as one that is

- "[E]xclusively for the use of a financial institution or the United States Government, or, in the case of a computer not exclusively for such use, used by or for a financial institution or the United States Government and the conduct constituting the offense affects that use by or for the financial institution or the Government"

- "[U]sed in or affecting interstate or foreign commerce or communication"

In plain English, a *protected computer* is a computer used by the U.S. government or financial institutions, or one used for interstate and foreign communications and financial transactions. It's important to note here that this definition is broad enough to apply to any computer that is "used in or affecting" government and commerce — a computer does not need to be directly used or targeted by a cybercriminal to be considered protected under this definition.

The CFAA establishes seven criminal offenses related to computer fraud and abuse and identifies the penalties for each:

- **Obtaining national security information:** §1030(a)(1) describes the felony act of knowingly accessing a computer without or in excess of authorization, obtaining national security or foreign relations information, and willfully retaining or transmitting that information to an unauthorized party.

- **Accessing a computer and obtaining information:** §1030(a)(2) describes the misdemeanor act of intentionally accessing a computer without or in excess of authorization and obtaining information from a protected computer. This crime is upgraded to a felony if the act is committed to gain commercial advantage or private financial gain, if the act is committed in furtherance of any other criminal or tortious act, or if the value of the obtained information exceeds $5,000.

■ **Trespassing in a government computer:** §1030(a)(3) extends the definition of trespassing to the computing world and describes a misdemeanor act of intentionally accessing a nonpublic protected computer, without authorization, and affecting the use of that computer by or for the U.S. government. §1030(a) (2) applies to many of that same cases that §1030(a)(3) could be charged, but §1030(a)(2) may be charged even when no information is obtained from the computer. In other words, section 1030(a)(3) protects against simply trespassing into a protected computer, with or without information theft.

■ **Accessing to defraud and obtain value:** §1030(a)(4) was a key addition to the 1984 act, and it describes the felony act of knowingly accessing a protected computer without or in excess of authorization with the intent to fraud. Under §1030(a)(4), the criminal must obtain anything of value, including use of the information if its value exceeds $5,000. The key factor with §1030(a)(4) is that it allows information theft (described in §1030(a)(2)) to be prosecuted as a felony if there is evidence of fraud.

■ **Damaging a computer or information:** §1030(a)(5) was originally written to describe the felony act associated with altering, damaging, or destroying a protected computer or its information, or preventing authorized use of the computer or information, such that it results in an aggregate loss of $1,000 or more during a one-year period. This provision was later rewritten and now more generally describes a misdemeanor act associated with knowingly and intentionally causing damage to a computer or information. §1030(a)(5) upgrades the crime to a felony if the damage results in losses of $5,000 or more during one year, modifies medical care of a person, causes physical injury, threatens public health or safety, damages systems used for administration of justice or national security, or if the damage affects 10 or more protected computers within 1 year.

■ **Trafficking in passwords:** §1030(a)(6) establishes a misdemeanor and prohibits a person from intentionally trafficking computer passwords or similar information when such trafficking affects interstate or foreign commerce or permits unauthorized access to computers used by or for the United States. The term *traffic* here means to illegally transfer or obtain control of a password with the intent to transfer it to another party. This definition is important because it excludes mere possession of passwords if there is no intent to transfer them.

■ **Threatening to damage a computer:** §1030(a)(7) describes a felony offense associated with the computer variation of old-fashioned extortion. This provision prohibits threats to damage a protected computer or threats to obtain or reveal confidential information without or in excess of authorization with intent to extort money or anything else of value.

The U.S. Computer Fraud and Abuse Act of 1986 has seen numerous amendments over time, both directly and through other legislations. Minor amendments were made in 1988, 1989, and 1999, with major amendments being issued in 1994, 1996, and 2001 through various other acts discussed later in this chapter.

U.S. Electronic Communications Privacy Act of 1986

The Electronic Communications Privacy Act (ECPA) was enacted by the U.S. Congress in 1986 to extend restrictions on government wire taps to include computer and network-based communications (rather than just telephone calls). The ECPA complements the CFAA by prohibiting eavesdropping, interception, and unauthorized monitoring of all electronic communications (including those sent over computer networks).

The ECPA does, however, make certain exceptions that allow communications providers (like an ISP) to monitor their networks for legitimate business reasons if they first notify their users of the monitoring. This sets up a legal basis for network monitoring, which has been criticized over the years. The USA PATRIOT Act (discussed in a later section) made several extensive amendments to the ECPA in 2001.

U.S. Economic Espionage Act of 1996

The Economic Espionage Act (EEA) was enacted by the U.S. Congress and signed into law by President Clinton in 1996. The EEA was the first federal law to broadly define and establish strict penalties for theft or unauthorized use of trade secrets. The EEA makes it a criminal offense to copy, download, upload, alter, steal, or transfer trade secrets for the benefit of a foreign entity. The EEA establishes penalties for economic espionage that include fines up to $10 million and imprisonment up to 15 years, as well as forfeiture of any property used to commit economic espionage or property obtained as a result of the criminal act.

U.S. Child Pornography Prevention Act of 1996

The Child Pornography Prevention Act (CPPA) was issued in 1996 to restrict and punish the production and distribution of child pornography on the internet.

U.S. Identity Theft and Assumption Deterrence Act of 1998

The Identity Theft and Assumption Deterrence Act was enacted in 1998, and formally established identity theft as a criminal act under U.S. federal law. Under the act, *identity theft* is "knowingly transfer[ring] or us[ing], without lawful authority, a means of identification of another person with the intent to commit, or to aid or abet, any unlawful activity that constitutes a violation of Federal law, or that constitutes a felony under any applicable State or local law." Prior to the act, identity theft was not regulated or investigated as a crime, which made it difficult to prosecute the growing number of identity theft claims stemming from the rise of the internet.

USA PATRIOT Act of 2001

The Uniting and Strengthening America by Providing Appropriate Tools Required to Intercept and Obstruct Terrorism (USA PATRIOT) Act, commonly known as the Patriot Act, was signed into law in 2001 in response to the terrorist attacks that took place in the United States on September 11, 2001. The act was initially issued as a temporary measure, but most measures were reauthorized in 2006.

The Patriot Act amends many of the provisions within the CFAA and the ECPA with both new definitions of criminal offenses and new penalties for previously and newly defined computer crimes.

The Patriot Act attempts to strengthen provisions in the CFAA and ECPA to give law enforcement further authority to protect the United States against terrorist acts. The act has been heavily debated since its inception, with some of the act's provisions having been declared unconstitutional by various federal district courts. Of the act's remaining provisions, the following are particularly relevant to the CISSP exam and to you as a security professional:

- **Section 202 — Authority to intercept wire, oral, and electronic communications relating to computer fraud and abuse offenses:** This section amends the CFAA to authorize investigators to obtain a wiretap for felony violations relating to computer fraud and abuse.

- **Section 209 — Seizure of voicemail messages pursuant to warrants:** This section authorizes investigators to seize voicemail messages with a search warrant. Prior to the Patriot Act, voicemail was only authorized for seizure with a harder-to-obtain wiretap order.

- **Section 210 — Scope of subpoenas for records of electronic communications:** This section updates previous law and grants access to additional information when filing a subpoena for electronic records.

- **Section 212 — Emergency disclosure of electronic communications to protect life and limb:** This section grants special provisions to allow a communications provider (like an ISP) to disclose customer information to law enforcement in emergency situations, such as imminent crime or terrorist attack. Prior to this amendment, communications providers may have been subject to civil liability suits for providing such information without the customer's consent.

- **Section 214 — Pen register and trap and trace authority under FISA:** A *pen register* is a device that shows the outgoing calls made from a phone, while a *trap and trace device* shows incoming numbers that called a phone; these capabilities are often consolidated into a single device called a *pen/trap device*. This section of the Patriot Act authorizes use of these devices nationwide (as opposed to an issuing court's jurisdiction) and broadens authority to include computer and internet-based communications.

- **Section 217 — Interception of computer trespasser communications:** This section amends previous law to allow communications providers and other organizations to allow law enforcement to intercept and monitor their systems. Prior to this amendment, companies were authorized to monitor their own systems, but were not permitted to allow law enforcement to assist in such monitoring.

- **Section 220 — Nationwide service of search warrants for electronic evidence:** This section authorizes nationwide jurisdiction for search warrants related to electronic evidence, such as email.

- **Section 808 — Definition of federal crime of terrorism:** The official definition of terrorism includes, among other things, "destruction of communication lines, stations, or systems."

- **Section 814 — Deterrence and prevention of cyberterrorism:** This section strengthens penalties associated with violations in the CFAA, including doubling the maximum prison sentence from 10 to 20 years.

- **Section 815 — Additional defense to civil actions relating to preserving records in response to government requests:** This amendment absolves an organization from civil penalties associated with violations of the ECPA if the organization is responding to "a request of a governmental entity."

- **Section 816 — Development and support for cybersecurity forensic capabilities:** This section requires the U.S. Attorney General to establish regional computer forensic laboratories to support forensic examinations on seized or intercepted computer evidence. Section 816 also requires these laboratories to provide forensic analysis training and education to federal, state, and local law enforcement personnel and prosecutors. This section also includes open-ended language authorizing these forensic labs "to carry out such other activities as the U.S. Attorney General considers appropriate."

U.S. Homeland Security Act of 2002

The Homeland Security Act was enacted in 2002, building off the Patriot Act's response to the September 11, 2001, terrorist attacks in the United States. The

Homeland Security Act sparked the largest U.S. government reorganization since the creation of the Department of Defense in 1947. Under the Homeland Security Act, dozens of government agencies, offices, and services were consolidated into the newly created U.S. Department of Homeland Security (DHS). With the creation of the DHS, a new cabinet-level position, Secretary of Homeland Security, was also created. Title X of the Homeland Security Act identifies several standards, tactics, and controls that should be used to secure U.S. federal government information. Title X and its subsections establish the authorities, responsibilities, and functions associated with information security.

U.S. Controlling the Assault of Non-Solicited Pornography and Marketing Act of 2003

The U.S. Controlling the Assault of Non-Solicit Pornography and Marketing Act was signed into law in 2003. This law established the United States' first national standards for sending commercial emails in response to the growing number of complaints over spam (unwanted) emails. The law requires companies to allow email recipients to unsubscribe or opt out from future emails and establishes a variety of requirements around email content and sending behavior. CAN-SPAM designates the Federal Trade Commission (FTC) as responsible for enforcing the provisions within the Act.

U.S. Intelligence Reform and Terrorism Prevention Act of 2004

The Intelligence Reform and Terrorism Prevention Act of 2004 established the National Counterterrorism Center (NCTC) and the position of the Director of National Intelligence (DNI). Under this law, the Department of Homeland Security and other U.S. government agencies are required to share intelligence information to help prevent terrorist acts against the United States. This act also established the Privacy and Civil Liberties Oversight Board with the intent of protecting the privacy and civil liberties of U.S. citizens.

The Council of Europe's Convention on Cybercrime of 2001

The Convention on Cybercrime, also known as the Budapest Convention, is the first international treaty established to address cybercrime. The treaty was first signed in 2001 and became effective in 2004, and has since been signed by more than 65 nations (the United States ratified the treaty in 2006). The treaty aims to increase cooperation among nations and establish more consistent national laws related to preventing and prosecuting cybercrime.

The Computer Misuse Act 1990 (U.K.)

The Computer Misuse Act came into effect in the United Kingdom in 1990 and introduced five offenses related to cybercrime:

- Unauthorized access to computer material
- Unauthorized access with intent to commit or facilitate commission of further offenses
- Unauthorized acts with intent to impair, or with recklessness as to impairing, operation of computer, etc.
- Unauthorized acts causing, or creating risk of, serious damage
- Making, supplying, or obtaining articles for use in other offenses

Information Technology Act of 2000 (India)

The Information Technology Act was passed by the Indian Parliament in 2000 and amended in 2008. The act established legal recognition of electronic documents and digital signatures, while it also established definitions and penalties for cybercrimes such as data theft, identity theft, child pornography, and cyber terrorism.

Cybercrime Act 2001 (Australia)

The Cybercrime Act 2001 was Australia's response to the September 11, 2001, terror attacks in the United States. The Cybercrime Act 2001 defined serious computer offenses such as unauthorized access, unauthorized modification, and unauthorized impairment of electronic communication, and also established penalties for such crimes.

Licensing and Intellectual Property Requirements

Despite the growing list of cybercrime laws that exist today, it's still fairly difficult to legally define and prosecute computer crimes. As a result, many prosecutors fall back on traditional criminal law concepts such as theft and fraud. No matter what organization you work for, there is a good chance that you have some sort of IP that needs to be protected against theft and fraud. IP may include software, data, multimedia content like music and movies, algorithms, drawings, and so much more. As a CISSP, it is your job to protect all forms of IP.

There are various organizations around the world that establish and protect IP rights; among them are the World Trade Organization (WTO), World Customs Organization (WCO), and the World Intellectual Property Organization (WIPO).

There are numerous intellectual property laws and regulations in the United States, and they fit into five categories:

- Licensing
- Patents
- Trademarks
- Copyrights
- Trade secrets

Licensing

Legal protections over intellectual property allow creators and inventors to profit from their work. Unfortunately, the ease with which information can be duplicated and transmitted has made it easier for people to copy information in violation of the legitimate owner's rights.

From an economic perspective, the effect is tremendous. By 2022, the global trade in counterfeited and pirated products, both physical and online, will grow to between 1.9 and 2.8 trillion dollars. Estimates by the Business Software Alliance (BSA) suggest that more than 40 percent of the software in use worldwide is not properly licensed.

Counterfeit goods also present significant economic as well as physical risks. A $460 billion–a–year industry, counterfeiting has been simplified by the e-commerce platforms and expedited international shipping, which has accompanied the lowering of trade barriers. The secondary impacts of illegal use of intellectual property are equally surprising. One estimate suggests that 23 percent of all bandwidth is consumed by activities that infringe on intellectual property.

While emerging technologies present opportunities for improving licensing methods, lack of enforcement remains one of the largest hurdles. With more applications transitioning to a cloud-enabled model, ensuring legal software licensing goes hand in hand with software as a service.

The use of unlicensed software increases the risk of software vulnerabilities, as the users are unable to get patches and updates. This leaves the users of bootleg software at risk when compromises are found in the software. While the vendors patch their legitimate versions, the unlicensed versions don't get the updates. It is somewhat ironic that by illegally using unlicensed software, individuals are more likely to be targeted by other illegal actors. The effect of this was seen most clearly in the rapid distribution of the WannaCry malware in China, where estimates suggest that 70 percent of computer users in China are running unlicensed software, and state media acknowledged that more than 40,000 institutions were affected by the attack.

Patents

A *patent* is a government-issued license or grant of property rights to an inventor that prohibits another party from making, using, importing, or selling the invention for a set period of time. In the United States, patents are issued by the United States Patent and Trademark Office (USPTO) and are usually valid for 15 or 20 years. To qualify for a patent, an invention must be new, useful, and nonobvious. Patents issued by the USPTO are only valid in the United States and its territories; inventors must file patent applications in all countries where they want to be protected under national patent law. There is a European Patent Office (EPO), Eurasian Patent Organization (EAPO), and African Regional Intellectual Property Organization (ARIPO), among others. As a CISSP, you should familiarize yourself with the local IP laws in your jurisdiction.

United States patent law is codified in 35 U.S.C. and 37 C.F.R. and enforced by the U.S. legal system (not the USPTO). For international violations of a U.S. patent, a patent holder may pursue action by the U.S. International Trade Commission (ITC) instead of or in addition to the court system; the ITC can issue exclusion or cease and desist orders to restrict the infringed product from entering the United States. The most robust remedy for international infringement of a U.S. patent may only be achieved through the courts.

Trademarks

According to the USPTO, a *trademark* is "a word, phrase, symbol, and/or design that identifies and distinguishes the source of the goods of one party from those of others." A *service mark* is a similar legal grant that identifies and distinguishes the source of a service rather than goods. The term *trademark* is commonly used to refer to both trademarks and service marks. Think of the brand name Coca-Cola as a popular trademark; the word Coca-Cola distinguishes that specific brand from Pepsi or any other brand of cola/soda/pop. In addition to 35 U.S.C., trademarks are protected under the Trademark Law Treaty Implementation Act (U.S. Public Law 105-330). Unlike patents, a trademark does not expire after a set period of time. Instead, trademark rights last as long as the mark is used in commerce, which can be as long as forever.

Copyrights

A *copyright* is a legal protection granted to the authors of "original works of authorship" that may include books, movies, songs, poetry, artistic creations, and computer software, among other categories. Copyrights created by an individual are protected for the life of the author plus 70 years. Copyright law in the United States was last generally revised by the Copyright Act of 1976 and codified in 17 U.S.C. The U.S. Copyright Office handles registration, recording, and transferring of copyrights, although an original work does not need to be registered to receive copyright protections.

Trade Secrets

A *trade secret* is a proprietary formula, process, practice, or combination of information that a company has exclusive rights to. Using an earlier example, the recipe that Coca-Cola has maintained since 1886 is a trade secret because it is proprietary and has economic value to the company only because of its secrecy. In the United States, trade secret laws are generally left up to the states, although most states have adopted the Uniform Trade Secrets Act (UTSA), which was last amended in 1985. In addition, the Economic Espionage Act of 1996 (discussed earlier in this chapter) and the Defend Trade Secrets Act (DTSA) of 2016 both establish the theft or misappropriation of trade secrets as a federal crime.

Import/Export Controls

Many countries closely regulate the movement of technology through their borders. This might be done to protect local industries from external competition, limit the exportation of sensitive technologies (like encryption), or meet other policy goals of a particular nation. As a CISSP, you should be aware of the implications of any import/export controls in which your organization operates or to which your company's employees may travel.

NOTE The United States, European Union, and other jurisdictions sometimes issue *sanctions* (government edicts that prohibit doing business with a given person, group, organization, or country) against particular countries or particular entities. These sanctions come and go much more frequently than import/export laws and can pose challenges for security teams that operate in or do business with sanctioned entities. As a CISSP, you should be aware of sanctions that impact your organization and help ensure your organization's IT systems meet relevant legal requirements.

One of the most well-known regulations that establishes import/export controls is the U.S. International Traffic in Arms Regulations (ITAR). ITAR regulates the export of defense articles and defense services to keep those sensitive materials out of the hands of foreign nationals. ITAR applies to both government agencies and contractors or subcontractors who handle regulated materials outlined in the United States Munitions List (USML). Regulated products and technical data include satellites, aircraft, spacecraft, missiles, and much more. Merely sending an email containing ITAR-controlled data (like a blueprint or 3D design file) is considered an export under ITAR. As such, it's important that your organization maintains proper security controls to restrict the flow of ITAR data to legitimate people and locations.

The European Union also places restrictions on dual-use technology. ECPA No. 428/2009 of May 5, 2009, requires member states to participate in the control of exports, transfer, brokering, and transit of dual-use items. In 2017, these regulations were updated to reflect controls over cyber weapons.

A number of countries have adopted laws or regulations that require security reviews to be conducted or, in some cases, denied companies the authority to import products to their countries altogether. In 2016, China passed a broad cybersecurity law that requires information technology vendors to submit their products to the Ministry of State Security for technical analysis. The law allows the ministry to demand source code for inspection as part of the review process. Similar expectations have been placed on software products by Russia and other nations. In 2017, the U.S. government, citing security concerns, singled out Kaspersky Labs, legislating that the company's products would not be allowed on any U.S. government computer system.

Transborder Data Flow

The concept of transborder data flow is closely related to the previously discussed topic of import/export controls. More specifically, this concept focuses on requirements around restricting certain data to or from specific geographic locations or jurisdictions. The ITAR discussed in the previous section is a great example of a legislation that restricts the flow of data. Under ITAR, data must remain within the United States; otherwise, it is considered an export (which may or may not be permitted). Further, ITAR specifically prohibits regulated data from being sent to Iran, Syria, North Korea, and other specified countries. ITAR requirements are particularly noteworthy for public cloud infrastructures that have a global footprint. Many cloud providers have developed the concept of "GovCloud" or similar regionalized cloud offerings to support ITAR and other import/export requirements that restrict transborder data flow.

Many jurisdictions require that certain types of data must be processed inside their borders. This trend has been increasing in recent years, on the assumption that the information, by default, will be more secure, will be available to governments on legal request, and will have the economic benefit of inducing operators of data processing centers to locate facilities within their countries. More than 34 countries have some sort of data localization requirement.

Data localization law took on greater importance following the Snowden disclosures of the range of collection activities performed by the National Security Agency (NSA). Data localization laws were seen as providing some protection against the intelligence activities of foreign powers.

The economic argument for data localization is not necessarily convincing. A substantial body of research suggests that the costs of barriers to data flows in terms of lost trade and investment opportunities, higher IT costs, reduced competitiveness, and lower economic productivity and GDP growth are significant. The estimates suggest that localization reduces the GDP by 0.7 to 1.7 percent in Brazil, China, the European Union, India, Indonesia, Korea, and Vietnam.

Nevertheless, many countries (in addition to the United States, as already mentioned) have adopted such laws.

Russia

In 2015, Russia became one of the first regimes to require all data collected inside Russia on Russian citizens to be stored inside Russia. The regulations implementing the law may not require localization if the information service is not directed at Russia (i.e., use of Russian language, use of Russian top-level domains, etc.); this has still had significant impact on information providers. Some providers, including Google, Apple, and Twitter, have acquired computing capabilities in Russia to comply with the law. Others, most notably LinkedIn, have resisted the law, and their services have been blocked or curtailed inside Russia.

China

In China, the enforcement of the Cybersecurity Law will place new restrictions on the movement of information. China has asserted sovereignty over the internet operating within its borders and has installed network protections, including limiting access points and strict firewall rules to censor data made available inside China. Article 37 of the Cybersecurity Law requires network operators in critical sectors to store all data that is gathered or produced by the network operator in the country on systems in the country. In particular, the law requires data on Chinese citizens gathered within China to be kept inside China and not transferred abroad without the permission of the Chinese government.

Privacy

Privacy and information security go hand in hand. As discussed earlier in this chapter, privacy is effectively the security principle of confidentiality applied to personal data. There are several important regulations around the globe that establish privacy and data protection requirements. As a security professional, it's important that you understand each privacy regulation that governs your jurisdiction. As a CISSP, you may be familiar with the following regulations, among others, depending on your jurisdiction:

- U.S. Federal Privacy Act of 1974
- U.S. Health Insurance Portability and Accountability Act (HIPAA) of 1996

- U.S. Children's Online Privacy Protection Act (COPPA) of 1998

- U.S. Gramm-Leach-Bliley Act (GLBA) of 1999

- U.S. Health Information Technology for Economic and Clinical Health Act (HITECH) of 2009

- Data Protection Directive (EU)

- Data Protection Act 1998 (UK)

- Safe Harbor

- EU-US Privacy Shield

- General Data Protection Regulation (GDPR) (EU)

NOTE The Asia-Pacific Economic Cooperation (APEC) Privacy Framework is intended to provide member nations and economies with a flexible and consistent approach to information privacy protection without unnecessarily stifling information flow. Although it's not a law or regulation, the APEC Privacy Framework aims to improve information sharing with a common set of privacy principles and is worth reading if you do business in an APEC member economy.

U.S. Federal Privacy Act of 1974, 5 U.S.C. § 552a

The Federal Privacy Act is a U.S. law that was enacted in 1974. The Privacy Act establishes and governs practices related to the collection, maintenance, use, and dissemination of PII by U.S. government agencies. The purpose of the Privacy Act is to balance the government's need to maintain information about citizens and permanent residents with the rights of those individuals to keep their personal information private. Among its provisions, the Privacy Act states that "no agency shall disclose any record which is contained in a system of records by any means of communication to any person, or to another agency, except pursuant to a written request by, or with the prior written consent of, the individual to whom the record pertains." Although the Privacy Act of 1974 substantially predates the internet, the provisions within the act continue to remain relevant and manifest in the form of online privacy consent forms and other mechanisms used to serve as "written consent of the individual."

NOTE Criminal violations of the Federal Privacy Act are deemed misdemeanors and may be subject to penalties of up to $5,000 per violation.

U.S. Health Insurance Portability and Accountability Act of 1996

HIPAA was signed into law in 1996, while the HIPAA Privacy Rule and Security Rule each went into effect in 2003. Organizations that must comply with HIPAA requirements are known as *covered entities* and fit into three categories:

- **Health plans:** This includes health insurance companies, government programs like Medicare, and military and veteran's health programs that pay for healthcare.

- **Healthcare providers:** This includes hospitals, doctors, nursing homes, pharmacies, and other medical providers that transmit health information.

- **Healthcare clearinghouses:** This includes public and private organizations, like billing services, that process or facilitate the processing of nonstandard health information and convert it into standard data types. A healthcare clearinghouse is usually the intermediary between a healthcare provider and a health plan or payer of health services.

The HIPAA Privacy Rule establishes minimum standards for protecting a patient's privacy and regulates the use and disclosure of individuals' health information, referred to as *protected health information*. Under HIPAA, an individual's PHI is permitted to be used strictly for the purposes of performing and billing for healthcare services and must be protected against improper disclosure or use.

The HIPAA Security Rule establishes minimum standards for protecting PHI that is stored or transferred in electronic form. The Security Rule operationalizes the Privacy Rule by establishing the technical, physical, and administrative controls that covered entities must put in place to protect the confidentiality, integrity, and availability of electronically stored PHI (or e-PHI).

Civil penalties for HIPAA violation may include fines that range from $100 to $50,000 per violation, with a maximum penalty of $1.5 million per year for similar violations. Criminal penalties include fines up to $250,000 and potential imprisonment up to 10 years.

U.S. Children's Online Privacy Protection Act of 1998

The Children's Online Privacy Protection Act of 1998 is a U.S. federal law that establishes strict guidelines for online businesses to protect the privacy of children under the age of 13. COPPA applies to any organization around the world that handles the data of children residing in the United States and also applies to children that reside outside of the United States, if the company is U.S.-based. The law sets requirements for seeking parental consent and establishes restrictions on marketing to children under the age of 13.

According to the Federal Trade Commission (FTC), civil penalties of up to $43,280 may be levied for each violation of COPPA.

U.S. Gramm-Leach-Bliley Act of 1999

The Gramm-Leach-Bliley Act, also known as the Financial Services Modernization Act of 1999, is a U.S. law that requires financial institutions to safeguard their customer's PII. Among the provisions within GLBA, the Financial Privacy Rule requires that financial institutions provide each customer with a written privacy notice that explains what personal information is collected from the customer, how it is used, and how it is protected. The GLBA Safeguards Rule requires organizations to implement proper security controls to protect their customers' personal data.

Penalties for noncompliance with GLBA can include civil fines of up to $100,000 per violation for an organization, and up to $10,000 for officers and directors of a financial services company. In addition, criminal violations of GLBA can include revocation of licenses and up to five years in prison.

U.S. Health Information Technology for Economic and Clinical Health Act of 2009

The Health Information Technology for Economic and Clinical Health Act, referred to as the HITECH Act, was enacted under the American Recovery and Reinvestment Act of 2009. The HITECH Act was created to promote the expanded use of electronic health records (EHRs). Along with increased adoption, the act anticipated an increase in security and privacy risks. As such, the HITECH Act extended HIPAA privacy protections by improving security and privacy protections for healthcare data by imposing tougher penalties for HIPAA compliance violations. Under the HITECH Act, maximum financial penalties were raised to $1.5 million per violation category, per year.

The HITECH Act also introduced a new HIPAA Breach Notification Rule. Under this rule, covered entities are required to disclose a breach of unsecured protected health information to affected parties within 60 days of discovery of the breach. In addition to notifying affected individuals, the Breach Notification Rule requires covered entities to report breaches affecting 500 or more people to the U.S. Department of Health and Human Services and a major media outlet servicing the jurisdiction of the affected parties.

Data Protection Directive (EU)

The Data Protection Directive, officially known as Directive 95/46/EC, was enacted by the European Parliament in 1995. The Data Protection Directive aimed at regulating the processing of the personal data of European citizens. Although it has since been superseded by the GDPR (discussed in a later section), the Data Protection Directive was the first major privacy law in the European Union and is considered the foundational privacy regulation in all of Europe.

Data Protection Act 1998 (UK)

The Data Protection Act was established by the United Kingdom Parliament to enact the provisions within the EU's Data Protection Directive. The Data Protection Act established that UK citizens held the legal right to control their personal information and was designed to enforce privacy of personal data stored on computing systems. The Data Protection Act 1998 was later superseded by the Data Protection Act 2018, which was designed to enforce and supplement provisions within the GDPR (discussed in a later section).

Safe Harbor

The International Safe Harbor Privacy Principles, often short-handed as just "Safe Harbor," is an agreement between the United States and European Union, established between 1998 and 2000, that was developed to reconcile differences between U.S. and EU privacy laws. Under Safe Harbor, a U.S. company could self-certify that it met data privacy requirements agreed upon by the United States and European Union. Safe Harbor was ruled invalid by the European Court of Justice in 2015 and replaced with the EU-US Privacy Shield soon after.

EU-US Privacy Shield

The EU-US Privacy Shield was the second attempt by the European Union and United States to agree upon principles to mutually regulate the exchange of personal data between the two jurisdictions. The agreement was reached in 2016, less than a year after Safe Harbor was ruled invalid by the European Court of Justice. By 2020, however, the same court declared the EU-US Privacy Shield invalid.

General Data Protection Regulation (EU)

The GDPR is considered by most to be the world's strongest data privacy law. GDPR was established in 2016 and replaced the EU's 1995 Data Protection Directive with hundreds of pages of regulations that require organizations around the world to protect the privacy of EU citizens. With this sweeping regulation, companies around the world that do business with European customers have been forced to rethink their approach to data security and privacy. As a CISSP and information security leader, this is one legislation that you'll likely need to be familiar with.

NOTE If your organization stores or processes the personal data of EU citizens or residents, then GDPR applies to you, whether or not your company is located in the EU.

GDPR Article 5 establishes and describes seven principles for processing personal data:

- **Lawfulness, fairness, and transparency:** Obtain and process personal data in accordance with applicable laws and fully inform the customer of how their data will be used.

- **Purpose limitation:** Identify "specific, explicit, and legitimate" purpose for data collection, and inform them of such purpose.

- **Data minimization:** Collect and process the minimum amount of data necessary to provide the agreed-upon services.

- **Accuracy:** Ensure that personal data remains "accurate and where necessary kept up-to-date."

- **Storage limitation:** Personal data may be stored only long as necessary to provide the agreed-upon services.

- **Integrity and confidentiality:** Ensure appropriate security of personal data, and provide protection against unauthorized access, and accidental loss or destruction. This includes implementing data anonymization techniques to protect your customers' identities, where necessary.

- **Accountability:** The *data controller* (i.e., the party that stores and processes the personal data) must be able to demonstrate compliance with all of these principles. Many customers pursue industry-standard certifications, like ISO 27001, to demonstrate accountability and commitment to security and privacy.

TIP Article 17 within the GDPR establishes a person's "right to be forgotten." This provision grants the *data subject* (i.e., the person whose data is being used) the right to have their personal data deleted if one of several circumstances exists and is a critical concept that information security professionals must consider when developing their data storage and retention policies.

GDPR Chapter 4 contains several articles that establish requirements related to the data controller and processor and requires that *data processors* (i.e., an organization that stores and processes PII on behalf of a data controller) prioritize security and privacy. Of particular interest, Article 25 requires "data protection by design and by default"; this is a huge directive that codifies what security professionals have been recommending as best practice for years.

NOTE GDPR Article 33 establishes rules that require data controllers to notify proper authorities within 72 hours of becoming aware of a personal data breach.

✔ GDPR Fines

The GDPR imposes stiff fines on data controllers and processors for noncompliance.

Determination

Fines are administered by individual member state supervisory authorities (83.1). The following 10 criteria are to be used to determine the amount of the fine on a noncompliant firm:

- **Nature of infringement:** Number of people affected, damage they suffered, duration of infringement, and purpose of processing

- **Intention:** Whether the infringement is intentional or negligent

- **Mitigation:** Actions taken to mitigate damage to data subjects

- **Preventative measures:** How much technical and organizational preparation the firm had previously implemented to prevent noncompliance

- **History:** Past relevant infringements, which may be interpreted to include infringements under the Data Protection Directive and not just the GDPR, and past administrative corrective actions under the GDPR, from warnings to bans on processing and fines

- **Cooperation:** How cooperative the firm has been with the supervisory authority to remedy the infringement

- **Data type:** What types of data the infringement impacts; see special categories of personal data

- **Notification:** Whether the infringement was proactively reported to the supervisory authority by the firm itself or a third party

- **Certification:** Whether the firm had qualified under-approved certifications or adhered to approved codes of conduct

- **Other:** Other aggravating or mitigating factors, including financial impact on the firm from the infringement

Lower Level

Up to €10 million, or 2 percent of the worldwide annual revenue of the prior financial year, whichever is higher, shall be issued for infringements of:

- Controllers and processors under Articles 8, 11, 25–39, 42, 43

- Certification body under Articles 42, 43

- Monitoring body under Article 41(4)

Upper Level

Up to €20 million, or 4 percent of the worldwide annual revenue of the prior financial year, whichever is higher, shall be issued for infringements of:

- The basic principles for processing, including conditions for consent, under Articles 5, 6, 7, and 9

- The data subjects' rights under Articles 12–22

- The transfer of personal data to a recipient in a third country or an international organization under Articles 44–49

- Any obligations pursuant to member state law adopted under Chapter IX

- Any noncompliance with an order by a supervisory authority

UNDERSTAND REQUIREMENTS FOR INVESTIGATION TYPES

In this section, we compare and contrast different investigation types, including administrative, criminal, civil, and regulatory investigations. For each investigation type, we discuss who performs the investigation, the standard for collecting and presenting evidence, and the general differences between the types.

In discussing legal matters, it is important to stress that laws and courts vary significantly across the globe; there are a great many particular distinctions between how law enforcement, courts, lawyers, and judges behave and perform, depending on where you live, where the events leading to the investigation occurred, and other variables. The information presented in this book is largely based on traditions of English common law, strictly as an example; however, it is absolutely essential that you, as a security professional, familiarize yourself with the laws and regulations relevant to your locale and customers so you can provide adequate, informed service.

Burden of proof is the requirement that the criminal prosecutor or civil plaintiff/claimant prove the claims they are making against the accused, or defendant. The party making a claim must demonstrate the truth of that claim, with compelling evidence; the entity defending against the claim, in most modern societies, is presumed innocent or without fault — that is, the court will not recognize the validity of a claim against anyone until that claim is substantiated and the defendant is proven guilty. The amount and strength of proof required to sway the judgment away from this presumption of innocence differs depending on which kind of claim is being made; for instance, whether the claim is being made by one private party against another or whether the claim is being made by the government against a person or organization (more on this distinction in just a moment). In the U.S. legal system, the two predominant standards of proof that must be met are called preponderance of the evidence and beyond a reasonable doubt.

Preponderance of the evidence is the lower standard of the two and is used primarily in civil actions. It essentially means that the evidence shows that the defendant is more likely to have caused the damage than not. In other words, the evidence convinced the judge, jury, or ruling body that there was at least a 51 percent chance that the defendant caused the damage.

The second standard, *beyond a reasonable doubt*, is much harder to prove and is used primarily in criminal actions. It is insufficient for the evidence to merely make the judge or jury *lean* more toward guilt than not. In this case, the evidence has to be so clear and compelling that a "reasonable" person has no doubt or reservation about the defendant's guilt after seeing it.

Administrative

When discussing investigations, for (ISC)² purposes, the term *administrative* will refer to actions constrained to those conducted within a single organization — that is, the organization performs an administrative investigation of itself. Internal investigations are typically performed when the matter involves some violation of organizational policy and does *not* involve any external entities such as law enforcement, investors, third-party suppliers, or attackers.

NOTE   To avoid confusion, it is important to distinguish how the term *administrative* is used in a variety of ways to avoid confusion. For (ISC)², it means an internal investigation. In the United States, *administrative law* refers to a set of laws made by regulatory bodies (such as the Drug Enforcement Agency, the Food and Drug Administration, and the like). For the purposes of the CISSP Body of Knowledge, an administrative investigation will *only* refer to an internal investigation.

The organization itself can task anyone to perform activities for administrative investigations. This can include staff and employees within the organization (physical and IT security personnel, auditors, management, etc.) or might involve specialized contractors hired by the organization to perform investigative tasks.

The burden of proof for administrative investigations is the lowest of all investigation types. Management can use whatever criteria they choose to believe evidence.

Punitive measures that may result from administrative investigations include employee termination, loss of privilege, reassignment, and so forth. Management might also choose to change the type of investigation as a result of findings made during the administrative investigation; if the administrative investigation reveals that the parties involved engaged in intentional/malicious or criminal activity, management may escalate to civil actions (lawsuits) or filing criminal charges, both of which would require investigatory actions relevant to those situations.

Despite the low burden of proof required for management to act in an administrative investigation, care should still be taken during the process. Occasionally, evidence gathered during an administrative investigation may lead to or be used in a civil or criminal investigation, as stated earlier. If evidence is mishandled during an administrative investigation, it may compromise the ability to use that evidence in later proceedings. If there is any uncertainty about whether an administrative investigation may ultimately escalate, a discussion of this concern with management or in-house or outside counsel is prudent.

Consider this example of an investigation: The IT department contacts the security office to make a report of an employee misusing the organization's internet connection to engage in unauthorized file sharing, in direct violation of the organization's policy. The security office makes the situation known to management; management instructs the IT and security departments to gather information about the user's online activity. Personnel in the IT and security departments work together to gather log data about the user's account and machine, and they present this information to management. Management consults with the legal and human resources departments to evaluate courses of action. Management decides to terminate the employee.

This is strictly an administrative investigation.

Criminal

Criminal investigations involve prosecution under criminal laws. The government, at the federal, state, or local level, prosecutes violations of its laws by imposing fines, imprisonment, or, in some extreme cases, even death for offenders. Criminal investigations are conducted by law enforcement organizations, which can include local, state, federal, or even international agencies. While some CISSPs are in law enforcement positions and conduct criminal investigations themselves, most of us will likely be reporting criminal incidents to law enforcement and helping to collect/provide evidence.

For a law enforcement agency to take part in prosecuting a criminal matter, jurisdiction must first be established. Jurisdiction, as we discussed in the section, "Determine Compliance and Other Requirements," is the legal authority of a governmental body (such as a court or enforcement agency) over a specific matter, often based on geography. With crimes that involve information assets, determining jurisdiction can be complicated and frequently may involve several different government bodies, locales, and laws.

Once jurisdiction has been established, the law enforcement investigator first tries to understand what happened, what damage was done, and what possible range of crimes apply for possible prosecution. In some cases, because of the global nature of IT, a case may be dropped or referred to another law enforcement agency due to a combination of jurisdictional issues, the cost of the investigation versus the scale and impact of the crime, and the likelihood of successful prosecution.

As the investigation progresses, law enforcement begins to understand who the potential suspects might be and what evidence is available, and the investigator must begin to narrow the focus to specific laws and statutes. Many countries, provinces, cities, and other jurisdictions have a variety of laws relating to the misuse and abuse of technology.

Typically, criminal courts have the highest legal standard for determining liability and guilt; this is often referred to as evidence that shows that the accused has caused harm beyond a reasonable doubt. With this standard, the overwhelming majority of evidence must show that the defendant is guilty, leaving the court with no other rational conclusion.

The criminal investigator collects evidence until the elements can be proven or until it is clear that they *cannot* be proven. They use investigative techniques, including digital forensics (covered in Chapter 7, "Security Operations"). The investigators may secure media and devices as necessary for evidence.

When gathering evidence, law enforcers may or may not be required to get a court order, allowing the government to access property, devices, and data that are owned by private entities. These court orders may be in the form of warrants or subpoenas; some must be issued by a judge, while others can be issued by any officer of the court (such as a government-commissioned prosecutor).

When a private organization requests law enforcement involvement with or in response to a suspected incident, that organization may give permission to the government to access the property/devices/data, and there is no need for a court order; the organization owns the property/devices/data and therefore can allow access to anyone it chooses. In criminal matters, the security professional in the employ of an organization requesting law enforcement response should *not* try to investigate without guidance from law enforcement personnel. In other words, if you, as a security professional, suspect a crime has been committed and are going to report this crime to the government, you should suspend investigative activity (beyond containment of immediate damage) until and unless otherwise instructed by the government/authority and immediately escalate the issue to management. It is possible that investigative actions by untrained personnel unfamiliar with legal procedure and the processes for proper evidence collection and handling can taint the evidence and otherwise impede an investigation.

Further, a security professional in the employ of an organization should not unilaterally make the decision to contact law enforcement. This can be a complex decision and should be made in consultation with management and in-house and/or outside counsel.

Lastly, additional rules apply to security professionals or investigators who are employed by law enforcement and prosecutorial agencies. While a company that owns evidence can simply choose to provide that evidence to law enforcement, stringent rules apply to the collection, handling, and analysis of evidence by law enforcement and the prosecution of employees. Government investigators must be conscious of and understand the legal requirements that apply to them; this will include (among other requirements) whether search warrants are necessary to seize evidence, a stringent adherence to chain of custody procedures, and the analysis of evidence that does not exceed what is legally permitted in a given situation.

Civil

Civil law governs relations and interactions between private entities. The plaintiff in a civil case sues for compensation for a loss or relief from some type of dispute. As information security practitioners, we may be called on to support our clients when they are either plaintiffs or defendants in civil suits. The following are examples of possible civil actions that a security professional, like you, may be involved in:

- **Your organization is the plaintiff:** If someone accesses your production environment without authorization and steals data, causing harm to your organization, your organization might sue the perpetrator for damages (restitution for the harm that was caused). You may be called on to oversee collection of evidence (e.g., logs from penetrated hosts, intrusion detection systems, and network appliances) proving the defendant caused the harm. (Note: This may be in *addition* to criminal action brought by the government against the defendant.)

- **Your organization is the defendant:** If a former employee accuses the organization of creating a hostile work environment, you may have to oversee collection of evidence (such as emails between managers and executives discussing how employees are treated), as well as preventing the destruction of potential evidence (referred to as *destruction hold notice, preservation notice, litigation hold,* or similar terms) upon request by courts or attorneys.

Unlike criminal law, in civil proceedings, the usual standard of proof is preponderance of the evidence, meaning it is a much lower burden of proof. Preponderance of the evidence is a simple majority of fault/liability; if the plaintiff can prove to the court that the defendant is even 50.1 percent culpable for the damages, the defendant will lose the civil case.

In a civil proceeding, there is no question of guilty versus not guilty but rather liable versus not liable. If the defendant is found liable, they may be ordered to pay for damages, to stop an activity that is harming the plaintiff, or to honor a contract or agreement into which they had previously entered. Unlike criminal sentences, a litigant cannot be jailed or put to death for liability in a civil lawsuit. However, if a civil litigant refuses to obey a court order, it can result in a contempt of court charge, which could eventually lead to jail time.

Because the burden of evidence and stakes involved in losing a civil case are much lower than they are in criminal cases, the level of effort in collecting and processing the evidence is likewise lower. This is *not* to say that evidence in civil cases can be handled in a haphazard or careless manner; due care must still be taken to perform actions in a suitable, professional way. However, in civil cases, investigation and evidence collection will not be performed by badged law enforcement personnel and government agents; instead, it is done by information technology and security professionals, such as CISSPs.

Similar to criminal trials, there are rules as to what evidence may be used in a civil trial. Collected evidence that is deemed unreliable may be excluded by a judge presiding over the trial. Care should be taken to retain original copies of evidence collected by an investigator, and chains of custody should be well documented. Original evidence should never be altered, with very few exceptions, and without direct instructions from counsel who is overseeing an investigation or handling the case. Spoliation of evidence (i.e., altering or destruction of the original) can lead to exclusion of evidence in a case or, in some situations, can lead to a separate lawsuit for the damages resulting from the spoliation.

If there is uncertainty about the rules surrounding the collection and handling of evidence for a civil lawsuit, consultation with a digital forensic expert or counsel can be helpful.

Regulatory

Regulatory investigations involve determining whether an organization is compliant with a given regulation or legal requirement. Regulations have the force of law; consequently, regulatory investigations are similar to criminal investigations. Regulations are written under the auspices of protecting the average citizen or consumer, protecting the environment, or making an industry safer and more equitable.

NOTE It is important to understand the (ISC)^2 definition of regulations, as it is used in the CISSP CBK. A regulation is not a standard, guideline, or suggestion — it is law, established by a government body. For instance, in the United States, the Environmental Protection Agency (EPA) is part of the federal government; the EPA writes regulations concerning activities that may impact the environment (such as handling hazardous/toxic waste, transportation of certain materials, and so forth). EPA regulations have the force of law: anyone violating these regulations may be prosecuted by the government. Conversely, the PCI-DSS is *not* a regulation, as defined by (ISC)^2; the PCI-DSS is a contractual standard, affecting only those parties that voluntarily choose to comply with it (i.e., merchants that accept credit card payment).

Government agencies perform regulatory investigations to determine whether sufficient evidence exists to prove some violation of rules or regulations. These agencies have the authority and discretion to decide when to perform investigations. These agencies have their own internal investigators, prosecutors, and courts for their proceedings. Regulators can also demand information from target organizations or utilize audit report data in addition to or instead of performing their own investigations.

The burden of proof for regulatory investigations is the preponderance of the evidence, and the penalties typically involve fines and injunctions. There are, however, instances where regulators call for referral to criminal law enforcement that may result in prison time.

Industry Standards

Investigation is a broad term. There are currently many standards and guidelines offered in this realm, some of which are dependent on the jurisdiction or industry in which the organization operates. This section takes a quick look at some of the most common standards and guidelines that are related to investigations.

ISO/IEC 27043:2015 recommends procedural steps for conducting security incident investigations. These guidelines cover many incident scenarios from the preparation phase all the way through to the conclusion of the investigation. The scenarios covered include incidents such as data loss or corruption, unauthorized access, and confirmed data breaches.

ISO/IEC 27037:2012 provides guidelines for handling digital evidence. This is covered through a four-step process of identification, collection, acquisition, and preservation. Evidence collection and handling is covered across many types of media and scenarios, including magnetic and optical storage media, mobile devices, camera systems, standard computers, and collecting network traffic data from network devices. This publication also covers chain of custody procedures and how to properly exchange evidence between jurisdictions.

NIST SP 800-86, "Guide to Integrating Forensic Techniques into Incident Response," overlaps significantly in terms of content with the two previous sources. It is the NIST perspective on the digital forensic process. It details how to build a forensic capability within your organization, what that means, and which tools and training your staff will need. The publication also describes how to structure forensic policies, standards, and procedures for your organization and what they should contain. Most importantly, NIST SP 800-86 describes the digital forensic process overall in four phases: collection, examination, analysis, and reporting.

NIST SP 800-101 Revision 1, "Guidelines on Mobile Device Forensics," has a self-explanatory title. It covers the unique requirements for acquiring, preserving, examining, analyzing, and reporting on the digital evidence present on mobile devices. The technical differences associated with mobile devices are discussed, such as differences in memory type and file structure that affect evidence collection. The publication also discusses sensitive areas that may arise when a mobile device is privately owned.

As you can see from this list of industry standards, evidence management and digital forensics are at the heart of conducting technology-based investigations. Domain 7 of the CISSP CBK covers Security Operations, and we further discuss understanding and complying with investigations in Chapter 7 of this book.

DEVELOP, DOCUMENT, AND IMPLEMENT SECURITY POLICY, STANDARDS, PROCEDURES, AND GUIDELINES

Although technical security controls like firewalls, encryption, and sophisticated access control mechanisms are incredibly important in maintaining the security of your organization's data, documents such as policies, standards, procedures, and guidelines are the most essential components of an information security program. Each of these documents is different, yet they are closely related and work together to guide your organization's behavior. Figure 1.3 shows the relationship that policies, standards, procedures, and guidelines have with each other.

Policies

A *policy* is a formal set of statements that establish a system of principles to guide decisions and actions. More specifically, a *security policy* is a set of statements that identifies the principles and rules that govern an organization's protection of information systems and data. Policies can be company-wide, system-specific, or issue-specific (e.g., an incident response policy). Some common examples of security policies include the following:

- Acceptable use policy
- Access control policy
- Change management policy
- Remote access policy
- Disaster recover policy

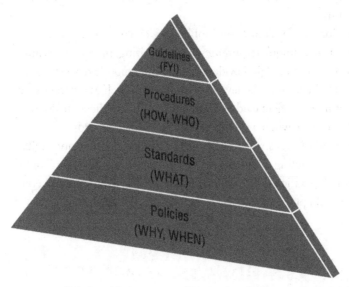

FIGURE 1.3 **Relationship between policies, procedures, standards, and guidelines**

Policies set the foundation for your organization's security program and are typically written to be broad enough to be applicable and relevant for many years. Much like the foundation of a building, security policies should survive long-term and are less likely to change than other documents, although they should be periodically reviewed and updated, as necessary. Standards, procedures, and guidelines are supporting elements that provide specific details to a complement an organization's policies.

Standards

Standards are specific and granular requirements that give direction to support broader, higher-level policies. Standards establish specific behavior and actions that must be followed and enforced to satisfy policies. Standards may be mandatory for a given organization, if mandated by contract or law. The Federal Information Processing Standards (FIPS), for example, are publicly announced standards that were developed by NIST to establish various security requirements for U.S. government agencies; FIPS 140-2, for example, is a standard that establishes security requirements for cryptographic modules.

Within this standard, there are specific encryption devices that are permitted and prohibited for use within U.S. government systems.

Baselines are related to standards and establish a minimum level of a security for a system, network, or device. For example, your organization might maintain individual baselines for each operating system that the company uses. Each of these baselines should identify what specific settings, applications, and configurations must be in place to meet your company's security standards and policies. While not specifically called out in the CISSP CBK, you should be familiar with baselines and understand how they fit into the bigger picture.

As a subset of baselines, *security baselines* express the minimum set of security controls necessary to safeguard the CIA and other security properties for a particular configuration. Scoping guidance is often published as part of a baseline, defining the range of deviation from the baseline that is acceptable for a particular baseline. Once scoping guidance has been established, then tailoring is performed to apply a particular set of controls to achieve the baseline within the scoping guidance. Scoping and tailoring is further discussed in Chapter 2, "Asset Security."

Procedures

A *procedure* is a detailed step-by-step guide to achieve a particular goal or requirement. Procedures tell you *how* to implement your policies and *how* to meet your standards and baselines. Some common examples of security procedures include the following:

- Vulnerability scanning procedures
- Backup and restore procedures
- Account provisioning procedures
- Patch management procedures

As a CISSP, you may be called upon to create, update, and manage information security policies at your organization. In addition, as a CISSP, you must ensure that other, noninformation security procedures (e.g., HR and transaction processing procedures) within your organization are safe, secure, and compliant with relevant policies and standards.

Guidelines

A *guideline* is similar to a standard but is a recommendation rather than a mandatory requirement. Guidelines refer to policy statements and offer flexible suggestions for meeting the intent of the policy or recommendations to implement the requirements in standards and baselines.

There are many sources of guidelines for information security practice. Certainly, the CISSP CBK is one, as it reflects a broad range of security practices but is not prescriptive inside an organization's information security environment. The ISO/NIST/ITIL frameworks are often leveraged as guidelines; however, they may become policies or standards if the organization has a compliance expectation. Other sources of guidelines include manufacturers' default configurations, industry-specific guidelines, or independent organizations such as the Open Web Application Security Project (OWASP) work in software development.

IDENTIFY, ANALYZE, AND PRIORITIZE BUSINESS CONTINUITY REQUIREMENTS

Business continuity (BC) and disaster recovery (DR) (discussed in detail in Chapter 7) are closely related concepts that help an organization continue essential operations during a security incident and recovery from a disaster (or major disruptive event) as quickly and securely as possible. Business continuity and disaster recovery are quite often referred to in the same breath, but it's important that you understand the role that each plays.

- A *business continuity plan* (BCP) is a methodology and set of protocols that deals with allowing an organization to keep their key business functions running in the event of a crisis; this is sometimes referred to as *continuity of operations* (COOP). Business continuity includes all of the preventative controls and the management of employees that help preserve the functionality of the overall business during a disaster.

- A *disaster recovery plan* (DRP) is the set of processes that deal with restoring your information systems and operations, securely and efficiently, after a disruptive event occurs. DR is the subset of BC whose primary objective is to minimize business downtime and reclaim normal operations as soon as possible.

NOTE   Generally speaking, BCP is broadly focused on all critical business functions and operations, while disaster recovery is more narrowly focused on systems, applications, and data. For example, BCP covers everything from DDoS and ransomware attacks (discussed in Chapter 3) to natural disasters that shut down entire datacenters. DRP, on the other hand, focuses on getting things back to "normal" — "things" here includes both IT systems and business processes.

When a disaster occurs, BC and DR activities are each kicked off simultaneously — business continuity tasks keep essential business functions running while disaster recovery actions work toward getting things back to normal. For both BC and DR planning, a business impact analysis (BIA) can help identify critical business functions.

Business Impact Analysis

According to the ISO, a *business impact analysis* is "the process of analyzing the impact over time of a disruption on the organization." In other words, a BIA helps an organization identify its essential business functions and understand the impact that a disaster would have on each of those functions; the BIA provides the primary justification for the business continuity plan and its requirements. The BIA helps an organization identify which of its business functions are more resilient and which are more fragile.

To complete the BIA, you should begin by establishing your BC project team, scope, and budget; we cover this step in the next section, "Develop and Document the Scope and the Plan." You should ensure that you have executive support for BCP activities. BCP does not yield an immediate or tangible return, so you need senior leadership's support for financial resources, staffing, and overall strategic vision.

The next step is one of the most important: identify all your critical business functions (CBFs) and other essential business elements. The key word here is *business*, as you should be focused on identifying the essential functions that are critical to your business operations, whether your business involves selling widgets or saving lives.

Identifying CBFs requires input from a broad range of stakeholders. The perspectives of the system owners, subject-matter experts, customers, and suppliers all help in identifying an organization's potential CBFs. A list of CBFs and essential business elements should include the following:

- Personnel
- Business processes
- Information systems and applications
- Other assets

For each CBF that your organization identifies, you should perform a risk analysis to identify any vulnerabilities that exist, along with steps to mitigate those weaknesses. In addition, you must determine the likelihood of adverse events affecting your CBFs and the level of impact the business is willing to accept due to disruption to any one of the critical business functions. Determining the level of impact of a disaster is done in several ways, and there are a few metrics that you should be comfortable with:

- *Maximum tolerable downtime* (MTD), or maximum acceptable outage (MAO), expresses the total length of time a critical business function can be unavailable without causing significant, long-term harm to the business; it is the longest time a CBF can remain disabled before it threatens the organization's long-term survival. MTD must be defined by the system owner, who is ultimately responsible to the organization for the proper operation of the CBF. Exceeding the MTD is an expression of unacceptable risk by the business owner.

- *Recovery time objective* (RTO) is the planned time necessary to restore a system to the point where it meets the minimum service expectations of the system owner. In other words, RTO is the maximum period of time within which a CBF must be restored after a disruption to avoid unacceptable business consequences. Since unacceptable disaster occurs when the MTD is exceeded, the RTO, by definition, must be less than or equal to the MTD. The RTO must be adjusted by the application of additional controls to bring it within the MTD. At the point where the business owner is no longer willing to apply control, they have accepted the risk of operation.

- *Recovery Point Objective* (RPO) represents the measurement of tolerable data loss, represented as a period of time. As with the MTD, this must be defined by the business, and the business is responsible for resourcing the controls to achieve the RPO.

MTD, RTO, and RPO are essential thresholds for business continuity planning. Figure 1.4 visually represents these concepts and how they fit together.

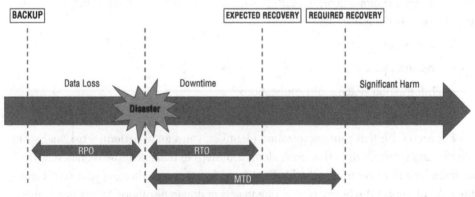

FIGURE 1.4 **Relationship between MTD, RTO, and RPO**

NOTE   MTD, RTO, and RPO are important planning horizons and estimates that are strongly linked to an organization's risk tolerance. During an actual recovery event, organizational leaders can and usually do adapt in real time, making these thresholds more guidelines than strict survival limits.

Develop and Document the Scope and the Plan

The BCP itself is the organization's commitment to maintaining the operations of the business, and the steps the organization takes to do so. This plan focuses on the people, processes, and technologies on which the business relies to deliver goods and services to its customers. The information derived from your BIA activities should be used to document the scope of your business continuity plan.

The BCP must protect an organization's critical business functions and its customers and provide the capability for an organization to continue effective business operations at a service level and in a time period that meets any legal and regulatory requirements in addition to the organization's defined MTD, RTO, and RPO (discussed in the previous section).

The scope of the BCP must encompass all of the organization's operations, including each business area and within every geographic region that the organization does business. While there is no one-size-fits-all for business continuity planning, the scope of most plans includes the following:

- Critical business functions
- Threats, vulnerabilities, and risks
- Data backup and recovery plan
- BCP personnel
- Communications plan
- BCP testing requirements

Once your organization has completed a business impact assessment, you should have a list of CBFs and an understanding of your organization's threshold for downtime and loss for each of them. The next phase of continuity planning involves identifying the specific mechanisms and procedures to mitigate risks to your CBFs and maintain compliance with your established MTD, RTO, and RPO.

As with any good plan, a BCP involves people, processes, and technologies — in that order. In next three sections, we cover some of the requirements and techniques involved in protecting these three categories of assets.

People

People are always, without exception, your most valuable and critical asset. The first goal of any BCP must be to ensure the safety of your people during and after an emergency. In the context of BCP, "people" include your employees, contractors, customers, vendors, and any other living human being that may be affected by an adverse event.

After ensuring the safety of your people, you must ensure that they are provided with the resources necessary to continue working as normally as possible. This may include shelter (e.g., an alternate work site) and food they require to survive and complete their BCP and operational tasks.

A well-designed business continuity plan must include protocols for notifying all affected people (internal and external) that an adverse event has occurred. You must ensure that multiple methods of communications are in place to notify critical BCP personnel, in case one or more methods are unavailable due to the disaster. Further, management and key BCP stakeholders must receive regular status updates during a disaster to provide awareness and allow strategic decisions to be well-informed.

Processes

The BCP team must evaluate every critical business function and determine what resources must be available during a disaster. Your continuity plan should identify the critical supplies and logistics required to maintain critical operations, and it should establish a process to ensure those resources remain continuously available.

One of the most essential BCP processes assures an organization that its critical data processing facilities and capabilities remain operational during a disaster. Your organization should identify where and how you will continue your critical data processing functions. The most relevant method of addressing this topic is by developing processes for the use of alternate sites during a disaster. The primary recover site types are hot sites, cold sites, and warm sites. We cover these in Chapter 7.

Technologies

Hardware and software failures — that's just part of the reality of technology. A business continuity plan must anticipate these failures and outline controls and procedures to mitigate the risk of technology failure. System and data backups are the most tried-and-true way that organizations address this risk. You must have a comprehensive backup process to ensure your critical systems and data are captured, stored, and available for recovery when necessary. You should maintain multiple copies of your most critical information. If your organization maintains on-premise systems (e.g., if you run a data center), for, one set of your backups must be stored offsite; this serves to protect at least one replica of your data in case a disaster destroys your primary location. If you use cloud-based systems, you should maintain backup copies in multiple *cloud regions* (or geographic locations where datacenters are located) so that your data is recoverable at any given time.

Aside from information backup, your BCP should establish a protocol for maintaining redundant systems to continue supporting your business during a significant negative event. Redundant electrical supplies, water supplies, telecommunication systems, and network connectivity systems are required to ensure continued operations during a disaster. Many organizations lease two or more internet service providers (ISPs), multiple utility providers, and at least two banking providers, in case the disaster originates with one of these providers rather than internal to the organization.

CONTRIBUTE TO AND ENFORCE PERSONNEL SECURITY POLICIES AND PROCEDURES

The Security and Risk Management domain of the CISSP CBK covers many of the foundational concepts necessary to build and manage secure systems and data. Because hardware, software, and technical controls tend to get all the attention, it's important that you keep in mind that the human element is perhaps the biggest part of information security. An essential part of your organization's security planning should be focused on policies and procedures to ensure the security of your employees. In this section, we cover topics such as candidate screening and hiring, employee onboarding and offboarding, managing external personnel (i.e., vendors, consultants, and contractors), and other important personnel security considerations.

Candidate Screening and Hiring

Candidate screening and hiring the right employees is a critical part of assuring the security of your company's systems and data. Not only do you need to make sure to hire the right fit for the job, but it's also critical that you are familiar with a candidate's background and history before bringing them into your organization and giving them access to your sensitive information.

There are a couple things your organization must do before beginning to recruit candidates for a position. First, the hiring manager should work with HR to clearly and concisely document the job description and responsibilities. Having a job description with well-documented responsibilities can help you recruit the right person for the job and can later be used as a measuring stick to assess the employee against the expectations set before they were hired. Next, you should identify the classification or sensitivity of the role, based on the level of damage that could done by a person in that role who intentionally or negligently violates security protocols. The classification or sensitivity assigned to a role (referred to as a *risk designation* by NIST, for example) should inform the types of authorizations an employee will receive once they are hired; as such, the thoroughness of your candidate screening process should match the security of the position that you're filling. As a CISSP, risk designation (or the equivalent in your jurisdiction) should be considered prior to granting any employee access to sensitive information.

Once a potential employee or contractor is identified, your organization should verify the information in their application and confirm their suitability for the position by conducting a background check. Generally speaking, an employment background check may include the following checks and verifications:

- Education
- Work history
- Citizenship
- Criminal record
- Credit and financial history
- References

In addition to the previous list, candidate screening may include drug testing and/or further investigation for highly sensitive roles, or positions requiring a special security clearance (this is especially relevant for employment with a government agency). As a CISSP, you should ensure that your organization has policies and procedures in place to screen and hire candidates in accordance with any relevant regulations in your jurisdiction.

NOTE   While background investigations used to be strictly handled by organizations specifically created to conduct them, many employers have added online background screening to their standard procedures. In these circumstances, an employer may choose to research a potential candidate's social media and online presence to gain a fuller picture of that person's attitude, intelligence, professionalism, and general character. Organizations should have clear policies that define the appropriate uses of internet and social media research, standardize which information is to be taken from the social media sites, verify the accuracy of the information, and disclose to applicants the potential use of internet and social media in deciding which applicants to consider.

Employment Agreements and Policies

When joining an organization, an employee generally signs an employment contract that may include one or more employee agreements that make certain stipulations by which the employee must abide. The most common employee agreements are nondisclosure agreements and noncompete agreements.

A *nondisclosure agreement* (NDA) is an agreement that restricts an employee or contractor (or anyone else with access to sensitive information) from disclosing sensitive information they obtain through the course of their employment or relationship with an organization. An NDA is designed to protect the confidentiality of the organization's data (such as trade secrets or customer information) and is often a lifetime agreement (even after the employee leaves the company).

A *noncompete agreement* is an agreement that restricts an employee from directly competing with the organization during their employment and, in most cases, for a fixed time after employment. Noncompetes are one-way agreements that are designed to protect organizations from unfair competition by former employees or contractors. As an example, if you are hired as a hardware engineer for a mobile phone designer, you may be required to sign a noncompete stating that you will not work for other companies that design mobile phones for at least 18 months after termination of your employment; the idea here is that your inside knowledge of the company will present less of a disadvantage after those 18 months.

In addition to NDAs and noncompete agreements, employees may be responsible for reviewing and/or signing various employment policies such as acceptable use policies, code of conduct, or conflict of interest policies.

Onboarding, Transfers, and Termination Processes

Onboarding, transfers, and termination are three stages of employment that each comes with its own security considerations. The processes that bring people into an organization set the tone for their work behavior. Similarly, employee termination processes should clarify people's obligation to respect the protection of the organization's intellectual property and data security as they leave the company. As a security professional, you should be actively engaged with the business to ensure that onboarding, transfer, and termination processes are clearly documented and set behavior expectations during all stages of employment.

Onboarding

Setting good expectations for work behavior should start before the employee walks in the door. Part of the employee orientation program should address information security expectations and requirements. Employees should be reminded of their obligations to protect information and current threats to the organization's information assets, particularly if they are likely to be the targets of malicious actors. Further, orientation practices should inform new employees of the processes for reporting security incidents, their role in maintaining the security of their work area, and the company's classification and categorization processes so they can identify the level of control necessary for particular information.

Employees should also be made generally aware of the existence of controls that monitor their use of the organization's assets. Not only does this provide them with assurance that the organization does indeed take action to protect its information, but the information alone may act as a deterrent to inappropriate behavior. The intent is not to provide the employee with sufficient technical detail to defeat the controls, but to make sure they understand that their actions may be scrutinized.

Transfers

Organizations should have well-defined policies and procedures for handling an employee transferring from one role to another. Part of this process should involve reviewing the employee's existing access to information and evaluating the need for continued access to the same information. Where possible, your organization should seek to remove access that will no longer be needed in the employee's new role; this enforces the principle least privilege, which we discussed earlier in this chapter. In addition, you should have a process in place to identify any role-based training that the employee needs to take prior to the transfer; this is particularly critical when the employee's new role comes with new responsibilities or access to information at a higher sensitivity.

Termination

Taking appropriate care when people depart an organization is just as important as ensuring they are properly brought into the organization. Terminations may be voluntary (i.e., an employee retires or finds a new job) or involuntary (i.e., an employee is fired, furloughed, or otherwise "let go"). These former insiders represent a risk to the organization, and appropriate actions must be taken to ensure they do not compromise the operations, intellectual property, or sensitive information with which they have been entrusted.

When an individual leaves an organization on good terms, it is relatively easy to go through the standard checklist: suspending electronic access, recovering their access badges and equipment, accounting for their keys, and changing the key codes on cipher locks that the departing employee used are among many other standard practices. Most organizations have well-structured off-boarding processes to ensure the removal of access when an individual is no longer entitled to organizational information or resources.

Involuntary termination of employment is an emotionally charged event for all involved. In virtually all cases, an involuntary termination forces the employer to assume the terminated individual is a threat to the organization, and appropriate action should be taken to protect organizational assets. Termination procedures at most organizations include specific processes to notify the information security organization to disable access to electronic and physical systems.

Where possible, recovery of property that an involuntarily terminated employee used should be attempted. Where appropriate, the recovered material should be tracked as evidence and retained for subsequent forensic analysis. Finally, once the individual has left the organization, remaining staff should be informed that the terminated individual is no longer allowed access and that any attempts by that individual to access resources or property should be reported.

TIP It is not unusual for individuals to have taken steps to harm the organization in the event that they were terminated. The most obvious forms of this are the theft of data by the terminated individual, who hopes to sell back the key to the organization (i.e., ransomware), use the information to begin or join a competing organization, or disclose the information to discredit the organization. Strong data security practices and a well-developed insider threat program are essential in defeating malicious activities by terminated employees. User and Entity Behavior Analytics (UEBA), for example, can help detect a disgruntled employee who is heading toward a rage quit.

Vendor, Consultant, and Contractor Agreements and Controls

Many organizations require expertise or talent that does not exist inside their organizations. These relationships may exist for goods or services, but both types of acquisition open the organization to risk. Information security policies should be in place to ensure that these relationships do not expose the organization's sensitive information to an unreasonable amount of risk. NDAs and other employment agreement policies play a big part in establishing expectations with third parties and can lead to additional compliance burden on the organization who must enforce them.

Compliance Policy Requirements

Responsibilities for compliance with applicable policies and regulations should be clearly documented and understood by all employees within an organization. In many cases, employees may be required to sign an attestation stating that they have reviewed and agree to comply with all company policies and applicable regulations.

Employees and other parties with access to systems and information must undergo initial and periodic training that includes security awareness and job-based training. Generally, annual recertification is a good way to ensure that all parties with access remain in compliance with employment policies.

Privacy Policy Requirements

Your organization's *privacy policy* is an explanation of your company's personal data collection and use practices. Privacy policies should link back to applicable privacy laws and regulations, such as HIPAA in the United States and GDPR (discussed later in this chapter) for companies that handle EU residents' information.

Your privacy policy should explain what kind of personal data is collected, how your organization will or won't use it, and how the personal data will be stored, maintained, and secured. The privacy policy should be made available to all personnel, and many organizations require a signed acknowledgment from each employee.

UNDERSTAND AND APPLY RISK MANAGEMENT CONCEPTS

The topic of risk management, and all the concepts within it, is at the heart of information security and is the core of every strong information security program. *Risk management* includes all the processes associated with identifying threats and vulnerabilities and quantifying and addressing the risk associated with those threats and vulnerabilities. Risk management processes provide a structured method for making security decisions such as purchasing and implementing security tools and hiring people. This section covers the key concepts behind risk management and guides you through applying these concepts in your organization.

Identify Threats and Vulnerabilities

In security, a *risk* is the potential for negative impact on the organization, its goals or objectives, or its assets (including people, systems, and data) due to a threat exploiting a vulnerability. You should note that there are dozens of definitions for each of these terms (i.e., risk, threat, and vulnerability) across different industries. We'll discuss these terms further, but it's important to understand that risk lies at the intersection of the three components shown in Figure 1.5.

NOTE   There are two classifications of risk that you should be familiar with: inherent risk and residual risk. Simply put, *inherent risk* is the risk present *before* any controls are applied, while *residual risk* is the level of risk that remains *after* controls are in place. The concept of security controls is discussed later in this chapter.

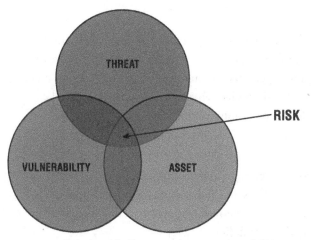

FIGURE 1.5 **Relationship between threats, vulnerabilities, assets, and risks**

Threats

A *threat* is a negative event that can lead to an undesired outcome, such as damage to, or loss of, an asset. A threat is posed by a *threat actor*, which is a person or entity that is capable of intentionally or accidentally compromising an asset's security. As security professionals, threats are the people and events that we work to protect our information and systems from.

Examples of security threats include the following:

- A hacker who wants to encrypt your data and charge you a ransom for it

- A disgruntled employee who wants to steal or sell corporate information

- A fire or other natural disaster that may damage or destroy your datacenter

Vulnerabilities

A *vulnerability* is a weakness or gap that exists within a system that may be exploited (by a threat actor) to compromise an asset's security or trigger a risk event. Vulnerabilities are the things within our systems that we try to fortify and improve.

Examples of security vulnerabilities include the following:

- Unpatched software applications

- Weak access control mechanisms (e.g., weak passwords)

- Faulty fire suppression systems

Assets

An *asset* is anything of value, which may include people, property, and information. Assets are the things that we, as security professionals, are trying to protect. People assets may include your company's employees, contractors, and vendors, as well as your customers. Property assets include tangible things like servers and equipment, as well as intangible things like software code and other intellectual property.

Risk Assessment

Remember that risks are the intersection between threats, vulnerabilities, and assets, as shown in Figure 1.5. A *risk assessment* is the set of activities that involve identifying the threats and vulnerabilities that exist and determining the impact and likelihood of those threats exploiting the identified vulnerabilities.

There are numerous risk frameworks (as discussed in the "Risk Frameworks" section) that provide guidance on conducting risk assessments, but generally speaking, risk assessments include the steps shown in Figure 1.6.

FIGURE 1.6 **Steps for assessing risk**

NOTE The NIST CSF and other modern risk frameworks are recognizing the need for the small to medium business (SMB) community to start with the first risk they identify and manage it, rather than going through the stepwise cycle in Figure 1.6. It's important that you consider your organization's resources and identify a risk management process that works for you.

Risk Identification

The first step in a typical risk assessment process is to identify your assets and determine the value of those assets; this includes identifying and classifying your sensitive data, based on its sensitivity or value to your organization. During the risk identification phase, you find the systems, applications, and information that need protecting and then identify and describe the vulnerabilities and threats that pose a risk to each of those assets.

Risk Analysis

Risk analysis should always begin with a vulnerability assessment (discussed in Chapter 6, "Security Assessment and Testing") and a threat analysis (discussed in the section

"Understand and Apply Threat Modeling Concepts and Methodologies" later in this chapter). This stage of risk assessment is focused on evaluating the likelihood of identified threats exploiting weaknesses (i.e., vulnerabilities) in your environment and determining the impact to your assets if that happens. *Likelihood* describes the probability that an event will occur, and *impact* defines how disastrous the event would be if it were to happen.

Likelihood can be identified by evaluating each threat and assessing the probability that the threats might actually exploit a vulnerability, or weakness. For example, you might determine that the risk associated with a destructive fire is relatively low if you have redundant fire suppression systems that are tested monthly; if you have mechanisms in place to detect and extinguish fires and if you are testing those mechanisms regularly, then the likelihood, or probability, of a fire destroying everything is reduced. Similarly, you might identify insider threat as high likelihood if you've contracted with a large organization without conducting thorough background checks — in this situation, there is a greater probability that something bad will happen.

Impact can be identified by establishing the value associated with each potentially affected asset and determining how that value will be destroyed or otherwise affected by an adverse event. An asset's value can be both *quantitative* (i.e., determined by its cost or market value) or *qualitative* (i.e., determined by its relative importance to you or your organization). By establishing an asset's value, you can better determine the impact of that asset's security being compromised — this allows informed decision-making when determining how much to spend on safeguarding a given resource, as you never want to spend more protecting an asset than the asset itself is worth.

✔ Quantitative Risk Calculation

Risk analysis can be either qualitative or quantitative (or a combination of the two). *Qualitative risk analysis* avoids the use of numbers and tends to be more subjective. *Quantitative risk analysis* is far more precise and objective, because it uses verifiable data to analyze the impact and likelihood of each risk. Quantitative risk calculation involves making measurements to mathematically determine probability (likelihood) and impact. Qualitative risk analysis involves assigning less precise values (like critical, high, medium, and low) to likelihood and impact.

While some risks can be hard to quantify, keep in mind that qualitative analysis can often be vague, imprecise, and even misleading. For example, pandemics were a pretty "low" probability of occurrence prior to 2019, but COVID-19 demonstrated that the overall risk associated with pandemics could be very high.

One important concept in quantitative risk analysis is *annualized loss expectancy* (ALE), which is a metric that helps quantify the impact of a realized threat on your organization's assets. ALE is measured in dollars and is the product of single loss expectancy (SLE) and annual rate of occurrence (ARO), which are each discussed here:

- SLE is a measure of the monetary loss (calculated in dollars) you would expect from a single adverse event. In other words, SLE estimates how much you would lose from one occurrence of a particular realized threat. SLE is calculated by multiplying an asset's value (AV) by its exposure factor (EF). EF is the estimated percentage of loss to a specific asset if a specific threat is realized.

- ARO is the estimated annual frequency of occurrence for a given adverse event. In other words, ARO is the number of times that you expect a particular risk event to occur every year.

Here are the two formulas to keep in mind:

$$ALE = SLE \times ARO$$

$$SLE = AV \times EF$$

Risk Evaluation

During risk evaluation, you compare the results of your risk analysis to your organization's established risk profile or risk tolerance (i.e., how much risk your organization is willing to take on). In doing so, you are able to determine the best course of action for each of your identified risks. We cover the various options for risk response in the following section.

Risk Response/Treatment

Once you identify and assess your organization's threats, vulnerabilities, and risks, you must determine the best way to address each risk; this is known as *risk treatment* (or *risk response*). There are four main categories of risk treatment, as we describe in the following sections: avoid, mitigate, transfer, and accept. Each of these are ultimately leadership/management decisions that should have CISSP input and awareness.

Avoid

Risk avoidance involves eliminating an identified risk by stopping or removing the activity or technology that causes the risk in the first place. Organizations use risk avoidance when a particular risk exceeds their acceptable risk tolerance, but complete avoidance is often difficult to achieve without business disruption. While this type of risk treatment can often mean simply not doing something, policies that ban the use of removable media or personal cloud storage services are avoidance steps that require upfront investment and action.

Mitigate

Risk mitigation (sometimes called *risk reduction* or *risk modification*) is a strategy that involves reducing the likelihood of a threat being realized or lessening the impact that the realized threat would have on the organization. Risk mitigation is the most common treatment option for identified risks and involves implementing policies and technologies to reduce the harm that a risk might cause. Moving from single-factor to mutifactor authentication is an example of a mitigation treatment for sensitive data access.

Transfer

Risk transference (also known as *risk assignment*) involves shifting the responsibility and potential loss associated with a risk onto a third party. Insurance is the most common form of risk transference. For example, if a company loses customer data due to a cyber breach, the company may rely on their cyber insurance to cover any monetary losses associated with the breach. In this case, the breached organization has transferred financial risk to their cyber insurer, but the company still must manage through some level of reputational risk. It's hard to completely transfer *all* risk, so many people instead use the term *risk sharing*. Using cloud-based services or managed security services is a great example, because risk is split between you, as the customer, and the third-party provider.

Accept

Risk acceptance unsurprisingly involves accepting the risk associated with a particular threat. Risk acceptance is the way to go if avoiding, mitigating, or transferring the risk would cost more than the expected losses of the realized threat. In theory, a risk should be accepted only if it is completely within an organization's risk tolerance. In practice, organizations are often forced to accept potentially painful risks associated with normal business operations.

Countermeasure Selection and Implementation

Mitigation is the most common risk treatment method of the four treatment approaches in the previous section. Risk mitigation involves the selection and implementation of one or more countermeasures (or "security controls") with the goal of reducing the likelihood of an adverse event or the impact of that event occurring. Countermeasures generally fall into three categories:

- **Personnel-related:** As people are commonly considered to be an organization's "weakest link," these countermeasures often prove invaluable. Hiring (or firing), organization restructuring, and awareness training are some common personnel-related countermeasures. Despite our potential as weaknesses, people in high-performing organizations with strong security awareness programs can often prove to be the greatest security asset.

- **Process-related:** Policy, procedure, and other "workflow-based" mitigations generally fall into this category. As an example, consider the implementation of separation of duties on invoice approval and payment as a process-related mitigation against cyber fraud.

- **Technology-related:** This is the category that typically gets the most attention. Encryption, modifying configuration settings, and other hardware or software changes are common examples of technology-related countermeasures.

When selecting countermeasures, you must consider factors such as security-effectiveness, cost-effectiveness, and operational impact.

Security-Effectiveness

Measuring the security-effectiveness of a security control is an essential step in the selection and implementation process. When selecting your countermeasures, you want to be certain that the specific policy, technology, or operational control that you select is able to directly address a risk identified during your risk analysis process. To do this, one must consider what kind of security risks one wants to prevent, detect, or correct, and then identify countermeasures that specifically target those risks. For example, many security teams choose to throw encryption at everything, but if you are concerned with risks that encryption cannot fix (like availability risks), you are better off using those resources for other countermeasures (such as backups).

Cost-Effectiveness

Perhaps even more important than security-effectiveness (believe it or not), cost-effectiveness is a primary consideration for security teams and the management teams that oversee them. Cost-effectiveness can be calculated by performing a cost-benefit analysis that compares the cost of a countermeasure (or multiple countermeasures) to the costs that would be realized by a compromise of the risks that the countermeasures are intended to mitigate.

A countermeasure can be considered cost-effective if the annual loss expectancy (ALE) *with* the countermeasure plus the cost of countermeasure is less than ALE *without* the countermeasure. For example, if the ALE associated with theft of sensitive data is $500,000, you can theoretically spend up to $499,999.99 on countermeasures to reduce the ALE of such data theft to $0.01. Of course, you'd want to gain more than a single penny from all your troubles, but this demonstrates the point. Another way to look at it is if the ALE due to ransomware attacks on your company is projected at $200,000 and you spend $50,000 on a sophisticated backup system, the selected countermeasure has a value of $150,000 to your organization, which is quite clearly cost-effective.

> **NOTE** Countermeasures generally have an initial acquisition and implementation cost, followed by recurring (e.g., annual) operating and maintenance costs. You should consider both sets of costs when determining whether a countermeasure makes financial sense for your organization.

Operational Impact

Beyond cost-effectiveness and pure security-effectiveness, you must be sure to evaluate the potential operational impact that a countermeasure may have on your organization. If a countermeasure is too difficult to implement or use, it may have a counterintuitive effect and actually increase risk because it is not being used properly (or at all). For example, some organizations require the use of third-party email encryption platforms to send sensitive information, and some of these platforms are not user friendly at all. Without careful selection of a platform and proper user training, some users may circumvent this countermeasure and send sensitive emails in the clear. Understanding your organization's culture and strategy is an important part of selecting countermeasures that don't have a negative operational impact.

Applicable Types of Controls

A *security control* is any safeguard that is put in place to positively impact security. Security controls may be automatic or manual, and they can be technical (i.e., implemented and executed through hardware, software, or firmware), operational (i.e., related to day-to-day operations and tangible things like security guards, gates, etc.), or management (i.e., implemented by people and related to administrative methods — things like policies, procedures, and guidelines). There are five major types of controls, and you'll notice that some countermeasures (like security guards) may fit into multiple categories:

- **Preventative:** These are the first-line controls that are designed to keep adverse security events from occurring. For example, software applications typically have some form of "input validation" to avoid invalid inputs from being executed and causing an issue. Firewalls, system backups, and security awareness training are other common examples of preventative controls.

- **Detective:** These controls are designed to identify a negative security event while it is in progress or soon after it occurs. Much like a human detective, this type of control is intended to gather information and help security teams determine what happened, how bad the damage is, and what caused it to happen. Security audits, door alarms, and IDSs are common examples of detective controls.

- **Corrective:** These controls are designed to minimize and repair damages following an adverse security event; they are typically put in place after a detective control identifies a problem. Corrective controls include things such as software patches, configuration file modifications, and new policies that target the cause of the incident.

- **Recovery:** These countermeasures are designed to complement corrective controls, with the intent to get a system back to normal as quickly as possible. Examples include system and data backups and disaster recovery sites.

- **Deterrent:** These controls are designed to discourage attackers by making them think twice about their malicious intents. Wired fences, security guards, and guard dogs are some examples of deterrents.

TIP You should also be familiar with the concept of a *compensating control*, which is a safeguard used in addition to or in place of a primary control; compensating controls are often implemented if a primary control cannot be fully implemented for some reason. For example, if a technical security control is too expensive, you may opt for policies that *encourage* rather than *enforce* a desired behavior. The compensating control may not fully mitigate the risk, but it provides some level of security that wouldn't exist without any control being implemented. PCI-DSS provides some good examples of compensating controls usage.

Control Assessments

Periodic assessment of your security controls is equally as important as the selection and implementation of those controls. In many cases, your organization may have legal or regulatory requirements that dictate how and when to conduct security control assessments (SCA), but in all cases, you should routinely conduct control assessments to ensure that your security and privacy controls remain effective.

SCAs may take the form of self-assessments or external assessments conducted by third parties. There are many different SCA methodologies, but they generally include some form of the following assessment methods: examine, interview, and test. NIST 800-53A, "Assessing Security and Privacy Controls in Federal Information Systems and Organizations," lays out some helpful guidelines for conducting controls assessments and describes the three assessment methods as follows:

- **Examine:** This method is "the process of reviewing, inspecting, observing, studying, or analyzing one or more assessment objects (i.e., specifications, mechanisms, or activities). The purpose of the examine method is to facilitate assessor understanding, achieve clarification, or obtain evidence." Assessors often begin an SCA by requesting a list of artifacts or evidence (such as security policies, configuration files, etc.) that they can examine to form an initial perspective.

- **Interview:** This method is "the process of holding discussions with individuals or groups of individuals within an organization to once again, facilitate assessor understanding, achieve clarification, or obtain evidence." After reviewing any evidence provided during the examine phase, assessors meet with key stakeholders to gain additional clarity on what security controls are in place and how they work.

- **Test:** This method is "the process of exercising one or more assessment objects (i.e., activities or mechanisms) under specified conditions to compare actual with expected behavior." In this stage, an auditor or assessor is seeking to confirm that security controls are implemented as they are documented and that they are operating effectively and as intended.

Chapter 6 covers security assessment extensively.

Monitoring and Measurement

Monitoring and measurement of your controls is an important part of operating a risk-based security program. In addition to conducting periodic (e.g., annual or quarterly) security and privacy control assessments, you should actively and intentionally monitor your controls to measure their effectiveness and assess the health of your overall security program. Depending on your organization's needs, you should develop a set of key performance indicators (KPIs) that allow you to quantify and measure the long-term performance of your controls.

Reporting

Conducting SCAs and other monitoring and measurement activities is useless without a well-managed reporting function. Auditors and assessors generally create formal reports that detail their findings for each control that is assessed. In addition, your security team should have a process to document and report any important discoveries or metrics to senior leadership, regulators, and other stakeholders.

Some laws, regulations, and industry requirements come with specific reporting guidelines; as an information security leader, you must be familiar with any such requirements that are relevant to your organization. In general, a well-managed risk-based security program includes some level of reporting for the following:

- Internal audits (e.g., self-assessments)
- External audits (i.e., regulator or any other third-party audits)
- Significant changes to the organization's risk posture
- Significant changes to security or privacy controls
- Suspected or confirmed security breaches (or other incidents)

Continuous Improvement

A common goal among security leaders is to continuously improve their organization's security posture and measure their journey toward their desired end state. As a CISSP, you need to continuously identify whether your organization is improving its management of information security risks. You should also seek to continuously improve the return on investment (ROI) associated with the security tools, controls, and processes that your organization implements. There is a fine line between "not secure enough" and "perhaps too many security tools and processes." As a CISSP, you should seek to continuously improve the efficiency of your organization's security management program.

Risk maturity modeling is a process that allows an organization to assess the strength of its security program and create a plan for continuous improvement based on their results. By identifying the maturity of its program on a predefined scale, an organization may better focus on what types of behaviors are necessary to improve, rather than getting caught up strictly in individual security gaps. Maturity models are discussed further in Chapter 8.

Risk Frameworks

A *risk framework* is a structured process for identifying, assessing, and managing an organization's risks. A number of frameworks have been developed to identify and evaluate risk. These frameworks have evolved to address the unique needs of different industries and regulations. Individually, these frameworks address assessment, control, monitoring, and audit of information systems in different ways, but all strive to provide internal controls to bring risk to an acceptable level. While there are several internationally accepted risk frameworks, a number of industry-specific frameworks have also been developed to meet specific needs.

Regardless of the framework, to effectively address risk in an organization, standard processes to evaluate the risks of operation of information systems must take into account the changing threat environment, the potential and actual vulnerabilities of systems, the likelihood that the risk will occur, and the impact to the organization should that risk become realized.

From a governance perspective, the selection of a framework should create a controls environment that is as follows:

- **Consistent:** A governance program must be consistent in how information security and privacy are approached and applied.

- **Measurable:** The governance program must provide a way to determine progress and set goals. Most control frameworks contain an assessment standard or procedure to determine compliance and, in some cases, risk as well.

- **Standardized:** As with measurable, a controls framework should rely on standardization so results from one organization or part of an organization can be compared in a meaningful way to results from another organization.

- **Comprehensive:** The selected framework should cover the minimum legal and regulatory requirements of an organization and be extensible to accommodate additional organization-specific requirements.

- **Modular:** A modular framework is more likely to withstand the changes of an organization, as only the controls or requirements needing modification are reviewed and updated.

There are dozens of different risk management frameworks. While many of the frameworks address specific industry or organizational requirements, you should be aware of the broad characteristics of the more common frameworks.

International Standards Organization

The International Standards Organization has developed the ISO 31000 series of standards to identify principles for general risk management and to provide a set of guidelines for implementation. Developed using the consistent language contained in ISO/IEC Guide 73:2009, the ISO 31000:2018 is intended to be applicable to any organization, regardless of the governance structure or industry. The standard encourages the integration of risk management activities across organizational lines and levels to provide the organization with a consistent approach to management of operational and strategic risks.

ISO 31000:2018 is based on a set of eight principles that drive the development of the risk framework shown in Figure 1.7. That framework, in turn, structures the processes for implementing risk management.

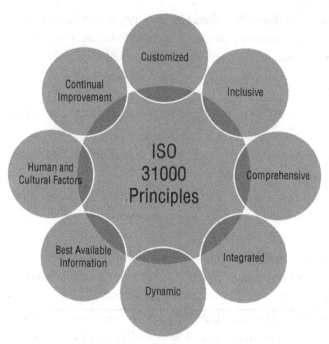

FIGURE 1.7 **ISO 31000:2018**

The eight ISO 31000 principles are described here:

- **Customized:** The framework should be customized and proportionate to the organization and the level of risk.

- **Inclusive:** The appropriate and timely involvement of stakeholders is necessary.

- **Comprehensive:** A structured and comprehensive approach is required.

- **Integrated:** Risk management is an integral part of all organizational activities.

- **Dynamic:** Risk management anticipates, detects, acknowledges, and responds to changes in a timely fashion.

- **Best available information:** Risk management explicitly considers any limitations of available information.

- **Human and cultural factors:** Human and cultural factors influence all aspects of risk management.

- **Continual improvement:** Risk management is continually improved through learning and experience.

To assist organizations in implementing the ISO 31000 standard, ISO 31004, "Risk Management — Guidance for the implementation of ISO 31000," was published to provide a structured approach to transition their existing risk management practices to be consistent with ISO 31000 and consistent with the individual characteristics and demands of the organization.

While the 31000 series addresses general risk, information security practices are addressed in the ISO 27000 series. The use of the ISO/IEC Guide 73 allows for a common language, but ISO/IEC 27005:2011, "Information technology— Security techniques — Information security risk management," gives detail and structure to the information security risks by defining the context for information security risk decision-making. This context includes definition of the organization's risk tolerance, compliance expectations, and the preferred approaches for assessment and treatment of risk.

ISO 27005 does not directly provide a risk assessment process. Rather, it provides inputs to, and gets outputs from, the risk assessment practice used by the organization. In this framework, the assessment process may be performed in a quantitative or qualitative manner but must be done consistently so that prioritization can be performed. ISO 27005 further emphasizes the need for communication with stakeholders and for processes that continuously monitor for changes in the risk environment.

The ISO standards have seen broad adoption, in part because of the broad international process in the development of the standards. Further, the standards themselves, while constantly under review, connect to other standards managed within the ISO. This enables organizations to adopt those standards that are appropriate for their businesses and provides a more holistic view of an organizations' risk and compliance activities.

U.S. National Institute of Standards and Technology

Through a hierarchy of publications, the National Institute of Standards and Technology provides direction to U.S. government agencies in implementing information security practices. In the current incarnation, the Risk Management Framework (RMF) provides a structured analytical process to identify, control, evaluate, and improve the organization's information security controls. Documented in NIST Special Publication 800-37, "Guide for Applying the Risk Management Framework to Federal Information Systems," it prescribes a six-step process through which the federal government manages the risks of its information systems; the six steps are pictured in Figure 1.8. Though the steps in this framework are tailored to government agencies, they are widely applicable within just about every industry.

The first step of the NIST RMF involves categorizing all information systems based on the potential impact to the organization due to the loss of confidentiality, integrity, or availability. Implied in this process is that the organization must have a comprehensive inventory of systems to apply the categorization standard. Once security categorization has been performed, a baseline set of controls must be selected based on the identified categorization and impact.

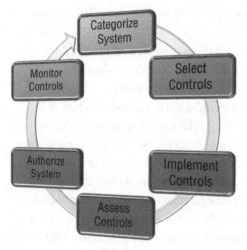

FIGURE 1.8 **NIST Risk Management Framework**

Once the system has been categorized and baseline controls are selected, the controls must be implemented and monitored to ensure that they "are implemented correctly, operating as intended, and producing the desired outcome with respect to meeting the security requirements for the system." This will produce a set of documents certifying the technical application of the controls.

After categorizing information systems, selecting and implementing controls, and assessing the effectiveness of those controls, organizational leadership then makes a formal decision whether to authorize the use of the system. This decision is based on the ability of the controls to operate the system within the organization's risk tolerance. Finally, the organization must continuously monitor the effectiveness of the controls over time to ensure that the ongoing operation of the system occurs within the organization's risk tolerance.

While focused on the computing activities of the U.S. government, the NIST standards and guidelines have had a pervasive effect on the security community because of their broad scope, their availability in the public domain, and the inclusion of industry, academic, and other standards organizations in the development of the standards. Further, the NIST standards often set the expectations for security practice that are placed on other regulated industries. This is most clearly shown in HIPAA legislation, where healthcare organizations must demonstrate that their controls align with the NIST security practice. Due to its broad reference, the NIST RMF is an important part of the CISSP CBK.

TIP NIST 800-30, "Guide for Conducting Risk Assessments," and the NIST Cybersecurity Framework (discussed in the "Security Control Frameworks" section) both provide practical guidance to help the CISSP frame, present, and inform management decisions about risk.

COBIT and RiskIT

In the late 1990s, the audit community in the United States and Canada recognized that there was a significant gap between IT governance and the larger organizational management structures. Consequently, IT activities were often misaligned with corporate goals, and risks were not comprehensively addressed by the control structure or consistently reflected in financial reporting. To address this gap, ISACA developed a framework through which the IT activities of an organization could be assessed.

The Control Objectives for Information and Related Technology framework differentiates processes into either Governance of Enterprise IT (five processes) or Management of Enterprise IT (32 processes). Each process has a set of objectives, inputs, key activities, and outputs, and measures to evaluate performance against the objectives. As the framework is closely aligned with other management frameworks and tools (ISO 20000, ISO 27001, ITIL, Prince 2, SOX, and TOGAF), it has gained wide acceptance as an encompassing framework for managing the delivery of IT.

Based on the ISACA COBIT governance framework, the RiskIT framework provides a structure for the identification, evaluation, and monitoring of information technology risk. This simplifies the integration of IT risk into the larger organization enterprise risk management (ERM) activities.

The RiskIT framework consists of three domains — risk governance, risk evaluation, and risk response — each of which has three processes. The framework then details the key activities within each process and identifies organizational responsibilities, information flows between processes, and process performance management activities. Additional detail on how to implement the framework and link it to other organizational management practices is contained in the RiskIT Practitioner Guide.

UNDERSTAND AND APPLY THREAT MODELING CONCEPTS AND METHODOLOGIES

Threat modeling is a technique by which you can identify potential threats to your systems and applications, as well as identify suitable countermeasures against those threats.

Threats may be related to overall system vulnerabilities or an absence of necessary security controls. Threat modeling is most often used during the application development phase, but you can also use threat modeling to help reduce risk in existing applications and environments.

The *attack surface* is the total range of areas where an attacker can potentially execute a compromise. With an information system, this might include the methods of communication, the access controls, or weaknesses in the underlying architectures. With a physical environment, the attack surface might include the construction techniques, the location, or the means of entrance and egress. Limiting the attack surface to the minimum number of areas of exposure reduces the opportunities for a threat to become a successful attack.

Threat Modeling Concepts

There are three general approaches to threat modeling. Different risk methodologies, compliance frameworks, or systems prefer one or another, but as a CISSP, you should be able to apply all three approaches to a particular environment. These approaches are attacker-centric, asset-centric, and software-centric (or system-centric), which are each covered in the following sections.

Attacker-centric

The attacker-centric threat modeling approach starts by identifying the various actors who could potentially cause harm to a system. With an attacker-centric approach, you start by profiling a potential attacker's characteristics, skillset, and motivation, and then use that profile to identify attackers who would be most likely to execute specific types of attacks. This approach can be helpful when narrowly approaching a problem by limiting the number of scenarios under analysis. Tactical military intelligence is typically driven by an attacker-centric threat model, as are many business continuity/disaster recovery planning processes. If you work in financial services, you may be familiar with attacker-centric modelling from anti-money laundering (AML) and other anti-financial crimes applications. AML processes involve using process models of how money launderers operate when they attack to identify steps to take in order to thwart such attacks.

Asset-centric

As opposed to an attacker-centric approach, an asset-centric threat model identifies the assets of value first. Assets should be characterized by their value to the organization as well as their value to potential attackers. The means by which the asset is managed, manipulated, used, and stored are then evaluated to identify how an attacker might compromise the asset. Many compliance regimes focus on protection of an asset (e.g., PHI under HIPAA, PII under the GDPR, or cardholder data under PCI-DSS), so this approach is helpful when establishing or verifying compliance. You'll also find this approach particularly useful when protecting other high-value assets such as intellectual property and security credentials.

Software-centric (or System-centric)

For many information systems environments, the software- or system-centric model is most useful. In this approach, the system is represented as a set of interconnected processes, using architecture diagrams such as dataflow diagrams (DFDs) or component diagrams. These diagrams are then evaluated by threat analysts to identify potential attacks against each component and to determine whether a security control is necessary, exists, and achieves the control effect.

Threat Modeling Methodologies

There are many different threat modeling methodologies. Some of the most important methodologies are STRIDE, PASTA, NIST 800-154, and DREAD — we discuss each of these in the following sections.

STRIDE

STRIDE is a threat modeling methodology developed by Microsoft in the late 1990s to help identify and classify computer security threats. The name itself is a mnemonic for six categories of security threats, discussed here:

- **Spoofing:** *Spoofing* is an attack during which a malicious party assumes the identity of another party (either a user or a system) by falsifying information. A common example of identity spoofing occurs when email spammers modify the "From:" field to depict the name of a sender that the target recipient is more likely to trust. Within applications, spoofing can occur if an attacker steals and uses a victim's authentication information (like username and password) to impersonate them within the application.

- **Tampering:** *Data tampering* is an attack on the integrity of data by intentionally and maliciously manipulating data. Tampering can include altering data on disk, in memory, over the network, or elsewhere. Applications that don't properly validate user input may allow malicious actors to modify values and have the manipulated data stored and used by the application.

- **Repudiation:** *Repudiation* is the ability of a party to deny that they are responsible for performing an action. The threat of repudiation occurs when a user claims that they did not perform an action, and no other party is able to prove otherwise. In the physical world, signing for a mail delivery is a common form of nonrepudiation — the delivery company maintains a record that you received and accepted the mail on a specific date. In the digital world, an example of a repudiation threat is a user claiming that they did not make an online purchase — even if they did, in fact, make that purchase. Comprehensive logging, digital signatures, and multifactor authentication can be integrated into applications to provide nonrepudiation for high-risk actions.

- **Information disclosure:** *Information disclosure* is when information is shared with an unauthorized party — such as during a data breach or when inadvertently sending an email to the wrong person. This threat compromises the confidentiality of data and carries a great deal of risk depending on the sensitivity of the leaked data. Organizations that store and process PII, PHI, cardholder data, or other confidential information should focus on this threat, and identify controls to mitigate against it. Data encryption, strong access control, and other data protection mechanisms are the keys to protecting against unauthorized information disclosure.

- **Denial of service:** A *denial-of-service* (DoS) attack is a common availability attack that denies access to resources by legitimate users. Controls should be put in place to monitor and detect abnormally high resource consumption by any single user; this may be an indication of either malicious or unintentional resource exhaustion. As a principle, applications should be developed with availability and reliability in mind.

- **Elevation of privilege:** *Elevation of privilege* (or *privilege escalation*) occurs when an unprivileged user is able to upgrade their privileges to those of a privileged user (e.g., a system administrator). Elevation of privilege can give an untrusted party the "keys to the kingdom" and grant them access to and control over sensitive data and systems. Strong access control is required to help protect against this threat. Systems should revalidate a user's identity and credentials prior to granting privileged access, and multifactor authentication should be used, wherever possible.

PASTA

The *Process for Attack Simulation and Threat Analysis* (PASTA) is a risk-based threat model, developed in 2012, that supports dynamic threat analysis. The PASTA methodology integrates business objectives with technical requirements, making the output more easily understood by upper management.

There are seven stages of the PASTA methodology:

- Define objectives
- Define technical scope
- Application decomposition
- Threat analysis
- Vulnerability analysis
- Attack enumeration
- Risk and impact analysis

NIST 800-154

NIST 800-154, "Guide to Data-Centric System Threat Modeling," was released in draft form in 2016. It explicitly rejects that best-practice approaches are sufficient to protect sensitive information, as best practice is too general and often overlooks controls specifically tailored to meet the protection of the sensitive asset. NIST 800-154 establishes four major steps for data-centric system threat modeling:

1. Identify and characterize the system and data of interest.
2. Identify and select the attack vectors to be included in the model.
3. Characterize the security controls for mitigating the attack vectors.
4. Analyze the threat model.

DREAD

DREAD is an older threat modeling technique, previously used by Microsoft but later abandoned. DREAD provides a mnemonic for quantitative risk rating security threats using five categories:

- **D**amage
- **R**eproducibility
- **E**xploitability
- **A**ffected users
- **D**iscoverability

Though it is sparsely used today, you should be familiar with the DREAD mnemonic and the categories that it represents.

Other Models

Other threat modeling methodologies include the following:

- Operationally Critical Threat, Asset, and Vulnerability Evaluation (OCTAVE) is an approach for managing information security risks, developed at the Software Engineering Institute (SEI).

- Trike is an open-source threat modeling approach and tool that focuses on using threat models as a risk management tool.

- Construct a platform for Risk Analysis of Security Critical Systems (CORAS), also open source, is a European project that relies heavily on Unified Modeling Language (UML) as the front end for visualizing the threats.

- Visual, Agile, and Simple Threat Modeling (VAST) is a proprietary approach that leverages Agile concepts.

Implementing a structured threat modeling program allows an organization to consistently identify and characterize the threats it faces and then apply appropriate control to the risks associated with those threats.

APPLY SUPPLY CHAIN RISK MANAGEMENT CONCEPTS

The interconnected nature of today's information systems places a high degree of reliance on the confidentiality, integrity, and availability of systems from multiple vendors spread across the globe. This ecosystem has been shown to be vulnerable to both accidental and intentional disruption and compromise. Securing your organization's assets requires that you evaluate the security risk of your entire supply chain and that you apply appropriate controls to manage that risk.

Risks Associated with Hardware, Software, and Services

Any time an organization considers using third-party hardware, software, or services, the organization must determine how the new hardware, software, or services may fit into the organization's existing environment, and evaluate how the additions may impact the organization's overall security posture. For example, if your organization considers using a public cloud provider, there may be compliance risks if the CSP stores data outside of your country, or other security risks if the CSP does not meet data security requirements that you are legally or contractually required to meet.

✔ Malicious Code in the Supply Chain

The widespread use of proprietary commercial off-the-shelf (COTS) software requires customers to trust the security practices of the vendors. However, many instances have been documented where that trust has been abused, and the COTS vendors become a vehicle to introduce vulnerabilities or compromise the CIA aspects of the customers' data.

This method has become increasingly popular for malware authors precisely because the updates are from a trusted source. In 2017, the developer of the antivirus product CCleaner distributed a routine update to its users that contained a remote-access Trojan. As the malicious software had been inserted into the code before it was signed, the entire update package was seen by most users as a legitimate update. More than 2 billion downloads of the compromised software were reported.

✔ SolarWinds and the SUNBURST Attack

One of the largest supply chain attacks in history became public in 2020 when FireEye disclosed a global attack, now known as the SUNBURST attack. SUNBURST is a vulnerability within the SolarWinds Orion Platform, which, if present and activated, allows an attacker to compromise the server on which the Orion product is running.

This widespread attack is particularly concerning because it impacted a SolarWinds product that is used for IT monitoring and management. What should be used to keep an eye on IT infrastructures ironically became the instrument of harm to those infrastructures.

With the SolarWinds Orion product being used by companies around the globe, large and small, this is a devasting example of how important supply chain management is. The victims of the SUNBURST attack include sophisticated tech companies, like Microsoft and Intel, numerous U.S. government agencies, and even the top-tier cybersecurity firm, FireEye (who initially disclosed the breach). In all, SolarWinds estimates that approximately 18,000 firms were affected around the world.

Third-Party Assessment and Monitoring

To minimize supply chain risk, appropriate controls must be applied to verify the security practices of all involved parties. In most cases, controls have been identified that would address security risks; the toughest challenge is to ensure that third parties actually do what they should to protect your organization's information from those risks.

Any organization that does business with contractors, vendors, or any other third parties should have a third-party risk management policy that establishes a third-party risk management program responsible for assessing, monitoring, and controlling risks associated with outsourcing to third parties. Governance and oversight activities should include onsite security surveys, formal security audits of third-party systems, and penetration testing, where feasible. Any new third party should be assessed against your organization's security requirements, and gaps should be documented and closely monitored. Further, vendors and other third parties should be regularly reassessed and continuously monitored to ensure that they continue to adequately protect your organization's information. We cover audits, audit standards, and other related concepts in detail in Chapter 6.

Minimum Security Requirements

Similar to baselines and standards (discussed earlier in this chapter), your organization should establish minimum security requirements (MSRs) that define the least acceptable security standards that vendors and other parties in your supply chain must satisfy. Of course, you should strive to ensure that your third parties have the strongest possible security postures, but MSRs, as the name suggests, describe the lowest level of security that your organization is willing to accept from a third party. To avoid issues, your MSRs should take into consideration any legal, contractual, or regulatory requirements that you are required to satisfy; you should not establish an MSR that is below any external security compliance requirement. You must also be prepared to audit and assess third parties' compliance with any MSRs that you have established and communicated.

Service-Level Requirements

A *service-level agreement* (SLA) is a contractual agreement between a service provider and its customers that establishes the minimum performance standards that the provider is obligated to meet. When dealing with vendors and other third parties, SLAs serve as documented and agreed-upon performance requirements that a customer can use to hold the third party accountable. For example, you may have an SLA with a public cloud provider that commits to a certain level of system uptime and availability. In the event of a sustained outage of the cloud service, you may be entitled to financial compensation or the right to terminate services with no penalty.

Frameworks

Several frameworks explicitly address supply chain risks. This is an evolving area of risk management, but the complexities of managing the information systems supply chain have been evident for many years.

NIST IR 7622

The U.S. government began directly addressing cyber supply chain risk as a separate issue with the publication of NIST IR 7622, "Notional Supply Chain Risk Management Practices for Federal Information Systems." This work recognizes that the actions required of the entities in the supply chain will change depending on their role, as will the level and type of control to be applied. The document identifies 10 practices that should be taken into account in addressing supply chain risk:

- Uniquely identify supply chain elements, processes, and actors.
- Limit access and exposure within the supply chain.
- Establish and maintain the provenance of elements, processes, tools, and data.
- Share information within strict limits.
- Perform supply chain risk management awareness and training.
- Use defensive design for systems, elements, and processes.
- Perform continuous integrator review.
- Strengthen delivery mechanisms.
- Assure sustainment activities and processes.
- Manage disposal and final disposition activities throughout the system or element lifecycle.

The U.S. government has a number of other supply chain risk management initiatives, including the Committee on National Security Systems Directive 505, "Supply Chain Risk Management," which specifically addresses security requirements for strategic national systems and the Comprehensive National Cybersecurity Initiative Number 11, which provides a set of tools to agencies to manage their cybersecurity supply chain through a risk-driven approach.

ISO 28000

ISO 28000:2007, "Specification for security management systems for the supply chain," provides a broad framework for managing supply chain risk. While not specific to cybersecurity, ISO 28000 is useful for organizations that leverage other ISO specifications (such as ISO 9001 and ISO 27001) to align supply chain risk with the organizations' audit processes or that seek to use a standardized, risk-based approach to evaluating supply chain risk.

ISO 28000:2007 relies heavily on the continuous process improvement model of plan, do, check, act (PDCA) to improve the security management system and to assure organizational conformance to the security practice. This approach facilitates the integration of supply chain risk with broader organizational risk management activities.

U.K. National Cyber Security Centre

The U.K. National Cyber Security Centre (NCSC) proposed guidance that attempts to provide organizations with improved awareness of supply chain risks, while also establishing 12 principles intended to help organizations establish and maintain effective control of their supply chain. The 12 supply chain principles are divided into these separate stages:

1. **Understand the risks:** The principles in this stage involve identifying your vendors in your supply chain and establishing what needs to be protected in that supply chain (and why).

2. **Establish control:** This stage involves establishing minimum security requirements (see the earlier section "Minimum Security Requirements") and communicating your security expectations to your suppliers.

3. **Check your arrangements:** This stage involves establishing assurance activities and building those into your supply chain processes. This includes establishing audit rights, key performance indicators, and other testing/validation activities.

4. **Continuous improvement:** This stage involves continually building trust with your suppliers and constantly encouraging security improvements for your supply chain.

ESTABLISH AND MAINTAIN A SECURITY AWARENESS, EDUCATION, AND TRAINING PROGRAM

No matter how many security tools you have in your arsenal, your organization's security is only as strong as its weakest link — and that tends to be your personnel. Information security is one of the few fields that is governed by relatively small teams but is the responsibility of every person within an organization. As such, all personnel within an organization need to be trained and made aware of security threats and attacker techniques so that they know what to look for and how to avoid common pitfalls that can compromise your organization's information security.

Methods and Techniques to Present Awareness and Training

A *security awareness program* is a formal program that includes processes to train users of the potential threats to an organization's information and systems, as well as educates those users on how to handle such threats. A standard security awareness program should include, at a minimum, new user orientation, lectures or computer-based trainings (CBTs), and printed materials like posters and handouts that share security tips. In addition, organizations can use phishing and other social engineering exercises, security champions, and gamification to help raise awareness of important security topics; each of these is discussed in the following sections.

Social Engineering

Social engineering is the practice of human manipulation that involves an attacker pretending to be someone else in an effort to retrieve sensitive data. *Phishing* is the most common form of social engineering, and it relates to social engineering activities that are conducted over email. Phishing is routinely at the top of the most common security concerns because it can evade many of your most sophisticated security tools and compromise an organization's weakest link — its people.

Simulated phishing campaigns are a popular component of security awareness programs. You should first start by educating your employees on why phishing is harmful and how to spot it. You should conduct randomized simulated phishing exercises to help reinforce the employee training and to help you understand where your risks are (i.e., which types of phishing are most successful on your employees and which employees need further training). Employees who click on a simulated phishing link should be notified and subject to further training that reminds them of how to identify and report signs of phishing.

Security Champions

A *security champion* is a liaison between an organization's security team and the rest of the company; they are tasked with raising security awareness within the organization. In this role, a security champion is an advocate of security best practices for employees who don't work on security as their primary job. The role of security champion was initially created to raise awareness of application security on software development teams, but nowadays, organizations may frequently choose to assign a security champion to any (or all) nonsecurity teams.

Gamification

Gamification is the use of game techniques in nongame applications to engage and educate an audience. In security awareness, gamification can provide a fun and engaging way to educate employees and promote strong security practices. Games like this allow companies to educate their employees on critical information security concepts in an interesting and engaging manner.

Periodic Content Reviews

Information security is a constantly evolving field, with security threats and vulnerabilities that are forever changing. As such, it's important that you regularly review the content within your security awareness, education, and training program to certify that it remains relevant. Content should be reviewed and updated annually, at a minimum, to ensure that there is no reference to obsolete or irrelevant technologies or terminology, and these reviews should validate that all security awareness and training materials reflect current security trends, concepts, and concerns that are relevant to your organization and industry. Ideally, security awareness content should be considered "live" material that evolves even more frequently than these periodic reviews. As a CISSP, you should ensure that such security training content includes all the relevant and current information that your organization's employees should know.

Program Effectiveness Evaluation

Conducting security awareness, education, and training activities is not enough; it's equally important to evaluate and measure the effectiveness of your security education activities. Although the effectiveness of your security awareness program may be gleaned through the evaluation of your organization's overall information security posture, a formal evaluation should be conducted to target deficiencies within the awareness program itself.

There are several methods by which you can evaluate the effectiveness of your security awareness program. Some examples include the following:

- **Training metrics:** Simple metrics like training completion rates are a great place to start when evaluating the effectiveness of your security awareness program. These types of metrics can tell you whether your training resources are reaching a sufficient percentage of your employees and may alert you if alternate delivery methods are necessary.

- **Quizzes:** This is one of the most effective methods of measuring program effectiveness through knowledge retention. Quizzes are most reliable when measuring the effectiveness of security policies and related information. Analysis of quiz results should be conducted to identify trends that reveal necessary modifications to your training materials; if a substantial number of your employees get the same question wrong, it likely means you need to provide further (or clearer) information about that topic.

- **Security awareness days or weeks:** By sponsoring security awareness days or weeks, you not only have an opportunity to provide security education, but you can also use this as an opportunity to solicit feedback from your employees on the program itself. You can provide attendees with anonymous questionnaires that allow them to express their opinion about the current program and propose new ideas on content delivery.

- **Inherent evaluation:** As previously stated, you can also measure the effectiveness of your awareness program by evaluating your organization's overall security posture. Certain metrics, such as the number of phishing emails and other security issues reported to IT, can provide a great deal of insight into the effectiveness of your program. As your company's employees are increasingly educated on security risks, you should start to see the number of self-reported security issues rise. It's better to see a rise in reported suspected issues than a rise in successful compromises.

SUMMARY

The breadth of information security demands that security professionals possess a wide range of knowledge and skills. You must fully grasp concepts such as confidentiality, integrity, and availability, and understand how to develop, document, and implement security policies, standards, procedures, and guidelines that enforce these concepts. Good security practices must be aligned with an organization's business objectives, strategy, and goals. As a security professional, it's important that you fully understand these business concepts and grasp how you can apply security governance principles to help your organization achieve its mission.

Risk management is at the heart of information security, and every security program should strive to be based on risk management concepts. Identifying threats and vulnerabilities and evaluating security risks is the key to identifying the right security controls to implement in your environment. Controls should be continuously monitored for their effectiveness at reducing risk, and your organization should maintain a program to regularly measure and report on the company's risk posture. There are several industry-standard risk frameworks available to guide your development and management of a risk-based security program.

Legal, regulatory, and compliance requirements play a big role in security. An important component of the CISSP CBK revolves around understanding such laws and other requirements that impact your organization, based on jurisdiction, industry, or other factors.

Tools and technologies often get the majority of the attention, but it's essential to remember that people are the weakest link when it comes to maintaining information security. Candidate screening, background investigations, and other personnel security policies play a critical part in ensuring that your organization's data stays in the right hands. Further, establishing and maintaining a robust security awareness program is an essential way to educate your employees and measure the risk they present to your organization's assets.

Asset Security

TO APPLY AND ENFORCE effective asset security, you must concentrate on inventorying all sources of value, called *assets*. Assets can be tangible or intangible, existing in the form of information stores, databases, hardware, software, or entire networks.

In this domain, we cover significant elements of strategy to identify, categorize, secure, and monitor those assets throughout the information lifecycle. Although assets can also be buildings and real estate, those are not within the scope of this domain — physical security is substantially addressed in Chapter 7, "Security Operations." This chapter will focus on the best policies, practices, and methods to properly assure the confidentiality, integrity, and availability of an organization's information and technology assets.

IDENTIFY AND CLASSIFY INFORMATION AND ASSETS

Identifying and classifying information assets is a critical first step toward ensuring the security of your systems and data. Without giving careful consideration to these tasks, you will not know where your assets are — much less know how to secure them! Without information classification, you will not be able to determine which assets are more valuable than others, and which assets require additional security controls. The result will be an inefficient, costly information security program attempting to secure all assets, with an assumption that sensitive assets are located in all parts of the organization (local storage, shared storage, in the cloud, etc.). Worse, some assets requiring minimal protection, like public information, will be secured the same as confidential information. A mature security program begins with asset identification and classification, which allows you to locate and categorize your assets and differentiate the security approaches for each of them.

Creating an inventory of what assets an organization has, where the assets are located, and who is responsible for the assets are foundational steps in establishing an information security asset management program. Locating data has become more difficult because data has proliferated throughout the organization due to inexpensive local storage, cloud technologies, and the "work from anywhere" movement. Mapping where data resides is a tough task, but necessary.

Laws and regulations are often the driving source for an organization's asset identification and classification policies. The following are some of the common regulations and guidelines that formalize the classification and categorization of information assets:

- **Canada:** Security of Information Act
- **China:** Guarding State Secrets
- **European Union (EU):** General Data Protection Regulation (GDPR)
- **United Kingdom:** Official Secrets Acts (OSA)
- **United States:** NIST Federal Information Processing Standard 199, "Standards for Security Categorization of Federal Information and Information Systems"
- **United States:** NIST Special Publication (SP) 800-60, "Guide for Mapping Types of Information and Information Systems to Security Categories" (this is considered the "how-to" manual for FIPS 199)
- **United States:** Committee on National Security Systems (CNSS) Instruction No. 1253, "Security Categorization and Control Selection for National Security Systems"

The content of the previous regulations and guidelines varies, but each concentrates on one or more aspects of data protection. The UK OSA, for example, is concerned with protection of state secrets and official information, and it informs data classification levels of such information. The EU GDPR strengthens and unifies data protection and informs data flow policy. In the United States, NIST FIPS 199 can be used for asset classification within the overall risk management process. Depending on the region(s) in which your organization does business, one or more of these regulations or guidelines may be used as a foundational step in developing your asset classification requirements.

Data Classification and Data Categorization

Data classification and categorization are closely related processes that allow organizations to sort and organize their data for more effective analysis and security control implementation. The following sections introduce these concepts and lay the groundwork for classifying and categorizing data assets in your organization.

Data Classification

Data classification is the process of organizing data into groups or categories that describe the data's sensitivity, criticality, or value. Data classification helps to determine the security controls necessary to manage and safeguard the confidentiality, integrity, and availability of the data, and is a cornerstone of data security and risk management. In addition, data classification is often necessary to remain compliant with legal and regulatory requirements.

There are three primary types of data classification:

- **Context-based:** Derived from metadata like ownership, location, or other values that can indirectly indicate sensitivity or criticality.

- **Content-based:** Derived by inspecting the contents of files and directly identifying sensitive data, rather than inferring it from metadata. Compliance authorities, such as the Health Insurance Portability and Accountability Act of 1996 (HIPAA), Payment Card Industry (PCI), or contract-related terms (e.g., nondisclosure agreements) involve content-based classifications, as the type of information itself drives classification.

- **User-based:** Involves manual assignment of data classification and is based on users' understanding of the data and your organization's classification scheme.

Although it is always a best practice to classify data, the concept is most formalized in military or government organizations or in heavily regulated organizations, such as banks. The actual labels will differ in each organization.

✔ Examples of Classification Schemes

Commercial organizations might use this scheme:

- **Confidential:** Generally considered the highest level of classification outside of government or military organizations. The loss or theft of this data can cause serious risk to the organization. This category of data is usually subject to regulation or controlled by contractual agreement.

- **Sensitive:** A level of relative value less than confidential but still important to protect. Losing the data will raise the risk to the organization, even if it is just reputational damage. Strategy documents or interorganizational correspondence can be considered sensitive.

- **Private:** Usually compartmental data that might not do the company damage but must be kept private for other reasons. Employee retention statistics or salary ranges are often classified as private.

- **Proprietary:** Data that is disclosed outside the company on a limited basis or contains information that could reduce the company's competitive advantage, such as the technical specifications of a new product.

- **Public:** Data that if lost would have little or no impact to the company. A briefing on proper anti-phishing techniques that does not disclose specific results may be considered public information and is suitable for sharing outside the organization.

NOTE   Other labels used to designate documents (but not considered classifications) include For Official Use Only (FOUO) and Limited Official Use. If you do not work in a military or government organization, you will want to collaborate with your organization's legal department to determine proper terminology to establish document designation based on one or more of the primary types of data classification listed earlier.

Having a data classification policy and procedure in place allows your organization to begin designing security controls for the most efficient and effective protection of the information. Without locating and properly classifying your data, you run the risk of under-protecting critical data or over-protecting noncritical data. Once you have thoroughly classified your data, you are better equipped to classify the assets that store and process that data.

Data Categorization

Often confused with data classification, data categorization is a closely related, but different technique. *Data categorization* is the process of grouping types of data with comparable "sensitivity labels" (classifications). According to NIST SP 800-60, "Information is categorized according to its information type. An information type is a specific category of information (e.g., privacy, medical, proprietary, financial, investigative, contractor sensitive, security management) defined by an organization or, in some instances, by a specific law, Executive Order, directive, policy, or regulation." By categorizing data into buckets of similarly classified sensitivity, your organization is better equipped to apply similar security controls to assets with similar sensitivities.

Asset Classification

Whereas data classification is focused on the identification of the sensitivity, criticality, and value of data, *asset classification* is more broadly related to identifying the sensitivity, criticality, and value of the information systems and assets that store, process, and transmit that data, as well as the data itself. Assets include the data of value, the hardware that processes it, and the media on which it is stored — they may take either electronic or physical form and include things like servers, hard drives, databases, cloud storage, or paper-based records. Asset classification involves grouping assets based on their relative level of sensitivity and the impact to the organization should the assets be compromised. When considering the classification of an asset, it is important to consider the classification of the information stored on or processed by that asset, as data is often the greatest asset of them all (e.g., intellectual property).

Asset classification begins with conducting an inventory of assets and determining the responsible people, or owners, for the assets. Assets contain data or provide information-handling capabilities, and the asset inventory allows management to understand what kinds of sensitive assets exist in the organization and who is responsible for it. With this inventory, security teams and asset owners are able to categorize and group assets by the respective level of sensitivity, which then dictates the minimum set of security controls the organization will use to protect the information. A formal data policy is the primary mechanism through which an organization should establish classification levels, and then management can develop controls that provide sufficient protections against specific risks and threats to assets.

Benefits of Classification

Because it provides valuable insight into an environment, classification is a critical first step to better and more secure asset and data management. For a relatively simple process, the benefits are significant. Figure 2.1 depicts the major benefits of classification. The list is not comprehensive, and some organizations will find varying levels of benefit.

Asset Classification Levels

Assets should be identified and controlled based on their level of sensitivity. This allows similar assets to be grouped according to the value the organization places on the assets. The evaluation criteria can include the types of data the assets handle, the processes the assets perform, or both. There is no mandatory formula or nomenclature for asset classification categories. Each organization will have to establish names and sensitivity levels. Table 2.1 shows an example of types of asset classification. This is a notional framework for asset classification to illustrate how a portfolio of assets in an organization can be segmented into criticalities that map to high, medium, and low. The terms *tier* and *significant systems* are used as examples here and are not prescribed by a regulatory authority.

 Make an accurate asset inventory

 Gain insight into the environment

 Optimize change, vulnerability, and patch management programs

 Determine the best maintenance windows

 Improve security controls and segmentation

 Tailor protection of sensitive data

 Identify rogue assets

 Understand potential risks posed by vulnerabilities

 Identify proprietary assets and intellectual property

 Forecast costs of protection

 Compliance / Regulatory controls

FIGURE 2.1 **General benefits of asset classification**

TABLE 2.1 **Examples of Asset Classifications**

CATEGORIES	ASPECTS	EXAMPLES
Tier 0	Essential to several business units. May handle or include data that is extremely sensitive. Compromise could have a critical impact on the business's ability to function. Required to be available 100 percent of the time.	Domain controllers. Databases. Email servers. File shares. Client web servers. Gateway network devices (firewalls, routers, and network-critical infra-structure). Anything else that shuts down business for a day if it breaks or turns off.

(Continued)

TABLE 2.1 **(Continued)**

CATEGORIES	ASPECTS	EXAMPLES
Tier 1	Important but not necessarily critical to the organization.	Development environments with critical data.
	Essential to specific departments but not to the entire business.	Redundant backup systems with critical data.
		Department file shares.
	Compromise of any of these assets would have a moderate impact on the business's ability to function.	Local network devices (switches, routers, firewalls, and segmentation devices).
Tier 2	Neither essential nor critical to daily operations.	Workstations.
		Laptops.
	These systems and data are typically only used by a few people or a single individual.	Mobile phones and tablets.
		Printers.
	The compromise of any of these assets may inconvenience a few people but would not be a major disruption to business processes.	Desk phones.
Significant Systems	Any assets that handle or store data subject to compliance standards.	Cardholder data (CD) — any system that stores, processes, or transmits CD must align to PCI DSS.
	Significant systems may fall into more than one category or may stand alone for categorization, because loss of the system would not disrupt operations, even if it is damaging to the business.	Protected health information (PHI) — medical data must be protected per the standards outlined in HIPAA.
		Financial data — this data may fall under certain privacy requirements outlined in the Financial Industry Regulatory Authority (FINRA).
		U.S. federal government data (FISMA/FIPS) — for U.S. military and government.

ESTABLISH INFORMATION AND ASSET HANDLING REQUIREMENTS

There are various forms of technical, operational, and management controls that assist security professionals in enforcing handling requirements for sensitive information and valued assets. Organizations should establish and maintain policies and procedures that govern the marking and labeling, handling, declassification, and storage of sensitive information and other important assets.

NOTE Information and asset handling requirements tend to vary by security level (i.e., asset classification and categorization) and should consider all applicable laws, regulations, and standards; PCI and HIPAA, for example, contain specific requirements for handling cardholder data and PHI, respectively. In addition, your organization should conduct a risk assessment (discussed in Chapter 1, "Security and Risk Management") to identify specific threats and vulnerabilities that impact your assets and identify the specific handling requirements and controls required to mitigate risks to your assets.

Marking and Labeling

Marking an asset involves placing relevant information in plain view directly on the asset, such that a person can easily identify applicable security levels and classifications of the information contained on the asset, as well as any distribution limits and handling caveats. This is pretty straightforward for physical assets (like paper documents or hard disks), but for information assets (i.e., data), the logical structure or metadata must contain a place where labeling can be written, such as a document header. Another term for this process is labeling, because the information used to mark the asset is most effective when grouped together and easily accessed on a digital or physical label, depending on the asset. Electronic assets can include markings and labels in document headers or footers, for example, while hard assets can include a physical tag affixed to the asset. When users know the value of an asset (including data), they are better equipped to properly safeguard the asset based on its classification.

TIP While data classification is the most important element on a data label, asset labels may contain other information, such as the title of the asset, the data owner, and the data retention period (if applicable).

With a label in plain view, it is much easier to identify the importance of individual assets and manage the assets to assure confidentiality, integrity, and availability based on their classification levels.

NOTE Marking and labeling of public data or unclassified information helps to keep asset handling efficient and cost-effective. For example, if an unmarked data asset is found, a handling decision must be made. Best practice is to apply the highest level of security until the data can be determined as not sensitive or proprietary. Until proper classification is determined, elevated handling requirements may cause an organization to use additional resources, applying unnecessary controls to less-sensitive data assets.

TIP Data loss prevention (DLP) systems (discussed later in this chapter) are aided by using digital markings to identify and prevent sensitive information from leaking out of an organization.

Handling

Your organization should have established policies and procedures in place that govern the handling of each category and classification of asset. These policies and procedures provide rules for accessing, transmitting, transporting, and using sensitive data and other critical assets.

Employee awareness and training regarding responsibilities for proper information handling is a critical part of any asset security program. Training should educate your employees on the risks associated with becoming complacent about asset handling requirements. It is likely that, over time, employees handling even the most restricted information will become complacent, and data loss may be the result. The insider threat of an employee sending proprietary information to the wrong person or accessing sensitive data in a public coffee shop happens when employees become indifferent about data handling policies and procedures.

Storage

Similar to information handling guidelines, information storage guidelines are critical to your organization's overall asset security management. When sensitive information was all paper-based, information storage security was as simple as keeping assets locked up and behind adequate physical barriers. With digital information stored in data centers, on removable hard drives, on mobile phones, and in the cloud, asset storage can be a bit complicated. In the digital age, there are too many easy ways for stored data to be stolen, leaked inadvertently because of mismanagement, or accessed by unauthorized individuals through identification credential theft.

A primary consideration for secure asset storage of digital information is encryption. Sensitive data at rest should be encrypted, whenever feasible. Additional consideration must also be given to the storage and safeguarding of the encryption keys themselves. This usually requires the use of multiple-person integrity controls, such as those built into many hardware security module (HSM) systems (which we discuss in Chapter 3, "Security Architecture and Engineering").

An additional consideration for secure storage is limiting the volume of data retained. Making sure to only store data that is needed limits risk to the organization and reduces operational costs. In terms of risk, limitations on data storage also improve disaster recovery and business continuity because access to data on short notice is more feasible if excess data does not impinge on the overall recovery process.

A final consideration related to data storage is backups. Your organization must establish clear policies and procedures that specify what data to backup and how it should be backed up. In addition, you should establish and provide guidance related to how backup media must be secured and protected.

Declassification

Declassification is the process of modifying the assigned classification of an asset to a lower level of sensitivity. As data moves throughout the data lifecycle, there may come a time when it no longer holds the same value or maintains the same sensitivity as when it was originally classified; your organization must have a process to declassify data to account for such evolution. When data sensitivity changes from confidential to public, for example, marking, handling, and storage requirements have to be adjusted accordingly. If declassification does not happen properly, excessive and costly controls remain in place, leading to both financial and work efficiency impacts.

The declassification of assets is a process that requires thorough documentation and often multiple levels of approval. The data owner plays a central role in this process, as they determine the classification level of the data and when it can change. There should be a data governance process within your organization to determine whether there will be a manual review adjustment of data classifications. The organization could opt to automate the process using rules and applications to find and reclassify data assets. The rules may be based on the occurrence of a specific event as determined by the data owner or the expiration of a maximum time frame.

Methods to declassify assets include altering data to remove or obfuscate identifying or sensitive elements of the data. A couple of these methods are described in the following sections: de-identification (including anonymization and masking) and tokenization.

De-identification

Data de-identification is the process of removing information that can be used to identify an individual (i.e., personally identifiable information (PII)). De-identification is used to protect the confidentiality of sensitive data, particularly when the data is being used in test or development environment or other use cases that may not have the required security mechanisms in place. This process involves taking any personally identifying data fields and converting them to masked, obfuscated, encrypted, or tokenized data fields. For instance, a "Name" data field may change from a person's actual name to a random unique number under *anonymization* (see Figure 2.2), while all but the last four digits of your credit card number may be replaced by a series of "X" characters under a *masking* protocol (see Figure 2.3).

Gradebook

Name	Exam 1
Alice	85
Brandon	92
Cesar	79
Donna	77

Original Data

Name	Exam 1
#661243	85
#207510	92
#833384	79
#562099	77

De-identified Data

FIGURE 2.2 **Data de-identification via anonymization**

2222 5555 6666 7890

Original Card Number

XXXX XXXX XXXX 7890

Masked Card Number

FIGURE 2.3 **Data de-identification via masking**

Some data fields in a file may remain in their original form, but the de-identification process makes the remaining original information less useful to an unauthorized individual. Fields like age or race may still be useful for analytics, even if names and other personally identifiable information is de-identified. If encryption is used, a re-identification key is required to decrypt the database. No matter what process is used to de-identify the data, guidelines must be followed to keep the data from being easily re-identified by combining data fields or guessing the algorithm used to anonymize the data.

Tokenization

Tokenization is a specific form of de-identification that has been around for as long as there have been ciphers. However, it has gained popularity as security threats have changed and limitations have been identified with technical controls like encryption. *Tokenization* is the process of substituting a sensitive data element with a nonsensitive set of characters or numbers, called a *token*. Usually, the token has the same field length as the data that was replaced but is otherwise not meaningful in relation to the original data. In other words, unlike encryption, the token cannot be reverse engineered back to the value of the original data. A lookup table is used as a re-identification key. The original data and re-identification keys are stored securely, separately from the production system and the original data.

PROVISION RESOURCES SECURELY

An organization's security posture is constantly evolving as resources come and go. So, provisioning (and deprovisioning) of information technology (IT) resources can have a significant effect on your organization's overall security. There are many elements involved in securely provisioning information resources. These topics are discussed throughout this book, such as supply chain management in Chapter 1. This section addresses asset ownership, asset inventory, and overall asset management concepts.

Information and Asset Ownership

Information and asset ownership is central to proper information security. Within an organization, depending on the mission and the sensitivity levels of data and assets, there may be a data policy and an information asset security management policy. Data that is protected by law, contract, or other compliance structures must be addressed by the organization's data governance practice. However, a common part of each policy will be assigning responsibility and guidelines for asset ownership. Data owners and data processors (discussed later in this chapter) should have clearly defined roles and responsibilities. Data governance, including access, acceptable use, and data retention, must be performed or overseen by the right individuals in the organization.

Within an organization, the chief executive officer or authorized delegates have formal ownership responsibility, as defined and directed by the organization's formal governance documents, and within compliance limits of law and regulation. This responsibility includes the authority to represent the organization for the protection and security of the information asset.

Additional responsibilities of asset owners may include the following:

- Keeping the information asset inventory up-to-date
- Identifying the classification level of the information asset
- Defining and implementing appropriate safeguards to ensure the confidentiality, integrity, and availability of the information asset
- Assessing and monitoring safeguards to ensure compliance and reporting situations of noncompliance
- Authorizing access for those who have a business need for the information
- Ensuring that access is removed from those who no longer have a business need for the information
- Continually evaluating the environment and the legal/compliance landscape to determine if changes to the above are necessary

Asset Inventory

Any organization needs, as a foundation to its security and compliance programs, effective tools and processes to track its asset inventory. The asset inventory includes all physical and virtual assets, including hardware, software, and data.

Having a current and complete inventory is the absolute bedrock for implementing and monitoring technical security controls. Without a thorough and accurate asset inventory, you cannot be certain that you are properly securing all your critical assets.

TIP   Asset inventory appears at the top of the popular CIS 20 Controls list, because managing an inventory of all hardware, software, and data assets is foundational for just about every other security function.

Robust asset inventory tools and processes will also inform the organization of unauthorized (or "rogue") assets. In addition to knowing what to protect, of course we also want to know what doesn't belong, so any unwanted assets can be removed or isolated as soon as possible.

Inventory Tool/System of Record

Because of the size, complexity, and frequency of the task, an organization should use automated tools to assist in creating and maintaining the asset inventory. These system enumeration tools and other endpoint management tools should have awareness of all assets in the organization's enterprise and the ability to discover new assets introduced to the environment that have not been properly documented in the inventory.

This data comes from either an asset management agent or a client installed on each asset or "baked in" to each system image, through integrations with various scanner and sensor tools, or, in the case of hosted or cloud assets, from a data feed or recurring report from the vendor (which may or may not be shared with clients, depending on the contract). System enumeration tools, like the ones described in this paragraph, provide an organization with great visibility of the assets in their environment and can help support configuration management activities, as described in Chapter 7.

An asset inventory tool should have a way to distinguish authorized assets from unauthorized devices and applications and the ability to send alerts when the latter are discovered. The tool should also collect and track individual asset details necessary for reporting, audits, risk management, and incident management. These details need to cover technical specifications, such as the following:

- Hardware
  - Manufacturer
  - Model number
  - Serial number
  - Physical location
  - Number and type of processors
  - Memory size
  - Network interfaces and their MACs and IPs
  - Hostname
  - Hypervisor, operating systems, containers, virtual images running on this device
  - Purchase date, warranty information
  - Last update dates (firmware, hypervisor, etc.)
  - Asset usage metrics
- Software
  - Publisher
  - Version number, service pack/hotfix number
  - License information
  - Purchase date
  - Install date

In addition, operational security details should be collected, such as the type of data stored and processed on the asset, the asset classification and special handling requirements, the business processes or missions it supports, and the owner and administrators and their contact information.

There are, of course, many tools available that do these tasks or portions of these tasks. Most organizations already own many such tools. Consider the following:

- An Active Directory (AD) and Lightweight Directory Access Protocol (LDAP) server can provide a large portion of this information.

- Vulnerability scanners, configuration scanners, and network mapping tools can find and provide basic information about all the hosts in the organization's IP ranges.

- Tools that manage/track software licenses can perform a large portion of this task.

- DLP solutions typically have a discovery capability that can serve this purpose.

In addition to the previous list, organizations may need to utilize specialized systems enumeration and asset management tools to discovery, track, and manage their asset inventory. For gaps in their available tools, organizations can and do compensate with manual efforts, spreadsheets, and scripting to pull and tabulate asset data. Dedicated asset inventory tools usually provide this functionality and preclude the need for manual data pulls and tool integration.

Regardless of the tool or combination of tools used, there should be one the organization deems authoritative and final so that it can be referenced throughout the organization — this is the *system of record*. The information in this tool needs to be definitive. This is the data source to trust if there is conflict between what other tools are reporting. The system of record should also be the source used for official reports and other data requests, such as part of an audit. With the advent of next generation security systems that auto-map environments, organizations are more able to dynamically track agile environments that may see multiple software drops per day and endpoints that come and go. Continuous integration and continuous delivery (CI/CD) and other software development concepts are covered in Chapter 8, "Software Development Security."

Process Considerations

Now that we've discussed the tools needed, we will discuss inventory management best practices. First, the organization must define the authoritative inventory list or system of record and the process by which the inventory should be refreshed or updated; this includes defining an appropriate frequency for updating the inventory, although many agile organizations will do this on an as-needed basis. In addition to the regular interval inventory updates, it is also a good practice to manually notify the inventory tool administrator when an asset is installed or removed or when the components are updated/changed in a significant way, just to verify that those changes were captured by the inventory tools.

Inventory management can be accomplished in a different way for environments that make heavy use of virtualized components, including managed cloud service implementations. In these cases, use of automated tools to seek out, tabulate, and provision assets is often preferable; popular brands include Puppet, Chef, and Ansible.

For on-premises assets, it is often helpful to augment the inventory process with the use of geolocation information/geotags or the use of radio-frequency identification (RFID) inventory tags. This can increase the speed and accuracy of locating an asset, especially during an incident, when time is critical.

Asset Management

Figure 2.4 depicts a typical asset lifecycle that is helpful in understanding the continuum of phases relevant to asset management. Organizations should track, manage, and report on information assets throughout their entire lifecycle. Doing so can ultimately increase cyber resilience by enhancing the visibility of assets, identifying vulnerable assets, enabling faster response to security alerts, revealing which applications are actually being used, and so on. When properly implemented, an asset management process helps reduce costs, improve services, and mitigate risk.

FIGURE 2.4 **Typical asset management lifecycle**

Helpful guidance for proper management of physical assets (including non-IT infrastructure, such as power and plumbing utilities) can be found in ISO 55000.

Activities critical to implementing a formal asset management program include assignment of ownership (discussed earlier in this section), IT asset management (ITAM), configuration management, and change management.

NOTE It's important to remember that not every asset worth managing is one whose existence was planned to occur. Many (especially agile) organizations create ad hoc assets to support development and other dynamic tasks, and many of those ad hoc assets may remain in the environment for months or even years. While Figure 2.4 depicts a "typical" asset management lifecycle, you should keep in mind that even unplanned, discovered assets must be appropriately managed.

Information Technology Asset Management

Information technology asset management (also known as *IT asset management*, or just ITAM) is a set of business practices related to governing and managing IT assets, including hardware, software, data, and related processes. ITAM helps an organization ensure that its assets are accounted for, maintained, upgraded, and retired when appropriate. Simply put, ITAM is all about making sure that your valuable IT assets, tangible and intangible, are tracked and used efficiently.

The International Standards Organization (ISO) has established an official set of standards related to ITAM. ISO 19770 is a family of standards, last updated in 2017, that aims to assist organizations with managing risks and costs associated with IT assets.

ISO 19770 consists of five major parts, discussed here:

- **ISO/IEC 19770-1:** Establishes a process framework that outlines best practices and allows an organization to demonstrate compliance with an ITAM standard.
- **ISO/IEC 19770-2:** Establishes an ITAM data standard for *software identification* (or SWID) *tags*, which provide authoritative identifying information for installed software or other licensable items. SWID tags allow your organization to uniquely identify software that's deployed on your hardware assets.
- **ISO/IEC 19770-3:** Provides an ITAM data standard that establishes common terminology to be used when describing software entitlement rights, limitations, and metrics.

- **ISO/IEC 19770-4:** Establishes a data standard that supports standardized reporting of resource utilization. This standard is especially important when managing cloud-based systems or other complex assets and licenses.

- **ISO/IEC 19770-5:** Provides an overview of ITAM and defines related vocabulary.

Configuration Management

Configuration management is discussed in detail in Chapter 7, but it's important to introduce here as it relates to asset management and asset security. Related to keeping the inventory current, system and software configurations must be tightly controlled and thoroughly documented — that's the role of *configuration management*. Configurations made without direction can lead to problems in other security areas, like vulnerability management, because hardware and software requirements for upgrades and patching might be unknown and missed.

There are two types of baselines with which you should be familiar. A *system baseline* identifies the versions and settings of all configuration items (CIs) in a product, system, or subsystem; system baselines answer the question "what do I need to build the system correctly?" A security *baseline* is a minimum set of safeguards (e.g., security controls) required to protect a given system. Organizations commonly establish a baseline for every category of system within their enterprise (for example, they may establish a Windows baseline, a RedHat Linux baseline, and a macOS baseline) to describe the minimum acceptable configurations that must be in place for each of these systems. Many organizations use guides or checklists to accomplish and maintain a secure baseline configuration for their assets. A leading source that is publicly available is the National Checklist Program (NCP), defined by NIST SP 800-70. This is the U.S. government repository for up-to-date and detailed guidance for security configurations. Similar guidance exists in other countries, for both broad and specific application. A popular example in the EU is the "Baseline Security Recommendations for IoT" guidance that establishes a set of recommended configurations for critical information infrastructures.

Some organizations automate much of the baseline security configurations through the metadata available in the NCP and using the *Security Content Automation Protocol* (SCAP). SCAP enables validated security products to automatically perform configuration checking using NCP checklists. Domain 7 of the CISSP CBK goes deeper into configuration management, and we explore the concepts of provisioning, baselining, and automation in Chapter 7.

Change Management

Change management is an IT discipline focused on ensuring that organizations employ standardized processes to make changes to their assets. Organizations must develop policies and procedures to prevent arbitrary and unexpected modifications to their hardware and software inventory. Change management includes all activities that allow your organization to roll out and prioritize changes in a controlled manner that does not adversely impact your production environment or customer expectations. This includes change control (which is the set of processes and tools that allow you to verify that authorized changes are implemented correctly), enforcement (i.e., prevention of unauthorized changes), verification of changes, and audit.

If change management is not handled properly, a variety of issues can arise. For example, significant gaps can gradually emerge between your inventory record and the reality in your environment. Because any change to your IT environment can potentially impact your organization's security posture, all significant IT changes should go through a formal change process that includes an assessment of the security impact of the change. Change management is further discussed in Chapter 7.

TIP   The Information Technology Infrastructure Library (ITIL) calls for the use of a configuration management database (CMDB) to document the inventory and account for planned deployment of changes.

MANAGE DATA LIFECYCLE

Maintaining data security requires that you understand where the data is in the overall data lifecycle. Figure 2.5 depicts the secure data lifecycle, and each step is described in the list that follows.

FIGURE 2.5 **Secure data lifecycle**

1. **Collect:** Data is generated or aggregated.
2. **Store:** Data is saved into a storage system or repository.
3. **Use:** Data is processed and/or analyzed, by users or systems, for its intended purposes.
4. **Share:** Data is shared with authorized external users and systems.
5. **Retain:** Data is kept (e.g., archived) for a predefined period of time.
6. **Destroy:** Data is deleted and permanently removed from storage, making it inaccessible and unusable.

The data lifecycle is a high-level process that describes how data can flow through an organization, and the specific steps may vary slightly from one organization to the next. For example, some data may go straight from step 1 to step 6, never being stored or retained, while some data may never reach step 6, instead being archived (i.e., retained) in cold storage forever.

Understanding the differences between each phase in the secure data lifecycle is critically important to define efficient security processes and effective data security controls. The data lifecycle model can be used to help your organization think through the security needs of your data during each phase. We discuss each phase and the relevant data roles in the following sections.

Data Roles

A key factor in managing the security of your organization's data is being able to identify the parties that control or may access your data and understanding their roles and responsibilities throughout the entire data lifecycle. Some regulations (GDPR, for example) set strict requirements for organizations to identify specific individuals for specific data roles. The meaning of each title may vary slightly from one regulation to another or from one organization to the next. A general description of each data role is discussed throughout the rest of this section.

Owners

Not surprisingly, data owner is one of the most important roles in an organization. A *data owner* is an individual or group of individuals responsible for dictating how and why data should be used, as well as determining how the data must be secured. Data owners can have legal rights and complete control over information and can authorize or deny access to their data — the data owner is ultimately responsible and accountable for their data. In many organizations, this responsibility may be a senior leader, potentially the chief executive officer (CEO) or a company president, but particular data-related tasks can be delegated. The data owner can be held liable for negligence in the event that sensitive data that they own is misused or disclosed in an unauthorized way; even when day-to-day tasks are delegated, the data owner remains ultimately accountable. The extent of a data owner's responsibility can be established and enforced through legal or regulatory measures. The organization's data policy will outline the manner in which the data owner may use, collect, share, and store data that they own. All data, but especially data with a sensitivity level, must be assigned to an owner.

TIP   A data owner sets data use and asset protection rules. In collaboration with information system owners, the data owner will determine the security controls for access and use for data within the system.

NOTE   Data owner has synonymous terms used in various guidelines and regulations. Consider information owner or steward as interchangeable terms, for instance.

Expectations for the data owner are to provide due care and due diligence. These are primarily legal terms that guide information protection activities. These concepts were introduced in Chapter 1 and are detailed later in the chapter.

Due care, in terms of asset management, is using reasonable measures and efforts to protect assets deemed valuable or assigned sensitivity levels. An example of providing due care is keeping and maintaining an accurate asset inventory. Additionally, due care extends to ensuring that all assets are classified appropriately, and the classifications are accurate based on the information contained on the asset.

Due diligence is taking all expectable or practical steps to maintain due care, including verifying that everything is being done as intended by due care. An example of due diligence begins with an acknowledgment that valuable assets are found throughout an organization and significant effort must be made to account for and assess them. This will allow the organization to properly evaluate risk and protection strategies. Assets are no longer relegated to stationary boundaries. Assets like laptops, thumb drives, and portable devices are mobile. As data moves to the cloud, tangible and intangible assets and, therefore, due diligence extend to the cloud environment too.

The importance of due care and due diligence is seen during incident response activities or data breach investigations. Organizations that demonstrate due care and due diligence may be able to reduce culpability and liability, whereas lack of due care and due diligence is grounds for civil or even criminal penalties.

Controllers

The *data controller* is the person, agency, company, or other body that, alone or jointly with others, determines the purposes and means of data processing. Made increasingly relevant with the advent of GDPR regulations (discussed in Chapter 1), the data controller is responsible for adhering to all principles relating to processing personal data. To that end, the controller has to be able to demonstrate compliance with the principles of lawfulness, fairness, transparency, data minimization, accuracy, storage limitation, integrity, and confidentiality of personal data. Data controllers negotiate privacy protections for personal data with data processors via secure contractual terms and assurances, called *data processing agreements*.

NOTE   Data controllers are often the same parties as the data owners, but not always. In many cases, such as with cloud services and managed service providers, the data owner may outsource the responsibility to establish data processing requirements to a third party. Even in these situations, the data owner remains ultimately responsible and accountable for the security of the data.

Custodians

In an organization, the data governance process should include a role for the data custodian. A data custodian is responsible for maintaining data on the IT infrastructure, in accordance with requirements established by the data owner and the business. Data custodians are responsible for maintaining the technical environment that ensures safe custody, transport, and storage of data.

NOTE   Whereas data owner, data controller, and other data roles tend to be business-focused, the data custodian role is very much a technical role that is typically housed in an organization's IT department.

Processors

The value in data is often in the sharing or exchange of the information between authorized entities. The party responsible for transferring, transmitting, or otherwise handling data on behalf of a data owner is a *data processor*. Data processors have a distinct role in the protection of data. In a healthcare setting, data exchange can be important in the safe and proper conduct of patient care, appropriate treatment, managing billing, and other organizational operations. In banking, the data supports business and individual investments as well as creditworthiness. The regulatory focus in GDPR and HIPAA, as examples, reflects the importance of data processing responsibilities.

NOTE A data processor is not synonymous with a data controller. The key difference is a data processor does not have legal responsibility and accountability for the data, as does a data controller. The processor performs data manipulation on behalf of the data controller. A data controller is an entity that determines the purposes, conditions, and means of processing the personal data. Figure 2.6 depicts the relationship between data processors and data controllers.

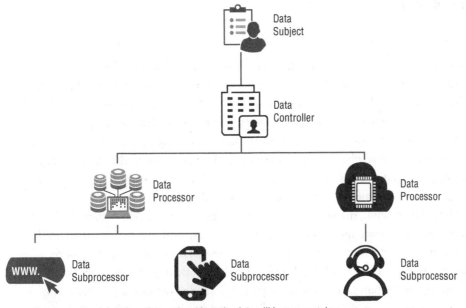

- *Data controller determines the need and how the data will be processed.*
- *Data processor is a separate legal entity processing data for the controller.*
  - *Cloud providers are generally considered data processors, as are market research firms, payroll companies, accountants.*

FIGURE 2.6 **Relationship between data processor and data controller**

In some instances, people in organizations play both roles as data processor and data controller. For instance, a human resources firm would have data about their own employees and would be a data controller in this sense. However, if the firm provides outsourced human resource actions for other clients, the human resources firm would be a data processor for the client data, while the individual clients remain the data controllers.

Users

Arguably the easiest to understand, a *data user* is the party who consumes the data; the data user is the customer or intended recipient of data. Data users may hold data processors accountable to service-level agreements (SLAs) and other contractual agreements that require a specific level of performance (e.g., data availability).

Subjects

Data subjects, as defined by GDPR, are "identified or identifiable natural people" — or just human beings, in plain English, from whom or about whom information is collected. The overall purpose of GDPR is to protect the privacy of data subjects and their personal information.

Data Collection

The data lifecycle (refer to Figure 2.5) begins with data collection. This phase may include data creation, acquisition, aggregation, or any circumstance where data is "new" to your system. New data may be freshly generated content, data that is newly introduced to your environment, or content that has been updated/modified into a new state.

Secure defaults, privacy by design, and other secure design principles are most important during this initial phase of the data lifecycle. Rather than introducing security at a later stage, regulations and best practice recommend (and often require) data protection principles to be designed and integrated right from the start.

Data classification, discussed earlier in the "Identify and Classify Information and Assets" section, is most appropriate to occur during data collection or creation; this helps ensure that the right security controls are implemented from the beginning. In addition to establishing data classification, this phase is also a good opportunity to tag data with any important attributes, and also assign proper access restrictions to your data. Any decisions made during data collection follows your data throughout its lifecycle. So, sufficient consideration must be given to how collected/created data must be managed and secured throughout its lifecycle.

TIP   From a privacy perspective, best practice and regulations like GDPR recommend or require data collectors to first obtain consent, or have other legal authority, prior to actively or passively collecting data from a subject.

Data Location

With the growth of cloud-based storage, data location is an increasingly discussed topic. Many jurisdictions or governments have laws that require a citizen's (or resident's) data be collected, processed, or stored inside the country. The data may still be transferred internationally, but it has to originate from the country and can be transferred only after local privacy or data protection laws are met. An example of these conditions is notifying a user how the information will be used and obtaining their consent. This is data localization or residency before the data is exchanged outside of the jurisdiction. In some cases, data localization or residency mandates that data about a nation's citizens or residents must be deleted from foreign systems before being removed from systems in the data subject's nation. Some regulations prohibit certain data (like military secrets, for example) from leaving the country of origin under any circumstances.

A prominent example of data location requirements can be examined in China's Cybersecurity Law. This law was passed in 2016 and increases the national government's jurisdiction over the business of cybersecurity. All critical information infrastructure (CII) is subject to the law. The government has interest in key industries that maintain data that could pose a national security or public interest risk if damaged or lost. Some of the Chinese businesses that are contemplated by the law are in the industries of energy, finance, transportation, telecommunications, electricity, water, gas, and medical and healthcare. As part of this law, impacted foreign companies must either build servers and data centers in China or outsource data management to locally managed Chinese companies, such as Alibaba or Tencent.

With the use of a cloud provider, data localization or residency highlights several important considerations, including knowing where your data will reside (or where it might travel) and the contractual obligations the cloud provider has to support the data owner's requirements. Data localization or residency is another valid reason to mandate that the data controller holds the encryption keys to cloud data stores. If the nation requires international organizations to destroy data before the nation does, deleting the encryption key can be a compensating control to make sensitive data unreadable and unusable.

Data Maintenance

After collecting and storing data, it is likely moved throughout your organization and used for its intended purpose. The "Use" phase of the secure data lifecycle involves all manners of processing, analyzing, and sharing data. During this phase, you should actively manage and maintain the security of your data by controlling access to the data and applying the proper security controls along the way. Data maintenance involves continuously monitoring your data and applying principles like least privilege and defense in depth (both discussed in Chapter 3).

Data maintenance during the "Use" phase of the data lifecycle is often a challenge for companies because it requires careful balance between functionality and security. For example, encryption is a core security mechanism, but it often gets in the way when data needs to be analyzed or used. Careful consideration must be given to these types of tradeoffs, and your organization must continuously evaluate your policies and controls to ensure your business needs are met securely.

Data Retention

Whether your data is stored in a local datacenter or hosted by a third party (e.g., a cloud provider), you need to consider how long the data will be retained before being securely destroyed. Having data retention policies and procedures, which define what to keep and how long to keep it, is not only standard practice, but likely a legal, regulatory, or contractual requirement. For example, NIST SP 800-53 outlines requirements that federal agencies and government contractors need to meet for compliance with the Federal Information Security Management Act (FISMA); these NIST guidelines require data retention for a minimum of three years. Similarly, HIPAA data retention requirements mandate that covered entities keep HIPAA-related data for a minimum of six years from creation. Knowing how long you should keep certain types of data can quickly become complicated. Your organization's security and legal teams should work closely together to ensure that data retention policies satisfy all legal and regulatory requirements.

Data retention policies should also specify the maximum retention periods for sensitive or personal data. Whereas retention minimums are designed to help support incident response and other types of investigations, retention maximums are typically enforced to protect the privacy of personal data. For example, GDPR Article 5 states that personal data should be retained for only as long as it is required in order to achieve the purpose for which the data was originally collected; in other words, GDPR requires that organizations retain personal data for as long as necessary, but no longer than that. Again, the variety of regulatory requirements, oftentimes conflicting, can make establishing and following data retention policies very challenging. Nonetheless, this is a critical part of every asset management program and requires thoughtful consideration.

TIP The less data you have, the less damaging a security breach will be. If you don't need data, securely destroy it. Retention policies and various data management solutions can help archive, secure, and delete old or unnecessary data.

NOTE   Your data retention policies and procedures, as with your other enterprise policies and procedures, should be reviewed and updated on a regular basis to ensure continued effectiveness and compliance with the latest regulations.

Data Destruction

The final stage of the data lifecycle is also the most often neglected: *data destruction*. If data is no longer needed, by regulation or for functionality, then you should get rid of it. Stale data is a magnet for hackers and is often the least protected resource in an environment. By logically or physically destroying unneeded data, you can both reduce your risk exposure and decrease your storage and data maintenance costs. Anything but complete physical destruction of storage media may allow residual pieces of data to remain. We discuss this phenomenon, and ways to address it, in the following section.

Data Remanence

Although many popular crime shows on TV depict a fictitious ability to recover any digital data on any medium, it is true that insufficient deletion of data can result in the compromise of the information. Residual data can remain on media if not disposed of properly, and recovery of that data by unauthorized viewers is possible. *Data remanence* occurs when data destruction efforts were insufficient to prevent the reconstruction of the data.

NOTE   Temporary files (e.g., cache), transient partial results in CPUs, GPUs, communications equipment, cryptographic systems, and other objects with storage all have a risk of data remanence when power is turned off. Those responsible for systems maintenance must consider this, along with disposal of obsolete or abandoned equipment.

The underlying principle of data remanence is that data simply deleted from a hard drive or other storage medium is not sufficiently discarded; in using an operating system's deletion command, only pointers to the data are removed, not the data itself. Regulated data (such as PHI) and data with higher sensitivity classifications (e.g., confidential or Top Secret) must follow rigorous destruction methods. The destruction must be certified, and evidence of the destruction/certification must be kept as proper documentation of the process. A certificate of destruction from the entity that destroyed the data, signed by the people who oversaw the data destruction, is usually sufficient.

NOTE   The specific requirements for mitigating data remanence vary by data type and by regulation. Make sure you understand what processes you're required to follow and what evidence of data destruction you may need to maintain.

The use of cloud providers has introduced some challenges with respect to data remanence. It takes significant collaboration between a cloud provider and cloud customer to make secure data destruction possible. Cloud users or tenants are not given access to the physical drive, only to a higher-level abstraction like file systems. Techniques such as overwriting file sectors are not possible as they are with on-premises data centers that the organization owns and operates. In software as a service (SaaS) and platform as a service (PaaS) environments, access happens only at the data level. In cloud environments, the alternative is to encrypt the data and keep the key outside the cloud environment where the data resides. When the data is no longer needed and the key is deleted, the data is rendered unusable and unreadable — this is known as *cryptographic erasure*. This is not a perfect solution, but because cloud providers allocate resources and cloud users cannot control where the physical assets that house the data reside, overwrite methods are typically impossible.

The rules and regulations that govern the destruction of data often dictate the level of protection that must be applied to various types of sensitive information. Several U.S. federal laws are potentially applicable to organizations relative to data destruction, including the Gramm-Leach-Bliley Act (GLBA, discussed in Chapter 1), which limits the disclosure and use of customer information and imposes a security rule for financial institutions. HIPAA regulates the handling of customer medical records and information. The Fair Credit Reporting Act governs the use, disclosure, and disposal of information in reports about consumer credit and credit ratings. The approved European standard BS EN 15713, "Secure Destruction of Confidential Information," defines the code of practice for securely and effectively destroying such data. It applies to any organization that collects, transports, and destroys confidential materials. BS EN 15713 can be integrated with other management system standards, most commonly ISO 9001.

There are many frameworks and regulations that recommend or require specific mitigations against data remanence. For example, in the U.S. National Security Agency (NSA) Central Security Service (CSS) Policy Manual 9-12, requirements begin with removing all labels and markings that indicate previous use and classification. After that, the requirements vary depending on the type of medium being used. Some of the requirements include the following:

- Sanitize magnetic tapes and disks by degaussing using an NSA/CSS–evaluated degausser and/or incinerating by burning the material, reducing it to ash. In doing so, the following criteria apply:
    - It is highly recommended to physically damage the hard disk drive by deforming the internal platters prior to release by any means or by using a hard disk drive crusher.

- Hard disks can be degaussed by using a degaussing wand, disassembling the device, and erasing all surfaces of the enclosed platters.

- Disintegrate the hard disk into particles that are nominally 2 millimeter edge-length in size. It is highly recommended to disintegrate hard disk drive storage devices in bulk with other storage devices.

- Shredding of smaller diskettes is allowed using an approved crosscut shredder. Remove the diskette cover and metal hub prior to shredding.

- Optical storage devices including CDs, DVDs, and Blu-ray disks (BDs) can be sanitized in the following ways:

  - The only way BDs can be sanitized is by incinerating the material and reducing it to ash. The other methods listed here do not work for them. Incineration also works for CDs and DVDs.

  - CDs and DVDs can be disintegrated.

  - CDs and DVDs can be shredded.

  - CDs and DVDs can be embossed/knurled by using an approved optical storage device embosser/knurler.

  - CDs can be sanitized by approved grinders. DVDs or BDs cannot be sanitized by grinding.

- For solid-state storage devices, including random access memory (RAM), read-only memory (ROM), Field Programmable Gate Array (FPGA), smart cards, and flash memory, the following methods are acceptable:

  - Disintegrate into particles that are nominally 2 millimeter edge-length in size using an approved disintegrator; it is recommended to do this in bulk with multiple storage devices together.

  - Incinerate the material to ash.

- Smart cards can be sanitized using strip shredding to a maximum of 2 millimeters or cutting the smart card into strips diagonally at a 45-degree angle, ensuring that the microchip is cut through the center. Also, make sure that the barcode, magnetic strip, and written information are cut into several pieces and the written information is unreadable. Cross-cut shredders are *not* allowed for this shredding.

The requirements of BS EN 15713 are similar and include the following:

- There must be a confidential destruction premises.

- A written contract covering all transactions should exist between the client and the organization; subcontractors must follow the guidelines too.

- Personnel doing this work must be trained, be certified, and have passed a Criminal Records Bureau (CRB) check or Disclosure or Barring Service (DBS) check.

- Confidential material to be collected should remain protected from unauthorized access from the point of collection to complete destruction.

- The trucks that are used to collect and transport protected material have specific requirements, including being box-shaped, having the ability for drivers to communicate to base stations, being lockable, not being left unattended, and so on.

- In addition to the destruction focus, there is consideration for environmental issues, and recycling is allowed under certain conditions.

There are two general approaches to data destruction. The first approach is to render the actual device or object containing the media useless. Physical destruction of the media, electromagnetic degaussing, and incineration are common tactics.

The other type of asset disposal is by cleansing or sanitizing the media/drive. The physical media can therefore be reused, but there is no trace of data remanence after the data-wiping action. There are numerous validated processes for this objective.

Your asset disposal policy should differentiate between assets being reused within your organization and those to be repurposed outside of the organization (or discarded completely). For example, an asset to be reallocated internally may be sufficiently sanitized by a lower level of sanitization (e.g., reformatting or re-imaging the hard drive). This scenario does not preclude the organization from mandating the highest levels of sanitization if the assets are deemed critical or the data is sensitive. Some different tactics to achieve desired levels of security assurance with specific steps and instructions are available in NIST SP 800-88, "Guidelines for Media Sanitization," at https:// nvlpubs.nist.gov/nistpubs/SpecialPublications/NIST.SP.800-88r1.pdf.

To achieve a level of assurance of adequate asset sanitization, the following techniques can be used:

- **Clearing:** This involves digitally wiping data or overwriting it with zeros or ones. This is the least effective method of data deletion and may allow data to be recovered.

- **Purging:** This includes methods such as *degaussing*, which is the destruction of data by exposing its storage media to a strong magnetic field.

- **Destruction:** This includes physically destroying media through shredding, burning, or pulverizing, and also includes the use of strong encryption to logically destroy data.

Examples of specific techniques to achieve the desired level of assurance in sanitization requirements include the following:

- **Zeroing:** This erases data on the disk and overwrites it with all zeros.

- **Overwriting:** Data is written to storage locations that previously held sensitive data. It is typical to use random passes of 0 and 1 combinations, not patterns, to overwrite. The number of times an overwrite must be accomplished depends on storage media, sometimes on its sensitivity, and sometimes on differing organizational requirements.

- **Degaussing:** This is a process whereby the magnetic media is erased (i.e., returned to its initial blank state through the use of strong magnetic fields).

ENSURE APPROPRIATE ASSET RETENTION

Data retention programs serve many purposes. Organizations need to preserve intellectual property. A proper data retention process will support institutional memory. In legal or forensic examinations, evidence can be preserved through data retention. In many cases, data retention is an obligation resulting from regulatory and compliance requirements.

The information security professional must address the confidentiality, integrity, and availability of information throughout its existence. Absent a mature data retention process, an organization will experience more incidents of record tampering, data loss, and inappropriate access. Several considerations must be made to establish which types of information should be maintained and for how long. Regulations may establish guidelines based on the category or sensitivity of the data. While it may seem like some regulations mandate seemingly excessive retention requirements, keep in mind that the costs associated with noncompliance (e.g., legal penalties, litigation fees, etc.) may far exceed the costs associated with retaining the data.

Where a regulation or other compliance requirement does not give a specific mandate, organizations must establish asset retention guidelines. These timelines should be relevant to the type of asset (critical, production, etc.) and sensitivity of the data (confidential, public, etc.).

Asset and data retention is essential for organizations to protect and preserve records as evidence of actions. An asset management system results in a source of information about business activities that can support subsequent activities and business decisions. The process also ensures accountability to present and future stakeholders. Several good references exist for the practice of records management. One is ISO 15489-1:2016, "Information and Documentation — Records Management — Part 1: Concepts and Principles." Another is DoD Instruction 5015.02, "DoD Records Management Program."

The steps necessary to build a data retention policy are important. The first action is to have a designated person of authority or a steering committee decide what electronic and physical documents the business produces and assign ownership. Next, the person or committee should review relevant regulations regarding asset and data retention to make sure the policy will align. Then, the team is ready to actually write the policy. Once the policy is published in the organization, it is important to train employees on the plan. Continued communication will help ensure success for the processes. On a periodic basis, review the data retention policy and update it as needed.

The list that follows is a general outline to help establish an initial data retention policy. In an organization that already has a data retention policy, this template of actions can be used to review the current policy:

- Document the purpose of the policy.
- Identify who is affected by the policy.
- Identify the types of data and electronic systems covered by the policy.
- Define key terms, especially legal and technical terminology.
- Describe the requirements in detail from the legal, business, and regulatory perspectives.
- Outline the procedures for ensuring data is properly retained.
- Outline the procedures for ensuring data is properly destroyed.
- Clearly document the litigation exception process and how to respond to e-discovery requests.
- List the responsibilities of those involved in data retention activities.
- Build a table showing the information type and its corresponding retention period.
- Document the specific duties of a central or corporate data retention team if one exists.
- Include an appendix for additional reference information.

The policy should make it clear that during all phases of the data management lifecycle, including destruction, proper secure handling procedures are required.

NOTE   Data retention requirements also apply to security and IT operations audit logs. NIST SP 800-92, "Guide to Computer Security Log Management," offers guidance on log archival, log retention, and log preservation. Data retention requirements are based on factors such as operational need, legal requirements, and, in some cases, a specific incident or event that requires an exception to log management policy.

TIP   Most data should have retention limits, although some data may have permanent value to an organization or society. Keep in mind that indefinite storage may create unnecessary cost, and disclosure of stored data can be required by subpoena in the event of litigation, even if the data is useless to the organization. Unlike data classification where the highest classification is applied to all data in a group as a precautionary best practice, the organization must tailor the data retention length specific to the data sensitivity (in addition, of course, to any legal or compliance drivers for the retention length).

The most important role a security practitioner might have in asset retention is to create and maintain a policy that is informed by and adheres to regulations, meets business objectives, and is understood and followed throughout the organization. Conducting training and testing of the policy are important measures of program performance. Users have to be made aware of their responsibilities in maintaining safeguards during the entire asset lifecycle. Audits should be conducted to assure the organization that the policy and procedures are being followed.

Determining Appropriate Records Retention

Security professionals have to stay aware of the various local, national, and international developments that can impact record retention requirements. An example is the enactment and enforcement of the EU GDPR's Article 17, "The Right to Erasure," commonly called the *right to be forgotten*. This causes organizations to evaluate previous record retention requirements against the right to be forgotten considerations introduced by Article 17. This provision gives explicit rights to individuals to have their records erased without undue delay. There is an exception for instances where the business or data controller must keep the data for the purposes for which it was collected (i.e., the original business requirement). In this instance, a business requirement can create an exception to regulatory guidance.

There are also regulatory requirements that cause an organization to establish and maintain record retention policies that exceed the internal useful life of the record. An example of this scenario is HIPAA, which requires subject healthcare organizations to maintain documentation related to HIPAA compliance, such as log records pertaining to electronic protected health information (ePHI) review, for six years. While HIPAA mandates a six-year record retention requirement for documentation required to maintain the policies and procedures relevant to HIPAA, U.S. state law generally covers the record retention requirements for patient medical records. See U.S. Code of Federal Regulations (CFR) Section 164.316(b)(1) and 164.316(b)(2)(i) for more detail. The U.S. Department of Health and Human Services (HHS), which has oversight of HIPAA, recommends the six-year record retention minimum in the absence of more specific federal and state-level guidance. Consult organizational legal counsel for clear guidance when multiple jurisdictions are involved. Let them be the gatekeepers on notifying you of changes, rather than the security team needing to be the subscribers to legal news services.

Record retention requirements should also be complemented with de-identification and obfuscation processes. The record retention schedule can include a date when the personal data is no longer needed, but other elements are useful for data analytics and trend analysis. This can extend the useful life of the record while protecting the personal information of the individual. Regulatory compliance is met as files are regularly sanitized and personal data is not retained any longer than is necessary.

Records Retention Best Practices

Each organization must handle and retain records in accordance with applicable laws, directives, policies, regulations, standards, and operational requirements. While the requirements may be different according to geographic jurisdiction or industry-specific considerations, there are several summary-level best practices the security professional can use to model a compliant and effective records management program:

- Maintain records according to the organization's record retention schedule.
- Conduct regular evaluations of the system. There may be triggers to start a review, such as a merger or acquisition. Otherwise, consider a scheduled, periodic review of records in the organization. These reviews should include legal and compliance teams, as well as any relevant application and data owners.
- Conduct a review of the actual record retention schedule every year to make sure the schedule is relevant to business requirements and regulatory requirements.
- Label electronically maintained records.
- Create backup electronic file copies.
- Retain paper copies of records that cannot be accurately or completely transferred to the electronic recordkeeping system.
- Do not keep records longer than is necessary to accomplish the original purpose for which the information was collected.

- Make sure records have valid dates of origin. Movement and use of records can change electronic file dates, but not the date that determines the retention period.

- A reasonable attempt should be made to remove unnecessary electronic records, per the retention schedule, in all identified electronic repositories.

- Maintain information-handling controls over the full lifecycle of information, in some cases extending beyond the disposal of the records.

- Ensure that records remain persistently accessible for the length of the time they are retained according to the frequency with which they are retrieved.

- Deduplicate records to avoid unnecessary storage of multiple copies that increase risk and storage costs.

- Remember to classify and retain emails that are official records. Create an email retention schedule as a subset of the records retention schedule.

- Ensure that records remain accessible for the required retention period by periodically converting and migrating records from media sources, because digital media can degrade or become obsolete over time.

- Securely delete data in accordance with written retention periods and information security and retention policies.

Your record retention schedule may be distinct to your organization, but it is foundational to follow best practices to have an effective electronic records retention program. Your organization needs to defend its intellectual property rights and provide protection in times of litigation. Appropriate record retention enables organizations to be able to verify the authenticity of the records they keep. As the surge in criticality, value, and volume of digital information continues to grow, records retention is important to prevent organizations from being overwhelmed and records becoming unavailable or unprotected. In sum, while there is no universally applicable records management plan, security professionals need to examine specific requirements at their own enterprises and consider best-practice approaches that best serve their organization.

DETERMINE DATA SECURITY CONTROLS AND COMPLIANCE REQUIREMENTS

After assets have been identified, inventoried, and classified, it is important that you lend careful consideration to the data security controls that are best suited for your organization. These security controls will vary based on the classification of each asset, the data state (discussed next), and any compliance requirements or industry standards that your organization has selected to align with.

To start, there are three categories of controls with which you should be familiar: technical, administrative, and physical. A deeper understanding of each type of control is needed to emphasize the role each plays in securing organizational assets.

- **Technical controls:** The category of controls grouped as *technical controls* serve to use computer capabilities and automation to implement safeguards. The technical controls defend against misuse or unauthorized access to valuable information. In most organizations, a combination of technical controls is needed to work together to protect, detect, and respond to potential and actual security incidents and events. A few examples of technical controls related to asset management are access control systems that prevent unauthorized reading, writing, moving, or executing of assets, as well as filters that allow or restrict access to URLs, IP addresses, or the loading/execution of software.

- **Administrative controls:** *Administrative controls* are the people-facing policies, procedures, standards, and guidelines that an organization uses to implement technical and physical controls. The sources of administrative controls can be laws and regulations, industry best practices, and organizational mandates. Administrative controls inform the organization on roles and responsibilities, proper information protection practices, and enforcement actions if controls are not followed.

- **Physical controls:** As information and technology assets continue to digitize and become more interconnected, *physical controls* remain highly important. Controlling physical access to information assets is often the least expensive and most effective prevention control we can use. Designing asset protection programs that include guards and receptionists, entry access controls, area lighting and surveillance, closed-circuit television (CCTV), and physical intrusion detection systems provides a layered defense approach.

NOTE   When thinking of the three types of controls, remember that technical controls shape the behavior of hardware and software, administrative controls shape the behavior of humans, and physical controls shape the behavior of anything that moves (which may include humans, robots, IoT devices, etc.).

Physical, technical, and administrative controls are also defined by their protective purpose. Each type of control can be described as deterrent, preventative, detective, corrective, or recovery. Depending on the control, it may serve multiple functions in the overall security program. Each of these is discussed in detail in Chapter 1, in the section "Applicable Types of Controls."

Data States

Data is a volatile asset. As the use of data changes in an organization, the security controls to protect it must change. Depending on the value of the data, it has to be protected no matter what state it is in. Data can be in storage or at rest on backup tapes, on hard drives, or in the cloud. Data is often in use temporarily by applications and web pages. When data is transferred between users or computing assets, it is considered in transit. Some key methods for protecting data as an asset specifically are encryption and access control, to include proper authorization limits. Encryption prevents data visibility in the event of unauthorized access or theft. Figure 2.7 provides examples for data in the various states. Detailed coverage of appropriate security controls for each data state can be found in Chapters 3, 5, and 7.

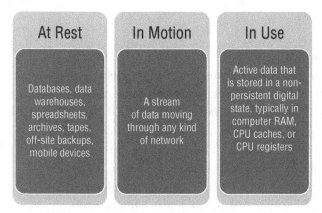

At Rest

Databases, data warehouses, spreadsheets, archives, tapes, off-site backups, mobile devices

In Motion

A stream of data moving through any kind of network

In Use

Active data that is stored in a non-persistent digital state, typically in computer RAM, CPU caches, or CPU registers

FIGURE 2.7 **Data states and examples**

Data at Rest

Data at rest refers to data that is stored on a system and not actively being written to, read from, transmitted, or otherwise processed. The data is "at rest" because there is no active processing or transfer from device to device or across networks.

Data-at-rest protection often begins with access control. It's important that you consider what data asset you're trying to protect, who should have access to it, and who should absolutely be denied access to it. Proper access control, including multifactor authentication for sensitive data, is an important starting point to achieving secure data at rest.

Encryption (discussed at length in Chapter 3) is another common security control for data at rest. Encryption can be employed across an entire volume of storage, called *full disk encryption*. A couple of approaches to encrypting an entire hard drive are worth noting.

- A *Trusted Platform Module* (TPM) is a microcontroller chip integrated into the computer hardware that provides a crypto processor. The cryptographic keys are incorporated in the device itself and can help authenticate the platform upon booting.

- A *self-encrypting drive* (SED) is a hard disk drive or solid-state drive that automatically encrypts and decrypts drive data without the need for additional encryption software. SEDs continuously encrypt drive data without the need for user input.

A more granular approach allows encryption to be applied at the individual file level, called *file-level encryption*. File-level encryption is a tailored data protection strategy that may provide additional protection from unauthorized access to a file on a hard drive in the event the full disk is decrypted. For even more granularity, *field-level encryption* allows the encryption of specific data fields within a single file.

Data in Transit

Data in transit refers to data that is actively being transmitted across a network, between multiple networks, or from one location to another. Also described as *data in motion*, data in transit is any data that is actively moving from a point of origin to a destination across networks, including trusted, private networks. The data can also be transferred across untrusted networks through the internet and to the cloud, as examples. transport layer security (TLS) (including HTTPS) and virtual private networks (VPNs) are key encryption-based technologies that help secure data in transit.

Link encryption is a method of data-in-transit security where the traffic is encrypted and decrypted at each network routing point (e.g., network switch or node through which it passes). This process continues until the data arrives at its final destination. The routing information is discovered during the decryption process at each node so the transmission can continue. The message is then re-encrypted. Link encryption offers a couple of advantages:

- There is less human error because the process of encryption is automatic.

- Traffic analysis tools are circumvented, and attackers are thwarted because a continuous communications link with an unvarying level of traffic maintains the encryption protections.

End-to-end encryption is another data-in-transit method. This type of system of communication ensures that only the sender and recipient can read the data. No eavesdropper can access the cryptographic keys needed to decrypt the conversation; this means that even telecom providers, internet providers, or the provider of the communication service cannot access the cryptographic keys needed to decrypt the conversation.

Data in Use

Data in use is the third, often-forgotten, state of digital data and refers to data that is actively being processed by an application being used by a user (either human or system). While an authenticated user is accessing a database or an application, data is in a volatile state. Data in use is typically used in RAM, CPU caches, or CPU registers to perform the transactions and tasks the end user requires. Encryption is not necessarily relevant here, nor is it a primary control used with data in use, but it can be complementary to other controls. Data in use, presumably by an authorized user, underscores the importance of authentication, authorization, and accounting to control and monitor access to sensitive assets. Once a hacker has stolen valid credentials, many controls like encryption are rendered ineffective because the intruder has access like an insider. These types of issues are discussed further in Chapter 3.

Scoping and Tailoring

Establishing the baseline of security controls begins the scoping and tailoring process. Because every organization has unique factors that impact how it values assets, the threats it faces, and what level of security it can afford, in terms of both resources and business operation impact, refining individual controls is an important role for the security professional. A CISSP has to help build the plan to clarify and limit the general recommendations of guidelines and frameworks to be applicable to the organization.

Scoping and tailoring are not synonymous, but the concepts work together to build the security baseline. *Scoping* is the process the organization undertakes to consider which security controls apply and what assets they need to protect. *Tailoring* is the process of modifying the set of controls to meet the specific characteristics and requirements of the organization. As each organization is different, some controls in a framework may not apply; those controls can be removed from the baseline. Sometimes a security control does apply, but implementation should be altered based on the information asset or information use within the organization. In that case, tailoring the controls is done to eliminate unnecessary requirements or to incorporate compensating controls when needed based on organizational variables. The scoping and tailoring activities must be well documented with appropriate justification. Figure 2.8 illustrates the tailoring process according to best practices, including NIST SP 800-53.

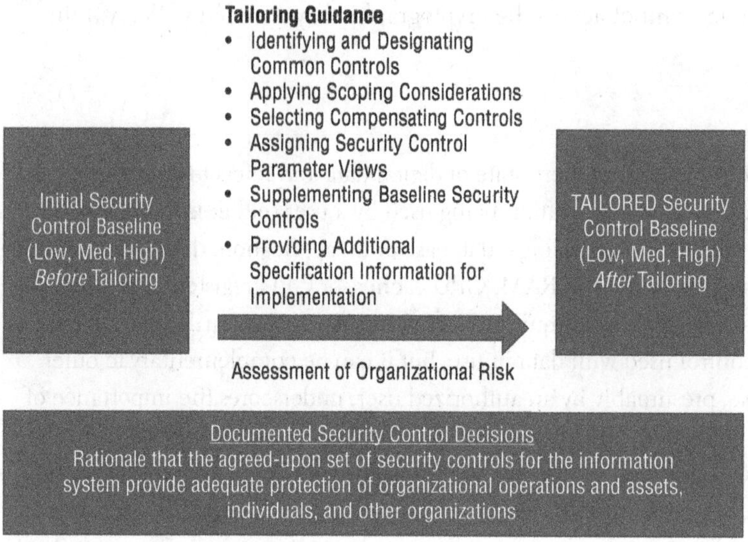

Tailoring Guidance
- Identifying and Designating Common Controls
- Applying Scoping Considerations
- Selecting Compensating Controls
- Assigning Security Control Parameter Views
- Supplementing Baseline Security Controls
- Providing Additional Specification Information for Implementation

Initial Security Control Baseline (Low, Med, High) *Before* Tailoring

TAILORED Security Control Baseline (Low, Med, High) *After* Tailoring

Assessment of Organizational Risk

Documented Security Control Decisions
Rationale that the agreed-upon set of security controls for the information system provide adequate protection of organizational operations and assets, individuals, and other organizations

FIGURE 2.8 **Tailoring process**

TIP Convenience is not a factor for removing or altering security controls. Make sure any changes to baseline requirements are rationalized against operational requirements and are analyzed for impact to risk.

Common Controls

In any enterprise, security controls may safeguard multiple assets. These controls are considered *common controls* and are typically implemented as part of the organization's security architecture. The security benefits of implementing common controls are inheritable across the assets in scope for the baseline assessment. Effective use of common controls can potentially reduce the overall resource expenditures by organizations. The following are examples of common controls within the types of controls described earlier:

- **Technical controls:** Firewalls, intrusion detection systems, and data loss prevention appliances are types of security devices that provide network boundary defense for all assets. Public key infrastructure (PKI) and network security monitoring are also examples of inheritable technical controls from which all assets benefit.

- **Administrative controls:** Data protection policies and nondisclosure agreements are common examples of administrative controls.

- **Physical controls:** The access controls for physical entry are shared by all systems located in a data center. The environmental controls maintain proper conditions and suppression of fire for all computing equipment.

Compensating Security Controls

In some cases, the prescribed or recommended security controls are applicable but cannot be scoped or tailored sufficiently to meet the control objective. When baseline controls have potential to degrade or obstruct business operations or are cost-prohibitive, we have to explore compensating controls. *Compensating controls* augment a primary control's ability to achieve a control objective or replace the primary control to meet the given control objective.

To illustrate this point, separation of duties for security personnel is a prescribed security control. In some organizations with small security staffs, separation of duties may be too costly in terms of needing more employees (i.e., it's really hard to separate duties between employees when there are very few employees). In this case, a compensating control can be increased collection and review of security activity logs.

TIP   Integrating compensating controls into a security baseline requires documentation of why the compensating controls are necessary and how they provide equivalent mitigation of the risk.

NOTE   As a reminder, a security baseline is the minimum set of security controls that is required. You may want to implement additional security controls. *Supplemental controls* are based on specific threats or regulatory requirements of an organization or an industry.

Standards Selection

Many organizations find that laws, regulations, contracts, and market requirements force them to comply with a set of standards. Those organizations that are not required to be compliant have the flexibility to choose a recognized framework or a combination of parts of recognized frameworks to establish their baseline requirements. If a standard is recognized by regulators or security industry entities, that most likely means expert practitioners in the field developed the standards. The following sections cover some U.S. and internationally recognized frameworks.

Leading Security Frameworks

One approach to establishing a security control baseline is to choose an existing framework. A *security framework* is a collection of documented policies and procedures that define how to manage an enterprise's security. In general, security frameworks focus less on specific controls and more on overall processes and best practices. The use of a framework to establish the security baseline is appropriate to assess and improve the organization's ability to prevent, detect, and respond to cyber attacks. A few examples that can be used in government and private organizations are included here:

- **U.S. Department of Defense Instruction (DoDI): DoDI 8510.01, "Risk Management Framework (RMF) for DoD Information Technology (IT)"** (www.esd.whs.mil/Portals/54/Documents/DD/issuances/dodi/851001p.pdf): This directive applies to DoD information systems and manages the lifecycle cybersecurity risk to all DoD IT. The use of this framework assists DoD security professionals in establishing a baseline and tailoring security controls as it relates to the DoD mission.

- **NIST SP 800-37, "Risk Management Framework"** (csrc.nist.gov/publications/ detail/sp/800-37/rev-2/final): Similar to the DoD RMF, the NIST RMF has broader access and applicability to both public and private-sector organizations. Federal government agencies outside of the DoD are subject to the FISMA framework, of which NIST SP 800-37 is a cornerstone directive.

- **NIST Cybersecurity Framework (CSF)** (www.nist.gov/cyberframework): This provides security and privacy guidelines that are primarily targeted at helping private-sector companies improve their security. The NIST CSF is broken into five functions: identify, protect, detect, respond, and recover.

- **UK 10 Steps to Cyber Security** (www.ncsc.gov.uk/guidance/10-steps-cyber- security) This is an example of a government-published advice document that is meant to help organizations focus on the main threats to reduce the greatest amount of risk. This document is intended for UK organizations and is considered official. It is insufficient alone but is valuable in a portfolio of security controls to make up the baseline control set.

Security Standards

In addition to the security frameworks listed in the previous section, there are a number of regional and industry-specific standards (such as PCI DSS, HIPAA, and GDPR) that take matters a step further and recommend or even require specific security controls. Some common security standards are listed here, but this is not an exhaustive list:

- **U.S. National Institute of Standards and Technology Special Publications:**

  - **NIST SP 800-53 Rev 5, "Security and Privacy Controls for Federal Information Systems and Organizations"** (csrc.nist.gov/publications/detail/sp/800-53/rev-5/final): This is a catalog of security controls for all U.S. federal information systems except those related to national security (e.g., DoD). It is used by organizations to establish the baseline security controls, tailor security controls, and supplement security controls based on assessment of risk for the organization.

  - **NIST SP 800-53A Rev 4, "Assessing Security and Privacy Controls in Federal Information Systems and Organizations: Building Effective Assessment Plans"** (csrc.nist.gov/publications/detail/sp/800-53a/rev-4/final): Used as a complementary guide, it provides a set of procedures for conducting assessments of security controls and privacy controls employed within U.S. federal information systems and organizations. The assessment procedures, executed at various phases of the system development lifecycle, are consistent with the security and privacy controls in NIST SP 800-53, Revision 5. It is applicable to private-sector organizations too.

- **U.S. NIST Federal Information Processing Standards:**

  - **FIPS Publication 199, "Standards for Security Categorization of Federal Information and Information Systems"** (nvlpubs.nist.gov/nistpubs/FIPS/NIST.FIPS.199.pdf): This provides a standard for categorizing U.S. federal information and information systems according to a government agency's level of concern for confidentiality, integrity, and availability and the potential impact on agency assets and operations, should their information and information systems be compromised through unauthorized access, use, disclosure, disruption, modification, or destruction. This is another directive primarily aimed at U.S. government agencies, but it can be applicable and useful for private-sector organizations.

  - **FIPS Publication 200, "Minimum Security Requirements for Federal Information and Information Systems"** (nvlpubs.nist.gov/nistpubs/FIPS/NIST.FIPS.200.pdf): An integral part of the NIST RMF, this standard emphasizes more security during the development, implementation, and operation of more secure information systems. FIPS 200 defines the 17 families of security controls covered under confidentiality, integrity, and availability of U.S. federal information systems and the information processed, stored, and transmitted by those systems. This is another U.S. government standard that is a useful reference for any country or industry.

- International Organization for Standardization (ISO):

  - ISO 27001, "Information technology – Security techniques – Information security management systems – Requirements" (www.iso.org/isoiec-27001-information-security.html): This specifies the requirements for establishing, implementing, maintaining, and continually improving an information security management system within the context of the organization. It also includes requirements for the assessment and treatment of information security risks tailored to the needs of the organization. The requirements set out in ISO/IEC 27001 are generic and are intended to be applicable to all organizations, regardless of type, size, or nature. It is applicable to global organizations independent of national jurisdiction and industry. For example, although not focused on HIPAA, the information security management system framework in ISO 27001 is relevant for use in U.S. healthcare organizations.

  - ISO 27002, "Information Technology: Security techniques – Code of practice for information security controls" (www.iso.org/standard/54533.html): This gives guidelines for organizational information security standards and information security management practices including the selection, implementation, and management of controls, taking into consideration the organization's information security risk environment(s). The code of practice is designed to be used by organizations that intend to select controls within the process of implementing an information security management system based on ISO 27001. It can also be tailored for organizations that want to implement commonly accepted information security controls and develop their own information security management guidelines, but as a modification of the ISO 270001 framework.

NOTE The scope of this text is not to enumerate and evaluate all available control frameworks (or to recommend any one over the others). You should be aware of recognized frameworks and understand how to evaluate the applicability and effectiveness of each for your organization. You will want to use evaluation criteria such as the following:

- Sensitivity of assets to be protected
- Industry requirements
- Regulatory factors (e.g., jurisdiction)
- Cost/benefit

The common theme is that there are many good security frameworks. They all have advantages and disadvantages. Each can be customized to solve specific information security problems. The choice of cybersecurity frameworks depends on the particular variables present in an organization, such as regulatory and compliance requirements, cost, risk tolerance, and business mission. The security practitioner must be able to evaluate the frameworks against organizational requirements and implement the solutions that drive the level of asset security desired.

Data Protection Methods

An organization's data is one of its most highly valued assets (generally considered second only to its people). Financial information is central to the business operations of banking institutions, while healthcare information is important to hospitals and medical organizations. Generally speaking, protecting data and assuring confidentiality, integrity, and availability are central not only for IT teams, but to the entire business. Several commonly used methods may suit different needs your organization has.

Digital Rights Management

Digital rights management (DRM) is a set of tools and processes focused on controlling the use, modification, and distribution of intellectual property (IP) throughout its lifecycle. DRM allows you to restrict access, editing, copying, and printing of your digital assets. Here is one common use case: DRM technology allows movie studios and music producers to prevent pirated content from being viewed on a device that isn't associated with a legitimate purchase of that content. The technology became hugely relevant in the early 2000s, amidst the growth of peer-to-peer filesharing applications like Napster and LimeWire.

Information rights management (IRM) is a related technology that more broadly protects data from unauthorized access by controlling who can view, copy, delete, or otherwise modify data. IRM technologies can be used to protect files, emails, web pages, and other forms of information.

Data Loss Prevention

Data loss prevention (DLP), sometimes referred to as *data leakage prevention*, is the set of technologies and practices used to ensure that sensitive data is not lost or accessed by unauthorized parties. DLP technologies can be used to identify and classify sensitive data and apply protections that prevent the data from being "lost" or stolen.

DLP is a foundational component of data protection programs, and it can help restrict the flow of both structured and unstructured data to authorized users, locations, and devices. Simply put, DLP analyzes data storage, identifies sensitive data elements, and prevents users from accidentally or intentionally sending that sensitive data to the wrong recipient.

DLP implementations generally consist of three core stages: discovery and classification, monitoring, and enforcement.

- **Discovery and classification:** The first stage of DLP is discovery and classification. Discovery is the process of finding all instances of data, while classification is the act of categorizing that data based on its sensitivity and value to the organization. While you should have classified your data as part of your information asset inventory, many DLP tools are capable of applying signature-based logic that determines the classification of data. In many cases, your existing classification information can be used to "tune" the DLP to know what you consider sensitive. Examples of classifications might include "PCI data" (or "cardholder data"), "Social Security numbers," "PHI," and so on. Comprehensive discovery and proper classification is critical to the effectiveness of the remaining stages and to the success of your overall DLP implementation.

- **Monitoring:** The monitoring stage involves inspecting data as it moves throughout the data lifecycle. During this stage, DLP technologies seek to identify data that is being misused or mishandled. DLP monitoring should happen on workstations, servers, networking devices, and other endpoints, and it should evaluate traffic across all potential exfiltration paths (such as email, internet browsers, messaging applications, etc.). Be mindful that standard DLP implementations cannot monitor encrypted traffic. (See "DLP in transit" in the following list for more details on these limitations.

- **Enforcement:** The final DLP stage, enforcement, is where action is taken to prevent policy violations identified during the monitoring stage. These actions are configured based on the data classification and the potential impact of its loss. For less sensitive data, violations may be automatically logged and/or alerted on, while more sensitive data can actually be blocked from unauthorized exposure or loss. As with any monitoring tool, you must monitor for false negatives and false positives, and constantly tune your DLP implementation to avoid enforcement issues, such as blocking legitimate/authorized data sharing.

When creating a DLP implementation strategy, it's important that organizations consider techniques for protection in every data state (as discussed earlier in this chapter). DLP considerations for each of the data states are discussed here:

- **DLP at rest:** For data at rest, the DLP implementation is located wherever the data is stored. This can include workstations, file servers, or just about any other endpoint with storage. Because data at rest is static, it does not require data loss prevention, in the purest sense. Data in this state is most commonly protected via encryption, access control, and other mechanisms. Although DLP monitoring is still important in this state, it is most effective when combined with other DLP technologies.

- **DLP in transit:** *Network-based DLP* is data loss prevention that involves monitoring outbound network traffic, typically near the perimeter. This DLP implementation monitors traffic over HTTP, FTP, SMTP, and other network protocols. It's important to note here that one limitation of standard DLP implementations is that they cannot effectively monitor encrypted traffic, such as HTTPS. If attempting to monitor encrypted network traffic, organizations must integrate encryption and key management technologies into the overall DLP solution; this may significantly increase the complexity of a DLP implementation but is required for certain use-cases.

- **DLP in use:** *Host-based (or endpoint-based) DLP* is data loss prevention that involves installation of a DLP application on a workstation or other endpoint device. This DLP implementation allows monitoring of all data in use on the endpoint and provides insights that network-based DLP systems are not able to provide (such as attempts to transfer data to removable media). DLP systems that monitor data in use can protect against unauthorized copy/paste, screen capture, and other operations that involve active use of sensitive data.

When creating a DLP strategy, organizations must consider how the technology aligns with their existing architecture and processes. DLP controls need to be thoroughly evaluated and applied in a manner that aligns with the organization's overall enterprise architecture to ensure that only the right type of data is blocked from being transmitted. DLP that is incorrectly implemented can lead to false positives that result in legitimate traffic being blocked or false negatives that permit sensitive data to be sent to unauthorized parties.

Cloud Access Security Broker

With the growth of cloud-based data storage, designated methods for protecting data in the cloud have become essential. A *cloud access security broker* (CASB) is a software application that sits between cloud users and cloud services and applications; CASBs actively monitor all cloud activity and implement centralized controls to enforce security. A CASB may be used to enforce security policies, stop malware, and alert security teams of potential security events — all important contributions to an organization's data security program.

Generally speaking, a CASB aims to serve four primary functions:

- **Visibility:** Provide insight into an organization's cloud usage, including which users use which cloud applications, and which devices are used to connect to cloud resources. CASBs can also help detect, monitor, and secure shadow IT.

- **Data security:** Monitor an organization's data security and help prevent data exfiltration through cloud services. They can also help enforce specific security policies based on the data being used.

- **Threat protection:** Guard against insider threats by providing a comprehensive view of cloud usage.

- **Compliance:** Help organizations demonstrate compliance with regulatory requirements like GDPR, HIPAA, and PCI DSS.

There are three primary types of CASB solutions:

- **Forward proxy:** This type of CASB generally resides on a user's device (e.g., a computer or mobile device) and uses an encrypted man-in-the-middle technique to securely inspect and forward all cloud traffic for the user. This type of CASB requires you to install certificates on every endpoint that needs to be monitored, making it difficult or tedious to deploy in large, distributed organizations.

- **Reverse proxy:** This type of CASB integrates into identity services, such as Okta, to force all traffic through the CASB for inline monitoring. This removes the need to individually install certificates on user endpoints but poses compatibility challenges for client-server applications that have hard-coded hostnames.

- **API-based:** This type of CASB allows organizations to protect any user accessing cloud resources from any device, from any location. API-based CASBs monitor data within the cloud itself, rather than on a perimeter-based proxy. There's no need to install anything on user devices, but a potential drawback is that not all cloud applications provide API support for these types of CASBs.

SUMMARY

In any organization, the most important assets (aside from people) are most likely found in the IT and data inventory. Protection of these assets is incredibly important to security professionals as well as executive leadership, governing boards, and customers of these organizations. Because of the sensitivity and value of these assets, governments and industries across the globe have put legislations and regulations in place to protect them. Along with the loss of revenue or recovery costs if assets are lost or stolen, significant privacy concerns exist when sensitive assets are mismanaged. This chapter covered a great many of the important concepts and guiding principles a security practitioner is expected to know and implement in their daily work. Beginning with constructing an asset management policy, the organizational policy must be informed by prevailing law, directives, and best practices but be customized to each organization's mission and unique risk profile. The process for asset management will include multiple stakeholders within the organization, so roles and responsibilities must be clearly documented, and people should be trained adequately.

At the core of asset management are the standards and frameworks that have been developed by industry experts and cohorts of practitioners that should be used to build the asset management program in an organization. The choice of standards or frameworks and the individual security controls put in place to protect confidentiality, integrity, and availability of assets will also differ from one organization to the next. How a security practitioner will scope and tailor asset management controls depends on measuring and evaluating risk based on variables such as legal jurisdiction, industry, and considerations like compensating and alternative controls. Keep in mind, security controls work best when working together, not managed independently. The proper acquisition, inventorying, monitoring, and security management of assets in organizations around the world is a significant undertaking. Information systems are highly interconnected and dependent on each other, information is valuable and requires protection, and the impact of doing it wrong can be disastrous to an organization and/or its customers. Security professionals have to master the proper security management of information through proper marking, storing, handling, and destruction of assets within their organizations to minimize risk and protect the assets throughout the entire data lifecycle.

Security Architecture and Engineering

SECURITY ARCHITECTURE IS THE design and organization of the components, processes, services, and controls appropriate to reduce the security risks associated with a system to an acceptable level. Security engineering is the implementation of that design. The goal of both security architecture and security engineering is first and foremost to protect the confidentiality, integrity, and availability of the systems or business in question, in addition to ensuring other important principles such as privacy. This is generally done by following an industry- or government-accepted enterprise or security architecture methodology.

Before designing security architecture, a comprehensive risk assessment must be conducted so that the security architect has an accurate idea of the risks to be addressed. In Chapter 1, "Security and Risk Management," risk management, risk assessment, threat modeling, and other approaches are used when determining the risks to the system. Once properly identified and assessed, each risk must eventually be found acceptable by the organization, either as is or after an action is taken. What that action is depends on a number of factors, but it generally occurs in one of four ways:

- Avoid
- Transfer or share (i.e., insurance or contract)
- Mitigate (e.g., through security architecture)
- Accept

Risk assessment is an iterative process. First, the initial risk assessment identifies the risks to be reduced through the design of a security architecture to incorporate appropriate security controls. Then, an assessment must be made to confirm that the resulting system's risks have been reduced to an acceptable level. This is done in line with the principles outlined next.

It may be that during the security architecture process, the costs associated with certain controls are prohibitive relative to the anticipated benefit of the system. As a result, the decision to reduce certain risks may need to be reconsidered, and those risks treated in another manner, avoided through a system redesign, or the project simply abandoned.

Also, security serves to protect the business. The work of the security architect is to ensure the business and its interests at the very least are protected according to applicable standards and laws, as well as meeting any relevant regulatory compliance needs. At times, the organizational leadership's goal to achieve its objectives may appear to be in conflict with compliance. As an essential technical member of the security team, there is a tendency to concentrate on technical security controls and attempt to address all known security issues or requirements. Security for security's sake, while intellectually satisfying, is a disservice to the organization. We must always remember we first serve as subject matter experts, aware of relevant regulations or laws and capable of ensuring our organization's compliance wherever change is required. As for the organization, the same expertise works together with leadership to securely advance the goals of the organization.

It's important to remember that an organization's security strategy must align with its mission, goals, objectives, and compliance environment. Success in security architecture is much more likely when one is aligned with the business and taking a risk management approach to security architecture.

RESEARCH, IMPLEMENT, AND MANAGE ENGINEERING PROCESSES USING SECURE DESIGN PRINCIPLES

System and application development generally consists of the following stages:

- Design
- Development
- Testing
- Implementation
- Maintenance
- Decommissioning

Secure development principles should be considered at each of the previous stages, but addressing security up front in the Design phase is most critical. Security engineers are often called in to retrofit an existing system with security features designed to protect the confidentiality, integrity, and availability of the system and its data. While this is often necessary, it is best that security be incorporated into the design process (and updated over time, as necessary) for two primary reasons:

- It is less expensive to incorporate security when the overall functional system design is developed rather than trying to add it on later (which will often require redesign, if not reengineering, of already developed components).

- The need for security controls is not just to prevent the user from performing unauthorized actions, but to prevent components of the system itself from violating security requirements when acting on the user's requests. If security is not intrinsic to the overall design, it is not possible to completely mediate all the activities that can compromise security.

Fundamental to any security architecture, regardless of the design principles employed, are the basic requirements outlined in 1972 by James Anderson in *Computer Security Technology Planning Study* (USAF):

- Security functions need to be implemented in a manner that prevents their being bypassed, circumvented, or tampered with.

- Security functions need to be invoked whenever necessary to implement the security control.
- Security functions need to be as small as possible so that defects are more likely to be found.

ISO/IEC 19249

In 2017, the International Organization for Standardization (ISO) published its first revision of standard 19249, "Information technology — Security techniques — Catalogue of architectural and design principles for secure products, systems and applications." The aim of ISO 19249 is to describe architectural and design principles to be used to foster the secure development of systems and applications. ISO 19249 specifies five architectural principles and five design principles.

The five architectural principles from ISO/IEC 19249 are as follows:

- Domain separation
- Layering
- Encapsulation
- Redundancy
- Virtualization

The five design principles from ISO/IEC 19249 are as follows:

- Least privilege
- Attack surface minimization
- Centralized parameter validation
- Centralized general security services
- Preparing for error and exception handling

These architectural and design principles build on existing concepts and reflect a number of new approaches to security theory. The following sections examine each of these architectural and design principles.

ISO/IEC 19249 Architectural Principles

In the introductory text of ISO/IEC 19249's architectural principles section, the technical specification describes the primary challenge that all information security professionals know well: finding the difficult balance between security and functionality. The specification proposes that the way to secure any system, project, or application is to first adopt its five architectural principles and then approach the easier challenge of finding the balance between functionality and security for each principle. ISO/IEC 19249's architectural principles are examined in the following five sections.

Domain Separation

A *domain* is a concept that describes enclosing a group of components together as a common entity. As a common entity, these components, be they resources, data, or applications, can be assigned a common set of security attributes. The principle of *domain separation* involves the following:

- Placing components that share similar security attributes, such as privileges and access rights, in a domain. That domain can then be assigned the necessary controls deemed pertinent to its components.

- Only permitting separate domains to communicate over well-defined and (completely) mediated communication channels (e.g. application programming interfaces, or APIs).

In networking, the principle of domain separation can be implemented through network segmentation — putting devices that share similar access privileges on the same distinct network, connected to other network segments using a firewall or other device to mediate access between segments (domains).

Of particular concern are systems in which privileges are not static — situations in which components of a single domain, or entire domains, have privileges and access permissions that can change dynamically. These designs need to be treated particularly carefully to ensure that the appropriate mediations occur, based on the specific system requirements at any given point in time.

Examples where domain separation is used in the real world include the following:

- A network is separated into manageable and logical segments. Network traffic (inter-domain communication) is handled according to policy and routing control, based on the trust level and workflow between segments.

- Data is separated into domains in the context of classification, categorization, and security baseline. Even though data might come from disparate sources, if that data is classified at the same level, the handling and security of that classification level (domain) is accomplished with like security attributes.

Layering

Layering is the hierarchical structuring of a system into different levels of abstraction, with higher levels relying upon services and functions provided by lower levels, and lower levels hiding (or abstracting) details of the underlying implementation from higher levels. Layering is seen in network protocols, starting with the classic OSI seven-layer model running from physical through to application layers.

In software systems, one encounters operating system calls, upon which libraries are built, upon which we build our programs. Within the operating system, higher-level functions (such as filesystem functions) are built upon lower-level functions (such as block disk I/O functions).

In web applications we see this principle in the *n*-tier architecture illustrated in Figure 3.1.

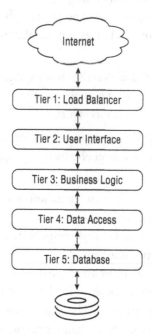

FIGURE 3.1 **N-tier architecture**

The purpose of layering is to do the following:

- Create the ability to impose specific security policies at each layer
- Simplify functionality so that the correctness of its operation is more easily validated

From a security perspective:

- Higher levels always have the same or less privilege than a lower level.
- If layering to provide security controls, it must not be possible for a higher level to bypass an intermediate level. For example, if a program is able to bypass the filesystem layer and issue direct block-level I/O requests to the underlying disk storage device, then the security policies (i.e., file permissions) enforced by the filesystem layer will be for naught.

Layering and domain separation are related techniques and work well together. A single domain might have multiple layers to assist in structuring functions and validating correctness. Alternatively, different layers might be implemented as different domains. Or a combination of these might apply.

An example where layering is used in the real world is a filesystem. The lowest layer, access to the raw disk, provides only basic protection to the disk sectors. The next layer might be the virtual or logical partitioning of the disk. Still higher layers would be the filesystems as users browse the data, employing advanced access control features.

Encapsulation

Encapsulation is an architectural concept where objects are accessed only through functions that logically separate functions that are abstracted from their underlying object by inclusion or information hiding within higher level objects. For example, raw disk reads/writes are abstracted away from the user through several layers of encapsulation (as discussed in the previous section). The functions might be specific to accessing or changing attributes about that object. The encapsulation functions can define the security policy for that object and mediate all operations on that object. As a whole, those functions act as sort of an agent for the object.

Proper encapsulation requires that all access or manipulation of the encapsulated object must go through the encapsulation functions, and that it is not possible to tamper with the encapsulation of the object or the security attributes (e.g., permissions) of the encapsulation functions.

Device drivers can be considered to use a form of encapsulation in which a simpler and consistent interface is provided that hides the details of a particular device, as well as the differences between similar devices. Forcing interactions to occur through the abstract object increases the assurance that information flows conform to the expected inputs and outputs.

An example where encapsulation is used in the real world is the use of the *setuid bit*. Typically, in Linux or any Unix-based operating system, a file has ownership based on the person who created it, and an application runs based on the person who launched it. A special mechanism, setuid, allows for a file or object to be set with different privileges. Setting the setuid bit on a file will cause it to open with the permission of whatever account you set it to be. The setuid bit controls access, above and beyond the typical operation. That is an example of encapsulation.

Redundancy

Redundancy is designing a system with replicated components, operating in parallel, so that the system can continue to operate in spite of errors or excessive load. From a security perspective, redundancy is an architectural principle for addressing possible availability and integrity compromises or issues.

In the case of replicated data stores, the particular challenge is to ensure consistency. State changes to one data store must be reliably replicated across all redundant data stores, or the purpose of redundancy is defeated and potential security vulnerabilities may be created.

For redundancy to work, it must be possible for the overall system to detect errors in one of the replicated subsystems. Once an error is detected, that error may be eliminated or the error triggers a failover to the redundant subsystem. How any particular error is handled depends upon the capabilities of the overall system. In some cases, it is sufficient merely to reject the operation and wait for the requester to reissue it (this time on one of the working remaining redundant systems). In other cases, it is necessary to reverse (roll back) intermediate state changes so that when the request is reattempted on a correctly functioning system, the overall system state is consistent.

An example of the first is a load balancer to a website. If it fails and cannot process a request for a web page, it may be sufficient to fail the request and wait for the user to reload the page.

In a situation in which the request involves, for example, transferring funds from an account at one bank to another, if the funds have been deducted from the first account before the failure occurs, it is necessary to ensure that the deduction is reversed before failing and retrying the request.

Examples where redundancy is used in the real world include the following:

- High availability solutions such as a cluster, where one component or system takes over when its active partner becomes inaccessible

- Having storage in redundant array of inexpensive disks (RAID) configurations where the data is made redundant and fault tolerant

- Cloud-based storage, where data is replicated across multiple data centers, zones, or regions

Virtualization

Virtualization is a form of emulation in which the functionality of one real or simulated device is emulated on a different one. (This is discussed in more detail in the "Understand Security Capabilities of Information Systems" section later in this chapter.)

More commonly, virtualization is the provision of an environment that functions like a single dedicated computer environment but supports multiple such environments on the same physical hardware. The emulation can operate at the hardware level, in which case we speak of virtual machines (VMs), or the operating system level, in which case we speak of containers. In either example, virtualization involves abstracting the underlying components of hardware or software from the end user.

Virtualization is used extensively in the real world to make the most cost-effective use of resources and to scale up or down as business needs require. Cloud computing environments are the most common examples of virtualization today.

ISO/IEC 19249 Design Principles

The following design principles are meant to help identify and mitigate risk during system design. Some of these five fundamental ideas can be directly associated with security properties of the target system or project, while others are generally applied. The following sections explain the five ISO/IEC 19249 design principles.

Least Privilege

The principle of *least privilege* asserts that access to information should only be granted on an as-needed basis (i.e., a subject should only be granted the privileges needed to complete an assigned or authorized task). Every process, service, or individual ought to operate with only those permissions absolutely necessary to perform the authorized activities and only for as long as necessary and no more. By limiting permissions, one limits the damage that can be done should a mistake, defect, or compromise cause an undesired action to be attempted.

Granting permissions based on the principle of least privilege is the implementation of the concept of need-to-know, restricting access and knowledge to only those items necessary for the authorized task.

TIP   *Just-in-time*, or *JIT, access* is a principle that complements the principle of least privilege. JIT enforces true least privilege by enforcing granular time limits on privileged access. We discuss JIT privileged access management in Chapter 5, "Identity and Access Management (IAM)."

We see this in practice, for example, with the Linux `sudo` command, which temporarily elevates a user's permission to perform a privileged operation. This allows the user to perform a task requiring additional permissions only for the period of time necessary to perform the task. Properly configured, authorized users may "sudo" as a privileged user (other than root) to perform functions specific to certain services. This is especially valid when it is restricted to privileged accounts related to specific services, but not used to access the root account. The increased security comes from not allowing the user to operate for extended periods with unneeded permissions.

Attack Surface Minimization

A system's *attack surface* is the sum of all possible security risk exposures through which an attacker may compromise the system — think of this as the number of doors and windows on a house through which a burglar may enter. The more entry points, the greater the attack surface.

System hardening, the disabling and/or removal of unneeded services and components, is a form of attack surface minimization. This can involve blocking network ports, removing system daemons, and otherwise ensuring that the only services and programs that are available are the minimum set necessary for the system to function as required. In our house example, hardening may include adding locks to doors, bars to windows, and a guard dog out front.

Reducing the number of unnecessary open ports and running applications is an obvious approach. Another, less frequently observed strategy for minimizing the attack surface is to reduce the complexity of necessary services. If a service or function of a system is required, perhaps the workflow or operation of that service can be "minimized" by simplifying it.

Centralized Parameter Validation

As will be discussed later in this chapter in the discussion of common system vulnerabilities, many threats involve systems accepting improper inputs. Since ensuring that parameters are valid is common across all components that process similar types of parameters, using a single library to validate those parameters enables the necessary capability to properly review and test that library.

Full parameter validation is especially important when dealing with user input, or input from systems to which users input data. Invalid or malformed data can be fed to the system, either unwittingly, by inept users, or intentionally by malicious attackers.

Examples where centralized parameter validation is used in the real world include the following:

- Validating input data by secure coding practices
- Screening data through an application firewall

Centralized General Security Services

The principle of centralizing security services can be implemented at several levels. At the operating system level, your access control, user authentication and authorization, logging, and key management are all examples of discrete security services that can and should be managed centrally. Simplifying your security services interface instead of managing multiple interfaces is a sensible benefit.

The centralized general security services principle is a generalization of the previously discussed centralized parameter validation principle: by implementing commonly used security functions once, it is easier to ensure that the security controls have been properly reviewed and tested. It is also more cost-effective to concentrate one's efforts on validating the correct operation of a few centralized services rather than on myriad implementations of what is essentially the same control.

Examples where centralized security services are used in the real world include the following:

- Centralized access control server
- Centralized cryptographic processing
- Security information and event management (SIEM)
- Security orchestration, automation, and response (SOAR)

Preparing for Error and Exception Handling

Errors happen. Systems must ensure that errors are detected and appropriate action taken, whether that is to just log the error or to take some action to mitigate the impact of the issue. Error handling should not leak information, for example, by displaying stack traces or internal information in error reports that might disclose confidential information or provide information useful to an attacker. Systems must be designed to fail safe (as discussed later) and to always remain in a secure state, even when errors occur.

Errors can also be indicators of compromise. Detecting and reporting such errors can enable a quick response that limits the scope of the breach.

An example of where error and exception handling are used in the real world is developing applications to properly handle errors and respond with a corresponding action. For example, an automated teller machine (ATM) may use error handling to validate that a withdrawal request does not exceed the account balance, and respond with an informative message if such a withdrawal is attempted.

Threat Modeling

Threat modeling is a process by which potential security threats and vulnerabilities can be identified, and mitigations can be prioritized. Threat modeling can be used to help securely develop applications or to help reduce risk in an already deployed application.

There are numerous approaches to threat modeling, but three of the most commonly used are called STRIDE, DREAD, and PASTA.

STRIDE

STRIDE is a model developed at Microsoft in the late '90s to help identify and classify computer security threats. The name itself is a mnemonic for the following six categories of security threats:

- **Spoofing:** *Spoofing* is an attack during which a person or system assumes the identity of another person or system by falsifying information. Strong passwords, multifactor authentication, and digital signatures are common controls to protect against spoofing.

- **Tampering:** *Data tampering* is an attack on the integrity of data by maliciously manipulating data. Strong access controls and thorough logging and monitoring are good ways to prevent and detect data tampering.

- **Repudiation:** *Repudiation* is the ability of a party to deny that they are responsible for performing an action. Repudiation threat occurs when a user claims that they did not perform an action, and there is no evidence to prove otherwise. Digital signatures and secure logging and auditing are the primary controls to provide nonrepudiation.

- **Information disclosure:** *Information disclosure* — commonly referred to as a *data leak* — occurs when information is improperly shared with an unauthorized party. Encryption, data loss prevention (DLP), and strong access controls are common controls to protect against information disclosure.

- **Denial of service (DoS):** A *denial-of-service (DoS)* attack involves a malicious actor rendering a system or service unavailable by legitimate users. System redundancy, network filtering, and resource limits are common protections against DoS attacks.

- **Elevation of privilege:** *Elevation of privilege* (or *privilege escalation*) occurs when an unprivileged application user is able to upgrade their privileges to those of a privileged user (such as an administrator). Strong access control and input validation are common protections against privilege escalation.

The STRIDE model can be used as a starting point to answer the question "what can go wrong?" as systems are being developed or analyzed. The six security threats cover a broad range of potential issues that can compromise confidentiality, integrity, and availability, as well as authenticity and authorization.

DREAD

The DREAD model, developed in 2002, is a quantitative risk analysis model that involves rating the severity of security threats by assigning numeric values (typically from 1 to 10) that represent different levels of severity. DREAD is a mnemonic that describes the five key points and associated questions that you must answer for any given threat:

- **Damage:** What is the total amount of damage the threat is capable of causing to your business?

- **Reproducibility:** How easily can an attack on the particular threat be replicated?

- **Exploitability:** How much effort is required for the threat to be exploited by an attacker?

- **Affected users:** How many people, either inside or outside of your organization, will be affected by the security threat?
- **Discoverability:** How easily can the vulnerability be found?

Once each of these categories is rated, the sum is then calculated. The sum of all ratings for a given risk can be used to prioritize different risks.

TIP There are many opinions on the relative importance of each of the categories within DREAD, and many security professionals disagree with a model that weights each category equally. Some modified applications of the DREAD model involve using higher or lower rating scales for the particular categories that are more or less important to a particular organization.

PASTA

The *Process for Attack Simulation and Threat Analysis* (PASTA) is a seven-step risk-based threat model, developed in 2012, that supports dynamic threat analysis. Unlike STRIDE, which is strictly intended as a framework for threat identification, the PASTA methodology provides a robust process for identifying and mitigating threats. PASTA integrates business objectives with technical requirements, system risks, and attack modeling. The PASTA model is intended to provide an attacker-centric perspective of the application and infrastructure and help security teams develop a mitigation strategy based on threat enumeration and impact analysis.

These are the seven stages of the PASTA methodology:

1. **Define objectives.**
   During this first stage, key business objectives are defined, and critical security and compliance requirements are identified. In addition, a preliminary business impact analysis (BIA) is conducted to identify potential business impact considerations.

2. **Define technical scope.**
   During this stage, the boundaries of the technical environment and the scope of all technical assets for which threat analysis is needed are defined. In addition to the application boundaries, you must discover and document all infrastructure, application, and software dependencies. The goal is to capture a high-level but comprehensive view of all servers, hosts, devices, applications, protocols, and data that need to be protected.

3. **Application decomposition.**
   During this stage, an evaluation of all assets (i.e., the application components) needs to be conducted, and the data flows between these assets need to be

identified. As part of this process, all application entry points and trust boundaries should be identified and defined. This stage is intended to establish a clear understanding of all data sources, the parties that access those data sources, and all use cases for data access within the application — in other words, who should perform what actions on which components of the application.

4. **Threat analysis.**

    This stage is intended to identify and analyze threat information from within the system, such as SIEM feeds, web application firewall (WAF) logs, etc., as well as externally available threat intelligence that is related to the system. Threat-attack scenarios that are relevant to the specific application, environment, and data should be identified and understood. The output of this stage should include a list of the most likely attack vectors for the given application or system.

5. **Vulnerability analysis.**

    During this stage, all vulnerabilities within the application's code should be identified and correlated to the threat-attack scenarios identified in step 4. Operating system, application, network, and database scans should be conducted, and dynamic and static code analysis results should be evaluated to enumerate and score existing vulnerabilities. The primary output of this stage is a correlated mapping of all threat-attack vectors to existing vulnerabilities and impacted assets.

6. **Attack modeling.**

    During this stage, attacks that could exploit identified vulnerabilities (from step 5) are modeled and simulated. This helps determine the likelihood and impact of each identified attack vector. After this stage, your organization should have a strong understanding of your application's attack surface (i.e., what bad things could happen to which assets within your application environment).

7. **Risk and impact analysis.**

    During this final stage, your business impact analysis (from step 1) should be refined based on all the analysis performed in the previous six steps. Risks should be prioritized for remediation, and a risk mitigation strategy should be developed to identify countermeasures for all residual risks.

Secure Defaults

The concept of *secure defaults* (or *secure-by-default*) essentially means that systems should be designed with the best security possible without users needing to turn on security features or otherwise think about security configurations. Secure-by-default means that a system's default configuration includes the most secure settings possible, which may not always be the most highly functioning settings. A new server, for example, may have ports 80 and 443 disabled by default. While this hardened configuration is certainly the most secure, it would not make for a very good web server without opening port 443, which is used for secure web traffic. The point here is that systems and applications should be designed such that the end user (or system admin) must actively choose to override secure configurations based on the business's needs and risk appetite.

Fail Securely

It's essential to consider how your systems will behave if an error or exception should occur. For some systems, a *fail-open* design, where systems continue to allow access when exceptions occur, may be preferable to ensure that access to important information remains readily available during a system error or exception. Conversely, a *fail-secure* (also known as a *fail-safe* or *fail-closed*) system blocks access by default, ensuring that security is prioritized over availability.

For systems with sensitive data, security controls should be designed such that in the absence of specific configuration settings to the contrary, the default is to not permit the action. Access should be based on permission (e.g., allowed list), not exclusion (e.g., blocked list). This is the principle behind "deny all" default firewall rules and also relates to the concept of least privileged (discussed in an earlier section). Generally speaking, it is best to design systems so that if an error is detected, the system fails in a deny (or safe) state of higher security rather than failing in an open, less secure state.

Separation of Duties

Separation of duties (SoD) requires two (or more) actions, actors, or components to operate in a coordinated manner to perform a security-sensitive operation. This control, adopted from the financial accounting practice, has been a foundational protection against fraud for years. Breaking up a process into multiple steps performed by different individuals or requiring two individuals to perform a single operation together (known as *dual control*) forces the malicious insider to collude with multiple insiders to compromise the system.

Security controls that require the active participation of two or more individuals are more robust and less susceptible to failure than those that do not. While not every control is suitable for separation of duties, nor does every risk mandate such security, the redundancy that comes from separation of duties makes security less likely to be compromised by a single mistake (or rogue actor).

TIP   Separation of duties can also be viewed as a defense-in-depth control; permission for sensitive operations should not depend on a single condition.

Keep It Simple

Complexity is the enemy of security. The simpler and smaller the system, the easier it is to design, assess, and test. When the system as a whole cannot be simplified sufficiently, consider partitioning the problem so that the components with the most significant risks are separated and simplified to the extent possible. This is the concept behind a *security kernel* — a small separate subsystem with the security-critical components that the rest of the system can rely upon.

Information security and cryptography expert Bruce Schneier stated the following (`www.schneier.com/news/archives/2016/04/bruce_schneier_build.html`):

> *Complexity is the worst enemy of security. The more complex you make your system, the less secure it's going to be, because you'll have more vulnerabilities and make more mistakes somewhere in the system. . . . The simpler we can make systems, the more secure they are.*

By separating security functionality into small, isolated components, the task of carefully reviewing and testing the code for security vulnerabilities can be significantly reduced.

Trust, but Verify

U.S. President Ronald Reagan first started using the English translation of the old Russian adage "trust, but verify" in the late 1980s. At that time, President Reagan used the phrase to describe his cautious approach to nuclear disarmament talks between the United States and the Soviet Union. Several decades later, the "trust, but verify" mantra is widely used to describe situations that require an extra layer of verification and accountability.

In the information security world, "trust, but verify" has been used to describe the use of perimeter firewalls and other controls that use a party's identity, location, and other characteristics to verify that they are a trusted user or system from a trusted location — in other words, "trust, but verify" assumes everything behind your corporate firewall is safe and verifies that anything passing through that firewall into your network is safe to allow in essentially, "verify once, trust forever." This model of security has become less-preferred in recent years, in favor of the zero trust model (discussed in the next section).

The phrase "trust, but verify" may also be used colloquially when dealing with third parties or when describing the need to validate the operation and effectiveness of internal security controls. If there is a single security concept that comes to mind when discussing "trust, but verify," it might be the concept of auditing. When working with third parties (such as partners, cloud providers, or anyone else outside of your organization), a certain level of trust is required in order to execute day-to-day business operations. The notion of "verify" comes in when you consider the need to periodically audit those relationships to ensure they continue operating as agreed upon and expected. This is why cloud providers, for example, share compliance reports and other artifacts with customers who wish to periodically validate the CSP's security posture.

When looking inward, "trust, but verify" also plays a large role in how we assess and monitor our security architecture to ensure ongoing compliance and secure functionality — there should never be a "set-and-forget" approach to security controls. "Trust, but verify" also shows up in our use of threat intelligence products and information to determine whether a potential threat is viable. Ultimately, the concept of "trust, but verify" is yet another reminder that maintaining security is a never-ending task.

Zero Trust

Zero trust architecture was first described in the early 2010s and has since become a mainstream approach to secure system architecture, with the National Institute of Standards and Technology (NIST) formalizing guidance, in 2020, in NIST SP 800-207, "Zero Trust Architecture." *Zero trust* is a security model that is predicated on the idea that an organization should not automatically trust anything outside *or* inside its perimeters — instead, they must verify anything and everything trying to connect to its systems before allowing access. This model is a drastic departure from the previously mentioned "trust, but verify" model that involves fiercely defending your perimeters while assuming anything inside your network is safe.

NOTE The term *zero trust* was coined in 2010 by security expert John Kindervag while he was at Forrester Research. Kindervag's viewpoint that risk is inherent both inside and outside the perimeter was groundbreaking and has changed the way security teams approach security architecture.

The zero trust model preaches a "never trust, always verify" mindset that requires every access request to be fully authenticated, authorized, and encrypted before granting access. With this approach, an attacker who successfully breaches your perimeter is much less able to move laterally within your network, because every device is protected from the others, thus reducing the blast radius (or total impact) of a successful compromise.

The zero trust model is based on the following core principles:

- **Always verify.** Authenticate and authorize every access request based on user identity, location, system health (e.g., patch levels), data classification, user behavior analytics, and any other available data points.

- **Use least privilege access.** Always assign the minimum rights required for the specific access requested, on a Just in Time (JIT) basis.

- **Assume breach.** Instead of trusting devices on your network, assume the worst-case scenario (i.e., that you've already been breached) and minimize the blast radius to prevent further damage.

Prevention is the biggest goal of zero trust, and "always verify" is huge part of that. Identities should always be verified and secured with strong multifactor authentication, or MFA, wherever possible. Devices that access your network should be inspected both for identity verification and also to ensure their health status and compliance with your organization's security requirements prior to granting access.

Remember that users and devices shouldn't be trusted just because they're on an internal network. All internal communications should be encrypted, access should be limited to least privilege, by policy, and microsegmentation should be employed to contain threats. *Microsegmentation* is a network security technique that involves dividing large network segments into smaller zones to isolate resources from one another and minimize lateral movement by users. If a breach occurs, microsegmentation restricts a hacker to a single microsegment, making containment and detection easier. In addition to the network security changes, zero trust architectures move from perimeter-based data protection to data-focused protection that relies on strong data classification and tagging. The most effective zero trust architectures have well-classified data that provides additional insight for trust-based decisions to be made.

Despite a heavy bias toward preventative measures, detective controls play a big part in a successful zero trust architecture. Organizations should deploy real-time monitoring to help detect and stop attacks and other anomalous behavior. Real-time analytics can also help inform access decisions by providing real-time context for access requests and supporting JIT permissions (discussed earlier in this chapter).

✔ BeyondCorp at Google

BeyondCorp is Google's implementation of a zero trust architecture and was one of the earliest corporate implementations of the zero trust model. BeyondCorp started in 2011 as an internal Google initiative with the mission "to enable every Google employee to work successfully from untrusted networks without the use of a VPN." Today, that mission is fulfilled — and BeyondCorp is one of the largest demonstrations of zero trust in action — with nearly every one of their employees (known as "Googlers") relying on the BeyondCorp architecture to access Google's infrastructure and corporate resources from anywhere, without relying on virtual private networks (VPNs).

BeyondCorp provides Googlers with single sign-on (SSO) access to Google's infrastructure, based on contextual factors from the user and their device — access is not determined based on the network from which a user is connecting. As a zero trust architecture, BeyondCorp requires resource access to be authenticated, authorized, and encrypted.

Privacy by Design

Privacy by Design (abbreviated PbD) is a systems engineering approach, initially developed by former Information and Privacy Commissioner of Ontario, Ann Cavoukian, in the 1990s and later formalized into a framework in 2009; the framework focuses on extending the use of privacy-enhancing technologies and establishes seven foundational principles (discussed next). *Privacy-enhancing technologies* (PETs) are technologies that support data protection and PbD by minimizing personal data use and maximizing data security.

PbD involves building privacy directly into the design, operation, and management of a system or process, rather than considering privacy after the fact. The seven PbD principles aim to ensure privacy of personal data while also giving users more control over their personal information. Those seven principles, as identified by Cavoukian, are summarized here:

1. **Proactive not Reactive; Preventative not Remedial:**
    Design systems and processes to proactively take action before a privacy incident, not afterward. In other words, anticipate and prevent invasive privacy events before they happen, rather than relying on detecting and responding to them once they already occur. As you design and develop your systems, you should determine what privacy risks exist and plan for them, rather than putting out privacy fires later.

2. **Privacy as the Default Setting:**
    Ensure that all personal data is automatically protected in all IT systems or business processes, with no added action required by any individual. This principle places the responsibility for privacy on the system, rather than on the individual. Practical examples include anonymizing or masking personal information, restricting access to personal information to those who absolutely need it (i.e., least privilege), and deleting such information when it is no longer needed.

3. **Privacy Embedded into Design:**
    Privacy measures should be fully integrated components of the system and associated processes, rather than added on after the fact; privacy should be treated as a core functionality of the system. Examples of this principle include building encryption and authentication mechanisms into your system, rather than finding ways to add these functionalities in afterwards.

4. **Full Functionality — Positive-Sum, not Zero-Sum:**
    PbD encourages a "win-win" approach to all legitimate system design goals and discourages unnecessary trade-offs being made. Both privacy and security are

important — both can and should be achieved. For example, internet cookies provide necessary web functionality, and they can be implemented in a secure and private manner.

5. **End-to-End Security — Full Lifecycle Protection:**
Ensure security and privacy of personal data from cradle to grave; data should be created, managed, and destroyed in a secure fashion. Encryption and authentication are standard at every stage, but you should pay close attention to what security and privacy mechanisms may be required throughout the data lifecycle.

6. **Visibility and Transparency — Keep it Open:**
This is a "trust, but verify" principle (discussed earlier) that seeks to assure all stakeholders that the system operates securely and maintains data privacy as intended. The clearest example of this principle is establishing a well-documented privacy policy that is shared with all impacted parties.

7. **Respect for User Privacy — Keep it User-Centric:**
When it's all said and done, privacy is about the user, and this principle reinforces that notion. System architects, developers, and operators must keep the interests of the individual as their utmost priority by providing strong privacy defaults, appropriate notice, and a user-friendly experience. One of the most practical ways to keep privacy user-centric is by requiring the user to take action (e.g., by clicking a button or ticking a check box) in order to give consent.

As users' personal data continues to proliferate across various systems and platforms, PbD continues to become a foundational concept in secure system architecture and development. Numerous private companies have committed to PbD principles, while companies like Deloitte offer services to evaluate and even certify an organization's compliance with PbD principles.

In the United States, the Federal Trade Commission (FTC) has recognized PbD as one of three recommended practices for protecting online privacy, while the European Union General Data Protection Regulation (EU GDPR), the largest privacy regulation around the world to-date, includes "data protection by design" and "data protection by default" as part of its requirements.

Shared Responsibility

The *shared responsibility model* is a cloud security framework that describes the obligations of a cloud service provider (CSP) and its customers in keeping cloud systems and data secure. In a traditional data center model, your organization is responsible for security across your entire environment — all applications, servers, physical assets, and so on. In a cloud environment, the CSP takes on much of the operational burden, including a great deal of security responsibility — but not all of it. The specific breakdown of responsibility varies by cloud provider and by cloud service type. We discuss the concept of shared responsibility in detail later in this chapter (in the "Cloud-Based Systems" section).

Defense in Depth

Defense in depth (or *layered security*) is the concept of applying multiple, distinct layers of security technologies and strategies to achieve greater overall protection. In the context of information security, the U.S. National Security Agency (NSA) first used the phrase to describe the use of multiple types, locations, and layers of defense combined with the ability to detect and analyze breaches for prompt reaction and mitigation.

By using combinations of security controls, the impact from the failure of any single control can be reduced if not eliminated. Many of the security principles mentioned earlier are types of defense in depth. For example, separation of duties ensures that sensitive operations require the active cooperation of two (or more) individuals. The compromise (via rogue or malicious intent) of one individual is not sufficient to compromise the system.

Layering is another method of separating system components: security controls are placed between the layers, preventing an attacker who has compromised one layer from accessing other layers.

While redundancy is primarily a method of protecting against loss of availability through replicated systems or components that operate in parallel, it is also a way to avoid security single points of failure by replicating security controls serially. This means having overlapping security controls such that the failure or compromise of one does not by itself result in an exposure or compromise. An example would be using Linux iptables to block access to certain ports even though the server is behind a firewall that is configured to block the same ports. Should a configuration change to one control (the firewall or iptables) accidentally remove a *deny* rule (or add an inappropriate *allow* rule), the "redundant" control in the iptable or firewall will continue to provide the necessary protection.

Defense in depth is related to the concept of *assumption of breach*, which means managing security on the assumption that one or more security controls have already been compromised. The assumption of breach mindset shifts thinking from being simply focused on defending the perimeter (or perimeters) to a balanced approach of establishing multiple defenses so that the compromise of one control does not immediately lead to a successful breach and of considering detection and mitigation to be as important as prevention. As an example, consider that anti-malware systems and email scanning applications are no longer sufficient. Endpoint security applications, such as Carbon Black, are capable of blocking any executions not previously identified as trustworthy — this second layer of security demonstrates the importance of defense in depth.

UNDERSTAND THE FUNDAMENTAL CONCEPTS OF SECURITY MODELS

A *model* is a hypothetical abstraction of a system, simplified to enable analysis of certain aspects of the system without the complexity and details of the entire system being analyzed. A *security model* is a model that deals with security policy.

Security models can be formal, intended for mathematical analysis to assist in the verification that a system complies with a specific policy, or they can be informal, serving to illustrate and simplify the assessment of a system without the rigor of a proof. Security models can be useful tools during requirements development, information asset classification and categorization, and also during system analysis and testing.

The structured approach of codifying security requirements in a security model can help reduce ambiguity and potential misunderstanding as to what, exactly, a security architecture is trying to accomplish. It distills the essential requirements into clear rules and analyzes the design to ensure that those rules are adhered to at every step in the process. Ensuring that a security architecture conforms to a well-designed security model greatly strengthens it.

Interestingly, the differences of emphasis between models can be attributed to each model's origin. Security models developed to address the concerns of the military and government emphasize confidentiality as the prime objective. Meanwhile, models designed for commercial entities or safety systems might focus on the integrity of the data as key to preventing fraud or misleading financial reporting. Despite their differences, each of the security models discussed in the rest of this section focuses on access control rules.

Primer on Common Model Components

In examining security models, it is helpful to understand some concepts common across many security models, particularly finite state machines and lattices.

A *finite state machine* (or just *state machine*) is a conceptual computer that can be in one of a finite number of states. The computer implements a state transition function that determines the next state, given the current state and the next input and that can, optionally, produce output. Figure 3.2 depicts a generic example of a finite state model. In this model, evaluating the confidentiality-integrity-availability (CIA) properties of each state can ensure the system operates in a secure manner.

A *lattice* is a finite set with a partial ordering. A partial ordering is a binary relation that is reflexive, anti-symmetric, and transitive. Reflexive means that each item in the set is comparable to itself. Anti-symmetric means that no two different elements precede each other. Transitive means that if *a* yields *b*, and *b* yields *c*, then *a* yields *c*.

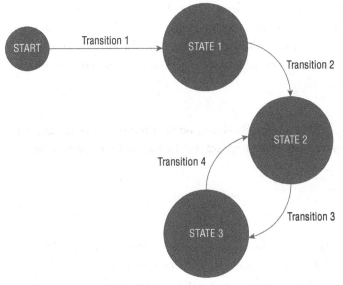

FIGURE 3.2 **Finite state model**

In short, a lattice security model does the following:

- Defines a set of security levels
- Defines a partial ordering of that set
- Assigns every subject (e.g., user or process) and object (e.g., data) a security level
- Defines a set of rules governing the operations a subject can perform on an object based on the relationship between the security levels of the subject and object

Information Flow Model

An *information flow model* is a type of access control model that defines the flow of information — from one application to another or even one system to another. In these models, objects are assigned a security classification, and the direction or type of flow of these objects is controlled by security policy. The Bell–LaPadula and Biba integrity models, each discussed in upcoming sections, are common examples of information flow models.

Noninterference Model

A *noninterference model* is an evolution of the information flow model designed to ensure that objects and subjects on a system don't interfere with other objects and subjects on the same system. Under this model, any activities that take place at a higher security level must not impact (or interfere) with activities occurring at a lower level. In other words, the actions of subject A (higher classification) should not affect subject B (lower classification), nor should those actions even be noticed by subject B, in a way that might inform subject B of subject A's actions. Without the protection of a noninterference model, subject B might be able to glean the activities of subject A, which may result in information leakage (for example).

NOTE   The noninterference model was first defined by Goguen and Meseguer in 1982, and the Goguen–Meseguer integrity model is often considered the foundation of the conceptual theory behind noninterference.

Bell–LaPadula Model

One of the first, and the best known, of the lattice security models was published by David Bell and Leonard LaPadula and is aptly known as the Bell–LaPadula (BLP) model. The BLP model is a confidentiality model that specifies the following three rules:

- **Simple Security Property (ss property):** Sometimes referred to as *no read up*, this rule prevents a subject from reading an object at a higher security level.

- **Star Property (* property):** Sometimes referred to as *no write down*, this rule prevents a subject from writing to an object at a lower security level.

- **Discretionary-Security Property:** A subject can perform an operation on an object if permitted by the access matrix (discussed later in this section).

NOTE   A *trusted subject* is an entity that can violate the star property after it has been shown to be trustworthy based on the security policy. A trusted subject may transfer information from a high-sensitivity object to a lower-sensitivity object.

The Simple Security Property rule protects against unauthorized subjects accessing sensitive information that they are not permitted to read. The Star Property rule prevents an authorized subject from breaching security by writing sensitive information to an object at a lower security level.

For a real-world scenario, imagine an intelligence officer in the military who has "Secret" access, a mid-level classification between "Confidential" and "Top Secret." According to the Simple Security Property rule, the officer can only read Secret and Confidential material. According to the Star Property rule, the officer can only write to Top Secret and Secret. The first rule doesn't make unauthorized material accessible to the officer, while the second rule prevents the officer from accidentally revealing unauthorized material to staff with a lower clearance. Figure 3.3 provides a graphical view of these two rules.

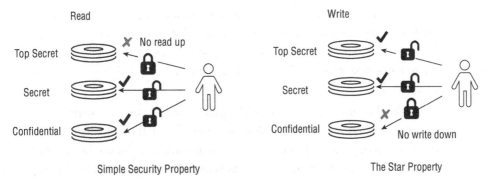

FIGURE 3.3 Simple Security Property and Star Property rules

The Discretionary-Security Property rule is useful when, for example, there are different departments. Let's say our same officer can read Secret and Confidential in one department, but can only read Confidential in other departments. Likewise, other intelligence officers in various departments might have higher clearance levels for their respective areas, but not for all. In this case, the model allows for an access matrix, and the Discretionary-Security Property comes into effect.

An *access matrix* has a row for each subject and a column for each object, and the element in a cell where a subject row and object column intersect defines what operation (i.e., access), if any, is to be permitted. Table 3.1 provides an example of an access matrix.

TABLE 3.1 An Example Access Matrix

SUBJECTS	OBJECT 1	OBJECT 2
Subject A	Read only	Read/Write
Subject B	No access	Write only (append)

The Discretionary-Security Property operates in conjunction with the other two mandatory access controls. The subject can access the object only if all three properties hold.

There are two other issues that are not well addressed by the Bell–LaPadula model:

- The model focuses on confidentiality, as one would expect from a model developed to meet the requirements of military and government organizations. It does not consider risks to the integrity of information. Protecting the integrity of objects means preventing the unauthorized, possibly malicious, modification of an object.

In the commercial world, preventing tampering with financial records, which could facilitate fraud, is more important than maintaining the confidentiality of those records. Likewise, in safety-critical applications, such as autonomous vehicles, robotics, and some medical systems, integrity is often a higher priority than confidentiality.

■ The model does not deal with covert channels or the possibility of performing permitted operations in a manner that reveals confidential information through side channels (e.g., by performing operations in a manner that can be detected by other, less secure, processes — such as consuming bursts of CPU or forcing abnormal levels of VM paging).

Biba Integrity Model

To address the integrity issue, Kenneth Biba developed what has become known as the Biba integrity model that, in a manner similar to the BLP model, posits the following:

■ **Simple Integrity Property:** Sometimes referred to as *no read down,* this rule prevents compromising the integrity of more secure information from a less secure source. In other words, higher integrity processes could produce untrustworthy results if they read and use data from lower integrity sources.

■ **Star Integrity Property (* integrity property):** Sometimes referred to as *no write up,* this rule prevents the corruption of more secure information by a less privileged subject.

Figure 3.4 illustrates these concepts.

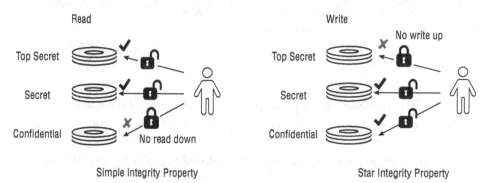

FIGURE 3.4 **Simple Integrity Property and Star Integrity Property rules**

Clark–Wilson Model

David Clark and David Wilson argue that a lattice model, such as the Biba model, is not sufficient to protect the integrity of data. Their proposed approach is to base the security model on two concepts that the commercial world developed to protect against fraud long before computers:

- Well-formed transactions
- Separation of duties

In contrast to the Bell LaPadula and Biba models, which permit a subject to make any changes to an object, if they are permitted to make any (i.e., have write permission), the Clark–Wilson concept of a well-formed transaction is that subjects are constrained to make only those changes that maintain the integrity of the data.

The example from the original paper outlining this model is the handwritten ledger when bookkeepers wrote in ink, and mistakes were corrected by entering a correcting or reversing entry. Signs that the entries in the ledger had been erased (which would be obvious given the use of indelible ink) would be detected as a violation of the ledger's integrity and a possible indication of fraud.

The practice of separation of duties in the commercial world aims to make sure that the certifier of a transaction is a different party from the initiator or implementer of the transaction.

The following concepts are important components of the Clark–Wilson Model and are worth being familiar with:

- **Constrained data item (CDI):** This is the key data type in the Clark–Wilson model, and it refers to data whose integrity must be preserved.

- **Unconstrained data item (UDI):** This includes all data other than CDIs, typically system inputs.

- **Integrity verification procedures (IVPs):** These procedures check and ensure that all CDIs are valid.

- **Transformation procedures (TPs):** These procedures enforce a system's integrity policy and maintain the integrity of CDIs.

Brewer–Nash Model

The Brewer–Nash model was developed to implement an ethical wall security policy. In the commercial world, there are regulatory requirements designed to prevent conflicts of interest arising from insider knowledge. These rules require that organizations establish barriers to prevent those with confidential information from being placed in a position where that knowledge could improperly influence their actions.

For example, a financial analyst working for a bank cannot provide advice for a client company when he has insider knowledge related to another client who is a competitor. Similarly, in countries in which a law firm is permitted to represent adversarial clients, the regulations require an ethical wall to exist between the two legal teams within the same company.

Recall that in the BLP security model, access to data is determined based on attributes of the subject and the object. In contrast to BLP, the Brewer–Nash security model is based on segregation of duties, like erecting an ethical wall. Access to the data must be limited by what data the person is already permitted to access.

The Brewer–Nash model defines a hierarchical model for information:

- Individual pieces of information related to a single company or client are called *objects*, in keeping with BLP's usage.

- All objects related to the same company (or client) are part of what is called a *company data set*.

- All company data sets in the same industry (i.e., that are competitors) are part of what is called a *conflict of interest class*.

The objective of an ethical wall security policy is that people are only permitted to access information (objects) that does not cause a conflict of interest due to information they already have access to (for example, you wouldn't want your red team knowing what your blue team is planning to do, or vice versa). As such, Brewer–Nash is a dynamic access control model that changes instead of relying on static state tables.

For example, let's say a new financial analyst who has not accessed any information held by his newer employer and therefore, under Brewer–Nash (BN), is free to access any company data set. The analyst already accessed ACME Finance information, and he is free to access information that exists in a different conflict of interest class, say, BETA Chemicals. But if he tries to access an object associated with Ajax Finance, which is in the same conflict of interest class as ACME, the BN security model would bar that access. See Figure 3.5.

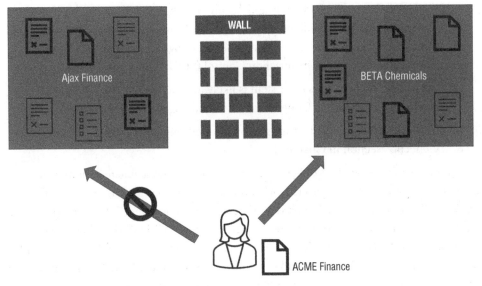

FIGURE 3.5 **Brewer–Nash security model**

Take-Grant Model

The *Take-Grant model* (also called the *Take-Grant protection model*) is a security model that specifies the rights of an entity (subject or object) to obtain rights from one entity and give them to another entity. There are four rules, or operations, in this model, and the first two will be no surprise:

- **Take:** Allows a subject to obtain (or take) the rights of another object
- **Grant:** Allows a subject to give (or grant) rights to an object
- **Create:** Allows a subject to generate (or create) a new object
- **Remove:** Allows a subject to revoke (or remove) rights it has on an object

SELECT CONTROLS BASED UPON SYSTEMS SECURITY REQUIREMENTS

Selecting the security controls appropriate for an information system starts with an analysis of the security requirements. The security requirements are determined by the following:

- An analysis of any regulatory or compliance requirements placed on the system (e.g., regulatory frameworks such as the Federal Information Security Management Act (FISMA) in the United States; privacy legislation such as GDPR in the EU or the Health Insurance Portability and Accountability Act (HIPAA) in the United States; contractual obligations such as Payment Card Industry Data Security Standard (PCI DSS); or voluntary compliance programs such as ISO 27001 certification or Service Organization Control (SOC) 1/2/3 audits)

- An analysis of the threats the system is likely to face (see the "Understand and Apply Threat Modeling Concepts and Methodologies" section in Chapter 1)

- A risk assessment of the system (see the "Understand and Apply Risk Management Concepts" section in Chapter 1)

In some cases, the analysis of both the threats and any applicable regulatory compliance requirements will specify exactly what minimum set of controls is necessary. For example, the organization that processes primary account numbers (PANs) and handles bank card transactions understands their systems must be PCI DSS compliant. In other cases, such as GDPR compliance, the requirements are more nebulous, and the security architect must analyze the threats, risks, and affected stakeholders to determine an appropriate set of controls to appropriately protect systems and data.

If an organization has not yet adopted a certain framework, it is beneficial to start with an established information security framework such as ISO 27001, NIST Special Publication 800-37 "Risk Management Framework," or the NIST Cybersecurity Framework (CSF), ISA624443, or COBIT 5 (to name a few), as this will help ensure that you have considered the full spectrum of controls and that your process is defined, repeatable, and consistent.

There are a few things to understand about these security frameworks:

- They are not mandatory.

- They are not mutually exclusive of each other.

- They are not exhaustive (i.e., they don't cover all security concerns).

- They are not the same as a standard or a control list.

Now let's expand on each of those points.

Frameworks are not mandatory. But as an organization adopts or follows a framework, some of the subsequent documents or steps may involve taking mandatory action. Take, for example, a company seeking to secure their systems that process credit card data. When they act according to a framework prompting them to identify their systems and the risks to those systems, the organization will understand they must adhere to the PCI DSS, not a framework but a compliance standard. From here, the organization can gain insight into some required security controls.

Information security frameworks are not mutually exclusive. Many organizations such as the Cloud Security Alliance, ISACA, and the Unified Compliance Framework have developed mappings between the controls in different frameworks, making it easier to achieve compliance with more than one framework at the same time. This might be necessary, for example, when a specific system must meet PCI DSS requirements, but the organization as a whole has selected, say, ISO 27001 as the framework for its information security management system. The NIST Cybersecurity Framework (CSF) is one such example of a useful mapping between multiple different frameworks. Understanding how security frameworks complement each other is essential to avoiding duplicative efforts and redundant security controls.

Certainly frameworks are not intended to be completely exhaustive. Frameworks can be specialized in either an industry or a scope, or they can be broadly applicable. However, even those broadly applicable frameworks are not intended to cover 100 percent of your security controls. Take, for example, the NIST CSF, which is widely recognized as a general security framework that is applicable for basically any industry. Despite its breadth, the CSF does omit one huge security concern: physical security. Understanding that security frameworks are only a piece of the puzzle is an important part of selecting your security controls.

Lastly, remember not to confuse a framework with a standard or a control list. Frameworks, control lists, and standards are three different concepts. While a framework is an approach or strategy to take, a standard is a set of quantifiable directions or rules to follow. In most organizations, the standard would logically follow the policy, just as mandatory instructions would follow a decree stating what is mandatory. In any case, keep these differences in mind when selecting your organization's security controls.

What all frameworks have in common is an all-embracing, overarching approach to the task of securing systems. They break that task down into manageable phases or steps. For example, at the highest level, NIST SP 800-37, "Risk Management Framework," breaks down the task of securing a system this way: tstarts with categorizing the system (based on the impact if that system's security were affected), identifying the proper security controls, implementing those controls, assessing their effectiveness, and then managing and monitoring the system. From this breakdown, security controls are the obvious central point involved in securing the system. These controls are the real tangible work performed from adopting a framework.

Once you have selected your framework, you need to review all of the controls to determine which are appropriate to address the risks you have identified. In some cases, the framework itself will provide guidance. For example, NIST SP 800-53 provides three levels of controls, called *initial control baselines*, based on the risk assessment. Threat modeling and risk assessment will also provide information on which controls are most important and need to be implemented with higher priority than other controls that address vulnerabilities with a low likelihood and impact. Implementing all of the controls in your selected framework to the same level of depth and maturity is a waste of time, money, and resources. The general objective is to reduce all risks to a level below the organization's risk threshold. This means some controls will have to be thoroughly and completely implemented while others may not be needed at all.

Often, the framework will incorporate a security standard with a minimum set of security controls forming a recommended baseline as a starting point for system security. Scoping guidance within the baseline identifies the acceptable deviation from control and results in a tailored system deployment that meets the organization's risk tolerance.

Implementing a defined, repeatable, and industry-accepted approach to selecting controls is one way your organization can demonstrate due care and due diligence in security decision-making.

Of course, selecting controls is just the beginning. You need to do the following:

- Consider the control and how to implement and adapt it to your specific circumstances (the "Plan" phase)

- Implement the control (the "Do" phase)

- Assess the effectiveness of the control (the "Check" phase)

- Remediate the gaps and deficiencies (the "Act" phase)

This Plan-Do-Check-Act cycle (also known as PDCA or the Deming cycle) is, of course, an iterative process. This was explicitly pointed out in ISO 27000:2009, but only implied in later editions. Other frameworks, such as the NIST Risk Management Framework, also leverage the continuous process improvement model to shape the efficiency and effectiveness of the controls environment. See Figure 3.6.

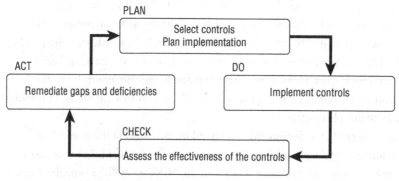

FIGURE 3.6 **Plan-Do-Check-Act cycle**

On a more frequent basis, you need to (re-)assess the effectiveness of your controls, and on a less frequent basis (but still periodically), you need to reexamine your choice of controls. Business objectives change. The threat landscape changes. And your risks change.

The set (and level) of controls that were appropriate at one point in time is unlikely to be the same a year or two later. As in all things related to information security, it is certainly not a case of set and forget.

In addition to the periodic review of the control selection, the following specific events warrant taking a fresh look at your security controls:

- A security incident or breach
- A significant change in organization structure or major staffing change
- A new or retired product or service
- A new or significantly changed threat or threat actor
- A significant change to an information system or infrastructure
- A significant change to the type of information being processed
- A significant change to security governance, the risk management framework, or policies
- A widespread social, economic, or political change (e.g., COVID-19)

The preceding list includes examples of "lessons learned" process triggers. It's highly advisable that your organization follow a periodic and event-driven process to evaluate your controls for suitability and effectiveness.

Security frameworks are also periodically updated, and when they are, one needs to consider the changes and adjust as appropriate.

UNDERSTAND SECURITY CAPABILITIES OF INFORMATION SYSTEMS

The information systems that store and process your organization's data generally include an assortment of security capabilities that you should be familiar with. It is important that you understand these capabilities in order to properly evaluate them and effectively implement them. Some of the most foundational information system security (ISS) capabilities include the following:

- Memory protection
- Trusted Platform Modules (TPMs)
- Cryptographic modules
- Hardware Security Modules (HSMs)

Memory Protection

One of the basic foundational security controls on all systems that allows multiple programs to run simultaneously is *memory protection*. This feature enables the operating system to load multiple programs into main memory at the same time and prevent one program from referencing memory not specifically assigned to it. If a program attempts to reference a memory address it is not permitted to access, the system blocks the access, suspends the program, and transfers control to the operating system. In most cases, the operating system will terminate the offending program. See Figure 3.7.

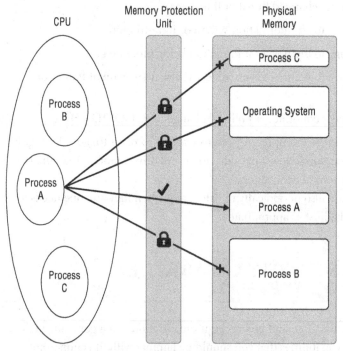

FIGURE 3.7 **Operating system memory protection**

A related hardware feature that is required to support memory protection is *dual-mode operation*. This means the processor can operate in one of (at least) two modes: privileged (or kernel) mode and unprivileged (or user) mode. The operating system runs in privileged mode, which grants it permission to set up and control the memory protection subsystem. Privileged mode also permits the operating system to execute special privileged instructions that control the processor environment.

Once a program has been loaded into memory and the memory protection is configured to limit that program's access to those areas of memory assigned to it by the operating system, the operating system transfers control to the program and simultaneously transitions to unprivileged mode.

The program runs in unprivileged mode, which limits it to accessing only the specific memory area dictated by the operating system. Should it make an illegal memory reference, attempt to execute a privileged CPU instruction, or use up the time slice granted to it by the operating system, control is returned to the operating system (running in privileged mode).

The operating system determines if control has been returned to the operating system because of an illegal operation by the user program, and decides how to handle the transgression (i.e., returning control to the user program with an error indication or terminating the program).

Another security control, *address space layout randomization* (ASLR), seeks to mitigate the risks of predictable memory address location. The location in memory for a known instruction becomes a risk when there is a threat of exploiting that location for an attack. For example, a buffer overflow attack requires knowing two things: the exact amount by which to overflow the memory to facilitate executing malicious code, and where exactly to send the overflow. ASLR defeats the second item by randomizing the location.

Whatever the approach or specific technical control, the need to protect memory is both fundamental and critical to securing information systems.

Potential Weaknesses

Proper memory protection relies upon both the correct operation of the hardware and the correct design of the operating system that uses the underlying memory protection hardware to prevent programs from accessing memory they have not been given permission to access. A defect in either can compromise the security provided by memory protection.

Note that this protection prevents the direct disclosure of memory contents that are blocked from an unauthorized program, but does not necessarily prevent side-channel exploits from revealing information about memory that is protected from access.

Attacks that leverage ineffective isolation and memory protection can have catastrophic effects. As the Spectre and Meltdown exploits in 2018 revealed, flaws in the design of Intel and some other CPU chips permitted clever programming techniques to deduce the contents of memory locations that those programs were not permitted to access directly.

The roots of how Spectre and Meltdown began date back more than five years before the two famous vulnerabilities were publicly revealed together in January 2018. Most affected hardware vendors were told six months earlier, and due to the highly specula-tive nature of the vulnerability, one vendor coined the vulnerability as Spectre.

To understand Spectre and Meltdown, it helps to consider some aspects of how CPUs operate. CPUs sometimes run instructions speculatively, meaning they run instructions out of order in an effort to potentially save time. Sometimes it's worthwhile, and other times it's not. CPUs keep track of those speculative attempts in what's called a *branch history buffer* (BHB).

Unfortunately, two widespread misperceptions about speculative execution and the BHB created a major vulnerability. The first was that when CPUs scanned instructions out of order and acted on them and the speculation turned out to not be worthwhile, the understanding was the CPU's cache memory was then emptied of that effort. That belief was incorrect. The second erroneous perception involved how the BHB works. The addressing of memory locations in the BHB is not absolute (full). Instead, the BHB uses only partial addressing to save space. While that could lead to overwriting of multiple memory locations sharing a single BHB position, CPU designers understood it was only addressing speculative execution, so no harm was done if something went awry. Bet-ween those two bad assumptions, Spectre and Meltdown are possible.

Understanding that the CPU's cache is not emptied of a bad attempt to do some things in parallel, consider what could be read if you specifically told the CPU to access something secret, such as a password, or whether the system was actually a VM. With the BHB addressing being vulnerable to collisions as well, well-designed malware could send sensitive information to the CPU cache and then use a completely different speculative instruction to locate the secret sent earlier. A good explanation can be found at `meltdownattack.com/`.

Secure Cryptoprocessor

The challenge with standard microprocessors is that code running with the highest priv-ilege can access any device and any memory location, meaning that the security of the system depends entirely on the security of all the software operating at that privilege level. If that software is defective or can be compromised, then the fundamental security of everything done on that processor becomes suspect.

To address this problem, hardware modules called *secure cryptoprocessors* have been developed that are resistant to hardware tampering and that have a limited interface (i.e., attack surface), making it easier to verify the integrity and secure operation of the (limited) code running on the cryptoprocessor.

Cryptoprocessors are used to provide services such as the following:

- Hardware-based true random number generators (TRNGs)
- Secure generation of keys using the embedded TRNG
- Secure storage of keys that are not externally accessible
- Encryption and digital signing using internally secured keys
- High-speed encryption, offloading the main processor from the computational burden of cryptographic operations

The following are features of cryptoprocessors that enhance their security over standard microprocessors (that could do most of the above in software):

- Tamper detection with automatic destruction of storage in the event of tampering, and a design that makes it difficult to tamper with the device without leaving obvious traces of the physical compromise. These protections can range from tamper-evident stickers that clearly show attempts to access the device's internal components to secure enclosures that detect unauthorized attempts to open the device and automatically erase or destroy sensitive key material.
- Chip design features such as shield layers to prevent eavesdropping on internal signals using ion probes or other microscopic devices.
- A hardware-based cryptographic accelerator (i.e., specialized instructions or logic to increase the performance of standard cryptographic algorithms such as AES, SHA, RSA, ECC, DSA, and ECDSA, which are discussed in detail later in this chapter).
- A trusted boot process that validates the initial boot firmware and operating system load.

There are many types of secure cryptoprocessors such as:

- Proprietary, such as Apple's "Secure Enclave" found in iPhones
- Open standard, such as the TPM as specified by the ISO/IEC 11889 standard and used in some laptops and servers
- Standalone (e.g., separate standalone device with external communications ports)
- Smartcards

Some of these are discussed further in the following sections.

Trusted Platform Module

A TPM is a secure cryptoprocessor that provides secure storage and cryptographic services as specified by ISO/IEC 11889 (see Figure 3.8).

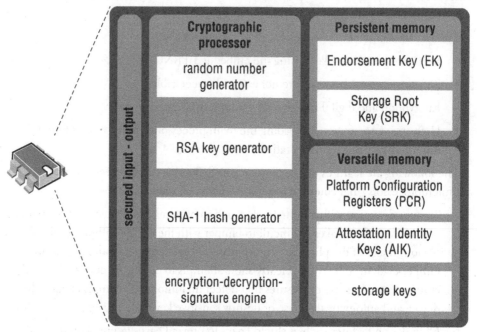

FIGURE 3.8 Trusted Platform Module processes

A TPM is essentially a security chip that is hardwired into a system (e.g., on a motherboard). At its core, a TPM is responsible for the following functions:

- **Attestation:** Creates a cryptographic hash of the system's known good hardware and software state, allowing third-party verification of the system's integrity
- **Binding:** Encrypts data using a cryptographic key that is uniquely associated with (or bound to) the system
- **Sealing:** Ensures that ciphertext can be decrypted only if the system is attested to be in a known good state

A TPM can be used by the operating system, processor BIOS, or application (if the OS provides access to the TPM) to provide a number of cryptographic and security services such as:

- Generate private/public key pairs such that the private key never leaves the TPM in plaintext, substantially increasing the security related to the private key. (Public/private keys are discussed in more detail later in this chapter.)

- Digitally sign data using a private key that is stored on the TPM and that never leaves the confines of the TPM, significantly decreasing the possibility that the key can become known by an attacker and used to forge identities and launch man-in-the-middle (MITM) attacks. (Digital signatures are discussed later in this chapter.)

- Encrypt data such that it can only be decrypted using the same TPM.

- Verify the state of the machine the TPM is installed on to detect certain forms of tampering (i.e., with the BIOS) and ensure platform integrity.

Potential Weaknesses

The *endorsement key* (EK) is a fundamental component of a TPM's security. This key is generated by the TPM manufacturer and burned into the TPM hardware during the manufacturing process. Because of this, the user/system owner depends upon the security of the TPM manufacturer to ensure that the PEK remains confidential.

We also depend on the quality of the TPM manufacturer's processes. In late 2017, it was revealed that a defect in the software library used by Infineon for its line of smartcards and TPMs contained a flaw that made it possible to deduce the private key stored internally. As a result, there were millions of cryptographic keys made unreliable and vulnerable. Attackers were able to calculate the private portion of an account holder's key from having access to only the public portion. What happened, unfortunately, is that hackers impersonated legitimate users with the assurance and nonrepudiation provided by having their private keys. This bug and others are constant reminders of the importance of supply chain risk management programs that assess the security risk of vendors and other third parties. Be mindful of where your software and hardware come from, and ensure you take proper precaution (i.e., due diligence) to keep your data secure.

Cryptographic Module

A *cryptographic module* is typically a hardware device that implements key generation and other cryptographic functions and is embedded in a larger system.

The advantages of using a cryptographic module as opposed to obtaining the equivalent functionality from a cryptographic software library include the following:

- By performing critical cryptographic functions on a separate device that is dedicated to that purpose, it is much harder for malware or other software-based attacks to compromise the security of the cryptographic operation.

- By isolating security-sensitive functionality in an isolated device with limited interfaces and attack surfaces, it is easier to provide assurances about the secure operation of the device. It also makes it easier to provide secure functions to larger systems by embedding a cryptographic module within the larger system.

- By separating cryptographic functions into a separate module, you gain increased availability of noncryptographic dedicated resources.

- Most secure cryptographic modules contain physical security protections including tamper resistance and tamper detection, making it difficult to compromise the security of the device even if the device has been physically compromised.

- Some cryptographic modules can enforce separation of duties so that certain sensitive operations, such as manipulating key storage, can be done only with the cooperation of two different individuals who authenticate to the cryptographic module separately.

Some government organizations have issued standards related to the security of cryptographic modules and have established evaluation and certification processes so that manufacturers can have the security of their devices validated by an independent third party, and users can have confidence in the security that using the module will provide their larger system.

For example, the U.S. government's FIPS 140-2, "Security Requirements for Cryptographic Modules," specifies the requirements for cryptographic hardware and software to meet four different levels of security. It also provides for certification of products to validate they meet the requirements.

Internationally, the "Common Criteria for Information Technology Security Evaluation," documented in the ISO/IEC 15408 standard, provides an alternate set of requirements and certification processes to validate information security products.

Hardware Security Module

A *Hardware Security Module* (HSM) is a type of cryptographic module designed to stand alone as an appliance and to provide cryptographic services over an externally accessible API (typically over a network or USB connection).

HSMs are frequently found in certificate authorities (CAs) that use them to protect their root private keys, and payment processors that use them to protect the symmetric encryption keys used to protect cardholder data. HSMs are also used in many national security applications or other environments where proper management of cryptographic material is critical to the business process. In addition, HSMs are used by enterprise network backbones as part of encryption management of archives, east-west data movement, and even VPN traffic. CAs, digital signatures, certificates, and asymmetric/symmetric encryption are discussed later in this chapter.

ASSESS AND MITIGATE THE VULNERABILITIES OF SECURITY ARCHITECTURES, DESIGNS, AND SOLUTION ELEMENTS

Assessing information security vulnerabilities can be done by inspection or testing. Inspection can be manual (e.g., reviewing the design and implementation, looking for vulnerabilities) or automated (e.g., using software to analyze the configuration or code). Testing can be white-box, in which the tester knows the details of the system's design and implementation; black-box, in which the tester knows nothing about the internals of the system; or gray-box, in which the tester has some knowledge of the system, but not all.

In practice, a combination of some or all of the above methods is usually employed in order to try to reduce the probability that an unidentified (and unmitigated) vulnerability will remain in the system when it is put into production. These activities, combined with threat modeling, increase the level of assurance that the system will operate in a secure manner.

In the case of secure software development, code is usually manually reviewed at least once, sometimes twice: first, a peer review process that requires the approval of a second developer before any code changes or additions can be committed to production; and later, a code inspection of the most sensitive and critical components, conducted by developers unrelated to those who developed the original code, to carefully examine the code looking for vulnerabilities or security defects. (We discuss secure software development further in Chapter 8, "Software Development Security.")

Once you have analyzed the system and identified the potential vulnerabilities, you need to consider the impact should the vulnerability be exploited by a threat actor, and the likelihood of the vulnerability being exploited. This risk analysis (as we discussed in Chapter 1) is a requirement for prioritizing your mitigation activities.

Different architectures (e.g., distributed versus centralized) and systems (e.g., databases, servers, applications, etc.) require controls that address the unique security challenges they present, but in all cases, the underlying platform (e.g., operating system) needs to be secure, which includes ensuring that the underlying system has been appropriately hardened (unnecessary services disabled, unneeded ports blocked, etc.) and updated as part of a vulnerability management process, both discussed in Chapter 7, "Security Operations."

Client-Based Systems

In a traditional client-server system, client-related vulnerabilities can be grouped into two broad categories: those related to the client application itself, and those related to the system on which the client runs. It matters little how well implemented and configured the client software is if the underlying operating system or hardware is vulnerable.

Broadly speaking, software vulnerabilities in client-based systems involve weaknesses in client-side code that is present in browsers and applications.

Client-based vulnerabilities may fall into the following categories:

- Vulnerabilities related to the insecure operation of the client:
  - Storing temporary data on the client system in a manner that is insecure (i.e., accessible to unauthorized users through, for example, direct access to the client device's filesystem)
  - Running insecure (e.g., out-of-date or unpatched) software versions
- Vulnerabilities related to communications with the server, such as client software that connects to remote servers but does not take appropriate steps to do the following:
  - Validate the identity of the server
  - Validate or sanitize the data received from the server
  - Prevent eavesdropping of data exchanged with the server
  - Detect tampering with data exchanged with the server
  - Validate commands or code received from the server before executing or taking action based on information received from the server

To address these vulnerabilities, one can consider the following:

- Evaluate your operating systems and applications for unpatched software or insecure configurations
- Using a recognized secure protocol (e.g., transport layer security (TLS)) to validate the identity of the server and to prevent eavesdropping of, and tampering with, data communicated with the server
- Using appropriate coding techniques to ensure that the data or commands received from the server are valid and consistent
- Using digital signing to verify executable code received from the server prior to execution

In many cases, the client may use software libraries, applets, or applications to process data received from the server. For example, the client may rely upon image display components to permit the viewing of files. These components (e.g., Flash, Java Development Kit, etc.) will typically be provided by third parties and, as such, will need to be part of a vulnerability management program so that vulnerabilities that are discovered later can be patched in a timely manner.

If the client is a browser, then the browser ought to be configured in accordance with hardening guidelines available for the major web browsers. Similarly, the appropriate steps to protect and patch the underlying system that runs the client software need to be taken. Excellent sources of such guidance for browsers and client operating systems include The Center for Internet Security (CIS) and the Defense Information Systems Agency's Security Technical Implementation Guides.

The client system also needs to be protected from other threats as appropriate, based on the risk assessment and threat modeling. This could include firewalls, physical security controls, full-disk encryption, and so on.

If the software has been developed specifically for this application, then the appropriate secure software development process as described in Chapter 8 must be employed.

NOTE   While much of this and the following sections focus on software security, it is important to remember that overall endpoint security is paramount. In addition to software security, your endpoint security must address hardware security, physical security, work process and workflow design security, as well as user issues.

Server-Based Systems

Server vulnerabilities mirror many of the same vulnerabilities described earlier, just from the server's perspective. It's important to remember that client and server systems are usually similar; the terms *client* and *server* only indicate the role a system plays in the overall system operations.

The server needs to validate the identity of the client and/or the identity of the user of the client. This can be done using a combination of Identity and Access Management (IAM) techniques along with a secure communications protocol such as TLS, using client-side certificates. TLS will also protect the server from eavesdropping and tampering, such as might happen from a MITM attack. The server also must validate all inputs and not assume that simply because the commands and data coming from the client are originating from (and have been validated by) the corresponding client-side software, they are valid and have been sanitized. The client must be considered untrusted, and it must be assumed that the client-end can insert or modify commands or data before being encrypted and transmitted over the secure (e.g., TLS) link. Depending on the nature of the environment, it might be appropriate to protect the server from DoS attacks by using techniques such as rate-limiting, CAPTCHA, and other approaches.

Certainly, a vulnerability management program is needed to ensure that updates and patches are applied in a timely fashion. This holds true regardless of whether the server-side software is developed in-house or is based in part or completely on software obtained from a third party (such as commercial off-the-shelf software, or COTS).

If the software has been developed specifically for this application, then the appropriate secure software development process must be employed. This includes ensuring that the server application runs only with the minimum permissions necessary, commonly understood as the "principle of least privilege." If and when privilege escalation is needed, the period during which the server operates with elevated privileges is minimized. Best practices include the server using filesystem ownership and permissions to avoid data leakage, logging and monitoring appropriate information (such as successful and failed login attempts, privileged access, etc.), and capturing forensic information to permit analysis of a possible or actual security incident.

Finally, threats to the server itself need to be addressed. This may include physical and environmental threats, threats to the communications infrastructure, and server hardening as per industry recommendations such as those promulgated by the CIS (`www.cisecurity.org/cis-benchmarks`) or collected and indexed in NIST's National Checklist Program Repository (`nvd.nist.gov/ncp/repository`).

✔ Server Hardening Guidelines

The details of the specific issues that need to be addressed when hardening a specific operating system will vary slightly depending on the OS, but generally involves the following:

- Installing updates and patches

- Removing or locking unnecessary default accounts

- Changing default account passwords

- Enabling only needed services, protocols, daemons, etc. (conversely, disabling any not needed)

- Enabling logging and auditing

- Implementing only one primary function per server

- Changing default system, filesystem, service, and network configurations as needed to improve security (including full-disk encryption if appropriate)

- Removing (or disabling) unneeded drivers, executables, filesystems, libraries, scripts, services, etc.

Database Systems

Securing database systems is a special case of the more general server-based system security discussed in the previous section. If the database is accessible over a network, then all the security controls discussed there apply as well as those outlined below. If the database is not network accessible, then there are fewer risks, and some server security controls may not be necessary. Database-specific security controls include the following:

- Consult the CIS's hardening guidelines for the database system being used. These guidelines include several of the recommendations below, and many others.
- Only install or enable those components of the database system that are needed for your application.
- Place data stores and log files on nonsystem partitions.
- Set appropriate filesystem permissions on database directories, data stores, logs, and certificate files.
- Run database services using a dedicated unprivileged account on a dedicated server.
- Disable command history.
- Do not use environment variables, command line, or database configuration files to pass authentication credentials.
- Do not reuse database account names across different applications.
- Disable "anonymous" accounts (if supported by the database).
- Mandate that all connections use TLS if access or replication traffic travels over untrusted networks.
- Use unique certificates for each database instance.
- Use restricted views.
- Ensure that all DBMS vendor-provided sample or test databases are removed or not accessible from user endpoints and clients.
- Change all default passwords, ensure all accounts have secure passwords, and consider enabling multifactor or certificate-based authentication (where supported).
- Ensure user account permissions have been assigned using the principle of least privilege and in alignment with enterprise-wide access control policies and procedures. Database privileges can be complex and interact in unexpected ways—avoid default roles and define those you need with only the permissions needed for each.
- Disable or remove unneeded accounts, especially those with administrative permissions.

- Manage all accounts according to best practices (see Chapter 5).

- Enable logging of sensitive operations and route logs to your log monitoring and alerting system.

- Use *bind* variables where possible to minimize injection attack surfaces.

- Assign unique admin accounts for each administrator (i.e., do not share admin accounts between more than one admin). Carefully consider a risk-based, role-based approach that supports a least-privilege and separation-of-duties model in which each admin only has those admin permissions necessary to discharge their specific responsibilities. Where possible, ensure that critical operations require the cooperation of two admins.

- Enable logging at a sufficiently detailed level to provide the forensic information needed to identify the cause of events related to security incidents (but ensure logging does not include passwords), and protect the logs from tampering by database admins, either through permissions on the database system itself or by transmitting the log data in real time to a separate secure logging system.

- Consult vendor database documentation for database-specific security controls. For example, Oracle supports a control known as *data dictionary protection*, which provides an additional level of least-privilege control, restricting certain operations to a subset of those with database admin privileges).

- For databases that are only accessed through application software (e.g., the typical *n*-tier web server application), run the database on private networks only accessible to the business logic servers that need access.

Database encryption deserves special attention. The encryption of data at rest can happen at any (or all) of several different levels:

- Full-disk encryption (FDE) at the lowest level protects all the data on the storage media, protecting against the physical theft or loss of the drive itself. It provides no protection from threat actors who have logical access to the system, as the operating system or drive itself will decrypt all data that is read from the storage media before it is passed to the application without regard to the identity of the requester (other than the permission to access the file). This can be implemented through firmware (self-encrypting drives) or through the operating system (e.g., BitLocker).

- Filesystem-level encryption allows the encryption to occur at the filesystem level. This can be done at the volume, directory, or file level, depending on the capabilities of the operating system.

- Transparent data encryption (TDE) protects the data from those who have direct access to the filesystem (i.e., the "root" user), but do not have permission to access the database system and the specific database item. It does not protect against malicious database administrators or attacks, such as SQL injection, that are able to bypass the application-level controls and issue database access commands directly. While TDE provides protection beyond FDE, there are significant vulnerabilities it does not mitigate, so it is not meant to be used alone. Note also that with some database systems, if the attacker can obtain both the operating system image and the TDE-protected database, the unencrypted contents can be extracted. Cell-level encryption (CLE) or application-level encryption (covered next) are necessary to protect against threats that TDE does not address.

- CLE encrypts database information at the cell or column level. With this approach, data remains encrypted when read from the database and is decrypted only when requested. It also permits the user to exert very granular control over the cryptographic keys. This additional security and flexibility is not without its drawbacks. Key management, and handling the decryption/encryption requests can add considerable complexity to the application, and depending on the types of queries (and whether they include CLE-protected data), the performance can be affected, sometimes drastically.

Application-level encryption is a high-level approach that provides protection even if access to the database system is compromised. In this case, the business-logic or application layer is responsible for encrypting the data to be protected before it is passed to the database and for decrypting it once it has been retrieved. The database itself sees only binary data and does not have any access to the encryption keys. This approach is the most complex, but provides greater security (if properly implemented and managed) than the other approaches. To maximize the benefit of this approach, applications ought to encrypt as early as possible and decrypt as late as possible. Or to put it another way, handle the encryption/decryption as close to the point of use as possible. For example, if your server-side application has a number of layers (refer to Figure 3.1), then the cryptographic component ought to be called from the *business-logic layer*, not the storage management layer. Note, however, that performing the decryption completely externally to the database will make certain database functions unavailable (certain types of search, for example). The decision as to which combination of database encryption approaches to use will be influenced by considerations such as the following:

- Performance, especially if searches reference data encrypted using CLE.
- Backups, which will be protected using TDE or CLE, but not necessarily when using FDE (unless the backup is on another FDE-protected drive).
- Compression as encrypted data does not compress, so the use of encryption may significantly increase the size of backups. Some databases support decrypting the data prior to compression, and then re-encrypting so the backup is compressed and encrypted. That may, however, introduce other vulnerabilities in the process.

Cryptographic Systems

As American cryptologist Bruce Schneier famously stated, "All cryptography can eventually be broken — the only question is how much effort is required." The challenge then becomes one of weighing the value of the encrypted information to the attacker against the level of effort required to compromise the cryptographic system. In making this decision, the potential attacker has a number of avenues that can be followed to compromise a cryptographic system. These include the following:

- Algorithm and protocol weaknesses
- Implementation weakness
- Key management vulnerabilities

As a side note, there are countries that strictly regulate the use of cryptography, and countries that, while permitting the unrestricted *use* of cryptography, regulate the export of cryptographic technology. A detailed discussion of these issues is beyond the scope of this text, but they need to be considered by the security architect who must be familiar with the legislative constraints that apply. See Chapter 1 for more information on legislative compliance issues relevant to information security.

The following sections will explore these vulnerabilities of cryptographic systems, and the "Select and Determine Cryptographic Solutions" section later in this chapter will examine cryptography further.

Algorithm and Protocol Weaknesses

Designing a secure cryptographic algorithm or protocol is difficult, and only those algorithms that have been carefully examined by many experts and have stood the test of time ought to be used. A good pool of cryptographic algorithms with strong potential to be secure are those examined during the open public multiyear competitions to select cryptographic algorithms run by organizations such as NIST. Winners of these contests are carefully examined by cryptographers around the world. Such algorithms are scrutinized to identify any weaknesses or backdoors. Of course, the harsh reality that necessitates much scrutiny is that the threat actors that are most capable and well-funded often position themselves as advocates for secure algorithms. For an example, please see the upcoming sidebar "The Dual Elliptic Curve Deterministic Random Bit Generator (Dual EC DBRG)." As an example of how true peer scrutiny can be done, consider the progress made for symmetric cryptography as the current recommended algorithm (Advanced Encryption Standard, or AES) was developed by a group of Belgian cryptographers and subjected to many years of intense scrutiny before being approved.

✔ The Dual Elliptic Curve Deterministic Random Bit Generator (Dual EC DBRG)

Between 2004 and 2007, ANSI, NIST, and the ISO published standards (in draft and, later, final form) that included a cryptographically secure pseudo-random number generator (CSPRNG) known as Dual EC DRBG. Research at that time indicated that this algorithm might not be secure and, in fact, may have a secret backdoor that would enable the decryption of TLS Hypertext Transfer Protocol Secure (HTTPS) traffic that used this algorithm. Subsequent analysis, combined with revelations by Edward Snowden in 2013, strongly suggested that the U.S. NSA had constructed the Dual EC DBRG to have a backdoor and then worked to have it adopted by the various standards organizations (ANSI, NIST, and ISO). All three organizations have subsequently removed EC DBRG from their standards.

What is a security architect to do if the world's standards bodies can be compromised? First, do your research. Not all standardized algorithms are equally secure. Read the literature. The weaknesses in EC DBRG were openly discussed well before the algorithm was standardized. Second, do not blindly accept defaults. The prime reason EC DBRG was widely deployed is that a commonly used cryptographic library provided by RSA made it the default CSPRNG.

✔ WEP: A Design Flaw Case Study

Wired Equivalent Privacy (WEP) was the first approach to encryption used for WiFi networks. It had a number of design flaws that made it possible to decrypt most traffic, sometimes after only eavesdropping for as little as three minutes. It has been superseded by far more secure protocols (WPA3 being the current standard) and should not be used.

The primary weakness is that WEP used an *initialization vector* (IV) that was too short (24 bits). An IV is a number that is used by a stream cipher to ensure that two identical strings encrypted by the same key do not produce the same ciphertext. It is critical that the IV never be reused because if it is, the two messages encrypted with the same IV reveal information about how the data was encrypted. With such a short IV, it is unavoidable that an IV will be reused given sufficient network traffic.

A second major weakness is a combination of two flaws: the underlying stream cipher that was used, RC4, has known "weak" keys, and part of the key is based on the IV (which is transmitted in plaintext). By looking for intercepted packets with certain IVs, one could more easily extract the full key.

The net result is that WEP traffic on a busy network can be compromised after eavesdropping for only a few minutes.

Next, realize that as computing power increases and more time is spent analyzing algorithms and protocols, weaknesses in what were previously robust approaches to cryptology will be found. Cryptology never gets stronger; it only gets weaker with the passage of time, so managing cryptologic products through their lifecycle is essential. There are many examples. The first symmetric cryptographic algorithm selected by NIST, the Data Encryption Standard (DES), was developed by IBM in the early 1970s, approved in 1977, and publicly broken in 1999. The Secure Hashing Algorithm (SHA-1) was approved in 1996 and first deprecated in 2011. In early 2020, security researchers announced that they had fully and practically broken the SHA-1 algorithm by identifying a collision attack, deeming it unfit for any practical use.

In the future, there is the threat that the performance advances inherent in quantum computing will enable certain cryptographic algorithms currently resistant to brute-force attacks to be compromised. Quantum computing was complete fantasy until only recently, and practical application is still new. However, the future will arrive quickly, as experts are claiming widespread commercial use could easily happen within the next several years. Given that quantum computing will have the capability to solve problems in seconds, quantum computing poses a significant threat to the sustainability of encryption.

Researchers are working to develop quantum-resistant algorithms. NIST runs a post-quantum cryptography program and competition seeking to establish post-quantum cryptography standards by 2024. As of July 2020, the competition was in its third round, with seven encryption and signature schemes still under evaluation. There are also European organizations (such as ETSI and the EU's PQCrypto project) working on post-quantum approaches to cryptology.

The story for cryptology protocols is similar. The original protocol to protect HTTPS web traffic was Secure Sockets Layer (SSL). The first version was found to be vulnerable and so was not even released publicly. Version 2.0 fixed that problem, was released in 1995, and was found to be vulnerable the next year. Its replacement, 3.0, fared slightly better, thought to be secure until the disclosure of the POODLE vulnerability in 2014. These are the conclusions to be drawn:

- Cryptology is hard, and even the experts get it wrong.
- The cryptographic attack surface includes not only the algorithm, but the people, processes, and technology that implement the cryptographic protections, all of which are potentially vulnerable to attack.
- Cryptanalysis becomes more effective over time, owing to advances in computing, mathematical breakthroughs, and other improvements in cryptanalytic methods.

Because time erodes the security of cryptographic protections, the security architect must consider the lifecycle of the encrypted data when choosing cryptographic methods, particularly in the selection of an appropriate algorithm and key length. An appropriate choice for data that has a lifetime of only one or two years might not be the right choice if the data to be encrypted will remain sensitive for decades. In such a case, applying a compensating control for systems that must archive data for longer periods of time might be to design the system to allow for changing the cryptographic algorithm and re-encrypting the data as required by the risk assessment for the information.

Implementation Weaknesses

Not only is designing a secure cryptographic algorithm or protocol hard, securely implementing an algorithm is no easier. Use industry-standard and tested algorithms, implemented in published libraries. Don't invent or implement algorithms yourself.

✔ Heartbleed: An Implementation Flaw Case Study

Heartbleed was an implementation flaw in the TLS protocol used to secure web traffic (HTTPS). Part of the protocol defined a "heartbeat" packet that contains a text message and a length field. The computer receiving the message is simply to send the message back. The defect was that the size of the message sent back was not based on the actual size of the received heartbeat packet, but on the length parameter sent by the requester. So, a malicious actor could send a heartbeat packet containing the message "Hello, world!" but with a length field of, say, 64,000. The reply would contain "Hello, world!" plus the next 63,987 bytes of whatever happened to be in memory beyond that message. That memory could contain the private key used to secure the website, or copies of previous messages containing confidential information. Access to a web server's private keys would enable an attacker to decrypt past and future web traffic, as well as spoof the identity of the website, enabling phishing attacks.

The flaw existed in the widely used library for two years before being reported and patched. At least half a million secure websites were estimated to have been affected, not to mention the hundreds of thousands of devices with an embedded web server used to manage the device. In one example, a curious computer science student used the flaw to exfiltrate 900 social insurance numbers from the Canada Revenue Agency, earning an 18-month conditional sentence in prison for his efforts. Cybersecurity columnist Joseph Steinberg wrote in *Forbes*: "Some might argue that Heartbleed is the worst vulnerability found (at least in terms of its potential impact) since commercial traffic began to flow on the Internet."

More information may be found at `heartbleed.com`.

A *side-channel attack* is the analysis of artifacts related to the implementation of the algorithm, such as the time the algorithm takes to execute, the electrical power consumed by the device running the cryptographic implementation, or the electromagnetic radiation released by the device. More details are available in the "Understand Methods of Cryptanalytic Attacks" section.

Defeating side-channel attacks is often difficult since detecting an attack that does not interfere with the operation of the cryptosystem is difficult. The best defense is to use standard cryptographic libraries that have been tested over time for side-channel information leakage.

There are also a number of steps one can take to minimize the possibility of leaking information via side channels. For example (and this is only a partial list of implementation traps lying in wait for the unsuspecting developer):

- Compare secret strings (e.g., keys, plaintext, unhashed passwords) using constant-time comparison routines
- Avoid branching or loop counts that depend upon secret data
- Avoid indexing lookup tables or arrays using secret data
- Use strong (i.e., "cryptographic grade") random number generators

One also needs to be aware that compiler optimizations can change or remove code to introduce side-channel vulnerabilities. The system security requirements need to identify these possible weaknesses, and the testing and code validation need to verify that they have been adequately addressed.

Vulnerabilities can also be introduced by misusing an otherwise securely implemented, sound cryptographic algorithm.

With algorithms that use an IV (refer to the "WEP: A Design Flaw Case Study" sidebar to learn what an IV is), the IV must be properly selected to protect the encrypted data stream. Typically, this means it must be cryptographically random and unique, and of enough length (i.e., not reused for subsequent messages).

Block ciphers can be used in a number of different modes (discussed later in this chapter), some of which may leak significant information when used with certain types of data. Selecting the correct mode is as important as selecting the block cipher itself.

Key Management Vulnerabilities

There are a number of vulnerabilities that can be introduced through the incorrect use, storage, and management of cryptographic keys.

Keys should be generated in a manner appropriate for the cryptographic algorithm being used. The proper method to generate a symmetric key is different from a public/

private key pair. NIST SP 800-133, "Recommendation for Cryptographic Key Generation," provides specific guidance.

Keys should not be reused and should be rotated (replaced) periodically to ensure that the amount of data encrypted using a single key is limited, and the lifetime of data encrypted using a given key is likewise limited.

Symmetric and private keys depend upon confidentiality to be effective. This means great care must be taken with how the keys are stored to reduce the possibility of their becoming known to unauthorized entities. There are a number of approaches to secure key storage. These are some common examples:

- Key management software

- Key management services provided by cloud service providers

- Dedicated hardware devices that keep the keys stored internally in a tamper-resistant secure device

Keys that have reached the end of their lifetime (and all properly managed keys ought to have a defined lifetime) must be securely destroyed to prevent their misuse in the future.

Another vulnerability can arise from insider threats. A rogue employee with access to key material can use that access to defeat the security of encrypted material (or enable another to do the same). Dual control or segregation of duties can be employed to ensure that at least two people must be actively involved before any key management operation that might compromise the security of the keys or the system can be completed.

The final leg of the CIA Triad must also be considered: availability. If the key management system cannot provide access to the key material to authorized processes when required, then access to the encrypted material will be denied, even if the encrypted data is readily accessible.

Key operations must be logged in a manner that ensures accountability and traceability so that should a compromise be suspected, the forensic evidence will be available to analyze the possible breach.

Finally, where possible, key management functions ought to be automated. Manual processes are more prone to error (either of commission or omission), leading to weaknesses in the system that depends upon the keys for security.

Obviously, a key management system needs to be properly designed in the first place before it can be used. The "Key Management Practices" section later in this chapter further discusses the key management lifecycle, including HSMs and various other aspects of key management.

Industrial Control Systems

Industrial control systems (ICSs) are used to automate industrial processes and cover a range of control systems and related sensors. Security in this context concentrates mostly on the integrity and availability aspects of the CIA Triad: integrity of the data (e.g., sensor inputs and control setpoints) used by the control system to make control decisions, and availability of the sensor data and the control system itself. In addition to integrity, safety is a huge consideration for modern industrial control systems, such as those that steer aircrafts, treat our drinking water, and power biomedical systems.

The importance of this can range from ensuring the proper operation of a building's heating, ventilation, and air-conditioning (HVAC) systems to the safe production of dangerous chemicals to the reliable distribution of electricity to large areas of entire cities and countries.

Historically, ICSs communicated using proprietary methods and were not connected to local area networks (LANs) or the internet, so security was not a design consideration. Today, many industrial control systems have been attached to internet protocol (IP) gateways without much consideration as to the threats such access enables.

There are a number of organizations that provide guidance or regulations related to ICS security:

- ISA/IEC-62443 is a series of standards, technical reports, and related information that define procedures for implementing electronically secure Industrial Automation and Control Systems (IACS).

- The North American Electric Reliability Corporation (NERC) provides a series of guides referred to as the Critical Infrastructure Protection (CIP) standards. NERC CIP standards are mandatory in the United States and Canada for entities involved in power generation/distribution.

- The European Reference Network for Critical Infrastructure Protection (ERN-CIP) is an EU project with similar aims to those of NERC CIP.

- NIST and the UK National Centre for the Protection of National Infrastructure (CPNI). See, for example, NIST publication SP800-82.

The importance of security to critical public infrastructure (such as electrical power distribution, water systems, and other public utilities) has come to the attention of governments because vulnerabilities in such systems are considered prime targets for economic warfare in times of conflict with foreign states.

✔ Ukraine Power Grid Cyber Attack

In the aftermath of Russia's annexation of Crimea in 2014, unknown attackers launched a coordinated and sophisticated attack against three different electrical utilities in Ukraine, taking almost 60 substations offline and disrupting power to more than 230,000 residents. This is the first confirmed successful cyber attack on an electrical power grid.

The compromise appears to have started with a successful spear phishing attack using malicious Word or Excel documents, which enabled the attackers to obtain the information and credentials necessary to access the control systems (which were not protected by two-factor authentication).

Then, in addition to taking control of systems that enabled the attackers to start turning off breakers, they uploaded malicious firmware into various components of the ICS so that even when the utilities regained control of their supervisory control systems, many of the substations would not respond to remote commands and had to be operated manually by technicians dispatched to each site.

Finally, the attackers used a piece of malware called KillDisk to erase essential system files on operator stations.

Although this attack was limited in its impact (the power interruptions lasted between 1 and 6 hours and affected only about 0.5 percent of the country's population), the analysis showed the attackers had access to the control systems for at least six months prior and could have done a lot more damage if they had wanted. Some suspect this attack was intended to send a message rather than inflict heavy damage.

✔ Israel Water Supply Cyber Attacks

In April 2020, an attempted cyber attack targeted the industrial control systems of the Israel Water Authority's water treatment station. Hackers successfully gained access to Israel's water treatment systems and tried altering water chlorine levels, before ultimately being detected and stopped. If the attack had been successful, it's likely that attackers would have caused poisoning of local residents served by the targeted water treatment facility.

Following the April attacks, Israeli authorities issued an alert urging water treatment facilities and other ICS operators to change their passwords and consider additional security measures on their publicly accessible operational systems. The attack, though thwarted, is a great demonstration of what could happen if security is not treated as a priority for ICSs.

Israel's water supply experienced two additional failed attacks within months of the initial April 2020 compromise, indicating that ICS attacks are likely just getting started.

ICS security shares many of the same threats, vulnerabilities, and risks as any information system, and a review of the controls outlined in the standards described earlier shows strong similarities to other information security frameworks.

These are the challenges specific to industrial control:

- The difficulty of patching device firmware to address vulnerabilities in the software discovered after placing the device into production in the field

- Failure to change factory-default settings, especially those related to access controls and passwords

- The long production lifetime of industrial systems as compared to IT systems

- The reliance on air-gapped networks as a compensating control without proper supervision of network connections

Let's consider each of these in turn.

As has been discussed earlier, patching software (including firmware) to address security defects discovered after the initial release of the software is a critically important aspect of security.

With ICSs, patching can be difficult or impossible:

- With industrial systems operating nonstop, it may not be feasible to remove an ICS device from operation to update its firmware.

- Similarly, with continuous production being important, the risk of an update breaking something (such as patching the underlying operating system and interfering with the ICS app running on that OS) can be too great (and greater than the perceived risk of running obsolete software). Consider an air traffic control system or an oil and gas pipeline, for example. These systems are hugely important and rely on nearly 100 percent uptime. Often, organizations must weigh the risk of operating an unpatched system with the risk of a patch disrupting service.

- Finally, the location of the ICS device in the field may make the simple matter of reaching the device physically to connect a laptop to install the firmware update a significant undertaking.

Obviously, a proper ICS design would accommodate the need to update components, but unfortunately, many production systems were installed before there was an understanding of the security vulnerabilities inherent in ICSs. These systems are constantly being upgraded and modernized, and as an on-duty CISSP, you can help your organization manage ICS-centric elements while balancing functionality with security.

Many IT departments plan to replace systems every three to five years. Most computer vendors stop supporting devices five to seven years after their first release, and no longer provide patches to address security issues. Most industrial process equipment is designed to operate for 10 to 20 years and longer. Further, the greater reliance on commercial off-the-shelf operating systems increases the known attack surface for many ICS implementations, especially once those COTS operating systems have reached end-of-life while the ICS remains in service.

If the physical security of the ICS is adequate, then the primary threats are from the internet. In that case, a reasonable and common compensating control is to air-gap the networks used by the industrial control devices. This can provide adequate security if properly enforced, but keeping the air-gapped network safe requires careful diligence and technical controls to prevent foreign equipment from being connected. If external equipment must be connected periodically, say for maintenance purposes, consider using a firewall or proxy between the maintenance laptop and ICS network to provide an additional layer of security.

The classic example of compromising an air-gapped ICS was Stuxnet, which was used to cause considerable damage to Iran's uranium enrichment facility. It has been reported that the air-gapped network was compromised by a virus-infected USB thumb drive being plugged into a computer on the ICS network.

At a minimum, computers used to maintain and manage industrial systems must never be used for any other purpose (or removed from the facility). They must be regularly updated, employ anti-malware protection, and carefully scan any removable media (e.g., USB thumb drives) before being used. See the guidance published by the organizations listed earlier for more specifics.

If complete isolation from the corporate LAN and the internet is not an option, then it is essential to limit and screen permitted traffic accessing the ICS network through the use of carefully configured firewalls and network proxies. Consideration ought to be given to further segmenting the ICS network itself to limit the lateral spread of a compromise.

For ICSs that must be remotely accessible, compensating controls such as installing a web proxy or VPN should be considered to add an additional layer of security on top of whatever access controls are implemented on the ICS itself.

Security awareness training is also particularly important, and advocating security principles among all the technicians and plant operators is critically important. If those personnel burdened with the need to observe security controls understand the importance and rationale associated with those controls, they are less likely to view them as an impediment to their job of running the plant and something to be avoided or circumvented.

Cloud-Based Systems

According to NIST, "*Cloud computing* is a model for enabling ubiquitous, convenient, on-demand network access to a shared pool of configurable computing resources (e.g., networks, servers, storage, applications, and services) that can be rapidly provisioned and released with minimal management effort or service provider interaction." In short, cloud-based systems are remotely located, separately managed systems that are accessible by the internet.

NIST SP 800-145 and ISO/IEC 17788 define a number of characteristics that describe cloud computing:

- **Broad network access:** Resources (physical and virtual) are accessible and managed over the network.

- **Measured service:** Users pay only for the services they use.

- **On-demand self-service:** Users can provision and manage services using automated tools without requiring human interaction.

- **Rapid elasticity and scalability:** Services can be rapidly and automatically scaled up or down to meet demand.

- **Resource pooling and multitenancy:** Physical or virtual resources are aggregated to serve multiple users while keeping their data isolated and inaccessible to other tenants.

There are three primary *cloud service models*, as shown in Table 3.2.

TABLE 3.2 Cloud Service Models

CLOUD SERVICE MODEL	SERVICE PROVIDED	SERVICE PROVIDER RESPONSIBILITIES	CUSTOMER RESPONSIBILITIES
Software as a service (SaaS)	Software application accessible to the customer over the internet (via a browser or API)	Provide and manage all infrastructure from server and network hardware to applications software	Provide the client device and manage user-specific configuration settings
Platform as a service (PaaS)	Web-based framework for developers to create customized applications	Provide and manage all infrastructure from server and network hardware to the libraries and runtime services necessary to run applications	Provide the application and manage the hosting environment
Infrastructure as a service (IaaS)	Infrastructure, including servers, network, storage, and operating systems, delivered through virtualization technology	Provide network and server infrastructure to support VMs and other virtualized resources	Provide and manage all components that run on the VM as well as limited aspects of network services

NOTE IaaS, PaaS, and SaaS are the three most common service models, but you may come across dozens of others. Anything as a service (XaaS) simply refers to anything hosted and operated by a cloud provider or third party. While "XaaS" has become popular marketing jargon, you should be familiar with the concept of a service model, as well as the three most common service models described in Table 3.2.

With each service model, there is obviously a different division between the components supplied by the cloud service provider and those provided by the customer. This gives rise to the cloud shared responsibility model, as illustrated in Figure 3.9. Security of cloud deployment is shared between the customer and the provider. The cloud service provider is responsible for the security of the cloud, and the customer is responsible for the security in the cloud. This also means that one has to consider the security capabilities and commitments of the provider when assessing the risk of a cloud deployment.

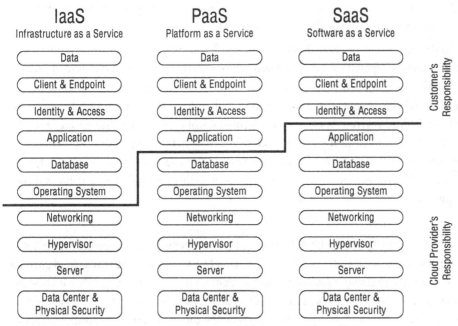

FIGURE 3.9 The cloud shared responsibility model for IaaS, PaaS, and SaaS

In particular, the cloud service provider is exclusively responsible for the following:

- Physical security
- Environmental security
- Hardware (i.e., the servers and storage devices)
- Networking (i.e., cables, switches, routers, firewalls, and internet connectivity)

The cloud service provider and the customer share responsibility for the following:

- **Vulnerability and patch management:** Using Figure 3.9 as a guide to determine which organization is responsible for which activities, the cloud service provider is responsible for patching the software below the responsibility dividing line, the customer is responsible for everything above the line (i.e., in the case of SaaS, the customer is responsible only for the computers and browsers used to access the cloud).

- **Configuration management:** The cloud service provider is responsible for the infrastructure, the customer for everything above. Network configuration and security is a special case, as the customer of an IaaS provider typically has configuration control over significant aspects of the network routing and firewalls through APIs and web-based management consoles. As these network controls are a key component of the security of an IaaS cloud deployment, the customer must take great care in ensuring their proper configuration.

- **Training:** Both the cloud provider and customer are responsible for the specific training required for their own personnel.

In the IaaS situation, in which the customer has responsibility for many aspects of network security, providing perimeter and interior security requires a different approach from traditional data center security. In the cloud, the customer rarely has the ability to install actual networking or security devices (such as firewalls, routers, switches, and the like), but instead is given API access to a limited number of firewall and router functions that they can use to control access to their VMs. Also, depending on the cloud service provider, access to network traffic, as one might expect in a data center using a network tap or a SPAN (mirror) port, may or may not be available, or might be available only on a sampled basis such as NetFlow or sFlow.

NOTE   Failure to fully comprehend the shared responsibility model is a primary contributor to insecure cloud-based systems. Far too often, cloud customers assume that a cloud provider handles *all* security configurations and management for their cloud service. While it's true that a cloud provider handles *most* security tasks for IaaS services (like patching and configuring the underlying infrastructure), even this service model comes with customer responsibility. As you move "up the stack" to PaaS and even SaaS, the customer's responsibility is decreased, but never fully goes away. Customers should work with their cloud providers, request appropriate compliance reports (such as PCI and SOC reports), and understand what security requirements they are required to implement and manage for a given cloud service.

Finally, cloud service can be deployed in a number of ways (known as *deployment models*):

- **Public cloud:** Available to any customer
- **Private cloud:** Used exclusively by a single customer (may be in-house or run by a third party, on-premise or off)
- **Community cloud:** Used exclusively by a small group of customers with similar interests or requirements (may be managed by one or more of the customers, or a third party, on-premise or off)
- **Hybrid cloud:** A combination of two or more of the above deployment models

---

NOTE Since many government agencies share similar interests and requirements, the notion of a government cloud (or "GovCoud") has become an important community cloud concept.

The deployment model will have a significant effect on the nature of the risk assessment for the cloud deployment. That said, do not assume that private or on-premise cloud deployments are intrinsically more secure than public clouds. The major cloud providers have invested heavily in security, as attested to by their many security audits and certifications, and they can typically provide better security for their clients than those companies can for themselves.

NOTE Not all cloud providers are able to meet all security standards. As a CISSP, you must not only understand what security features a cloud provider offers, but first what capabilities you need and which features are enabled by default versus those that require additional configuration. Too many cloud-based systems are breached because customers wrongly assume that an advertised security feature is enabled without their action.

Distributed Systems

A distributed system is a collection of systems designed to appear as a single system to users. Distributed systems are built to achieve a number of objectives, including reliance, performance, and scalability.

Because a distributed system, by definition, involves multiple subsystems, possibly distributed geographically, and interconnected in some manner, the attack surface is much larger than that of a single system.

It is important to model threats to the overall system and identify the relative risks that need to be addressed.

Consider the following:

- The need for encryption and authentication on the connections between the subsystems to ensure attackers cannot intercept, eavesdrop, or spoof communications between subsystems

- The need to protect against DoS attacks against the communications links or the subsystems themselves

- The risks from a lack of homogeneity across subsystems (e.g., different versions and patch levels of operating systems, middleware, and application software; difficulty of maintaining consistent configurations across disparate and distributed systems) and mechanisms to mitigate those risks

- The need to maintain consistency should communications be disrupted (delayed or interrupted) between groups of (normally) connected subsystems (sometimes referred to as the "split-brain" problem)

- The challenge of ensuring comparable security controls in the case of geographically distributed components (e.g., physical, environmental, and personnel)

- The requirements of privacy and data sovereignty regulations that may limit the transfer of personal data across international borders

These risks are not unique to distributed systems, but the nature of distributed systems can make their mitigation much more complex than for nondistributed systems.

Internet of Things

The term *Internet of Things* (IoT) describes a network of physical objects that are embedded with technologies (e.g., sensors and software) that enable them to connect to and exchange data with other devices over the internet. These physical objects — or "things" — include all manner of devices in business, government, and commercial use. Examples include household appliances, medical equipment, smart home devices, and so on. Estimates are that the number of such devices in 2020 was somewhere between 20 and 50 billion, and the rapid expansion of 5G networks is expected to continue to drive IoT growth.

The importance of IoT security can be demonstrated through the infamous Mirai distributed denial of service (DDoS) attack.

The Mirai attack (Figure 3.10) involved a worm that searched for vulnerable IoT devices (typically consumer routers and IP-enabled closed circuit television (CCTV) cameras), infected them with a copy of the malware, and then waited for instructions from a command and control (C&C) server as to which target to attack with a DDoS attack. In late 2016, this botnet took the Krebs on Security blog offline and later attacked the Dyn DNS service, which in turn seriously impacted many of their customers including GitHub, Twitter, Reddit, Netflix, and Airbnb.

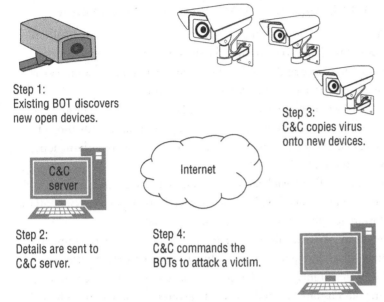

Step 1:
Existing BOT discovers
new open devices.

Step 3:
C&C copies virus
onto new devices.

C&C
server

Internet

Step 2:
Details are sent to
C&C server.

Step 4:
C&C commands the
BOTs to attack a victim.

FIGURE 3.10 **Components of the Mirai DDoS BotNet attack**

✔ Smart Lightbulb Hack

In early 2020, researchers from security firm Check Point announced that they had successfully compromised a home network by attacking the popular Philips Hue smart lightbulb.

The firm's researchers identified vulnerabilities in the ZigBee low-power WiFi protocol used by Philips and many other IoT vendors. Using a remote exploit, Check Point researchers were able to compromise the smart lightbulb, install malicious firmware on it, and used the lightbulb as a pivot to take over the lightbulb's control bridge. From there, the attackers are able to cause the bulb to appear to glitch, prompting the victim to reset the compromised lightbulb. Upon adding the compromised bulb back to the user's network, vulnerabilities in the ZigBee protocol enable the hacker to install malware on the network bridge, thus creating a backdoor from the target network back to the hacker.

Prior to releasing their report, Check Point worked with Philips to identify solutions to the vulnerabilities. Philips has since remediated this particular weakness, but the vulnerable ZigBee protocol is still used by several other vendors in many other IoT devices. This case study is a quick example of how the proliferation of IoT devices is leading to a broader attack surface for commercial businesses and consumers alike.

IoT Security from an Equipment Manufacturer's Perspective

During development, you will want to conduct threat modeling to determine likely vulnerabilities and to ensure that appropriate mitigations are deployed. You must review their product's security architecture to determine if the general guidelines outlined earlier in this section have been observed in the design of the firmware.

The development team will need to pay particular attention to secure software development guidelines such as those from the open web application security project (OWASP) and SANS. And the quality assurance (QA) team will need to perform active white- and black-box penetration testing.

Many of the vulnerabilities that have been exploited in IoT devices in the past could have been mitigated through basic security hygiene such as changing default credentials and updating the firmware to patch known vulnerabilities.

As an IoT product developer, apart from trying to design and develop as secure an IoT device as you can, you need to make implementing the previous two security controls as easy as possible. You can make your device the most secure IoT device on the planet, but once it's in your customers' hands, it is out of your control. You need to make it as easy as possible for them to properly secure and maintain the device.

This means that your device should refuse to connect to the internet until the user has changed the default admin credentials. It means that your device should update itself automatically (with the consent of the user), and if auto-update has not been enabled, possibly refuse to operate (after sufficient notice) should a patch be available for a high-severity vulnerability being actively exploited in the wild. In some cases, IoT devices may refuse to operate without first connecting to the internet for initialization. In these cases, it's best that you keep potentially insecure IoT devices isolated from critical systems or sensitive areas on your network.

While ease of use is a key factor in the commercial success of IoT devices, one has to draw the line where ease of use is directly connected to ease of compromise.

IoT Security from a User's Perspective

As a user of IoT devices, there are steps you can take to mitigate the risks related to devices with poor design or support so that you do not become part of a botnet used to attack others, and your IoT devices are not used as a beachhead from which your other information systems can be attacked.

To start, you can protect yourself (and others that might be a target of your compromised devices) through the same two basic security controls previously mentioned:

- Change default credentials as soon as possible, and before you connect the device to the internet.

- Keep your device updated with the current firmware release, either by enabling auto-update (if supported by your device) or by periodically checking with the manufacturer's website for firmware updates.

In addition, you can employ security in depth through additional controls:

- Do not place IoT devices on the open internet, but rather behind a firewall so that they are not directly accessible externally.

- Segment your network so that your IoT devices do not have access to other sensitive devices or servers on your internal networks.

- If you have to be able to access your IoT device externally, then at the very least put the device behind a router that does reverse NAT mapping. Recall that reverse NAT provides network address translation, but from an external source to an internal private address. Hence, it is NAT but in reverse. Preferably, put the device behind a proxy that can perform its own user authentication before providing access to the IoT device.

Note, of course, that the router or proxy is also a potential vulnerability and must itself be operated securely: it must be properly configured (change default credentials) and maintained (patched and updated).

Relying on the security of an IoT device is unwise given the history of unpatched vulnerabilities in such devices. By placing the device behind another that acts as an access gateway, one implements security in depth and security layering, requiring the compromise of two different devices before the IoT device can be breached. And if you have properly segmented your network, even the compromise of your IoT devices will have limited impact on the confidentiality and integrity of your information systems (the availability of those systems in the face of an IoT DDoS attack is another matter). In fact, taking network segmentation to the extreme leads to Google's BeyondCorp paradigm: a network in which access to resources is not granted based on network location but by user privileges.

✔ UK Report on Consumer IoT

Many governments have realized the threat that IoT poses, not only to their citizens, but to their nations' infrastructures. The UK government published a report in March 2018 called "Secure by Design: Improving the cyber security of consumer Internet of Things Report" that included a proposed code of practice, the main points of which are listed here:

- No default passwords

- Implement a vulnerability disclosure policy

- Keep software updated

CONTINUES

- Securely store credentials and security-sensitive data (and avoid hard-coded credentials)

- Communicate securely

- Minimize exposed attack surfaces

- Ensure software integrity

- Ensure that personal data is protected

- Make systems resilient to outages

- Monitor system telemetry data

- Make it easy for consumers to delete personal data

- Make installation and maintenance of devices easy

- Validate input data

Microservices

Microservice architecture is a modular software development style that involves developing a single application as a collection of loosely coupled smaller applications or services (*microservices*), each running its own processes. The microservices are built to be independently deployable and work together through lightweight communications protocols. Microservices can be contrasted with the more traditional *monolithic architecture*, which involves developing an application as a single, indivisible unit, typically with a large codebase that lacks modularity. Figure 3.11 depicts the difference between monoliths and microservices.

As an example, consider Microsoft O365. This is a suite of monolithic applications. You cannot just invoke the "change font" feature or the "sort a table" feature without loading the entire monolithic application. On the other hand, Amazon Web Services started out as a monolithic architecture, but has moved into a more service-oriented architecture using microservices.

Microservice architectures are highly distributed and dynamic and present unique security concerns that must be considered from the first stages of design and throughout the entire development lifecycle. Two key principles to consider when securing microservices are: isolation and defense in depth.

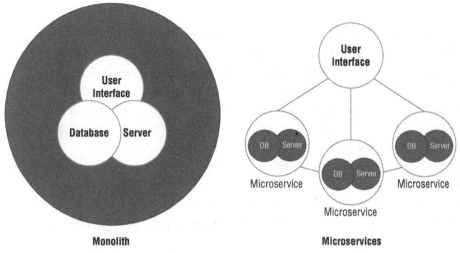

FIGURE 3.11 **Monoliths and microservices**

Isolation is a core principle of microservices, and each microservice must be able to be deployed, modified, maintained, and destroyed without impacting the other microservices around it. By architecting microservices with the principle of isolation in mind, you can better ensure that weaknesses in one microservice are contained and cannot negatively affect other microservices in the application.

The principle of defense in depth, while important in any architecture, is particularly critical when dealing with microservices. Defense in depth is a security strategy that calls for multiple layers of security controls to be implemented throughout an application or system. It is essential in a microservice architecture to independently monitor and protect each microservice and the communications between each microservice in the overall environment.

NOTE   Among the most vulnerable parts of a microservice architecture are the APIs used to communicate with and between the microservices. When securing your microservice architecture, ensuring API security is essential. An API gateway is an API management tool that sits between a client and multiple backend services, and aggregates all API calls to and from those services. A security best practice for microservices is to use an API gateway to establish a single interface for all your microservices, allowing you to secure your microservices behind a firewall and use the API gateway as a proxy that handles all requests to the microservices behind that firewall. API gateways are a great tool to block a client's direct access to your microservices and prevent potential attacks from bad actors.

Containerization

A *container* is unit of software that packages up an application and its dependencies so that the application can be decoupled from its environment and developed, deployed, and run consistently across multiple environments (e.g., public cloud, private cloud, local systems, etc.). Instead of running an entire operating system (like a VM does), a container uses the operating system's kernel and only the resources required to operate the given application. Thus, by design, containers are lightweight and flexible, allowing faster application development than noncontainerized applications.

Containers were made popular with the development of the open-source Kubernetes platform. Kubernetes and other container platforms are particularly useful in hybrid cloud environments, as they allow developers and users to seamlessly move applications from one cloud to another, or even between cloud and on-prem environments.

NOTE   Containers can sometimes be confused with microservices, but they are not the same. A microservice may run in a container, but it could also run as a full-featured VM. It's possible to have a single monolithic application deployed as a container, and it's also possible to have multiple microservices without using any containers. In other words, microservices can be built, deployed, and run with or without containers, and containers can be built with or without any microservices inside them.

Security Concerns

Containerization comes with its own set of security challenges, as container technology is inherently flexible and open. Because containers allow you to rapidly scale up and down resources, asset management and configuration management are perhaps even bigger security concerns than traditional systems.

Container security risks generally fall into two major categories:

- Compromise of a container image or the entire container repository
- Misuse of a container to attack other containers or the host OS

Careful management of your container images is the key to container security. Your base container image is the most important, because it is used as a starting point for derivative images. Container security begins with using signed base images from trusted sources. Follow careful configuration management practices when adding applications or other variables to your images. In addition, all container images should adhere to strict vulnerability scanning and patching requirements.

NOTE Containers running with the "privileged flag" can do almost anything the underlying host can do. This is a powerful configuration, and should be avoided whenever possible, based on the principle of least privilege. If a privileged container is compromised, an attacker can easily compromise the host OS and any other containers hosted on it. Use with caution!

In addition to managing secure image baselines, you must also ensure proper access controls to all of your container images. Use role-based access controls, where possible, to manage access to your container images.

Securing the host OS that runs your containers is a foundational part of securing your containers. Host operating systems should run only the minimally required services necessary to operate the containers and exclude applications like web servers, databases, and others that increase the attack surface. Proper configuration is also important, and host OSs must be included in your configuration management plans. In addition, communications between containers should be restricted based on the principle of least privilege — only allow containers to communicate with those containers that are absolutely required for operation. Container orchestration and management tools, like Kubernetes, allow you to implement network controls that restrict communication paths, where appropriate.

Serverless

Serverless computing is a cloud computing model that involves the cloud provider managing servers, and dynamically allocating machine resources, as needed. With serverless computing, infrastructure management tasks like provisioning and patching are handled by the cloud provider, leaving the customer primarily responsible for writing the code that executes on these servers. AWS Lambda, Azure Functions, and Google Cloud Functions are popular serverless frameworks available from public cloud providers.

Serverless computing comes with some notable security benefits. To start, serverless functions are typically ephemeral (i.e., short lived). These functions typically spin up for a few seconds, run their code, and then die. This short-lived nature creates a moving target that adds a high degree of difficulty for attackers to compromise. In addition, serverless functions are commonly much smaller codebases than even the smallest containers. Given this fact, you are able to apply much more granular access control rules to each function, rather than relying on container-level rules that might require granting excessive permissions to achieve the same functionality. Finally, with serverless architecture, your responsibility (as a cloud customer) for security is drastically reduced, and largely transferred to the cloud provider, who is responsible for all OS hardening, patching, and runtime security. Of course, this is only a security benefit if the cloud provider executes these tasks reliably.

Security Concerns

Despite its benefits, serverless computing is not without its security challenges. In 2019, the Israel chapter of the Cloud Security Alliance (CSA) drafted a paper titled "The 12 Most Critical Risks for Serverless Applications." Among the risks cited include broken authentication, over-privileged function permissions and roles, and other issues related to attack surface complexity and nuances associated with serverless architectures. The publication can be found by visiting `cloudsecurityalliance.org/artifacts/ the-12-most-critical-risks-for-serverless-applications`.

Effective serverless security is built on ensuring code integrity, tight access permissions, and proper monitoring. You should maintain least-privileged access for serverless functions, as you do other services — serverless functions should be granted only the access and permissions necessary to execute their task. Code should be routinely scanned for vulnerabilities and configuration issues. In addition, runtime protection should be used to detect suspicious events or errors that may lead to unexpected behavior or compromise. Most large cloud providers offer features to achieve these goals, and there are various third-party vendors with additional support for serverless security.

Embedded Systems

Embedded systems are dedicated information processing components built into larger mechanical or electrical systems, intended to provide a limited set of functions. Embedded systems can be found in a wide range of technologies, including the following:

- Domestic appliances (e.g., dishwashers, clothes washers and dryers, refrigerators, and televisions)
- Office equipment (e.g., printers, scanners, and fax machines)
- Networking devices (e.g., routers, switches, and firewalls)
- Cars and other automobiles
- ATMs
- Medical devices (e.g., heart monitors, glucose meters, and IV infusion pumps)
- Mass transit vehicles, stations, and systems
- Building automation and control systems
- Traffic control and monitoring systems

The healthcare industry has innovated with embedded systems that provide great benefit to both care providers and patients. One example is the tracking of patients and healthcare staff through a real-time location system (RTLS), fulfilled by active radio frequency identification (RFID) tags and proximity sensors. Another example that truly embraces IoT-capable embedded devices is what's now known as *telemedicine* or remote health monitoring and care. Most helpful for patients who cannot easily travel to a hospital, IoT-capable devices are brought to the patient's home and communicate remotely with healthcare staff.

Assessing the vulnerabilities in an embedded system ought to start with an enumeration of the attack surfaces available and then examining each. As described in greater detail earlier in this chapter, this examination can be done in a number of ways, including code inspection, threat modeling, and white- or black-box penetration testing.

Generally, these attack surfaces will fall into the following categories:

- User interface (UI, which are buttons or other methods of user input)
- Physical attacks
- Sensor attacks
- Output attacks
- Processor attacks

UI attacks involve manipulating the controls of the device in a manner that causes the device to malfunction. This can involve pressing buttons in the wrong order or in ways not expected or anticipated by the designer (multiple times, multiple buttons at the same time, etc.).

Depending on the nature of the user interface, there may be functions that are restricted and accessible only through special means. This can be as simple as special combinations of button presses to "unlock" administrative or privileged features, or user login processes (which can be vulnerable to all the standard user authentication problems such as default or poorly chosen passwords). Keep in mind that these restricted functions are often leaked on the internet, which requires special precautions when you're securing such devices and systems.

Mitigations for these attacks include careful review of the security-critical parts of the firmware as well as penetration-type testing of the embedded system's UI. Obviously, pen testing a vending machine takes a slightly different approach than a web app, but the concept is very similar. Consider all of the methods available to send data or commands to the device and then try invalid or unusual data or commands, or sequences of data or commands (both intentionally selected and random, as in fuzzing) in an attempt to get the embedded system to malfunction. Working "hacks" for vending machines are widely available online in the form of odd sequences of button presses that in turn cause a machine to dispense product. Similar to how pen testing a web app is dependent on the underlying language, the vending machine vulnerabilities depend on the underlying programming and thus the button sequences differ per vendor.

Physical attacks involve the compromise of the embedded system's packaging, either to directly compromise the device (i.e., breaking the glass front of a vending machine and grabbing the contents) or to gain access to parts of the embedded system in order to expose other attack surfaces that may be vulnerable (discussed later in this section). Particularly prone to causing vulnerabilities are the ports or interfaces intended for managing or servicing that machine. A real-world example involves voting machines, where a proof-of-concept demonstration can be found online as someone defeats the on-screen access control by exploiting the voting machine through its management port.

Defenses for physical attacks can range from increasing the strength of the physical protection (e.g., thicker steel container, strong locks, or epoxy embedding/soldering of components to make access difficult) to adding forms of tamper detection. Depending on the type of tampering, detection might merely mean building the device so that attempts to physically manipulate it (e.g., by adding a credit card skimmer) are easily apparent or cause the device to take defensive measures (from triggering an alarm to erasing sensitive memory to self-destructing).

Sensor attacks involve manipulating, or intercepting data from, the sensors the embedded system uses to detect external conditions that are relevant to its operation. For example, in a vending machine, the coin accepter is a sensor that tells the processor what coins have been deposited. Attacks on the sensor (e.g., using slugs or inserting wires or other thin implements to trip coin detectors) can fool the device into thinking payment has been made and that the product ought to be dispensed.

Much more costly than a vending machine hack are the sensor attacks on keyless entry cars. One well-known example is the viral video feed from an external security camera that shows two men approach a parked and locked Tesla Model S in the home-owner's driveway. A man with a laptop scans close to the home's external walls, hoping to come within distance of the Tesla's key fob. The other man stands very near the car door with a signal relaying device. By triggering the key fob, the first thief can relay the signal to his accomplice. The relay attack allows them to unlock the car and ultimately steal it.

Credit card skimmers and shimmers are forms of sensor attack. A skimmer is when the attacker eavesdrops on the data from the magnetic stripe reader in a credit card terminal. The card's magnetic data might be read by a portable device carried by, for example, a malicious wait server. Or the reading device could be a stationary point-of-sale terminal, where the attacker installed a second sensor to read the same data and record it.

A shimmer is another device that also lifts data from bank cards, but, unlike a skimmer, the shimmer intercepts data from the card's embedded EMV (Europay, MasterCard, Visa) chip. On bank cards with the EMV chip, the chip is enclosed within the card, but it has familiar gold-plated contacts on the surface to provide conductive touchpoints for when the bank card is inserted at a point-of-sale (POS) reader. The attacker's shimmer is a thin plastic sleeve or plate, shoved completely inside the POS reader. The shimmer as a plastic sleeve is little more than a surface to hold electrical contacts and a small integrated circuit (IC) chip for recording the inserted bank card. The shimmer's contacts are placed in a position to be "sandwiched" between the bank card and the legitimate POS reader.

Output attacks involve manipulating the actuators controlled by the embedded system to bypass the controls imposed by the system. Imagine an electric door lock in which the cabling is exposed, so all the attacker needs to do is strip the insulation and apply the appropriate voltage to cause the door to unlock.

Processor attacks involve compromising the processor directly, through means that can range from connecting directly to the processor or memory chips to carefully removing the tops of integrated circuits and using ion beams to probe the chip to obtain or manipulate information within the processor. Processor attacks are normally preceded by a physical attack to gain access to the processor.

Embedded systems that support firmware updates may be vulnerable to accepting rogue or unauthorized firmware. The attacker loads their own version of the firmware (either written from scratch or reverse engineered from code extracted from the device or downloaded from the manufacturer) that causes the device to behave as the attacker desires.

Protection against firmware attacks can include digital signatures to prevent unauthorized firmware from being accepted and executed, and cryptography to protect against reverse engineering of firmware updates.

As with IoT devices, a problem is that it is difficult, if not impossible, to upgrade the software in many embedded systems. This means that vulnerabilities that are discovered after the product has shipped may be difficult or impossible to patch. The result may be the need for compensating controls to mitigate the risk from the unpatched vulnerability or the need to replace the unit entirely.

High-Performance Computing Systems

High-performance computing (HPC) refers to the use of one or more supercomputers, generally for the purpose of highly complex computational science and other mathematically involved applications. Supercomputers have been around since the 1960s, but they continue to evolve, with most modern HPC systems leveraging cloud-based technologies to increase their distributed computing capabilities.

Generally speaking, HPC systems experience many of the same security concerns as traditional systems and other cloud-based systems (as discussed in earlier sections). They typically run Linux-based operating systems and are subject to software vulnerabilities, configuration issues, and compromised credentials. All of the traditional security measures should be considered here. A distinction, however, may come in the form of highly specialized, purpose-built hardware and software that supports the HPC environment. Any customized hardware and software present an added threat vector that must be secured. In the case of high-performance computing, the challenge becomes ensuring secure operation without adversely impacting performance.

As a best practice, HPC systems should be moved to their own physical enclave or logical security zone that is separate from traditional systems. Doing so segregates HPC systems from other types of computing systems that may have different security needs or regulations. The separate enclave provides a single point for ingress and egress monitoring of the HPC environment.

Accommodating the high volume of data traffic that passes through HPC systems requires a modified approach to network monitoring. Instead of using stateful firewalls for deep packet inspection, it's typically best to use firewalls that inspect packet headers, but not the payloads themselves. Separately, deep packet inspection may be used for intrusion detection, because stateful IDSs are not used inline, thus not introducing throughput delays. Here, using separate tools allows achieving traditional security intentions that accommodate for the uniqueness of HPC systems.

Edge Computing Systems

Edge computing is a distributed computing model that brings compute and storage resources closer to the location where it is needed, improving response times and reducing bandwidth. The concept of edge computing dates back to the content delivery networks (CDNs) of the 1990s and now extends into the world of cloud computing. CDNs are covered in detail in Chapter 4, "Communication and Network Security."

Today, edge computing helps manage the tremendous growth we're seeing with IoT devices. Edge computing allows pseudo-local data processing to minimize data sent over the internet. For example, imagine a factory with 5,000 internet-connected video cameras that send video to a remote location. This many live streams being sent over the company's network would be both slow and costly. Edge computing addresses this by processing the camera data locally and sending only necessary information over the internet. As opposed to all 5,000 continuous live streams being transmitted, your edge device might use artificial intelligence (AI) to identify anomalous behaviors in the factory and send 30 second clips when something needs to be investigated.

Security Concerns

From a security standpoint, edge computing presents a few challenges.

Devices located at the edge, rather than centrally managed in a data center or other tightly managed facility, may not always receive the same diligence as their peers. You must be sure to apply the same security rigor to edge devices as your centrally managed devices. This includes hardening, patching, and providing the right level of physical security for edge computing systems. SOAR (covered in Chapter 7) can help organizations observe and harden their devices, including those located at the edge.

Data must be encrypted when in transit between edge devices and centralized systems (or the cloud), and VPN tunneling may also be advisable for sensitive data when managing remote systems.

There are also availability concerns for edge devices. Redundancy and failover management of edge computing systems is important to ensure that data continues to be processed and transmitted in the event a single edge node fails. In addition, edge devices must be monitored for such failures so that errors and failures can be remedied as quickly as possible.

Virtualized Systems

Operating systems provide programs with a set of services to enable them to operate more efficiently (and to be more easily designed and run) than if the program had to run on the computer directly. For example, instead of an application reading and writing disk storage blocks directly, the operating system provides a level of abstraction that manages the details of files and directories. Furthermore, most operating systems also enable multiple programs to run concurrently, with each application able to operate oblivious to the presence of other apps on the same system.

In some sense, an operating system provides a type of virtual computer, a computer that does not exist in reality (i.e., hardware) but that is much easier for applications to use than the physical hardware and that makes more efficient use of the hardware by sharing it among different programs (see Figure 3.12).

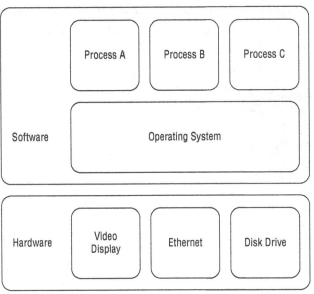

FIGURE 3.12 **An operating system efficiently allocates hardware resources between multiple processes.**

Virtualization takes this concept a step further. *Virtualization* is the act of creating virtual (i.e., not real) compute, storage, and network resources — in other words, virtualization allows you to create software versions of hardware. VMs, for instance, are software instances of actual computers. Likewise, software-defined networks (SDNs) are software instances of physical networks.

Instead of just one operating system enabling multiple application programs running on the same hardware, virtualization enables multiple operating systems to run on the same computer, each unaware of and unable (in a properly designed system) to affect the other operating systems. Virtualization is the primary technology behind cloud computing (discussed earlier in this section).

The most common implementation of virtualization is a hypervisor. A *hypervisor* is a computing layer that allows multiple operating systems to run simultaneously on a single piece of hardware, with each operating system viewing the machine's resources as its own dedicated resources. A hypervisor allows multiple guest virtual machines to run on a single physical host.

There are two types of hypervisors, commonly referred to as Type 1 and Type 2 hypervisors. The primary difference between them is whether an underlying operating system is used to bridge the hardware with the VMs. A Type 1 hypervisor is the sole installation, acting as a bridge between hardware components and VMs. For this reason, Type 1 hypervisors are also called *bare-metal* hypervisors. They are commonly found when flexibility and efficiency are most required. This is especially the case when the virtualized servers are running the same or similar services, making the most efficient use of the underlying hardware. In production environments, you are more likely to find virtualized machines sitting on Type 1 hypervisors. With a bit more overhead comes the Type 2 hypervisor, relying on a *host* operating system installed on the hardware. The virtualized machines running within the host OS are then called *guest* machines. Figure 3.13 depicts the differences between a Type 1 and Type 2 hypervisor.

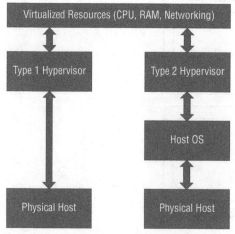

FIGURE 3.13 **Type 1 and Type 2 hypervisors**

Virtualization is the foundation upon which cloud providers such as AWS or Google Cloud Platform (GCP) provide VMs to different clients who may well end up running on the same physical computer, unknown to each other.

The advantages of virtualization include the following:

- More efficient use of the underlying hardware (just as operating systems permitted a single computer to be shared by multiple programs and users)
- Dynamic scaling of infrastructure in response to demand
- Additional separation and isolation between programs and applications running on different operating systems (as opposed to running on the same OS) — supporting the security principles of defense in depth and layers of security outlined earlier

Potential Weaknesses

As with memory protection, virtualization depends on the correct operation of both the hardware and the hypervisor (which may include hardware and/or software). Hardware defects such as Meltdown break the underlying assumption that the hardware will prevent an unauthorized program (and possibly a completely unrelated client) from accessing memory assigned to another program (and client).

NOTE   Type 2 hypervisors generally have a greater attack surface because of the additional vulnerabilities associated with the host operating system and associated software. OS and application vulnerabilities can be used to compromise a Type 2 hypervisor and the virtual systems it hosts. Type 1 hypervisors generally have embedded operating systems that are hardened and tightly controlled by the vendor. Despite this additional layer of security, Type 1 hypervisors are not immune to attack.

Similarly, software defects in hypervisors can improperly permit software running on one VM to access data on a different VM on the same computer. An exploit known as *virtual machine escape*, for example, occurs when a program is able to break out of its VM and directly interact with the underlying host operating system; once able to access the host OS, an attacker may be able to pivot into other VMs or cause service outages for tenants of the host system. When such defects are discovered, they are usually disclosed to the largest cloud service providers so that they can be patched before the vulnerability becomes widely known.

There is always the possibility that these unpatched defects in the hardware or hypervisor might be known to a threat actor who is then able to compromise the protections that are supposed to prevent unrelated clients on VMs from interacting. To mitigate this risk, some IaaS cloud providers offer dedicated hosts that guarantee that only VMs assigned to your account will be permitted to run on the dedicated host.

SELECT AND DETERMINE CRYPTOGRAPHIC SOLUTIONS

Cryptography is the mathematical manipulation of data so as to protect its confidentiality and/or integrity. Cryptography is arguably one of the most powerful tools in the arsenal of the security architect, yet a tool that can be so easily misapplied, resulting in a false sense of security.

Cryptography can be used across your environment to accomplish several objectives of information security, including two of three core principles from the CIA Triad (confidentiality and integrity), among others (namely, privacy, authenticity, nonrepudiation):

- **Confidentiality (and privacy):** One of the main uses of cryptography is to protect the confidentiality of information, both at rest and in transit. This offers the critical feature of "privacy" when applied to personally identifiable information (PII) and protected health information (PHI).

- **Integrity:** Another common application of cryptography is the use of hashing algorithms and message digest to provide assurance of data integrity (or accuracy). These cryptographic applications help ensure that data being accessed is intact and as expected.

- **Authenticity (and nonrepudiation):** Cryptography can also be used for authentication services as well as nonrepudiation through digital signatures and digital certificates.

Each of these applications are discussed throughout the rest of this section.

NOTE   Cryptography does very little to provide the "A" in the CIA Triad: availability. Even so, authenticity and nonrepudiation are two important principles that cryptography does support. This is an important reminder that information security is bigger than the traditional CIA Triad!

It is hard to think of an aspect of our use of computers that does not touch upon some aspect of cryptography. When you log in to a system, your password is protected using cryptography (at least we hope it is). When you connect to a website using an https: URL, your traffic is protected using cryptography. If you store PII with a responsible service provider, it ought to be protected using cryptography. In short, at every step of the process, cryptography can help secure sensitive information.

In the following sections, we will provide an overview of the various aspects of cryptography that the security architect needs to be familiar with. Earlier, in the section on assessing and mitigating vulnerabilities, we discussed potential weaknesses from the incorrect application of cryptography.

NOTE A critical concept in cryptography, *work factor* describes the amount time, effort, and resources required to break a cryptosystem. With enough time, effort, and resources, any cryptosystem can be broken, and any ciphertext can be decrypted without knowing the key or algorithm. Given this, the goal of any cryptographic solution is to ensure a work factor great enough to protect information until after the need for protection has lapsed (data has been destroyed, declassified, etc.).

What's an acceptable encryption algorithm today may not be acceptable five years from now, as computing continues to advance and work factors decrease. For that reason, we must stay vigilant and ensure that we are using the right algorithms and solutions to keep our data protected.

Cryptography Basics

Before jumping into some complex topics, let's begin with the basics. The following definitions from (ISC)² are core to the topic of cryptography, and you will see (and likely use) them frequently:

- **Plaintext:** The message in its natural format, which has not been turned into a secret.
- **Cleartext:** The message in readable, usable form that is not intended to be obscured by cryptographic means.
- **Ciphertext:** The altered form of a plaintext message, so as to be unreadable for anyone except the intended recipients (in other words, something that has been turned into a secret).
- **Encryption:** The process of converting the message from its plaintext to ciphertext.
- **Decryption:** The reverse process from encryption — it is the process of converting a ciphertext message back into plaintext through the use of the cryptographic algorithm and the appropriate key that was used to do the original encryption.
- **Cryptographic algorithm:** A mathematical function that is used in the encryption and decryption process.

- **Key:** The input that controls the operation of the cryptographic algorithm; it determines the behavior of the algorithm and permits the reliable encryption and decryption of the message. Symmetric/private keys (discussed later in this chapter) must be kept private, while public keys (also discussed later in this chapter) are shared to enable authentication and other use cases.

For additional helpful definitions, visit the (ISC)² CISSP Glossary: www.isc2.org/ Certifications/CISSP/CISSP-Student-Glossary#.

NOTE The notion of key strength is critical in cryptography. The strength of encryption is related to the difficulty of discovering the key, which is largely determined by the length of the key: larger key lengths offer greater encryption strength than shorter key lengths.

Cryptographic Lifecycle

The cryptographic lifecycle involves algorithm selection, key management, and the management of encrypted data at rest, in transit, and in use.

Algorithm selection involves a number of choices:

- The type of cryptography appropriate for the purpose (e.g., symmetric, public key, hashing, etc.)
- The specific algorithm (e.g., AES, RSA, SHA, etc.)
- The key length (e.g., AES-256, RSA-2048, SHA-512, etc.)
- The operating mode (ECB, CBC, etc.)

Symmetric encryption is best for storing data at rest that has to be recovered (decrypted) before being used. Symmetric encryption is also far more efficient than public key cryptography, so it's appropriate for protecting data in transit. The problem, as explained in detail later in this section, is that for symmetric cryptography to be used for data in transit, both ends of the communications link must have knowledge of the secret key. There are a number of methods for securely exchanging keys over an insecure channel, the most widely used of which uses public key cryptography (also discussed later).

There are some types of data that need to be protected but that do not need to be decrypted. In fact, for security, it is best that some data never be able to be decrypted. For example, to protect the confidentiality of passwords used for user authentication, they obviously have to be encrypted. But there is no need to be able to decrypt them. To verify an entered password against the previously stored password, all one need do is encrypt the entered password and compare the two ciphertexts. In fact, being able to decrypt passwords significantly weakens their security. So, for this purpose, we use a one-way encryption function, otherwise known as *cryptographic hashing*. To be clear, cryptography is not exclusively encryption and decryption. Cryptography uses an algorithm that, regardless of its level of complexity, deals with an input and an output. Cryptographic hashing inputs a string to produce an output, which is generally assumed to be an output of fixed length, regardless of the input length.

Another example is the use of credit card numbers within a billing system. While the system that submits the transaction to the payment processor obviously has to be able to access the account number in plaintext, there are many databases and logs in which the account number needs to be stored. For most of those, it is sufficient to store a cryptographic hash of the account number. This hash can be stored and communicated without significant risk should it be disclosed. Only a limited number of systems need store the account number using a symmetric cipher that can be decrypted. In this manner, the attack surface is sharply reduced.

Another technique to protecting the PAN is to disassociate the number from the account holder and any information that can identify that account holder. In and of itself, the PAN is like a token. Only when the PAN can be linked to PII does the credit card number become sensitive information. Translation vaults are being used to generate a random token with which the PAN is securely linked. This process (known as *tokenization*) helps separate account numbers from the PII by providing an encrypted relationship between the two.

Having chosen the type of cryptography, one must select the appropriate algorithm. In some cases, the set of algorithms is constrained by protocol standards. For example, if one is using cryptography to protect data in transit, then there is a finite list of supported algorithms, and your choice is limited by this list as well as a desire to remain compatible with as wide a range of browsers as reasonably possible. For IoT and edge devices, you'll generally want algorithms that are lightweight and can be supported by devices that are usually resource constrained. This is one example of how performance and other system factors make cryptography an important factor in overall system architecture and design.

Symmetric cryptography is the use of a single key, shared between two or more parties. Symmetric algorithms are broadly divided into block and stream ciphers. As the names imply, block ciphers take a block of data (typically 8, 16, or 32 bytes) at a time. Stream ciphers take either a single bit or a single byte at a time. Block ciphers are typically used in bulk encryption, such as with data at rest, while stream ciphers are optimized for encrypting communications links. Stream ciphers frequently have the property of being able to quickly resynchronize in the face of dropped or corrupted bits. Block ciphers, in certain chaining modes, are unable to resynchronize, and the loss or corruption of the data stream will make the remainder of the transmission unable to be decrypted. It is possible, at the cost of some (or considerable) efficiency to employ a block cipher as a stream cipher and vice versa.

On communications links in which lower levels of the protocol handle error detection and retransmission, block ciphers are typically used (e.g., in TLS and WiFi).

In other cases, such as encrypting data to be stored in a database, one could choose any symmetric block algorithm. In this case, one ought to turn to the guidance provided by national research organizations (such as NIST in the United States, the National Cyber Security Centre in the UK, or the International Standards Organization). These agencies make recommendations on appropriate algorithms based on an analysis of their relative strengths.

Other considerations include the efficiency of the algorithm. If the code is to be implemented on a system that has limited processing power or will have to encrypt large amounts of data, small differences in algorithm efficiency have a big impact on performance. Consider also that some processors include coded support for certain algorithms. Having support in the processor instruction set for certain algorithms makes their operation much faster than without the processor support. For example, most Intel, AMD, and ARM processors include instructions to speed up the operation of the AES algorithm. One study found an 800 percent speedup from using CPU-accelerated cryptography.

The longer the key, the more secure the cipher. But longer keys mean more processing time. You have to balance the security of long (strong) keys with the impact on system performance. An important consideration is the lifetime of the encrypted data. If the data can be re-encrypted periodically (say, every year or two years), then selecting a key that is likely to withstand advances in brute-force attacks over the next two decades is not important. Conversely, if the data is likely to be archived for long periods of time, a longer key may be required. (The details of key management and key lifetimes are discussed at greater length later in this chapter.)

With symmetric block encryption, there are a number of ways to use the algorithm. Figure 3.14 shows the main variants from the simplest, Electronic Code Book (ECB) mode, to the more complex Cipher Block Chaining (CBC) and Cipher Feedback (CFB) modes. These are discussed further in the next section.

One final note: the choices outlined earlier are only optimal at a point in time. Weaknesses in cryptographic algorithms are discovered, more powerful processors make brute-force attacks more viable, and the development of quantum computing may make certain algorithms obsolete. There have been countless examples in the past of previously considered secure algorithms being deprecated because of advances in cryptanalysis, such as DES, RC4, SHA-1, and others.

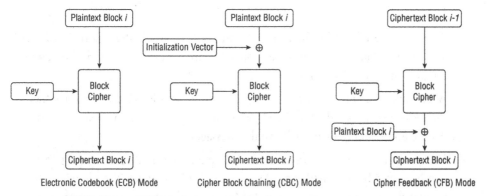

FIGURE 3.14 **ECB, CBC and CFB block encryption implementations**

TIP   Not only do cryptographic keys have finite lifetimes, so do cryptographic algorithms. It is periodically necessary to revisit the choices made to determine if they still provide the security necessary. This also means that systems need to be designed so that changing the cryptographic algorithm can be done with a minimum of disruption.

Cryptographic Methods

There are a number of cryptographic tools available to the security architect to protect the confidentiality and integrity of data, the choice of which depends on the threat being defended against, the nature of the communications, and the sensitivity of the information. See Table 3.3 for cryptographic approaches that can be used for different scenarios.

TABLE 3.3 **Cryptographic Approaches**

USE CASE	TYPE OF CRYPTOGRAPHY
Protect confidentiality of stored data	Symmetric
Protect confidentiality of data in transit	Symmetric (possibly aided by asymmetric)
Verify identity	Public key Infrastructure
Protect integrity (detect tampering)	Hashing (e.g., Message Authentication Code)
Protect passwords	Hashing (with salt and pepper)
Nonrepudiation	Digital signature

Consider the following different situations:

- Two people (Alice and Bob) want to communicate confidential information over an insecure channel without unauthorized people being able to eavesdrop on or tamper with the information.

- Alice wants to send a message to Bob in a manner that Bob has confidence that the message originated with Alice (and not an impostor) and in a manner that Alice cannot later deny having sent the message.

- Bob wants to store passwords and wants to make sure that the original passwords cannot be obtained even if someone is able to access the file where the passwords are stored, even if the intruder knows the method used to encrypt the passwords.

The following sections will discuss the various categories of cryptographic algorithms and how they can address the situations described in the preceding list.

Symmetric Encryption

Symmetric encryption is the most common approach and the one most people think of when speaking of cryptography. Symmetric encryption takes a message (referred to as the *plaintext*) and an encryption key and produces output (called the *ciphertext*) that does not reveal any of the information in the original plaintext. The output can be converted back into the original plaintext if a person has the encryption key that was used to perform the original encryption.

The objective is to make it difficult for an eavesdropper who does not know the key to extract any information about the original plaintext from the ciphertext. It is also a necessary property of a secure symmetric cipher that an attacker who comes into possession of examples of plaintext and the related ciphertext cannot deduce or determine the key that was used to encrypt the messages through reverse engineering, back-calculation, or any other analytical technique. If an attacker could do so, all other messages encrypted by that key would then be at risk.

For symmetric encryption to work, both the sender and the receiver must share the key. For the message to remain confidential, the key must be kept secret. For these reasons, symmetric cryptography is sometimes referred to as *secret-key* or *shared-secret encryption*.

The basic types of symmetric cryptography include stream ciphers and block ciphers.

A *stream cipher* is an encryption algorithm that works one character or bit at a time (instead of a block). They are typically used to encrypt serial communication links and cell-phone traffic and specifically designed to be computationally efficient so that they can be employed in devices with limited CPU power, or in dedicated hardware or field programmable gate arrays (FPGAs). See Figure 3.15 where the plaintext flows through the cipher function as a stream, out into ciphertext. At the top of Figure 3.15 is the keystream generator, a constant flow of random bits that are generated one bit at a time. The keystream is a necessity for a stream cipher, relying on these random bits to convert plaintext to ciphertext through an Exclusive OR (XOR) function.

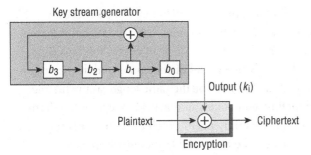

FIGURE 3.15 **Stream cipher encryption algorithm**

NOTE An Exclusive OR (XOR) function is a binary operation applied to two input bits. If the two inputs are equal to one another, the result is zero. If the two bits are different, the result is 1.

Block ciphers use a deterministic algorithm that takes a fixed-sized block of bits (the plaintext) and a key value, and produces an encrypted block (the ciphertext) of the same size as the plaintext block. Different key values will produce different ciphertexts from the same plaintext. See Figure 3.16.

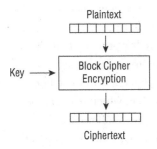

FIGURE 3.16 **Block cipher encryption algorithm**

Although block ciphers are a useful way of dividing ciphers, it is possible to convert nearly all block ciphers into a stream cipher, or vice versa.

Stream Ciphers

An example of a simple and provably unbreakable stream cipher is to take a message of length n (the plaintext) and a truly random string of digits of the same length (the key) and combine them as shown in Figure 3.15 to produce the ciphertext.

American cryptographer Claude Shannon proved in 1949 that if the key is truly random, the same length as the plaintext, and used only once, then the system is secure and unbreakable (assuming the key remains secret). This type of encryption is called a *one-time pad* because the key is used for only one round of encrypting and decrypting. The problem with this approach is that the key must be the same length as the message and cannot be reused, making the method completely impractical except for the shortest of messages or for situations (typically government) in which the cost of securely delivering large amounts of key material can be justified. Developments in quantum cryptography (see the section "Quantum Cryptography"), however, will provide methods of securely delivering large amounts of random data that can be used for one-time pad cryptography.

Practical ciphers use a fixed-length key to encrypt many messages of variable length. As we will see in the section on cryptanalysis, some ciphers can be broken if the attacker comes into possession of enough ciphertexts that have been encrypted with the same key. Changing the key periodically so that the amount of ciphertext produced with each unique key is limited can increase the security of the cipher.

Stream ciphers are divided into two types: synchronous and self-synchronizing.

Synchronous ciphers require the sender and receiver to remain in perfect synchronization in order to decrypt the stream. Should characters (bits) be added or dropped from the stream, the decryption will fail from that point on. The receiver needs to be able to detect the loss of synchronization and either try various offsets to resynchronize or wait for a distinctive marker inserted by the sender to enable the receiver to resync.

Self-synchronizing stream ciphers, as the name implies, have the property that after at most N characters (N being a property of the particular self-synchronizing stream cipher), the receiver will automatically recover from dropped or added characters in the ciphertext stream. While they can be an obvious advantage in situations in which data can be dropped or added to the ciphertext stream, self-synchronizing ciphers suffer from the problem that should a character be corrupted, the error will propagate, affecting up to the next N characters. With a synchronous cipher, a single-character error in the ciphertext will result in only a single-character error in the decrypted plaintext.

Block Ciphers

Block ciphers process blocks of n bits at a time, using a key of size k. The output of the processed block then becomes the input for the next iteration of the cipher function. The number of iterations that occur are referred to as *rounds*. Table 3.4 provides an overview of block ciphers.

TABLE 3.4 **Overview of Block Ciphers**

BLOCK CIPHER	BLOCK SIZE (N)	KEY SIZE (K)	ROUNDS
DES	64	56	16
AES-128	128	128	10
AES-192	128	192	12
AES-256	128	256	14

The DES cipher is no longer considered secure because of its short key size, but it introduced the modern age of cryptography and so is historically important. Because DES was no longer secure, finding its replacement was crucial. AES was selected after a five-year process to evaluate and select an algorithm from over a dozen candidates. Triple DES (3DES) is an important evolution of DES and is discussed later in this section.

Most block ciphers, including DES and AES, are built from multiple rounds of mathematical functions, as illustrated in Figure 3.17. While more rounds mean greater security, it also slows down the algorithmic process, so the choice is a trade-off between security and speed.

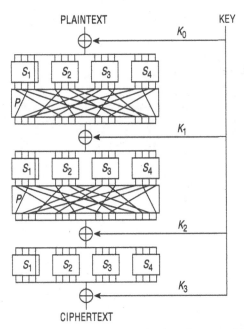

FIGURE 3.17 **Multiple rounds of mathematical functions in block ciphers**

The differences between different block ciphers are in the transformations performed during each round, and the manner in which the encryption key is stretched and then divided to provide a unique key for each round.

There are a couple of standard building blocks used to construct block ciphers:

- Substitution or S-boxes (Figure 3.18)
- Permutations or P-boxes (Figure 3.19)

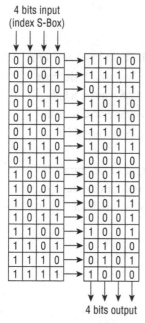

FIGURE 3.18 **Block cipher with substitution of S-boxes**

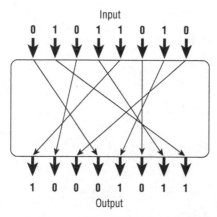

FIGURE 3.19 **Block cipher with permutation of P-boxes**

AES uses multiple rounds of substitutions and permutations, while DES uses a 16-round Feistel network.

Block Cipher Modes of Operation

A block cipher such as AES takes eight bytes of plaintext and produces eight bytes of ciphertext. But what if your message is shorter than eight bytes, longer than eight bytes, or not a multiple of eight bytes?

To handle messages that are not a multiple of the cipher's block length, one mechanism is to add padding before encryption and remove the padding after encryption. There are many ways to do this, but one approach is to add bytes to the end of the message, with each byte containing the count of the number of bytes that have been added (see Figure 3.20). Because the decryption process will examine the last byte of the last block to determine how many padding bytes have been added (and thus need to be removed), if the plaintext is a multiple of the block size, then a final block that just contains padding must be added.

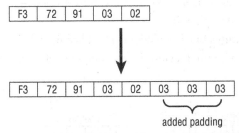

added padding

FIGURE 3.20 **Adding padding at the end of a message in a block cipher**

Padding is not without its own risks, such as the Padding Oracle Attack described later in the "Side-Channel Attacks" section.

Once the message has been padded to be an exact multiple of the cipher's block size, it can be encrypted. The easiest, obvious, and least secure method (for longer messages) is the ECB mode of operation. In this mode, each block of plaintext is processed independently by the cipher. While this may be adequate for messages that are no greater than the block size, it has serious weaknesses for longer messages, as identical blocks of plaintext will produce identical blocks of ciphertext (Figure 3.21).

Even in situations in which the data to be encrypted is the same or smaller than the block size (e.g., a numeric field in a database), use of ECB may be ill-advised if revealing that different rows of the table have the same value might compromise confidentiality. As a trivial example, if one were to use ECB to encrypt the birthdate field, then one could easily determine all the people in the database born on the same day, and if one could determine the birthdate of one of those individuals, you would know the birthdate of all (with the same encrypted birthdate).

Original image   Encrypted using ECB mode

FIGURE 3.21 **ECB padding produces serious weaknesses for longer messages**

The advantage of ECB, apart from its simplicity, is that encryption can be done in parallel (i.e., divided up across multiple processors), and so can decryption. Consequently, an error in one block does not affect subsequent blocks.

With CBC, the first block of data is XORed with a block of random data called the IV. Every subsequent block of plaintext is XORed with the previous block of ciphertext before being encrypted. (See Figure 3.22.)

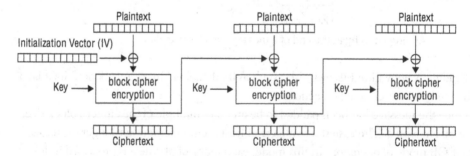

Cipher Block Chaining (CBC) mode encryption

FIGURE 3.22 **CBC mode encryption**

With CFB mode, the IV is encrypted and then XORed with the first block of the plaintext, producing the first block of ciphertext. Then that block of ciphertext is encrypted, and the result is XORed with the next block of plaintext, producing the next block of ciphertext. (See Figure 3.23.)

Because with both CBC and CFB the encryption of block Pn_{+1} depends on the encryption of block Pn, neither mode is amenable to the parallel encryption of data. Both modes can, however, be decrypted in parallel.

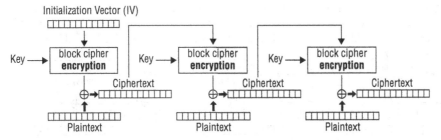

Cipher Feedback (CFB) mode encryption

FIGURE 3.23 **CFB mode encryption**

The following are the main differences between CBC and CFB:

- With CBC, a one-bit change in the IV will result in the same change in the same bit in the first block of decrypted ciphertext. Depending on the application, this could permit an attacker who can tamper with the IV to introduce changes to the first block of the message. This means with CBC it is necessary to ensure the integrity of the IV.

- With CFB, a one-bit change in the IV will result in random errors in the decrypted message; thus, this is not a method of effectively tampering with the message.

- With CBC, the decryption of messages requires the use of the block cipher in decryption mode. With CFB, the block cipher is used in the encryption mode for both encryption and decryption, which can result in a simpler implementation.

The problem with both modes is that encryption cannot be parallelized, and random access is complicated by the need to decrypt block C_{n-1} before one can decrypt the desired block Cn.

Counter (CTR) mode addresses this problem by not using previous blocks of the CBC or CFB in producing the ciphertext. (See Figure 3.24.) By using an IV combined with a counter value, one can both parallelize the encryption process and decrypt a single block of the ciphertext. You'll note that Figure 3.24 includes a nonce value. That unique, randomly generated value is inserted into each block cipher encryption round. Similar to how a random "salt" value is used to ensure different hash values (to prevent comparing to Rainbow tables), a nonce is unique and is intended to prevent replay attacks.

With all the modes other than ECB, you need an IV, which must be communicated to the receiver, or the message must be prefixed by a throwaway block of data (since decryption of a CBC or CFB stream of data without knowing the IV will only cause problems for the first block).

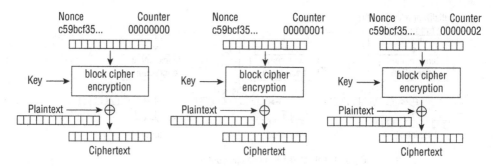

Counter (CTR) mode encryption

FIGURE 3.24 **CTR mode encryption**

The IV need not be secret (it can be transmitted in plaintext along with the cipher-text), but it must be unpredictable. If an attacker can predict the next IV that will be used and is able to launch a chosen plaintext attack, then that may enable launching a dictionary attack on the ciphertext.

Coming back to the overarching concept of symmetric encryption, both block and stream ciphers do what most people envision when thinking of cryptography. They turn intelligible text into an unintelligible representation and vice versa. This functions as a closed box without the need for distinguishing between encryption keys and decryption keys, as is the case with asymmetric algorithms.

Some of the more common symmetric-key algorithms include DES, 3DES, AES, and Rivest's cipher (RC).

Data Encryption Standard

The Data Encryption Standard (DES) is a symmetric-key encryption algorithm developed in the early 1970s. The algorithm uses a rather short, 56-bit key length, which ultimately led to it being deemed insecure in the 1990s and later superseded by the AES algorithm (discussed in a moment). Despite being an insecure algorithm, DES holds some important historical context as it introduced encryption to the business community and general public, making it one you should be aware of.

Triple DES

As you might surmise from its name, the 3DES algorithm applies the DES algorithm three times to each data block. The 3DES algorithm was devised to extend the life of the DES algorithm by increasing the 56-bit key length to a theoretical length of 168 bits. Theory aside, some practical limitations of the algorithm reduce the effective key size of the 3DES algorithm to about 112 bits. In addition, 3DES was found to be vulnerable to chosen-plaintext and known-plaintext attacks, further reducing the effective key length to 80 bits. With these weaknesses, 3DES is also considered insecure and was deprecated by NIST in 2017.

Advanced Encryption Standard

The AES, originally known as the Rijndael Block Cipher, was announced by NIST in 2001 and adopted by the U.S. government to replace DES as the standard for sensitive and classified data.

The AES algorithm uses three different key lengths: 128, 192, and 256 bits. The algorithm was designed to be simple, fast, and easy to implement and operate in either hardware or software. As of the writing of this book, AES is still considered a secure algorithm.

Rivest Ciphers

Dr. Ron Rivest (the "R" in the RSA algorithm discussed in the next section) developed a number of symmetric-key algorithms, collectively known as the Rivest ciphers. These algorithms are annotated RCn, and you should be familiar with these four:

- **RC2** is a block cipher, developed in 1987, that uses a 64-bit block size and a variable-length key. RC2 is vulnerable to chosen-plaintext attacks and should not be used.

- **RC4** is a stream cipher that is commonly used in internet protocols such as TLS and SSH. RC4 keys are variable length, ranging from 40 to 2048 bits. RC4 is not considered secure and should not be used, although it still is in many places.

- **RC5** is similar to the RC2 block cipher, but with a variable block size (32, 64, or 128 bits) and variable key size (0 to 2040 bits). RC5 is considered secure with sufficient rounds of encryption.

- **RC6** is a derivative of RC5 that uses a 128-bit block size and variable-length keys (128, 192, or 256 bits). The RC4 cipher was a finalist in the AES competition. RC6 is an improvement upon RC5 and is considered to be a secure algorithm.

Asymmetric Encryption (Public Key Cryptography)

The problem with symmetric encryption is that both parties to the communication (Alice and Bob in our examples) must each know the secret key used to encrypt the data, and if the encrypted data is to remain confidential, no one else must know or be able to guess the secret key. The difficulties of managing and sharing secret keys can make symmetric encryption prohibitively complex as soon as the number of people involved increases beyond a handful.

If there are n people who need to communicate securely using symmetric cryptography, there must be n $(n$-1$)$ / 2 unique keys, and each person must manage (and arrange to share) n - 1 keys. This is not feasible.

The solution is asymmetric or public key cryptography. The magic of public key cryptography is that instead of having a single secret key that is used to both encrypt and decrypt information, you have two keys: a secret private key and a nonsecret public key. Data encrypted using a public key cryptography algorithm using one of the keys can only be decrypted using the other key. For example, if Alice encrypts a message to Bob using Bob's public key, only Bob can decrypt it with his private key. Conversely, if Alice encrypts a message using her secret private key, then anyone can decrypt it since Alice's public key is, well, public.

Obviously, encrypting a message with a private key alone does nothing to protect the confidentiality of Alice's message, but it serves a different purpose: it proves that the message originated from Alice (because who else could have produced it?). This, of course, assumes that Alice's private key has remained private. But what if it hasn't? That leads us to the next section on PKI and how public and private keys are managed.

There are a number of public key cryptography algorithms, all based on mathematical functions that are easy to perform in the forward direction but extremely time-consuming to perform in the reverse direction unless a secret is known.

A trapdoor function, as they are called, is one for which computing $f(x)$ is easy, but calculating the inverse function (e.g., determining x if one only knows the value of $f(x)$) is extremely difficult unless one knows the value of a second variable, y.

The most well-known encryption algorithm based on a trapdoor function is the one first published by Ron Rivest, Adi Shamir, and Leonard Adleman. It is called RSA and is based on the difficulty of factoring large integers.

Choose two large primes p and q and compute this:

$$n = pq$$

These three numbers are then used to produce the public exponent e and private exponent d. The numbers e and n are made public; e, p, and q are kept secret.

Messages are encrypted with integer modular math on the message using e and n (the public key). Messages are decrypted with similar math but using d (the private key) and n.

The method works because deriving d from n and e is equivalent to finding the two prime factors of n, and if n is a very large semiprime number (i.e., the product of two primes of similar size), this is computationally infeasible (at least for nonquantum computers). The largest semiprime factored to date had 232 decimal digits and took 1,500 processor years in 2009. The semiprimes used in RSA have 600 more digits.

Some of the more common asymmetric-key algorithms include Diffie–Hellman–Merkle, RSA, ElGamal, and Elliptic Curve Cryptography (ECC).

Diffie–Hellman–Merkle Key Exchange

Diffie–Hellman–Merkle key exchange is a method of securely exchanging cryptographic keys. Developed in 1976 by Whitfield Diffie and Martin Hellman, this is the first known implementation of public key cryptography. Like many of the asymmetric key algorithms that came after it, the Diffie–Hellman–Merkle algorithm is based on logarithmic mathematics. Unlike the encryption algorithms before it, the Diffie–Hellman–Merkle algorithm is not used for encryption or decryption, but instead is used to enable two parties to securely generate a shared secret key to use for their (symmetric-key) encrypted communications.

RSA

RSA (Rivest-Shamir-Adleman) is an asymmetric-key algorithm used for encrypting and signing data. The security of the algorithm is based on the difficulty of factoring two large prime numbers. The RSA algorithm was first developed by Dr. Ron Rivest, Adi Shamir, and Len Adleman in 1978, and continues to be one of the most commonly used public key encryption algorithms.

ElGamal

ElGamal is an asymmetric-key algorithm used for transmitting digital signatures and key exchanges. The ElGamal algorithm is derived from the Diffie–Hellman–Merkle algorithm (discussed earlier) and is again based on discrete logarithmic problem solving.

Elliptic Curve Cryptography

ECC is an approach to public key cryptography that is based on far more complex computations than other public key algorithmic approaches. Whereas the security of earlier public key systems was based on the difficulty of factoring sets of large prime integers, ECC is based on the algebraic structure of elliptic curves (see Figure 3.25), which can become quite complex.

A key benefit of ECC is that it allows smaller keys to be used for equivalent security. For example, a 256-bit ECC key would be equivalent to a 3,072-bit RSA key. Using smaller keys leads to faster computations; as such, ECC is more efficient than other public key algorithms, allowing it to be used in more applications — particularly applications with resource constraints.

Several discrete logarithm-based algorithms have been adapted to ECC. While it is often discussed with RSA, there is the Elliptic Curve Diffie–Hellman–Merkle (ECDH) scheme based on the traditional Diffie–Hellman–Merkle scheme, the Elliptic Curve Digital Signature Algorithm (ECDSA) based on the Digital Signature Algorithm, and several others.

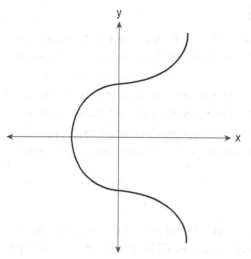

FIGURE 3.25 **Elliptic curve**

Quantum Cryptography

One property of quantum mechanics that lends itself to cryptography is that any attempt to observe or measure a quantum system will disturb it. This provides a basis to transmit a secret encryption key such that if it is intercepted by an eavesdropper, it can be detected. So, Alice first sends Bob a secret key using quantum key distribution (QKD), and Bob checks to see if it has been intercepted. If it has, he asks for another key. If it hasn't, he signals Alice to start sending messages encrypted using a symmetric cipher or a one-time pad and the key, knowing that only Alice and he have access to the key and therefore the communications will remain secret. QKD infrastructures continue to grow in popularity around the globe. The European Telecommunications Standards Institute (ETSI) offers a great resource to learn more about QKD: `www.etsi.org/technologies/quantum-key-distribution`.

As this relies upon a fundamental property of nature, it is immune to advances in computing power or more sophisticated cryptanalytic techniques.

With the advent of quantum computing and its application to encryption and decryption, there is growing concern that today's secure algorithms may be broken at any moment. Post-quantum, or "quantum-safe," devices are becoming prevalent in the security market to prepare for a post-quantum world. Quantum safe devices claim to be resistant to eavesdropping and compromise based on the current state of cryptographic research and quantum computing research. The ETSI Quantum-Safe Cryptography (QSC) Working Group aims to assess and make recommendations for quantum-safe protocols and implementations.

Public Key Infrastructure

In the "Asymmetric Encryption (Public Key Cryptography)" section, we discussed the concept of public keys, a method for Alice to send to Bob a message that only Bob can decrypt, without Alice having to first confidentially share a secret symmetric cryptography key with Bob. For this to work, Alice needs to trust that the public key she is using is really and truly owned by Bob. Obviously, she could obtain the public key directly from Bob, but it is not feasible for Alice to directly and securely obtain the public key of every person and organization she wants to securely communicate with. Public keys solve the problem of everyone having to share unique secret symmetric keys with everyone else (the $n(n-1)/2$ problem described earlier), but unless we have a scalable method of establishing trust, we have merely replaced the problem of sharing $n(n-1)/2$ symmetric keys with a problem of establishing $n(n-1)/2$ trust relationships.

Enter the trusted third party — an intermediary that is trusted by both parties to the asymmetric transaction: Alice, the person claiming ownership of her public key, and Bob, who needs to be sure that the public key Alice claims is hers actually belongs to her (and not to Michelle pretending to be Alice).

The process starts with Alice creating a certificate-signing request (CSR). This is a file that contains the details of Alice's identity (name, location, and email address) and her public key. The CSR is signed by Alice using her private key. Requiring the CSR to be signed prevents someone other than the public key owner from requesting a certificate for that key.

Alice sends her public key to a certificate authority, along with such proof of her identity as the CA may require. The CA verifies Alice's identity and then digitally signs her public key and sends back a file (certificate) that includes Alice's public key and the CA's attestation that this key indeed belongs to Alice.

The standard for public key certificates (also known as *digital certificates*) is X.509, defined by the International Telecommunications Union (ITU). An X.509 certificate contains the following:

- Version number
- Serial number
- Signature algorithm ID
- Issuer (CA) name
- Validity period (not before, not after)
- Subject name
- Subject public key (algorithm, public key)
- Key usage

- Optional extensions
- Certificate signature (algorithm, signature)

In PKI certificates used for encrypted email, code signing, or digital signatures, the subject of the certificate is an individual or organization. For PKI certificates used to secure TLS (the protocol that protects secure HTTPS browser connections), the subject is the server (e.g., domain name of the website).

For web certificates, the owner of the website generates a public/private key pair and then prepares a key signing request that contains the folowing:

- The domain name of the website (with or without wildcards)
- The identity of the website owner
- The public key of the website owner
- A digital signature of the website owner

The certificate is digital proof that the issuing certificate authority (the CA) has certified (to the extent implied by the type of the certificate) that the subject's identity has been verified. By signing the certificate with the issuer's private key, the issuer binds the subject's identity with the subject's public key in a manner that cannot be tampered with and that can only have been produced by the issuer (but see the following caveat).

Who is this certificate authority who bestows certificates? Well, anyone. Alice can be her own CA and can sign her own certificate. These are called *self-signed certificates* and are useful in situations where trust can be directly established. For example, a company might sign its own website certificates for its internal corporate intranet and configure the browsers on its employees' computers to trust those certificates.

But if Alice wants to communicate with the larger world, that won't suffice. Commercial CAs have been established that offer the service of verifying identities and signing individual keys and producing digital certificates.

These certificates work because the CAs that produce them have been vetted by the major web browser companies (e.g., Apple, Google, Microsoft, Mozilla, etc.), who have configured their browsers to trust certificates signed by these CAs.

For this to be secure, the website owner's private key must remain secret. If an attacker is able to obtain (or guess) that key, then communications with the website can be compromised, either by spoofing the website or by a MITM attack.

Similarly, if the private key used by the CA is compromised, then the attacker can generate a private/public key purporting to be that of the website owner and spoof or MITM the website.

So the security of PKI depends entirely on the secrecy of the private keys — both the participants' keys as well as the CA's keys.

Several methods exist to verify the validity of a certificate prior to its use in a cryptographic session. Every protocol that relies upon PKI includes some check of the certificate to determine if it has been reported as compromised (and therefore no longer to be trusted). There are several methods of validating certificates.

The original approach was for the browser to download a certificate revocation list (CRL) from the CA. Before accepting the certificate (even if it is properly signed), it is checked against the CRL to see whether it has been revoked, and if it has, the user is warned that the communications link is not secure.

Problems with CRLs, not the least of which being their substantial size, led to the development of the Online Certificate Status Protocol (OCSP), defined in RFC 6960, which provides a real-time status of a certificate from the CA, returning a "Good," "Revoked," or "Unknown" reply from the CA.

At least one browser (e.g., Google Chrome) has decided that problems with both CRLs and OCSP require a different approach and instead relies upon an internal list of revoked certificates that is updated regularly by Google.

There is one final detail to consider regarding PKI. To decrease the possibility of a CA's root private key becoming compromised, it is never used to sign website certificates. It is used to sign a limited number of subordinate or intermediate certificates, and it is these certificates that are used to sign website certificates. Or, in some cases, subordinate certificates can be used to generate third-level subordinate certificates and on and on, creating a certificate chain (see Figure 3.26). Verifying a website requires following the chain from the website's certificate, through any number of subordinate certificates, until reaching the CA's root certificate.

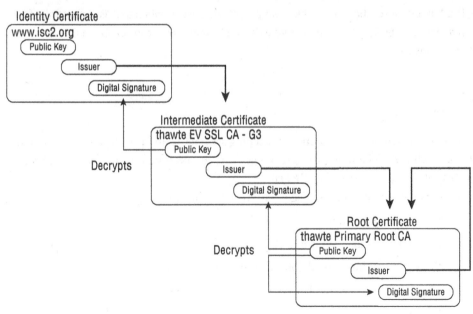

FIGURE 3.26 **A certificate chain protects a CA's root private key**

The need for a chain of trust and CAs complicates the use of public key cryptography considerably. There is a protocol called DNS-based Authentication of Named Entities (DANE), which would eliminate the need for CAs, but this protocol is not widely supported by browsers and hence has not been adopted by websites.

> ✔ **DigiNotar: When a Trusted CA Is Compromised**
>
> In July 2011, an attacker used DigiNotar's systems to issue a wildcard certificate for Google, allowing an Iranian MITM attack against Google services. Once this issue came to light, DigiNotar discovered quite a few fraudulent certificates for major services. DigiNotar also found that it wasn't able to ensure that all of the fraudulent certificates were revoked, resulting in Google, Mozilla, and other companies like Apple removing them as a trusted CA from their browsers and other products.
>
> The collapse of trust had quite a dire impact for DigiNotar as a CA. The Dutch government, which used DigiNotar as part of its PKIoverheid system, removed DigiNotar's intermediate certificate for the system and replaced untrusted certificates with new ones from trusted alternate providers.
>
> Not long after the issue came to light, DigiNotar declared bankruptcy and shut down. A report released after the bankruptcy showed that their systems were seriously compromised, indicating major security problems for the CA.
>
> DigiNotar is one of the most visible examples of what occurs when a CA is compromised, highlighting how important trust is for a CA and how quickly it can collapse if that trust is lost.

Key Management Practices

Secure use of cryptography depends on keeping symmetric and private keys confidential. Attackers who can obtain or guess a secret key can compromise the confidentiality and integrity of the data protected by that key.

Proper cryptographic key management includes the following:

- Secure key generation
- Secure key storage and use
- Separation of duties, dual control, and split knowledge
- Timely key rotation and key change
- Key destruction

Secure Key Generation

There are two factors that make for a secure cryptographic key: length and randomness. Long, random keys have a higher "key strength," as discussed earlier in this section.

Generally, the longer the key, the more difficult it is to attack encrypted messages — but what constitutes a secure key length changes with time as computer power increases and cryptanalysis techniques become more sophisticated. In 1977, the U.S. government selected a symmetric block cipher it dubbed the DES, which was considered secure for nonclassified use (e.g., banking, e-commerce, etc.). In 1999, it was demonstrated that DES-encrypted messages could be cracked in less than 24 hours.

Estimates are that, using modern computers, a brute-force attack on a 128-bit key would take longer than the age of the universe (~14 billion years) to crack. Of course, as computing power continues to increase, and with the growing maturity of quantum computing, these estimates will someday be shattered, and the need for additional key length will surface.

The strength of a symmetric key also depends on its being unpredictable (i.e., unguessable). Even if only some of the bits can be guessed, that can significantly reduce the strength of the cipher. Using a mechanism that will generate high-quality (i.e., cryptographically secure) random numbers is essential for key generation. The best method is to use hardware-based true random number generators that rely on physical phenomena known to be truly random. Such devices are embedded in various cryptographic hardware devices such as TPMs and HSMs, discussed earlier, as well as some microprocessors.

Software-based random number generators (RNGs), best referred to as *pseudorandom number generators*, are hard to get right. For example, from 2006 until 2008, a defect introduced into the OpenSSL package in the Debian and Ubuntu Linux distributions caused all keys generated to be weak because of a bug in the random number generator (CVE-2008-0166).

Secure Key Storage and Use

Once you have generated a nice long and random key, how do you keep it secret? Obviously, the first step is to encrypt your data encryption key (DEK) with another key, the key encryption key (KEK). That solves the problem but creates another: how do you secure your KEK? This depends on the sensitivity of the underlying data being encrypted and the mechanisms that are appropriate for the system you are designing.

An HSM is specifically designed to securely generate and store KEKs and is among the more secure methods of protecting keys. HSMs also provide for secure ways of replicating the KEKs between redundant HSMs and for enforcing controls so that no one individual can use the KEK to decrypt a data encryption key.

Compliance regimes on banks, payment processors, and other highly regulated organizations often require the use of an HSM. As a CISSP, you should understand your organization's compliance requirements and determine if an HSM is required (or beneficial) for your company.

For systems that are deployed in the public cloud, the major cloud providers offer cloud implementations of HSM technology. Numerous HSM as a Service (HSMaaS) vendors are also available in the marketplace, often as a service offered in conjunction with other cryptographic functionality such as key escrow and cryptographic acceleration.

For less demanding applications, the approach must be tailored to the specific requirements and risks. One could store the master key in any of the following:

- A hardware-encrypted USB key
- A password management app
- A secrets management package

Another factor to consider is how your keys are (securely) backed up. Losing access to your keys can cause you to lose access to significant amounts of other data (and backups of that data).

Separation of Duties, Dual Control, and Split Knowledge

Some keys and data are so sensitive that the risk of an insider threat (e.g., a rogue or disgruntled employee) is too great to permit a single individual to have access to the key encryption key, the data encryption key, and the encrypted data, or sole access to administrative functions of the HSM.

These are three types of controls used to mitigate the risk of a rogue employee:

- Separation of duties
- Dual control
- Split knowledge

These three concepts are related but different.

Separation of duties (sometimes called *segregation of duties*) means that certain processes should require at least two different individuals to complete from beginning to end. In the financial world, this might involve ensuring that the person who has authority to write checks is not the person who reconciles the bank statements. In the cryptography world, it might dictate that the person with access to the encryption keys does not have access to the encrypted data. Another form of separation of duties is ensuring that the people who administer a system do not have the authority to interfere with the logging system or tamper with the logs.

Dual control means that a specific step in a process requires two or more individuals. In the financial world, this would be the requirement that two signatures be present on every check. In the cryptography world, it might require that two or more individuals present their credentials to be able to use the key encryption key to decrypt a data encryption key.

For access to a system that supports multifactor authentication, dual control could involve entrusting the password to one individual, and the MFA device to a different individual.

Note that dual control is often incorrectly referred to as the separation of duties. Be aware of the difference and examine the control to determine if it is truly separation of duties or dual control.

Split knowledge is when a key (or password) is split into two or more pieces such that each piece is unusable by itself, and it requires that two (or more) pieces be brought together to decrypt the data (or access the system).

For example, a vendor might generate a large key and split it into (say m) multiple pieces. In this model, a minimum of n pieces are required to recreate the key encryption key. The numbers n and m are configurable so that one can, for example, split the key into a dozen pieces, but only require any three of the key holders to come together to unlock the key.

Timely Key Rotation and Key Change

Keys should have a limited lifespan. If there is evidence or even suspicion that a key has been compromised, it ought to be rotated as soon as feasible. Even if the confidentiality of the key has been maintained, it ought to be replaced periodically. Further, best practice is to also perform key rotation when essential personnel with access to cryptographic material leave their positions.

Although industry standards vary, current guidance from NIST and the Payment Card Industry (PCI) is to rotate data encryption keys at least annually. In practice, the key used to encrypt new data is changed each year, and all of the previously encrypted data is decrypted using the retired key and re-encrypted using the new key within the year following the key rotation. Thus, by the end of a year after the key rotation, there is no data encrypted using the retired key, at which time it can be destroyed. In cases in which backups must be maintained for longer than one year, either a process for securely archiving retired keys must be instituted or backups will have to also be re-encrypted with the new key.

Why rotate keys?

- To limit the damage should the key be discovered by an attacker
- To limit the amount of data encrypted by the same key (the more data encrypted using the same key, the easier it is to crack the encryption)

- To limit the time available to the attacker to crack the cipher (if none of your data is encrypted with the same key for longer than one year, then any brute-force attack must be able to be completed within a year of the key's generation)

Key Destruction

Once a key has been retired and it has been determined that there is no data that has been encrypted using that key that will need to be decrypted, then the key must be securely destroyed. This involves locating every copy of the key and deleting it in a manner appropriate for the media on which it was stored to ensure that it cannot be recovered.

Depending on the media and the risk of it becoming accessible to unauthorized individuals, this may require overwriting the storage, degaussing of the media, or physical destruction of the media or device containing the media.

Records ought to be kept that document the locations of the destroyed keys and the means used to ensure secure destruction.

Digital Signatures and Digital Certificates

Digital signatures use cryptographic techniques to replicate the intent of a signature: authentication (to give the recipient confidence that the message originated with a specific entity), nonrepudiation (evidence that the originator did, in fact, compose the message), and integrity (confidence the message has not been altered after it was signed). *Digital certificates* are electronic documents used to prove ownership of a public key; this concept is discussed in the "Public Key Infrastructure" section earlier in this chapter.

Figure 3.27 illustrates the basic process. The message to be signed is passed through a cryptographically secure hash function that produces a fixed-length output (typically between 160 and 512 bits) called a *Message Digest*. This hash value is then encrypted using the message author's private key to produce a digital signature. The digital signature is transmitted as an appendix to the message.

When a recipient wants to verify the document, they compute the Message Digest for the message, as received. They then decrypt the digital signature using the author's public key to produce the originator's Message Digest. If the two are identical, then the recipient knows the following:

1. The message has not been tampered with (i.e., integrity has been preserved).

2. The message has originated with the owner of the public/private key pair (i.e., authentication and nonrepudiation).

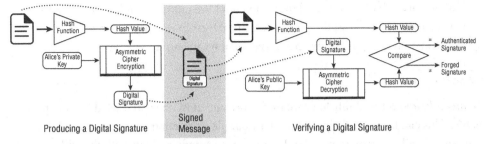

Producing a Digital Signature | Signed Message | Verifying a Digital Signature

FIGURE 3.27 **Producing and verifying a digital signature**

NOTE   A digital signature, in and of itself, does not protect the confidentiality of the message. If that is required, the sender must also encrypt the message itself.

Assertion 2 requires that the recipient has sufficient reason to trust that the public key used to verify the digital signature is owned by the originator. This can be done either by direct key sharing (i.e., prior to communicating, the originator provides the recipient with the originator's public key in a secure manner that precludes tampering) or by registering the public key with a CA (as discussed in the section on PKI earlier) who assumes the responsibility of verifying the identity of the originator.

To protect the security of digital signatures, it is strongly recommended that the private key used to sign messages only be used for digital signing and not for any other purpose (such as general message encryption).

There are a number of possible vulnerabilities with digital signatures:

- Hash collision

- Private key disclosure

- CA compromise

The security of a digital signature depends upon any changes in the body of the message resulting in a change to the Message Digest. If the attacker can create two messages that generate the same Message Digest when put through a hashing algorithm (called a *hash collision*), then the digital signature is no longer reliable.

For the recipient to have confidence that a message actually originated with the author, the sender's private key must remain secure, because with access to the key, an attacker can sign any message (including a tampered message), destroying any validity of the digital signature. To mitigate this situation, all PKI models include the concept of a key revocation list that records all keys that have been (or are suspected of having been) compromised or retired.

Finally, checking a message against the sender's public key depends upon knowing the public key is actually the sender's. Usually, this is done by having the owner's identity tied to the public key by a CA, and the recipient of the public key relies upon the trust they place in the CA to trust the public key. But if the CA is compromised, attackers can spoof the identity of a public key and "forge" digital signatures.

Nonrepudiation

Nonrepudiation is the ability to prove that a message must have originated from a specific entity. This can be critically important, for example, with contracts or other legal documents, as well as instructions to banks or orders to suppliers. Only with the ability to demonstrate nonrepudiation of the received communication can the recipient act on the message with confidence that the originator is accountable for the content of the message.

Nonrepudiation is accomplished by the originator's signing the message using a private key known only to the originator, and which the originator commits to protecting. Protecting a private signing key means keeping it confidential and, if the key is compromised, promptly revoking the matching public key.

The primary risk to the nonrepudiation property is the disclosure of the originator's private key. As mentioned earlier, if the private key can be obtained (or guessed), an attacker can sign any message and have it accepted as if the owner of the private key sent the message (e.g., "Transfer $100,000 to Bank Account XXX").

To ensure that digital signatures retain nonrepudiation even after the compromise of the private key used for signing, one can use a trusted timestamp that proves the message was signed before the time when the private key was compromised. IETF standard RFC 3161 defines the protocol to be used with a Time Stamping Authority (TSA) to provide trusted timestamps. A TSA, like a CA, is a trusted third party that provides assurances. The TSA asserts that a specific datum existed at a point in time, in a manner that the recipient of the timestamp has confidence (if the TSA is trusted) that the assertion is correct and the timestamp has not been, and cannot be, tampered with.

A secondary risk is from weaknesses in the PKI that lead to recipients of the message being fooled into thinking a certain public key is associated with a certain entity, when, in fact, the attacker generated the public key and managed to spoof the identity associated with it. This, for example, is what happened when the DigiNotar CA was compromised and attackers were able to generate public keys purporting to be from Google and other companies. (See the "DigiNotar: When a Trusted CA Is Compromised" sidebar earlier in this chapter.)

Blockchain and Nonrepudiation

Another approach to nonrepudiation is to use a blockchain. Blockchain is a form of a decentralized and distributed ledger in which records are recorded and linked together, using cryptographic hashes, meaning that to change any record in the blockchain, one must change every subsequent block. Since the blockchain is distributed (i.e., stored by multiple systems), it requires the collusion of a majority of the blockchain participants. For a sufficiently widely (and independently) operated blockchain, this is infeasible. For example, Bitcoin currently (early 2021) has approximately 12,000 nodes across 100 countries.

Benefits like nonrepudiation have driven the adoption of the technology in business applications such as supply chain management. Organizations like Ford Motor Company have begun exploring blockchain technology for their supply chain management because it enables faster and more cost-efficient delivery of products and enhances products' traceability (i.e., nonrepudiation).

NOTE   Not all distributed ledgers require blockchain, and not all blockchains need to be "coin-based" like Bitcoin and Ethereum.

Integrity

Cryptographic methods can do more than just protect the confidentiality of messages and help prove the identity of the originator. They can also be used to protect the integrity of messages by detecting tampering. Integrity, a core security concept, is part of the well-known CIA Triad and is introduced in Chapter 1. See the section titled "Understand and Apply Security Concepts" in that chapter for more information on integrity and how it can be achieved and validated.

A *hash function* is an algorithm that takes a block of data (i.e., a message or file) and computes a derived value such that any change to the data will result in a change to the hash value. Effective hashing functions need additional properties too, as will be covered in this chapter.

This function can be used to verify the integrity of the data by comparing the hash value of the original data with the hash value of the data at some later point in time.

Using a cryptographic hash to detect tampering of a message involves the following three steps (as illustrated in Figure 3.28):

1. Generate the hash value (H_1) by applying the hash function to the original block of data or message (M_1).

2. Generate the hash value (H_2) by applying the hash function to the block of data or message (M_2) to be verified.

3. If (H_1) is the same as (H_2), then that indicates that the two messages are likely to be identical and have not been tampered with. As we shall shortly see, however, the key question is "how likely?" What degree of confidence should we have that two messages are identical if their hash values are identical?

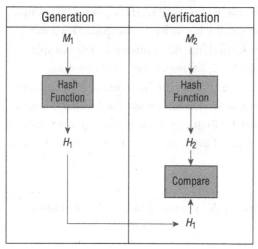

Generation	Verification
M_1	M_2
Hash Function	Hash Function
H_1	H_2
	Compare
	H_1

FIGURE 3.28 **Steps for using a cryptographic hash to detect tampering of a message**

From NIST Special Publication SP800-175B, "Guideline for Using Cryptographic Standards in the Federal Government: *Cryptographic Mechanisms*"

To understand hashing, let's consider a simple example, the checksum. A *checksum* is a mathematical function that takes a block of data and calculates a number (the checksum) in a manner such that any single change to the block of data will cause the checksum number to change. As the name implies, a checksum is typically calculated by taking the sum of each byte in the message, as an unsigned integer, and ignoring any overflow.

When the primary threat was from noise or other defects in the communications channel, data packets carried a checksum that could be used by the receiving party to determine if the data had been corrupted in transit. The receiving party recalculated the checksum for the packet, compared it with the checksum calculated by the sender and appended to the message, and if they did not match, the recipient would know the message had been received with errors.

In a situation in which the changes to the message are random and not malicious, a simple checksum can be sufficient to protect the integrity of the message. But imagine a situation in which a threat actor wants to tamper with the message. Instead of an order to transfer $100, the malicious agent wants to change the message to transfer $100,000. Obviously, if just the amount field is changed, then the checksum is unlikely to match, and his tampering will probably be caught.

That's not a problem for our attacker, however, who understands the algorithm used to calculate the checksum and can further tamper with the message, either by making other changes to the message content so that the checksum remains the same or by calculating the new checksum and overwriting the original checksum. With either approach, the checksum will validate, and the fraudulent message to transfer $100,000 will be accepted as valid.

For example, consider the following transmission, where [0x116c] is the checksum appended to the message by the sender:

```
TRANSFER $100.00 TO JANE DOE FOR OFFICE AND MISC EXPENSES IN DECEMBER
[0x116c]
```

Our attacker wants to send a slightly different message (but copies the checksum from the original message):

```
TRANSFER $100,000.00 TO JANE DOE FOR OFFICE AND MISC EXPENSES IN DECEMBER
[0x116c]
```

The problem is the actual checksum of the new message (0x1228) doesn't match the claimed checksum (0x166c), so his tampering would be detected.

One possible attack would be to make other changes to the message so that the checksum is the same as the original message:

```
TRANSFER $100,000.00 TO JANE DOE FOR OFFICE MISC EXPENSES IN DECEMBER7
[0x116c]
```

which has the same 0x116c checksum as the original. Alternatively, the attacker could overwrite the checksum that is appended to the message to be the checksum of the message after being tampered with:

```
TRANSFER $100,000.00 TO JANE DOE FOR OFFICE AND MISC EXPENSES IN DECEMBER
[0x1228]
```

Clearly, using a simple checksum and including it in the message is not going to work to detect malicious tampering, but it is useful to help avoid nonmalicious errors in transmission or data entry. Checksums are often used to prevent accidental errors for credit card, government ID number, and other types of verification processes. One of the most commonly used algorithms is the Luhn algorithm, which is specified by ISO/IEC 7812-1.

When checksums aren't sufficient, we need a method of verifying message integrity that the attacker cannot easily circumvent. To protect the integrity of data, we need a hashing function sufficiently complex that it is essentially not possible to create a message with the same hash as another message. When two different messages generate the same hash value, it is called a *collision*, so we need a hashing function that makes it almost impossible to create an intentional collision.

In our previous example, two factors made it trivial to create a collision:

- The simplicity of the algorithm made it easy to determine what changes need to be made to the modified message to change the hash (checksum) to match the original message's.

- Even if the algorithm had been complex, the shortness of the hash (16 bits) means that, with only 65,536 possible hash values, it would not take long to repeatedly make random changes to the end of the message until one happened upon a collision.

Cryptographically secure hash algorithms must therefore be sufficiently complex that it is not possible to determine what changes need to be made to a message to create a specific hash result, and the length of the hash value (i.e., number of bits) must be sufficiently large to make brute-force attacks computationally infeasible.

NOTE   Message Digest 5 (MD5) is a very well-known and widely used algorithm that was initially developed as a hashing function, until it was later discovered to be susceptible to collisions. The algorithm is now considered "cryptographically broken" by private and public institutions around the world, but widely remains in use. Despite its flaws, MD5 can still be safely used as a checksum — however, it is not suitable for use in hashing applications.

One of the organizations responsible for researching and recommending suitable cryptographic algorithms is NIST. One of their guidelines, FIPS 202, recommends a family of algorithms known as Secure Hash Algorithm-3 (SHA-3). The SHA-3 set of functions includes hashing functions that produce hash values varying in length from 224 to 512 bits.

Using SHA-3, we can compute a hash value that is very difficult to attack by creating an intentional collision — but how do we protect against the attacker simply calculating a new hash value for the changed message and overwriting the original hash? For this, we need to use a cryptographic hash that incorporates a secret key known only to the sender and receiver. The value of the hash depends not only on the contents of the message, but on this secret key.

One method, known as Hash-based Message Authentication Code (HMAC), was developed by Bellare, Canetti, and Krawczyk and formalized in RFC-2104. This algorithm concatenates a secret key (which has been XORed with a string to pad it to a fixed length) and hashes that. It then takes that hash, combines it with the key again, and hashes it a second time, producing the HMAC value (see Figure 3.29). If the attacker changes the message without knowing the secret key K, the HMAC value will not match. This enables the recipient to verify both the integrity and origin (i.e., authentication or nonrepudiation) of the message.

Among other uses, HMAC functions are found within the IPsec and TLS protocols. The problem with this, however, is similar to the problem discussed in the context of symmetric encryption. Securely sharing keys between the sender and the receiver can be difficult and cumbersome. What then? Just as the solution to the shared secret problem with symmetric encryption was to use public/private keys and asymmetric encryption, with cryptographic hashes, we can encrypt the hash using the sender's private key, which anyone can validate by using the sender's public key, but which no one can spoof without access to the private key. And that is a digital signature (discussed in the "Digital Signatures" section earlier in this chapter).

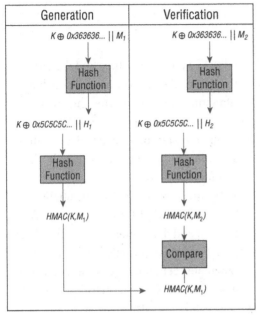

FIGURE 3.29 **HMAC process**

HMAC is a less complex method of ensuring message integrity and authentication, but with the overhead of sharing a symmetric cipher key. Digital signatures eliminate the need to share a secret but require the overhead of PKI. Each has its application.

UNDERSTAND METHODS OF CRYPTANALYTIC ATTACKS

It is important to understand how cryptography can be attacked so that you understand where vulnerabilities might be found and how the incorrect application of cryptography can result in vulnerabilities.

As a security architect, you will need to understand architectural weaknesses that can be exploited by attackers so that you can ensure that your design avoids or mitigates those risks. But as a security architect, you don't need to worry about subtleties such as related key attacks on symmetric ciphers. This is the concern of cryptographers charged with developing new cryptographic algorithms or testing existing ciphers. As a security architect, your interest is more to follow the news from agencies such as the European Union Agency for Cybersecurity (ENISA) and NIST who are responsible for making considered recommendations on which algorithms to use (and how), so that should new attack vectors be found by cryptanalysts, you can take their findings into account when you select (or update) the ciphers you are using.

Brute Force

In a *brute-force attack*, the attacker tries all possible key values until they find the one that works. In the case of a symmetric cipher, this means the attacker tries all possible keys until they have decrypted the ciphertext into something that matches the known plaintext. In many cases, full knowledge of the plaintext is not needed. If one knows the general format of the message or the language of the message, one can check the output of the decryption against certain heuristics to determine if the output is likely to be the original plaintext (i.e., reading the output to see if it makes sense).

If the encryption algorithm uses 64-bit keys, the attacker starts with 00 00 00 00 00 00 00 00$_{16}$ and continues until they reach FF FF FF FF FF FF FF FF$_{16}$. This can take a while. If your system can decrypt a block of ciphertext and determine if the result is likely to be the desired plaintext in 1 microsecond, going through all possible keys will take roughly 5,800 centuries. Unfortunately for cryptography, computers get faster every year.

Obviously, the primary defense against brute-force attacks on symmetric ciphers is key length, which is why the minimum key length for AES is 128 bits.

In the case of cryptographically secure hashes (such as are used for securing passwords), the attack scenario assumes one has a dump of the system's password file containing all the passwords encrypted using a secure hash. The attacker then tries to compare the password hashes with guesses to see which passwords can be determined.

The naive approach is to start with "a" and try every combination up to, say, "ZZZZZZZZZZ." A more sophisticated approach is to have a dictionary of commonly used passwords, typically made up of entries from language dictionaries, combined with combinations of words, letters, and numbers frequently used as passwords (e.g., Password123). After trying all of the entries in a password-cracking word list (or dictionary), the attacker can then start with every possible six-character combination (assuming the system's minimum password length was six), then every seven-character password, etc., until one runs out of patience (or budget).

This is the method used to analyze the 177 million hashes leaked in the 2016 LinkedIn password breach. Roughly 50 million unique passwords, representing more than 85 percent of the passwords in the file, have been cracked.

There are two defenses against such attacks, neither of which was used by LinkedIn at the time:

- Hashing complexity
- Salting

The LinkedIn password file used SHA1, a fast and efficient hashing algorithm. When it comes to protecting passwords, fast and efficient is exactly what one does *not* want. An eight-GPU password cracking system using 2016 technology can test 69 billion SHA1 hashes per second!

When it comes to password hashing, slower is better . . . much better. One of the currently recommended algorithms is the Password-Based Key Derivation Function 2 (PBKDF2) — using the same eight-GPU engine, one can generate only 10,000 hashes per second (i.e., roughly 7 million times slower).

The counterattack to slow hashing is a precomputed database of hashes. The attacker takes a dictionary of common passwords (hundreds of millions of passwords from past breaches are freely available online) and every possible password up to, say, eight characters, and runs it through the hashing algorithm in advance. When coming into possession of a breached password file, there is no need to lumber through 10,000 hashes per second; if the password hashes are already known, all that is needed is just to look up each hash.

If the storage space it would take to store these hashes is too large, to compress the hashes at the cost of slightly longer lookup times, the technique called *rainbow tables* can be used.

The defense against stored dictionary or rainbow table attacks is to combine the password with a unique large random number (called the *salt*) and then store the combined hash of the password and salt. In this manner, one would have to precompute 2^n rainbow tables (if the salt has n bits), so the attack is not feasible.

So, the password file contains two fields (in addition to the user's login name and other metadata):

- The salt
- The output of HASH (salt + password)

To be secure, the salt must be the following:

- Long (at least 16 bytes, and preferably 32 or 64 bytes)
- Random (i.e., the output of a *cryptographically secure* pseudo-random number generator)
- Unique (calculate a new salt for every user's password, and a new salt every time the password is changed)

Some go one step further and encrypt the hash using a symmetric cipher, but this is considered to be unnecessary and adds little additional security. In keeping with the nomenclature used in password cryptography, this step is called *pepper*.

Following the defense-in-depth principle outlined at the beginning of this chapter, one should not rely upon a single security mechanism to provide security. In the world of passwords, defense in depth typically means multifactor authentication so that a compromise of a password in and of itself does not lead to the compromise of the access management system.

Ciphertext Only

In this situation, an attacker only has access to the encrypted traffic (ciphertext). In many cases, some information about the plaintext can be guessed (such as the language of the message, which can lead to knowledge of the character probability distribution or the format of the message, which can give clues to parts of the plaintext). WEP, the original security algorithm for WiFi, is vulnerable to a number of ciphertext-only attacks. By capturing a sufficient number of packets (which typically can be gathered within minutes on a busy network), it is possible to derive the key used in the RC4 stream cipher.

Known Plaintext

In this situation, the attacker knows some or all of the plaintext of one or more messages (as well as the ciphertext). This frequently happens when parts of the message tend to be fixed (such as protocol headers or other relatively invariant parts of the messages being communicated). An example of a known-plaintext attack is the famous German Enigma cipher machine, which was cracked in large part by relying upon known plaintexts. Many messages contained the same word in the same place, or contained the same text (e.g., "Nothing to report"), making deciphering the messages possible.

Chosen Plaintext Attack

In this situation, the attacker is able to submit any plaintext the attacker chooses and obtain the corresponding ciphertext. The classic example of a chosen-plaintext attack occurred during WWII when the U.S. intercepted messages indicating the Japanese were planning an attack on a location known as "AF" in code. The United States suspected this might be Midway Island, and to confirm their hypothesis, they arranged for a plaintext message to be sent from Midway Island indicating that the island's water purification plant had broken down. When the Japanese intercepted the message and then transmitted a coded message referring to "AF," the United States had the confirmation it needed.

Frequency Analysis

In cryptanalysis, *frequency analysis* is the study of the frequency of characters (letters, numbers, or groups of either) in ciphertext. This attack works best against rudimentary cryptographic approaches such as substitution ciphers that map each character in a given set (e.g., alphabet) to another character (for example, a = z, b = y, and so on). By understanding the typical distribution of characters in a given language, frequency analysis can help a cryptanalyst deduce plaintext equivalents of commonly occurring ciphertext characters. Most modern cryptographic algorithms are not susceptible to frequency analysis.

Chosen Ciphertext

In this situation, the attacker is able to submit any ciphertext and obtain the corresponding plaintext. An example of this was the attack on SSL 3.0 developed by Bleichenbacher of Bell Labs, which could obtain the RSA private key of a website after trying between 300,000 and 2 million chosen ciphertexts.

Implementation Attacks

Implementation attack is a broad term used to describe any attack that exploits implementation weaknesses, such as in software, hardware, or the encryption algorithm itself. (See the "Select and Determine Cryptographic Solutions" section for more details.)

Side-Channel Attacks

Side-channel attacks involve measuring artifacts of the cryptographic process to deduce information to assist with compromising encrypted information. These artifacts can include the following:

- Timing
- Cache access
- Power consumption
- Electromagnetic emanations
- Error information

The time taken to encrypt or decrypt a block of data can vary depending on the key or plaintext, and a careful analysis of the time taken to encrypt or decrypt the data can reveal information. The time to perform a cryptographic operation can vary for a number of reasons:

- Conditional branches within the code, which can change the time of execution depending on the branches taken, which in turn depend on the value of the key or plaintext

- CPU instructions that take variable time to complete depending on the operands (e.g., multiplication and division)
- Memory access, which can vary depending on where the data is located (type of memory) or the access history (thus affecting the cache and thus the speed of memory access)

Cache attacks typically involve processes running on different virtual machines on the same physical processor. As the VM performing the encryption is time sliced with the VM running the attacker's processes, the attacker can probe the processor's cache to deduce information about the plaintext and the key, and thus compromise the encryption process.

NOTE   A cache-timing attack was at the heart of the Spectre and Meltdown attacks revealed in 2018 as methods of extracting data from protected regions of a processor's memory (e.g., keys or plaintext messages).

The power consumed by the device performing the cryptographic operation may vary depending on the instructions executed, which in turn depend on the key and data being encrypted. By carefully monitoring the power consumed by the device, it can sometimes be possible to extract information about the key or plaintext. This type of attack has been most successfully demonstrated against smartcards because of the relative ease with which the device's power consumption can be monitored, but the attack mechanism has wide applicability.

All electronic systems emit electromagnetic radiation, and it is possible to capture this, sometimes at some distance from the device. These radio signals can sometimes be analyzed to reveal information about the data being processed by the device. Early examples of this type of attack involved analyzing the emanations of cryptographic devices that printed the decrypted message on teletypewriters to determine which characters were being printed.

Countermeasures exist, but in some cases, they can be very difficult to implement or can exact a considerable performance penalty. In the case of timing attacks, it is necessary to modify the algorithm so that it is isochronous, which is to say it runs in constant time regardless of the key and data being processed.

Error information provided (or leaked) by decryption software can provide useful information for attackers. In the Padding Oracle Attack, a system that can be sent any number of test messages, and which generates a distinctive error for encrypted messages that are not properly padded, can be used to decrypt messages without knowing the key. The defense is to report generic errors and not to distinguish between padding errors and other errors.

Fault Injection

Fault injection attacks are side-channel attacks that involve deliberately injecting faulty or erroneous inputs and observing the errors and outputs. See the "Side-Channel Attacks" section for more detail.

Timing Attacks

A *timing attack* is a side-channel attack that involves the attacker attempting to compromise a cryptosystem by monitoring the time taken to execute algorithmic functions. See the "Side-Channel Attacks" section for more detail.

Man-in-the-Middle

An MITM attack requires that the attacker be able to intercept and relay messages between two parties. For example, Michelle wants to compromise communications between Alice and Bob. Alice wants to communicate securely with Bob using public key cryptography. Michelle is our attacker. With that in mind, the following takes place:

1. Alice sends Bob a message requesting Bob's public key.

2. Michelle relays the message to Bob.

3. Bob replies with his public key, but Michelle intercepts that message and replaces it with Michelle's public key.

4. Alice, thinking she has Bob's public key, uses Michelle's key to encrypt a message (e.g., "Please transfer $10,000 from my account to Acme Company").

5. Michelle intercepts the message, decrypts it (since it was encrypted using her key), tampers with it (e.g., "Please transfer $10,000 from my account to Michelle"), encrypts the tampered message using Bob's key, and sends the message on to Bob.

To defend against such attacks, Alice needs to have confidence that the message containing Bob's key actually originated from Bob (and not the MITM attacker, Michelle). In the case of encrypted HTTPS web traffic, this is done by relying upon public key certificates attested to by a CA (as described earlier in the "Public Key Infrastructure" section). But if the CA is compromised, the attacker can circumvent the identity authentication protections of HTTPS.

In 2011, the compromise of the Dutch CA DigiNotar led to successful MITM attacks against an estimated 300,000 Gmail users.

Pass the Hash

Pass the hash is an attack that occurs when an attacker obtains a password hash and passes it through for authentication. With this type of attack, the attacker does not need to decrypt the hash or otherwise obtain the plaintext password. This type of attack targets the authentication protocol, as opposed to the hash or any other cryptographic elements.

A least privilege security model can help limit the likelihood and impact of a potential pass-the-hash attack by reducing an attacker's ability to gain and use elevated privileges. Password management processes and tools that rotate passwords (preferably automatically) can also help fight against this attack.

Kerberos Exploitation

Kerberos is a network authentication protocol that uses symmetric-key encryption to provide strong authentication for client/server environments. The protocol operates on the basis of tickets that allow nodes (systems) on a network to prove their identity to one another.

As with any widely used protocols, hackers have sought and found ways to compromise Kerberos. Most of successful Kerberos exploits take advantage of system vulnerabilities (such as using weak algorithms), malware, or weak passwords. A common exploit, called pass the ticket, is the process of an attacker forging a ticket and passing it along to authenticate to a resource.

Multifactor authentication should be used to defeat phishing attacks and password weaknesses in Kerberos implementations. Logging and monitoring of your Active Directory domains should also be enabled to detect access to resources without proper authentication (e.g., via pass the ticket).

Ransomware

Ransomware is malicious software that infects a system, encrypts the victim's files, and renders them unavailable until a ransom is paid. In a typical ransomware attack, the victim is given instructions on how to pay a fee to get the decryption key required to recover their data. Attackers will often request payment in Bitcoin, due to its anonymity.

Protection against ransomware is similar to best practices for protecting your systems against any type of malware. Keep your operating systems and applications patched and up-to-date, limit use of administrative privileges (i.e., least privilege), and use trusted antimalware software with updated signatures, among the other system hardening best practices.

Aside from maintaining overall good security hygiene, backing up your data frequently is the best way to recover from a ransomware attack — without paying the fee! With routine backups stored securely, you will be able to revert to a known good state, should you be faced with such an attack.

APPLY SECURITY PRINCIPLES TO SITE AND FACILITY DESIGN

The general security principles outlined earlier for information security also have application to site and facility design. The CIA Triad and supporting security principles apply here and guide our application of security principles to this challenge:

- **Confidentiality and Integrity:** The primary physical threat to confidentiality and integrity is unauthorized access (e.g., intruders and theft).

- **Availability:** In addition to the threat to availability from unauthorized access, availability can also be compromised intentionally or accidentally by a range of events:

  - Environmental events such as fire, floods, storms, or earthquakes

  - Infrastructure events such as power outages, cooling (HVAC) failure, floods (from burst water pipes)

The following sections will outline controls that can be employed to reduce the risk from the above vulnerabilities but as with all risks, the security architect must consider all methods of handling risk: avoid, mitigate, transfer, and accept.

One can avoid physical threats by selecting facilities that are unlikely to be vulnerable to certain risks (e.g., locating a data center in an area of known geological stability can effectively eliminate the risk of earthquakes, just as avoiding areas of known tornado and hurricane activity can reduce the risk from meteorological events).

One can mitigate threats by implementing the security controls (administrative, technical, and physical) outlined in the sections that follow.

One can transfer (or share) many physical risks through insurance (fire, theft, business interruption, etc.) or by contractual means (e.g., contract with a colocation or data center hosting provider to provide a secure site and facility, thus relieving your organization of some those responsibilities).

Once one has applied the chosen risk management approaches (avoid, mitigate, transfer), then one assesses the residual risk to determine if it is within the organization's risk appetite, or is acceptable to the risk owner. If not, then additional steps must be taken to further reduce the residual risk.

DESIGN SITE AND FACILITY SECURITY CONTROLS

All the thought and effort put into ensuring that the operation of your systems protects the confidentiality, integrity, and availability of your data is for naught if the threat actor can simply walk into your data center and walk out with your servers. Designing a data center or engaging the services of a third-party data center requires careful consideration of the risks and appropriate controls to mitigate those risks.

Similarly, the physical and environmental controls protecting your place of work are critical to ensure the security of your information.

In this section, we will examine a range of vulnerabilities and outline appropriate mitigations to be considered.

Remember, however, as we pointed out in the beginning of this chapter, a fundamental principle of security architecture is defense in depth. This means that you must not rely just on physical security to protect physical assets. We must employ other controls so that, to the extent reasonably possible, a failure of a physical security control by itself does not lead to a failure of confidentiality, integrity, or availability.

Wiring Closets/Intermediate Distribution Facilities

The vulnerabilities related to networking distribution differ slightly between a data center and an office. In a data center owned and managed for a single company (or cloud-hosting provider), usually the network distribution will be within the same perimeter as the servers themselves, so the physical and environmental security controls will apply to both. In a colocation facility, different clients will have access to different areas of the facility (to access the equipment owned by or assigned to them for their exclusive use). In this situation, the wiring closets are managed by the hosting provider and must not be accessible to clients, as it would permit even authorized clients to access or affect service to other clients. In an office, intermediate distribution facilities need to be protected from both malicious outsiders and insider threats, not to mention environmental risks.

Not all insider threats are malicious — well-meaning staff trying to troubleshoot a networking problem can wreak havoc in a wiring closet. Too often, network switches and other pieces of intermediate distribution equipment are placed in any convenient out-of-the-way location, sharing space with other building infrastructure (e.g., electrical, plumbing, heating, or ventilation). When this is being contemplated, consider the additional risks from environmental impacts (flooding, overheating, or electromagnetic interference from electrical equipment). A small wiring closet full of network switches with poor (or no) ventilation can overheat, at a minimum shortening the life of your equipment, causing random resets, errors, and even total failure in the worst case.

Wiring closets can also be at risk from threats such as burst or leaking pipes that pass through or near the space or overflowing washrooms on the floors above. Again, if the obvious solution (moving the location of the wiring closet) is not an option, one must consider compensating controls — in this case a shield over the top of the equipment to deflect any falling water, and a rack (to keep all equipment and wiring sufficiently high off the floor) to prevent any pooling of water from affecting the equipment.

One must consider not just network infrastructure that you install for your internal purposes, but also cabling for other services (telephone, alarm, electronic door locks, etc.) that may transit spaces outside of your control. How useful are your electronic door locks if the cables powering them are in the suspended ceiling in the hallway outside your office? What good is your alarm going to be if the signal is carried on telephone wires that can be found behind an unlocked panel in the public hallway and easily tampered with?

Server Rooms/Data Centers

Just as with office space, the physical security of your data center can span a wide range of controls. You need to determine the risks in order to ensure you secure, but do not over-secure, your data center.

Security controls need to be selected to address the following:

- Physical access risks (see the "Apply Security Principles to Site and Facility Design" section)
- HVAC (see the "Utilities and Heating, Ventilation, and Air Conditioning" section)
- Environmental risks (see the "Environmental Issues" section)
- Fire risks (see the "Fire Prevention, Detection, and Suppression" section)

It is not enough to design and build your server room or data center properly, one must also have the proper procedures in place to ensure the data center continues to operate properly and securely. These controls should cover, at a minimum, the following:

- Personnel (e.g., background checks, training, or access procedures)
- Maintenance
- Logging, monitoring, and alerting
- Control testing and auditing

For example, it is not enough to have a diesel generator to take over should a power outage last longer than the capacity of your uninterruptible power supply (UPS) to carry the load. You must also test and maintain the generator regularly, as well as ensure a sufficient supply of fuel (and attend to the deterioration of that fuel over time).

The art and science of data center design is well understood. Anyone charged with the responsibility of working on such a project (or selecting a vendor to provide hosting or colocation) ought to review the guidance available from organizations such as the following:

- American Society of Heating, Refrigerating and Air-Conditioning Engineers (ASHRAE)
- ANSI / BICSI: ANSI/BICSI 002-2014, Data Center Design and Implementation Best Practices

- Electronic Industries Association and Telecommunications Industries Association (EIA/TIA): ANSI/TIA-942, Telecommunications Infrastructure Standard for Data Centers

- European Union (EU): EN 50600 series of standards

- International Organization for Standardization (ISO): ISO/IEC 30134 series, "Information technology – Data centres – Key performance indicators"

- Uptime Institute: Tier Standards

These documents cover the entire range of issues that need to be considered. Our treatment here will focus on threats to the security of your systems and data, and the privacy of your customers.

Media Storage Facilities

In addition to the usual threats to confidentiality, integrity, and availability faced by any facility containing information technology equipment, media storage facilities must implement additional environmental controls to ensure that the stored media do not degrade over time (or at least degrade as slowly as can reasonably be provided for).

The specific controls will depend on the media being stored, the manufacturer's recommendations, and the specific threats anticipated, but typically they will include the following:

- Controlled and stable temperature and humidity

- Air filtration and positive air pressure to minimize infiltration by airborne dust and microfine particulate matter or contaminants (such as corrosive fumes and engine exhaust from diesel generators or nearby vehicles)

- Appropriate floor covering to minimize static electricity

- Careful siting of the media storage facilities to avoid magnetic fields that might arise from electrical equipment (e.g., transformers or motors)

Other considerations with respect to media storage include the following:

- If the environment of the media storage facility is different (in temperature or humidity) than the production environment in which the tape will be read, then time must be allowed for the tape to acclimate to the different environment before being processed.

- Some tape media needs to be "retensioned" (i.e., unspooled and respooled), depending on the tape manufacturer's recommendations (e.g., every three years).

- For longer archival storage, it is advisable to read the data from the stored media and rerecord on new media. Again, the tape manufacturer's recommendations ought to be followed with respect to the appropriate frequency (e.g., every six years).

- Appropriate procedures are necessary for the tracking of media that are placed in, and removed from, storage. This may include bar code scanning and separation-of-duties controls requiring two people to sign in and sign out media items.

- Fire detection and suppression systems may need to be installed.

- Proper housekeeping is required to reduce the possibility of fire and to reduce the fuel available should a fire break out. On a related note, media storage facilities ought to be used only to store media and should not be shared with other general storage.

- Depending on the risk analysis and costs associated with managing on-premises media storage, it may be appropriate to retain the services of an off-site media storage service that will handle the physical security and environmental concerns related to secure long-term storage of media. This can be used for all media, or a portion, in order to provide disaster recovery should the primary media storage facility be damaged by fire or other calamity.

- Appropriate media end-of-life procedures must be enforced to sanitize (e.g., by degaussing magnetic media) and securely destroy media before disposal so that sensitive information cannot be extracted from the media once it leaves the control of the organization.

Evidence Storage

In addition to the security controls appropriate for other facilities (including media storage, should you be storing evidence in the form of magnetic media), evidence storage requires attention to physical controls that can assist in protecting the chain of custody necessary to prove that evidence used in court has not been tampered with or contaminated.

These controls include, at a minimum, a logbook that indelibly records every item that has been placed in, or removed from, evidence storage. Additional controls that can increase the confidence in the chain-of-custody log with respect to the evidence storage room include the following:

- Strict policies surrounding who is permitted access to the evidence storage room, the information that is to be entered into the log, and procedures governing the management of the access keys to the evidence storage room

- Video monitoring

- Double locks on the evidence storage room doors, or a locked storage cabinet inside the locked evidence storage room, with separation of duties surrounding the control of the keys, so that two people are required to access the evidence storage

With respect to video monitoring, consideration ought to be given to a system that incorporates motion detection or is linked to door sensors so that the recording is performed only while people are in the evidence storage room. The reason is that evidence frequently must be kept in storage during long periods while awaiting trial, and either continuous video recording will consume too much storage, or the storage period will be much shorter than the typical time an item of evidence is stored.

Restricted and Work Area Security

Work area security must be designed in response to a risk assessment (including threat modeling) and in accordance with security principles and the appropriate controls to mitigate risk. The considerations to be addressed include least privilege, need-to-know, separation of duties, dual control, defense in depth, and compliance obligations. This is especially important in the context of implementing facility security controls. No other facet of site security controls more directly affects the people of an organization.

Least Privilege and Need-to-Know

Access to restricted and secure areas must be granted only to the extent necessary for individuals to carry out their responsibilities, in accordance with formally approved policies and procedures. Access also must be periodically reviewed to ensure that the justification for access has not changed. Furthermore, detailed auditable records attesting to the previous must be maintained.

Separation of Duties and/or Dual Control

Depending on the risk assessment, it may be appropriate to require more than one authenticated staff member to be present in order to obtain access to the secure work area. This can be an administrative control, verified through guard records or video surveillance, or it can be enforced through multiple locks or electronic access controls.

Defense in Depth

The facility ought to be designed with layers of security controls supporting a hierarchy of security levels, from public on the exterior of the building (and possibly including common entrance areas), to low security areas such as reception, all the way to the highest security zones where the most sensitive or high-risk assets or work are located.

Passing from an area of lower security to an area of higher security ought to be obvious to the knowledgeable insider and must require successfully authenticating with an access control system (be it a receptionist/guard, door lock, card reader, biometric scanner, or other device for identifying the individual transitioning the security boundary). The appropriate rigor and tolerable rate of false positives depend on the security level of the area being protected.

Furthermore, different types of security controls ought to be considered for the higher security zones. For example, in addition to preventive controls such as door locks, detective controls such as video monitoring and corrective controls such as motion detectors and alarms can be used as compensating controls should the primary preventive control (e.g., the door lock) fail or be compromised.

Multifactor authentication techniques are as valuable for physical access as for logical (e.g., login) access. Requiring a user to have an access card as well as enter a personal identification number (PIN) to unlock the door to higher security zones protects against loss of the access card and its use by an impostor. Requiring the card (and not the PIN alone) protects against shoulder-surfing by a threat actor observing staff enter their PINs.

Compliance Obligations

Organizations handling government or military classified data will have to institute such security controls as required to meet the obligations of their facility security clearance. The organization responsible for certifying compliance will provide detailed documentation on the controls that are necessary for the level of security clearance being sought, including requirements for the following:

- Personnel identification
- Guards
- Electronic access control
- Electronic intrusion detection
- Video monitoring
- Interior access controls

One solution for having confidential discussions is the Sensitive Compartmented Information Facility (SCIF). *SCIF* is a common term among U.S. and British military and governmental agencies with a need for isolated space to preserve confidentiality. Typically, at least a room, if not a secured, hardened building, the SCIF can be temporary or permanent. If you watch any movie where the military leaders are briefing the president on an important and sensitive situation, they are in a SCIF.

GDPR, HIPAA, PCI DSS, and other regulations or contractual obligations may impose security requirements that may affect the design of your physical work area security controls.

For related concerns, see the section "Control Physical and Logical Access to Assets" in Chapter 5.

3SECURITY ARCHITECTURE AND ENGINEERING

Utilities and Heating, Ventilation, and Air Conditioning

Utilities (such as power) and HVAC are equally important to the reliable operation of your data center. It matters little if you can maintain power to your server racks if your cooling system fails and the room temperature passes 105° F (40° C). As with all aspects of data center design, you start with a risk assessment and then consider the relevant controls that can be used to reduce the risk to an acceptable level. You also need to balance building a single particularly resilient data center versus two geographically separated, less resilient data centers.

Having only sufficient (say N) UPS units to handle the load means some equipment will have to be disconnected during maintenance.

Having a spare UPS (N+1) and appropriate switching gear means that units can be removed from service for maintenance without disrupting operations. But should a unit be out of service when the power fails, each of the other UPS units is a single point of failure. It also means that the switching gear is a single point of failure.

Having completely redundant UPS systems from separate utility feeds all the way to the rack is referred to as 2N and eliminates any single point of failure.

The degree of redundancy within a single data center is typically characterized by a tier level. The exact requirements for each tier vary somewhat between the different standards but generally provide availability and redundancy similar to what is shown in Table 3.5.

TABLE 3.5 **General Data Center Redundancy Tier Levels**

TIER LEVEL	AVAILABILITY %	REDUNDANCY
1	99.671	None. Multiple single points of failure.
2	99.741	Some. Nonredundant (e.g., N) UPS.
3	99.982	N+1 UPS. Able to take equipment out of service for maintenance without affecting operation.
4	99.995	2N UPS. No single point of failure, able to automatically compensate for any single failure.

Smaller data centers or server rooms without direct and dedicated connections to the power utility's distribution network need to consider who their neighbors (electrically speaking) might be. A server room located near a pump room, air conditioning, or refrigeration compressor, or an industrial facility with large electrical motors, might need special power conditioning equipment to remove the interference and voltage spikes introduced into the power circuits by the noisy neighbors.

There are many types of UPS systems that vary in their design and features. Battery UPS systems can differ in a number of important aspects:

- **Load:** The capacity of the unit to deliver a specified level of continuous power

- **Capacity:** The time during which the unit can maintain the load

- **Filtering:** The ability of the unit to isolate the equipment from noise, surges, and other problems with the utility power

- **Reliability:** Some designs trade low cost for reliability

Nonbattery UPS systems exist that use large-mass rotating flywheels connected to provide short-term backup. These are appropriate for larger loads (> 200KW) and can provide higher reliability and lower lifetime costs than comparable battery UPS systems.

Typically, a UPS is intended only to carry the load during short outages, and for the short time it takes for a backup generator to start and be able to take the full load. So, most data centers or server rooms will need a generator to handle the load, should the power interruption last longer than that which the UPS can handle.

Generators are available in a wide range of capacities and use different fuels (gasoline, diesel, natural gas, and hydrogen). The advantage of natural gas is the elimination of the need to store fuel. The risk is that certain natural disasters can cause both power and gas distribution outages.

Cooling systems must be designed so that there are multiple units with sufficient capacity so that the data center not only can be maintained below the maximum safe operating temperature even in the face of the failure (or maintenance) of one or more units, but also the maximum rate of temperature change is kept within permitted limits (for example, less than 5°C/hour if magnetic tapes are being used, 20°C/hour otherwise), even if a unit is taken out of service for maintenance.

Finally, humidity also needs to be managed. Low humidity leads to increased static electricity, and high humidity can lead to condensation. Both conditions will lead to lower equipment reliability.

With both power (UPS and generator) and HVAC systems, due consideration has to be made for the following:

- Regularly scheduled maintenance

- Regular testing under full load (of UPS and generators, and backup HVAC equipment if not used in production)

- System fault detection and alerting (and regular tests of those subsystems)

- Periodic checks and audits to ensure all of the above are being properly and regularly performed

Without the previous items, the risk mitigations from your expensive backup systems might be more imaginary than real.

✔ Generator Failure Takes Out Major Data Center

In 2008, in downtown Vancouver, a large underground fire destroyed a significant amount of the power infrastructure serving a large area of the business district. Included in this outage was the Vancouver location of a major multinational colocation provider.

The UPS units cut in immediately and functioned as expected. After 10 minutes or so, when the power had not been restored and the UPS battery capacity was draining, the diesel generators fired up, also as expected. The transition from UPS to diesel power was smooth and the servers kept running.

Roughly 30 minutes later, however, one of the diesel generators carrying the entire load of one of the three floors of the data center failed and stopped. The UPS had recharged slightly, so the servers ran for another 5 minutes — then silence. A thousand servers stopped as if a switch had been flipped.

What happened? It depends on who you talk to. The official announcement claimed that the firefighters' use of water caused a drop in water pressure resulting in generator 7 overheating. Not explained was why generators 1 through 6 continued to work, serving other floors in the office tower.

The other explanation widely discussed at the time was that the generator had overheated because a $30 coolant thermostat had failed. While the generator had been routinely tested every month, the tests had run for only 15 minutes — not long enough to cause the generator's coolant to heat to the point where the thermostat had to function.

Whichever story is true, there are valuable lessons to be learned:

- A generator can be a single point of failure; proper redundancy requires N+1 generators (when N generators can carry the entire load).

- Testing of disaster response plans (DRP) ought to mimic real-life scenarios as closely as possible (e.g., generators that have to run for longer than 15 minutes).

- External dependencies (such as external water pressure) on DRP components need to be identified and assessed.

As discussed in the "Industrial Control Systems" section earlier in this chapter, the system that monitors and manages your HVAC or UPS system can be a vulnerability itself. If an attacker can remotely access your HVAC and disrupt its operation, possibly on a weekend when your data center is not staffed, causing the cooling to be disabled and servers to overheat, that can be just as effective a DoS as one launched by a 100,000 bots.

Similarly, unauthorized remote admin access to your UPS can result, at best, in your UPS being disabled and the next power outage not being mitigated; at worst, a direct power outage triggered by taking the UPS offline.

A variety of industry, national, and international standards cover HVAC, utilities, and environmental systems.

- The Uptime Institute's Data Center design certification tiers assess areas including facility mechanical and electrical systems, as well as environmental and design considerations. Specifications for the tiers can be found at `uptimeinstitute.com/resources/`.

- The International Data Center Authority (IDC) provides open standards for data centers, facilities, and infrastructure at `www.idc-a.org/data-center-standards`.

- The ASHRAE standards for ventilation, refrigeration, building automation, and a variety of other related topics can be found at `www.ashrae.org/technical-resources/standards-and-guidelines`.

Other standards including the LEEDS standard, BICSI-001, and those created by one of the three European standards organizations (CEN, CENELEC, or ETSI) may all be useful or even required in the design of utilities and HVAC systems.

Environmental Issues

Environmental issues that need to be considered include the likelihood of the following:

- Major storms (hurricanes, lightning, blizzards, ice storms, typhoons, tornadoes, blizzards, etc.)
- Earthquakes
- Floods and tsunamis
- Forest fires
- Internal building risks
- Vermin and wildlife
- Volcanoes

Some vulnerabilities can be mitigated through selecting the appropriate location for the data center, others through building and site design. In fact, areas with specific common threats like earthquakes, floods, tornadoes, or hurricanes, like Japan, California, and others around the world, often have building codes that require new structures to be designed to survive these environmental threats.

Consider not placing any critical infrastructure components in the basement, as they may be prone to flooding (either from external sources such as storms or broken water mains, or internal causes such as burst pipes). Recall that one of the main causes of the Fukushima Daiichi Nuclear Power Station disaster was the flooding of batteries, electrical switching gear, and cooling pumps installed below the level of the reactors.

In the cases of major threats, a decision has to be made as to how resilient to make the data center, as well as which events to accept as beyond the ability of the data center to withstand and which will be handled through a remote backup data center and a disaster recovery plan.

You must also consider that even if you invest the money in a data center that could handle the worst storm or earthquake, like investing in a super-strength link to connect two chains, the ability of the data center depends on external suppliers to continue.

At some point, it makes more sense to invest in your disaster recovery plan than to try to make your data center able to withstand environmental threats that your suppliers and your staff cannot cope with.

As discussed in Chapter 6, "Security Assessment and Testing," selecting your alternate data center involves considering the threats that might take out your primary data center to determine if they are likely to affect your alternate too. If the two data centers are too close together, or potentially in the path of the same hurricane, they might not provide the redundancy your DRP depends upon.

Internal building risks include things such as water leaks from burst pipes; condensate from water, sprinkler pipes, or HVAC equipment in the suspended ceiling; and overflowing washroom or kitchen facilities on the floors above.

Mitigations include appropriate routing of pipes within the building relative to equipment, or if moving into an existing building, appropriate location of equipment relative to plumbing. In some circumstances, installing a canopy over some equipment may be the best option.

Vermin and wildlife can do astounding damage to communications cabling and power distribution, either from eating through the insulation or wires themselves or from physically short-circuiting powerlines. Electrical disruptions caused by squirrels are sufficiently common as to warrant an entry in Wikipedia!

Another risk that might be considered to be environmental is an epidemic or pandemic that prevents your employees, or your suppliers' employees, from working or that places an extra strain on your organization because of service demands triggered by the outbreak of disease. The COVID-19 pandemic was a major event for every company around the world and has forced businesses to rethink their approach to operating.

The analysis must consider the risk level your employees face (obviously those in the healthcare industry or with frequent contact with the public will be more exposed, while those with minimal contact are less likely to be affected).

Mitigations include the following:

- Monitoring announcements from public health authorities
- Having a sick-leave policy that does not incentivize employees to come to work ill

- Developing a plan to operate with: a reduced workforce; employees working from home; or work shifted to office locations less affected (in the case of larger companies with multiple offices)

✔ Cloud Computing and Availability

Designing to handle environmental issues can often mean ensuring that local environmental issues do not interrupt services or systems. Widespread availability of remote hosting and cloud services has allowed many organizations to move critical services to locations and data centers that aren't threatened by the same environmental concerns. An organization located in a hurricane-prone coastal area may opt to have their alternate operations in an area that isn't likely to be impacted by a weather event. Organizations that want to take availability a step further use hybrid/multicloud deployments so that they don't rely on a single CSP for their operations.

The same concepts that apply when assessing environmental risks for an onsite facility apply to choosing cloud or third-party hosting, so simply outsourcing to another location doesn't prevent organizations from having to do the work. The advantage is that there is a broader range of choices than a single geographic area may provide, allowing risks to be balanced or influenced in ways that can't be done onsite.

The availability increases that highly redundant data centers can provide are impressive, with cloud providers claiming 99.99 percent or higher availability. That number is useful only if organizations also ensure that they will be able to access cloud providers that are highly available. Redundant network routes and hardware that can stay online through a local or regional disaster are a necessary part of cloud hosting availability designs that can take full advantage of these highly available remote infrastructures.

Fire Prevention, Detection, and Suppression

There are a range of fire suppression technologies that can be deployed to protect technology infrastructure, facilities, and people. The process, as with selecting any set of security controls, is to perform a risk assessment to determine the appropriate mitigation strategy.

As always, human safety is paramount, and any fire safety system must be designed first and foremost to protect the lives and health of those who work in the facility. Enabling occupants to safely exit the building and ensuring that fire suppression systems are unlikely to compromise health or safety are more important than protecting systems and buildings.

Next, one has to balance the costs of the following:

- Downtime
- Restoration costs
- Fire suppression system costs (capital and ongoing maintenance)

Typically, there will be a trade-off between the first two and the third. In other words, reducing downtime and restoration costs will require a more expensive fire suppression system. Selecting a less expensive approach is likely to increase the time it will take to return the data center to operation after a fire event.

Fire needs three things to start: heat, fuel, and oxygen (more generally, an oxidizing agent). Fire prevention and suppression involves reducing one or more of these three elements such that fire cannot start or be sustained. A more complete model adds the chemical reaction between the fuel and the oxidizing agent, creating the fire "tetrahedron." This model is useful in that some fire suppression systems block the chemical reaction itself rather than reducing one of the three components necessary for that reaction.

Fire safety is subject to many regulations, informed by centuries of experience. It is the realm of trained professionals who ought to be consulted prior to the installation of any fire suppression system. While this section provides the information security professional with general information, it is no substitute for expert advice specific to a given situation.

Most jurisdictions have standards and guidelines for the fire protection systems for IT equipment:

- **Canada and the United States:** NFPA 75, "Standard for the Fire Protection of Information Technology Equipment," and NFPA 76, "Fire Protection of Telecommunications Facilities."

- **UK:** BS 6266:2011, "Fire protection for electronic equipment installations." Code of practice.

- **Germany:** The VdS series of guidelines for fire protection and suppression.

Fire suppression systems work by applying a fire suppressant to the area of the fire, removing one or more of the four components needed to sustain the fire.

The simplest and most widely used system is the wet-pipe water sprinkler system. These systems have water in the pipes at all times, and the sprinkler heads each have valves held closed either by a heat-sensitive glass bulb or a metal link, both designed to release the water at a specific temperature. The advantages of wet-pipe systems include low installation and maintenance costs and relatively high reliability. These systems also only release water through those sprinkler heads closest to the fire, thus limiting water damage. The risk from wet-pipe water sprinklers is the damage that occurs due to accidental release from faulty sprinkler heads or physical damage (hitting a sprinkler head with a rack or ladder while working in the facility).

Dry-pipe systems have, as the name implies, no water in the supply pipes until a sprinkler head is triggered by fire. These are used in warehouses and parking garages exposed to freezing temperature and are not relevant to data centers or most office buildings. The advantage is that the pipes do not contain water, which can freeze and damage the pipes. The disadvantages are increased corrosion and a delay in response time, as the air must be forced out of the sprinkler heads before the water reaches the fire.

Another specialized sprinkler system not usually deployed in data centers or office buildings is the deluge sprinkler. This is a variant of the dry-pipe sprinkler but with open sprinkler heads. Once a fire is detected (using a smoke, heat, or manual alarm), a valve opens to let water into the supply pipes and through all sprinkler heads (without regard to the specific location of the fire). These systems are appropriate in certain industrial situations in which a large volume of water is required to prevent the spread of the fire.

Pre-action systems are a combination of one of the previous three types of sprinkler systems (wet-pipe, dry-pipe, or deluge) with a more sophisticated triggering mechanism. A single-interlock pre-action system is a dry-pipe system with pressurized gas in the pipes, in which the activation of a smoke or heat detector causes water to be released into the supply pipes, essentially converting the dry-pipe system to a wet-pipe system. The water, however, is released only if the sprinkler head is triggered. This system sharply reduces the chance of an accidental release of water because should a sprinkler head trigger accidentally, the system will detect a drop in air pressure and set off a trouble alarm but not release any water. A double-interlock pre-action system requires both the activation of a smoke or heat detector and the activation of sprinkler heads before water is released into the supply pipes. This can be an advantage in refrigerated spaces but delays the release of water in the case of an actual fire event.

Proper design of any sprinkler system requires professional advice and continued vigilance to ensure that later developments (such as the addition of suspended cable trays) do not impair the effectiveness of the system. A limitation of sprinklers is that they do not work well in the confined space of a raised floor or suspended ceiling. These require either water mist or clean agent fire suppression systems.

An alternative to standard sprinkler heads that can discharge high quantities of water per minute are water mist sprinklers, which release a much smaller amount of water in the form of microscopic water droplets. These extinguish the fire both through removing heat (as a standard sprinkler does) as well as by displacing oxygen when the mist is converted to steam.

In situations in which the impact of water damage would be significant, various "clean agent" extinguishants can be used. These have the advantage of causing little or no damage to the equipment being protected. The disadvantage is their much higher installation and ongoing maintenance costs.

The original clean agents included carbon dioxide and halon. Carbon dioxide works primarily by displacing oxygen and additionally by removing heat. Unfortunately, it can cause asphyxiation in concentrations well below that required for fire suppression and so requires pre-discharge alarms to ensure the space about to be flooded with CO_2 is evacuated prior to discharge. Halon gas works by interfering with the chemical reaction (the fourth part of the "fire tetrahedron") and has the advantage of being nontoxic at concentrations well above those needed. This resulted in its widespread use in data centers and other facilities for several decades where sprinklers might cause more damage than a contained fire. Halon, however, is very damaging. In Canada, the Montreal Protocol in 1994 phased out its use.

Newer clean agents that are ozone-friendly have been developed, each with specific advantages. These include HFC-227ea, fluorinated ketone, and various gas mixtures (e.g., argon, nitrogen, and carbon dioxide). These newer clean agents are more environmentally friendly and less toxic than earlier alternatives.

Just as network segmentation can limit the damage of a security breach in one part of the network, physically separating critical communications facilities in a separate room with a two-hour fire wall (literally) from less critical data processing facilities can also limit the damage by preventing a fire (and the water from the fire suppression system) in one area from affecting equipment in another.

Similarly, backup media that must be stored onsite can be stored in a separate room or in a fireproof storage vault.

The use of gaseous fire suppression is made more complicated by the need to be able to automatically isolate the affected areas from the normal ventilation and cooling systems so that the HVAC system does not dilute or remove the fire suppression gas.

Fire extinguishers are mandatory, but staff need to be trained in their purpose and proper use. While they may serve to put out very small fires caught in their early stages, they are primarily there to enable staff in the server room to reach an exit should fire block their path. Fires are categorized by the type of fuel:

- **Class A:** Ordinary solid combustibles (e.g., paper, wood, and plastic)
- **Class B:** Flammable liquids and gases (e.g., gasoline)
- **Class C:** Energized electrical equipment
- **Class D:** Combustible metals (e.g., lithium metal, but not lithium-ion batteries, which are considered Class B, although water will also work well with Li-ion battery fires)
- **Class F or K:** Cooking oils and greases

Fire extinguishers are rated based on the classes of fires they are designed to combat and the amount of extinguishant they contain. A fire extinguisher rated 5BC may be used on Class B or C fires. A 10BC extinguisher would have twice the capacity of a 5BC extinguisher.

Use of the incorrect extinguisher not only can make the fire worse (e.g., using water on a gasoline fire can spread the fuel), it can be a grave safety hazard to the person using the extinguisher (e.g., using water on an electrical fire can result in a risk of electrocution).

Training does not end with knowledge of how and when to use the fire extinguishers. All staff who will normally be present in the data center need to be properly trained and rehearsed on how to respond to a fire alarm or fire event.

Make sure they know the following information:

- Where all the exits are (so they know the closest, and if blocked, the alternates)

- Where all the fire extinguishers are located as well as how and when to use them (different types of fire extinguishers are appropriate for different types of fires)

- How to disable (or delay the discharge of) the fire suppression system should a false fire detection be suspected

- How to manually trip the fire suppression system (in the case of gaseous suppression and some sprinkler systems) should early signs of fire be detected by staff before the fire detectors are triggered

- Where the fire alarm pull stations or call points are

- How to manually shut off power to the data center

Finally, good housekeeping is an important part of fire suppression. The data center or server room must not be used for storage. Cardboard boxes of computer parts or wooden reels of Cat 5 cabling must be stored in a separate part of the facility. Wastepaper receptacles should be outside the facility or, if they must be inside the data center, small and frequently emptied. The less fuel there is available, the less likely there will be a fire, and if there is a fire, less damage will result.

SUMMARY

In discussing security architecture and security engineering, this chapter has taken a path through the third domain of the CISSP Common Body of Knowledge. The discussion of secure design principles and security models introduced both historical significance and a foundation for understanding security architecture. Further discussion centered on hardware, from the security capabilities of information systems to securing a variety of platforms.

The middle of the chapter was focused on vulnerability management, namely the process of assessing and mitigating those vulnerabilities. Vulnerability management covered several types of systems and architectures, including client- and server-based systems, cloud-based systems, industrial control systems, and others.

The chapter ended with cryptography being covered, from the lifecycle, through methods, to various practices and applied uses. Last, site and facility design was discussed, both how to apply security principles to facility design and their application through several solutions.

Communication and Network Security

AS A CISSP, YOU should have a thorough understanding of networking fundamentals and secure network design principles. In this chapter, we examine various
aspects of computing networks, interconnections, networked devices, and communication processes as they relate to information security. We detail common networking protocols, services, and models, and also introduce various design principles
as they relate to secure network architecture and secure communication channels.

ASSESS AND IMPLEMENT SECURE DESIGN PRINCIPLES IN NETWORK ARCHITECTURES

A solid understanding of networking principles and concepts is essential for creating
and managing secure network architectures. This section introduces the key models,
protocols, and network topologies that lay the groundwork for designing secure network
architectures.

Recall that there are many different types of networks:

- **Local area network (LAN):** A *local area network* is a group of devices that communicate on a single localized network, typically (but not always) within the same
building. Office networks are common examples of LANs.

- **Metropolitan area network (MAN):** A *metropolitan area network* is a connection of multiple LANs throughout an entire city. An example would be a citywide Wi-Fi network.

- **Wide area network (WAN):** A *wide area network* is a larger network that covers a broader space than a LAN, typically larger than most MANs. The internet is the largest, most commonly used WAN.

- **Personal area network (PAN):** A *personal area network* connects devices within a narrow distance of each other (typically within 10 yards). Bluetooth networks are common examples of PANs.

- **Internet:** The *internet* is a globally connected WAN that enables people, systems, and entities to share information and communicate across vast geographical regions.

- **Intranet:** An *intranet* is a local or restricted network that enables users to store and share information within their organization.

- **Extranet:** An *extranet* is an externally facing web portal that allows an organization to share select information with vendors, customers, and other external parties.

Two security principles that directly affect network architecture are layering and domain separation. *Layering* involves designing something in increasingly abstract terms, with each layer offering some aspect of security or assurance. In the context of hosts communicating over a network, the Open Systems Interconnection (OSI) model is the prevailing example. The OSI model is one of increasing abstraction, with each layer making room for varying methods of ensuring security.

Domain separation, as an architectural principle, applies to secure network design. Separating network traffic at the collision domain helps avoid network congestion. Separating network traffic into broadcast domains further inhibits an adversary from sniffing valuable clues to the network topology. Going further, separating a network into segments isolates local network traffic from traveling across routes. This again mitigates the risk of a potential adversary learning about the network design.

NOTE   A *collision domain* is the part of a network where packet collisions can occur. A network collision happens when two devices send a packet at the same time on a shared network segment. The packets interfere with each other (or "collide"), and both devices are required to resend their packets, reducing network efficiency. Each port on a bridge, switch, or router is in a separate collision domain, but all ports on a hub share the same collision domain.

A *broadcast domain* contains all devices that can reach each other at the data link layer (discussed later in this section) by broadcast. All ports on a router are in different, isolated broadcast domains.

As a CISSP, you must understand a range of relevant subjects to adequately implement secure design principles in network architectures.

You must understand the OSI model in detail, and you must also understand how Transmission Control Protocol (TCP) and Internet Protocol (IP) each function. Another significant subject is multilayer protocols, where several protocols make up a group, spread across multiple OSI layers. By comparison, converged protocols involve a specialized protocol that is grouped with a commonly used protocol.

In addition to protocols, networking concepts are significant, beginning with the benefits of virtualized networking, termed *software-defined networking* (SDN). Wireless networking is also important, including its security implications. Beyond wireless, there are commonly accepted divisions of a network as defined by areas of control, including an intranet, extranet, and the internet. If a section of an intranet is public-facing yet partially controlled between the internet and the fully protected intranet, that section is the *demilitarized zone* (DMZ). Lastly, the concept of a virtual local area network (VLAN) is essential, as VLANs form isolated broadcast zones to segment a network. This section and its subsections examine all these topics.

Open System Interconnection and Transmission Control Protocol/Internet Protocol Models

The OSI and TCP/IP models define and set the standards for network communication and interoperability by using a layered approach (see the earlier definition of *layering*). Using these layered models allows network architects and security professionals to divide complex networks into simpler functional components that can more easily be architected and secured.

We use networking models to reduce complexity, standardize interfaces, assist understanding, promote rapid product development, support interoperability, and facilitate modular engineering. In this way, a series of complex and geographically dispersed networks can be interconnected securely and relatively seamlessly. The prevailing networking models, TCP/IP and OSI, support interoperability and reduce proprietary incompatibilities where there are competing vendor or supplier product lines. Keep in mind that the models are guidelines, not requirements. There may still be some variations among vendors.

The OSI Reference Model

The OSI reference model is a conceptual model made up of seven layers that describe information flow from one computing asset to another, over a network. Each layer of the OSI model performs or facilitates a specific network function. The layers are listed in numerical order here, but you may also see them arranged from top to bottom (with layer 1 being at the bottom):

- Layer 1: Physical
- Layer 2: Data Link
- Layer 3: Network
- Layer 4: Transport
- Layer 5: Session
- Layer 6: Presentation
- Layer 7: Application

The specific layers are described in greater detail in the following subsections. The OSI model, defined in ISO/IEC 7498-1, is a product of research and collaboration from the International Organization for Standardization (ISO). As the standard has proven reliable, the consensus is that OSI is the primary architectural model in networking and communications. As such, many networking concepts and technologies refer directly to OSI and its individual layers.

Figure 4.1 details the seven layers of the OSI reference model, in the "bottom-up" view (where layer 1 is at the bottom).

LAYER	DESCRIPTION	PROTOCOL DATA UNIT (PDU)	Applied Use
Application	— Coding and conversion functions on application layer data — Ensures information sent from one system's application layer is readable at destination system's application layer	Data	HTTP, HTTPS, DICOM, LDAP, MIME, SMTP, FTP, SFTP
Presentation	— Establishes, manages, and terminates communication sessions between presentation layer entities — Communication sessions consist of service requests and service responses between applications on different network devices	Data	In many references, no distinction between Presentation and Application layer protocols & TLS, SSL
Session	— Session management capabilities between hosts — Assists in synchronization, dialog control, and critical operation management — Remembers session information like password verification so a host does not have to repeatedly supply credentials on subsequent access requests	Data	RPC, SMB, SSH, NFS, NetBIOS, H.245, PAP, PPTP, SCP, ZIP
Transport	— Reliable internetwork data transport services transparent to upper layers — Functions include flow control, multiplexing, virtual circuit management, and error checking and recovery	Segment	TCP, UDP, BGP, DCCP, FCP, RDP
Network	— Provides routing and related functions that enable multiple data links to be combined into an internetwork — Uses logical addressing versus physical addressing of devices	Packet	ATM, Routers, IP, IPSec, ICMP, OPSF, IPv4, IPv6, IPX, DDP, SPB
Data Link	— Provides reliable transit of data across a physical network link	Frame	Ethernet, FDDI, Frame Relay, VLAN, MAC, Switches, SPB
Physical	— Bit-level transmission between different devices; electrical or mechanical interfaces; activates, maintains, and deactivates the physical link between communicating network systems	Bits	Volts, PINS, bit-rate, serial or parallel, USB, Ethernet 10Base varieties

FIGURE 4.1 The OSI reference model

Layer 1: Physical Layer

The physical layer is responsible for the transmission and reception of raw data across a transmission medium (e.g., network cabling or wireless link) from one device to another. This layer converts digital bits into electrical signals (or other form of energy) that can be transmitted across the given transmission medium.

As mentioned, the physical layer consists of transmitting raw bits, rather than logical data packets, over a physical link that connects devices across a network. Physical layer specifications relate to electrical signals, optical signals (optical fiber, laser), electromagnetic waves (wireless networks), or sound. Some common physical layer implementations are Ethernet, Bluetooth, and USB. See the "Transmission Media" section later in this chapter for additional coverage of physical layer components.

Physical network topologies are also defined at this layer. The *physical topology* of a computer network is the structure and arrangement of the various nodes and their connections depicted as links between the nodes. Physical topology is not always the same as *logical topology*, which describes how data flows across the network. There are four basic physical network topologies: ring, bus, star, and mesh. Each of these is discussed later in this chapter, in the "Network Topologies" section.

Layer 1 Attack Vectors

Physical layer attacks are attempts to penetrate devices and connection media or interfere with their operation. This may include passive sniffing, either over the cable or wireless, causing excessive electrical interference, or simply cutting a cable. Technical specifics on attacks such as sniffing and interference are discussed later in the chapter. However, at the physical layer, attacks that may cause destruction or denial of service are plentiful.

Layer 2: Data Link Layer

The data link layer is the second layer in the OSI model, and it transfers data between network nodes on the physical link. This layer encodes bits into packets before transmission and then decodes the packets back into bits. The data link layer is where the protocols for the network specifications are established. Specifically, how devices are to be connected, such as in a bus or a ring topology, is set at this layer. Data link provides reliability because it establishes capabilities for synchronization, error control, alerting, and flow control. These services are important because if transmission or packet sequencing fails, errors and alerts are helpful in correcting the problems quickly. Flow control at the data link layer is vital so the devices send and receive data flows at a manageable rate.

NOTE   Switches are layer 2 devices.

There are two sublayers of the data link layer as established by the Institute of Electrical and Electronics Engineers (IEEE) per the IEEE 802 series of specifications. These are the logical link control (LLC) and the media access control (MAC).

The LLC controls packet synchronization, flow control, and error checking. This upper sublayer provides the interface between the MAC sublayer below and the network layer (layer 3) above. LLC facilitates node-to-node flow control and error management, such as automatic repeat request (ARQ).

The MAC sublayer is the interface between the LLC above and the physical layer (layer 1) below. The MAC sublayer is responsible for controlling how devices on a network gain permission to transmit data. MAC provides an addressing mechanism and channel access so nodes on a network can communicate with each other. MAC addressing works at the data link layer (layer 2). It is similar to IP addressing except that IP addressing applies to networking and routing performed at the network layer (layer 3). MAC addressing is commonly referred to as *physical addressing*, while IP addressing (performed at the network layer) is referred to *logical addressing*. Network layer addressing is discussed in the next section.

A MAC address is unique and specific to each computing device. It is a 12-digit hexadecimal number that is 48 bits long. There are two common MAC address formats,

MM:MM:MM:SS:SS:SS and MM-MM-MM-SS-SS-SS. The first half of a MAC address, called a *prefix*, contains the ID number of the adapter manufacturer. These IDs are regulated by the IEEE. As an example, the prefixes 00:13:10, 00:25:9C, and 68:7F:74 (plus many others) all belong to Linksys (Cisco Systems). The second half of a MAC address represents the serial number assigned to the adapter by the manufacturer. It is possible for devices from different manufacturers to have the same device portion, the rightmost 24-bit number. The prefixes will differ to accomplish uniqueness.

Layer 2 Attack Vectors

An example attack vector unique to the data link layer would include forging the MAC address, otherwise known as *Address Resolution Protocol (ARP) spoofing*. By forging ARP requests or replies, an attacker can fool data link layer switching to redirect network traffic intended for a legitimate host to the attacker's machine. ARP spoofing is also a common precursor to man-in-the-middle (MITM) attacks and session hijacking attacks.

TIP   Another name for man-in-the-middle is *machine-in-the-middle*. You may see either of these terms used to describe similar attacks.

Layer 3: Network Layer

The network layer provides routing and other functions that enable data packets to be sent from one node to another, either on the same network or between interconnected networks. The network layer receives service requests from the transport layer and issues service requests to the data link layer. Network layer functions include logical connection setup, data forwarding, routing, packet fragmentation, and delivery error reporting.

At this layer, the logical addressing of devices is necessary to structure the flow of traffic across and between networks; logical addressing, perhaps more familiar as IP addresses, is a network layer concept. IP addresses are discussed in detail in the upcoming section titled "Internet Protocol Networking."

There are connection-oriented and connectionless network layer protocols. In connection-oriented protocols, a logical connection is established between two devices before data transfer begins. Connection-oriented protocols also exist at other, higher layers of the OSI model. In connectionless protocols, as soon as a device has data to send to another device, it just sends it.

The primary responsibility of the network layer is routing traffic around the network. Routing protocols specify how routers communicate with one another on a network, while routed protocols are used to send data from one network to another. In short, routing protocols transmit routing protocol messages across networks. Routing protocols learn routes (or paths) for routed protocols and are used to transmit packets across those routes (paths).

Several routing protocols are defined at the network layer: Border Gateway Protocol (BGP), an internet interdomain routing protocol; Open Shortest Path First (OSPF), a link-state, interior gateway protocol developed for use in TCP/IP networks; and Routing Information Protocol (RIP), an internet routing protocol that uses hop count as its metric. Logical addressing is accomplished at this layer through routed protocols like Internet Protocol (IP) and Internetwork Packet Exchange (IPX).

There are several noteworthy functions that occur at the network layer:

- **Internet Protocol (IP):** IP is a set of requirements for addressing and routing data across networks, including the internet.

- **Addressing:** IP facilitates transmission of data from host to destination IP address, traversing the network until the destination address is located and reached.

- **Host addressing:** Each host has a unique address to provide its logical location on the internet. That address is the IP address.

- **Message forwarding:** Gateways or routers are special-purpose devices or hosts on the network that forward data between networks that are segmented, partitioned, or interconnected across a WAN.

- **Fragmentation:** Packet sizes can be large and complex. The network layer facilitates the subdivision of a data packet into a manageable or allowable size without the loss of data integrity.

- **Internet Protocol Security (IPSec):** When implemented, secure communications using virtual private networks (VPNs) and encryption is made possible by this set of protocols that provides security for IP. IPSec is further discussed in the next section, "Internet Protocol Networking."

A range of protocols operate at the network layer. BGP provides much of the backbone for the internet's routing. RIP (also mentioned earlier) is an early protocol that is still occasionally used. OSPF is a fast, scalable protocol used in large enterprise networks. The Internet Control Message Protocol (ICMP) is used for troubleshooting and error control purposes. The Internet Group Management Protocol (IGMP) is used to simultaneously transmit messages to multiple recipients. The following sections examine more closely how these protocols work at the network layer.

Border Gateway Protocol

An *autonomous system* (AS) is a large network or group of networks managed or controlled by a single entity or organization. BGP is a path-vector routing protocol used between separate ASs. It is the most prevalent and scalable of all routing protocols, as it is the routing protocol of the global internet and private networks of service providers too. When BGP operates between autonomous systems (such as between internet service providers, or ISPs), it is called external BGP (eBGP). When it operates within a single autonomous system (e.g., within a large private network), it is called internal BGP (iBGP).

NOTE   Individual autonomous systems are assigned a globally unique autonomous system number (ASN) by the Internet Assigned Numbers Authority (IANA).

BGP operates by choosing the shortest path through the internet by navigating the least number of ASs along the route. The paths are stored in a Routing Information Base (RIB). Only one route per destination is stored in the routing table, but the RIB is aware of multiple paths to a destination. Each router determines which routes to store from the RIB, and the RIB keeps track of possible routes. When routes are deleted, the RIB silently removes them without notification to peers. RIB entries never time out.

BGP was initially designed to carry internet reachability information only, but it has expanded in capability to carry routes for Multicast, IPv6, VPNs, and a variety of other data.

NOTE   While BGP functions on top of TCP (layer 4), its core functionality is that of a routing protocol. While you may encounter BGP discussed in layer 4 or even layer 7, for the purposes of this book, we discuss it as a layer 3 routing protocol.

There is a vulnerability inherent in the task of determining the optimal path. The vulnerability is that a network in one region can negatively influence the path that traffic takes far outside that region. Countries with an authoritarian view on controlling network traffic within their borders take advantage of that vulnerability. An example of this happened with China and Russia in 2018, when both countries abused how BGP operates to redirect traffic away from and through their borders. Western countries experienced availability outages for several minutes, while the core internet routers fought conflicting messages and converged path updates.

Routing Information Protocol Versions 1 and 2

Assignment of logical addresses (i.e., IP addresses) to networks requires a mechanism to inform the routers of which networks are directly or indirectly accessible. In the past, manual entries in routing tables created static routes, forcing traffic between two locations to travel on a designated path. As more networks were added, maintaining these tables efficiently required the adoption of standards-based protocols to automatically share this information. The evolution of routing protocols reflects the growth of the internet in order to address the scope and increasingly complex interconnected infrastructure.

Routing Information Protocol (RIP) is one of the earliest routing protocols and the first to use the distance-vector routing method. RIP uses the count of hops that a signal makes along the network path. RIP allows a maximum of 15 hops, and, at hop number 16, the distance is considered infinite and the destination unreachable. This constraint limits the size of networks RIP can support, but also is the reason RIP prevents routing loops (which occur when a data packet is continually routed through the same routers over and over). In addition to hop count, RIP implements split horizon, route poisoning, and hold-down timers to prevent routing loops.

- **Split horizon:** This routing configuration prevents a route from being advertised back in the direction from which it came.

- **Route poisoning:** When a router detects that one of its connected routes has failed, the router sets the hop count on the failed route to 16, establishing the route as unreachable.

- **Hold-down timers:** When a router receives information that a route is bad, it establishes a hold-down period during which the router will neither advertise the route nor accept advertisements about the route.

A RIP router transmits full updates every 30 seconds. When this technology was originated, this was not expected to be a problem. Over time, the volume of routing devices on the network created the potential for high volumes of traffic bursts. The theory was that random implementation of new devices would help to normalize the traffic flow over time.

Because time to converge and scalability issues are prevalent in RIP, it is not the preferred choice in most networking environments. However, RIP is still a potential choice in smaller networks because it is widely supported, is easy to configure, and does not require any parameters, unlike other protocols.

RIP uses the User Datagram Protocol (UDP) as its transport protocol and is assigned the reserved port number 520.

NOTE   For support of Internet Protocol version 6 (IPv6), RIP next generation (RIPng) is an extension of RIPv2. RIPng sends updates on UDP port 521 using the multicast group FF02::9.

Open Shortest Path First Versions 1 and 2

The OSPF protocol is common in large enterprise networks because it provides fast convergence and scalability. Convergence refers to how routing tables get updated. OSPF is a link-state protocol, specifically one of the interior gateway protocols (IGPs) standardized by the Internet Engineering Task Force (IETF). Link-state protocols gather information from nearby routing devices and create a network topology, making the protocol very efficient. OSPF monitors the topology, and when it detects a change, it automatically reroutes the topology. Within seconds, OSPF is able to reroute from link failures and create loop-free routing.

OSPF supports Internet Protocol version 4 (IPv4) and IPv6 networks. The updates for IPv6 are specified as OSPF version 3. OSPF computes traffic load and seeks to balance it between routes. To do so, several variables are included, such as the round-trip distance (measured in time) of a router, data throughput of a link, or link availability and reliability. OSPF encapsulates data directly in IP packets at protocol number 89. It does not use a transport protocol like UDP or TCP.

Internet Control Message Protocol

The ICMP message has three fields distinguishing the type and code of the ICMP packet, and those values never change in the header while in transit. They are followed by ICMP-specific information and then the original IP header information. The most common uses for ICMP traffic are manual troubleshooting (the ping utility) and network diagnostics (the traceroute utility) and system-generated error messages during IP transmissions.

ICMP information is used for troubleshooting and control purposes when there are errors in the IP transmissions. In ICMP utilities, every device forwards an IP packet, and an ICMP message can be subsequently sent to the source address. Using ping and traceroute, for example, the source IP address can ascertain several useful network mapping messages such as Destination Unreachable, Echo Request and Reply (Ping), Redirect, Time Exceeded, and Router Advertisement and Router Solicitation. All are important in the daily operations of security personnel.

Ping and traceroute can also be used by attackers to identify the location of hosts (ping) and, for malicious reasons, to map the network for future attacks of all types (traceroute).

Internet Group Management Protocol

The IGMP operates at the network layer but is specific to a host or a router within the group. IGMP is the key protocol necessary for doing IP multicast transmissions. Multicast becomes useful when you have an application needing to perform a one-to-many transmission, such as a video multicast from the CEO to her employees. Likely, an attack on IGMP begins with an attack on the multicast routing software or hardware device itself utilizing IGMP.

NOTE IGMP is used only on IPv4 networks. IPv6 networks manage multicast transmissions through Multicast Listener Discovery (MLD), which is part of ICMPv6. The differences between IPv4 and IPv6 are discussed later in this chapter.

Layer 3 Attack Vectors

Network layer attacks are generally specific to how network traffic is routed. A MITM attack, involving traffic being redirected to a malicious actor, is an example of an attack at the network layer. Spoofing or forging of a network address is another common form of network layer attack. Assuming the attacker has access to the resources, the simplest attack to execute may be a denial-of-service (DoS) attack that involves simply overwhelming the target's resources.

Layer 4: Transport Layer

The transport layer is responsible for providing reliable data transport and end-to-end transmission control. The protocols of this layer provide host-to-host communication services and manage the transfer of packets from one host to another, across networks. The transport layer provides the upper layers (layers 5 through 7) standardized access so that they do not need to be concerned with the details of the lower layers (layers 1 through 3).

Some of the functions that happen at the transport layer are flow control, multiplexing, virtual circuit management, and error checking and recovery.

- Flow control manages data transmission and keeps the sending device from overwhelming the processing capability of the receiving device.
- Multiplexing allows several applications to transmit data along a single physical link.
- Virtual circuits are established, maintained, and terminated by the transport layer.
- Error checking involves creating various mechanisms for detecting transmission errors.
- Error recovery resolves errors such as a request that data be retransmitted.

There are two primary transport layer protocols that every security professional must be familiar with: TCP and UDP.

Transmission Control Protocol

TCP is a connection-oriented protocol, which means that communicating devices must establish a reliable connection before any data is transmitted (and possibly lost); this connection must also be closed after data transmission is complete. TCP establishes connections via a three-way handshake. Figure 4.2 illustrates the typical three-way handshake process.

In addition to being connection-oriented, TCP provides extensive error checking mechanisms through flow control and acknowledgment of data. The protocol enforces data sequencing, such that packets arrive at the receiving host in the order that the sending device sent them, and it supports packet retransmission if packets are lost.

NOTE   You may come across the term *socket*, and you should understand what that is. A socket is one logical endpoint on a communication link between two applications running on a network. A socket is bound to a port number so that the TCP layer can identify exactly where to send the data. Sockets are typically expressed as a combination of an IP address and a port number, such as 192.168.100.10:22 (i.e., port 22 on IP address 192.168.100.10).

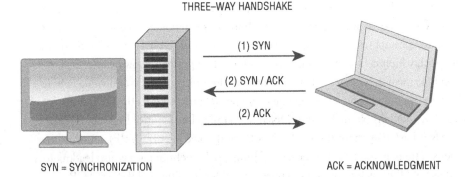

THREE–WAY HANDSHAKE

(1) SYN

(2) SYN / ACK

(2) ACK

SYN = SYNCHRONIZATION

ACK = ACKNOWLEDGMENT

(1) A client node sends a SYN data packet over an IP network to a destination node on the same or an external network. The SYN packet is asking if the destination is open for new connections.

(2) The target node must have open ports that can accept and initiate new connections. When the destination target receives the SYN packet from the client node, it responds and returns a confirmation receipt, specifically the ACK packet or SYN/ACK packet.

(3) The client node receives the SYN/ACK from the destination and responds with an ACK packet.

Upon completion of this process, the connection is created and the host and target can communicate.

FIGURE 4.2 **TCP three-way handshake**

TCP's connection-oriented nature makes it a reliable protocol, because it is guarantees delivery by acknowledging packets, checking for missing or corrupted packets, and requesting retransmission, when necessary. Due to the additional overhead associated with the three-way handshake, acknowledging packets, and error checking and correction, TCP is generally a slower protocol than connectionless protocols like UDP. TCP is used by Hypertext Transfer Protocol (HTTP), Hypertext Transfer Protocol Secure (HTTPS), and File Transfer Protocol (FTP), and other protocols that require reliable data transfer and extensive error checking.

User Datagram Protocol

In contrast with TCP, UDP is a connectionless protocol. There is no overhead associated with establishing a connection, maintaining a connection, or terminating a connection, making UDP simpler, faster, and more efficient than TCP.

NOTE   *Datagram* is the connectionless sibling of *packet*. *Datagram* is a combination of the words *data* and *telegram* and is essentially used to describe a basic unit of data that is capable of being transmitted from one location (source) to another (destination) on a network via UDP or other connectionless protocols.

UDP is often referred to as a "best-effort" communications protocol. It offers none of the features of TCP — no error detection or correction, no sequencing, no flow control mechanisms — and does not use a pre-established session. In short, UDP is considered an unreliable protocol, which is fine for certain applications. The protocol's low overhead permits quick data transmission, which is ideal for real-time streaming of audio and video, where speed is more important than ensuring that every packet arrives perfectly. UDP is also commonly used by Domain Name System (DNS), Dynamic Host Control Protocol (DHCP), Simple Network Management Protocol (SNMP), and Voice over IP (VoIP), among other applications. The ongoing rise of Internet of Things (IoT) technologies is also leading to an increased use of UDP, as sensor data is typically ideal for sending via UDP vs. TCP.

Layer 4 Attack Vectors

Attack vectors unique to the transport layer would include attacks utilizing TCP and UDP. One specific example would be the SYN flood attack that drains a target's network memory resources by continuously initiating TCP-based connections, but not allowing them to complete; this creates a DoS that prevents legitimate connections to the target. Trojans and other malware also tend to target specific TCP and UDP ports. Session hijacking is another common attack that can operate at layer 4 (as well as other layers).

Layer 5: Session Layer

The session layer facilitates the logical, persistent connection between systems on a network. This layer controls the dialogue (connection) between a local application and a remote application. The session layer is responsible for establishing, coordinating, and terminating a session efficiently and effectively between end-user application processes.

The session layer is commonly implemented in applications that use remote procedure calls (RPCs) to handle requests and responses that occur between applications. RPCs are the mechanism for application environments to make service requests and service responses between applications on various networked devices. In other words, RPCs allow a procedure (a sequence of tasks or instructions) to be created on a client and performed on a server device — the session layer manages this process.

There are three primary modes of operation to choose from when a session is established:

- **Full-duplex mode:** This is when data is sent over a connection between two devices in both directions at the same time. Full-duplex channels can be constructed either as a pair of simplex links or using one channel designed to permit bidirectional simultaneous transmissions. If multiple devices need to be connected using full-duplex mode, many individual links are required because one full-duplex link can connect only two devices.

- **Half-duplex mode:** Half-duplex has the capability of sending data in both directions, but in only one direction at a time. While this may seem like a step down in capability from full-duplex, it is widely used and successful across single network media such as cable, radio frequency, and Ethernet, as examples. The communications work well when the devices take turns sending and receiving.

- **Simplex mode:** This mode involves using a communication channel that operates as a one-way street. An example of simplex construction is where a fiber optics run or a network cable as a single strand sends data and another separate channel receives it.

Layer 5 Attack Vectors

What sorts of attacks target the session layer? This layer and the presentation layer aren't popular targets for common attacks. Routing or packet-based attacks (lower on the OSI model) and application-level attacks (higher on the OSI model) offer "low-hanging fruit" for attackers, leaving the session and presentation layers at an awkward level of abstraction for identifying vulnerabilities. Still, given the layer's functions, you can hypothesize an attack where authentication to establish a session across the network is compromised. There are also specific session layer protocols, such as NetBIOS and Network File System (NFS), that may be vulnerable to DoS and root privilege attacks, for example. Weaknesses in the deprecated Secure Sockets Layer (SSL) protocol and less secure versions of Transport Layer Security (TLS) are also prime targets at the session layer.

Layer 6: Presentation Layer

The purpose of the presentation layer is to translate data between the lower layers and the application layer. At lower levels, data is sent as datagrams and packets. The presentation layer is the first layer in the OSI model at which data structure and presentation are evident, as this layer is responsible for applying coding and conversion functions to data being presented to the application layer.

Here are some examples of the coding and conversion at this layer:

- Common data representation formats, such as the use of standard image, sound, and video formats

- Common data compression schemes, such as JPEG and MPEG

- Common data encryption and decryption schemes

These functions enable the interchange of application data between different types of computer systems. In short, the presentation layer ensures that formats are converted and presented to the application layer as needed.

Encryption and decryption can be used at other layers with distinct advantages and disadvantages. However, encryption and decryption involve the SSL protocol and its replacement, TLS. While encryption through SSL is generally done at the presentation layer, SSL/TLS is more complex and shares functionality with the session layer. Ultimately, the OSI model, as a layered stack of abstraction, cannot cleanly confine to one layer where TLS functions, but the model places encryption broadly on the presentation layer.

Layer 6 Attack Vectors

The most common attacks at this layer involve attacks on the encryption schemes themselves. Cryptography and cryptanalytic attacks are covered in Chapter 3, "Security Architecture and Engineering."

Layer 7: Application Layer

The application layer is the highest layer of the OSI model and the closest layer to the end user. This layer supports network access for software applications and provides an interface for the user. The software applications do not reside at the application layer. Instead, this layer facilitates communication through the lower layers to establish connections with applications at the other end of the network connection. Web browsers (e.g., Chrome, Safari, Firefox), HTTP, FTP, and Telnet all rely on the application layer to function properly.

NOTE Application layer functions typically include identifying communication partners, determining resource availability, and synchronizing communication.

Layer 7 Attack Vectors

Attack vectors specific to the application layer vary wildly, and most security breaches occur at this layer. To begin the list, consider weaknesses in application layer protocols such as HTTP, FTP, Simple Mail Transfer Protocol (SMTP), and SNMP. Every attack on the user interface falls into this category, as well as web-based attacks such as HTTP flooding or input validation attacks. SQL injection and cross-site scripting (XSS) are among the most common attacks that operate at the application layer.

At the application layer, where services support user applications, user authentication takes place. In addition to these attack vectors, authentication weaknesses (such as weak or poorly managed passwords) also provide a critical attack vector at this OSI layer.

The TCP/IP Reference Model

The TCP/IP reference model is a four-layer conceptual model that was initially developed in the 1960s by the U.S. Defense Advanced Research Projects Agency (DARPA). The four layers of the TCP/IP model are Application, Transport, Internet, and Link (or Network Access), as illustrated in Figure 4.3.

TCP/IP Model

Application Layer Application programs using the network
Transport Layer (TCP/UDP) Management of end-to-end message transmission, error detection, and error correction
Internet Layer (IP) Handling of datagrams: routing and congestion
Link Layer Management of cost-effective and reliable data delivery, access to physical networks

FIGURE 4.3 **The TCP/IP reference model**

Each layer in the TCP/IP model corresponds to one or more layers of the seven-layer OSI model. See Figure 4.4 for the comparison.

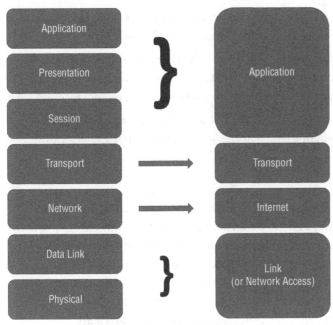

FIGURE 4.4 **Comparison of the OSI and TCP/IP models**

Link (or Network Access) Layer

The link layer is called by several other names, including the network access layer or the data link layer (and, indeed, the TCP/IP model's link layer includes some of the same functionality as the OSI model's data link layer). Think of it as the physical interface between the host system and the network hardware. The role of this layer is to facilitate TCP/IP data packets across the network transmission channel in a reliable manner. This layer can detect transmission errors. This layer determines how common data link standards like IEEE 802.2 and X.25 format data packets for transmission and routing. The way TCP/IP was designed allows the data format to be independent of the network access method, frame format, and medium that establishes TCP/IP to interconnect across disparate or different networks. It is this independence from any specific network technology that makes both the TCP/IP and OSI 7 layer models scalable to newer networking technologies like Asynchronous Transfer Mode (ATM).

NOTE   The TCP/IP link layer corresponds to the data link and physical layers of the OSI model.

There are several important services that the link layer provides:

- **Data frame:** This is a defined sequence of bits or symbols from a sender that the receiver uses to find the beginning and end of the payload data within the overall stream of other bits or symbols it receives.

- **Checksums:** Data is used within a data frame to manage the integrity of data and allow the receiver to know the data frame was received error-free.

- **Acknowledgment:** This enables reliability in data transmission because a positive acknowledgment is made when data is received. A timeout notice or a negative acknowledgment is received when data is expected but not received.

- **Flow control:** To maintain traffic and avoid errors due to congestion, the link layer supports buffering data transmissions to regulate fast senders with slow senders.

TIP   There are several types of hardware that are associated with the link layer. Network interface cards (NICs) are typically associated with this layer. The NIC is hardware, ranging from a small circuit board to only additional surface layer components added to a motherboard. The NIC provides the physical coupling that interfaces the physical layer media, be it a copper cable, fiber, or a wireless antenna, with the system. Other hardware at this layer would include the various pieces of networking hardware, such as a switch, bridge, or hub. These three differentiate from each other by how they do or do not separate signals between ports.

Internet Layer

Using core protocols like IP, ARP, ICMP, and IGMP, the internet layer is responsible for addressing, packaging, and routing functions of data packets. Unlike the link layer, the internet layer does not take advantage of data sequencing and acknowledgment services.

The internet layer performs several invaluable functions. To transmit packets from host to host, IP selects the next-hop or gateway for outgoing packets across the link layer. It transfers data packets up to the transport layer for incoming packets if the data meets transmission parameters. To that end, the internet layer helps with error detection and diagnostic capability, so data is not transferred in error.

These are the main protocols residing at this layer:

- IP is the principal routable communications protocol responsible for addressing, routing, and the fragmentation and reassembly of data packets.

- ARP resolves the hardware address of a host from a given IP address.

- ICMP provides diagnostic functions and error reporting when there is an unsuccessful delivery of packets.

NOTE   The TCP/IP internet layer corresponds to the network layer of the OSI model.

Transport Layer

At the transport layer, services are provided to the application layer for session and data-gram communication. You may also hear this layer referred to as the *host-to-host transport layer*. In the TCP/IP model, the transport layer does not make use of the features of the link layer. It assumes an unreliable connection at the link layer. Therefore, at the transport layer, session establishment, packet acknowledgment, and data sequencing are accomplished to enable reliable communications. The core protocols of the transport layer are TCP and UDP, both discussed in the earlier "Layer 4: Transport Layer" section of the OSI 7 model.

NOTE   The TCP/IP transport layer corresponds to the transport layer of the OSI model.

Application Layer

So that applications can access the services of the other layers of the TCP/IP model, the application layer defines the data exchange protocols used by applications. This is the highest layer in the model, and many application layer protocols exist, while new protocols are constantly being developed.

The TCP/IP application layer corresponds to the session, presentation, and application layers (often collectively referred to as the *upper layers*) of the OSI model.

The most widely known application layer protocols are those used for the exchange of user information:

- HTTP/HTTPS is the foundation of file and data transfer on the World Wide Web that comprises and supports websites.

- FTP/FTPS enables file transfer in the client-server architecture.

- SMTP/SMTPS allows email and associated attachments to be sent and received.

- Telnet is a bidirectional interactive text-oriented communication protocol used to access or log on to networked computers remotely. Telnet has no built-in security, so it should be avoided in use over the public internet. It is an unsecured terminal emulation protocol.

NOTE   Instead of Telnet, a secure alternative is the Secure Shell (SSH) protocol, which uses encryption to protect data transferred between a client and a server. The categories of data that are encrypted are credentials, commands, output, and file transfers.

Internet Protocol Networking

IP networking is the main protocol of the internet. The protocol resides at the OSI model's network layer and the TCP/IP model's internet layer. For all intents and purposes, IP makes the internet a reality because the protocol makes it possible to relay datagrams across network boundaries. IP exists in two versions: IPv4 (version 4), which is currently the main version used, and IPv6 (version 6), to which internet-connected devices are evolving.

Internet Protocol Version 4

IPv4 uses 32-bit IP addresses, often written as four decimal numbers called *octets*, each in the range 0–255, such as 172.16.8.93. The IPv4 address space is partitioned into five network classes of 32-bit IP addresses. Classes A, B, and C each correspond to a maximum number of networks and number of hosts per network, while class D is used for multicasting, and class E is reserved for experimental use.

Refer to Table 4.1 to see the network classes that subdivide IP addressing.

TABLE 4.1 IPv4 Network Classes

CLASS	RANGE OF FIRST OCTET	NUMBER OF NETWORKS	NUMBER OF HOSTS PER NETWORK
A	1–127	127	16,777,214
B	128–191	16,384	65,534
C	192–223	2,097,152	254
D	224–239	Multicast	
E	240–255	Reserved	

When IPv4 was first established in the 1980s, the roughly 4 billion IP addresses it provided seemed like a lot. With the growth of IoT devices and the proliferation of network-enabled systems, the need for additional IP addresses is now greater than ever. IPv6 is the long-term solution to this problem, but you should be familiar with the current leading solution, which is *network address translation* (NAT), discussed next.

Network Address Translation

NAT is a technique used to map (or translate) one or more local (internal) IP addresses to one or more global (external) IP addresses, and vice versa.

NAT can be implemented on a variety of different devices such as firewalls, routers, gateways, and proxies. It can be used only on IP networks and operates at the network layer (layer 3). Originally, NAT was designed to extend the use of IPv4, since the pool of available addresses was quickly being exhausted. To that point, NAT is a legacy technology that comes with advantages and disadvantages.

First, consider its advantages. NAT is used to accomplish network and security objectives to hide the identity of internal clients, mask the routable design of your private network, and keep network addressing costs at a minimum by using the fewest public IP addresses possible. Figure 4.5 shows an example of how you might find NAT implemented on a perimeter firewall. Through NAT processes, the organization assigns internal IP addresses, perhaps even a private addressing scheme. The NAT appliance catalogs the addresses and will convert them into public IP addresses for transmission over the internet. On the internal network, NAT allows for any address to be used, and this does not cause collisions or conflict with public internet hosts with the same IP addresses. In effect, NAT translates the IP addresses of the internal clients to leased addresses outside the environment. NAT offers numerous benefits, including the following:

- NAT connects an entire private network to the internet using only a single or just a few leased public IP addresses.

- NAT uses private IP addresses (10.0.0.0 to 10.255.255.255) in a private network and retains the ability to communicate with the internet as the NAT translates to a public, routable address.
- NAT hides the IP addressing scheme and network topography of an internal, private network from the internet.
- NAT ensures that connections originated from within the internal protected network are allowed back into the network from the internet.

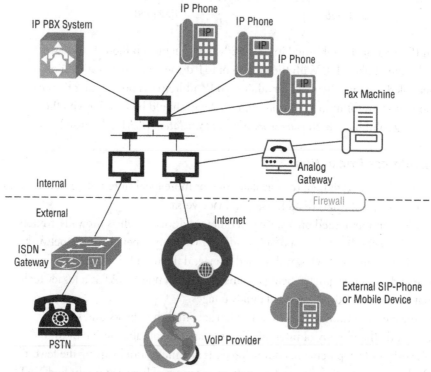

FIGURE 4.5 **NAT implemented on a perimeter firewall**

Public IP addresses are essentially all allocated after the remaining class A (see Table 4.1) addresses were exhausted years ago. This explains the upward trend in the popularity of NAT. Security concerns also favor the use of NAT, which mitigates many intrusion types of attacks. With roughly only 4 billion addresses available in IPv4, the world has simply deployed more devices using IP than there are unique IP addresses available. The fact that early designers of the internet and TCP/IP reserved a few blocks of addresses for private, unrestricted use is becoming a good idea. These set-aside IP addresses, known as private IP addresses, are defined in the standard RFC 1918.

Now, consider some of NAT's disadvantages. Again, remember that NAT was developed to help deal with the fact that IPv4 addressing was being exhausted. To that end, NAT was assumed to be a temporary solution. Because it was considered only temporary, the IETF, responsible for defining protocol standards, didn't pursue creating an in-depth official standard for NAT. In fact, while the IETF recognized the benefits of NAT and published a general specification, it avoided developing a technical specification to discourage NAT's widespread adoption. For that reason alone, the biggest disadvantage to NAT is how inconsistent its implementation in devices is.

A few technical disadvantages of NAT have been recognized, but solutions to those problems were discovered or developed without needing to reinvent NAT. For example, consider how peer-to-peer communication is handled. Without NAT, an initiator communicates with a target. This is not a problem provided both the initiator and the target have routable addresses. With NAT implemented, an initiator on the internet seeking to connect with a target behind NAT cannot connect with a nonroutable address. One way to solve this is for the peer-to-peer session to begin "backward," with the target first connecting with the initiator for the purpose of discovering NAT in place. Then, once NAT's outside public address is known, the originator can begin a new peer-to-peer session. Services such as Skype, which rely on peer-to-peer or VoIP protocols, needed to create innovative ways to sidestep how NAT would otherwise break their service. Skype, for example, employs "SuperNodes" on public addresses to permit a peer-to-peer connection, even if both the target and the initiator are behind NAT.

Another disadvantage is how IPSec checks integrity. IPSec computes a hash value for the purpose of ensuring the integrity of each packet. That hash value is computed using various parts of the packet, and since NAT changes the packet's values, that hash value is no longer valid. To address this, the technology of NAT-Traversal (NAT-T) was developed. NAT-T ensures that IPSec isn't broken when one or both ends of the IPSec tunnel cross over a NAT device.

While NAT is a critical technology for IPv4 networks, the technology is no longer needed in IPv6. This is one of several improvements offered by the latest version of the Internet Protocol, which is discussed in the following section.

Internet Protocol Version 6

As opposed to IPv4's 32-bit IP addresses, IPv6 uses 128-bit IP addresses to support a significantly larger number of addresses than its older peer. Each IPv6 address is portioned into four hexadecimal digits, which are separated by colons for addressing, and segmented into two parts: a 64-bit network prefix and a 64-bit interface identifier. An example IPv6 address looks like 2607:F0F0:1002:00B1:0000:0000:0000:0004. The added complexity allows IPv6 to support 1,028 times the total number of IPv4 addresses, allowing for internet-connected devices to expand for the foreseeable future. The IPv6 scheme intends also to improve network addressing and routing.

Some of the principal benefits of IPv6 over IPv4 include the following:

- **Scoped addresses:** This adds a layer of security and access control for administrators who can group and then deny or allow access to network services, like file servers or printing.

- **Autoconfiguration:** This removes the need for both DHCP and NAT, thanks to the much larger public address space.

- **Quality of service (QoS) priority values:** Based on the content priority, traffic management is conducted according to preset QoS priority values.

IPv6 was developed by the IETF to manage the anticipated problem of IPv4 address exhaustion, but adoption of IPv6 has been slow. Operating systems since about 2000 have had the ability to use IPv6, either natively or via an add-in. Adoption hurdles include added cost of some IPv6-capable devices and the fact that IPv4 works well. Decision-makers are reluctant to either make a change for the sake of change itself or make process improvements that provide a minimal financial return on investment (ROI). Early adopters of IPv6 are found in private, internal networks in large corporations, research laboratories, and universities.

Network Attacks

Networking protocols were designed long before the necessity of security was fully recognized. Consequently, even today, networked hosts remain vulnerable and networked systems fail to implement mitigating controls. Systems that are hardened against attacks that exploit misconfiguration and unnecessary services can still be vulnerable from attacks exploiting network services. Several updates and revisions to networking protocols have been adopted, but weaknesses remain due to security being designed as an afterthought, although progress continues to be made.

The "Open System Interconnection and Transmission Control Protocol/Internet Protocol Models" section earlier in this chapter explored the OSI model and how its layers continue in the abstract from physical to application. It examined where established protocols fall within those layers. The section also touched on what attack vectors exist at each OSI layer to expose some of the vulnerability therein.

By knowing how networked hosts communicate with each other, security professionals can better understand how network attacks can occur and be successful. Armed with that information, the following sections delve into a variety of network attacks.

Distributed Denial-of-Service Attacks

When an attacker does not have the skills or tools for a sophisticated attack, they may use a brute-force attack, which can be just as effective. Simply flooding the targeted system with UDP packets from infected machines has proven successful, especially as IoT devices have been used, unwittingly, to help launch these distributed denial-of-service (DDoS) attacks. A typical DDoS attack consists of a large number of individual machines that are subverted to bombard a target with overwhelming traffic over a short period of time. The individual contribution of any one compromised machine — be it a PC, IoT device, networking hardware, or server — would amount to no damage, but the collective sum creates a crushing amount of traffic to the end target.

TIP To produce the volumes of machines needed for a DDoS, a botnet is created and used. A *botnet* is a number of internet-connected and commandeered devices that communicate in a command-and-control manner.

SYN Flooding

In an attempt to overload a system, this type of attack bombards the recipient with an overwhelming number of SYN packets, and the sender or senders do not acknowledge any of the replies. SYN flooding is a form of DoS attack, exploiting properties of TCP at the transport layer (layer 4). TCP initiates a connection by sending a SYN packet, which when received and accepted is replied to with a SYN-ACK packet. The SYN flooding DoS attack is executed by sending massive amounts of those SYN packets. The SYN packets accumulate at the recipient system, and the software crashes because it cannot handle the overflow. The attacker attempts to consume enough server resources to make the system unresponsive to legitimate traffic. Some refer to this attack as the half-open attack because of the partial three-way TCP handshake that underlies the attack. Eventually, given enough connection attempts, the capacity of the network card to maintain open connections is exhausted.

Even though these types of attacks have such a long history and the mitigations have been in existence for almost as long, SYN flooding is still a common attack. There are some ways to mitigate a SYN flood vulnerability. A few of the most prevalent approaches are the following:

- **Increasing backlog queue:** This involves raising the allowance for the number of half-open connections a system will sustain. It requires additional memory resources to increase the maximum backlog. Depending on the availability of memory resources, mitigating the SYN flooding threat can degrade system performance. A risk-benefit analysis is required against unwanted DoS impact and slower performance.

- **Recycling the oldest half-open TCP connection:** This is a first-in, first-out queueing strategy where once the backlog queue limit is reached, the oldest half-open request is overwritten. The benefit is fully establishing legitimate connections faster than the backlog can be filled with malicious SYN packets. However, if the backlog queue is too small or the attack too voluminous, this mitigation can be insufficient.

- **SYN cookies:** The server responds to each connection request (SYN) with a SYN-ACK packet. The SYN request is dropped from the backlog. The port is open to new, ideally legitimate, new connections. If the initial connection is legitimate, the original sender will send its ACK packet. The initial recipient, which created the SYN cookie, will reconstruct the SYN backlog queue entry. Of course, there will be some limitations as some information about the TCP connection can be lost. This is more advantageous than the full DoS outage.

DDoS and the Internet of Things

As an emerging technology, IoT devices deserve a little more attention in this chapter. From a security perspective, these devices offer a soft target for potential attackers. They are delivered with default settings that are easily guessed or, in fact, publicly well known. Administrative credentials and management access are wide open to internet-facing interfaces. Attackers can exploit the devices with a relatively simple remote access code. What compounds the vulnerabilities is that users do not interact with the devices the same way as they do with office automation or other endpoint computing assets. The default settings are rarely changed, even if the end user has the ability to make changes. Vendors are typically slow to provide upgrades and patches, if they supply post-sale manufacturing support at all. For these reasons, the devices are easy prey, and users often have no idea the devices are being hacked until it is too late.

The volume of IoT devices generates a lot of concern from security professionals. It is estimated that there are already tens of millions of vulnerable IoT devices installed or in use today. That number is growing. The interconnections are usually always on, left unprotected to ingress and egress unlike a typical LAN or WAN, but they enjoy high-speed connections. These variables explain why a botnet of huge groups of commandeered IoT devices presents a serious problem. Common attack sequences consist of compromising the device to send spam or broadcast messages. If spam filters block that attack, a tailored malware insert may be tried, like fast flux, which is a DNS technique to hide spamming attacks. If that does not accomplish the disruption, a brute-force type of DDoS might be launched. Increasingly, well-resourced websites have sufficient bandwidth and can expand capacity above baseline or normal usage levels to withstand most attacks. However, just the threat of launching an attack can be enough to convince website owners to pay a ransom to extortionists to avoid testing the limits of the targeted site's ability to remain responsive.

Man-in-the-Middle Attacks

In a communication where sender and receiver believe they are connected, a MITM attack can be hard to detect and presents a significant threat to unprotected communications. In a MITM attack, the attacker intercepts the signal and secretly relays (and possibly alters) the communication before stopping the transmission or allowing the message to reach the intended recipient.

Eavesdropping is a specific type of MITM attack. In that scenario, the attacker relays the message to complete the circuit. The entire conversation is overheard, and in some instances controlled, by the attacker, while the sender and receiver think the message is private. Figure 4.6 depicts the general concepts of a MITM attack.

Man-in-the-Middle Attack (MITM)

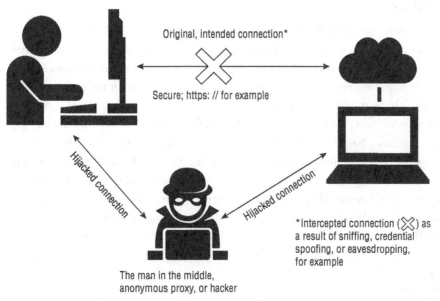

FIGURE 4.6 **Man-in-the-middle attack**

Another type of MITM attack is impersonation. This happens when the attacker circumvents the authentication process and compromises the credentials of one account. The endpoint communicating with the attacker is not aware that the communication has been intercepted.

There are two main ways to prevent or detect MITM attacks: authentication and tamper detection. Authentication provides some degree of certainty that a given message has come from a legitimate source. Tamper detection merely shows evidence that a message may have been altered.

- **Authentication:** To prevent MITM attacks, cryptographic protocols are used to authenticate the endpoints or transmission media. One such technique is to employ a TLS server paired with X.509 certificates. The X.509 certificates are used by the mutually trusted certificate authority (CA) to authenticate one or more entities. The message and an exchange of public keys are employed to make the channel secure.

- **Tamper detection:** One way to detect MITM attacks is through examination of any latency in the transaction above baseline expectations. Response times are checked, and normal factors like long calculations of hash functions are accounted for. If a delay is not explained, there may be unwanted, malicious third-party interference in the communication.

Packet Sniffing

Administrators often use packet sniffing tools for legitimate purposes, like trouble-shooting. But attackers conduct MITM packet sniffing to gain information for adversarial purposes. Any unencrypted protocols are subject to passive attacks where an attacker has been able to place a packet sniffing tool on the network to monitor traffic. The monitoring might be used to determine traffic types and patterns or to map network information. In any case, packet sniffing greatly benefits the attacker in preparing for other types of attacks. Say, for example, that an attacker using packet sniffing discovers that a company still uses deprecated SSL ciphers or discovers the IP address of the Active Directory (AD) controller. The attacker is now set up to exploit that outdated protocol or server. Packet sniffing can also include grabbing packets in transit and attempting to extract useful information from the contents. Contained in some packets are usernames, passwords, IP addresses, credit card numbers, and other valuable payload. Encrypting sensitive traffic is the best way to protect against network sniffing.

Hijacking Attacks

Hijacking attacks describe many different types of MITM attacks. A hijacking attack is any attack that involves the exploitation of a session, which is an established dialogue between devices. Normally, a session is managed by a control mechanism, such as a cookie or token. An attacker might try to intercept or eavesdrop on the session token or cookie. In the case where an attacker has sniffed the cookie or token, the attacker may connect with the server using the legitimate token in parallel with the victim. Or the attacker may intercept the session token to use as well as to send a specially formed packet to the victim to terminate their initial session.

Many websites require authentication and use cookies to remember session tracking information. When the session is terminated as the user logs out, the cookie and credentials are typically cleared. Hijacking a session and stealing the token or cookie while the session is active can provide an attacker with valuable, sensitive information, such as unique details on what site was visited. Even worse, hijacking the session cookie may allow the attacker an opportunity to continue a session, posing as the victim.

TIP Promiscuous mode is a setting that packet sniffers enable to stop a device from discarding or filtering data unintended for it. The packet sniffer can gain access to the additional traffic and data packets that otherwise would have been filtered.

MITRE ATT&CK Framework

This chapter is not intended to present an exhaustive list of network attacks, but the MITRE Organization (usually just called MITRE) maintains quite an extensive knowledge base of adversary tactics and techniques known as MITRE ATT&CK. This knowledge base is a globally accessible reference that includes hundreds of real-world attack tactics and techniques, which is intended to serve as a foundation for security professionals to develop threat models and methodologies in their organizations. You can learn all about MITRE ATT&CK at `attack.mitre.org`.

Secure Protocols

Secure protocols provide security services for communications channels as well as secure authentication services.

Some common secure communications protocols include SSH, TLS, Kerberos, IPSec, and Internet Key Exchange (IKE).

Secure Shell

SSH is a replacement for Telnet, which supports interactive, text-oriented communication over TCP. SSH is a cryptographic network protocol that creates a secure tunnel that protects the integrity of communication, preventing session hijacking and other MITM attacks.

SSH is also a client-server architecture that is often used to accomplish remote command-line login and remote command execution. Any network service can be secured with SSH. The protocol specification distinguishes between two major versions, referred to as SSH-1 and SSH-2. SSH-1 is considered insecure, while SSH-2 provides more secure and efficient protections against eavesdropping, DNS and IP spoofing, and MITM attacks.

Transport Layer Security

TLS is a secure protocol that replaced SSL as the primary protocol for secure web traffic. SSL is a session-oriented legacy protocol that was commonly used to secure web, email, FTP, or even Telnet traffic. SSL is still in broad use despite having known security weaknesses, but it is insecure and should be replaced by TLS whenever possible. TLS functions in the same general manner as SSL, but it uses stronger authentication and encryption protocols. Rather than establishing a VPN using IPSec at the network layer and requiring each remote user to have a client installed, SSL or TLS is used to create an on-demand tunnel. Remote users need no client installed, and access to the private network is via a web browser.

SSL and TLS both have the following features:

- Support secure client-server communications across an insecure network while preventing tampering, spoofing, and eavesdropping
- Support one-way authentication using digital certificates
- Support two-way authentication using digital certificates
- Often implemented as the initial payload of a TCP package, allowing it to encapsulate all higher-layer protocol payloads
- Can be implemented at lower layers, such as the network layer (layer 3) to operate as a VPN. This implementation is known as OpenVPN.

In addition, TLS can be used to encrypt UDP and Session Initiation Protocol (SIP) connections. TLS encrypted sessions are the preferred mechanism for secure e-commerce.

Kerberos

Kerberos is a communication protocol that provides protection for logon credentials. It uses the concept of tickets to allow systems communicating over an unsecured network to prove their identity to one another securely. Kerberos is discussed further in Chapter 5, "Identity and Access Management."

Internet Protocol Security

IPSec is a suite of protocols developed to provide confidentiality, integrity, and authentication (note: this *a* is authentication, not availability) of data sent over an IP network. IPSec uses several security services to accomplish authentication and encryption:

- **Authentication header (AH):** This authenticates the sender, and it discovers any changes in data during transmission.
- **Encapsulating security payload (ESP):** This not only performs authentication for the sender, but it also encrypts the data being sent.

- **Security associations (SAs):** These provide the bundle of shared security attributes or keys and data that provide the parameters necessary for AH and/or ESP operations.

There are two modes of IPSec:

- **Transport mode:** This only encrypts and authenticates the IP payload, which is the data being transmitted in the packet, to ensure a secure channel of communication.

- **Tunnel mode:** This will encrypt and authenticate the whole IP packet, which includes the data as well as routing information, to form a new IP packet with a new IP header to provide secure communication between two places (i.e., establish a VPN).

Internet Key Exchange

IKE is a secure protocol that is part of IPSec suite and is used to establish a secure, authenticated communications channel between two entities. The IKE protocol typically uses X.509 PKI certificates for authentication and the Diffie–Hellman–Merkle key exchange protocol to establish a shared session secret.

There are two versions of IKE: IKEv1 and IKEv2, where IKEv2 was designed to solve a number of configuration and security issues that exist within the first version. Even still, both versions of IKE are vulnerable to offline dictionary attacks, which requires a high entropy password to protect against. In addition, IPSec VPN configurations that support both IKEv1 and IKEv2 may be vulnerable to downgrade attacks that force the less secure version 1. This can be mitigated by segmenting systems that require IKEv1 from those that are suitable for the stricter IKEv2 configurations.

Implications of Multilayer Protocols

TCP/IP is an example of a multilayer protocol, in which multiple individual protocols are located across the various protocol stack layers. Encapsulation is an important capability and benefit of multilayer protocol schema. In the context of networking communication between two hosts, *encapsulation* means to envelope one protocol's contents as the payload for the subsequent protocol. To illustrate the process of encapsulation, consider a web server to web browser data transfer, which is HTTP-encapsulated in TCP. TCP is encapsulated in IP, and that packet is encapsulated in Ethernet. TCP/IP can also add additional layers of encapsulation. SSL/TLS encryption can be added to the communication to provide additional confidentiality.

There are instances of TCP/IP encapsulation used for adversarial purposes. Some attack tools can hide or isolate an unauthorized protocol within an authorized one. Using a technique like HTTP tunneling, FTP can be hidden within an HTTP packet to get around egress restrictions.

Virtual Local Area Networks

Attackers can also use multilayer protocol encapsulation to provide an ability to fool interior switching devices to gain access to a VLAN. VLANs are used to isolate network traffic to its own separate broadcast domain. (See Figure 4.7.) The switch knows what VLAN to place that traffic on according to a tag identifying the VLAN ID. Those tags, per IEEE 802.1Q, encapsulate each packet. Where a VLAN is established through logical addressing, VLAN hopping is an attack using a double-encapsulated IEEE 802.1Q VLAN tag. To be clear, that is one VLAN tag encapsulating a packet already encapsulated with a different VLAN ID. The first VLAN tag is removed by the first switch it encounters. The next switch will inadvertently move traffic according to the second layer VLAN encapsulated tag.

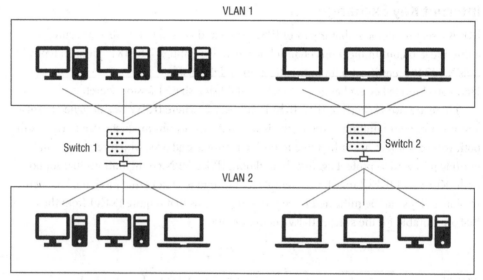

FIGURE 4.7 **Virtual local area network**

Supervisory Control and Data Acquisition Systems

An implication of multilayered protocols is the enablement of particular communication protocols across more ubiquitous transport protocols, chiefly TCP/IP. Probably the most salient examples of that are the industrial control in energy and utility industries using supervisory control and data acquisition (SCADA) systems. SCADA is a control system architecture that uses computers to gather data on processes and send control commands to connected devices that comprise the system.

SCADA systems utilize a legacy protocol called Distributed Network Protocol (DNP3). DNP3 is found primarily in the electric and water utility and management industries. Data is transported across various components in industrial control systems like substation computers, remote terminal units (RTUs), and SCADA master stations (control centers). DNP3 is an open and public standard. There are many similarities between DNP3 and the TCP/IP suite, as they are both multilayer protocols that have link and transport functionality in their respective layers.

Ultimately, to provide some connectivity to these SCADA systems over public networks, there is the solution of encapsulating DNP3 over TCP/IP. This encapsulation, while obviously bridging a connection between disparate standards, does introduce great risk. Perhaps the most common exploitation of this risk is through MITM attacks.

Proprietary technologies established the SCADA systems, but recently they have moved to more open and standardized solutions. With this evolution comes security concerns. Initially, the systems were designed for decentralized facilities like power, oil, gas pipelines, water distribution, and wastewater collection systems. Connections were not a primary concern as the systems were designed to be open, robust, and easily operated and repaired. Any security was a secondary concern. Increasingly, there have been more connections between SCADA systems, office networks, and the internet. The interconnectedness has ushered the systems into vulnerabilities like all other IP-based LANs and WANs. Although sensitive personal information is not necessarily the focus of information protection in SCADA systems, the primary concerns with SCADA cybersecurity are system disruption, sensitive configuration information, and national security.

NOTE Another protocol worth noting in industrial control systems is Modbus. It is a de facto standard of application layer protocol. It is used in several variations from plain Modbus to Modbus+ and Modbus/TCP. The protocol enables a Modbus client to send a request to a Modbus server with a function code that specifies the action to be taken and a data field that provides the additional information.

Converged Protocols

Converged protocols differ from encapsulated, multilayer protocols. Converged protocols are what happens when you merge specialty or proprietary protocols with standard protocols, such as TCP/IP suite protocols. With converged protocols, an organization can reduce reliance on distinct, costly proprietary hardware, as well as create variations of performance, depending on which converged protocol is being used.

Some common examples of converged protocols are described here:

- **Fibre Channel over Ethernet (FCoE):** Fibre Channel solutions usually need separate fiber-optic cabling infrastructure to deliver network data-storage options, such as a storage area network (SAN) or network-attached storage (NAS). Fibre Channel is useful because it allows for high-speed file transfers achieving

128 Gbps and today reaching 256 Gbps. FCoE was developed to enable Fibre Channel to work more efficiently, while using less expensive copper cables over Ethernet connections. Using 10 Gbps Ethernet, FCoE uses Ethernet frames to support the Fibre Channel communications.

NOTE   FCoE is capable of running over copper cables (not just fiber-optic) and uses the British spelling Fibre to differentiate it from a fiber-only perception of the service.

- **Internet Small Computer System Interface (iSCSI):** iSCSI is often viewed as a low-cost alternative to Fibre Channel. It is also a networking storage standard but based on IP. It facilitates the connection of a remote storage volume over a network as if the device were attached locally. The iSCSI transmits SCSI commands over IP networks and performs like a virtual SATA (or SCSI) cable.

- **Multiprotocol Label Switching (MPLS):** MPLS is a high-throughput, high-performance network technology that directs data across a network based on short path labels rather than longer network addresses. Compared with IP routing processes, which are complex and take a longer time to navigate, MPLS saves significant time. Using encapsulation, MPLS is designed to handle a wide range of protocols. An MPLS network can handle T1/E1, ATM, Frame Relay, synchronous optical networking (SONET), and DSL network technologies, not just TCP/IP and compatible protocols. MPLS is often used to create a virtual dedicated circuit between two stations. In the context of the OSI model, MPLS is commonly labeled a layer 2.5 protocol since it operates squarely between the common definitions of data link (layer 2) and network (layer 3) protocols.

- **Voice over Internet Protocol (VoIP):** VoIP is a method using several technologies to encapsulate voice communications and multimedia sessions over IP networks. VoIP has become a popular and inexpensive way for companies and individuals to operate telephony solution using a TCP/IP network connection. VoIP is further discussed later in this chapter, in the section "Implement Secure Communication Channels According to Design."

Microsegmentation

Microsegmentation is a method of creating zones within a network to isolate resources from one another and secure each segment individually. Microsegmentation requires re-authentication when viewing or otherwise accessing resources across zones.

Network architects can use microsegmentation to create policies that limit network traffic between resources, based on the principles of zero trust architecture (discussed in

Chapter 3). Doing so offers reduced attack surface, streamlined policy management, and improved visibility over your networks.

Microsegmentation is a growing practice, with NIST releasing related zero trust architecture guidance in August 2020 and ENISA releasing several microsegmentation-related papers since 2020.

Software-Defined Networking

SDN is an approach to network management that enables a network to be centrally managed (or programmed), offering holistic management across various vendors, applications, and technologies. SDN architectures allow dynamic network configuration and management that improves network performance and gives organizations (most notably cloud providers) a centralized view of their entire network architecture.

SDN separates hardware and hardware-based settings from the network services of data transmission. In other words, SDN abstracts network control from network forwarding capabilities (like routing), creating two layers (infrastructure and control) out of what is traditionally a single function.

These are the three layers of an SDN architecture:

- **Infrastructure layer (data plane):** Network switches and routers and the data itself as well as the process of forwarding data to the appropriate destination

- **Control layer:** The intelligence in devices that works in true intermediary fashion, determining how traffic should flow based on the status of the infrastructure layer and the requirements specified by the application layer

- **Application layer:** Network services, utilities, and applications that interface with the control layer to specify needs and requirements

---

TIP *East-West* is typically used to denote traffic flow within a data center or within a network. *North-South* is commonly used to describe data flow from the outside world (North) to inside the network (South). In SDN terminology, *North* usually refers to the Application plane, while *South* denotes the two layers below it (Control and Infrastructure).

NOTE The three layers of SDN architecture are closely related to the three-plane view that network engineers are familiar with: data, control, and management. These three network planes exist at the circuit level in routers and in the protocols used for managing network traffic.

Using SDN removes the traditional networking concepts of IP addressing, subnets, routing, and the like from needing to be programmed into or deciphered by hosted applications. It also improves the ability to respond to changes in threats, to adapt quickly to dynamic physical and business conditions, and to take advantage of the best available technology (regardless of the vendor).

Of course, using SDN has security implications along with its benefits. With this architecture being so flexible and scalable, it is not uncommon for SDN to be configured incorrectly. The consequence of misconfiguring SDN leads to unexpected flows of network traffic. Traffic intended to be on one area of the network is discovered to be on another part of the network.

Another perceived weakness of SDN is the lack of one common standard or implementation. Again, given its extreme flexibility, the absence of one way of doing things is not a surprise. Still, there are standards. One of the first SDN standards is OpenFlow. OpenFlow started out as a way of defining how the control plane works with the data plane. OpenFlow divides its interaction with the data plane into two separate "directions." OpenFlow works with the switches and routers (whether virtual or physical) through southbound application programming interfaces (APIs). Along the same lines, OpenFlow works with the network's business logic through northbound APIs.

Software-Defined Security

As microsegmentation continues to grow in popularity, new ways of implementing security controls continue to be developed and implemented. *Software-defined security* (SDS) is a security model in which security mechanisms are controlled and managed by security software. SDS is software-managed, policy-driven security that consists of network segmentation, intrusion detection and prevention, user and device identification, application controls, and more. Whereas traditional security architectures may fail to meet the complex security needs of physical infrastructures, SDS enables the implementation and management of more advanced and automated security controls for software-defined networks and environments.

Software-Defined Wide Area Network

Software-defined wide area network (SD-WAN) is an extension of SDN practices to connect to entities spread across the internet to support WAN architecture, especially related to cloud environments. SD-WAN solutions offer an alternative to traditional WAN routers and are agnostic to WAN transport technologies. Much like SDN, SD-WAN decouples the control plane from the data plane. SD-WAN uses software to control connectivity and management of services between data centers and remote networks, such as cloud service providers (CSPs).

According to Gartner, SD-WAN has four characteristics:

- Must support multiple connection types (e.g., internet, MPLS, LTE, etc.)
- Can perform dynamic path selection to support load sharing across WAN connections
- Provides a simple interface for managing the WAN
- Must support VPNs and other third-party services

Virtual eXtensible Local Area Network

Virtual extensible local area network (VXLAN) is a network virtualization technology that uses encapsulation techniques to encapsulate layer 2 Ethernet frames within layer 4 UDP datagrams. VXLAN technology allows network architects to segment their large networks (much like VLANs do) with scale that VLANs cannot support. For example, one can theoretically create as many as 16 million VXLANs in a domain, whereas one can only create a maximum of 4,094 VLANs. This added flexibility for large-scale segmentation allows VXLANs to meet the needs of large multitenant public cloud providers.

Encapsulation

As discussed earlier, encapsulation involves wrapping one protocol around the contents (or payload) of a subsequent protocol. More broadly defined, encapsulation is a method of logically separating functions in a network from their underlying structures (e.g., hardware). All the microsegmentation methods in this section use some form of encapsulation.

TIP   In addition to using encapsulation techniques, microsegmentation zones can be created through the expanded use of firewalls and routers.

Wireless Networks

By eliminating the dependency on cabling to the endpoint, wireless technologies have expanded networking capabilities significantly. Deploying a wireless network is relatively easy and has become the preference in many home and corporate environments. With the rapid growth of IoT adoption, the demand for wireless capabilities is consistently increasing.

Wireless networks face the same vulnerabilities, threats, and risks as any cabled network, but they also have additional security considerations. One of the principal issues with wireless technology is the insecure nature of the technology in the default configuration. For instance, wireless devices are sometimes shipped with default credentials that can be guessed or found on the internet (such as *admin* for the username and *password* for the password). This is acceptable if the recipient changes the credentials or establishes a multifactor authentication process before the device goes into the production environment, but a massive risk if they don't. Wireless networks also face an increased risk of MITM types of eavesdropping and packet sniffing using devices that capture and read data emanating across electromagnetic signals. Recently, with the proliferation of IoT devices, wireless DDoS attacks have become headline-making attacks of disruption. The configuration weaknesses of wireless connected devices permit attackers to insert malicious bots in things like web cameras, intelligent personal assistant devices, and smartphones to create a botnet to send out almost limitless signals to bring down critical services and highly visible web targets.

NOTE When electrons move, they create emanations and a magnetic field. These data emanations can be picked up by devices that scan for them. Attackers use such devices to capture and re-create these emanations elsewhere to reproduce the electron stream on, for example, the attacker's screen. The obvious result is that your data is exposed to the attacker.

Whereas wireless attacks were once limited to wardrivers with cantennas, Wi-Fi and cellular surveillance and attack tools are now readily available and very discreet. Modern wireless networks must be protected against an array of threats that include everything from your organization's janitors conducting radio frequency (RF) mapping.

To be properly prepared to deal with wireless networks, you must understand the standards and protocols that govern wireless technology. You also need to understand the variety of technologies, techniques, and obstacles involved with securing wireless access points (WAPs) and wireless technology in general. This knowledge is essential in preparing to adequately understand how to address wireless attacks. The following sections will examine these topics in more detail.

Wi-Fi

Wi-Fi (or wireless fidelity) is the most common family of wireless protocols today, with Wi-Fi network communications being governed by the IEEE 802.11 family of standards. Evolutions of the standard are published through amendments that document updated versions of the original standard. These are highlighted in Table 4.2, and it should be noted that each version or amendment to the 802.11 standard has offered improved maximum data rates. 802.11x is often used to indicate all of the specific implementations as a collective whole, but that is not preferred over a general reference to 802.11.

TIP Do not confuse 802.11x with 802.1x, which is an authentication technology and not related to wireless.

TABLE 4.2 **802.11 Standard Amendments**

STANDARD	FREQUENCY	MAX DATA RATE
802.11	2.4 GHz	2 Mbps
802.11a	5 GHz	54 Mbps
802.11b	2.4 GHz	11 Mbps
Wi-Fi 3 (802.11g)	2.4 GHz	54 Mbps
Wi-Fi 4 (802.11n)	2.4 GHz and 5 GHz	600 Mbps
Wi-Fi 5 (802.11ac)	5 GHz	3.5 Gbps
Wi-Fi 6 (802.11ax)	2.4 GHz and 5 GHz	9.6 Gbps
Wi-Fi 6E (802.11ax)	6 GHz	9.6 Gbps

NOTE   In April 2020, the U.S. Federal Communications Commission (FCC) voted unanimously to open the 6 GHz band of radio frequency for unlicensed use, which prompted the Wi-Fi alliance to release the revised Wi-Fi 6E standard. The increase from 5 GHz to 6 GHz dramatically increases the amount of airwaves available for routers and smart devices, which greatly reduces signal interference as wireless devices continue to proliferate. As of this writing, a similar release of the 6 GHz frequency band has not been finalized in the European Union (EU), but it is believed to be imminent. Similar decisions are being made on a region-by-region basis, as Brazil recently released the 6 GHz band in February 2021.

Wired Equivalent Privacy and Wi-Fi Protected Access

Wired Equivalent Privacy (WEP) and Wi-Fi Protected Access (WPA) are the two most used encryption standards for Wi-Fi communications. Today, WEP is considered a highly insecure standard and should not be used. WPA continues to evolve, with WPA3 being the current standard that should be used to protect Wi-Fi communications. We introduce WEP, WPA, WPA2, and WPA3 through the remainder of this section.

The IEEE 802.11 standard defines two methods that wireless clients can use to authenticate to WAPs before normal network communications can occur across the wireless link. These two methods are open system authentication (OSA) and shared key authentication (SKA).

- OSA provides no confidentiality or security because no real authentication is required. Communication happens if the radio signal is strong enough to reach a compatible receiver. All OSA transmissions are unencrypted.

- SKA enforces some form of authentication, and if the authentication is not provided, the communication is blocked. The 802.11 standard defines one optional technique for SKA known as Wired Equivalent Privacy (WEP), with subsequent amendments to the original 802.11 standard adding WiFi Protected Access (WPA), WPA2, WPA3, and other technologies. WEP, WPA, and WPA2 should all be moved away from in favor of WPA3, wherever possible.

WEP was designed to protect against eavesdropping for wireless communications. The initial aim of WEP was to provide the same level of protection against MITM attacks that wired networks have. WEP implemented encryption of data in wireless transmissions using a Rivest Cipher 4 (RC4) symmetric stream cipher. Message integrity verification is possible because a hash value is used to verify that received packets weren't modified or corrupted while in transit. It also can be configured to prevent unauthorized access. Knowledge or possession of the encryption key provides a basic form of authentication; without the key, access to the network itself is denied. WEP is used at the two lowest layers of the OSI model: the data link and physical layers. It therefore does not offer end-to-end security. Over time, WEP has been shown to have major security weaknesses. For instance, WEP uses static encryption keys, the same key used by every device on a wireless network. It is possible, therefore, that if an eavesdropper intercepted enough encrypted packets, the key could be deduced. In fact, WEP was cracked almost as soon as it was released. It takes less than a minute to hack through WEP protection, yielding WEP completely useless in wireless security.

To improve wireless security, a group known as Wi-Fi Alliance developed a new encryption standard called WPA. As a replacement for WEP, WPA could be retrofitted to WEP firmware on wireless NICs designed for WEP already in the computing environment. That feature proved to be more problematic than it was worth. The required changes to the WAPs were extensive, and hardware replacement was a better option.

WPA was intended as an interim solution until the IEEE published the promised 802.11i standard (discussed in the following section). That process lingered for years, so WPA was implemented independent of the 802.11 amendment. The WPA protocol implements the Lightweight Extensible Authentication Protocol (LEAP) and Temporal Key Integrity Protocol (TKIP), which support a per-packet key that dynamically generates a new 128-bit key for each packet. WPA negotiates a unique key set with each host. It improves upon the WEP 64-bit or 128-bit encryption key that had to be manually entered on WAPs and devices and did not change.

WPA uses LEAP and TKIP to perform message integrity check, which is designed to prevent an attacker from altering and resending data packets. This replaces the cyclic redundancy check (CRC) that was used by the WEP standard. CRC's main flaw was that it did not provide a sufficiently strong data integrity guarantee for the packets it handled. Researchers have identified a flaw in WPA similar to the weaknesses in WEP. WPA often employs a static yet secret passphrase for authentication. A brute-force attack theoretically can result in a guessed passphrase. The likelihood of a sufficient passphrase (no fewer than 14 characters) succumbing to this attack is low, but not impossible. Collaterally, the message integrity check hash function can then be exploited to retrieve the keystream from short strings of packets to use for injection attacks or spoofing. Basically, attacks specific to WPA — coWPAtty and a GPU-based cracking tool, to name two — have rendered WPA's security unreliable. Both the LEAP and TKIP encryption options for WPA are now considered crackable using a variety of available and easy-to-use cracking techniques.

WPA2 (or IEEE 802.11i)

The next evolution of Wi-Fi security was WPA2, which replaced WPA. Originally, it was meant to replace WEP, but as mentioned, the 802.11i standard lingered, and WPA was implemented independently. This amendment deals with the security issues of the original 802.11 standard. WPA2 is backward compatible to WPA. It provides U.S. government–grade security by implementing the National Institute of Standards and Technology (NIST) FIPS 140-2 compliant AES encryption algorithm and 802.1x-based authentications, and Counter Mode Cipher Block Chaining Message Authentication Code Protocol (CCMP). There are two versions of WPA2: WPA2-Personal and WPA2-Enterprise. WPA2-Personal protects unauthorized network access by utilizing a setup password. WPA2-Enterprise verifies network users through a server using Network Access Control (NAC).

The selection of the name WPA2 is because WPA was already published and in widespread use. However, WPA2 is not the second version of WPA. They are distinct and different. IEEE 802.11i, or WPA2, implemented concepts similar to IPSec to improve encryption and security within the wireless networks.

In late 2018, shortly after the newer WPA3 (discussed next) was announced, researchers identified a weakness in WPA2 that would allow an attacker to steal pre-shared login passwords, eavesdrop on communications, and perform MITM attacks.

WPA3

The Wi-Fi Alliance announced WPA3 as a replacement for WPA2 in January 2018. The newer standard uses 192-bit encryption and individualized encryption for each user. It also offers weak password mitigation and simplified setup processes for devices with no human interface. As of July 2020, any device certified by the Wi-Fi Alliance must support WPA3. As a standard practice, you should check your wireless-enabled devices to determine which Wi-Fi standards are supported. If your network is either WEP or WPA, you must upgrade to a WPA2-compatible or preferably WPA3-compatible router to secure your organization's network.

IEEE 802.1X

WPA, WPA2, and WPA3 support the enterprise authentication known as 802.1X/EAP, a standard NAC that is port-based to ensure client access control to network resources. Effectively, 802.1X is a checking system that allows the wireless network to leverage the existing network infrastructure's authentication services. Through the use of 802.1X, other techniques and solutions such as RADIUS, TACACS, certificates, smart cards, token devices, and biometrics can be integrated into wireless networks providing techniques for multifactor authentication.

Extensible Authentication Protocol

Extensible Authentication Protocol (EAP) is an authentication framework versus a specific mechanism of authentication. EAP facilitates compatibility with new authentication technologies for existing wireless or point-to-point connection technologies. More than 40 different EAP methods of authentication are widely supported. These include the wireless methods of LEAP, EAP-TLS, EAP-SIM, EAP-AKA, and EAP-TTLS. Two significant EAP methods that bear a closer look are Protected Extensible Authentication Protocol (PEAP) and LEAP.

TIP   EAP is not an assurance of security. For example, EAP-MD5 and a prerelease EAP known as LEAP are known to be vulnerable.

Protected Extensible Authentication Protocol

Using a TLS tunnel, PEAP encapsulates EAP methods to provide authentication and, potentially, encryption. Since EAP was originally designed for use over physically isolated channels and hence assumed secured pathways, EAP is usually not encrypted. So, PEAP can provide encryption for EAP methods.

Lightweight Extensible Authentication Protocol

LEAP is a Cisco proprietary alternative to Temporal Key Integrity Protocol (discussed next) for WPA, but it should not be used. An attack tool known as Asleap was released in 2004 that could exploit the ultimately weak protection provided by LEAP. Use of

EAP-TLS is preferred. If LEAP must be used, a complex password is an imperative. LEAP served the purpose of addressing deficiencies in TKIP before the advent of 802.11i/ WPA2.

Temporal Key Integrity Protocol

TKIP was designed as the replacement for WEP without requiring replacement of legacy wireless hardware. TKIP was implemented into the 802.11 wireless networking standards within the guidelines of WPA. TKIP improvements include a key-mixing function that combines the initialization vector (IV) (i.e., a random number) with the secret root key before using that key with RC4 to perform encryption; a sequence counter is used to prevent packet replay attacks, and a strong message integrity check (MIC) is used.

Counter Mode with Cipher Block Chaining Message Authentication Code Protocol

CCMP was created to replace WEP and TKIP/WPA. CCMP uses AES with a 128-bit key. CCMP is the preferred standard security protocol of 802.11 wireless networking indicated by 802.11i. To date, no attacks have yet been successful against the AES/CCMP encryption. CCMP is the standard encryption mechanism used in WPA2 and WPA3.

NOTE   The impact that security requirements can have on business and technology is not trivial. For instance, data encryption and filtering, like WPA3 and IPSec VPN, has to be tested and refined to optimal configurations to minimize any performance degradation.

Securing Wireless Access Points

A wireless access point (WAP), sometimes just referred to as an *access point* (AP), is a networking device that allows wireless-enabled devices to connect to a wired network. WAPs connect directly to a wired LAN and then provides wireless connections into that wired LAN using Wi-Fi or other wireless technologies (e.g., Li-Fi).

This section on how to secure WAPs assumes only that the need for wireless access is there, but no action has been taken to create it. Creating wireless access does not start with placing hardware arbitrarily. The first action to take is to conduct a site survey. A site survey is useful for assessing what, if any, wireless access exists currently. It also helps in planning for the future. Once the survey is complete, decisions on where to place WAPs can be made. This section also covers deciding on the correct type of antennas to broadcast from the chosen hardware.

Configuring your access points comes next. We first examine why the broadcast channels matter. Next, there is discussion on what modes the hardware may be set to, such as whether to centralize the communication or form a type of transmission mesh. Additional consideration is given to how the network is labeled and broadcasted, using *service set identifiers* (SSIDs). Finally, additional methods of securing access are covered, from the low-level filtering of MAC addresses to the higher-level use of captive portals.

Conducting a Site Survey

Site surveys are useful techniques for both identifying rogue APs and defining the placement, configuration, and documentation of APs. They are often required for compliance reasons but should generally be conducted on a periodic basis or whenever your physical environment changes.

Rogue WAPs are WAPs that are installed on an otherwise secure network, but without explicit authorization. These rogue APs make it difficult for organizations to track and monitor their authorized assets, and they also pose security risks to devices that connect and transfer data over them. Sometimes, a rogue AP is implemented by an employee for a perceived access or performance need. Even more concerning are cases where a malicious attacker installs a rogue AP to try to fool end users to connect to it. Such attacks harvest credentials, help launch DDoS attacks, or lead to data theft. It is important for security personnel to conduct searches and scans to be on the lookout for these unwanted devices.

A physical walk-through, or site survey, is a way to discover rogue APs in the physical environment. During the site survey, security personnel investigate the presence, strength, and reach of WAPs deployed in an environment, while looking for unsanctioned signals. As the walk-through is conducted, a normal endpoint client with a wireless NIC can be used to simply detect signals. Another approach is to use one of a variety of wireless intrusion detection devices to scan the environment.

Site surveys also provide operational benefits, as the review helps define optimal placement and configuration and generate documentation for APs. Optimal placement and configuration consist of ensuring sufficient signal strength is available at all locations where access is desired. At the same time, where access is not wanted, like in public areas or outside of the facility, the signal availability should be minimized or eliminated. A site survey is useful for evaluating existing wireless network deployments (such as when there is a change in the external environment), planning expansion of current deployments, and planning for future deployments.

Determining Wireless Access Placement

Using information determined by site surveys, optimal WAP locations can be identified. It is not recommended to commit to specific locations until the placements are informed by the walk-through. Conduct the proper testing of configurations and signal strength

---

with multiple WAPs in place. There will most likely be movements and adjustments in this phase. Once an optimal configuration and location pattern is reached, make the locations permanent.

Here are some general considerations for wireless access placement:

- Use a central location.
- Avoid solid physical obstructions.
- Avoid reflective or other flat metal surfaces.
- Avoid the use of electrical equipment (interference).
- Position external omnidirectional antennas pointing vertically.
- Point a directional antenna toward the area of desired use.

An essential consideration for wireless technology is the impact of the environment on the broadcast signal. Wireless signals are impacted by various types of interference — physical and electromagnetic. Distance and obstructions are physical concerns. Electricity and other radio signals can conflict with or impede the effectiveness of the wireless signals. Network administrators will manipulate directional antennas and tune signal strength to accommodate the physical and electromagnetic obstacles to reach the desired areas of access.

A primary security concern for antennas is understanding how the signal pattern (or *lobe pattern*) extends from the antenna. This is particularly true with directional antennas where the lobe reaches far beyond the typical unidirectional antenna in one focused direction while being attenuated (i.e., reduced) in the other directions. Even without special equipment, one can walk concentric circles around an AP and use a mobile device to measure radiation strength.

Antenna Types

The antenna is an integral component in wireless communication systems. The antenna transforms electrical signals into radio waves, and vice versa. Signal transmission requirements and reception quality dictate the choice of antenna from the various kinds available. Standard antennas can be upgraded to signal-boosting, stronger antennas. Some of the most common types of antennas used are as follows:

- The standard straight, pole-dipole, or vertical antenna sends signals in all directions away from the antenna. This radiation pattern is omnidirectional and is the prevalent type of antenna on base stations and endpoint devices.
- Many other types of antennas are directional. Instead of broadcasting in every direction, the signal is focused to one direction.

There are a few key antenna considerations with regard to securing the wireless network. Most importantly, recognize that directional antennas significantly extend the network's reach in one focused direction. This is the case for both receiving and transmitting. Therefore, care must be taken in pointing directional antennas such that the network's visibility and vulnerabilities are not cast out too far. For choosing antennas and their placement, bear in mind how the broadcast extends well past walls and through floors, particularly when the organization is in a multitenant building.

Wireless Channels

Wireless signals are subdivided within a frequency range in increments called *channels*. These channels are like the lanes on a road or highway. As an example, for the 2.4 GHz frequency, there are 11 channels in the United States, there are 13 in Europe, and there are 17 in Japan. In the United States, the FCC regulates the frequencies and has allocated 11. In the other countries and jurisdictions, the frequencies are regulated by national or the member states' union and explains why there are differences in the number of frequencies.

Normally, a wireless connection is a communication signal between an endpoint client and a WAP. This occurs over a single channel. It is possible to have interference with devices on separate channels when two or more APs are located too closely together or the radio strength of WAPs is too high.

Security professionals should note that channel selection has little to no impact on mitigating wireless risks such as spoofing, jamming, or the visibility of the network. Instead, channels get chosen to minimize the interference between APs or other Wi-Fi networks outside their control.

Infrastructure Mode and Ad Hoc Mode

When deploying wireless networks, WAPs can be deployed in one of two modes: ad hoc or infrastructure. It is generally better to configure WAPs in infrastructure mode rather than ad hoc mode to enforce restrictions supported by the WAPs. Ad hoc mode allows wireless devices to communicate without centralized control. Infrastructure mode prevents the devices or the NICs from interacting directly.

There are four distinct variants of infrastructure mode:

- **Standalone:** A WAP connects multiple wireless clients to each other but not to any wired resources.

- **Wired extension:** The WAP acts as a connection point, or hub, to link the wireless clients to the wired network.

- **Enterprise extended:** Multiple WAPs, all with the same extended service set identifier (ESSID), are used to connect a large physical area to the same wired network. This allows for physical device movement without losing connection to the ESSID.

- **Bridge:** A wireless connection is used to link two wired networks, often used between floors or buildings when running cables or wires is infeasible or inconvenient.

Service Set Identifiers

Anyone who has connected to a wireless network knows to ask for the network name, the technical term for which is SSID. The SSID is that string of characters that identifies the wireless network. It represents the logical wireless network, not the unique AP, as there can be multiple access points to provide coverage for one or multiple SSIDs.

There are two types of SSID, namely, ESSID and basic service set identifier (BSSID). An ESSID is the name of a wireless network in infrastructure mode when a wireless base station or WAP is used. A BSSID is the name of a wireless network when in ad hoc or peer-to-peer mode. In a scenario where multiple different base stations or WAPs are used in infrastructure mode, the BSSID is the MAC address of the base station hosting the ESSID to differentiate multiple base stations in the overall extended wireless network.

In securing the SSID wireless network, regardless of the types, note that the SSID is comparable to the name of a workgroup. When an endpoint client discovers an SSID, the wireless NIC is configured to communicate with the associated closest or strongest WAP. The SSID has secure access features so that discovery does not necessarily equate to access. There are additional steps before the client can communicate, such as enabling encryption and ensuring that discovered SSIDs are legitimate. With enabling encryption, the client is required to enter a password to permit access. Ensuring the legitimacy of the SSIDs that clients might see requires the organization to periodically monitor for rogue access points.

TIP   It is important to reconfigure the SSIDs of new devices before deployment, as many default settings are supplied by the vendor and, therefore, widely known.

A step that can be taken to better secure WAPs is to disable the SSID broadcast of the beacon frame. A *beacon frame* is a special broadcast transmission that the SSID sends regularly from the WAP. Discovery by end-user clients occurs as any wireless NIC finds this radio signal. In fact, with a detect and connect NIC feature, the connection can be automatic. Network administrators can disable, or silence, the broadcast; this is recommended as a security best practice. Disabling SSID broadcast makes connection

COMMUNICATION AND NETWORK SECURITY

Assess and Implement Secure Design Principles in Network Architectures   329 a little more difficult, as the end user must know the SSID address to search. Keeping the beacon off and the SSID hidden is not foolproof. Attackers have tools to discover SSID via wireless sniffer technology to capture SSID information used in transmissions between wireless clients and the WAPs, as the SSID is still needed to direct packets. Disabling SSID is a good first step. Hiding the existence of the network is a best practice, but it is not in itself sufficiently strong security. Not broadcasting the SSID, coupled with using WPA3, will provide a reliable authentication and encryption solution with fewer failed attempts.

Using Captive Portals

Captive portals are authentication safeguards for many wireless networks implemented for public use, such as at hotels, restaurants, bars, airports, libraries, and so on. They are a common practice on wired networks, too. The process is to force a newly connected device to a starting page to establish authorized access. The portal may require input of credentials, payment, or an access code. It is also a good location to publish or provide a link to privacy policies and acceptable use terms and conditions. If end-user consent for tracking and information collection is required, the captive portal allows for that as well. Once the end user satisfies the conditions required by the starting page, only then can they communicate across the network.

NOTE   While captive portals offer some security benefits, they may also pose some security risks. Captive portal authentication provides an easy point of entry for malicious actors seeking entry into a user's device or an organization's network. If a captive portal is compromised, it can be used to automatically load malware or execute unauthorized scripts on a victim's machine. For this reason, it is essential that you routinely monitor and conduct application scanning of your captive portal applications and infrastructure.

MAC Filters

A MAC filter is a list of authorized wireless client MAC addresses that are permitted to access a WAP. Devices not on the list are blocked. The downsides are that the list is difficult to manage and does not scale to large environments with many changes.

There are two approaches to utilizing MAC filters. In one approach, someone, such as a network security analyst or a security professional tasked with securing wireless access, would determine through asset management what devices are permitted to connect. The other approach would be using a software solution such as intrusion detection. Some access point vendors offer such features, including the ability to detect MAC address spoofing to mitigate the risk of someone forging a known whitelisted MAC.

Wireless Attacks

In spite of increasing attention and capability for securing wireless networks, they remain attractive targets for attackers. The types of attacks continue to grow, and many attacks are effective on wired networks as well as wireless ones. Attacks such as packet sniffing, MITM, and password theft are common to both wireless and wired networks and are discussed earlier in the chapter. A few types of attacks focus on wireless networks alone, like signal jamming attacks and a special collection of wireless attacks called *war driving*.

Signal jamming is the malicious activity of overwhelming a WAP to the extent that legitimate traffic can no longer be processed. Even though this is illegal in most places, there are inexpensive jamming products available for sale online.

War driving is a bit of a play on words. The term has roots in a form of attack in the 1980s called *war dialing*, where computers would be used to make large numbers of phone calls searching for modems to exploit. War driving, in contrast, is when someone, usually in a moving vehicle, actively searches for Wi-Fi wireless networks using wireless network scanning tools. These scanning tools and software are readily available and often free. When a wireless network appears to be present, the attacker uses the tools to interrogate the wireless interface or a wireless detector to locate wireless network signals. Once an attacker knows a wireless network is present, they can use sniffers to gather wireless packets for investigation. The next step in the attack is to discover hidden SSIDs, active IP addresses, valid MAC addresses, and even the authentication mechanism the clients use. MITM attacks may progress, or the attackers may conduct advanced attacks with specialized tools, like AirCrack and AirSnort, to attempt to break into the connection and gather additional sensitive information. When using no security protocols or older ones, like WEP and WPA, attackers have very little difficulty being successful.

NOTE   With the advancement of drones and the ability for private citizens to use them, a newer attack vector known as *war droning* is now a threat. Scanning and cracking activities are accomplished with a drone instead of by a person in a vehicle within proximity of the WAP.

War drivers often share the information they gather. Not all war driving attacks are meant to disrupt or be particularly malicious. It is likely the attackers are trying to simply get internet access for free. Using the information obtained from their own tools, they combine data with GPS information about location. Then they publish the information to websites like WiGLE, openBmap, or Geomena. Other people access the maps of various networks to find locations where they can hijack the wireless and access the internet or conduct additional attacks.

War driving is not explicitly prohibited in most countries. Some consider it ethically wrong, but at a high level, it is somewhat analogous to neighborhood mapping in the physical world with house numbers and phone numbers publicly listed. In fact, the reporting of war driving information on the Web could be considered an expanded version of what WAPs are meant to do: broadcast. However, as security professionals know, not all WAPs are broadcasting publicly, as they are hidden.

Li-Fi

Li-Fi (short for light fidelity) is a wireless communication technology that uses light to transmit data. Li-Fi is similar in use to Wi-Fi, except it uses visible, ultraviolet, or infrared light to transfer data, rather than the radio frequency transmission that Wi-Fi technology relies on.

Because Li-Fi uses light for transmission, it cannot transfer data through walls or other physical barriers. As a result, Li-Fi offers a security benefit over Wi-Fi, in that it can be contained within a physical space. Li-Fi is a disruptive technology that is still not widely adopted, as of this writing. Li-Fi's security benefits and speed improvements (roughly 100x the max bandwidth of today's Wi-Fi) have many projecting mass adoption in the near future and even potentially replacing Wi-Fi in the next 10 years.

Bluetooth

Bluetooth is a wireless technology standard that supports point-to-point wireless transmissions over a short distance. In general use, the maximum effective distance is about 30 feet. However, there are industrial or advanced versions of Bluetooth that can reach 300 feet. Many types of endpoint devices support Bluetooth, such as mobile phones, laptops, printers, radios, and digital personal assistants, along with an increasing number of other IoT devices.

One benefit of Bluetooth is that it does not require base stations, as it is a direct connection between devices. It also requires very little power, which is good for use with the battery-operated end devices that typically feature Bluetooth.

There are also a few downsides. The transmission speed is slower than the 802.11b wireless standard. It conflicts and interferes with existing 802.11b and 802.11g networks as it uses the 2.4 GHz broadcasting spectrum, causing problems for endpoint devices relying on the transmissions. Another significant downside is Bluetooth's inherent weakness because of its lack of encryption. Using Bluetooth to create a PAN carries security implications, too, since a PAN most likely has vulnerabilities that are not easily identified by corporate sweeps. The reason is that a PAN is a nonroutable section or extension of an existing LAN or WAN, so it is not easily assessed.

ZigBee

ZigBee is a standard (based on IEEE 802.15.4) for low-cost, low-power, and low-latency wireless communication. ZigBee's protocols were designed to be simpler than other wireless technologies (like Wi-Fi) and used in applications that require short-range, lower-bandwidth data transfer. Common applications include medical data collection, industrial control systems, building automation, home energy monitors, and other home automation uses.

ZigBee's widespread use in IoT applications has brought a lot of scrutiny over its security. The ZigBee standard includes security features such as access control lists (ACLs), frame counters, and encryption (using 128-bit AES keys). Despite these security features, the protocol is not without its flaws, as introduced in the "Smart Lightbulb Hack" sidebar in Chapter 3.

Cellular Networks

Cellular or mobile networks are wireless communications that traverse across cells. The cells are geographically dispersed areas that consist of one or more cell sites or base stations. The cell site or base station is a transceiver fixed to a location. The user of a cell network uses a portable device over a specific set of radio wave frequencies to connect to the cell site and other cellular devices or the internet. The standard descriptors to differentiate cellular technology refer to the generation when the technology was introduced. This can be confusing. For instance, 4G and 5G mean fourth- and fifth-generation, respectively. It does not indicate a specific frequency or signal strength. Table 4.3 provides an overview of the most recent wireless technologies.

TABLE 4.3 **Basic Overview of Cellular Wireless Technologies**

GENERATION	3G	4G	5G
Timeline	2002 to 2005	2010 to present	2018 to present
Messaging features	Graphics and formatted text	Full unified messaging	Full unified messaging
Data support	Packet switched	Native IPv6	Native IPv6
Target data rate	2 Mbps	1 Gbps	20 Gbps

While 4G has been the leading cellular technology available since about 2010, 5G technology made its limited debut in 2018 and has seen dramatic growth since 2020. The key difference between 4G and 5G is the tenfold increase in speed provided by the latter. This dramatic speed increase brings new applications to cellular technology and is projected to further advance the growth of IoT technologies in the near future. More internet-connected devices with greater capabilities means greater attack surface and must be a consideration for CISSPs moving forward.

A security professional should keep some important considerations in mind when it comes to supporting and securing information sent and received in a cellular wireless network. Since 2G, cellular use has been used for much more than just voice. Cell phones today (smartphones) have higher-level computing power to run applications, transmit text, send images, stream video, and store significant amounts of sensitive data. For these reasons, communications that need to be secured will need additional technical controls in place. Cellular transactions are not inherently secure. There are numerous tools available for attackers to intercept wireless transmissions. A common attack scenario uses cell base stations to conduct MITM traffic capture. These attacks can take place whether the cellular connections are to the internet or just between two or more mobile devices. As a CISSP, you should consider these threats when developing or managing your organization's bring your own device (BYOD) policies.

Content Distribution Networks

A content distribution network (CDN), also called a *content delivery network*, is a collection of resource services, proxy servers, and data centers that are geographically distributed. The nature of the architecture model is to provide the low latency, high performance, and high availability of content, especially multimedia, e-commerce, and social networking sites across a large (often national or continental) area. Content is acquired as near to the requesting customer as possible, which results in the lower latency and greater throughput.

CDN content is distributed among many data hosts, not centralized in one location. While this positively affects availability, given that content distribution mitigates the impact of any one location going offline, the distribution of content among many hosts can also negatively affect confidentiality.

Organizations concerned with regulatory compliance must also be mindful of how content distribution affects their compliance requirements. Many CDNs provide licensed access to content through a variety of subscriptions or fees for service models, and protecting that licensed content as well as ensuring its legal crossing of borders can be an issue. Naturally, as data is stored or processed across multiple jurisdictions, the CDN and its users must be aware of how local regulations affect their business and their customers.

NOTE Examples of CDN service providers include Akamai, CloudFlare, Azure CDN, Amazon CloudFront, Verizon, and Level 3 Communications. The fact that many of the examples are CSPs is not accidental. The capabilities of cloud computing are often leveraged in a complex CDN, although a CDN does not necessarily have to be in a cloud environment.

SECURE NETWORK COMPONENTS

One of the most foundational concepts that you must understand, as a security professional, is how to securely operate and maintain network components. This section begins with an introduction to the key concepts associated with operating network hardware, followed by coverage of network transmission media and network components (such as firewalls, routers, and switches), ending with some foundational coverage of endpoint security. As a CISSP, you should have a general understanding of security concepts related to different types of network components, and this section covers those topics.

Operation of Hardware

Network hardware, such as routers, switches, and firewalls (all discussed in the following sections) must be securely implemented, operated, and maintained. Secure and proper operation of network hardware includes the following concepts:

- **Standards, policies, and procedures:** Your organization should establish standards that document a secure baseline for your hardware devices, policies that guide how you operate and manage these devices, and procedures that formalize routine operation processes to support consistent device management.

- **Training:** Network administrators and other personnel who manage or operate hardware should be trained on proper and secure operation, before they receive access to such devices and on a routine basis (e.g., annually).

- **Change Management:** Configurations, patches, and other changes should be properly documented and follow your organization's standard change management procedures.

- **Redundant power:** Redundant power should be deployed to critical network infrastructure to ensure availability in the event of an outage.

- **Monitoring:** Network devices should be monitored for failure, anomalies, or other security-related events.

- **Warranty and support:** Your organization should maintain a current and active warranty on all network devices to provide coverage in the event of a system malfunction. When necessary, you should have access to vendor or third-party support to help troubleshoot common or rare hardware issues.

There are several network devices that you are likely familiar with, and the remainder of this section covers the key ones. First, it's important to establish working definitions of a few key networking terms: data collision, broadcast domain, and collision domain.

- A *data collision* occurs if two systems transmit simultaneously, attempting to use the network medium at the same time, with the effect that one or both messages may be corrupted.

- A *broadcast domain* is a logical division of a computer network, in which all nodes can reach each other by broadcast at the data link layer (layer 2). The broadcast originates from one system in the group and is sent to all other systems within that group.

- A *collision domain* consists of all the devices connected using a shared media where a collision can happen between devices at any time.

With respect to the OSI model, collision domains are divided by using any data link layer (layer 2) or higher device, and broadcast domains are divided by using any network layer (layer 3) or higher device. When a domain is divided, it means that systems on opposite sides of the deployed device are members of different domains.

Firewalls

A firewall is used to prevent unauthorized data flow from one area of the network to another. Firewalls create a boundary that could be between a private network and the internet or between two parts of a private network. In any case, a firewall creates a boundary and is employed to prevent or allow traffic from moving across that boundary.

The capabilities of a firewall can be accomplished with software, hardware, or both. Data coming into and out of the private network or internal segments must pass through the firewall. The firewall examines and inspects each packet and blocks those that do not match specified security criteria. These activities and some other network events are captured on firewall logs. Reviewing and auditing of logs are extremely valuable security processes that security professionals use for incident detection and response, forensic analysis, and improvement of the performance of the security assets.

The term *firewall* is used because the networking versions have a function similar to that of a firewall in a physical structure. A firewall in a building is a barrier meant to prevent or delay the spread of an actual fire. However, unlike a building firewall that suppresses all fire, a firewall in a network environment is designed to permit approved traffic to transit between two environments and prevent unauthorized or unwanted traffic, or attempts for users and entities, to transit between environments.

For the network perimeter, firewalls are considered the first line of protection as part of an overall layered security architecture. Elsewhere, firewalls, as noted earlier, are used to establish a boundary for any area and to separate and control traffic flow across that boundary. They are foundational to networking and one of the most prevalent security technologies used to protect information systems and networks. In terms of security due diligence, firewalls are essential. However, firewalls alone are not enough. For instance, they do not provide capabilities for authentication. Other types of devices and techniques are needed to complement firewalls. Without other devices and technologies in the security portfolio, firewalls become a single point of failure.

NOTE The expression "behind the firewall" describes traffic that flows within a subnet. Firewalls govern traffic from one subnet to another and do not protect from malicious data or software within the subnet.

Firewalls require configuration and human management, which is why security professionals must understand how to best use them. They do not automatically provide benefit. Besides any technical vulnerabilities that may be found, configuration and oversight in firewall management help mitigate the risk of human error and misconfiguration. Security professionals have to configure filtering rules that define permitted traffic.

Also important is how a firewall acts when it fails. If a firewall ceases to operate properly (for example, if it becomes overwhelmed), then the firewall optimally should fail "closed"; this means the firewall should not allow *any* packets through. To make sure the rules remain in place, the firewall must be protected against unauthorized change, and configurations must be kept current over time. Like any other device or endpoint, firewalls have vulnerabilities to be patched, and security professionals also oversee firewall patching and upgrade procedures.

One of the most important roles of a security professional is to use the activity logs generated by firewalls. The logs should be analyzed for several types of events. Here are a few examples:

- The reboot or restart of a firewall
- Failure to start or a device crashing
- Changes to the firewall configuration file
- A configuration or system error while the firewall is running
- Unusual probes for access on ports
- Unsuccessful logins on devices

TIP Although the term can be used in other contexts about access control, the list of rules that govern a firewall is usually referred to as its *access control list* (ACL). An ACL contains rules for authorized ports, protocols, list of permissions, IP addresses, URLs, and other variables to establish acceptable traffic.

Along with where a firewall is positioned on a network, how they process and interrogate data differentiates types of firewalls. The principle of defense in depth applies here too. None of the different types of firewalls is sufficient alone; a combination is almost always required.

Along with the variety of traditional firewalls that exist, there is the more recent next-generation firewall. There are also special firewalls such as multihomed and bastion firewalls. The following sections explore each of these, as well as firewall deployment architectures.

Types of Firewalls

There are four basic types of firewalls:

- Static packet filtering firewalls
- Application-level firewalls
- Stateful inspection firewalls
- Circuit level firewalls

The key differentiator between all four firewall types is the OSI model layer at which each operates.

Static Packet Filtering Firewalls

The first, a static packet filtering firewall, is the earliest and the simplest of firewall designs. Also called a *screening router*, the packet filtering firewall is the fastest design. Operating at the OSI model's network layer (layer 3), it inspects each packet. If a packet breaks the established rules, the packet is dropped and/or logged. Able to work most quickly, a packet filtering firewall will mitigate the risk of a particular packet type. This type of firewall offers no authentication mechanism and can be vulnerable to spoofing.

Application-Level Firewalls

An application-level firewall examines packets and network traffic with much more scrutiny than do packet filtering firewalls. Operating at the higher OSI model application layer (layer 7), an application-level firewall seeks to identify what kind of application traffic wants to cross the boundary. Often used as a separator between end users and the external network, the application-level firewall functions as a proxy. Deep inspection takes time, making this firewall the slowest of all types.

Stateful Inspection Firewalls

The stateful inspection firewall has one primary differentiating factor from a simple packet filtering firewall: a stateful firewall monitors the state of network connections. This firewall operates at the network and transport layers of the OSI model (layers 3 and 4, respectively).

The connection state is based on how TCP operates and how TCP establishes a session through the three-way handshake discussed earlier in this chapter. That state is kept track of, and other connection attributes (such as destination and source details) are saved temporarily in memory. Over time, these details are used to smartly apply filters.

Circuit-Level Firewalls

The circuit-level firewall is functionally simple and efficient, operating most like a stateful inspection firewall. The primary difference is that this firewall works only at the session layer (layer 5) of the OSI model. For a circuit-level firewall, the only task is to ensure that the TCP handshaking is complete. No actual packet is inspected, nor would any individual packet be dropped. Traffic coming through a circuit-level firewall will appear as if it originated from the gateway, since the circuit level firewall's big benefit is to verify the session, while masking any details about the protected network.

Next Generation Firewalls

The previous four types of firewalls represent the span from the earliest to the most well-established firewall technology. But there is the next-generation firewall, often referred to as the *next-gen firewall* (NGFW). The NGFW combines the traditional features of those earlier four with the advanced features of other network-based security devices such as an intrusion detection system (IDS) or intrusion prevention system (IPS). In the context of the OSI model, a next-generation firewall operates at multiple levels.

Multihomed Firewalls

Multihomed describes a firewall having two or more network interfaces. These firewalls use a set of software-defined rules to determine what traffic can pass between networks it is connected to, minimizing the risk of data being inadvertently exchanged between the two networks.

Bastion Host/Screened Host

A bastion host is so named for its resemblance to the medieval structure used as a first-layer protection guard house at the entry of a castle. In computing, a *bastion host* is a special-purpose type of firewall or host computer positioned logically behind the services of a core network routing device or in a DMZ. That router separates the internal, private network from an untrusted network, which can be the internet.

The terms *bastion hosts* and *screened hosts* are used interchangeably. They are also sometimes referred to as *jump hosts* (or *jump boxes*). They act as a proxy, as the only device reachable from external sources. The bastion host adds a layer of protection by concealing the identities of the internal nodes.

A bastion host will have a limited number of applications, usually only one, to limit the possible impact of host compromise. Most commonly, the application is a proxy server to facilitate services and encapsulate data through the bastion host.

Firewall Deployment Architectures

A screened subnet is a combination of bastion hosts. The basic architecture distinctly separates public and private segments. On the private intranet, the local computers and system are located behind a protective device or application, screening them from public access. On the other segment, public services like web servers and proxy servers are accessible. The subnets are helpful for increased security and can improve performance in data throughput.

In today's complex computing environment, a single firewall in line between the untrusted and the private networks is almost always insufficient. There are some basic implementations for a firewall connected to a router to direct traffic to the internet. However, it is best practice to eliminate the reliance on a single firewall.

To improve protection among and between subnets and externally to untrusted networks, organizations use multiple firewalls in combination. Figure 4.8 illustrates an example of a hybrid deployment of firewalls at different networking tiers of a private LAN.

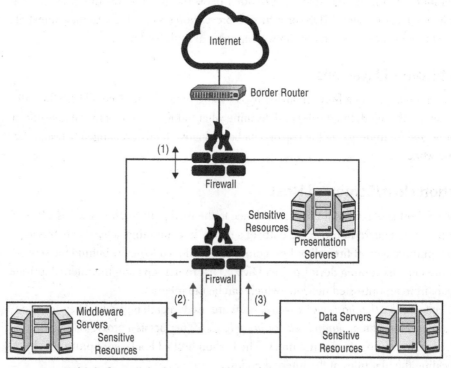

FIGURE 4.8 **Multiple firewall deployment architecture**

Today, traditional firewall models are not the steadfast solution that they once were. Cloud services have been disruptive to the typical firewall architecture. While firewall models and architectures have been around for years, cloud services are now common, and corporate dependency on the cloud dictates how protected network traffic moves through the public internet. One solution is using what Amazon Web Services (AWS) calls *security groups*. Virtual Private Cloud (VPC) security groups act as a virtual, stateful firewall for your Amazon Elastic Compute Cloud (Amazon EC2) instance to control inbound and outbound traffic.

Another approach is offering a firewall as a service (FWaaS), much like CSPs offer software as a service (SaaS). With FWaaS, filtering or screening packets is done virtually and offsite. FWaaS obviously requires more than your average trust in the CSP, but its benefits include dedicated management in terms of updates, configuration, and enforcing your agreed-upon rules and policies.

SDN also presents disruption to traditional firewall architectures. SDN makes managing a network more flexible. This is largely seen as a feature and an advantage for network engineers. However, SDN also makes maintaining firewall requirements more fluid, which can be a disadvantage. Again, SDN and cloud services have significantly affected how firewall services can be implemented, and you should take time to understand how these services work, if your organization uses them.

Repeaters, Concentrators, and Amplifiers

Repeaters, concentrators, and amplifiers operate at the physical layer (layer 1). These simple devices serve to extend the maximum length a signal can travel over a specific media type. They connect network segments that use the same protocol and are used to connect systems that are part of the same collision domain or broadcast domain.

Hubs

Hubs, also known as multiport repeaters, are a physical layer (layer 1) technology. They work only with interconnected systems using the same protocol, in the same domain. They simply repeat inbound traffic over all outbound ports to make the devices act like a single network segment. Because they offer little security-related capability, they are typically prohibited in organizations and are replaced with switches. Hubs are mainly a legacy technology that have little modern use.

TIP   The IEEE 802.3 Ethernet standard expresses disapproval for connecting network segments by repeaters or hubs due to their limited support for security.

Bridges

Bridges operate at the data link layer (layer 2). A bridge forwards traffic from one network to another. Unlike repeaters, which just forward received signals, bridges direct signals based on knowledge of MAC addressing. If a network uses the same protocol, a bridge can be used even if the networks differ in topologies, cabling types, and speeds. A buffer is used to store packets, using a store and forward capability until the packets can be released if the networks have differing speeds. Systems on either side of a bridge are part of the same broadcast domain but are in different collision domains.

Some bridges use a spanning tree algorithm (STA) to prevent bridges from forwarding traffic in endless loops, which can result in broadcast storms. STAs are an intelligent capability for bridges to prevent looping, establish redundant paths in case of a single bridge failure, uniquely identify bridges, assign bridge priority, and calculate the administrative costs of each pathway.

NOTE   Watch for broadcast storms on bridges, which can degrade network bandwidth and performance. The broadcast storms can happen when bridges are forwarding all traffic and become overwhelmed.

Switches

To combat the weaknesses of using hubs, switches are a better choice. A switch is an intelligent hub that operates at primarily the data link layer (layer 2), meaning the switch handles systems on the same broadcast domain, but different collision domains. However, switches with routing capabilities can operate at the network layer (layer 3), providing both are in different broadcast and collision domains.

Able to comprise a level of addressing intelligence for destination systems, switches can discriminate and forward traffic only to the devices that need to receive it. Switches also provide efficient traffic delivery, create separate collision domains, and improve the overall throughput of data where the segments operate on the same protocol.

Switches can create separate broadcast domains when used to create VLANs. The switch segments the network into VLANs, and broadcasts are handled within the VLAN. To permit traffic across VLANs, a router would have to be implemented; switches cannot accomplish this distribution.

Switches provide security services that other devices cannot. They look deeper into packets and can make granular traffic distribution decisions. By establishing and governing the VLANs, switches help to make it harder for attackers to sniff network traffic. Broadcast and collision information is contained, so the valuable network traffic is not continually traveling through the network.

Routers

Routers are network layer (layer 3) devices. A router connects discrete networks using the same protocol, whereby a data packet comes in from one host on the first network, and the router inspects the IP address information in the packet header and determines the destination and best path. The router is able to decide the best logical path for the transmission of packets based on a calculation of speed, hops, preference, and other metrics. A router has programmed routing tables or routing policies. These tables can be statically defined or manually configured. The other way the routing tables can be created and managed is dynamically through adaptive routing. A router has the ability to determine as it processes data how to best forward the data. The router can select and use different routes or given destinations based on the up-to-date conditions of the communication pathways within the interconnections. When a temporary outage of a node is present, the router can direct around the failed node and use other paths.

As previously mentioned, there are numerous dynamic routing protocols, including BGP, OSPF, and RIP. It should be noted that static routing and dynamic routing are best used together. Sometimes dynamic routing information fails to be exchanged, and static routes are used as a backup. Systems on either side of a router are part of different broadcast domains and different collision domains.

Gateways

An important function of a gateway device is that it connects networks that are using different network protocols. They may be hardware devices or software applications, and they operate at the application layer (layer 7), but arguably also at the presentation layer (layer 6, where formats change). The gateway device transforms the format of one data stream from one network to a compatible format usable by the second network. Because of this functionality, gateways are also called *protocol translators*. Another distinction, gateways connect systems that are on different broadcast and collision domains. There are many types of gateways, including data, mail, application, secure, and internet. Gateways are also commonly used when transitioning from a cloud-hosted virtual network to a physical world (or on-premises) system.

Proxies

A proxy is a form of gateway that performs as a mediator, filter, caching server, and even address translation server for a network. However, they do not translate across protocols. A proxy performs a function or requests a service on behalf of another system and connects network segments that use the same protocol.

NOTE SOCKS is a protocol used for networking through a proxy server. SOCKSv5 is the current protocol version that also provides authentication. While SOCKS as a protocol does not provide encryption, if the server employing it does, then SOCKS facilitates its use. It can be used with almost any application.

A common use of a proxy is to function as a NAT server. NAT provides access to the internet to private network clients while protecting those clients' identities. When a response is received, the proxy server determines which client it is destined for by reviewing its mappings and then sends the packets on to the client. NAT allows one set of IP addresses to be used for traffic within a private network and another set of IP addresses for outside traffic.

NOTE Systems on either side of a proxy are part of different broadcast domains and different collision domains.

Proxies can help maintain the security of your organization's internal network by keeping your network structure secret from external parties. They can also help anonymize web traffic, which supports confidentiality and privacy. Due to their role as security devices and because of their typical location on a network (i.e., between two zones of different security levels), maintaining the security of your proxy servers (e.g., through system hardening and strong access controls) is critical.

LAN Extenders

A LAN extender is a multilayer switch used to extend a network segment beyond the distance limitation specified in the IEEE 802.3 standard for a particular cable type. It can also be implemented as a WAN switch, WAN router, repeater, or amplifier.

Wireless Access Points

WAPs operate at the data link layer (layer 2). A wireless router is similar to a wired router in a network in that it also interrogates and determines the pathway and destination for a packet it receives. The wireless router also acts as an access point into the wireless network or wired network in integrated networks. However, the utility in wireless routers is their ability to allow portable endpoints (for example, notebooks, laptops, and smartphones) to access the network. Wireless routers can operate on the 2.4 GHz and 5 GHz bands simultaneously in a multiband configuration and provide data transfer rates of more than 300 Mbps on the 2.4 GHz band and 450 Mbps on the 5 GHz band. WAPs are discussed in detail earlier in the chapter in the "Wireless Networks" section and its subsections.

Transmission Media

There is more to securing a network than just implementing the hardware devices and software applications. In this section, we discuss the physical media that connect the various nodes within various networks.

Local Area Network Technologies

The most widely used LAN technologies are Ethernet and wireless LAN using IEEE 802.11. As a security professional, you should concentrate on understanding them. The differences between LAN technologies exist at and below the data link layer.

Ethernet

Ethernet is based on the IEEE 802.3 standard and is the most common LAN technology in use. It is so popular because it allows low-cost network implementation and is easy to understand, implement, and maintain. Ethernet is also applicable and flexible for use in a wide variety of network topologies. It is most commonly deployed with star or bus topologies. Another strength of Ethernet is that it can support two-way, full-duplex communications using twisted-pair cabling. Ethernet operates in two layers of the OSI model, the physical layer (layer 1) and the data link layer (layer 2). The protocol data unit for Ethernet is a frame.

Ethernet is a shared-media, or broadcast, LAN technology. As a reminder, broadcast and collision domains were introduced and defined earlier in this chapter. As a quick refresher, Ethernet as a broadcast technology allows numerous devices to communicate over the same medium. Ethernet supports collision detection and avoidance native to the attached networking devices. The design of an Ethernet LAN has network nodes and interconnecting media or links.

Ethernet is categorized by data transfer rate and distance. Some data rates for operation over optical fibers and twisted-pair cables are as follows:

- **Fast Ethernet:** Fast Ethernet refers to an Ethernet network that can transfer data at a rate of 100 Mbps.

- **Gigabit Ethernet:** Gigabit Ethernet delivers a data rate of 1,000 Mbps (1 Gbps).

- **10 Gigabit Ethernet:** 10 Gigabit Ethernet is the recent generation and delivers a data rate of 10 Gbps (10,000 Mbps). It is generally used for backbones in high-end applications requiring high data rates.

TIP   Data rates are often measured in megabits per second (Mbps), sometimes represented as Mbits/s. Note that Mbps as a rate differs from megabytes per second (MBps), sometimes represented as Mbytes/s. To convert data rates, know that there are 8 bits per byte and thus 80 Mbps/s is equivalent to 10 MBps.

Wireless LAN

Wireless LAN technology (Wi-Fi) follows the IEEE 802.11 standard and has ushered in a significant amount of mobility and flexibility in networking operations. There are two basic modes of Wi-Fi. In infrastructure mode, mobile APs, like laptops, connect via WAPs or wireless routers with APs. The connections serve as an entry point or bridge to a wired private network or directly to an internet connection. In ad hoc mode, mobile units transmit directly with each other or in a peer-to-peer interconnection.

TIP In Wi-Fi network design and implementation, encryption of the signal is important, as the communications are across a more open medium than a wired LAN. The encryption standards and their evolution to the present day are described earlier in this chapter (see the "Wireless Networks" section).

Network Cabling

Network cabling describes the connection of devices, hardware, or components via one or more types of physical data transmission medium. There are many types that exist, and each has particular specifications and capabilities. Which cabling is used in a network depends on physical and data requirements. Putting the correct network cabling in place is important, as cabling failures are among the most common causes of network malfunction. For instance, some types of network cabling have distance or span limitations and may not provide sufficient reach and availability of data across wide geographical areas. The security professional must consider the security impact of network cable selection, for instance the ease with which a potential adversary could wiretap copper network cabling as opposed to glass fiber.

Coaxial Cable

Coaxial cable, also called *coax*, was a popular networking cable type used throughout the 1970s and 1980s. In the early 1990s, its use as a data cable quickly declined because of the popularity and capabilities of twisted-pair wiring (explained in more detail later), but it is still widely employed for analog transmission. Coaxial cable has a center core of copper wire as an inner conductor surrounded by an insulating layer, surrounded by a conducting shield. There are some coaxial cables that have an additional insulating outer sheath or jacket.

Coax enables two-way communications because the center copper core and the braided shielding layer act as two independent conductors. The shielding design of coaxial cable makes it fairly resistant to electromagnetic interference (EMI) and less susceptible to leakage. Coax handles weak signals very well, especially as it can carry a signal over longer distances than twisted pair. Twisted pair is now preferred simply because it is less costly and easier to install. Coaxial cable requires the use of special tools, called *segment terminators*. Twisted-pair cabling does not. Coaxial cable is bulkier and has a larger minimum arc radius than twisted pair. The arc radius is the maximum distance the cable can be bent without damaging the internal conductors. Bending the coax beyond the minimum arc is, however, a relatively common cause of coaxial cabling failures.

Baseband and Broadband Cables

There is a naming convention used to label most network cable technologies, and it follows the pattern XXyyyyZZ. XX represents the maximum speed the cable type offers, such as 10 Mbps for a 10Base2 cable. The next series of letters, yyyy, represents whether it is baseband or broadband cable, such as baseband for a 10Base2 cable. Most networking cables are baseband cables. However, when used in specific configurations, coaxial cable can be used as a broadband connection, such as with cable modems. ZZ either represents the maximum distance the cable can be used or acts as shorthand to represent the technology of the cable, such as the approximately 200 meters for 10Base2 cable (actually 185 meters, but it's rounded up to 200) or T or TX for twisted pair in 10Base-T or 100Base-TX.

EMI is a key security implication when dealing with cabling. As the name implies, EMI is when an electromagnetic field interferes with the object's performance or functionality. The amount of EMI or its impact on the cabling naturally depends on the type of cabling. Table 4.4 shows the important characteristics for the most common network cabling types.

TABLE 4.4 **Important Characteristics for Common Network Cabling Types**

TYPE	MAX SPEED	DISTANCE	DIFFICULTY OF INSTALLATION	SUSCEPTIBILITY TO EMI	COST
10Base2	10 Mbps	185 meters	Medium	Medium	Medium
10Base5	10 Mbps	500 meters	High	Low	High
10Base-T (UTP)	10 Mbps	100 meters	Low	High	Very Low
STP	155 Mbps	100 meters	Medium	Medium	High
100Base-T/100Base-TX	100 Mbps	100 meters	Low	High	Low
1000Base-T	1 Gbps	100 meters	Low	High	Medium
Fiber-optic	2+ Gbps	2+ kilometers	Very high	None	Very high

Twisted Pair

As mentioned, twisted-pair cabling has become a preferred option because it is extremely thin and flexible versus the bulkiness of coaxial cable. All types of twisted pair are made up of four pairs of wires that are twisted around each other and then sheathed in a PVC insulator. There are two types of twisted pair, shielded twisted pair (STP), and unshielded twisted pair (UTP). STP has a metal foil wrapper around the wires underneath the external sheath. The foil provides additional protection from external EMI. UTP lacks the foil around the sheath. UTP is most often used to refer to 10Base-T, 100Base-T, or 1000Base-T, which are now considered outdated and are not used.

UTP and STP are both a collection of small copper wires that are twisted in pairs, which helps to guard against interference from external radio frequencies and electric and magnetic waves. The arrangement also reduces interference between the pairs themselves. The interference is called *crosstalk* and happens when data transmitted over one set of wires is pulled into another set of wires because the electric signal radiates electromagnetic waves that leak through the sheathing. To combat this, each twisted pair is twisted at a different rate, measured in twists per inch. The staggered twists prevent the signal or electromagnetic radiation from escaping from one pair of wires to another pair.

Conductors

The reason cabling is built upon copper wiring is because copper is one of the best materials to use for carrying electronic signals. It is also cost-effective and performs well at room temperature. Even though copper can carry signals a far distance, there is some resistance in the metal, so the signal strength does eventually degrade.

Fiber-optic cable provides an alternative to conductor-based network cabling over copper. Fiber-optic cables transmit pulses of light rather than electricity. This gives fiber-optic cable the advantage of being extremely fast and nearly impervious to tapping and interference. Fiber-optic cables can also transmit over a much longer distance before attenuation degrades the signal. The drawbacks are the relative difficultly to install and the initial expense of the line. The security and performance fiber-optic offers comes at a steep price.

Additional Cabling Considerations

Using more than four repeaters in a row is discouraged. The 5-4-3 rule has been developed to guide proper use of repeaters and concentrators to maximize cable lengths and remove as many attenuation problems as possible.

The 5-4-3 rule outlines a deployment strategy for repeaters and concentrators in segments arranged in a tree topology with a central hub, or trunk, connecting the segments, like the branches of a tree. In this configuration, between any two nodes on the network, the following must be true:

- There can be a maximum of five segments.
- The segments can be connected by a maximum of four repeaters and concentrators.
- Only three of those five segments can have additional or other user, server, or networking device connections.

TIP   The 5-4-3 rule *does not* apply to switched networks or the use of bridges or routers.

Network Topologies

The topology of a computer network is the structure and arrangement of the various nodes and their connections depicted as links between the nodes. The model can be described as a logical or physical design. Logical topology describes how the data flows on the network. Physical topology is the actual placement of the various components of a network. The physical topology is not always the same as the logical topology. The physical topology of networks has four basic variations: ring, bus, star, and mesh.

Ring Topology

In a ring topology, devices are connected, and data packets are transferred in a unidirectional circular loop pattern. The points are connected to make a circle. Figure 4.9 provides a basic illustration. Data is transmitted one system at a time, and if one system is down, the entire network is broken. A digital token is passed around the circle so that a system that needs to send out information can grab it. Only with the token can a system transmit data. When the data is sent, the token goes with the packet.

Each system on the ring is watching for the traffic. If a system registers as the intended recipient, it accepts and reads the data. If the system is not the intended recipient, it releases the token and data packet to the circle. The intended recipient releases the token but retains the data packet. The token is once again sent along the ring from system to system, searching for the next node that needs to send data.

This topology is seldom used today because it is not scalable to large organizations. However, in smaller networks, ring topology is efficient because a central server is not required to distribute traffic, and data transfer is relatively fast.

NOTE   In some ring topologies, a dual or redundant ring is constructed to prevent single node failure taking the entire network down.

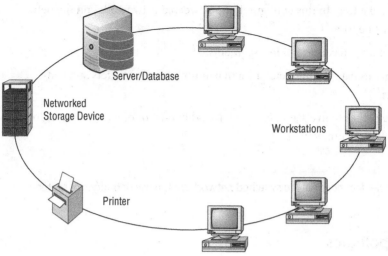

FIGURE 4.9 **Ring topology**

Bus Topology

Each node or system in a bus topology is connected by a single line or backbone cable. Unlike a ring topology, the bus configuration does experience data collisions, as multiple systems can transmit at the same time. The bus topology does have a collision avoidance capability because a system can listen to the cabling to determine whether there is traffic. When a system hears traffic, it waits. When it no longer hears traffic, it releases the data onto the cabling medium. All systems on the bus topology can hear the network traffic. A system that is not intended to be the recipient simply ignores the data. The bus topology, like the ring topology, has a single point of failure. If the bus is disconnected from a segment, the segment is down. However, within the segment, nodes can still reach each other.

The types of bus topology are linear and tree. Figure 4.10 shows a basic illustration of each. A linear bus topology employs a single trunk or main line (called the *backbone*) with all systems directly connected to it. The tree topology also has the backbone, but several segments to connected devices span from the backbone like branches on a tree. A bus topology is terminated at both ends of the network. That feature renders the bus topology impractical in modern interconnected networks.

Star Topology

In a star topology, the connected devices are attached to a central traffic management device, which is either a hub or a switch. Figure 4.11 shows how a dedicated line is run from each device to the central hub or switch. A benefit of star topology is that there is segment resiliency; if one link goes down, the rest of the network is still functional. Cabling is more efficiently used, and damaged cable is easier to detect and remediate.

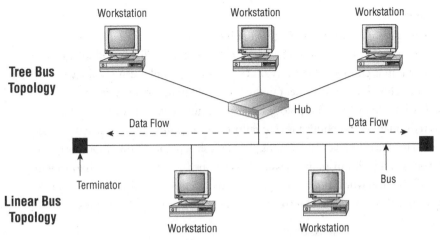

Tree Bus
Topology

Linear Bus
Topology

FIGURE 4.10 **Linear bus and tree bus topologies**

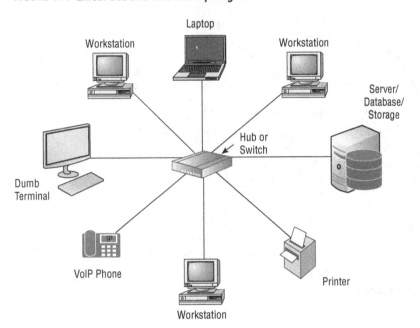

FIGURE 4.11 **Star topology**

Various logical configurations of a bus or ring topology can result in a star topology. An Ethernet network can be deployed as a physical star because it is based on a bus. The hub or switch device in this case is actually a logical bus connection device. A physical star pattern can be accomplished with a multistation access unit (also known as a media access unit, or MAU). An MAU allows for the cable segments to be deployed as a star while internally the device makes logical ring connections.

Mesh Topology

Putting it all together, a mesh topology is the interconnection of all the systems on a network across a number of individual paths. The concept of a full mesh topology means that every system is connected to every other system. A partial mesh topology stops short of total connection but does connect many systems to many other systems.

The key benefit of a mesh topology is the maximum levels of resiliency it provides, as redundant connections prevent failures of the entire network when one segment or device fails. The key disadvantage of a mesh topology is the disproportionate added expense and administrative hassle. This can be best appreciated when viewing Figure 4.12. It's also worth noting that the added cost and administration could lead to a security implication by virtue of resource strain and sheer network complexity.

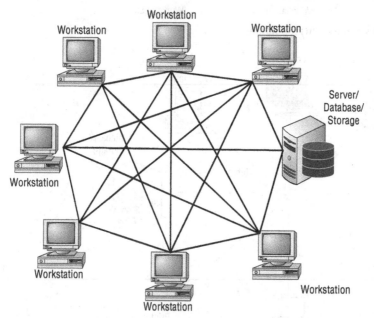

FIGURE 4.12 **Mesh topology**

Network Access Control

NAC solutions provide added security for your internal network infrastructure by enforcing security policies across all users and devices. NAC solutions are used to unify endpoint security methods (such as antivirus, host intrusion prevention, and vulnerability assessment), user or system authentication, and network security enforcement. NAC devices are designed to handle large enterprise networks that include a wide range of devices and technologies, making them particularly useful as mobile devices and IoT continue to proliferate.

There are several basic goals for the use of NAC:

- Mitigation of non-zero-day attacks

- Authentication and authorization of network connections

- Post-authentication role-based control of users and devices

- Encryption of traffic to the wireless and wired network using protocols for 802.1X such as EAP-TLS, EAP-PEAP or EAP-MSCHAP (EAP, CHAP, and other authentication protocols are introduced later in this chapter, in the "Remote Access" section.)

- Enforcement of network policy to prevent endpoints from network access if they lack up-to-date security patches or required configurations

- Ability to control access to the network based on device type and user roles

- Identity and access management based on authenticated user identities instead of just blocking IP addresses

When an unauthorized or suspicious device or user attempts to access the network, properly configured NAC automatically detects and responds instantly to block access and prevent attacks. The policies for NAC should be applied consistently for every device, user, or entity that attempts to connect. An effective NAC strategy is defined and continuously improved to better control, filter, prevent, detect, and respond to every internal or external communication.

TIP   802.1X, port-based NAC, is a simple form and just one component in a comprehensive NAC solution.

The following NAC concepts are worth remembering:

- **Pre-admission and post-admission:** In pre-admission, endpoints are inspected for policy compliance before they gain access (e.g., identifying and blocking endpoints or devices with out-of-date antivirus definitions or missing critical software updates). In post-admission, network access is granted, but user actions are regulated and decisions to remove access are made based on compliance with network behavior rules.

- **Agent versus agentless:** To make decisions about the endpoints, either NAC systems require a client application on the endpoint to report status upon access attempt or the NAC system can scan remotely and employ inventory techniques to determine access decisions.

TIP   Some software has network access protection agents built in. Microsoft Windows, Linux, and macOS have various NAC capabilities included.

- **Out-of-band versus inline:** Out-of-band devices separate the functions of analysis and enforcing, and they report to a central console for management. This approach uses (or reuses) existing infrastructure switches, gateways, and firewalls to enforce network policy. Some practitioners contend that out-of-band configuration can be disruptive. Inline devices sit in the middle of traffic flow, usually above the access switch level, and decide whether to admit or restrict traffic from each endpoint as it logs in. These can become bottlenecks if they become overloaded.

- **Remediation:** Remediation is necessary to resolve the problem that prevents access (e.g., update the antivirus software). There are two different approaches to remediation:

  - **Quarantine:** The endpoint is restricted to a specific IP network or assigned VLAN that provides users with routed access only to certain hosts and applications, like the patch management and update servers.

  - **Captive portals:** User access to websites is intercepted and redirected to a web application that guides a user through system remediation. Access is limited to the captive portal until remediation is completed.

TIP Address management techniques like Address Resolution Protocol (ARP) or Neighbor Discovery Protocol (NDP) are used for quarantine processing to reduce administrative overhead of manually managing quarantine VLANs.

Endpoint Security

Endpoints include the laptops, desktops, and servers we're all very familiar with, but also include mobile devices, IoT devices, industrial control systems, autonomous mobile systems, robots, and more. The concept of endpoint detection and response (EDR) is an emerging category of security solutions that addresses the need for continuous monitoring and response to advanced threats on all types of endpoints. EDR works by continuously monitoring endpoint and network events and analyzing those events to detect, investigate, and respond to suspicious activities.

Endpoint security is a significant line of defense, and it is important whether the device is attached to a network continuously, like servers, or intermittently, like mobile devices. Keeping infected or suspicious endpoints off the network makes sense. Allowing vulnerable or already corrupted devices access puts the entire networked environment at risk. Concepts like NAC and endpoint security used in tandem with other detection and response techniques (such as user and entity behavior analytics, or UEBA) are central to good security practices.

A defense-in-depth approach has always included endpoint security as part of the other layers like firewalls, proxies, centralized virus scanners, and even intrusion detection and intrusion prevention solutions (discussed in Chapter 7, "Security Operations"). However, the nature of the attack has changed. An attacker can gain access to valid credentials through social engineering, or they can bypass perimeter security controls through exposed remote access ports. Once the outsider becomes the insider, traditional perimeter and prevention controls are much less effective. Zero trust architecture (discussed earlier in this chapter), along with local host firewalls, advanced threat protection applications, multifactor authentication, auditing, client-based IDS/IPS, and other next-generation endpoint controls, are beneficial.

TIP   Endpoint security should at least consist of keeping antivirus and anti-malware software current and using a correctly configured host-based firewall, a hardened configuration with unneeded services disabled, and a patched operating system.

Mobile Devices

Mobile devices have special implications for security professionals:

- The small size and increasingly powerful compute and storage power of laptops, tablets, and smartphones make loss or theft of a mobile device a significant risk to an organization. The same amount of data that would fill an entire room in terms of physical storage of paper documents uses barely 5 percent of storage space on a modern laptop.

- Mobile devices are also easily and quickly lost, unlike desktop computers, mainframes, and other devices that are more difficult to remove from an organization.

- Mobile devices also present some risk as launching platforms for attacks. Either infected by malware individually or operated as botnets, mobile devices interact with the internet and are capable of facilitating attacks against corporate and government networks.

The proper security approach for mobile devices starts with guidance that is appropriate for all storage platforms: minimum data retention. If the data is not needed, do not keep it on the mobile device. Minimum data retention is centered around the minimum amount of data necessary for the phone's user. Periodically, remove any data that was once needed but has exceeded the data retention policy.

The next step in protecting mobile device data is to use password, biometric, or other available authentication mechanisms to lock the devices when not in use — multifactor should be used whenever possible. Another important step is to encrypt data at rest on mobile devices. Some devices, like those that use Apple iOS, have AES-256 level encryption built in. Other platforms have user-enabled encryption or support third-party encryption apps. If sensitive information is going to be used or potentially stored on a mobile device, encryption is at least a best practice and, for many organizations, a regulatory expectation.

For organizations keen on managing mobile devices in a consistent manner, centralized management of mobile devices is key. Additionally, NIST Special Publication 800-124 (currently at rev 2 draft) covers not only management but also aspects of improving secure access and authentication of mobile devices at a higher level. For example, a mobile security professional may reconsider granting access to the internal network by mobile devices solely by credentials. Smartphones, particularly personally owned devices, can be jailbroken or "rooted." Therefore, an organization should consider checking the connecting device's integrity before proceeding to grant full access to the network. To that effect, NIST 800-124 goes into depth on centralized management of mobile device security.

Another technique, growing in popularity in recent years, is the corporation permitting corporate data to be maintained on a personal device, in a "secure container" based on a BYOD policy. The corporation requires the container to periodically "phone home" to maintain access. In addition, an encryption and security protocol are used to further secure routine access to the container on the device. If the device is offline (i.e., does not phone home) for a set period of time (e.g., 30 days), the container is locked, and after another period of time, it is destroyed.

The techniques mentioned earlier to secure data, and people's strong preference for their own mobile devices, have made it more worthwhile for corporations to employ BYOD policies. There are several names that refer to the personal ownership of a mobile device. For example, personal mobile device (PMD), personal electronic device or portable electronic device (PED), and personally owned device (POD) are all synonymous.

With personal device proliferation, many organizations are using or considering BYOD initiatives. BYOD is a policy and a strategy by which employees are permitted to use their own equipment to perform work responsibilities. There are several options, which include one or more of the following actions:

- Unlimited access for personal devices
- Access only to nonsensitive systems and data
- Access, while preventing local storage of data on personal devices
- Access, but with IT control over personal devices, apps, and stored data

Some general technologies to understand related to security are mobile device management (MDM), containerization, and application virtualization. These are examples of software solutions and mobile device configurations that help identify, isolate, and layer protection processes on mobile devices, while preserving the need for personal privacy. In other words, in an effort to protect corporate sensitive information, it is not always necessary to track or ultimately delete personal information like photos or a personal health record that is not a corporate asset.

Your organization should request signed statements from employees acknowledging your BYOD policy and procedures, and the policy must include permission for the company to remotely wipe a lost or stolen mobile device. Device wipe is the process of using the MDM solution to remotely contact a mobile device and delete or remove all data from the device. Contrast that with corporate-owned, personally enabled (COPE) devices. With COPE, the corporation issues smartphones or mobile devices to employees, but allows them to alter the devices and use them as their own personal devices (within reason).

NOTE   Many organizations take a hybrid approach to allowing employees to use their own devices. To reduce the risk of unknown device compatibility with security policy and procedures, a choose your own device (CYOD) strategy allows employees to use one or more devices from an approved product list.

IMPLEMENT SECURE COMMUNICATION CHANNELS ACCORDING TO DESIGN

Earlier in this chapter, we provided examples and guidelines to properly analyze, design, implement, and monitor various network protocols, topologies, and infrastructure components. In this section, the particular aspects and concerns for voice, multimedia collaboration, remote access, data communications, virtualized networks, and third-party connectivity are addressed.

Voice

Voice communications have largely become integrated with many information technology platforms. Digital voice transmissions introduce their own set of vulnerabilities into a system. Authentication is important to stop eavesdroppers from capturing media, identities, patterns, and credentials — and possibly using those for subsequent unauthorized connections or other attempts to steal data. Integrity is a concern on two fronts: message and media integrity. The contents of the message, if intercepted, may be changed or reconstructed or the message can be rerouted. The actual media can be hijacked and degraded, or the attacker can insert new messages into the media.

To protect voice data in transit, encryption protocols can be used to encapsulate or even scramble voice traffic. However, as mentioned earlier in this chapter, end-to-end confidentiality cannot be provided in secure voice transmissions, as some portion of all traffic is decrypted to aid in government law enforcement. Although this is not mandated by overt law in the United States, China enacted the Cybersecurity Law in 2017. The Cybersecurity Law requires all network operators to cooperate with Chinese authorities for spot-checks and "technical support" to allow full access when requested.

Private Branch Exchange and Plain Old Telephone Service

A discussion on voice communication security starts with Private Branch Exchange (PBX) and Plain Old Telephone Service (POTS). PBX is the enterprise-class phone system, as opposed to a residential system. It includes an internal switching network and a controller. The problem with analog PBXs is that they are installed with default access configurations for ports, codes, and control interfaces. If these are not changed by the organization, attackers can easily exploit them. An example of a common method of exploiting these poorly configured systems is the massive toll fraud that occurs at the cost of billions of dollars annually. Toll fraud occurs when malicious actors make a high volume of calls to premium rate numbers (like international numbers) and take a portion of the revenue generated from these calls.

Some vulnerabilities, including default configurations, have been remediated as analog PBX has been largely replaced by digital PBX to support VoIP. However, some residual risk remains. The first step toward reducing the risk is identifying the problem. Identifying toll fraud typically comes from the department responsible for examining the organization's phone bills. Once fraudulent calls, particularly those from VoIP services, are identified, you can take steps to remediate. Figuring out how hackers are abusing the digital PBX systems or VoIP systems is difficult without strong vulnerability management on the relevant systems. Understanding the weaknesses in those systems helps identify what may be exploited to initiate the fraudulent calls. Subsequent use of strong policies and training will further minimize abuse by internal employees. Lastly, consider some specialized applications to monitor calls and alert if suspect calls are made.

POTS is still a predominant feature in residential networks and some businesses. It was designed to carry human voice over a bidirectional analog telephone interface. Over a POTS connection, voice communications are vulnerable to interception, eavesdropping, tapping, and other exploitations. Therefore, POTS and PBX security controls rely heavily on physical controls to limit access and protect the equipment. Additional ways to mitigate the risk include segregating network traffic and monitoring the more vulnerable areas. Many alarm systems and out-of-band network links for fax machines, some routers, and other network devices may keep PBX and POTS in organizations for years to come and are a concern for security professionals.

Voice over Internet Protocol

VoIP is a method using several technologies to encapsulate voice communications and multimedia sessions over IP networks. VoIP has become a popular and inexpensive way for companies and individuals to operate telephony solutions using a TCP/IP network connection.

VoIP technology is not automatically any more secure than analog. It is essentially plain-form communications and is easily intercepted and eavesdropped. With adequate configuration, highly encrypted solutions are possible, and attempts to interfere or wiretap are able to be deterred. Even then, VoIP still requires the attention of security professionals. Hackers have several vectors for VoIP attacks.

- Tools are available to spoof Caller ID, which facilitates vishing (VoIP phishing) or Spam over Internet Telephony (SPIT) attacks.

- Call manager systems and the VoIP phones themselves might be vulnerable to host operating system attacks and DoS attacks.

- MITM attacks may succeed by spoofing call managers or endpoint connection transmissions.

- Unencrypted network traffic may include VoIP, and therefore, decoding VoIP streams is possible.

The remediations for these issues center around employing encryption, increased authentication, and robust network infrastructure. As mentioned earlier, some vendors need to employ innovative means to safeguard their own service when protocols or vulnerabilities exist.

Multimedia Collaboration

"Work from anywhere" is an expression that underscores the impact multimedia collaboration has had on business, particularly since the start of the COVID-19 pandemic. Personal well-being has also changed with the growth of shared video, data, images, and audio platforms. Geographic distances have been bridged by the use of various multimedia-supporting communication solutions. When collaboration is done simultaneously, tools like email, chat, VoIP, video conferencing, digital whiteboards, online document editing, real-time file exchange, and versioning control, to name a few, can be used efficiently and effectively. Remote meeting technology has transformed the corporate world and changed the way every single business operates. With these changes, there are important security effects to address.

Remote Meeting

In this day and age, virtual meetings are a fact of life. As of this writing, many people around the world haven't seen the inside of an office in over a year. While we're sure that will change soon enough, the COVID-19 pandemic has shown us all that productive meetings can be held remotely with participants located in any number of geographically separated areas. To accomplish these remote meetings, several different types of technologies are used. There are hardware solutions like video cameras and VoIP telephony, and it's increasingly common for people's own personal or corporate-issued mobile devices to be used for teleconferencing. Software helps administer the meetings and allows for interaction between remote parties, like in the use of a shared screen whiteboard. Several terms are used to describe these technologies, such as digital collaboration, virtual meetings, video conferencing, software or application collaboration, shared whiteboard services, and virtual training solutions. The bottom line is that any service that enables people to communicate, exchange data, collaborate on materials/data/documents, and otherwise perform work tasks together is most likely performing or facilitating a remote meeting of some sort.

Multimedia remote meeting services have security implications. Because a person is not identified by virtue of being present in a physical meeting room, authentication must be assured in remote meetings. To provide that assurance, there needs to be a form of verification or validation of the attendee's identification, such as when the employee must preregister for the meeting using a unique password. The transmission of voice, data, or video might need to be protected via encryption. In a physical conference room where everyone is in the same location, voice does not need special protection sender to receiver, except for physical measures like closed doors and soundproofing the walls. To fully capitalize on multimedia collaboration, specifically remote meetings, security concerns must be addressed.

✔ Zoombombing

The term *Zoombombing* refers to the unwanted intrusion, by an outsider, into a video conference call. The term is derived from the popular Zoom videoconferencing software but has also been used to describe similar intrusions on other videoconferencing platforms.

Zoombombing was initially popularized in 2020, when the COVID-19 pandemic forced many people to stay at home, and videoconferencing became necessary for many businesses, schools, and other organizations. In many situations, these Zoombombing attacks involved the intruder inserting obscene, racist, homophobic, or otherwise inappropriate content into an existing meeting — prompting the meeting to be shut down.

The rise of Zoombombing in 2020 prompted Zoom to add various security measures to their application and also highlighted the need for security professionals to advise on the use of such software. Since then, access controls such as virtual waiting rooms, password-protected virtual meetings, and screensharing restrictions have become mainstream.

Instant Messaging

Instant messaging (IM), also referred to as *private messaging* (PM), is a collaboration tool that allows for bidirectional, real-time text-based chat between two users connected by the internet. Initially, the same client software had to be used by each user. In recent applications, JavaScript is more prevalent in IM, and users require only a modern browser. Some IM utilities allow for file transfer, multimedia, voice and video conferencing, screen sharing, remote control, and command scripting. Some forms of IM are based on a peer-to-peer service with direct communications. Other implementations use one or more centralized controlling servers inline. Peer-to-peer IM is vulnerable to several types of attack and potentially unauthorized access to data. However, it is easy to use and set up, which makes it popular in both corporate and personal use. Some of the common ways IM is vulnerable include the following:

- Where IM does not enforce strong authentication, account spoofing can threaten authenticity.

- Without encryption, IM is susceptible to packet sniffing, putting confidentiality at risk.

- File transfer and remote access add to the risk of malicious code deposit, infection, or data exfiltration.

- IM users are often subject to numerous forms of social engineering attacks, such as impersonation or convincing a victim to disclose sensitive information like passwords or classified data.

NOTE   IM traffic is sometimes invisible to firewall monitoring, as some IM clients embed traffic within an HTTP packet. Because IM uses ports that are typically open, like ports 80 (HTTPS) and 21 (FTP), blocking ports at the firewall to thwart IM attacks is not effective.

TIP   Spam is an attack vector for IM. When the attack is through IM, it is called SPIM.

Email

Securing email effectively is a large part of organizational information protection. Email is widely used and accepted as formal communication or a matter of record. It is one of the most used internet capabilities. Email infrastructure is predominantly mail-handling servers using SMTP. The servers accept messages from clients, transport those messages to other servers, and deposit them into a user's server-based inbox. The servers communicate with end-user destinations using mail delivery protocols such as Post Office Protocol version 3 (POP3) or Internet Message Access Protocol (IMAP). These protocols permit the clients to pull the email from their server-based inboxes. These protocols are used whether in a corporate LAN or with the plethora of web-based email services.

TIP   Many internet-compatible email systems rely on the X.400 standard for addressing and message handling.

Popular SMTP servers that should be familiar to security professionals are Sendmail for Unix systems and Exchange for Microsoft. As Google and Microsoft have gained market share with cloud-based email services, some security implications have changed. For the purposes of this chapter, understanding the fundamentals of SMTP servers in general is sufficient.

In fact, Sendmail and Exchange are just two of many alternatives. While they are popular in delivering business or private email services, there is growing popularity in using SaaS email solutions, with Gmail for business or Office 365 being two of the more popular email SaaS options. The key factor in deploying and securing SMTP servers is first to ensure that the protocols used provide the same basic functionality and compliance with internet email standards.

Securing SMTP servers begins with making sure the system is properly configured for strong authentication for both inbound and outbound mail. SMTP is designed to be a mail relay system. This means it relays mail from the sender to the intended recipient. Without proper authentication, the SMTP server is an open relay or an open relay agent. Open relays are vulnerable to attack as they do not authenticate senders before accepting and relaying mail. Therefore, it's important that relays are properly configured and have adequate controls in place.

Spam is a likely outcome, as floods of emails can be sent out because the infrastructure is wide open for piggybacking tactics by attackers. When authentication is present, SMTP attacks are harder to accomplish, but hijacked authenticated accounts do happen.

Email Security Goals

Email is convenient and has transformed the way we communicate. However, several security controls have to be implemented to assure the confidentiality, integrity, availability, nonrepudiation, and authenticity (CIANA) of email. That is most important at the application level.

At the hardware level, the secure placement of email servers and gateways is critically important, not just for proper functionality but for ensuring the security of the hardware.

The basic implementation of email on the internet does not include the required assurances. Security measures for email should generally accomplish several objectives:

- Secure placement of email servers and gateways on the network
- Ensure nonrepudiation, meaning that the sender is the sender
- Achieve privacy and confidentiality by restricting access through authentication mechanisms; verify the source of messages and delivery
- Classify sensitive content within or attached to messages

Email security should be defined by a policy that is supported by management. That policy should also be shared with employees or end users as part of initial and ongoing security training. Email attacks, such as phishing, remain a common and effective attack method. End users clicking a malicious link or infected attachment is often the first step in a cyber attack that can wreak havoc on an organization. A good email security policy has several main components:

- **Acceptable use:** These are general guidelines for what email can be used for, which may (or may not) include minimal personal use. As a business-owned asset, the expectation is that users accomplish business tasks and nothing illegal, immoral, or obscene. Acceptable use policies generally provide guidance on acceptable use of company data. For example, no personally identifiable information (PII) shall be sent via email.

- **Access control:** Access should be restricted to individual inboxes and archives. In some cases, a group email inbox is established with multiple recipients. Users with access should be prohibited from granting access to other people. How access control is implemented should be described so that users recognize the balance between legitimate access and some level of privacy. At least, access control deters or prevents unauthorized access.

- **Privacy:** Users of a corporate email system should generally be accustomed to having no expectation of privacy.

- **Email backup and retention policies:** Backups and archives are needed for data recovery, legal proceedings, and many audits. Retention rules are important to guide the organization from keeping records that are no longer valuable or needed for legal or regulatory reasons. Excessive record maintenance may lead to security issues of a different kind. Backups can be daily, weekly, or monthly, for example. Retention requirements range from several months of archive to several years. In either case, backup and retention rules must be based on risk, business requirements, and any legal or regulatory guidelines.

Email Security Solutions

As with all security approaches, a risk-reward (or cost-benefit) analysis must be performed. The cost of implementing and maintaining the security controls should not exceed the value of the information (or the cost of losing it). The security controls should preserve the ability of the business to operate and grow; otherwise, they will be unnecessary, as the business is potentially headed for obsolescence. In terms of email security, a critical consideration to underscore is confidentiality, as email messages may contain valuable and sensitive information to protect.

There are several techniques that organizations can employ to strengthen the protection of their email communications:

- Use digital signatures to combat impersonation attempts
- Subject all incoming email to anti-malware scanning
- Block suspicious attachments and potentially risky filename extensions (such as .zip and .exe) at the gateway to reduce phishing and similar attacks
- Employ filters to reduce spam and mailbombing problems
- Use encryption to prohibit eavesdropping efforts
- Train users in the importance of and methods for properly recognizing and handling spam or potentially malicious links in email
- Install, run, and update antivirus and endpoint protection

There are several protocols, services, and solutions to augment email infrastructure and provide security without an expensive and complete overhaul of the entire internet-based SMTP infrastructure. Some of these strategies are listed here:

- Secure Multipurpose Internet Mail Extensions (S/MIME)
- MIME Object Security Services (MOSS)
- Privacy Enhanced Mail (PEM)
- DomainKeys Identified Mail (DKIM)
- Pretty Good Privacy (PGP)
- Forced Encryption

S/MIME is an email security standard that uses public key encryption and digital signatures to enable authentication and confidentiality for emails. X.509 digital certificates are used to provide authentication. Public Key Cryptography Standard (PKCS) encryption is used to provide privacy. Two types of messages can be formed using S/MIME:

- **Signed messages:** To provide integrity, sender authentication, and nonrepudiation of the sender
- **Enveloped messages:** To provide integrity, sender authentication, and confidentiality

MOSS is another email security standard that can provide authentication and confidentiality, but also enables integrity and nonrepudiation services for email messages. MOSS employs Message Digest 2 (MD2) and MD5 algorithms; Rivest, Shamir, and Adelman (RSA) public key; and Data Encryption Standard (DES) to provide authentication and encryption services.

PEM is an email encryption mechanism that provides authentication, integrity, confidentiality, and nonrepudiation. Like the aforementioned services, PEM also uses RSA, DES, and X.509.

DKIM is a means to assert that valid mail is sent by an organization through verification of domain name identity. This adds a layer of nonrepudiation and authentication that is particularly helpful in identifying and filtering spoofed addresses in emails. Implementing DKIM relies on public keys and digital signing.

PGP is a public-private key system that uses a variety of encryption algorithms to encrypt email messages. PGP encryption can be used to protect files and other digital assets besides email. The first version of PGP used RSA, the second version, International Data Encryption Algorithm (IDEA), but later versions offered a spectrum of algorithm options. PGP encryption can be used to protect files and other digital assets besides email. PGP is not a standard, but rather an independently developed product that has wide internet appeal.

Forcing TLS for email encryption is another method to provide assurance. A few email service providers such as Apple and Google use TLS for @icloud and @gmail, their respective email services. It is not possible to force TLS as a sole option. In fact, RFC 2487 specifies that a public SMTP server must *not* force TLS since its implementation cannot (yet) be made mandatory. However, between email domains for business partners, forcing TLS is a viable option.

NOTE PGP started off as a free product open for public use and has since been developed into a commercial offering. OpenPGP and GnuPG are open-source products based on PGP that remain in the public domain.

Remote Access

Interconnected computing platforms, the strengths of multimedia collaboration, the globalization of business, and the "work from anywhere" movement are some of the forces that have made decentralized workplace arrangements more common. Telecommuting, or working remotely, occurs when a person separated from the main corporate compute and storage platforms accesses them from another location, such as their home, via a laptop. There is also a growing reliance on cloud-hosted resources, where employees on the protected LAN need to remotely access vital infrastructure hosted by a CSP.

When telecommuting or using cloud-based resources, the user might use one of the following access paths:

- Connecting to a network over the internet, with or without a VPN

- Connecting to a terminal server system or an access gateway through a thin-client connection

---

NOTE Telecommuting existed before the internet and multimedia made the practice a business imperative. The term has roots in the original description of telecommuting, which implied the use of telephony to connect workers and customers. Teleconferences over POTS, PTSN, and PBXs with geographically separated individuals conducting business meetings were an example of the first versions of telecommuting.

Remote Access for Telecommuting

For telecommuting to be productive and successful, employees need to have access to many of the same or comparable resources at a remote location as they would have at the primary office. Access to email, shared storage, and the capability to attend meetings virtually are necessary. Telecommuters use many remote access techniques to establish the required connectivity to the business office network. There are three main types of remote access techniques:

- **Service specific:** If a service such as email via Outlook Web Access (OWA) is needed, a service-specific remote access capability allows users to remotely connect to and use it. Service-specific capabilities are not limited to web-enabled versions of on-premises applications. Terminal service access can be limited to a time and attendance application, for example.

- **Remote control:** Common applications for remote control or remote access are help desk or Tier 1 support and employee training functions. Remote control allows an authorized user to gain remote access to another system and take full control as if they were physically in front of the remote system. There are significant security concerns with remote control. Potential threats include brute-force attacks hackers may use to exploit the proprietary Remote Desktop Protocol (RDP) that Windows environments use to enable Windows Remote Desktop and Terminal Server.

- **Screen scraping:** The process of *screen scraping* involves copying information that is displayed in one application so that it can be used or displayed in another application. Screen scraping technology has been commonly used within the financial sector to collect and reuse transaction data across analytics and other applications.

During screen scraping, there are risks of unauthorized disclosure or compromise, so security professionals will want to implement encryption with any screen-scraper solutions.

Remote Access Security Management

Organizations that allow for remote access are extending their risk beyond the figurative corporate walls. With the expansion of risk come additional security requirements. The private network can be compromised by remote access attacks. Figure 4.13 illustrates some common areas of increased risk of remote access. There are many security controls that can be put in place, and a few of the most important categories of control are as follows:

- A strong authentication system is required; multifactor authentication is the standard to protect sensitive information.

- Limit remote access to only those who need it and who routinely use it.

- Implement encryption across the transmission link, to include one or more of these examples: VPNs, SSL, TLS, SSH, and IPSec.

- Understand that a VPN is not a complete security solution; end users who can authenticate and establish a VPN may be accessing the network with an infected computer or mobile device.

As discussed throughout the chapter, endpoint security is also essential. Combinations of security controls are needed to manage and safeguard the remote access workforce.

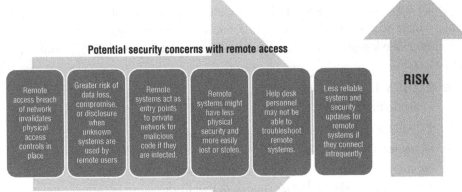

FIGURE 4.13 Common areas of increased risk in remote access

NOTE   A key point to remember is that any use of Wi-Fi or other mobile technologies is considered a remote access scenario. Even within a physically secure office building or campus, mobile device use comes with remote access concerns, which should be treated with care. UEBA and the security mechanisms mentioned throughout this section should be applied appropriately.

Authentication Approaches

Because remote access expands the private network beyond the corporate environment, invalidates many of the physical controls in place, and increases information risk for the organization, taking extra precaution with authentication of remote access users is worth exploring further. There are specific remote access protocols and services that an organization will use to strengthen credential management and permissions for remote clients and users. Most likely, the use of a centralized remote access authentication system should be in place. Some examples of remote authentication protocols are Password Authentication Protocol (PAP), Challenge Handshake Authentication Protocol (CHAP), Extensible Authentication Protocol (EAP, or its extensions PEAP or LEAP), Remote Authentication Dial-In User Service (RADIUS), and Terminal Access Controller Access Control System Plus (TACACS+).

Centralized Remote Authentication Services

Centralized remote authentication services add an extra layer of protection between the remote access clients and the private, internal network. Remote authentication and authorization services using a centralized server are different and separated from the similar services used for network clients locally. This is important because in the event a remote access server is compromised, the entire network's authentication and authorization services are unaffected. A few leading examples are RADIUS, Diameter, and TACACS+.

- **RADIUS:** Users pass login credentials to a RADIUS server for authentication, similar to the process used by domain clients sending login credentials to a domain controller for authentication.

- **Diameter:** Diameter is essentially the successor to RADIUS. One significant improvement Diameter provides is added reliability. Diameter is often used in prepaid and credit-based usage models in mobile device services, and similar applications.

- **TACACS:** This is an alternative to RADIUS. TACACS is available in three versions: original TACACS, Extended TACACS (XTACACS), and TACACS+. TACACS integrates the authentication and authorization processes. XTACACS keeps the authentication, authorization, and accounting processes separate. TACACS+ improves XTACACS by adding two-factor authentication. TACACS+ is the most current and relevant version of this product line.

Virtual Private Network

A VPN is a communication tunnel that establishes a secure, point-to-point connection over an untrusted network (such as the internet). Most VPNs use encryption to protect the encapsulated traffic, but encryption is not necessary for the connection to be considered a VPN.

The most common application of VPNs is to establish secure communications through the internet between two distant networks (such as a corporate network and a teleworker's home network). There are other examples and uses of VPNs that should be appreciated as well:

- Inside a private network for added layers of data protection
- Between end-user systems connected to an ISP
- The link between two entire private networks
- Provide security for legacy applications that rely on risky or vulnerable communication protocols or methodologies, especially when communication is across a network
- Provide confidentiality and integrity, but not availability, over insecure or untrusted intermediary networks

Tunneling

The concept of tunneling is fundamental to understanding how VPN works. Tunneling is the network communications process that encapsulates a packet of data with another protocol to protect the initial packet. The encapsulation is what creates the logical illusion of a communications tunnel over the untrusted intermediary network (i.e., the traffic is visible only to the systems on either end of the tunnel and hidden from the untrusted network). At the ends of the tunnel, the initial protocol packet is encapsulated and de-encapsulated to facilitate communication.

In situations where bypassing a firewall, gateway, proxy, or other networking device is warranted, tunneling is used. The authorized data is encapsulated, and the transmission is permitted even though access inside the tunnel is restricted. An advantage of tunneling is that traffic control devices cannot block or drop the communications because they cannot interrogate the packet contents. This can be useful in streamlining important content and connections. However, this capability is also a potential security problem, as security devices meant to protect the private network from malicious content cannot scan the packets as they arrive or leave. This is particularly true if tunneling involves encryption. The sensitive data will maintain confidentiality and integrity. However, again, the data is unreadable by networking and security devices.

TIP   Tunneling can be used to create a routable solution for nonroutable protocols because the nonroutable primary packet is encapsulated by a routing protocol.

The inability of security professionals to monitor the content of traffic within the tunnel is not the only concern with tunneling. There is an increased amount of message overhead when using multiple protocols. Each one probably has its own error detection, error handling, acknowledgment, and session management elements. This adds to complexity and processing time. The tunnel packet is larger in size or length than a normal data packet. This calls for more bandwidth resources that compete with other network resources. Network saturation and bottlenecking can happen quickly. In addition, tunneling is a point-to-point communication mechanism and is not designed to handle broadcast traffic.

Common VPN Protocols

VPNs can be implemented using software or hardware solutions. In either case, there are variations and combinations based on how the tunnel is implemented. There are three common VPN protocols that provide a foundational view of how VPNs are built:

- **Point-to-Point Tunneling Protocol (PPTP):** Data link layer (layer 2) used on IP networks.

- **Layer 2 Tunneling Protocol (L2TP):** Data link layer (layer 2) used on any LAN protocol.

- **IPSec:** Network layer (layer 3) used on IP networks; IPSec is covered in the "Secure Protocols" section earlier in this chapter.

NOTE   SSL/TLS can also be used as a VPN protocol, not just as a session encryption tool operating on top of TCP.

Point-to-Point Tunneling Protocol

This was developed from the dial-up protocol called Point-to-Point Protocol (PPP). It encapsulates traffic at the data link layer (layer 2) of the OSI model and is used on IP networks. PPTP encapsulates the PPP packets and creates a point-to-point tunnel connecting two separate systems. It protects the authentication traffic using the same authentication protocols supported by PPP:

- Microsoft Challenge Handshake Authentication Protocol (MS-CHAP)
- CHAP
- PAP
- EAP
- Shiva Password Authentication Protocol (SPAP)

TIP Microsoft used proprietary modifications to develop Microsoft Point-to-Point Encryption (MPPE). This protocol should not be confused with the version of PPTP in the RFC 2637 standard.

NOTE Something to be aware of is that session establishment for PTPP is not encrypted. The authentication process shares the IP addresses of sender and receiver in cleartext. The packets may even contain usernames and hashed passwords, any of which could be intercepted by a MITM attack.

Layer 2 Tunneling Protocol

L2TP was derived to create a point-to-point tunnel to connect disparate networks. This protocol does not employ encryption, so it does not provide confidentiality or strong authentication. In conjunction with IPSec, those services are possible. IPSec with L2TP is a common security structure. L2TP also supports TACACS+ and RADIUS. A most recent version, L2TPv3, improves upon security features to include improved encapsulation and the ability to use communication technologies like Frame Relay, Ethernet, and ATM, other than simply PPP over an IP network.

Data Communications

In previous sections of this chapter, we talked a lot about network topologies, media (wired or wireless), and protocols. Ultimately, data enters and leaves your premises over some form of communications path. In the rest of this section, we cover some of the most common data communications frameworks and standards.

Frame Relay

This framework uses packet switching to perform wide area networking, connecting networks operating at physical and data link layers of the digital communication channels. Frame relay has another utility: it often serves to connect LANs with major backbones.

It connects separate WANs and private network environments with leased lines over T-1 connections. Frame relay is sometimes used for video and voice, but it is not best suited for that because it does not provide steady flow transmission.

Frame Relay originated as an extension of ISDN in that frame relay integrates a packet-switched network capability over circuit-switched technology. The technology has become a standalone and cost-effective means of creating a WAN. Devices within the private network performing frame relay services are called *data circuit-terminating equipment* (DCE). Devices that connect to the frame relay DCEs are called *data terminal equipment* (DTE).

TIP Packet-switching technologies use virtual circuits instead of dedicated physical circuits. A virtual circuit is created only when needed, which makes for efficient use of the transmission medium and is extremely cost-effective. The confidentiality of virtual circuits is only as strong as the configuration and implementation. A virtual circuit still means physical circuits are shared among several customers. It is uncommon but very possible that, for example, a misconfigured frame relay can mean one customer's broadcast packets end up within another customer's internal network. The best way to ensure confidentiality is to utilize a VPN to encrypt traffic sent over a shared virtual circuit.

Asynchronous Transfer Mode

This is a high-speed networking standard that can support both voice and data communications. It was designed to integrate telecommunication and computer networks. ATM is normally utilized by ISPs on their private long-distance networks. ATM operates mostly at the data link layer (layer 2) and is utilized over either fiber or twisted-pair cable.

ATM is different from other data link technologies, in particular Ethernet. ATM utilizes no routing, but rather uses special-purpose hardware called ATM switches that establish point-to-point connections between endpoints. Data flows directly from source to destination. Another interesting difference is that Ethernet packets are variable in length.

The performance of ATM is often expressed in the form of optical carrier (OC) levels, written as "OC-xxx." Performance levels as high as 10 Gbps (OC-192) are technically feasible with ATM. More common performance levels for ATM are 155 Mbps (OC-3) and 622 Mbps (OC-12). ATM traffic has several components to ensure Quality of Service (QoS). There are four basic types:

- **Constant bit rate (CBR):** A peak cell rate (PCR) is specified, which is constant.
- **Variable bit rate (VBR):** An average or sustainable cell rate (SCR) is specified, which can peak at a certain level, a PCR, for a maximum interval before being problematic.

- **Available bit rate (ABR):** A minimum guaranteed rate is specified.
- **Unspecified bit rate (UBR):** Traffic is allocated to all remaining transmission capacity.

ATM has design capabilities for a network that must handle both traditional high-throughput data traffic and real-time, low-latency content such as voice and video. ATM operates at the three lowest layers of the OSI model: the network layer, the data link layer, and the physical layer. ATM is a core protocol used over the Synchronous Optical Networking (SONET) and Synchronous Digital Hierarchy (SDH) backbone of the PSTN and ISDN. SONET and SDH are standardized protocols that transfer multiple digital bit streams over optical fiber using lasers or light-emitting diodes (LEDs).

ATM provides functionality that is similar to both circuit-switching and packet-switching networks. It uses a connection-oriented model in which a virtual circuit must be established between two endpoints before the actual data exchange begins. These virtual circuits may be permanent (i.e., dedicated connections that are usually preconfigured by the service provider) or switched, meaning set up on a per-call basis using signaling and disconnected when the call is terminated.

Multiprotocol Label Switching

We have covered the advantages and strengths of ATM and frame relay. But MPLS seems to capture the benefits of both. MPLS is covered in the "Converged Protocols" section earlier in this chapter.

Virtualized Networks

Virtualization technology uses the memory of a single host computer to host one or more operating systems. Almost any operating system can be hosted on any hardware under this construct. The operating system in this scenario is called a *guest* operating system. There can be multiple operating systems running on one hardware host computer, all of which are considered guests. The operating systems, host, and guests can differ on the same virtual machine. Virtualization can be used to host servers, limited user interfaces such as virtual desktops, applications, and more.

NOTE   For more details on virtualization, refer to the "Virtualized Systems" section in Chapter 3.

As operating system virtualization has proven effective, virtualization has expanded to encompass other opportunities, such as virtualized networks. Network virtualization is the combination of hardware and software networking components into a single integrated entity. The system that results is managed by software control over all network functions including management, traffic shaping, address assignment, and more. A physical presence at all the hardware locations is no longer needed. A single management console or interface can be used to oversee every aspect of the network. Refer to the "Microsegmentation" section earlier in this chapter for coverage of SDN, SDS, and related concepts.

Third-Party Connectivity

Various connections with third parties are often required for many organizations to conduct business. Third parties can generally be broken down into three categories:

- Data and telecommunications providers, such as your ISP
- Cloud service providers
- Vendors, customers, partner organizations, and the like

Working with third parties comes with many risks, and you should generally hold such third parties to the same (or sometimes higher) security and privacy standards that you have established for your organization. Service-level agreements (SLAs), as discussed in Chapter 7, are an important mechanism to establish security expectations with an external party and hold them accountable if those expectations are not met.

Many of the considerations with third-party connectivity align with the topics covered in the "Remote Access" section of this chapter and throughout the rest of this book. You should follow best practices, such as encryption in transit, strong access control procedures, and strong email filtering. In addition, continuous monitoring of any third-party connections should be standard practice to identify new threats, unexpected behavior, or deviations from agreed-upon SLAs.

A major category of risk involved with third-party connectivity is compliance risk. As the owner of your and your customers' data, your organization is responsible for understanding how the external parties manage and secure your data. You must confirm that their controls meet your legal and regulatory obligations to protect the data, including (but not limited to) considerations around the location of the servers and systems that host and process the data. Compliance reports, such as SOC2 reports, can serve as a good starting point in assessing security and compliance risks associated with third-party connectivity, and SLAs are again pivotal in holding third parties accountable.

SUMMARY

Communication and network security used to be restricted to protecting assets and information within the physical confines of an organization. Today, the boundaries of a corporation have changed dramatically. Companies might have workers at home, in coffee shops, or in hotel lobbies. The boundaries of a company extend far beyond its physical buildings, so the structures, transmission methods, transport formats, and security methods used to provide confidentiality, integrity, and availability for transmissions over public and private communications networks and media have changed to accommodate those extended boundaries.

This chapter contains fundamental concepts such as telephony, data communications, the different layers of the OSI model, and transmission media and protocols. Understanding the historical development of communications technology interfaces, interoperability, and high-level approaches to leverage security controls to make everything work together and safeguard information is invaluable for network security professionals.

Security professionals need to develop skills in improving and administering remote access, virtualization, and cloud services to enable new business and workplace models. Along with these information technology changes come security challenges and opportunities. One of the foundational concepts that continue to underscore proper security management is that no single solution satisfies all gaps. A security professional has to understand the layered solution approach that describes defense in depth. Access control, authentication, and encryption, for example, work together to extend corporate computing borders, allow employees to work from anywhere, and reduce costs of providing information security. The nature of security attacks will also continue to evolve. In this chapter we discussed several types of attacks, like DDoS, MITM, and phishing, to underscore the importance and the dynamic nature of information security as a profession. As the threats change, so must our approaches to thwarting them.

Identity and Access Management

IDENTITY AND ACCESS MANAGEMENT (IAM or IDAM) is fundamental to information security. Controlling access to resources requires the ability to identify and validate the entities requesting access and to hold them accountable for the actions they take. Entities can be users, systems, applications, or processes, and IAM consists of four foundational elements: identification, authentication, authorization, and accountability (IAAA).

This chapter identifies each of the IAAA elements and how they can be configured and enforced, which forms the basis of many access control systems. Controlling physical and logical access to assets typically starts with establishing identities and providing users with credentials, which are then presented and authenticated whenever access is requested. From time to time, these credentials must be reviewed and updated, and at the end of their useful life, they are decommissioned. Creating and retiring access credentials is known as *provisioning* and *deprovisioning*, and the process for managing credentials can be viewed as a lifecycle.

IAM is involved in practically every aspect of an organization's security program, so a Certified Information System Security Professional (CISSP) is well served by ensuring adequate procedures and technical systems exist to support access control arrangements. This starts with understanding the requirements for identity information, choosing and implementing systems that meet those requirements, and ensuring administrative controls like access reviews support the technology controls to preserve security in systems.

CONTROL PHYSICAL AND LOGICAL ACCESS TO ASSETS

Physical access controls should be familiar to virtually all readers — doors, curtains, fences, etc., are common everyday objects used to control physical access to buildings like homes, schools, and office buildings. Logical access controls are similarly omnipresent, though they are not always as obvious to the untrained eye. Systems that require a password, personal identification number (PIN), or shared symmetric key for access are all examples of logical access controls. Both logical and physical access measures are designed to restrict which users or systems can access specific assets like data in a system or valuables stored in a safe.

There are a variety of access control methods, and choosing the correct combination requires a security practitioner to understand the organization's assets and priorities for controlling access. For example, valuable physical assets and a requirement for strong confidentiality demands strong physical access controls, while information systems with strict requirements for data integrity may require technical controls like application logic to meet requirements.

Access control systems typically enforce controls over subjects accessing objects. A *subject* can be a user or program, and an *object* is whatever the subject is trying to access, like a file, application, facility, or database. Controlling access via these systems is crucial for enforcing security concepts like confidentiality, integrity, and nonrepudiation.

Access Control Definitions

Access control models use a standard set of terms to discuss various concepts. These include the following, which are used throughout the remainder of this chapter:

- **Objects** are assets that require access control. Common objects include information like files or datasets as well as system objects like compute resources and networks. Physical access control models deal with facilities as objects, such as office buildings, computer rooms, and sensitive information handling facilities. All objects share a common need for protection of basic security attributes including confidentiality, integrity, availability, nonrepudiation, and authenticity (CIANA).

- **Subjects** can be human users or nonhuman entities like systems, processes, and devices. Subjects require access to objects like files, systems, and facilities, and the fundamental practice of access control defines how such access is granted, used, and monitored.

- **Access** is anything a subject is permitted to do with or to an object. For example, a human user can be allowed or denied entry to a facility, a system user can be allowed read access but denied write and update access to a file, and nonhuman users like system processes can be allowed or denied access to specific data objects based on the sensitivity level of the objects in question. Important concepts related to controlling access including authorization are discussed throughout this chapter.

Information

Information is typically an object in an access control model, and access control systems are designed to restrict access based on the credentials presented by a subject. The most obvious example is to preserve confidentiality — a system verifies a user's credentials before granting access, which prevents unauthorized users from gaining access to data. There are a variety of models that can be used to design access control systems for this purpose, and they are discussed later in this chapter.

Safeguarding the integrity of information can also be a goal of restricted access, if authorization controls are implemented such that only properly trained users are able to make changes. Security policies often utilize access control systems to enforce both confidentiality and integrity: only authorized users can access the policies, and only specifically authorized users, like trained members of a specific department, are able to make changes. If the system storing policy documents supports logging changes and version history, the security concept of nonrepudiation is also systematically enforced via access controls since a log entry is generated by any user making changes to the document.

Identifying the needs for information access control is a fundamental requirement for the security practitioner. Not all information needs the same type or level of protection, and the requirements for protecting a specific piece of information will change over time. For example, stock ownership is often public information, since stock trades are public information. Stock trades are usually kept secret before they are executed, which can provide a competitive advantage, so confidentiality requirements will be high. However, that need changes significantly once the trade is executed and becomes public; any access control system used in such an environment needs to understand this information lifecycle and ensure adequate, cost-effective protections are applied at every phase.

Systems

System is a term that can be difficult to define. Any collection of hardware, software, personnel, policies, procedures, and other resources may constitute a system, though the term is usually used to discuss electronic information systems. A security practitioner must understand the functions and objectives of the systems in use at their organization, as well as components like analog processes, hard-copy data, or electronic elements of the system, to design appropriate identity and access management controls.

Systems requirements may demand multiple security objectives, such as confidentiality, availability, or integrity of critical information, availability of the system itself, or authenticity and nonrepudiation of the system's users. Proper implementation of access controls, particularly within information systems where sensitive data and information objects exist, is a fundamental task for a CISSP to perform. Access controls are vital for both security and privacy of data and support the basic security concepts of CIANA, which are covered in Chapter 1, "Security and Risk Management." Common ways that the CIANA concepts can be implemented in system-level IAM include the following:

- **Confidentiality** requires information in a system to be kept secure from unauthorized access. Physical access controls at the facility level will be important, as will system- or component-level restrictions for both physical access controls, like a locked safe, and logical access controls, like full disk encryption (FDE).

- **Integrity** can be supported via access controls by preventing unauthorized users from making changes to information.

- **Availability** controls and integrity controls often share a common implementation; for example, locked server cabinets prevent unauthorized users from maliciously or accidentally shutting down a system. This can prevent data loss or corruption as well as loss of system availability.

- **Authenticity** leverages the use of authentication in IAM to prove the information, commands, or other information in a system can be trusted. It may be possible to make a decision about the trustworthiness of the subject or any data they supply, provided they have successfully proven an identity.

- **Nonrepudiation** shares commonality with authenticity. Nonrepudiation means a user or system is prevented from denying a specific action, and requires the IAM system to implement sufficient accountability to prove the action was taken by the specific subject. This rests on the ability of the IAM system to uniquely identify and authenticate subjects, as well as logging of system actions and identifying information.

Designing, implementing, and maintaining IAM for electronic data and systems access are frequent tasks performed by security practitioners. These tasks require a great deal of thought and analysis since each organization's processes and systems are unique. One major difference is the implementation of access control decision making and enforcement.

Centralized IAM administration uses a dedicated access control function, like a team or specific department to manage all access control, which offers the advantage of very strict oversight and monitoring. Centralized IAM has the disadvantage of a single point of failure. *Decentralized* IAM administration breaks the function out and typically assigns access control decisions to system or information owners. This can offer greater freedom and flexibility, with the potential downside of inconsistent enforcement and lack of unified oversight.

Devices

Devices are components of an information system, as well as systems themselves, and therefore they require adequate IAM. User workstations including laptops, desktops, and tablet computers are all full information systems with storage, processing, and networking abilities, and these capabilities create the need for appropriate security controls like restricted logical access. The increased use of cloud computing services to store and process data has also increased the number of devices that an organization must consider, since these services can be accessible from any internet-connected device.

A primary concern for device IAM is ensuring access is restricted to only authorized users. The explosion of new device types accessing data has led to IAM challenges, such as early smartphones that supported only four-digit PINs instead of complex passwords. The rapid evolution of these devices has also offered security benefits such as the commoditization of biometric sensors like fingerprint readers and facial geometry scanners. The lower cost and better effectiveness of these devices means they can be incorporated into a broader variety of systems, which provides additional options for multifactor authentication (MFA).

One element of effective IAM for devices is proper endpoint security. Practices like endpoint detection and response (EDR) are covered in more detail in Chapter 4, "Communication and Network Security," and Chapter 7, "Security Operations." It is essential that access controls be applied with respect to the security of these devices. For example, an asset inventory maintained in a mobile device management (MDM) system should indicate the owner, primary user, or custodian of each device. This supports incident response capabilities in the event a device is compromised.

Devices can be both objects and subjects in an access control model. If they contain sensitive data or grant access to sensitive functions, then it is important to control access to the device objects. Devices can also be treated as subjects or nonhuman users; a known workstation can be identified by a device fingerprint, digital certificate, cookie file, or the like. When the device attempts to gain access to sensitive objects, these identifiers may be presented to authenticate the device. If a new, untrusted device is used to sign in, the access control system should be configured to require additional authentication, such as MFA, before the device is granted access. This concept is applied in network access control (NAC), discussed in Chapter 4, which treats devices as objects and applies additional criteria to new devices joining a network. For example, a user's personal laptop may be placed in a quarantine network until its patch level and EDR software can be verified.

The portability of many modern computing devices also poses a challenge to confidentiality. Devices like laptops, tablets, smartphones, and even some powerful desktop computers are now small and light enough to be carried easily. This means they are vulnerable to being stolen, misplaced, or even accessed without the user's knowledge if a device is left unattended. Tools like MDM can counter risks to these devices and the data they contain, with features like these:

- **Device protection:** This enforces security policies on each device, including password complexity, software updates, and restricting what apps can be installed or used. EDR software can also be useful to identify suspicious or malicious activity and engage additional protections like quarantining, locking, or wiping a device.

- **Device restrictions:** This identifies hardware that is not supported or systems that have been *jailbroken*, which removes standard restrictions on the device and its operating system. Jailbreaking a device also removes standard protections imposed by the manufacturer, which can lead to unauthorized data access.

- **Remote lock or wipe:** If a device is reported stolen/missing, this allows the organization to prevent unauthorized users from gaining access. Remote lock can be reversed if the device is found, while remote wipe may either delete all data or render the device unusable; it is usually only used in situations where the device cannot be recovered.

- **Containerization:** Placing organization data into a logical contain isolates it from being accessed by other apps on the device. This is a common choice for organizations with a bring your own device (BYOD) policy that allows users to access organization resources from a personal device. Enforcing restrictions on the personal device may be difficult, so the restrictions are instead limited to the container, which can be locked or wiped if the user loses the device or leaves employment.

Physical access controls are a key element of device security controls. In a typical office environment, the organization's physical access controls provide shared protection for all devices inside the facility. Portable devices present a challenge because the devices often leave the secure facility. In this case, appropriate policies and training must be provided to users of the portable devices, such as never leaving them unattended in public places, or securing the devices in an unmarked bag or hotel safe when traveling.

Facilities

Facilities provide shared security for all the systems, devices, and information they contain, so ensuring adequate protections is vital. Physical security is particularly important when discussing information system security — if an attacker is able to gain physical access to a device, then even the best logical security controls may not be sufficient to prevent unwanted data access.

Traditional facility physical security measures often follow a secure perimeter paradigm, with layered defenses that provide increasing levels of security. Chapter 7 contains more detail and a diagram of how such a physical defense-in-depth strategy is implemented. This section presents the requirements for designing and supporting underlying IAM systems that can be deployed.

Physical Access Control Systems

Physical access control systems (PACSs) include physical security implementations like gates, fencing, turnstiles, security badges, and guards. They also include administrative procedures required to operate these controls, such as guard surveillance schedules, badge requirements, loading dock procedures, and visitor registration and escort.

When designing a PACS, it is critical to establish requirements for protection, as making changes to physical infrastructure is more difficult than changes like software upgrades. The first requirement that must be identified is who exactly needs access to a specified facility. Functional areas like computer rooms or wiring closets may require only limited, infrequent access, which makes the tasks of implementing physical security easier due to the small population of users. Other facilities, particularly office buildings, will have more complex access requirements as more individuals require access and the use of such facilities by visitors or business partners may be common.

Once the requirements for access have been determined, a PACS design can be developed and implemented. The complexity of the controls chosen must reflect the value of the assets being protected — a facility with no sensitive data or assets is unlikely to require 24/7 guards and advanced intrusion detection sensors. Elements might include one or more of the following:

- **User identification:** People, vehicles, and other resources entering or leaving a secured area should be identified. This may be accomplished via a badge, sticker, radio frequency ID (RFID) tag, barcode, etc., as appropriate. Human beings will typically be identified with an ID card, sticker, or badge, while vehicles or deliveries may be identified with RFID tags, barcodes, or Quick Response (QR) codes.

- **Device identification:** Nonhuman users may be tracked throughout the facility or at ingress and egress points using a variety of methods including identification stickers and RFID tags. This allows for tracking and controlling the flow of assets entering and leaving the facility and may be integrated with property and asset management systems.

- **Fences and gates**: Fences can prevent unwanted access or be designed to guide people to a controlled entry point, depending on the sensitivity of the facility. Gates offer the ability to implement additional checks, such as presenting an ID badge or entering a code, where identification and authentication occurs.

- **Secured doors**: Similar to gates, a secured door offers the opportunity to make an access decision — unauthorized users are denied access, while those who can present proper credentials are granted access. This could be done by presenting some form of ID or an authorization token like a smart card, smartphone app, or PIN code.

- **Locks and keys**: Although often implemented on gates or doors, locks can also be used to control physical access to individual assets such as hard-copy data in a filing cabinet, a sensitive laptop stored in a safe, or a locked server rack housing sensitive systems. Locks may be analog and require possession of a key or knowledge of a code to control access. Digital locks can provide unique identification of multiple users by requiring knowledge of a unique code or by utilizing biometrics.

- **Intrusion detection sensors**: These are a detective control and can be useful to identify if improper access has been gained. Examples include heat (infrared), sound (sonic), and weight or pressure sensors, which can detect an intruder based on body heat, sounds like breaking glass, or movement as the intruder walks about.

- **Turnstile or mantrap**: Turnstiles and mantraps are both designed to explicitly limit the rate of access to a facility. Turnstiles typically allow only one person through at a time, while a mantrap requires a user to enter a secure vestibule space by presenting one set of credentials and then requires a different set of credentials to move from the vestibule into the main space. These can be useful to guard against *piggybacking*, where one user attempts to gain access without presenting credentials by closely following an authorized user.

- **CCTV surveillance**: Video surveillance can serve multiple control functions. The presence of video cameras may be sufficient to deter or prevent some unwanted access, and footage captured can be used to detect and respond to situations. closed-circuit television (CCTV) footage typically requires review by a human for effectiveness. However, recent advances in artificial intelligence (AI) have provided the ability for cameras to detect motion or even specific objects like animals or people, which can be used to perform continuous monitoring and generate more intelligent alerts.

■ **Guards**: Guard staff are one of the most useful, flexible, and also most expensive forms of physical access control. Unlike technology systems that can only follow programmed responses, guards can respond dynamically, can think critically, and can mobilize to an incident location if needed. However, guards also incur additional costs that technology systems do not, such as benefits, time off, and an inability to work continuously.

Emergency considerations must also be taken into account when designing a PACS, since human life, health, and safety are always a primary concern. The goal of the PACS under normal circumstances is to restrict physical access; in an emergency such as a fire or workplace violence situation, access controls should be designed to allow quick and efficient egress. Secured doors may be integrated with fire detection systems and designed to fail open in the event of a fire alarm or may be equipped with an override that allows the door to open but also sets off an alarm.

An Expanded Definition of Facilities

A combination of forces has created a new definition of what an organization's facilities comprise. Rather than servers in a computer room communicating with an organization-controlled desktop workstation, a cloud service provider (CSP) and personally owned smartphones are the new "office" many organizations need to protect. Ensuring physical security for assets outside the organization's control is virtually impossible, so alternative, compensating controls may be required in place of a PACS.

As discussed in Chapter 1, asset owners and custodians share responsibility for proper security measures. Users are the owners of BYOD or personal devices used for work purposes, and custodians of organization-owned assets assigned to them for use. Training on proper security procedures for these devices should be mandatory for all users who are either owners or custodians. This training should cover common security measures like maintaining physical control over the devices, never leaving them unlocked or otherwise accessible when unattended, and preventing access by unauthorized parties to sensitive resources.

MDM and MFA can be combined to provide powerful compensating control for challenges arising from increased remote work, cloud-based systems, and BYOD. Traditionally, a user and the device they connect from were both considered to be trusted. The emerging paradigm of *zero trust* means that no users, devices, or processes are considered trusted; instead, all access must include proper authentication and may require the requesting party to meet certain criteria. MFA allows the organization to gain greater assurance about the entity requesting access, and MDM can be used to enforce security policy restrictions such as the use of a complex passcode or encryption on a user device.

Identity federation is also driving changes to the definition of facilities. Users in a federated identity system will not all belong to the same organization and are unlikely to work in the same facilities. In addition to the technical implementation of federated identity, which is discussed later in this chapter, the security practitioner should ensure that supply chain risk management practices are applied to any third parties sharing identities via federation.

Expanded use of cloud services is also driving IAM evolution. Organizations using cloud services share control over the data and systems in the cloud — the CSP is always responsible for physical security and aspects of logical security related to infrastructure, while the organization is always responsible for controlling logical access to its data in the cloud. Organizations moving to the cloud lose the capability to design, implement, and manage the physical and logical controls owned by the CSP.

Migrating to the cloud typically involves significant IT cost savings; a CISSP should ensure that risk assessments capture the increased risk inherent in this loss of control and that adequate compensating controls are in place. Compensating controls might include increased logging and oversight of activity, use of only approved CSPs or specific services at a given CSP, and additional data encryption prior to storage in cloud applications with organization control of the encryption keys. If the cost of the compensating controls is greater than the cost savings from migrating to the cloud, then it makes sense for the organization to instead pursue its own hosting.

Applications

Access to applications must be granted based on sound access management principles, like need to know and least privilege. Applications provide access to data, and designing an IAM strategy for them should consider access from the following perspectives:

- **Access to applications:** Not all users will require access to all applications in use at an organization — members of the sales team are unlikely to need access to Human Resources (HR) applications, while members of the HR team do not need access to internal accounting applications. A role-based access control (RBAC) model can be helpful in identifying common need-to-know criteria and granting access that is appropriate but not excessive.

- **Access by applications to specific data:** Access controls can be utilized to enforce restrictions on how data flows between applications. This is especially relevant in MDM where containerized apps are deployed to users' personal devices. These apps are logically isolated from other apps on the device, preventing unmanaged, unauthorized apps from gaining access to organization data.

- **Access within applications:** Applications typically offer multiple levels of user access, such as regular user and superuser or admin access. Large applications may also contain multiple datasets, like a document management system with unique folders for each project or department. *Granularity* describes the level at which access can be controlled — an application with high granularity supports tailoring each user's access to specific objects, while an application with low granularity allows only a basic allow/deny to the application and all data it contains. Inadequate granularity can cause a loss of security if a user, even an internal, non-malicious one, gains unauthorized access.

Applications can be treated as subjects in an access control system as well. They are nonhuman users who access other systems, applications, and data. This access often occurs without direct oversight from a human user, such as scheduled jobs or batch processes that run automatically. Applications may also be objects in access control, with a variety of needs for controlling access. The ability to run an application often permits access to data, so any subjects accessing the application have access to that data. The application itself can be a valuable object, since access may require a license. Managing licenses and users with access to all applications in use can be a full-time job in larger organizations.

MANAGE IDENTIFICATION AND AUTHENTICATION OF PEOPLE, DEVICES, AND SERVICES

All IAM systems must implement four crucial elements: identification, authentication, authorization, and accountability (IAAA). Creating user identities, granting them permissions on systems, authorizing users when they log in, and performing oversight of user actions all rely on adequate controls being implemented in IAM systems.

Identification is the process of a subject, like a user, system, or process, asserting an identity. This is often done by supplying a digital username or user ID, but may also utilize physical credentials like an ID card. It is important to note that identity management is a unique process that begins even before a subject attempts to access an object, and the process of identity management is covered in more detail in a later section. *Authentication* is the process of proving the asserted identity, which the subject does by supplying some information they are in control of. Factors that can be used for authentication include something a user knows, something a user has, or a measurement of something the user is. These are known as factors, and examples include the following:

- **Type 1:** This is something the user or entity knows, like a password, passphrase, or the answer to a security question.
- **Type 2:** This is something the user or entity has possession of, such as a preregistered mobile device or physical key card.

- **Type 3:** This is a measurement of one of the user's biological characteristics, such as hand geometry, fingerprint, iris scan, or facial geometry.

- **Type 4:** This is an emerging area of authentication, and formal definitions may vary. Access control systems can take into account details of how and where a subject is trying to authenticate from, such as whether the access is from a previously used device or a new device. Policy-based access controls can provide various authentication paths depending on this information such as if the user is on a known, trusted device then they are only required to provide a username and password. If the access is from a new device or location, then an MFA prompt is generated.

Authorization is a two-part concept. When an identity is created during provisioning, it must be granted access or permissions, which is an authorization action. Each time the subject makes requests for access, the system should again confirm authorization to ensure the subject is still authorized to access the given object. Additionally, systems should enforce *accountability* for system actions taken by a subject, which is often done by logging the actions for review.

Identity Management Implementation

Users in a typical organization will require access to multiple systems, such as email, collaboration tools, and external tools or systems from partners or service providers. Logging in to these systems requires users to have one or more identities, and managing these identities can prove difficult in any organization with more than a basic computing environment.

Identity management (IdM) systems are useful not only for managing the identities for user access, but the identities they manage enable the functions of authentication, authorization, and accountability as well, since these rely on a proven identity. Functionalities of an IdM can be provided by a standalone system or may be integrated with a larger IAM tool. These functions support critical tasks throughout the access management lifecycle and can include one or more of the following:

- **Provisioning:** The IdM tool may provide a method for initiating the access management lifecycle by requesting identity creation, as well as supporting access request review and approval processes. Requests may be initiated by a variety of parties, including the user, the user's manager, or even an HR department, depending on the IAM model implemented within the organization.

- **Deprovisioning:** Similar processes for deprovisioning users should also be supported by the IdM; requests to deprovision may be initiated by an access reviewer, HR, system owner, or the like. Deprovisioning actions can include suspending the user's account temporarily, as in the case of a leave of absence, or permanently if the user is retiring. Other actions may include deleting or disabling the identity. The choice of action should be driven by requirements for accountability — disabling a user account prevents the same identity from being reused in the future and possibly causing confusion if historical logs are needed.

- **Identity and account management:** The IdM can support centralized and decentralized functions for account management, such as password resets through a centralized authority (help desk) or decentralized service (self-serve).

- **Authorization management:** Once an identity is created, the IdM supports the initial authorization of access for the identity. For example, once a user account is created, it can be placed into a group that has specific permissions assigned.

- **Identity review:** IdM supports oversight of identities and access by providing key details about the authorizations that are granted to an identity. This list of accounts and access forms the basis of an access review — all current access is reviewed for appropriateness and deprovisioned if no longer needed.

IdM supports additional functions like identity federation, discussed elsewhere in this chapter, and single sign-on (SSO), which is an example of a feature that can offer both security and operational benefits. In an SSO environment, users are required to authenticate only once, possibly to an SSO portal or to a primary application like webmail. From there, access is granted to other resources by sharing a token generated by the initial authentication action. This offers a security benefit by reducing the number of passwords a user must remember, thereby reducing the likelihood the user will write down or choose bad passwords. The user benefits as well by having fewer passwords to remember.

Despite the benefits offered, SSO can also be a single point of failure in one of two ways. First, if the SSO is offline or unreachable, access to all SSO-enabled applications is also unavailable. Second, if a user's identity is compromised, the broad access granted through SSO is magnified — by contrast, in a non-SSO environment, if a user's identity is compromised, it grants access to only one system. Interestingly, this same capability makes recovering from an identity compromise easier, because an attacker using an SSO identity can be locked out of all systems once. Balancing benefits against potential risks of an SSO is a key task for a security practitioner when choosing an SSO. Specific benefits and drawbacks of various SSO solutions are discussed later in this chapter, including Kerberos and Open Authorization (OAuth).

Single/Multifactor Authentication

Authentication requires supplying information that proves the validity of an asserted identity; that is to say, the user truly is who they claim to be. There are three types of authentication factors, which are differentiated by what they utilize to prove the asserted identity.

These include something the user knows (Type 1), something the user has (Type 2), or a measurement of something the user is or does (Type 3).

Single-factor authentication requires just one factor to verify an identity. The best known example is the username, which is the identity, and a password, which is a Type 1 authentication factor. Virtually all systems support this combination, and users are well accustomed to using these when logging in. Multifactor authentication, as the name implies, requires the use of more than one authentication factor such as a username, password, and a randomly generated code from an authenticator app. In this example, both Type 1 and Type 2 authentication factors are utilized, so this is two-factor authentication (2FA). A system that requires a username, an authenticator app code, and a fingerprint is truly MFA, as it requires all three authentication factors.

NOTE   MFA does not simply mean that multiple pieces of authentication information must be provided. A system that requires a username, a password, and the answer to a secret security question is not truly MFA-enabled, since passwords and security questions are both Type 1 authentication factors.

MFA is useful to guard against account compromises like phishing attacks. Simply stealing a user's password is not sufficient, and the extra work to steal the additional authentication can make the attack less feasible or even impossible. The more information a user can provide to authenticate, such as a password and a code from an authenticator app on a trusted smartphone, the more trust a system has that the user is legitimate.

As with other security technologies, there is a requirement to ensure balance between security and usability objectives — requiring a user to open a smartphone app and type in a code every time they log in could become burdensome. In a facility where the organization can implement physical access controls, the risk of unauthorized access may be partially mitigated, meaning MFA could be required only once a day when a user first logs in. For users on mobile devices working from facilities outside the organization's physical control, more frequent MFA might be appropriate if the data or systems being accessed are sufficiently sensitive.

Sophisticated phishing attacks have been conducted in which a fake website is set up for users to log into with their username, password, and the randomly generated authenticator code from a smartphone app. Since these codes expire quickly (often 90 seconds or less), these sophisticated attacks rely on automation. The captured credentials must be used immediately on the legitimate website for the attackers to gain access.

Type 1 Authentication Factors

Type 1 authentication factors are something the user knows, such as a password, PIN, or the answer to a security question. Knowledge-based authentication is widely understood and accepted; passwords, passphrases, secret words, or similar are widely used in everyday life.

Passwords or passphrases are a common Type 1 authentication factor, and most operating systems, applications, and information systems support their use. Although widely accepted, there has been a recent paradigm shift in guidance for password security practices. Previous guidance, which was largely based on National Institute of Standards and Technology Special Publication (NIST SP) 800-63, will be familiar to both security practitioners and everyday users. So-called strong passwords should be at least eight characters, be changed frequently, and contain a mix of uppercase, lowercase, special, and numeric characters.

While this guidance was sound at a time when attackers employed largely manual means when attempting to circumvent access controls, in the era of cheap, high-powered computing hardware, it is demonstrably inadequate. The NIST SP 800-63 series of documents now contains guidance for managing digital identities, federating IdM, and authentication factor management. This updated guidance, specifically 800-63B, "Digital Identity Guidelines, Authentication and Lifecycle Management," applies a risk-based approach to managing authentication factors. This includes Type 1 factors, with specific guidance:

- **Emphasis on usability over complexity**: Requirements for complex passwords or passphrases lead to passwords that are difficult to remember, but easy for attackers to guess, like using a base word with changing numbers at the end like "password123" and "password 246." Updated guidance emphasizes allowing longer passphrases of common words without added complexity requirements, and more generous input attempts to account for a user mistyping.

- **Increased length over complexity**: Systems that implement passphrases over passwords are preferred, as they create more easily remembered authentication material. An example passphrase might be "RiskBasedSecurityIsTheFuture" in contrast to a complex password like "r!skB@s3d." The former is easier for a user to remember, while the latter is likely to result in more unintended user lockouts.

- **Less frequent changes**: Updated guidance requires password changes less frequently due to their increased complexity. A passphrase is harder to guess or crack, so current guidance requires changing it only if it has been compromised.

All Type 1 authentication factors share common strengths and weaknesses. Since they rely upon users to remember the secret information, they can be ineffective if a user has forgotten the secret. When used for system accounts where a program or script has the password stored, forgetting the information is not a concern; instead, a compromise of the authentication factor is the primary weakness, since a computer system is unable to determine if a valid user is supplying the password or if the information is supplied by an attacker who has compromised the authentication information.

✔ Password Managers

Although current password guidance places an emphasis on usability as well as security, many organizations and individuals find themselves with a multitude of passwords to create and manage. SSO can help in some cases, but a password manager is also an important tool.

A *password manager* is a software application that can manage authentication material like passwords, passphrases, and answers to secret questions. These tools offer support across desktop and mobile operating systems and can serve to offload the work of creating, remembering, and filling in passwords. When a user signs up for a new web application, service, or app, the password manager automatically creates a new random password, which is automatically saved in a vault. When the user logs in to the web application again, the password manager automatically supplies the password. Instead of remembering passwords for each service they have signed up for, the user is only required to remember the password needed to unlock their vault.

Password managers support good password hygiene by removing the need for users to create passwords manually, which often results in the creation of bad passwords, such as "MyPassword*ServiceName*," where *ServiceName* is replaced by the name of the service the user is signing up for. In this case, a user's password to other services can be easily guessed by simply replacing the service name when trying stolen credentials on another web application or service.

Password managers can also be used for important organizational functions such as password backup, recovery, and escrow, which allows administrators to retrieve passwords and gain access in the event a user is not available. The ability to access another user's credentials is risky due to the probability that it could be abused, so most password managers implement this ability as a centralized administrative function with additional auditing available.

Type 2 Authentication Factors

Type 2 authentication factors are something the user has, such as a digital certificate, identification badge, or smart card. Trusted devices are also an increasingly popular Type 2 factor, as portable computing devices have become ubiquitous. Physical authentication tokens and smartphone-based authenticator apps are also popular Type 2 factors. These provide additional authentication information in the form of a numeric code that the user must enter during login, further proving the authenticity of their asserted identity — only the specified user should have knowledge of their password and access to the authenticator token or app.

The use of trusted device authentication factors can be static or dynamic. A static example is an organization-issued workstation that is provisioned with a digital certificate used to log on to a virtual private network (VPN). During login, the user must provide their password, and the VPN client also provides the certificate for verification. While not foolproof, this approach reduces the usability of stolen user credentials and reduces user *friction*, or the difficulty users encounter when using the system. If the VPN requires a password and token code at each login, the user must remember to keep their token with them at all times. Storing a second authentication factor on the device reduces the workload for the user while also achieving a security objective.

Unlike Type 1 factors, there is no requirement for users to remember information related to Type 2 factors — a user who changes a password right before leaving on vacation may struggle to recall it, but using an authenticator app does not pose the same issue. However, some Type 2 factors do require the user to remember to physically bring a device, such as a token, smart card, or trusted smartphone. If the device is lost or stolen or requires power but has a dead battery, as in the case of a smartphone authenticator app, the user cannot authenticate successfully.

Safeguarding the confidentiality and availability of the physical devices is an important security consideration if they are used. Users should be trained in adequate security procedures related to these devices, such as maintaining physical control over them and reporting immediately if a device is lost or stolen. It is also important to have incident response scenarios and procedures defined to deal with these issues related to Type 2 authentication factors. Help desk personnel should be trained on how to handle a lost or stolen smartphone or authentication hardware, and adequate technical controls like a central console to deregister or deauthorize these devices must also exist.

NOTE   The use of SMS and email to deliver one-time passwords (OTPs) or two-factor authentication codes is not considered a security best practice, since both email and SMS are not secure delivery methods. Wherever possible, alternatives should be used.

CONDITIONAL MFA   Dynamic trusted device authentication can also be used to both increase security and provide greater usability. This is known as *conditional MFA* and is a key element of attribute-based access control (ABAC), which relies on a set of policies to make authentication decisions. If a user logs in on a previously unseen device at a new IP address, there is an increased likelihood this event is suspicious. For example, perhaps an attacker has successfully phished credentials. In this circumstance, additional authentication is a wise precaution, so a second authentication factor is required to prove the user's identity. If the user can successfully authentication, as software token such as a cookie is placed on their device and submitted with future logins to reduce the overhead on the user.

Type 3 Authentication Factors

Biometrics are measurements of a human user and are often referred to as something you are or do. The uniqueness of human physiological characteristics or behavior allows these to be used to prove an identity. These include measuring geometry of body parts by scanning, like with facial or fingerprint recognition, recording and comparing speech samples, or even monitoring the rhythm and cadence of the user typing a sample text like a passphrase. Type 3 authentication is not often used as a single factor but is often used as a second or third factor for MFA.

Biometrics provide one of the strongest methods to prove authenticity of an identity, as the characteristics measured are highly unique — only a small number of people in the world will have significantly similar fingerprints or retinas. Sophisticated biometric systems can also detect fake credentials, though all systems are subject to compromise or being spoofed, and some are subject to flaws or biases, such as facial recognition systems that have difficulty distinguishing users of certain ethnicities or skin colors.

Additional weaknesses of biometrics include the following, which require the security practitioner to balance the needs for authentication and acceptance of a biometric solution:

- **Cultural acceptance:** Although not invasive, biometric scanners do require visible skin and public access to body parts that may be culturally unacceptable. An exterior door that requires facial scans will be problematic in a country where facial coverings are common, so security practitioners must balance user and cultural requirements when designing authentication schemes.

- **Accessibility:** Disabled users may have difficulty using biometric systems or even lack the needed body parts — a user who is missing a right hand will not be able to utilize a hand geometry scanner that supports right-hand scans only. The use of biometrics also introduces concerns of disease transmission; if users must put body parts in contact with the scanner, the proper sanitization must also be considered.

- **Body changes:** Over time, some of the characteristics used for biometric authentication may change, such as a user losing their voice due to an illness, eye degeneration, or diseases that can change physical characteristics. The biometric system must support a way for users to update their authentication information if this is the case, as the changing biometric will cause false rejections.

- **No easy way to change:** Unlike Type 1 and Type 2 authentication factors, users do not have an easy way to change biometrics if the authentication system is compromised. It is not possible for human beings to easily change physical characteristics like fingerprints or facial geometry. These systems should always be classified as containing personally identifiable information (PII), since biometrics can be used to uniquely identify individuals. The choice to use such a system introduces additional risks due to the type of data it will store and process.

There are many issues related to the use of biometrics, including the relative difficulty of maintaining their secrecy. Human beings cannot easily prevent their fingerprints from being left on physical objects, and high-quality photographs are nearly ubiquitous due to social media and surveillance. An important test for biometric systems is their ability to determine the "liveness" of a subject or whether the biometric data being presented is from a live human being or a reproduction like a photograph. This concept was explored in detail in the work of Dorothy Denning and can be found here: liveness.com.

Common Access Control Errors

Authentication systems can suffer errors of either false rejection or false acceptance. False rejection occurs when a system denies access to a subject that is properly authorized, while false acceptance occurs when a system grants access to a subject that is not authorized. Access control systems can be measured for how frequently they exhibit these errors, and the measures are known as false rejection rate (FRR) and false acceptance rate (FAR), also known as Type 1 and Type 2 errors.

Access controls, like all security controls, incur costs to implement. More expensive systems may offer additional features, while adding more steps to user logins can decrease productivity as users spend more time performing security actions. A more costly system may include more sensitive authentication mechanisms like biometric sensors that increase FRR. By contrast, a cheaper system with a less-sensitive biometric mechanism might suffer from higher FAR, thereby granting access to unauthorized users. The crossover error rate (CER) is the point at which Type 1 and Type 2 errors are equal, and the CER is an important factor when choosing an authentication system. The risk of Type 2 (FAR) errors on a low-value asset is less severe than the impact on a high-value asset, as unauthorized access to the high-value asset would have a greater impact.

Accountability

A system that provides *accountability* provides a mechanism for users and processes to be held responsible for their actions and decisions. Knowing who (user or process) did what (action) is the foundation of accountability and relies on unique identification and proven authenticity of users or processes. Logging and monitoring actions are the most common way of enforcing accountability, and performing audits or reviews is a common way of utilizing the information gathered to verify activities performed in the system.

Strong authentication is required in order to enforce accountability. If all users share the same credentials, it is impossible to identify which user took a specific action even if all actions are logged. The level of accountability needed should be documented as a system requirement when choosing IAM tools. For example, a financial management system needs strong accountability like MFA for regulatory purposes, since many financial transactions are subject to auditing. A system designed for internal social interactions may only require a basic username and password, which serves to hold users accountable for material they share on the platform.

Designing processes or systems with separation of duties (SOD) can be useful for enforcing accountability. The requirement for a second user to review and approve or execute a request provides a method for holding a user accountable to specific policies or requirements. For example, if user expense reports require receipts for all expenses, the report reviewer can enforce this requirement by verifying the submitted information and returning any incomplete reports to the submitters.

Session Management

A *session* is an exchange between communicating devices, such as a client and server exchanging information when a user requests web pages or functions like filling an online shopping cart and placing an order. *Session management* is the practice of initiating, managing, and terminating sessions, and is critical because session information is an authentication method.

Hypertext Transfer Protocol (HTTP) is stateless — each request sent to a web server is handled without knowledge of any previous requests. Sessions can be used to maintain a persistent state, such as the items a user has placed in an online shopping cart, which in turn allow for more complex applications. Each user's session is identified uniquely, and the items they have browsed or placed in a cart are tied to a unique session identifier. The ability to create a stateful experience, where the context of interactions is tracked, has led to a multitude of security issues when implemented using the stateless HTTP.

In the shopping cart example, a session is created when a user logs in to the shopping application by providing their username and password. The session ID is provided to the user in a cookie file, which is then sent back to the web app when subsequent requests are made. This allows the application to place the request in context of previous actions for that specific user — for example, proceeding to check out with all the items in a shopping cart.

The implementation of session management by tracking a token has given rise to a number of security vulnerabilities, including the following:

- **Session hijacking:** A session is hijacked if one of the authentic communicating parties is impersonated by an attacker, often with the goal of misdirecting information. Man-in-the-middle attacks are often used to hijack sessions as information is flowing between the two parties. Session replay attacks are similar and involve an attacker intercepting a session token and later using it to impersonate an authorized user.

- **Session sidejacking:** A session can be sidejacked by a user on the same network performing packet sniffing to steal session cookie information, which allows the attacker to impersonate the authorized user.

- **Session fixation:** Fixation attacks occur against web applications that reuse session IDs. This reuse allows an attacker to use an existing session ID to trick a user's browser into authenticating with the specific session ID. Once authenticated, the credentials granted to that ID can also be used by the attacker.

The Open Web Application Security Project (OWASP) publishes a guide on session management best practices and ways to avoid, detect, or mitigate session management vulnerabilities in web applications. The Session Management Cheat Sheet can be found at `cheatsheetseries.owasp.org/cheatsheets/Session_Management_Cheat_Sheet.html`.

Guidance on securely issuing and managing session IDs includes ensuring they are sufficiently long and complex to avoid weaknesses like guessing valid session IDs and to ensure the session token does not contain obviously identifiable information like cleartext of a username and password. For web applications where session tokens take the form of cookies, it is also recommended to configure proper security such as setting the `Secure` attribute to force the browser to use HTTPS when sending the cookie.

Registration, Proofing, and Establishment of Identity

Provisioning user access begins with the creation of an identity, which requires some amount of information to be provided by the user and verified by the provisioning organization. This can be as simple as choosing a screen name to claim an identity when signing up for an online application or as complex as submitting government-verified proof of identity when gaining access to systems or facilities with sensitive data.

NIST SP 800-63-3, "Digital Identity Guidelines," details a process of identity proofing that a credential service provider (CSP) can use when creating identities. This framework comprises Identity Assurance Levels (IALs) that correspond to different levels of risk to be mitigated when performing identity proofing.

- **IAL1:** This is the lowest level and only requires the user to self-assert an identity. The CSP is not required to link the individual to a verified, real-life identity. IAL1 would be appropriate for systems where accountability does not extend to real-world consequences like the need to take criminal action in response to user actions.

- **IAL2:** This level requires submission of identity documentation and proofing either in-person or remotely by the CSP, and the evidence required must link the user to a real-world identity. IAL2 is frequently used in employment situations where valid identification documents must be submitted to the employer.

- **IAL3:** This is the highest level of assurance and requires physical presence for identity proofing, presentation of highly reliable identity evidence like government-issued ID, and formal review of the identity and supporting documentation by trained CSP staff. The CSP staff can verify the person's identity and documentation in person, and the in-person requirement provides extra confidence that the user is who they claim to be.

Once identity information has been presented, verified, and validated to the appropriate level, an identity can be established for the user. This often takes the form of creating a user account or username on a system, but may also result in the issuance of credentials like a facility badge or authentication token. If the facility allows visitor access, a streamlined process is likely to exist for visitors upon entering the facility: they must present credentials to be verified by a guard or receptionist, and a visitor badge is issued.

A CISSP responsible for architecting an identity management system must consider the security requirements of the system and its data, like authenticity, confidentiality, and integrity. A loss of one or more of these will cause different impacts, such as inconvenience or personal distress, loss of organization reputation, unauthorized disclosure of sensitive information, or possibly even personnel safety. Airline operations, as an example, will likely have different identification requirements for various employees based on the sensitivity of their job. A greeter who provides directions to passengers in the airport might not have any impact on life, health, and safety, and therefore require only IAL 2, while mechanics and maintenance personnel require more extensive vetting.

Federated Identity Management

Users in a *federated identity management* (FIM) scheme can authenticate to any one system participating in the federation and are then granted access to other federated systems. Organizations that need to share information and system access federate to reduce both the administrative and user overhead of managing multiple sets of credentials for each user. These organizations can be separate entities, like business partners who need to collaborate on a project, or even divisions within an organization where unique IT systems are maintained, and the purpose of federating the identity systems is similar to an SSO. It can simplify the administrative overhead of account creation and management, benefits the users by providing easier access, and allows for security benefits like simplified access deprovisioning.

The reduction in overhead is a primary advantage of federation and therefore provides a business justification for federating identity management across organizations. It is imperative for a security practitioner to properly assess the risk present in federating; however, another organization's identity management practices will now impact any systems where federation grants access. If the federated organization does not have commensurate security controls, the risk present to the federated system increases.

Credential Management Systems

A credential binds an authenticator, such as a password or digital certificate, to an identifier, like a username or process. Credential management systems (CMSs) provide tools to provision, manage, audit, and deprovision these credentials. Password managers are one common example of a CMS, as are the registration authorities (RAs) and certificate authorities (CAs) used in public key infrastructure (PKI) to manage digital certificates. The RA is a function designed to provide identity proofing in a PKI, and it is where users submit their identity information in order to prove an identity and acquire a digital certificate. The CA is used by any user who has received a digital certificate to verify its authenticity.

A CMS should support processes needed to enroll users, proof the identities they claim, issue credentials to verified users, and support management and oversight of existing credentials. These include the following enrollment steps:

- **Sponsorship:** An authorized entity, such as an employer, sponsors a user to request credentials from a service provider.

- **Enrollment:** The user enrolls for credentials and supplies the required information to claim an identity, which will depend on the IAL implemented by the credential service provider.

- **Credential production:** Credentials are produced by the service provider and may take the form of a digital certificate, identification badge, smart card, etc.
- **Issuance:** The credentials are provided to the user.
- **Credential lifecycle management:** It may be necessary to perform audits, oversight, or maintenance on the credential throughout its lifetime. This may include revoking credentials that are no longer needed, reissuing in response to events like a user changing names or roles, suspending credentials if the user resigns, or suspending and reinstating credentials as users take leave and return to the organization.

Single Sign-On

SSO describes a system where users have a unified login experience — they log in to a single service and are granted access to other tools or resources using the same credentials. There are a variety of ways to implement SSO, with these two popular approaches:

- **Web-based dashboard or portal:** Users log in to a specific website using a single set of credentials and are presented with links to access additional SSO-enabled applications. This type of SSO often supports legacy software or applications where identity federation is not possible; instead, the SSO software stores the user's credentials and transmits them to the target application when the user accesses it from the SSO portal.
- **Federated identity:** Users log in to a single work resource like the Microsoft 365 or Google Workspace collaboration platforms. Once authenticated, they are able to log in to other, outside resources such as web or smartphone apps using their organization credentials.

SSO has major advantages and disadvantages related to usability and security. SSO reduces the burden of users memorizing and managing passwords, which has two key benefits: fewer weak passwords will be chosen, and users have less overhead to remember a variety of passwords. However, the centralization inherent in SSO can be a disadvantage as well — if a user's SSO account is compromised, then all SSO-enabled applications are also compromised. This single point of failure is not entirely a drawback, however. A compromised SSO account does grant broad access, but also increases response speed, since suspending the compromised account also suspends access to all SSO-enabled apps. An SSO can also serve as a single source of access log data since all access is governed by one system. This centralized point of oversight can enable faster detection and response for compromised accounts or suspicious insider access since the log data is available for analysis in a single system.

Just-In-Time

Just-in-time (JIT) identity and access management has two primary use cases, and both focus on provisioning access only when needed. A user's account provides the same level of access to the legitimate user and an attacker who has compromised the credentials, and JIT identity is a way to reduce some of this insider threat.

The first use case for JIT identity is to create user identities only when access is requested. In a typical example, an employee joins an organization and has a primary account created, often to provide email access. Based on the user's role or job function, they may require access to other systems as well. In a legacy access management model, this access must be granted system by system. In a JIT model, the user is authorized to access resources based on a role, and Security Assertion Markup Language (SAML) is used to provision an identity and authorization upon the user first accessing a resource. This reduces management overhead with respect to user administration.

JIT is often implemented as an element of privileged account management (PAM), which deals with the management of credentials for privileged accounts such as system administrators. Due to the broad, and potentially disruptive, authorizations given to such users, it is advisable to follow the principle of minimum necessary access and heavily restrict these permissions. Rather than always being available to users, a JIT access management strategy places the credentials needed to access these functions into a secure vault. When a user needs access, they can elevate their permissions by accessing the vault, which provides additional control opportunities. Accessing credentials in the vault, sometimes known as privilege escalation, is an event that can be logged and trigger additional security oversight. This is often known as a *break the glass* process and refers to old-fashioned alarm systems that require a user to break a glass panel to access the alarm button, which reduced the likelihood of accidental activation. PAM tools can also implement time limits for credentials and automatically change them after the time limit expires, thereby limiting the amount of time the elevated privileges can be used.

FEDERATED IDENTITY WITH A THIRD-PARTY SERVICE

Identity as a service (IDaaS) is an extension of the federated identity concept, which addresses increased demand for collaboration across different teams, business units, and organizations. This may be driven by the increased sharing of data and information systems among business partners or by organizations adopting cloud services that are hosted outside the organization's direct control.

Rather than developing custom methods for extending the IAM scheme to external entities, a third-party IDaaS can provide native integration with both legacy systems and external or cloud-based systems. IDaaS implements federation solutions like SAML and OAuth by default, and these solutions are typically designed to meet the needs of enabling IAM across both internal and external systems.

The decision to use a third-party IDaaS requires a security practitioner to balance the operational need of access to external systems against two primary risks. First, the IDaaS can be a single point of failure — systems that rely on the IDaaS for access control are unavailable if it is down, though if the organization already uses a centralized IAM, this risk is minimal. IDaaS may actually decrease the risk if the chosen third party has more robust uptime capabilities than the organization's internal hosting, though of course if the IDaaS provider drops support for the target system or ceases operations, the organization will find itself in trouble.

The second risk to consider is the loss of control inherent in using a third party, which is common to any decision to use a cloud service. Identification is the foundation of access control, so the potential risk of outsourcing this function can be high. If the IDaaS provider suffers a data breach, the organization's identity and access management information could be compromised.

On Premises

On premises, sometimes shortened to *on-prem*, describes an architecture that exists in a facility controlled by the organization, such as a Lightweight Directory Access Protocol (LDAP) or Microsoft Active Directory (AD) system hosted in the organization's offices or data center. Many organizations have these systems deployed to support existing or legacy applications and infrastructure.

Key benefits of on-premises management systems include total control over the hardware and software used in the IAM system, unlike cloud or third-party systems where the organization gives up some control to the service provider. As a CISSP, it is important to review the benefit of total control against the additional costs incurred, such as full-time administrators needed to maintain a complex IAM system like Microsoft AD.

Extending an existing on-premise identity management system to cloud-based applications or federating it with external parties like business partners can prove difficult or impossible, if the tools in use were not designed to support this type of use. Retaining control over both the IAM system and the hardware offers security control opportunities, but limited federation capabilities can force organizations to seek alternatives. Many legacy IAM solutions can be quite complex to administer, which presents additional risk in the form of cost to maintain them and the potential for misconfiguration due to lack of adequate skills or understanding of a complex system.

The process of extending an existing IAM typically requires additional software and proper security configuration that allows the on-premise IAM to communicate with systems outside the organization's control. This might be achieved with native extensions or plugins to the IAM tool or with a separate application like a SAML gateway or SSO provider.

Cloud

Newer organizations may be "cloud-first" or "cloud-native," meaning they lack any on-premise or legacy infrastructure. Older organizations may pursue a strategy of migrating to cloud-only solutions due to the cost savings they provide. In both cases, a legacy IAM solution would be a poor fit due to significant costs to acquire hardware, software, and personnel skills to manage it; a cloud-based IDaaS is likely to be a more cost-effective solution.

Cloud-based IDaaS solutions act as an IAM broker and can be used to manage access controls for the organization's cloud-based systems and federated with other applications, services, or even organizations using the same IDaaS. Organizations migrating into the cloud can take advantage of hybrid IDaaS, which extends the IDaaS to support identity and access management for legacy applications, or SSO portal features, which allow users to access non-SSO applications by storing the credentials and facilitating automatic sign in.

Popular cloud services, including software as a service (SaaS) tools, offer native integration with popular cloud IDaaS platforms, which reduces administrative overhead associated with user provisioning. This can be used to implement JIT provisioning for new user accounts on cloud services; when a user attempts to log into a service for the first time, their authorization to use it is checked with the IDaaS provider. If they are authorized, an account is created; this benefits users and administrators, as it automates the process of checking authorizations and provisioning accounts.

Hybrid

Hybrid IDaaS is a combined deployment of IAM elements in both the cloud and on premises and is often used as part of a migration strategy in organizations where legacy infrastructure requires an on-premise solution. For example, this hybrid approach is commonly used in Windows environments that rely on legacy AD for current applications migrating to a cloud-based setup with Azure AD, which is a cloud-based IDaaS platform hosted in the Microsoft Azure cloud. Both the legacy AD and Azure AD run simultaneously and synchronize information, with the ultimate goal of total migration to the cloud-based solution once all legacy applications have been identified and migrated.

Other third-party IDaaS solutions can also integrate with existing on-premise IAM tools and act as a centralized point for credential management. Even if the organization does not plan to migrate completely to cloud solutions, legacy applications continue to use the on-premise IAM provider, while any cloud services or federated third parties can use the cloud-based IDaaS provider. This divided access control approach offers benefits to users, who are required to maintain only one set of credentials, and acts like an SSO to reduce management overhead.

The risks of a hybrid setup like this include the need to dedicate sufficient resources to maintaining dual IAM implementation. Many organizations assume a move to the cloud means no resources are required for on-premise maintenance, but the hybrid approach does not completely remove this need. Additionally, the hybrid approach introduces the same risk as cloud-based IAM due to a third party managing identities and can pose additional risk if a breach of the IDaaS grants access to internal resources that rely on on-premise IAM synchronized with the IDaaS provider.

IMPLEMENT AND MANAGE AUTHORIZATION MECHANISMS

Authorization can be the decision to grant a subject access to an object and confirmation that a subject is authorized to access an object when they attempt to access it. This implies decisions that are made before access, when a user is first enrolled in an IAM, as well as decisions made at the time of use when a user makes a request, such as trying to open a file or access a system. Authorization is simple to manage if a few subjects, like users or processes, require access to a few objects, like documents or an entire information system. However, complex organizations with hundreds or thousands of subjects accessing millions of objects are impossible to manage without a structured and orderly methodology. Even an organization with a hundred users and multiple information systems for various teams or departments will find that manually managing access on a per-user basis is inefficient at best, and at worst is totally impossible.

Access control models, which are described in the following sections, provide ways of identifying subjects and objects and establishing relationships to determine authorization. These relationships are foundational to access control systems, and the decision to allow or deny access supports fundamental security objectives like maintaining confidentiality, integrity, and authenticity of data. These models also provide a variety of methods for managing complex subject-object access needs, so they are useful to security practitioners in organizations with more than a few users and systems.

Modern information systems and IT environments often implement a mix of access control models, such as firewalls utilizing rule-based access control, file sharing systems with discretionary access control, and HR departments that identify specific job functions and associated permissions needed for role-based access control. NIST SP 800-192, "Verification and Test Methods for Access Control Policies/Models," provides definitions of these models and guidance on how to identify requirements for an access control model to apply to a specific system or organization.

Role-Based Access Control

RBAC is a model that maps subjects to a set of objects based on the user's role in the organization. A role is a set of job functions, often defined by a department or position, and the access granted is based on the needs of that particular role. Roles are mapped to object access authorizations, and all subjects granted a particular role are given the same access.

For example, a user with security responsibility might be given the role of security analyst. Users with the security analyst role are granted read/write access to the security information and event management (SIEM) platform, but are denied system adminis-trator privileges like Windows domain admin or Linux sudo. In this case, the role grants access to security logs, but prevents the analysts from accessing systems being monitored, which serves two purposes. First, the analysts do not require access to perform system admin functions, and nonanalyst users do not need access to the SIEM, so the roles implement least privilege.

Second, this role-based access can preserve data integrity, which supports account-ability. In a properly designed RBAC model, so-called toxic role combinations should be prevented. In this example, any user with a system admin role should be barred from the security analyst role, preventing an administrative user from taking malicious action on a system and also erasing evidence of their actions from logs on the SIEM.

RBAC reduces the management and overhead of creating and managing authoriza-tions for users. If members of the legal department need access to 15 systems, it is more efficient to create a role with access to these systems and then put new members in a group associated with that role. This supports important security objectives of access control, while also reducing resources required to implement security, which aligns with business or organization objectives.

Rule-Based Access Control

Rule-based access control, which is usually spelled out to avoid confusion with role-based models or shortened to RuBAC, is based on a list of predefined rules to determine autho-rization. In physical terms, a guest list is RuBAC model. If a person is on the guest list, they are granted access to the party; otherwise, they are denied entry.

Information systems often implement RuBAC via an access control list (ACL). Common examples include static firewall rulesets, which define allowed and blocked IP addresses or ports, and file ACLs, which define users who are authorized to access a file and their permissions like read or write. When an access attempt is made, the system performs a review against the ruleset. A traditional or nonstateful firewall reviews an incoming packet to determine if it comes from an IP address that is allowed, while a file-system reviews the current user against the file's ACL to determine if the requested action is allowed.

Rule-based systems also implement the concepts of implicit and explicit permissions. In an implicit allow system, all access is allowed unless a rule is defined to prohibit access, much like a shop is open to any member of the public except specific customers who are known to shoplift. These unwanted users are explicitly denied entry.

Implicit deny is the opposite — only people on an approved list are allowed entry, while everyone else is denied. This is sometimes known as *deny all* or *allow by exception* and is a fundamental security best practice as it reduces the chance of unauthorized access.

Mandatory Access Control

The mandatory access control (MAC) model is often associated with military or government organizations, and it employs a static and hierarchical approach to access control. MAC can be described as a *nondiscretionary access control* model, in which access control is enforced systematically and is not at the discretion of data owners or others.

MAC is achieved by applying security labels to both subjects and objects; for example, Top Secret, Secret, and Unclassified. When an object is created, the owner or creator is responsible for assigning a proper security label. When a subject attempts to access an object, the system verifies the security labels and enforces appropriate access control. For example, a user with a security label of Secret will be denied access to files with a security label of Top Secret, but will be granted access to files labeled Secret or Unclassified.

The Bell–LaPadula and Biba security models discussed in Chapter 3, "Security Architecture and Engineering," are examples of MAC and are often used as foundational principles in modern systems' access control features. The basic rules described by both models implement MACs using label-based descriptions of data confidentiality or integrity. The properties of each model describe how access to objects is restricted based on the subject security label of the subject and the label of the object they attempted to access.

Discretionary Access Control

Access decisions in a discretionary access control (DAC) model are made by a system or data owner, who decides at their discretion which subjects can access an object. In the case of a file, the file's owner can define other users who can access the file. This extends to the functions those users can perform, like reading or updating the file. This may take the form of granting public read access to a document, while specifying a small group of editors who can make changes to the file.

DAC is a distributed model and can be useful when no central authority has sufficient information to make access control decisions. Social media sites are a common example; the users who upload content like pictures are best suited to determine if the content should be accessible to any other user of the platform, or if it should be restricted to a specific group of users like close friends or family. In business settings, the owner is often the owner, creator, or custodian of a system or dataset. A centralized IT department may not be able to determine who needs access to specific files on a shared drive, but the owner of the folder does know which users need access to collaborate.

The flexibility and decentralized nature of DAC is also a potential security drawback. It is more difficult to enforce consistency when a large group of data owners is making access control decisions, and the ability for a data owner to make permission changes can be abused by an insider threat.

Attribute-Based Access Control

Attribute-based access control (ABAC), sometimes referred to as *policy-based access control*, is an emerging access control model that combines attributes about the subject and evaluates them against a policy to make an access control decision. For example, attributes might be the user's identity, role as a data entry professional, and the time of day. When a user attempts to access a system, these attributes are compared against a policy stating that access for data entry users is allowed only during standard business hours. If the data entry user attempts this access outside of normal business hours, the access request is denied.

ABAC provides more flexibility than other access control models and can be used to achieve more dynamic and risk-based access control. For example, users might be required to enter multifactor authentication only when logging in from a new device. ABAC is similar to RBAC models, but defines a complex policy to allow or deny access rather than a binary allow/deny decision. Stateful firewalls are one example of ABAC; incoming traffic to a host is allowed if it corresponds to a previously established session of communication; otherwise, traffic to the host is denied. A traditional or nonstateful firewall could be a hindrance to an organization if it blocked such traffic, which highlights the importance of choosing access control mechanisms with sufficiently robust capabilities to support organizational needs.

A system implementing ABAC utilizes a set of policy attributes to make access control decisions. Examples of attributes that can be tested include where the subject or object is located, when the request is being made, the role of the requestor, and whether the request is coming from a new device. For example, a routine user requesting access from their standard workstation to a sensitive production file outside of normal working hours can be allowed. If the same user attempts to access the same data, but the request comes from a previously unseen device in a foreign country, access should be denied. The user might be traveling and trying to stay productive, but there is a significant chance the user's credentials have been stolen.

Risk-Based Access Control

A risk-based access control model is designed around an assumption that risks change over time. Unlike other models that consider risks to be static and do not account for changing risks over time, risk-based models can provide dynamic access control using a variety of parameters to determine authorization. In other models such as RBAC or RuBAC, the dynamic nature of risks over time must be accounted for with manual updates to access controls, such as provisioning or deprovisioning access. Systems that implement these models cannot respond to these dynamic changes in real time.

For example, the IAM can integrate threat intelligence data and make dynamic authentication decisions based on the intelligence available. If another business unit or a partner organization has come under attack by a phishing campaign, then the IAM might temporarily increase the frequency of required MFA at login in response to the increased threat. Similarly, if the organization's SIEM has identified an increase in the number of failed login attempts, temporary firewall rules could be automatically implemented to block traffic associated with the failed logins, which could make a brute-force attack difficult or impossible.

Risk-based models can utilize a number of factors to dynamically define authentication requirements. Financial institutions often utilize this model to detect fraud at an individual account level. Accounts that belong to a person who rarely travels or makes online purchases have a different risk profile compared to frequent travelers or online shoppers, so writing static rules that apply to all account holders is nearly impossible. Instead, one account's fraud indicators are any purchases made outside a specific geographic region, while another account's indicators are purchases made in physical retail stores instead of online retailers.

MANAGE THE IDENTITY AND ACCESS PROVISIONING LIFECYCLE

The act of creating an account is known as *provisioning*. This encompasses actions such as reviewing proof that a user is who they claim to be before creating their account, as well as procedures designed to review and approve access requests. When an account is no longer needed, access is removed via *deprovisioning*, which happens when a user leaves or changes roles, or when a system account is terminated during decommissioning.

Reviews must be conducted periodically to identify if all provisioned accounts are still accurate. Any accounts that are not needed or permissions that are excessive should be terminated using appropriate deprovisioning actions like revoking, disabling, or deleting the account or authorizations. This deprovisioning typically focuses on removing access, but deprovisioning does not necessarily mean an account is deleted. Instead, it may be maintained for accountability purposes, since the user's actions are recorded in log files.

Reviews may also identify access that is needed but not currently granted, which can be addressed by provisioning new access. Figure 5.1 depicts this access management lifecycle.

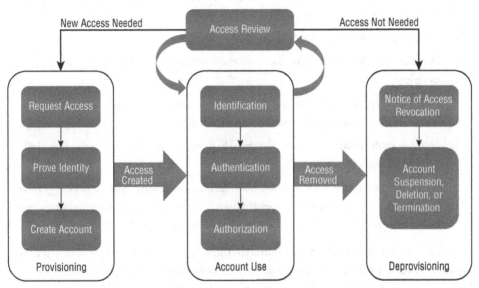

FIGURE 5.1 **The access management lifecycle**

Account Access Review

User accounts are associated with individuals, while system accounts are associated with nonhuman access needs. These often take the form of system or service accounts needed to perform crucial system functions like backups, database maintenance, or executing requests or processes on behalf of a user. Nonhuman accounts include devices as well, such as Internet of Things (IoT) or system Application Programming Interface (API) calls. Both user and system accounts must be periodically reviewed to ensure they are granted access only as needed to perform their intended functions.

When crafting an access review policy, a security practitioner must balance a number of important factors. Both the cadence of reviews and the accounts to be reviewed may be dictated by legal or regulatory obligations. For example, nonadministrative access might have an annual review cycle, while administrative accounts must be reviewed quarterly. The increased damage that could be caused by an improperly provisioned administrative account justifies the increased overhead of performing more frequent reviews.

Review procedures for user access must include identifying what systems, data, and permissions a user is granted. Once identified, these access attributes must be checked against the organization's access policies as well as IAM practices like least privilege. The review should encompass the following elements for each user, as well as a check of the appropriateness of the access:

- All accounts the user can access, whether by direct assignment or via shared credentials if used.

- All sensitive datasets or systems the user can access

- What actions the user can perform on each system or dataset, such as read, write, or delete.

- Identify any permissions that are excessive, such as a user who is not performing administrative actions but is granted administrative access.

- Inactive or dormant accounts, particularly those assigned to users who have left the organization or changed roles.

- Roles assigned to the user and any potential toxic combinations of access granted by roles. A toxic combination occurs when a user's role-based access violates controls like separation of duties or creates a conflict of interest.

Policies for system and service accounts should also be defined and must balance the frequency of review with the privileges granted. Nonhuman accounts will undergo less change than user accounts, as they are not subject to human actions like promotion or job change that require adjustment of privileges. However, they can still present a security risk due to inappropriate levels of access — for example, a default local administrator account might be enabled during troubleshooting. If it is not properly deactivated or disabled when troubleshooting is completed, it is at risk of being exploited.

In other cases, system or service accounts may be granted escalated privileges by default, but when implemented in a particular system, these permissions are not needed. Systems may include default local administrator accounts that are not needed if the computer in question is part of a remote management scheme like a Windows domain or MDM, or service accounts remain enabled even if the particular service is not active on the workstation. In these cases, access reviews are similar to configuration audits; they both share a goal of identifying system configurations, like default system account privileges, that are out of alignment with the secure baseline.

Performing access reviews can be time-consuming and potentially disruptive if an account is improperly flagged for inappropriate access. Implementing automation is critical to performing timely reviews, and some access management tools can be used to supplement the review with proactive controls like disabling accounts that are not used within a set time period. Security tools like SIEM or security orchestration, automation, and response (SOAR) can be useful to perform these automated reviews. The risk of not performing the reviews is inappropriate or unintended access, which can be exploited by insider threats or an attacker who has compromised a valid user account.

Account Usage Review

User, system, and nonhuman accounts should all be subject to review of the actions they have performed. This can help the organization identify unwanted or inappropriate use of permissions, as well as account permissions that are inappropriate. The usage review may be part of access reviews, may be performed using automated tools like a SIEM, or might even involve a process of occasional oversight like a random audit of system activity several times a year to spot unexpected or inappropriate usage.

A CISSP can achieve multiple security objectives with a usage review, though the primary reason is to enforce accountability for system usage. Automated system usage reviews should be integrated where JIT identity systems are in use, to perform reviews when privileges are used. For example, if a user accesses administrative credentials, it could be a legitimate support case or a privilege escalation by an attacker. Correlating the privilege escalation to a work ticket or support case demonstrates that the access was needed, while access to the administrative credentials for no reason is a suspicious incident worthy of investigation.

Provisioning and Deprovisioning

Provisioning is the action of enabling or creating access, and deprovisioning is the opposite action and may include suspending, terminating, or even deleting the access credentials. These processes are usually related to staff changes like onboarding or offboarding (joining or leaving an organization), job transfers, or role changes like promotions. These staff management processes are usually not handled by a security practitioner, so it is imperative that the security team properly coordinate the process with responsible teams like HR or IT to ensure security measures are designed, integrated into the process, and properly executed.

Deprovisioning is a particularly important task, as there is increased risk if users who no longer require access are still able to access data and systems. An access review must be performed to identify which systems and data the user has access to, and confirmation must be obtained when the access has been deprovisioned. The access management policy and procedures should account for user access changing under three main scenarios:

- **Hostile or involuntary** circumstances include a staff member being let go at the company's decision. This type of departure carries higher risk because employees may be disgruntled or act out in retaliation, and procedures will typically require faster deprovisioning and more oversight.

- **Friendly or voluntary** circumstances include a staff member resigning or retiring and generally carry less risk. Access deprovisioning in these cases may occur more slowly, and verification may be left until the next access review to catch any mistakes.

- **Job changes** are treated by some high-security organizations the same as a friendly deprovisioning as an extra precaution. The user's current access is entirely deprovisioned, and new access is requested and provisioned for the user's changed job role.

Systems that support self-provisioning or self-deprovisioning must have access control requirements addressed as part of the system development. For example, an online shopping site that allows users to register themselves for accounts will mostly likely implement RBAC. One role will be "customer," with permission to access information related to that specific user, while another role might be "customer support," which is for internal users who need access to limited information across all customers. The requirements for users to provision their own accounts will vary depending on the type of application, and the identity proofing requirements must be considered in light of any legal or regulatory compliance requirements associated with the identity proofing material that must be collected. Deprovisioning is likely to fall under privacy legislation or regulation, so appropriate methods for disabling and possibly deleting data associated with the user must be provided.

Role Definition

Roles simplify access management by providing a common set of access requirements for all users assigned the specific role. For example, an organization's roles might be defined according to department, so users with the IT role are granted access to all IT systems, while finance users are granted access to finance systems. When a new user joins, they are placed in a group or assigned a particular role, which grants them access to the appropriate systems. This simplifies the process of access provisioning and deprovisioning, as only one action needs to be performed instead of multiple actions to add the user to each system.

The process of defining roles must follow access management principles like least privilege and may also be used as a way to implement security controls like separation of duties. For example, if users are able to upload their own personal data into an HR system but should not be able to query the system, then non-HR roles can be granted write permissions and denied read permissions. A matrix of systems and roles can be useful to visualize these permissions.

Privilege Escalation

Escalating privileges is the process of gaining elevated permission. For example, if a user with read-only access finds a bug that allows them to write data, this escalates their privileges beyond what they should have. The escalation can lead to negative security outcomes like loss of confidentiality, integrity, authenticity, or even availability if the users' elevated privileges allow them to disrupt system operations.

There are valid use cases for privilege escalation. A user with authorization to perform administrative functions should not use their administrator account at all times, as they generally do not need access to all its functionality and could inadvertently execute commands. Features like sudo on Unix systems or credential vaults for other systems can be used to implement a *break-the-glass* process. When needed, the user can virtually break the glass and gain access to the credentials, which may trigger actions like a security alert or increased logging. If the access is inappropriate, these actions give defenders a greater chance of discovery.

A well-engineered IAM should limit user access to privileged accounts and allow access only when necessary. For example, even a system administrator does not need to use their administrative privileges to perform routine tasks like checking email or reading news in a web browser. Implementing restrictions to administrative privileges reduces the likelihood those privileges can be misused accidentally or intentionally. For instance, a drive-by download from a malicious website can be restricted from executing with administrative-level credentials if the user is not signed in as an administrator while performing casual web browsing. Examples of methods to implement this type of privilege escalation include the following:

- sudo on Linux and Unix systems allows an authenticated user to perform superuser actions for a limited amount of time if they can provide the proper credentials. The extra act of authenticating creates a barrier to accidental misuse of administrative privileges.

- Break-the-glass procedures or credential vaulting place administrative credentials in a restricted-access tool. Gaining access to the credentials requires a deliberate process and can be a trigger for alerts or alarms, thereby providing security with insight into the use of these credentials.

- Managed service accounts are nonhuman accounts designed to perform specific functions. They are typically configured to perform only their designated function and cannot be used to log in to a system, which makes attacks like phishing these account credentials nearly impossible.

Privilege escalation attacks are a common security threat as well. In a vertical escalation attack, the attacker is seeking to gain increased privileges on a system, such as using Structured Query Language (SQL) injection to gain direct database access when the user is only authorized to access data through a web front end. Horizontal privilege escalation, also known as lateral movement, is an attack method that grants access to systems or resources the user is not authorized for and may exploit improperly configured IAM tools or features like roles. Horizontal escalation is often targeted at accessing other systems using already compromised credentials; goals may include performing vertical escalation on another system or gaining access to additional sources or types of data.

IMPLEMENT AUTHENTICATION SYSTEMS

Once credentials are provisioned, subjects will use them to access resources. The credentials presented when the subject requests access must be authenticated, and a variety of authentication systems exist to support various use cases. These include local authentication functions that provide access to one computer or set of files and networked authentication systems like LDAP or IDaaS, which grants access to resources hosted across a network. Users are not always connected to the network or may need access across multiple networks, so authentication systems that support remote access or federated identities can also be useful to achieve access control security objectives, while still meeting user requirements.

OpenID Connect/Open Authorization

Open Authorization (OAuth) is an "open protocol to allow secure authorization in a simple and standard method from web, mobile, and desktop applications," as defined by the OAuth community website (`oauth.net`). The project is an Internet Engineering Task Force (IETF) working group, which lends its broad, global support, and, as the name implies, it is focused on authorization rather than authentication. The community website contains a variety of resources including specifications for platform-specific implementations and best-practice guides for using OAuth in various applications.

OAuth defines four key roles that systems in an OAuth federation must implement to exchange authorization information:

- **Resource owner:** Any entity that grants access to a protected resource, such as an information system or dataset.
- **Resource server:** Any server hosting the protected resource, which accepts and responds to access requests.
- **Client:** Any application making requests for access to protected resources.
- **Authorization server:** Any server issuing access tokens to clients after successful authentication; tokens are used across the federated system to gain access.

Open ID Connect (OIDC) adds authentication functions built on top of OAuth version 2.0 and federates identity management to provide users with an authentication experience similar to SSO. It is often implemented in web applications; and in OIDC, the user is presented with a choice of identity providers (IdPs), which are usually common email or social media platforms like Gmail, LinkedIn, or Twitter.

The user selects an IdP, which then provides authentication information to the relying party using OAuth. The authentication information in OIDC is passed from an OIDC provider (OP) to the relying party (RP) in the form of a token, which contains claims about the user and authentication of their asserted identity. IDaaS provider Okta has an illustrated developer blog highlighting the key steps of OIDC authentication (`developer.okta.com/blog/2019/10/21/illustrated-guide-to-oauth-and-oidc`).

As an example, a user registers for the eBay web application using a Twitter account; in the future, they can authenticate to eBay if they are able to successfully log in to Twitter. If they have authenticated to Twitter before opening eBay, then they may not even be required to perform any action — eBay can make an OIDC request to Twitter, which has an active, authenticated session for the user, and access is automatically granted. This user convenience can be beneficial to reduce the burden of user logins, but also carries risks similar to SSO. If the OP is unavailable, then all RPs will also lose availability. Other similar IdPs include Google, LinkedIn, Microsoft, and Apple, which provide user identification and authentication services that can be implemented in other websites, web apps, and many common smartphone apps.

Security Assertion Markup Language

SAML is a framework for different systems to exchange security assertions, which consist of information needed to enforce access controls. It uses Extensible Markup Language (XML) to format messages regarding identities, resources, and access information like authentication and authorization. In SAML, there are three roles: first is the user agent (like a web browser) that makes a request to the second role, which is a service provider (like a web application). The service provider relies on the assertion made by the third role, called an *identity provider* (IdP), for user identification, authentication, and authorization.

There are four components in SAML:

- **Assertions** define SAML attributes like how authentication and authorization message protocols or frameworks are to be used by the services.

- **Bindings** define the request-response pairs to be used by the three roles to communicate.

- **Protocols** include HTTP and simple object access protocol (SOAP), which are used to package and exchange messages between roles.

- **Profiles** are the combination of assertions, bindings, and protocols in use within a specific SAML implementation.

The current version of SAML, v2.0, is an OASIS standard. Documentation and best practices for SAML implementation are maintained on the SAML wiki (`wiki.oasis-open.org/security/FrontPage`). SAML is most often used to provide an SSO experience to end users. Users access resources using normal system functions like clicking links to access a web application. Security assertion information can be provided as part of a custom URL pointing to the web application or sent as a cookie to the web application. This information is based on the user's previously provided information, such as their login credentials entered when signing into their computer or a web portal, which then grants access to other SAML-enabled applications.

Kerberos

Kerberos is one of the earliest examples of an SSO designed to reduce the need for users to maintain separate accounts across multiple systems, and to reduce the overhead of individual information systems performing identification and authentication. It is widely implemented in modern information systems including Microsoft AD.

In a Kerberos environment, applications or systems that have been "kerberized" instead rely on the Kerberos server to authenticate users. Information is exchanged via tickets, which identify if a user is authentic and if they should be granted access to specific resources. User authenticity is proven using symmetric encryption, which requires users to maintain control over their secret key in order to authenticate identity.

A Kerberos realm comprises a set of services and resources, including the following:

- **Principals:** These are the parties using Kerberos for identification and authentication, including the users and services or applications.

- **Key Distribution Center (KDC):** The KDC is used to perform registration for new users and maintains the database of secret keys.

- **Authentication Server (AS):** The AS performs the function of authenticating principles by exchanging encrypted data. If the principal can successfully decrypt using a pre-shared symmetric key (a Type 2 authentication factor), they are authenticated.
- **Ticket Granting Server (TGS):** Kerberos operates using tickets, which are similar to tokens. A TGS provides a ticket to an authenticated principal, which allows them to make requests for service tickets. A service ticket is used by a kerberized application to grant access to a properly authenticated user.

A user requesting access to resources in a Kerberos realm follows a three-step process to identify, authenticate, and then gain access to resources:

1. The client authenticates to the AS, by passing a message encrypted with the client's secret key. If successful, the client is given a ticket-granting ticket (TGT), which grants the user the ability to request service tickets for a specific service.

2. The client requests a service ticket by providing the TGT. If they are authorized to access the service, a service ticket is issued.

3. The client provides service ticket to the target service and is granted access if the ticket is valid.

The Kerberos project was initiated and is maintained by MIT. Full documentation and code can be found at `web.mit.edu/kerberos`. Many popular IAM tools also implement Kerberos, such as Microsoft AD.

Remote Authentication Dial-In User Service/Terminal Access Controller Access Control System Plus

Remote authentication dial-in user service (RADIUS) was originally designed in the early 1990s, as evidenced by the name containing dial-in. At that time, remote access typically meant utilizing a modem and traditional phone line, but the authentication, authorization, and accounting (AAA) functions it provides are implemented in many modern systems like 802.1X authentication, which is both widely supported and used by modern desktop and smartphone operating systems. RADIUS accepts remote user credentials and performs authentication to enforce access control and also provides accounting of remote sessions like the amount of data transferred. The RADIUS standard is specified in IETF RFC 2865, available at `https://datatracker.ietf.org/doc/html/rfc2865`.

Another protocol that provides AAA functionality is the Terminal Access Controller Access Control System Plus (TACACS+), which was originally designed by Cisco systems. TACACS+ is generally implemented to control access to network infrastructure resources like routers and enables users logging in to perform maintenance and other administrative functions. It supports authenticating users and provides a centralized method for authorizing user access, as well as auditing of user access and actions. It is described in IETF RFC 8907 at `datatracker.ietf.org/doc/html/rfc8907`.

SUMMARY

Security is often equated with the confidentiality of data, so a totally secure system would simply provide no access, which also guarantees absolute integrity. However, availability is also part of security, so it is essential to grant access to systems. This presents risks to the other elements of security including authenticity, nonrepudiation, and confidentiality. IAM consists of processes and tools designed to restrict access to only properly authorized users. This restriction must balance the need for system availability with other requirements like preventing unwanted changes or unauthorized access to data.

IAM encompasses logical and physical access controls, administrative controls like identity proofing, the access provisioning lifecycle, and technical system implementations like federating identities or providing secure remote access. The lifecycle used to provision, review, and deprovision access should always be designed to manage the risk inherent in providing access to data and systems, and balance it with the organization's mission or objectives that are supported by users accessing and processing data.

Security Assessment and Testing

AN *ASSESSMENT* **IS AN** evaluation of an object, such as the likelihood of a specific risk occurring or the quality of an organization's security process documentation. An *audit* is similar but is a more formal process that involves a systematic analysis against a defined standard to determine if the object meets a set of criteria. Both are designed to measure a target, like the technology risk facing an organization or the security posture of a system. For example, a risk assessment identifies the assets an organization possesses and then measures or estimates the likelihood and impact of risks that could affect those assets. A system audit, by contrast, determines if the system in question meets specific, objective requirements set by an authority such as the Payment Card Industry Data Security Standard (PCI DSS).

Audit and assessment are terms that are often used interchangeably, but it is important for a CISSP to understand the differences and use each appropriately in designing or monitoring a security program. Both are used to gather information needed to perform oversight, and support efforts to identify the effectiveness of security controls and any necessary remedial action.

The output of an assessment or audit is a report detailing the actions taken and findings. This may include a specific list of gaps or issues, which represent risk to the organization. Controls that are not working as intended are known as *deficiencies* and identify a risk that is not being properly mitigated. Gaps are areas where the organization is missing risk mitigation, possibly due to new risks or insufficient controls in place. In both cases, these outputs should be treated just like any other risk — prioritized for fixing and given a defined plan of action to remediate them.

Testing is a method of gathering information. It can be used as part of performing audits or assessments, and it can also be used independently as part of security monitoring and oversight. Automated and routine testing can verify the effectiveness of security controls on an ongoing basis and can provide timely data needed to correct issues.

DESIGN AND VALIDATE ASSESSMENT, TEST, AND AUDIT STRATEGIES

Like all security measures, audits, assessments, and testing incur costs. A Certified Information Systems Security Professional (CISSP) should be aware of these and plan a strategy to make efficient use of resources to perform monitoring activities, since they can be useful in identifying and addressing risks. The scope of and targets for audit or assessment should be designed to ensure appropriate systems, processes, and services are evaluated based on their value to the organization, as well as to meet obligations like regulatory or contract requirements.

Various audit and assessment methodology standards exist and may be used as a starting point to guide the organization's strategy. Utilizing a standard methodology offers key benefits including repeatable testing and results that will be more comparable over time. Auditing against the same standard year over year can demonstrate return on investment (ROI) from the organization's spending on security efforts, as well as the increasing maturity of key security practices or processes. All concepts introduced here are revisited in more detail later in this chapter in the section "Conduct or Facilitate Security Audits."

Internal

Audits, assessments, and testing can be conducted from two perspectives. Internal evaluations are done inside the organization, with the staff and resources of the organization. Any use of third-party assessors or auditors constitutes an external perspective, which is discussed in the next section. When designing an audit strategy, different circumstances will drive the choice of internal, external, or even the use of both audit perspectives.

To conduct an internal audit, the organization must have adequate skills and knowledge on staff, it must have sufficient time and resources to perform the audit, and there must be no requirements for the audit or assessment to be performed by an independent observer who is totally free of conflicts. Assessments conducted from an internal perspective are appropriate as part of ongoing or continual assessment processes and are often used as part of continuous monitoring with a supplemental external audit performed less frequently.

✔ Preparing for External Audits

An audit conducted by internal personnel will never have the same objectivity as an audit conducted by external personnel. Internal audits are still a valuable tool, however, and are often used in preparation for an external audit. An organization preparing for an external audit may choose to perform an internal readiness audit prior to engaging external auditors. This offers the advantage of finding and correcting any deficiencies before they appear on an audit report, and conflict of interest is not an issue because the audience is the organization itself and not an external party.

Depending on the size of the organization, there may need to be a full-time staff member dedicated to assessment activities, or elements of the assessment may be distributed among multiple staff members. For example, access control reviews are often conducted once per quarter and may require only a few hours of work, so a single IT staff member can perform them in addition to other work assignments. In a large multinational organization with complex user access requirements, multiple offices, and hundreds or thousands of systems, access control reviews could be a full-time job.

There is a general saying that "Whoever wrote the policy shouldn't be the one to audit it," and mitigating conflicts of interest is an important element in an audit or assessment strategy. An internal auditor may be unintentionally blind to faults or may intentionally cover mistakes or deficiencies in the interest of maintaining their position. In some cases, this conflict of interest may be mitigated by using an internal audit team that does not report directly to any of the department heads being audited.

While conflict of interest can be an issue for internal audits, greater knowledge of skills, process, and systems in use at the organization is a potential positive. Internal testers can more accurately perform tests or assessments with the knowledge of an insider, which helps identify issues related to insider threat. Performing testing on complex systems with complex rules like separation of duties (SoD) can be challenging for an outsider.

These are some types of testing that may be best conducted internally:

- Vulnerability scanning, especially routine scans looking for unpatched software or unknown assets
- Process and procedure audits like change management or training completion
- Phishing simulations

External

The other perspective for conducing audits, assessments, and testing is external to the organization. An external auditor should have no conflicts of interest, since they are paid to perform an impartial assessment rather than to deliver a report that makes their department look good. External evaluations can also take advantage of specialized skills and knowledge that are valuable but not needed full-time. Performing penetration testing, often called pen testing, is an important and valuable skill, but due to the specialized skills and high salaries required, employing a full-time pen tester is not cost-effective for most organizations. Contracting an outside party to perform the test and sharing the costs with other organizations is a more sensible approach.

The use of an external firm for assessments, testing, or audits can identify issues the organization is unintentionally unaware of; a fresh pair of eyes can often spot a problem more quickly and offer insight the organization would otherwise miss. External testing may be advisable or even required in some cases, especially for legal or regulatory reasons, such as maturity assessments against a maturity model, which is covered in more detail in Chapter 8, "Software Development Security."

Audits for compliance purposes — for example, PCI-DSS, ISO 27001, and the U.S. government's Federal Risk and Authorization Management Program (FedRAMP) — all require the use of an independent, authorized third-party auditor or assessor. The results of these assessments also need to be reliable for any organization doing business with the audited firm, so the use of a third party with no conflict of interest increases the assurance provided by the audit.

Third-Party

Most organizations rely on a complex series of interconnected organizations, known as a *supply chain*, to support their operations. A standard office building with workers performing basic data processing and collaboration relies on hardware manufacturers, utility providers, and probably cloud services, just to name a few. Vulnerabilities in this supply chain can impact the organization, so an audit strategy is needed to identify risks and associated mitigations in the supply chain.

Supply chain audits are a topic introduced in Chapter 1, "Security and Risk Management," and are a vital part of any security risk management program. A sound third party audit strategy must be scoped to include any third-party critical to the organization's operations, handling any data valuable to the organization, or providing regulated services like payment processing. The audits may be performed by organizational resources or a third-party auditor retained by the organization to audit their suppliers. Some suppliers may be able to provide a report performed by a trusted third party, such as a Service Organization Control 2 (SOC 2) Type II report, which provides details about the supplier's security controls and their effectiveness. A CISSP must verify if the services their organization is using were in scope of the audit report provided by a supplier.

CONDUCT SECURITY CONTROL TESTING

Testing controls is essential to ensure they are implemented and operating as intended to mitigate risks. Over time, processes and systems change, and the risks facing the organization evolve, so a CISSP must design a control testing program to provide reliable and accurate data about the state of controls. This is a crucial piece of oversight that must support the ability to take action if a control is found to be deficient or no longer effective.

Testing may be done from internal or external perspectives and may target complex control implementations across people, process, and technology. For example, testing a media disposal control might entail policy and procedure reviews, staff interviews, examination of disposal records, and physical selection of disposed hard drives or other media to test by plugging them into a computer to see if data is recoverable.

Vulnerability Assessment

Vulnerabilities, which are weaknesses that could be exploited, are a major component of risk management and are discussed in detail in Chapter 1. Vulnerabilities are typically disclosed more frequently than risk assessments are performed, so ongoing vulnerability assessments are a key element of a continuous monitoring strategy. Hardware and software assets like servers, routers, operating systems, and applications can be vulnerable to attack, so technical testing is useful to identify vulnerabilities before an attacker does. Finding vulnerabilities is one step in the process — it is also important to assess the impact of the vulnerability and prioritize remediation, which is where the security practitioner's skills are valuable.

Assessing identified vulnerabilities includes analysis of their impact to the organization given the organization's unique configurations or circumstances. For example, a vulnerability that lets an attacker completely take over and delete data would be highly disruptive for an organization's financial system but would cause only a minor disruption to an internal company portal that shares news like the daily menu in the office café. Employees can always walk down to the café and see a printed menu! The output of vulnerability scanners can also identify the use of insecure protocols like File Transfer Protocol (FTP), which in general should be avoided. However, compensating controls may be in place that mitigate the risk, like network segmentation or the use of FTP for only publicly accessible, nonsensitive data.

Asset Inventory

Identifying the organization's critical assets is an important prerequisite to performing a vulnerability assessment. It is crucial to understand both the types of systems to be scanned and their criticality to choose appropriate scanning tools and prioritize scanning efforts. The asset inventory should capture data from other organizational processes like a business impact assessment (BIA), which identifies the criticality of each system, application, or data asset. Vulnerabilities in highly critical systems should be prioritized first since exploiting a vulnerability in a low criticality system is less likely to disrupt operations.

The asset inventory may also capture important data, like the system classification, needed to scope vulnerability assessments. Systems handling sensitive or regulated information may have specific requirements related to vulnerability assessments, like how frequently they must be scanned, the use of specific configurations to perform scans, or the baseline used for comparison. Scoping the scan targets can also be done using the asset inventory; for example, all assets marked as PCI in the inventory may be included in weekly scans using a PCI compliance configuration, while internal nonsensitive assets may be scanned monthly using the organization's secure baseline configuration.

Scanning Tool Functions and Considerations

Many popular scanning tools can identify vulnerabilities in hosts, networks, or applications. These include open-source tools that are free to use as well as commercial options; the choice to use open-source or commercial may include factors such as the availability of support, ability to scan specific systems or platforms, and the level of skill required to operate the tool. Proprietary tools may offer more features and support, but with a correspondingly higher price.

Most scanning tools offer a similar set of basic features and operate in a common manner. These automated tools identify targets, which may be a single network endpoint or a range of IP addresses, and then send network traffic and listen for a response to determine if an IP address is in use. Once an asset is discovered, the scan performs other automated actions to identify vulnerabilities, such as a port scan to identify active services like FTP or system-specific checks like querying the Windows Registry to identify installed software and patch levels. Some scanners can perform application-specific checks, like identifying a web server's supported encryption cipher suites.

Once the vulnerability scanner has identified relevant information, it can compare this information against a list of known vulnerabilities. For example, a Linux webserver running an outdated version of the Linux kernel can be cross-referenced with a list of known vulnerabilities in that version; this list of vulnerabilities is the output of the vulnerability scanner and can be used to identify remedial action needed to address the vulnerability — in this case, applying patches. Scan output should identify the criticality or severity rating for each finding, often using common standards like Common Vulnerability Scoring System (CVSS) scores or specific Common Vulnerabilities and Exposures (CVE) references.

When choosing and configuring a vulnerability scanner, there are several important considerations to ensure it provides valuable output. A CISSP should understand how these impact the output of the tool and strike a balance to ensure maximum benefit from the tool.

- **Obligations** such as legal, contractual, or regulatory, which may specify the scope, coverage, or frequency of scanning. A free vulnerability scanner might be appropriate for small environments without regulated data, but is likely insufficient for a heavily regulated financial services firm.

- **Depth, scope, or coverage** of the scanner, including the ability to perform advanced scanning by authenticating to targets being scanned with administrative credentials — sometimes known as *credentialed scanning*. Vulnerability scanners may generate false positives or provide low-resolution information by only looking at externally accessible information, but many can be configured with credentials like an administrator password or Secure Shell Protocol (SSH) key that allows the scanners to log in and perform additional checks.

- **Platform support** is a major consideration for organizations with mixed IT environments, such as Linux and Windows server operating systems or macOS and Windows workstation operating systems. Like all IT tools, the requirements for a vulnerability scanner should be defined, such as platform support or the ability to perform credentialed scans.

- **Cloud environments** may pose unique challenges for vulnerability scanning. Software as a service (SaaS) environments may prevent users from performing vulnerability scans due to the operational overhead it introduces, which can degrade system performance, and not all vulnerability scanners can be run against targets outside a local network. Some service providers share details of their own vulnerability scanning practices, which can be reviewed as part of a supply chain risk management.

Common Vulnerability Assessment Issues

Like many automated security tools, vulnerability scanners can cause issues or encounter problems. Avoiding these requires planning by security practitioners to develop a strategy. Here are some common examples:

- Excessive traffic and denial of service (DoS)
- Alerts or incidents
- Cross-functional ownership
- Data integrity pollution
- Network segmentation

Excessive Traffic and DoS

Vulnerability scanners can generate large volumes of traffic that consume network bandwidth and can lead to DoS conditions on both networks and systems that struggle to process the information. Proper configuration reduces the likelihood of these issues, such as implementing request throttling to limit the number of requests the scanner generates in a given time period. Credentialed scans can also help reduce the amount of traffic — a credentialed scan can read configuration information directly from a server's operating system to see what ports are open, rather than sending traffic to each port individually.

Scan scheduling may also be useful to ensure scans are conducted at times of low user activity. Spreading scans out over a larger time period can also be useful — scanning a few hosts per day reduces the impact of scanning an entire network.

Alerts and Incidents

Scanning hosts to identify open ports, well-known vulnerabilities, or other weaknesses is a common tactic used by attackers. When a vulnerability scanner performs the same actions, particularly if the scan triggers a DoS attack or unusual host activity, it will generate security alerts and possibly trigger incident response (IR) processes. Many security tools are designed to flag activity commonly used by both attackers and vulnerability scanners, like sequential port scans. An attacker might send a request to each port number in sequence to identify open services that could be exploited, which looks similar to a vulnerability scanner identifying open services. Configuring other security tools to ignore legitimate vulnerability activity is essential, such as marking port scans from the vulnerability scanner's IP address as nonsuspicious.

Cross-Functional Ownership

Cross-functional teams and ownership of scan results can be an issue that requires a CISSP to have not only security skills, but also project and business management skills. Vulnerability scanners are often owned by a security or IT team, while the applications and network assets where vulnerabilities are identified belong to another team. Fostering a relationship across those teams is crucial to ensure vulnerabilities are taken seriously and addressed; otherwise, asset owners may simply ignore emails from the security team alerting them to issues discovered by the scanner!

Even if the asset owner is receptive to the findings from a vulnerability assessment, there may be additional issues of communicating the context of any findings. For example, nonsecurity personnel typically do not understand CVSS scores, so those scores are not useful to prioritize the findings for remediation. Communicating context to the audience is important and may require formatting results in a way that is best suited to the asset owner.

Data Integrity Pollution

Vulnerability scanners can perform automated actions like filling in form fields on a web application to check for issues including Structured Query Language (SQL) injection or cross-site scripting (XSS). This testing data is obviously not real data that belongs in the system and can cause issues with reports or processes that expect valid data stored in the system. Some scanners can be configured to ignore certain types of fields, like email address (which could result in unintended messages being sent), or the scanner can be configured to put in a recognized type of test data that can be easily ignored or cleaned up after the scan. It may be necessary to conduct vulnerability assessments against a different environment altogether, such as a staging environment configured exactly like production but without live production data.

Network Segmentation

Segmenting or isolating different parts of a network with access controls like firewalls is a security best practice that may create problems when attempting to perform vulnerability scanning. The vulnerability scanner itself is a network endpoint, and it requires access to all other endpoints in scope for scanning; if the network is segmented using virtual LANs (VLANs), routers, or firewall rules, the scanner may not be able to reach its targets. Zero trust network architecture and microsegmentation are particularly challenging in cloud computing environments where these principles are the default and access follows a deny-all, allow-by-exception model. *Distributed scanning* is an architecture that places scanning agents inside network segments to allow the endpoints in that segment to be scanned, and then consolidates the results to a central console.

Penetration Testing

Penetration testing, or pen testing, is similar to vulnerability assessment but goes one step further. A vulnerability assessment merely identifies and reports on vulnerabilities in a system, while in a pen test, the tester will attempt to exploit identified vulnerabilities. The tester seeks to emulate the same process an attacker uses to identify and exploit vulnerabilities, and these testers are often known as *ethical hackers*. Ethical hacking has one key difference — the outcome is a report that the organization can use to fix vulnerabilities, while the outcome of a real attack is usually financial gain, theft, or disruption.

The exploitation of vulnerabilities in a pen test has both benefits and drawbacks. It may be difficult to prove whether results from a vulnerability scanner could actually be exploited, especially if compensating controls are in place. Pen testers often use vulnerability scanners to identify vulnerabilities and then attempt to exploit them, thereby proving or disproving the severity of the vulnerability. Potential drawbacks of this approach include the cost and the increased risk of disruption due to the testing activities. Engaging well-qualified pen testers is more expensive than simply running a vulnerability scanning tool, and the active exploitation of flaws can lead to system outages and downtime; although testers typically avoid causing disruption, accidents or unintended consequences can and will occur.

The amount of information provided to the pen tester varies depending on the organization's goal for the test. Different levels of information and the testing goals they support include the following:

- **White- or crystal-box** testing is total transparency. The pen testers have complete knowledge of the system or network to be tested, like IP addresses and system version numbers. This name implies transparency or illumination inside the "box" being tested, since the tester has details and knowledge. This allows more complete test coverage and simulates an insider threat, though controls designed to hide this information from outsiders, such as network address translation (NAT), are not evaluated.

- **Black-box** testing provides zero knowledge to the attacker and instead relies on them to perform reconnaissance to gather details. The name demonstrates how the interior of the system (the "box") is completely in shadow or dark to the tester. This can validate controls designed to hide information like internal network configurations, from outsiders, but risks missing assets that the testers are unable to discover.

- **Gray-box** testing combines elements of both white- and black-box methods. Some information is provided to the pen testers, but they are also charged with finding other information like internal network configurations.

Attackers, unlike pen testers, are not often constrained by time or the need to work billable hours in support of client services. A determined attacker can spend weeks, months, or even years observing an organization's network and resources, while a pen testing contract rarely lasts more than a few weeks. Even highly skilled pen testers can miss something in this limited time, so gray-box testing offers a hybrid benefit.

✔ Pen Test Scoping: It's Not Safe to Ignore Systems!

Many organizations scope pen tests to focus on a narrow set of systems or applications, usually as a cost-saving measure since pen testing an entire network is costly. In other cases, the pen test simply meets a compliance requirement, so only particular systems are in scope. While understandable, both approaches can create a false sense of security.

Networks are highly interconnected, which means a narrowly scoped pen test will likely miss vulnerabilities in out-of-scope systems that an attacker could exploit. As one major retailer discovered, a breach at a third-party vendor allowed attackers to access a contract management system. From there, attackers were able to access and compromise a payment card processing environment. Since the contract system did not process payments, it was outside the scope of many security controls like pen testing, but still proved a valuable pivot point to higher-value targets.

When defining a pen test scope, a CISSP should carefully balance available resources like time and budget to ensure optimum effectiveness of the testing. If a pen test does discover something on a system that is out of scope, the organization should never ignore the finding just because it is "out of scope." Attackers would certainly be happy to exploit that vulnerability.

Pen Testing Rules

Pen testing is an inherently dangerous activity with the possibility of internal incidents and even legal issues. If testing causes unintended consequences, many pen test contracts include indemnification for the individuals or organization providing the testing services; this prevents the organization who acquired the test from taking legal action like filing a lawsuit. Without such contracts in place, a penetration tester could be charged with criminal activity or business interruption if their testing activities cause a disruption.

Pen testing engagements should include defined rules of behavior, which document strict guidelines for what the pen testing team can do. For example, if a vulnerability is discovered and can be exploited to cause a denial-of-service attack, the pen testers should document it but may be barred from exploiting it. Crafting proper rules of behavior and managing the pen test engagement are key tasks for a CISSP to perform.

The rules of behavior document for a pen test should provide a set of ground rules for testers to follow and provide the organization with adequate information to coordinate necessary resources and plans. For example, if testing could cause a security incident to be triggered, then appropriate personnel may need to be briefed to ensure they calibrate the response accordingly. Rather than activating a contingency plan, the first step may be to confirm if the incident is the result of testing activity. In this instance, the organization's full response capability is not tested, and the penetration tester's results can be used to identify and address security deficiencies. Items that are typically defined in a rules of behavior document include the following:

- Which systems, offices, or other targets are in scope for testing?

- Are any systems, offices, or other targets specifically excluded from the scope of testing?

- Are any testing methods forbidden, such as social engineering or password cracking?

- Is physical security in scope? If yes, what facilities or targets are included?

- What level of access will testers be granted? Accounts may be provisioned for the testers in order to evaluate insider threats, or to perform verification activities if they are able to gain unauthorized access.

- What is the expected communication style and cadence? Some organizations may require immediate notice of any potentially critical security issues, while others may be satisfied to wait for a final report.

- Who is performing the test, what equipment and software is allowed, and when is testing to be conducted?

- What procedures are to be used for handling sensitive data like internal network configurations, customer records, etc.?
- How will sensitive data be securely disposed of at the conclusion of testing?
- What level of service is expected. For example, will testers perform re-testing immediately if a fix is implemented or wait for a defined re-test period?
- What are expectations for documentation, specifically details of any issues found, showing work done to verify the test results, and the format of any reports?

Pen Testing Phases

Pen testing activity can be broken down into a series of logically connected phases based on the pen tester's objective. The first goal is to gather information, which is utilized to find vulnerabilities that the testers then attempt to exploit. The final phase is documenting a report, which is where the pen testing and attack processes diverge — most attackers do not document their findings to help the organization improve cyber defenses! Figure 6.1 summarizes the phases, which are described in the following sections.

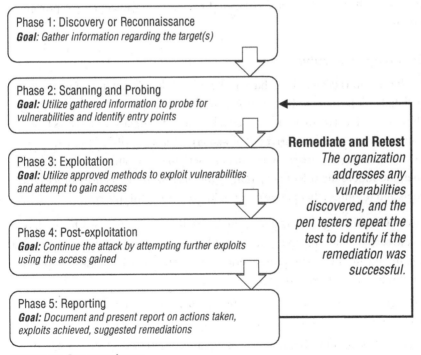

FIGURE 6.1 **Pen test phases**

Phase 1: Discovery or Reconnaissance

Discovery or reconnaissance requires the pen tester to gather information regarding the target. This often begins with open-source intelligence (OSINT), since the tester wants to emulate attackers and remain undetected. OSINT sources include the following:

- **Social media** to identify targets or useful personal details for phishing.

- **Public records** like Domain Name System (DNS) or company websites with information regarding services or locations.

- **Attack surface data** like enumerating the IP addresses associated with the target's DNS records and potential details about services in use. Publicly available tools Shodan or Have I Been Pwned can also be used.

- **Physical observations** like monitoring employee movements, photographing, driving by, or observing facilities, or dumpster diving to obtain hard copy.

Pen testers generally try to evade detection by the organization and seek information outside of the organization's monitoring abilities like DNS records, which are publicly accessible and maintained by a domain registrar. Not all pen testers will perform extensive discovery, especially in a white- or gray-box test where the organization has provided this information.

Phase 2: Scanning and Probing

Once basic information is gathered in Phase 1, the testers identify potential targets and gather more detailed information. For example, an IP address that leads to a marketing website with nonsensitive data may categorized a low-priority target, while URLs that clearly host high-value targets like `remote.*` or `webmail.*` are prioritized higher.

Scanning and probing require some traffic to be sent to the organization or target systems, which introduces the risk of detection by the organization's security processes. These are tools and resources that pen testers might use during this phase:

- **Network footprinting:** Testers define the footprint of a network, or what endpoints exist and services running on them. Tools like Nmap, nslookup, ping sweeps, and port scanning are used to perform queries that determine active network hosts and services running on a network.

- **Banner grabs:** Testers analyze information returned by endpoints, which often contains useful information including software names and versions.

- **Vulnerability scanning:** While an obvious approach, the use of a vulnerability scanner increases the pen tester's efficiency. These tools automate tasks like footprinting and parsing information from banners.

- **Exploitation toolkits:** Tools like Metasploit combine reconnaissance, footprinting, vulnerability scanning, and partially or fully automated exploitation into a single software interface. Since these tools combine multiple functions, they are utilized across multiple phases.

Phase 3: Exploitation

This third phase is self-explanatory — the testers exploit the identified vulnerabilities and attempt to gain access. They may use a variety of methods as defined by the rules of engagement, which are discussed in detail in a later section. The goal of exploitation is gaining access to systems or data that should not be accessible. These are some automated and manual exploitation tools:

- **Exploitation toolkits** like Metasploit, which can automate many aspects of pen testing
- **Password crackers** like John the Ripper, Hashcat, or Hydra, which are useful if the tester gathers hashed passwords and needs to identify a valid password
- **Monitoring tools and proxies** like Wireshark and Burp Suite, which allow the tester to capture, analyze, and modify network traffic
- **Application security tools** like Nikto or fuzzing tools, which can identify and attempt to exploit application vulnerabilities like buffer overflows or SQL injection

Although pen testers try to emulate attackers, they may have some limitations. Attackers usually do not work on timeframes or within budgets, which gives them more resources to use for hunting and exploiting vulnerabilities. Pen testers may be limited to a standard set of tools, while attackers may have more freedom to try new tools and processes.

Due to the risk of pen testing activities causing real operational and security incidents, it is important for the security practitioner to monitor the process closely. Although pen testers typically avoid causing major disruptions, they might discover a vulnerability that causes an application to crash or corrupt data. Unintended consequences like an operational outage should be disclosed to the testers quickly so the testing activity can be stopped, and internal communication may also be necessary to alert personnel to the testing activity and avoid drastic measures being taken, such as activating an expensive disaster recovery plan.

Phase 4: Post-exploitation

Once the testers have gained initial access, they will attempt to *pivot* or use that access to gain further access. For example, compromising a system in the demilitarized zone

(DMZ) is not highly valuable since sensitive data is typically not stored here. However, DMZ assets may be authorized to connect to endpoints on an internal network segment, which could grant the tester unauthorized access to something more valuable.

The compromised DMZ could even be used to iterate Phase 2 activities and perform network footprinting of internal resources that are not reachable from outside the network. Endpoints or assets discovered will be categorized, and attention will be paid to high-value targets. Once network endpoints have been enumerated, various techniques are used to fingerprint them — the goal is to discover useful details like operating system and application software versions. Exploits will be tried against these until the tester is discovered, runs out of time, or exhausts all identified possibilities.

Phase 5: Reporting

Throughout the testing process, documentation should be created to capture all activities performed, vulnerabilities found, and any access the testers achieve. These findings are compiled into a report, and it is typical for the testers to include recommendations for the organization to remediate any identified vulnerabilities. This report is usually presented in a formal meeting, which marks the end of the pen test engagement.

Different reports, or different parts of the report, may be designed for different audiences. An executive summary with the scope, high-level synopsis of tests performed, and number of findings is often prepared to share with management or users outside the organization, while more technically detailed parts of the report are in a separate document or appendix designed for internal IT staff.

Physical Penetration Testing

Physical security is a critical aspect of securing systems and data, so some organizations may need to conduct physical penetration testing. Testers attempt to gain unauthorized access to facilities like offices or data centers, with the goal of identifying potential weaknesses in physical security controls. Social engineering tactics like carrying a bulky item and asking someone to hold the door or showing up dressed as an official are often utilized.

Gaining unauthorized physical access to certain facilities is illegal in some circumstances, so physical pen testers should be given a *get out of jail free* card that details the purpose of their activity and a point of contact within the organization who can verify their story. In the event the tester is captured or detained, the test is concluded, since they failed to gain access and evade detection, and the card can be presented to help them avoid potential legal trouble like being arrested and charged with trespassing.

In high-security organizations, especially those with armed guards, it is important to properly coordinate penetration testing with stakeholders like the guard staff to ensure they are prepared to respond appropriately if a tester is discovered.

Log Reviews

The fundamentals of logging and monitoring are covered in Chapter 7, "Security Operations," but a CISSP should remember that logs play an essential role as detective controls in a security program. They can be generated by most systems, endpoints, devices, and applications, and the capability to generate logs should be turned on and configured to capture meaningful information. This information is made useful by reviewing it — if an attacker has gained access and the logs capturing the malicious activity are ignored, the attacker may evade detection.

Assessments and audits often rely on log entries as artifacts to directly prove that the organization's technical controls are in place and operating as intended. For example, if the organization's access control policy states that access to a critical system is available only during normal business hours, then auditors may look for both positive and negative enforcement of this control: system configurations that enforce this restriction, and logs that show users denied access when attempting access outside the defined hours.

The practice of log management is itself subject to auditing and assessment. Policies, procedures, and technical configurations for log generation, management, and review should be in place, and auditors may examine these to identify compliance with standards such as ISO 27001 control A.12.4, PCI-DSS Requirement 10.6, or the Audit and Accountability (AU) family of controls in NIST SP 800-53.

Synthetic Transactions

Synthetic transactions are automated activities run against a monitored target to measure its performance. For a web application, this might involve logging in with a test user account to verify if the application responds to the login request or returns data in response to queries. The term *transactions* does not necessarily mean financial transactions, but can be any system activity like querying for data or making a request for services. Monitored objects can be any system or application, such as a DNS or Dynamic Host Configuration Protocol (DHCP) server, and the synthetic transaction is a request for a DNS resolution or assignment of an IP address.

Synthetic transactions can be employed as a test mechanism for a variety of purposes:

- **SLA monitoring:** Hosted or cloud-based services may guarantee certain levels of service, such as a SaaS application that guarantees 99.9 percent uptime. Synthetic transactions can be used to log into the application every hour to verify if the service meets the agreed level.

- **Data integrity monitoring:** Systems with complex business logic may have dynamic rules for handling data. Synthetic transactions can be used to monitor these rules and alert administrators if processing a set of test data does not result in the expected outcome, which indicates issues with the business logic rules.

- **System or service monitoring:** Even in the absence of an Service Level Agreement (SLA), systems can be monitored to ensure they are online and responding as expected. This is often known as *heartbeat monitoring* and is a detective control that identifies services that are offline or unresponsive.

Real user monitoring (RUM) is often discussed along with synthetic transactions. RUM monitors users in real time as they interact with an application or service and can be useful for detecting issues like slow or unresponsive pages. Unfortunately, RUM tools also introduce privacy concerns as they often record every user interaction with an application or web page. This includes users entering sensitive data that may be captured by the RUM agent. Even if the application safeguards the data entered by users, the RUM tool may not; several RUM tools have caused data breaches by recording and storing sensitive or regulated information like financial data and user passwords.

Code Review and Testing

Code comprises software and is the foundation of information systems, so reviewing and testing this code to identify and remediate flaws is an essential security control. Bugs or vulnerabilities in the code can impact the security of the overall system and any data it stores or processes. Additional topics related to code reviews, testing, and software security are covered in Chapter 8, including common frameworks for assessing or describing software vulnerabilities like the Common Weakness Enumeration (CWE), CVSS, and the Open Web Application Security Project (OWASP) Top 10 security vulnerabilities.

Although a CISSP may not be directly responsible for writing or maintaining code in a system, which is the responsibility of a software developer, it is vital to understand the importance of adequate code review and testing measures. Code testing should be designed and implemented to detect and correct software vulnerabilities and ideally to detect flaws close to the time the code is written. It is generally easier to make changes while the code is still under development, and two main approaches may be used to support this goal:

- **Black-box testing:** The tester does not have access to the source code or internal workings of the application, modeling the perspective of an external attacker or user.

- **White-box testing:** The tester has access to the source code or knowledge of internal elements of the application like Application Programming Interface (API), which an outsider would not have.

Code testing may be done using automated tools or manual processes like code peer reviews, where developers manually review and edit the work of a peer to spot mistakes. Automated tools such as *static code analysis* use software to model the execution of code and identify potential vulnerabilities like buffer overflow or inconsistent data conditions that could result during program execution. *Dynamic analysis* tests the actual running program to observe the behavior of the system or application.

A CISSP should ensure that code review and testing controls meet the objectives of both security and business needs. For example, the testing should provide adequate coverage across the application code to detect flaws without introducing unacceptable delays into the software development process. Development practices in DevSecOps rely heavily on automated, repeatable testing in the continuous integration/continuous delivery (CI/CD) pipeline to balance delivery speed and security, and emerging security concepts like security orchestration, automation, and response (SOAR) apply a similar focus on automating security incident response; both topics are covered in detail in Chapter 8. These tests should be supplemented by manual testing like a penetration test or formal code testing on a less frequent basis to ensure deeper analysis is performed.

Misuse Case Testing

Misuse case or negative testing is designed to assess how a system or application responds to unexpected inputs or situations, and identifies vulnerabilities which might be exploitable under these unexpected circumstances. In the context of software development, a use case describes the expected interaction between an actor, typically a user or process, and a system. For example, a use case for system login would describe the steps the user takes to reach a login prompt, enter their credentials, and then be either granted or denied access as appropriate. A *misuse case* describes the opposite: what happens when the system is not used as expected?

Vulnerabilities have been found in several applications when users supply incomplete or unexpected information at a login prompt. The use case expects a user to enter a username and password; instead, a user enters a username but leaves the password blank. This might cause the applications to crash, or worse — Apple's macOS contained a bug where secure configuration settings could be accessed by supplying a username of "root" and leaving the password field blank, as documented in CVE-2017-13872.

Common elements of misuse case testing should be incorporated in system test plans and activities and often focus on system behavior when unexpected values are entered in application fields, such as incorrect data formats or data that is significantly different than what is expected. For example, how does the application behave when a string of text is entered into a field where a numerical value is expected, or the text of an entire book is pasted into a field designed to contain only a few words? Null or blank values should also be considered, as demonstrated in the previously described authentication bug where a username and blank password incorrectly granted access.

Misuse cases can test for application behavior in unintentional circumstances, such as a user accidentally entering their phone number in a field designed to hold their name. *Abuse case* testing models how a system or feature might be misused in a way that was not expected and specifically describes how an attacker might exploit this weakness. Modeling these cases can be useful to identify threats to a system or its data and assists in designing controls to mitigate the risk. OWASP has a cheat sheet for Abuse Case modeling and testing: `cheatsheetseries.owasp.org/cheatsheets/Abuse_Case_Cheat_Sheet.html`.

> ### ✔ Abuse Cases
>
> Unlike a misuse case, an abuse case is a specification of a deliberate, harmful interaction between a user and a system. They are often used to identify security requirements by specifying the ways a system could be abused by a malicious actor and are an integral part of threat modeling.

Test Coverage Analysis

Test coverage refers to the number of functions in a system or application that are tested and can be expressed as a percentage of the total system that has been tested or a specific number of things tested, such as functions or modules. Testing involves costs, so a key concern for the security practitioner is ensuring that adequate test coverage is achieved for critical system functions even if all functions cannot be tested due to cost. Since code testing may be the responsibility of other teams within the organization, a CISSP may be a stakeholder responsible for communicating requirements and validating test plan designs to ensure the chosen tools and test strategy achieve the desired level of coverage.

Test coverage analysis measures four main criteria to identify sub-elements of a program or system being tested:

- **Branch coverage** ensures that each branch in a control statement has been executed.

- **Condition coverage** requires each Boolean expression in the code to be validated for both true and false conditions.

- **Function coverage** makes sure that every function in the program is called.

- **Statement coverage** validates the execution of every statement in the program.

Additional coverage measurement includes more advanced criteria like *decision coverage*, which validates combinations of function and branch coverage to test various input and output scenarios, as well as *parameter coverage* to test the behavior of functions that accept parameter inputs. This can identify vulnerabilities related to unexpected or malformed inputs and is especially useful for applications that accept user-supplied data.

In an ideal scenario, test coverage would be 100 percent across the system or application, but costs and complexity associated with this level of testing may be prohibitive. A CISSP should identify criteria like the sensitivity of data handled by the system, impacts to human life or safety, and the organizational criticality of the system when developing requirements for acceptable test coverage, and should ensure test coverage is adequate. The definition of adequate will vary between systems and organizations, but in general, sensitive functions like user management, system administration, and sensitive data handling should be most thoroughly tested. Compensating controls may also be considered to mitigate untested system elements, such as an air-gapped system or additional continuous monitoring targets.

Interface Testing

An *interface* is an interaction point with a system. Examples include the user interface (UI), which provides a way for a human user to interact with a system, and APIs, which are used for system-to-system interaction. UIs often take the form of a graphical user interface (GUI) with windows and menus or text-based interaction using a command-line interface (CLI). APIs may be implemented using a variety of methods like Representational State Transfer (REST) APIs for web applications, inter-process communication (IPCs), and remote procedure calls (RPCs).

Evaluating interface functionality and security is a critical part of system testing. Security controls should be implemented in interfaces to support security goals of confidentiality, via access controls, or nonrepudiation, via logging of actions executed using the interface. Interface testing may be part of standard software development testing conducted by developers and is also a key element in security testing activities overseen by security practitioners, such as vulnerability assessments, penetration tests, and security testing like breach simulations.

Like many system testing functions, interface testing should identify if the interface behaves as expected under both typical use and abnormal circumstances like dealing with unexpected or malformed input. Interfaces, like all elements of a system, should have clearly documented requirements, test cases, and acceptance criteria to determine if they adequately implement the required levels of data protection.

Organizations with large and complex systems, or those with distributed components, may find server interface testing to be an appropriate area of focus. Interfaces between application servers, web servers, and databases are critical points of security control implementation and should be targeted to test the effectiveness of multilayered security controls. For example, if a web application accepts user-supplied input, then the application's input validation controls must be tested to ensure they reject incorrect data. In case this control fails, the interface to an application server may also incorporate logic to verify that incoming data conforms to expected parameters, providing a defense-in-depth input validation control.

Web application interfaces are particularly complex due to the possible inclusion of systems outside the organization's control. A web application with external users may require unique access management controls like session management to identify, authenticate, and track user interactions. If cookies are used to store information like session tokens or other identifying information, then the interface between outside user systems and the web application should be considered when defining interface testing requirements.

Breach Attack Simulations

Breach attack simulations or breach and attack simulations (BAS) are an emerging method of automated testing designed to simulate a realistic attacker attempting to gain unauthorized access. BAS combines elements of vulnerability scanning and automated penetration testing. BAS tools utilize a continuously refreshed database of attack methods and newly discovered vulnerabilities to test the ability for the organization to withstand newly evolved threats. Implementing a BAS solution allows this testing to be done more frequently to identify potential vulnerabilities sooner than legacy approaches like a quarterly vulnerability scan or yearly penetration test.

BAS tools perform automated attacks modeled after real attack vectors utilized when attempting to breach a network or system. If the simulated attacks are blocked, then the security controls functioned as intended. However, if an attack is successful, it could indicate a deficient control or a new risk that is not addressed by existing controls. The categories of attacks carried out by a BAS are often categorized by the target or vector and can include the following:

- **Endpoint:** The BAS performs action on or against a network endpoint, such as creating files or processes that match known malware signatures to test endpoint detection and response (EDR) capabilities. This may be accomplished remotely from a BAS appliance or console or may utilize a software agent running on the endpoint.

- **Network:** The BAS sends network traffic that should be blocked and generates an alert if known bad or malicious traffic is not blocked by controls like firewalls or routers.

- **Email:** Spam filters, email spoofing controls, and content filters can be tested by test messages generated and sent by the BAS. If messages reach inboxes or are opened, it indicates a deficiency in email security controls.

- **Behavior-based:** Advanced BAS functions can test behavior-based security controls like security tools monitoring for malicious network scans or complex interaction with applications that should be blocked by a web application firewall (WAF).

Compliance Checks

Compliance frameworks generally combine a set of risks specific to an industry or region, and the required security controls are designed to mitigate them. Compliance should be treated not as a security objective but as a starting point to help an organization's risk management program.

Compliance checks are a part of oversight designed to verify the status of controls in place to meet compliance objectives. Audits are a common method of checking this status; further details on conducting or facilitating audits are presented later in this chapter. Formal audits or assessments are conducted on a defined schedule, such as annual audits for PCI-DSS and SOC 2, or ISO 27001 audits once every three years.

Most compliance frameworks recognize that an audit at a single point in time is not an effective way to monitor security risk. The purpose of the scheduled audit is to evaluate the security program at a specific point in time, and the compliance frameworks typically include requirements for more frequent assessment of key controls or areas. Some compliance audits, like SOC 2 Type II and ISO 27001, require the evaluation of security over a period of performance, so the auditors will review data and artifacts from a specific time period (typically the last year) to determine if the organization's security program was functioning as intended during that time. Some examples of security and compliance frameworks that require compliance audits are identified here:

- **ISO 27001** audits are performed every three years by an external auditor to achieve certification, while the organization must perform continuous monitoring and oversight, including internal auditing and surveillance audits on an annual basis.

- **PCI-DSS** requires organizations to undergo an annual audit by a third-party auditor and perform routine internal activities such as quarterly vulnerability scans.

- **FedRAMP** requires an ongoing annual assessment after the initial full security assessment and also requires a continuous monitoring strategy for key risks in order to maintain Authority to Operate (ATO) status.

Compliance checks and continuous monitoring, which are discussed in Chapter 7, share a common goal: identify weaknesses as soon as possible and take corrective action before an attacker finds the weakness. Compliance checks can uncover controls that are deficient or ineffective due to changed risk circumstances, or controls that are no longer being properly executed. A CISSP should seek to balance the costs and operational overhead of performing these compliance checks against the threat landscape facing the organization, including the risk of noncompliance.

COLLECT SECURITY PROCESS DATA

Once an organization has identified risks and implemented appropriate controls to mitigate them, it is important to monitor the status of those controls and their effectiveness at achieving the desired risk mitigation. A CISSP must ensure that adequate data is collected and analyzed to support monitoring and oversight of how effective the organization's security controls are at mitigating risk. The strategy for and practice of continuous monitoring is discussed in Chapter 7, and the sources of data that should be monitored are discussed in the following sections.

Continuous monitoring is a complex task that requires an organization to have mature cybersecurity capabilities. Like any complex process, it is best to approach the implementation in stages, beginning with fundamentals like performing a thorough risk assessment and designing a security control program to mitigate the identified risks. Once these controls are in place, a logging and monitoring strategy can be developed, starting with basics like enabling logging on all systems, centralizing log files, and automating monitoring with tools like a security information and event management (SIEM) platform.

The volume of data generated by monitoring security processes and control implementations can make the task of monitoring overwhelming. Rather than looking at raw data, measurements or metrics can be useful to identify trends or useful information. Data trends can be analyzed using automated means to generate trending data such as key performance indicators (KPIs), and the emerging field of artificial intelligence and machine learning (AI/ML) offers some solutions to automate data analysis tasks.

A CISSP should be able to identify relevant information to monitor when looking at all possible sources of security process data. Reviewing every change request ticket individually is not an efficient use of time, but monitoring the number of changes that require a rollback can be a useful way to identify deficient change review processes. This metric supports obvious next steps — the change review process and changes that required rollbacks should be examined, and any findings can inform process changes.

Designing a security metrics program requires two key elements. First, an understanding of the security program objectives is essential, as this is the reference point for the metrics. Second, the security controls must provide a method of measurement or quantification. For example, if multifactor authentication is required for all logins, access control logs can be queried to determine if this requirement is enforced 100 percent of the time.

Technical Controls and Processes

Technical or logical controls are implemented with or by electronic systems, like username and password prompts to access an information system or the configuration of a firewall to reject traffic from a known malicious source. Collecting data from technical controls can be straightforward since electronic systems usually support logging natively. Technical process data may include information captured as part of the organization's logging and monitoring strategy, or it may be generated via analysis of that log data. Examples include application user access logs and logs from network devices like routers or firewalls.

Designing a technical metrics program should be done to measure the organization's effectiveness at implementing multilayered security. To do so, it is useful to capture metrics across categories like these:

- **Prevent:** Preventative technical processes include encryption of data and securing access to decryption keys, network access controls like virtual private networks (VPNs), and endpoint controls like host-based firewalls.

- **Detect:** These technical processes include any controls that detect incidents or deviations, such as EDR and SIEM. Detective security data may come from controls that overlap with operations, such as monitoring the status of hardware or software to detect unexpected outages.

- **Respond:** When something goes wrong, response controls are designed to correct the issue, and include EDR as well as network- and host-based intrusion prevention systems (IPSs).

Administrative Controls

Administrative controls are implemented in policies and procedures, like acceptable use policies, access review procedures, and personnel security controls such as job rotation. Unlike technical security processes, administrative processes do not automatically generate data like audit logs that can be easily monitored. Data regarding administrative processes may instead come from evaluation of process *artifacts*, which are objects created or used during process execution.

Artifacts are often indirect sources, like a guard recording that they performed a walkthrough of a facility at a particular time, or an incident report filed by the guard for an unlocked workstation discovered on the walkthrough. The record of the walkthrough indicates a process was executed, while the incident report provides details of a user who violated a clear screen policy. Direct sources often include documentation, which may prove confusing since documents are often managed in digital form using information systems. Even though the data comes from an information system, it still supports measuring an administrative control.

Take, for example, an organizational policy barring personal social media use on organization-issued equipment. This policy will have administrative components like an acceptable use policy and employee training and awareness, and it may comprise technical controls like web content filters or blocklists. Metrics about the implementation of this control could measure the following:

- **Policy reach:** How many users have read and acknowledged their understanding of the policy by signing it?

- **Education effectiveness:** How many users attempt to access restricted content?

- **Technology effectiveness:** Based on web traffic, how many users are able to reach restricted content, and how effective are technology controls at enforcing the policy?

Account Management

An account is a set of credentials used to access a resource. Usernames and passwords are a common example for user access, and there are other types of credentials like encryption keys, which can be used both to protect data and identify the user, system, or process accessing it. Identity and access management, including identification, authentication, authorization, and the account management lifecycle used to provision, review, and deprovision these access control elements are covered in Chapter 5, "Identity and Access Management."

Account management data is a critical area to focus on when collecting security process data, because access control is fundamental to information system security. Access controls are also a crucial example of blended control types — policies are implemented using process and procedure, implemented using technology systems, and may require physical controls like managing facility access or safeguarding account tokens like smart cards.

Take, for example, an information system's account management requirements. To restrict and monitor access, the following controls may be put in place. The data generated by these controls should be collected and analyzed to evaluate effectiveness.

- **Administrative process** for requesting user access, including formal request and approval before access is granted. This may require an access request ticket or hard-copy access request form. All user accounts must have corresponding request and approval documents, which must contain all required information like user role, justification for access, and necessary approvals. Audit and other assurance activities over these processes and artifacts are also a part of the administrative controls.

- **Technical implementation** might include the system for submitting the request, performing reviews and approvals, and the actual identity and access management tool where the user account is created like Active Directory, Okta, or a local computer operating system. A highly sensitive system may also utilize network access controls such as a segregated VLAN or restrictive firewall rules. If a system supports unique API login credentials, a secure method of distributing API keys, such as a secure API site, might also be needed to provision access.

- **Physical** controls will also be used to enforce the access control, such as placing information system components in access-restricted spaces. The implementation of user access controls may also utilize physical devices like tokens, smartcards, or trusted devices, which require policy, procedure, and training to ensure restricted physical access is maintained.

Key process data to collect from account management processes includes the following:

- Timely account management such as removal of access within specified timeframes after a user changes roles or leaves employment
- Timely notifications received for account provisioning or deprovisioning, like notification within 24 hours of a user joining or leaving the organization
- Proper account reviews performed according to the organization's defined schedule
- Proper process execution such as out-of-bound distribution of passwords, proper verification before password resets, or properly configured network access controls

Management Review and Approval

Management is responsible for defining and executing the mission of an organization, including supporting functions like security and privacy. In some organizations, a security practitioner like a CISSP will be in an executive role to manage mission objectives, while in others, a security practitioner will be tasked with providing data related to security and privacy processes to management. Management support and sponsorship of security initiatives is crucial, as it provides direction and support.

Each of the techniques and procedures discussed in this chapter play a role in management oversight of the security program. Assessments, audits, and ongoing monitoring of security process metrics provide timely data to management, and it is essential for decision-making like identifying organizational risks and the proper course of mitigating action. Examples include short-term decisions like a disaster necessitating activation of the business continuity plan (BCP), or long-term decisions like changing architecture from on-premises hosting to cloud-based systems due to the cost benefit of self-hosting compared to outsourcing.

Management review and approval of security process data should be performed to ensure that controls are functioning as intended; that is to say that they are reducing risks to an acceptable level and that previously accepted risks are still within acceptable parameters. Changes to the organization's operating environment can render controls ineffective, even if they were previously adequate to reduce risks. Examples including launching new lines of business, the addition of new systems or processes, new compliance or regulatory obligations, and organizational changes like mergers, acquisitions, and divestitures.

To perform adequate review and oversight of a security program, the organization's management will monitor a variety of sources. The continuous monitoring program should generate metrics and performance indicators, which are reliant upon security process data. These topics are discussed in another section in this chapter and are closely related to the continuous monitoring processes covered in Chapter 7.

Management Reviews for Compliance

There are several frameworks that formally define management review and approval processes related to security. This oversight task is a key element of governance and risk management, which is covered in Chapter 1. Specific security and compliance frameworks, and their requirements for management review, include the following:

- **ISO 27001** control 9.3 specifies that management must periodically review the information security program for "continuing suitability, adequacy and effectiveness."

- **NIST and FedRAMP** define management roles for assessment and authorization and continuous monitoring. Management must review the plans for assessing information systems and the results of assessments and then make a formal decision to authorize the system for use by issuing an authorization to operate (ATO). Management uses continuous monitoring data to ensure risk remediations remain effective.

- **Certification and accreditation** are similar to assessment and authorization. *Certification* is a formal process for evaluating a system or process against a set of criteria, and *accreditation* is a formal decision about the system's fitness to perform the specified function. Any organization can use this to develop management processes for formally evaluating and approving systems based on security capabilities and requirements.

- **SOC 2** requires management to establish "performance measures," as well as generate and use "relevant, quality information to support the functioning of internal control."

- **Control Objectives for Information Technologies (COBIT)** is a management framework for IT and cybersecurity, and it is geared toward high-level management tasks like planning adequate resources, capacity, and oversight tasks like reviews of the organization's control program.

Senior and executive managers are not the only stakeholders with responsibilities for reviewing and approving security control effectiveness. Information system owners, data owners, and custodians will also have responsibility for ensuring adequate controls are in place when handling data, as well as reporting any issues or deficiencies they encounter.

Key Performance and Risk Indicators

As a CISSP, it is important to measure not only existing performance, but also to maintain awareness of how situations may change in the future. Security metrics communicate the effectiveness of existing security controls at mitigating risk and monitor the state of risks that could impact the organization in the future. Key performance indicators (KPIs) are the monitoring tool for existing risk mitigations, while key risk indicators (KRIs) allow the organization to maintain awareness of potential future risks. Both are essential to a governance, risk, and compliance (GRC) program and provide proactive and reactive input to the GRC strategy.

Every organization will find different metrics useful and must take into account a variety of factors when determining which indicators are meaningful and worthy of monitoring. To use a nonsecurity example, a driver with cheap gasoline but poorly maintained roads is likely to monitor the health of a car's tires. A driver with the same car in a location with expensive gasoline but well-maintained roads might instead be concerned with the car's performance in miles per gallon or kilometers per liter. Both are useful indicators that provide usable information, but the circumstances dictate which is more applicable in a given situation. A CISSP must understand the business context of their security program and ensure that both KPIs and KRIs are chosen to provide this useful information. This requires coordinating with stakeholders including the user community, management, and possibly outside parties like regulators or business partners.

Key Performance Indicators

The terms KPIs and metrics are often used interchangeably, but there is a difference. Metrics are simply measurements, like the number of patches applied to a computing environment. A performance indicator uses metrics and provides context (an indication). For example, the number of patched endpoints divided by the total number of endpoints in the environment is an indicator of the effectiveness of a patch management program. If the organization expects 100 percent patch coverage after seven days, then this KPI can be used to gauge the performance of that program against the expectation. If the number is below the expectation, it indicates remedial action needed, such as manual application of patches or isolation of unpatched endpoints from the network until they have been properly remediated.

When designing KPIs for the organization's security program, it is helpful to understand the information needed by the organization and essential to ensure the KPIs provide clear information to support decision making. KPIs should exist to identify how effectively controls are operating to mitigate risks, and provide notice if a control is ineffective, which indicates a risk that may be more likely to occur. A performance baseline must be established, well as thresholds for upper and lower bounds on the process being monitored. Processes may have strict or loose requirements for performance, and the thresholds will reflect that — any deviation from the baseline is cause for concern in a strict process, with greater variation allowed for a loose process.

Patch deployment timeframes are a good example of a KPI. If the organization has set the baseline at seven days after the patch is released, then any patch deployed after the seven-day window is a negative indicator in a strict situation. In a loose example, patches deployed 8–10 days after release may be acceptable but do not require additional action. The KPI can even be used to measure the success of improvement efforts — if patches are consistently deployed in less than seven days, then the improvement worked.

Developing high-quality KPIs can be a challenge. Frameworks exist, including ISO 27004, "Security techniques — Information security management — Monitoring, measurement, analysis and evaluation," and NIST SP 800-55, "Performance Measurement Guide for Information Security." The Software Engineering Institute (SEI) at Carnegie Mellon University has also developed a framework called the Goal-Question-Indicator-Metric (GQIM) Method, which is designed to assist organizations in defining measurement strategies that provide meaningful information. The method documentation can be found at `resources.sei.cmu.edu/asset_files/ TechnicalNote/2016_004_001_455107.pdf`.

Determining targets and frequency of monitoring should be done by identifying organizational goals, critical systems, and the controls in place to mitigate risks to those goals or systems. As always, balancing the cost of measuring with the benefits is critical, as sampling a process or system every day can be costly. Examples of important metrics to track and define KPIs for include the following:

- **Mean time to detect (MTTD):** This measures the mean time required to detect a security incident or threat.

- **Mean time to resolve (MTTR):** This measures the time required to resolve incidents.

- **Security scores:** Many vendors provide security scorecards or grades, which can be an indicator of the maturity of an organization's security efforts. Note that these externally provided scores may not capture all the necessary details, so receiving an A or 100 percent, similar to passing a compliance audit, should not be interpreted as being entirely secure.

- **ROI:** This is a challenging area for many CISSPs, since business concerns like finances are often outside the scope of a technology or security practitioner. However, the risk-reducing effect of controls must always be balanced against their cost. Management may require an indicator showing how effective a particular security control or program is at reducing costs — for example, if phishing costs the organization 100 lost hours of productivity each month, then anti-phishing training must cost less than 100 hours *and* result in a reduction of lost productivity due to successful phishing attacks.

Key Risk Indicators

KRIs can provide the organization with a window into future risks and should be designed to capture how the changing risk landscape might impact the organization. The indications from KRIs can drive proactive mitigating action — for example, a rise in the volume of malicious traffic being blocked by a firewall can be an indicator to upgrade the firewall before it is overwhelmed. KRIs often support long-term management decision-making, like a firewall upgrade project requiring lead time for IT budget and resource allocation to avoid the risk of system disruption by malicious outsiders.

Sources of KRIs include common security practices like vulnerability scanning, auditing and assessments, security incident response, malware infection and containment rates, and other security process data. The indicators should measure the adequacy of existing security controls to deal with changing risks.

Continuing the example of patch deployments from earlier, a KRI might be set for the latest patches to be present on a specific percentage of endpoints. If patch deployments are delayed and the number of unpatched endpoints rises above the threshold, then the organization is at risk of any the unpatched vulnerabilities being exploited. Corrective action like initiating a security incident response and manually deploying patches could be an appropriate response. Examples of other valuable KRIs include the following:

- **Number of security incidents:** An increase in the number of security incidents could indicate that the threat environment has changed, and more robust security tools or additional staff are needed.

- **Number of findings:** An increase in findings from audits and assessments could indicate security program deficiencies that require additional attention or resources.

- **Number of phishing attempts detected or reported:** An increase in phishing attempts is often the precursor to an attack, as attackers seek to gain valid credentials to access the organization's resources. Additional system monitoring, multi-factor authentication (MFA), and user training could all be deployed in response to this threat.

Backup Verification Data

Data and system backups are an essential control for integrity and availability, so ensuring they are usable in the event of data loss or corruption is critical. The first step is identifying critical data or systems that the organization needs to continue operations and designing a backup strategy appropriate for the recovery needs, which is covered in more detail in Chapter 7.

Once procedures and systems are in place to perform backups, it is important to verify the integrity of both the backup process and the backup data. Both can be evaluated by performing a test restore from backup media to ensure that all required data is present and readable. If data is missing, it could indicate backup configuration issues like directories or systems that are excluded from the backup, or corruption of the backup media. Some backup systems include integrity checking as part of standard operations and can be configured to automatically verify backup integrity, generate alerts if integrity loss is detected, and automatically retry the backup process.

Training and Awareness

Establishing and maintaining a program to deliver security awareness, education, and training is vital, because users can be both a critical line of defense against attacks as well as a high-value target of attacks. Designing this program is a topic covered in more detail in Chapter 1. To test and evaluate the effectiveness of security training and awareness programs, the following metrics can be useful:

- **Training completion rates:** Users who do not complete training may be more liable to miss indications like a phishing email or unexpected system behavior.

- **Long-term information retention and habit building:** If users take a training, complete a quiz, and immediately forget the information, the program is ineffective.

- **Coverage:** Threats and risks are constantly evolving; training programs must be updated to address these.

- **Audience needs:** Some security practices are too technical or might be unimportant for all users, so it is important to deliver an appropriate level of knowledge and training material to the audience.

Disaster Recovery and Business Continuity

Business continuity and disaster recover (BCDR) topics, including strategies for gathering requirements, designing a plan to address them, and testing the plan, are discussed in Chapter 1 and Chapter 7. The output of the requirements gathering and testing processes are important sources to monitor and measure for effectiveness, as the BCDR activities support the goal of maintaining availability.

The information gathered when auditing, assessing, and monitoring BCDR activities should provide answers to the following questions. Insufficient or negative answers indicate weaknesses that might be addressed by updating the plan documents or iterating processes like business impact analysis (BIA) or plan exercises.

- Do appropriate plan documents exist, and are they updated? Examples include a BCDR plan, continuity of operations plan (COOP), or individual BC and DR plans.

- Are key personnel aware of their roles and responsibilities under the plan?

- Are new staff trained on key BCDR roles as part of onboarding? This can be a shared metric between security training and BCDR data collection.

- Is the current version of the plan readily accessible and securely stored?

- Are the organization's current critical functions captured in the plans?

- Have significant organizational changes occurred that are not reflected in the plan? Examples include major IT architecture changes and business activity like mergers, acquisitions, divestitures, or restructuring.

- Is the plan tested regularly, and have any deficiencies noted during testing been addressed?

- Does the organization rely on critical third parties or services? If so, have those dependencies been tested?

- Do other processes like change management integrate with the BCDR plans to ensure organizational changes are properly reflected in planning documents?

ANALYZE TEST OUTPUT AND GENERATE REPORT

Security evaluations such as vulnerability scans, penetration tests, gap assessments, continuous monitoring, and audits generate a large volume of data. Reviewing all output generated is time-consuming and may be impossible for nonsecurity practitioners, although users outside the security team do need to access data related to security processes. It is essential, therefore, to generate reports that summarize key details of testing and evaluation activities, including the circumstances or assumptions used to conduct testing, actions performed during testing, findings or issues discovered, and any recommended remedial steps to address the findings.

A security practitioner preparing a report must first identify the audience or user of the report, which is crucial to determine appropriate levels and types of details to include. The executive committee of a multinational corporation is unlikely to be interested in specific code issues that caused a buffer overflow vulnerability and might instead care about strategic risk management actions like increasing the developer security training budget or requiring more stringent application security testing. The developers responsible for fixing the vulnerability care more about the raw output of security testing tools like a code scanner, so a report that includes strategic process improvements is not appropriate.

The process of designing a report may require structuring content based on the needs of multiple audiences, and a modular structure can be useful. An executive summary and a high-level overview of the findings may be presented in a single section, to be shared with executives, business partners, or customers since these groups typically do not require highly detailed information. Technical details of testing can be presented in an appendix, which may be shared separately with appropriate technical audiences who need that level of detail to address any findings. Many security tools like vulnerability scanners can also be configured to present the same information in multiple formats — a dashboard for executives or a security practitioner to monitor, with more detailed information available via drill-down if a user chooses.

During testing, multiple copies of a report may also be generated that necessitates a lifecycle approach to managing the documentation. In formal security assessments, a draft report may be created and shared when testing is completed, in the interest of communicating information as quickly as possible. The assessors still have additional work to perform to finalize the report, like adjusting severity or criticality based on compensating controls and removing any false positives. Sharing the information contained in draft reports can be a tricky prospect, as "critical" findings in an initial report may be marked as "moderate" in a final report once compensating controls are considered; the initial rating can cause panic if shared without the full context.

Security evaluations performed with automated tools may automatically generate reports; however, these may be of limited use for several reasons. A security practitioner must decide whether the automated report provides appropriate information, or if manual reporting is required. Many tools provide information using standardized formats like base CVSS scores to define criticality, but do not account for CVSS environmental or temporal scores, which may be less severe. This distorts the criticality of the findings and may require a manual report to compensate.

Typical Audit Report Contents

A CISSP will likely need to read audit or assessment reports and may be called upon to write them as well depending on job assignments. Understanding common sections of these reports, as well as the contents they typically contain, is essential:

- **Executive summary:** This section contains a high-level overview of the testing activities and findings and typically takes up no more than one page.

  Dashboards present similar high-level information without a narrative and are often present in automated, repetitive testing tools like vulnerability scanners. They provide a summary of the findings and often support the ability to drill down into more technical data.

- **Assumptions or constraints:** Testing often involves constraints, such as a limited amount of time or scope of activities. Since this may lead to parts of a system not being tested, it is important to clearly state these assumptions to provide context for the report's findings.

- **Scope:** It is critical for a reader to understand the coverage of the findings and testing activities. For example, evaluations like pen testing or SOC 2 audits may be limited to specific systems, networks, or facilities, so the report does not include details about vulnerabilities related to objects outside that scope.

- **Summary of activities:** Tests, evaluations, or audit activities performed should be summarized to show the work performed by the evaluation team.

- **Findings or issues:** Findings, deficiencies, or issues are often presented in a table or bulleted list, and each one should include details like where it was found, the severity, and any evidence supporting the finding.

- **Recommendations:** Assessors may provide generic recommendations, like "Apply all current patches" or more detailed recommendations like which cipher suites to disable on specific webservers along with the relevant system configuration commands.

- **Appendixes:** Relevant information is often placed in an appendix for reference if needed, as raw data generated by security testing tools can be complex and lengthy. Placing such information in an appendix provides a more usable report for quick consumption, as well as providing details for a more technical audience might require if needed.

Remediation

Identifying deficiencies or issues with security controls is the main goal of performing security tests, evaluations, assessments, and audits. It is therefore essential that a CISSP implement a process, known as *remediation*, for addressing any findings. This requires project management skills like prioritizing work to be performed, identifying timelines and milestones, and tracking the work through to completion. Audit findings may be input to other areas of the security program like risk analysis and may be handled using the processes from that area. For example, an audit finding regarding a deficient control represents a risk that is not being fully mitigated. The risk management process typically involves documenting the mitigation effect of existing controls, so this audit finding should trigger a review of the relevant risk.

When presented with a set of assessment findings, the organization should create a plan to address them. The goal of these plans is the same, though various security and compliance frameworks use different names like plan of action and milestones (POAM), risk mitigation plans, or audit issue mitigation plans. Regardless of the name, they share similar features:

- Details of the finding
- Mitigating or other relevant circumstances
- Prioritization
- Timeframe for resolution
- Resources required
- Milestones (key dates) and expectations

Once a remediation plan has been executed, it may be prudent to perform the test again to verify the fix is sufficient, particularly for software or technological control vulnerabilities. Retesting is often a defined phase of penetration testing. The testers may even provide advance notice of confirmed findings even before a report is issued to give the organization additional time to address them before the retest. Routine evaluations like monthly vulnerability scanning can also be used to verify if implemented fixes were successful.

Exception Handling

When an audit or other security evaluation discovers an issue that cannot be remediated, it must be handled through an exception process. This is similar to and follows the same steps as documenting policy exceptions, used when a particular system is unable to meet the requirements specified in a policy. Although exceptions may be granted, it should be noted that they should be granted only on a temporary basis. If an exception is requested permanently, or the same issue frequently causes requests for exceptions, this is an indication that a policy or risk management decision is not properly aligned with the organization's objectives. Policy updates might be needed to achieve this alignment, or management governance decisions may need to be reviewed and updated.

Since these exceptions represent an inability to mitigate identified risks, they require specific attention from the organization's security function and management. This comes in the form of documentation of the exception along with relevant details and a formal review and approval, which explicitly states the organization's understanding and acceptance of the risk. This is information typically documented for exception handling:

- **Risk details:** The specifics of the risk, deficiency, or issue, including when it was found and by whom.

- **Reason(s) for exception:** The intended outcome of risk management is mitigation, so management will need details about why a particular risk cannot be mitigated.

- **Compensating controls:** Even if a risk cannot be directly treated to meet the organization's risk threshold, it may be possible to partially mitigate with compensating controls such as increased monitoring.

- **Exception approval:** Management must make an explicit decision to assume additional risk, and documenting the review and approval process provides accountability for this decision.

- **Time:** Most exceptions should be granted on a temporary basis. If the identified deficiency requires a long-term plan to address the risk, such as a major IT project, the exception should be granted only for the anticipated time required to complete the project.

Ethical Disclosure

Web applications, sites, and services like APIs will likely contain vulnerabilities. There is a growing community of security researchers who identify and report these issues to the organization responsible for the affected resource, with the goal of responsibly disclosing the vulnerability before a malicious actor can find it. These researchers are often ethical hackers, and this process is known as ethical or responsible disclosure.

Security practitioners at organizations with web resources should ensure they are prepared for ethical disclosure of vulnerabilities. This can be challenging, as the ethical hackers or security researchers are outside the organization and communication is often unexpected. One recommended practice is to develop and share a publicly available disclosure policy that outlines several key points:

- How to report vulnerabilities and what to expect, like details of when to expect an initial response, how long it will take to validate any findings submitted, and what types of requests for additional information might follow.

- Any payment or recognition made for reported vulnerabilities. Some researchers do not expect any recognition, while others may be satisfied with public recognition of their work in the form of thanks in a patch or security update when the vulnerability is fixed.

- Any security elements that are explicitly in scope or out of scope. Many organizations choose to exclude reports of missing "best practices" that do not fit the organization's operational needs or low-criticality items and vulnerabilities that result in only minor operational issues.

As a security researcher or ethical hacker, or as an organization providing these types of services, it is important to ensure the work you do follows the requirements of these policies. While there may be some areas that are open for respectful debate, such as the criticality of a particular vulnerability, there are several ethical disclosure rules that are not open to debate:

- Any vulnerabilities found should be reported to the responsible organization, and they should never be used exclusively for personal monetary or reputation gain.

- All work should be conducted in good faith, and organizations should be given the benefit of the doubt. Identified vulnerabilities are typically disclosed publicly after a specific period of time, which gives the organization time to address the vulnerability. If the organization has been responsive and asks for additional time to work on a remediation, it is not advisable to move ahead with disclosure before a fix is available.

- Act within the limits of the law.

- As an organization, be receptive to vulnerability disclosures, and do not act in a hostile manner unless a researcher is behaving in an abusive manner.

Many organizations are choosing to provide financial incentives to ethical hackers in the form of bug bounty or disclosure payouts. Since criminals are often motivated by profit, paying for responsible disclosure alters the economics to favor legitimate research and responsible disclosure. Third-party firms exist to manage the process of ethical disclosure and payment for identified bugs. These services offer the advantage of a pool of verified security researchers, and using a bug bounty provider can be a valuable addition to an organization's security testing and assessment strategy.

There are four circumstances related to ethical disclosure that a security researcher or organization needs to consider if they have discovered a vulnerability in a system they do not own or control. Rules, laws, and regulations for these security research and disclosure of vulnerabilities varies greatly across jurisdictions and is constantly evolving, so any individual or organization performing security research should seek legal guidance for their activities. The special circumstances for responsibly disclosing findings include the following:

- **Nondisclosure:** There may be contractual or legal obligations that prevent disclosure of a vulnerability; for example, when disclosing a vulnerability might compromise an active criminal investigation.

- **Full disclosure:** This is a philosophical argument that any time a weakness is discovered, it should be fully and transparently reported to the organization responsible for fixing it as soon as possible. While the goal of improving security is admirable, many vendors may be hostile to researchers who attempt to report vulnerabilities.

- **Responsible disclosure:** This principle defines a responsibility for the discoverer to report a weakness to the organization in a timely manner and give the organization time to fix the vulnerability before publicly disclosing it.

- **Mandatory reporting:** In certain circumstances, reporting a discovered vulnerability to law enforcement or other authorities may be mandatory. Legal and regulatory frameworks around the world vary, so this can be a difficult situation if the discoverer is in one jurisdiction but the organization responsible for the software or system is in another.

- **Whistleblowing:** A whistleblower is someone who feels ethically obligated to report a dangerous or illegal situation, and many jurisdictions have laws designed to protect whistleblowers from retribution for reporting. In the case of discovered security vulnerabilities, whistleblowers may be protected from prosecution for copyright infringement or other digital crimes if they follow proper channels for disclosing discovered vulnerabilities.

CONDUCT OR FACILITATE SECURITY AUDITS

Security practitioners are often in charge of either conducting or facilitating audits, and in both cases, the goal is the same: to compare some aspect of an organization against a standard. Conducting an audit, or being the auditor, requires a thorough understanding and knowledge of the processes, goals, and techniques used in auditing. Facilitating audits does not require as much knowledge, but being aware of the audit process can be helpful when preparing in advance of the audit.

Designing an Audit Program

An organization's audit program can be designed to conduct internal audits, facilitate external audits, or both if needed. Appropriate resources, oversight, and support from management are essential, as is a realistic schedule for performing audits. One-off, point-in-time audits provide a useful snapshot of a security program, but a recurring audit schedule allows the program to be tracked over time and show improvements.

Common Audit Frameworks

If an organization is pursuing a specific type of audit, such as FedRAMP or SOC 2, then the audit program will be dictated by the standard, as this is what external auditors are required to follow. The audit frameworks may also be used as a guide to best practices when designing an internal program. In fact, designing an internal program aligned to the same standard an external auditor uses makes sense, as it allows the organization to uncover the same issues an external auditor might find.

These are common information security frameworks that provide a standard against which to perform an audit:

- **SSAE 18** is the Statement on Standards for Attestation Engagements that is used by auditors when performing audits for SOC 2.

- **ISO/IEC 15408-1:2009**, "Information technology — Security techniques — Evaluation criteria for IT security," is the foundation for the Common Criteria certification, which is a formal assessment process for technology products against a defined set of security functional requirements. This document and ISO/IEC 18045 are available free of charge.

ISO/IEC 18045:2008, "Information technology — Security techniques — Methodology for IT security evaluation," is a companion to ISO 15048 and provides standards for consistent criteria and evaluation methods.

- **ISO/IEC 27006:2015**, "Information technology — Security techniques — Requirements for bodies providing audit and certification of information security management systems," is the official set of requirements and guidance for auditors performing certification audits against ISO 27001.

- **NIST Special Publication (SP) 800-53A**, "Assessing Security and Privacy Controls in Federal Information Systems and Organizations," is a guide to assessing the controls outlined in NIST SP 800-53. It introduces a simple set of testing procedures to assess control effectiveness: test, examine, or interview. Although applicable to U.S. government agencies, it is freely available and may be adapted for use by any organization.

The NIST Cybersecurity Framework (CSF) and **FedRAMP Security Assessment Framework (SAF)** are both freely available as well and may be used to perform assessments with evaluation methods similar to those in NIST SP 800-53A.

Sampling

When designing an audit program, the cost of work to gather information and gain assurance should be balanced against the benefit of risk visibility. Sampling is a technique utilized in audits to reduce work while maintaining assurance that deficiencies are identified. For example, a configuration audit might choose 100 servers out of a population of 1,000 to reduce the amount of work required. The sample should be representative — if the organization is evenly split between Windows and Linux, then 50 of each server type should be examined.

Internal Audits

An internal audit is conducted by the staff of an organization and offers the benefit of auditor familiarity with processes, tools, and personnel. This same familiarity can also be a drawback of internal audits, as someone familiar with an environment may unintentionally overlook issues — a second pair of eyes on a problem often identifies problems. A dedicated team member to perform audits and manage remediation, however, may be more effective than an external auditor who delivers a report and then has no further interaction.

Internal auditors may also lack sufficient independence to perform an objective assessment. Finding a major issue that could impact financial performance or the auditor's relationship with team members can create an incentive to downplay issues discovered. In some organizations, this can be solved by making auditors a separate team within the company, though for smaller organizations, that may not be a viable option.

Internal audits are often useful when preparing for an external audit to find and correct issues in preparation for the external audit. In situations where the external audit has significant business impacts, like PCI or other regulatory audit, an internal readiness assessment or mock audit is a prudent risk avoidance measure. Internal audits can play a key role in an organization's governance, as they provide reports to management showing how well policies and other governance are being implemented.

External Audits

An external audit is performed by personnel from outside the organization and is often a requirement for regulatory compliance audits. The key advantage of an external auditor is total independence from the organization being audited — the auditors are invested fully in the process of conducting the audit and should have no conflict of interest to overlook or suppress findings. They may also have highly specialized skills needed to perform audits, like SOC 2 audits performed using the SSAE 18 standard that require the skills of a Certified Public Accountant (CPA); this may not be a skillset most organizations have on internal teams.

The use of external auditors has two potential drawbacks. First is the cost, which can be significant for large and complex audits that may involve travel, hours billed by auditors, and service fees that match the skill level of the audit firm retained (generally firms with a higher reputation will charge more). The lack of knowledge about an organization's operations can also be a drawback, as an external auditor must spend more time learning than a similar internal auditor who is already familiar, or the external auditor may entirely miss a detail like specific policy language. This can lead to false positive audit findings.

The use of external auditors is a requirement in many compliance frameworks, such as PCI, ISO 27001, and the Cloud Security Alliance Security Trust Assurance and Risk (CSA STAR). The independent third party supports assurance that the findings in the report are reliable, which is beneficial to parties like business partners or customers. Regulatory bodies in some industries and governmental organizations may have their own auditors who assess organizations they regulate. In these cases, facilitating these external audits must be a high priority to a CISSP, as most of the regulatory bodies can take actions like issuing fines or suspending business operations for noncompliance.

Third-Party Audits

Third-party audits are a vital risk management tool used for external suppliers, vendors, and partners. A security practitioner may be in charge of conducting such an audit or be a consumer of an audit report provided by the external party. The goal in both is the same: to identify any of the third party's risks that could impact your organization, and the risk mitigations in place. Common examples include SOC 2 and CSA STAR audits, which are often conducted for the explicit purpose of sharing details about an organization's security program with third parties.

Auditing the security practices of third parties with access to your organization's sensitive data is especially crucial. Many privacy and data security laws explicitly place legal accountability for breaches on the data controller even if a data processor, like a cloud service, was the cause of the breach. These audits can identify the controls in place at the provider, and whether these mitigations reduce risk to a level acceptable by the organization.

Whether consuming a SOC 2 report or conducting an audit of a third party's controls, a security practitioner should seek to answer the following questions related to the security program:

- What standards do they use for selecting controls and auditing their effectiveness?

- What details are being shared? If only limited information is available, are there deficiencies being hidden?

- What findings exist, and what is the third party's response related to the risk?

- What plans exist to remediate any findings?

Third-party risk assessment can quickly become complicated due to the complexity of modern supply chains. An information system running in an organization's colocation provider inherits risks from the third-party hosting service, software used to run the system, and vendors of physical goods and services. Risk present in the supply chains of these third parties can also pose a risk to the organization, which is a fourth-party relationship. Identifying the suppliers in the supply chain and ensuring adequate coverage of audits and assessments are discussed in more detail in Chapter 1.

SUMMARY

Assessments, audits, tests, and evaluations all share similar goals of identifying issues in security control programs. The targets range from low-level items like individual hardware components all the way to high-level, organization-wide security programs. Gathering data from these components and comparing it to expected values provides the organization with insight into the effectiveness of the risk mitigation controls in place. These evaluations may be done using internal resources or external resources, or they may be furnished by third parties like service providers, vendors, and business partners.

Security assessment and testing relies heavily on collecting and managing data. Organizational processes like security awareness and BCDR should be inspected for data needed to support these oversight functions, but the data alone is not enough to prove valuable, so a CISSP should also review how to generate indicators, in the form of KPIs and KRIs, which identify actions needed to correct or avoid risks. These metrics should be tied to the organization's strategic, governance, and compliance needs.

DOMAIN **7** CISSP®

Security Operations

SECURITY OPERATIONS FOCUSES ON maintaining the various aspects of the organization's security controls in a functional state, as well as the processes and procedures needed to maintain security across people, processes, and technology. Organizations must identify and assess the risks they face and then apply appropriate risk mitigations in the form of security controls. Security operations (SecOps) covers a broad base of functions across the organization. Many of these areas will be outside the purview of the security practitioner, such as physical security, which is often handled by building or facility engineers, but the security function retains accountability for ensuring security is properly understood and addressed. After all, even the best logical access controls are worthless if an attacker can walk up to a workstation and access the data it contains!

SecOps encompasses disparate functions such as physical security of both data and operational facilities, incident response, supporting or conducting investigations, handling material and evidence collected during investigations, and performing digital forensics. Many of these areas are highly specialized, while the Certified Information Systems Security Professional (CISSP) is a general certification. Generalist security practitioners may not have the skills needed to perform all these functions, but it is important to have access to these skills, whether by hiring or training team members or through the use of a service provider.

If done correctly, SecOps should support business or organizational operations with a minimum of overhead, cost, or other impact. Having a comprehensive inventory of the organization's valuable assets and implementing a strategy for securing and monitoring them is the ultimate goal of the security function. This chapter presents an overview of important concerns to address when maintaining the various controls implemented to mitigate risk, including the most important: personnel life, health, and safety.

UNDERSTAND AND COMPLY WITH INVESTIGATIONS

Investigations, evidence collection/handling, and digital forensics requires highly specialized skills. It is similar to healthcare—you may be qualified to eat a balanced diet and take exercise without guidance from a professional, but if you need major surgery, a professional surgeon is required. Some security practitioners will specialize in digital forensics and incident response (DFIR) and hold credentials in these areas. For many CISSP credential holders, the process of supporting investigations and forensics will require coordination with appropriate experts to properly handle an investigation, as there are crucial concerns that require specialized skills and training to prevent corruption or destruction of evidence.

As this subdomain name implies, the security practitioner may not necessarily be responsible for managing an investigation but is required to comply with external requirements from appropriate professionals. This section presents elements of security incident investigations and the critical role a security practitioner must play; for a more technically detailed exploration, the book *Cybercrime Investigations: A Comprehensive Resource for Everyone* by John Bandler and Antonia Merzon is recommended.

Investigations usually follow from a security incident response (IR), and the IR process is where a security generalist is likely to play the most significant role. Any incident can be deemed serious enough to require a formal investigation, and likely scenarios include alleged criminal activity, severe violations of security policies, and inexplicable service interruptions or outages. The level of rigor applied and outputs such as documentation or witness testimony will vary depending on the type of investigation.

Evidence Collection and Handling

Evidence is any information that indicates a proposition is true or factual; put more simply, it is information that supports a statement. For example, a door access control record of Alice entering the building at 10 a.m. and CCTV footage of her accessing a restricted vault at 10:10 a.m. support an assertion that Alice entered a vault but does not necessarily support the assertion that Alice stole sensitive assets from the vault.

There are multiple types of evidence that could be collected while investigating a security incident. The most obvious is digital evidence like log files, recordings, computer files, and computer system components such as memory or hard drives. Hard-copy materials can be important evidence, too, though massive data sets are rarely printed. Depending on the type of crime, there may be physical evidence like fingerprints, hair, or DNA to be collected, which is not only outside the scope of most CISSP's knowledge but entirely outside the scope of digital forensics. Such an investigation is likely to involve a multidisciplinary team of professionals with law enforcement backgrounds, and the CISSP's role will be to support and comply with any requests from these professionals.

Collecting Digital Evidence

Collecting digital evidence can be particularly challenging due to the unique properties of digital information, and preserving the integrity of any evidence collected must be a primary concern when beginning an incident response. Digital evidence is often short-lived, like log files that are overwritten after only 24 hours or information in volatile RAM that is lost when the system is powered down. Cloud services have further confused the issue as they store information outside the organization's control and may not make digital evidence available. Virtually all digital information is easily changeable as well unless it has been written to specific media designed to prevent it from being altered. These factors make digital evidence collection a highly specialized endeavor—the investigator must take no actions that interfere with the integrity of the evidence they collect. Otherwise, the data cannot be relied upon as evidence to make an accusation, since the accused could raise doubt about the veracity of evidence if it was altered during collection or analysis.

Evidence collection may begin during initial incident response, well before a formal investigation is undertaken, so it is crucial to ensure information collected during the response is handled as if it could become evidence in the future. To achieve this, IR processes must be written to include the following best practices:

- **Record and document everything**, including dates, times, and locations of all actions taken, condition(s) of any evidence collected, and relevant personnel involved.

- **Always make copies** of digital evidence and perform an analysis or investigation of the copies wherever possible. A bit-level copy is preferred, as it makes an exact duplicate of not only the directories and files on a device but also any deleted files, data remnants, and slack space. This type of copy takes longer and uses more space than a logical backup that only copies directories and files, but it provides more complete evidence.

- **Prevent unwanted changes** by using copies of data, which can be discarded without losing evidence if an unwanted change is made, and using hardware or software to prevent changes to data. The simple act of plugging in a removable storage device to a modern computer causes data changes, as operating systems perform functions such as search indexing; the data written during these normal operations can irredeemably damage data that may be needed as evidence. Hardware devices and software known as *write blockers* should be used to prevent unwanted changes to media.

- **Verify integrity** to prove unwanted changes were not introduced during collection or analysis. This will usually involve calculating and comparing hash values to prove the data being used for analysis is the same as the data collected and that data is not changed during analysis leading to adulterated results.

- **Be aware of destructive changes** and avoid them at all costs. When something goes wrong, there is a natural inclination to power down a system or quit applications, but this risks destroying essential data stored in volatile memory like RAM or transient data like application caches. IR procedures should be written to balance the need to prevent further damage with the need to preserve potential evidence; rather than unplugging a compromised system, it is better to isolate it in a network segment where investigation can occur without evidence being destroyed.

Handling Digital Evidence

Once digital evidence has been collected, the highest priority is preserving its integrity as it is handled by the investigators, defined as the *chain of custody*. The chain of custody does not prove that information has not changed in any way; rather, it proves that the changes made to the evidence were done in a controlled manner that did not interfere with the information's integrity and authenticity, and therefore, its reliability as evidence. The mere act of collecting a mobile device and taking it to a lab for forensic analysis is technically a change, but so long as the evidence is in the custody of trained professionals and no changes were made during transport, any information those devices contain can be relied upon.

There are standards for collecting and handling digital evidence. For security practitioners who do not specialize in DFIR, the recommendations from these sources are likely best implemented in IR processes or procedures. In the International Organization for Standardization (ISO) 27000 series, there is ISO/IEC 27037:2012, "Information technology – Security techniques – Guidelines for identification, collection, acquisition and preservation of digital evidence," which provides guidance for collecting and handling evidence from desktop and laptop computers, mobile phones, personal electronic devices (including mobile navigation devices), and computer networks or equipment implementing Transmission Control Protocol / Internet Protocol (TCP/IP) networking. Although dated 2012, this ISO standard was reviewed in 2018 and remains current.

National Institute of Standards and Technology (NIST) Special Publication 800-86, "Guide to Integrating Forensic Techniques into Incident Response," also provides guidelines and suggestions for incorporating digital evidence collection into IR practices and covers data sources such as files, network traffic, computer apps, and operating systems. This document was last updated in 2006, and it provides a strategic level of for creating DFIR programs, which in turn require current skills and abilities relevant to the organization's IT environment. The NIST Computer Security Resource Center (CSRC) has a number of resources such as projects and publications addressing current forensics concerns like mobile devices, cloud computing, and analysis of advanced persistent threat (APT) activity, which can be found at `csrc.nist.gov`.

Cloud computing represents a specific challenge to the field of digital forensics due to the very nature of its operation. High availability features like global data replication and hosting can make it difficult to determine exactly where a crime or incident occurred, and if the incident occurred in a different legal jurisdiction, the options for investigating and collecting evidence may be limited. When choosing a cloud service model and cloud service provider (CSP), a CISSP must understand and provide input to balance business needs such as cost savings, operational functionality, and security capabilities such as digital forensics support.

Reporting and Documentation

Evidence, just like other data, will have important metadata crucial to its reliability. Details like who collected it, when, and what steps they used must be documented, though the level of metadata required will depend on the type of investigation being conducted. An internal administrative investigation requires evidence but not highly rigorous handling procedures, while information presented to a court will require thorough documentation and confirmed metadata to support the chain of custody.

Documentation should be created throughout the life of evidence, starting with initial detection of an incident, any investigation steps undertaken, information discovered during investigation, and all actions taken on the evidence. This documentation should allow for definitive determination of the time and person performing the actions, similar to the principle of accountability in access control. Any fans of crime investigation TV shows will be familiar—when an interview starts, the detectives state their names and the time on the recording to allow for identification, and any evidence found is bagged and tagged to preserve it and record the conditions of its collection. Investigation tools like ticketing systems and checklists should be designed to automatically capture this information or ensure the investigator properly documents it.

Reports of investigations and evidence should contain enough information to relate the details of events without the need for subjective interpretation. The information collected should be presented clearly and accompanied by all relevant metadata as required by the intended audience, such as a chain of custody required by a court.

Evidence being presented to a court is required to meet the most rigorous standards. Evidence deemed inadmissible that leads investigators to subsequent evidence can cause all the evidence to be useless. In general, all evidence should adhere to the following principles:

- **Accuracy**: Evidence and documentation must not contain errors, be in conflict with other evidence, or lack integrity. Since evidence is relied upon to prove a case, any inaccuracies weaken that ability.

- **Authenticity**: Authentic information or evidence is of undisputed origin, which is proven by the chain of custody. Inauthentic information runs the risk of, at best, demonstrating incompetence and, at worst, calling the presenter's credibility into question. Information that is falsified or adulterated should never be used. Excluding contrary information is also problematic and is not considered a good practice.

- **Comprehensibility**: This is a tricky subject, as digital information often requires specific technical knowledge to understand. Lawyers and judges in court or business professionals reviewing a case in a non-courtroom proceeding may lack the ability to interpret complex technical topics such as malware forensics or network traffic analysis. Expert witnesses can be a useful resource for translating or interpreting tech-speak into friendlier language.

- **Convincing**: A user logging in to a restricted workstation is not, by itself, sufficiently convincing evidence that a financial crime was committed. Presenting the user's actions along with evidence that they received large, unexpected bank payments is more convincing when telling a story of a particular user committing fraud.

- **Objective**: Evidence must stand on its own in support of an argument or assertion. Audit logs showing user activity are objective, while a security practitioner who "has a hunch" that a user has dubious morals is a subjective statement and does not definitively prove a case.

- **Admissible**: This applies mostly to evidence submitted to a court in civil or criminal trials. Evidence is admissible if it meets requirements set by the court to be introduced in support of a legal argument. For example, direct evidence like digital forensic examination is typically admissible, while hearsay such as "Sanjay heard a rumor that Lupita shared her password with a member of her team" is not.

Security practitioners are unlikely to be evidentiary experts, so it is crucial to seek advice from legal counsel, law enforcement, or other investigative professionals to ensure evidence you collect, handle, and prepare is adequate.

Investigative Techniques

The "examine, interview, and test" audit techniques discussed in Chapter 6, "Security Assessment and Testing," are similar to the techniques used to investigate security incidents and crimes. The fundamental idea is the same—gather and examine evidence to support a conclusion. In the case of investigations, there are some unique concerns, however, such as legal rights of a suspect when being questioned or investigated. A CISSP may be called upon to support or handle tasks in an investigation and, as with all evidence handling, should follow the guidance and advice of professionals.

These are the four main investigative techniques a security practitioner should be familiar with:

- **Data capture** includes gathering data such as audit logs or network traffic, as well as specialized techniques such as gathering photographic or video evidence of an incident scene and the associated investigation. *Automated capture* is done using traditional monitoring tools and may leverage the organization's continuous monitoring infrastructure like a security information and event management (SIEM) tool or recorded camera footage. *Manual capture* refers to techniques employed by forensic investigators like making copies of data and media and recording the scene of an incident or crime by photos or video.

- **Interviews** are a tool designed to solicit information from individuals, typically witnesses or those with knowledge of an incident. Interviews follow a question-and-answer format where the investigator is asking questions designed to elicit information and recording the answers, though interviewees may also give a statement. In general, interviews should be recorded, if permitted by local law and if appropriate permission from the interviewee has been documented. Multi-party interviews are also encouraged to provide greater reliability of information, whether by having multiple interviewers or an interviewee advocate present who can attest to the accuracy of information gathered. Interviewees typically have legal rights such as the ability to refuse or terminate an interview, and security practitioners must be careful to abide by all laws—a private citizen (like a CISSP) holding someone against their will without cause is illegal in most places!

- **Interrogations** carry more stringent requirements than interviews and are generally carried out by law enforcement professionals. An interrogation is conducted against an individual suspected of a crime and often takes place after that individual has been arrested. There are specific legal rights assigned to suspects that, if not observed, can render information gathered in the interrogation inadmissible.

- **External requests** can be made by investigators to gather information from third parties such as an internet service provider (ISP), government agency, or formal request for information from a specific party. These often require legal approvals and processes like warrants and subpoenas, so security practitioners may only be tangentially involved with originating them in an investigation. However, a CISSP may be subject to these processes if called upon to provide evidence. In these cases, guidance from appropriate legal counsel is key, either from a personal attorney or from corporate counsel.

Digital Forensics Tools, Tactics, and Procedures

Properly trained professionals are required to perform forensics tasks and must, of course, be given access to appropriate tools and resources. Organizations must decide if the analysts and investigators will be internal employees or contractors or will be external vendors that are called upon only when needed. The cost of retaining the needed talent and resources in-house must be weighed against the benefit of quicker response times and more customized procedures and should consider the frequency of incidents that require formal investigation.

An investigation and forensic team should include people with diverse skills and experience across computer networking protocols, security tools and platforms, system administrators, and the practices of threat and vulnerability management. Any investigation requiring forensic expertise is likely to be a critical priority for the organization, so forensic team members should be granted the ability to approach any member of the organization and expect cooperation, even if it interrupts the member's routine tasks. In some cases, organization members may be temporarily reassigned to support the investigation, similar to incident response teams.

Tools

There are physical forensic tools used by digital forensics experts, even though they are mainly interested in and deal with digital or electronic information. Forensics work requires tracking and case management software and equipment, workstations, and workspaces that are isolated and dedicated to forensics to prevent contamination of evidence under investigation. Additional tools include the following:

- **Write blockers and drive imagers** designed to allow examination or imaging of a storage device, typically a hard drive, without writing any data to the storage device, which would violate the integrity of the evidence.

- **Faraday containers** like bags or boxes, which are shielded to prevent radio communications to or from a physical device. These are especially useful when digital evidence exists on portable devices like smartphones, tablets, or even laptops, since these devices can send and receive commands using wireless protocols like Bluetooth, WiFi, or cellular connections. This can unintentionally alter data, such as an app update being installed that overwrites critical evidence, or the device can be tampered with to destroy evidence by remotely locking or wiping it.

- **Video and audio recording** tools can be used to document evidence of a crime or incident and can also serve to document the investigation team's activities to support the integrity of any evidence. Rather than taking extra time to document the steps taken when performing forensic analysis, the analyst can simply record a video or audio log of their work.

Once all physical evidence has been collected, it must be analyzed, and there are a variety of software tools available to the forensic investigator. These can be categorized based on their intended use or area of specialization:

- **Network traffic analysis** tools like Wireshark can be used for both network packet capture (pcap) and network traffic analysis, by reconstructing the communication sessions. With the rise of software-defined networks (SDNs) and virtualized cloud infrastructure, these software tools may replace physical network forensic tools like using a SPAN port to capture traffic; some of this capture and analysis may be performed proactively by tools like security orchestration, automation, and response (SOAR) or security information and event management (SIEM), as part of the organization's continuous monitoring strategy.

- **Log analysis tools** like SIEM tools are often useful to investigators as a way to reconstruct the series of events that led up to an incident. Less mature organizations may not have SIEM tools in place, in which case, logs can be manually collected and imported into a SIEM tool for analysis.

- **Data recovery tools** assist investigators in recovering files and information that have been deleted or overwritten. Most operating systems do not delete the actual data when a user deletes a file, but merely update an allocation table that tracks where files are stored on a disk and where free space exists. Deleted file contents still exist, but there is nothing preventing a new file from being written there if requested; if no new file has been written, it is easy to recover the information by reading the information on each sector of the drive. Depending on the type of media, it may even be possible to use highly specialized physical equipment to reconstruct data after a disk has been overwritten.

- **Virtual machines** (VMs) are not specifically a forensics tool, but they are useful for investigative purposes. Suspected malware can be copied to and run on a VM that is isolated from all other systems, which allows it to be observed and investigated without threat of infecting other systems. Such virtual lab or testing environments can be set up and torn down much easier than their physical counterparts.

- **Code analysis** tools include decompilers designed to reverse-engineer software, as well as binary analysis tools designed to observe the functioning of a program at the source-code level.

- **Hashing** tools are essential to investigators, not because they provide any insight into the data being analyzed, but due to their essential role in proving the continued integrity of data that is collected and analyzed. Hash values and message digests are useful to prove that data like an app or email has not been changed in transit, and hashing can also be used to prove the data was not altered by the investigator. This proves the data can be relied upon in support of any assertions or accusations made.

- **Toolkits** are suites of software that provide common tools for a specific purpose like forensic investigation, and there are many forensics toolkits that are made by commercial vendors, open-source projects, or even composed of tools chosen by a particular forensic expert to support their work. These toolkits combine multiple resources that are useful to forensic investigators, including system-specific analysis software like Windows Registry analyzers, data recovery and reconstruction apps, and tools discussed earlier like network traffic analyzers and software write blockers.

Techniques and Procedures

It is important to be prepared with training on forensics techniques and easily followed procedures, even with trained professionals conducting forensics and investigating an incident. The situation during an incident is frequently stressful and time sensitive in nature, so preparation and job aids will prove useful.

The first step is to define the process and procedure to be used during an incident, which is the realm of the IR plan. Many investigations begin as a response to an incident; details gathered during the response may require forensic analysis later if the cause of the incident is found to be a crime or other serious matter. Documented standards for the collection, handling, and investigation of digital evidence include ISO 27041, 27042, 27043, and 27050. SANS also provides a number of useful resources to aid investigators and responders, including cheat sheets, quick-start guides, and posters for common tasks like malware analysis using Linux or malicious document analysis. These can be found at `digital-forensics.sans.org/community/cheat-sheets`. NIST also provides resources for forensic investigators, focused on ensuring the quality of software forensic tools and on developing skills and training programs for investigators. These resources can be found at the NIST Computer Forensics Tool Testing Program (CFTT) site: `nist.gov/itl/ssd/software-quality-group/computer-forensics-tool-testing-program-cftt`.

A generic set of procedural steps for conducting a forensic analysis is presented here. These may be initiated proactively to investigate a suspected incident or be invoked by escalating an incident response for further investigation when the evidence points to a serious security issue.

- **Define priorities**: There are three possible priorities an organization might pursue when responding to an incident—return as quickly as possible to normal operations, minimize damage, or preserve the greatest amount of detail regarding the incident. Returning to normal operations by wiping and reimaging machines gets things running again quickly, but vital data is lost. Taking a system offline completely to conduct an investigation can cause business operations to cease completely or require expensive duplicate equipment purchases. The organization must ascertain the requirements of each situation and choose an appropriate set of actions.

- **Identify data sources**: All incidents require the discovery of relevant information, and certain actions will need to be taken in a timely manner based on the sources identified. Some log data, for example, is short-lived and must be captured before it is written over, and some memory may be frequently overwritten or volatile, meaning data stored there is available to be collected for only a short time. Some data may already be captured and stored long-term as part of continuous monitoring, making it easier to access. All data sources must be quickly identified and prioritized for collection.

- **Plan to collect data and execute**: Once data sources have been identified, a plan must be made and acted upon to collect the needed information. This plan should prioritize ephemeral data like temp files that are designed to be overwritten, as well as volatile memory storage like RAM that disappears when the machine is powered down. Executing data collection involves the use of investigative techniques discussed earlier and may require formal processes such as getting search warrants or subpoenas issued. Tools used in this step will vary based on the information source, such as specific programs needed for data recovery on different operating systems and physical collection and storage tools for different types of media.

- **Document and preserve integrity**: Data collection is the first link in the chain of custody, so documentation of the work done is essential. Details including the time a piece of evidence was collected and any handling it was subject to must be documented. In some cases, the evidence itself will already contain needed metadata, such as read-only log files in a SIEM tool that should contain date and timestamp information. In other cases, the integrity metadata must be calculated as part of the process, such as calculating hash values for files as they are collected to prove the evidence analyzed has not been changed since it was collected.

- **Look for hidden or erased data**: Vital information needed for the investigation may have been deleted, overwritten, or exist in hidden directories. In some cases, an attacker or malicious software will deliberately delete or obfuscate data to confuse the investigation, and in others, the data may have been deleted or overwritten during routine system operations or innocent user behavior. Unless extraordinary means like overwriting or cryptoshredding are employed, deleted data may be recoverable with hardware or software tools.

- **Perform analysis**: Once collected, forensic investigation of the data is performed. This may entail simple tasks such as reviewing documents, files, and communications for suspicious user activity, or more complex tasks such as network traffic analysis to determine how a piece of malware spread throughout a network. It may even require highly advanced tasks such as reverse-engineering malware to investigate the incident. Determining a timeline or sequence of events is also critical.

✔ Forensics in the Cloud

The very nature of cloud computing makes forensics much more difficult—even determining the scene of an incident can be difficult when VMs can move between geographically distributed data centers at any time. Issues of jurisdiction may arise, which prevent full access if investigations are required in a different country, and the level of access granted by the CSP may also be limited due to legal issues surrounding cloud customers accessing each other's data in the course of an investigation.

There are a variety of resources available for DFIR practitioners working in a cloud environment, as well as evolving software tools to address specific challenges. One factor driving proactive information collection like log centralization in a SIEM tool is the lack of reactive investigative options in the cloud—VMs are often configured to exist for only as long as needed to perform a specific task, so the logs they generate vanish and cannot be analyzed if an incident occurs. Some CSPs offer forensic and incident response services that support investigation without the risk of leaking data between cloud customers.

Industry groups also offer support for cloud forensics. The Cloud Security Alliance (CSA) has published a cross-reference of the ISO 27037 standard to common cloud scenarios, available at `downloads.cloudsecurityalliance.org/initiatives/imf/` `Mapping-the-Forensic-Standard-ISO-IEC-27037-to-Cloud-Computing.pdf`. CSA also publishes a Cloud Forensics Capability Maturity Model, which can be useful when designing a cloud forensics program and identifying improvement opportunities: `cloudsecurityalliance.org/press-releases/2015/10/13/cloud-forensics-` `capability-maturity-model-available-for-download`. NIST maintains a guide to cloud forensics with a specific focus on identifying common challenges and offering solutions to adapt existing DFIR tools, techniques, and practices to the cloud: `csrc` `.nist.gov/publications/detail/nistir/8006/final`.

Artifacts

Locard's exchange principle is a guiding idea in forensics and is named for a forensic scientist and criminologist who observed that a criminal will both introduce traces of their presence at a crime scene and remove something and that both can be used as forensic evidence. In the investigation of physical crimes, this is known as trace evidence like hair, fibers, and DNA. In computer crime, digital forensics often focus on *artifacts*, which are digital traces left behind when a user or program interacts with a device. Searching for these is one of the main goals of digital forensics, as these traces of activity tell the story of an incident and are vital in supporting any accusation or case made.

Given the specialized nature of digital forensics, there are advanced requirements for training and certification in the field. Many government organizations with law enforcement missions and dedicated DFIR providers have internal training and skills development programs that cover what artifacts to look for and how to recover them.

Computer

In almost all circumstances, using a computer will leave traces of the activities performed, and actions like installing programs or executing specific commands will leave evidence useful to an investigator. Log files will be created as system events like logins occur, system configuration files like the Windows Registry or Unix `.plist` files will be updated, and files will be written, altered, and deleted. Some information regarding an incident may be compiled by existing tools like endpoint detection and response (EDR) or host-based intrusion detection system (HIDS) agents, while other information will require manual investigation. The following list highlights a few common sources of artifacts across three major computing platforms. It is not exhaustive, and just like system administrators, it is often the case that forensic investigators will specialize in one of these platforms.

- **Windows**: Windows systems maintain a log that can be accessed using the Event Viewer, and they contain entries for vital system, application, and security events. Deleted files may be in the Recycle Bin if a user or malicious program has not taken extra steps, and hidden metadata or deleted-but-recoverable files may also be found. The Windows Registry is also a useful source of information, as it contains records of configuration changes and software installed.

- **macOS**: The Mac equivalents of the Windows Event Viewer and Recycle Bin are called the Console and Trash, respectively, and their investigation follows many of the same procedures. Some macOS-specific technologies can also prove useful investigation points such as the automatically generated Time Machine backup system, Spotlight indexing and systemwide search function, and configuration files known as property list (PLIST) files.

- **Linux**: Unlike desktop versions of Windows and macOS, many Linux systems are designed to be run solely using a command-line interface (CLI). Native graphical tools for accessing artifacts may not exist, so third-party toolkits are required, or the investigator must be familiar with the standard filesystem to find relevant data. Examples include the `/usr` folder where user files are stored, `/tmp` for temporary files (a vital source of volatile data, as most Linux systems will delete the data in this directory upon reboot), and `/var` where frequently changed files are stored including caches, log files, and information about currently running processes.

- **Browsers**: A user's browsing history contains enough data that it's now a common joke for an individual to be charged with the duty of deleting a person's browsing history upon their passing. However, if the root cause of a malware infection is the user visiting a particular website, records of activity like sites visited, cookies placed, and any data stored locally by websites could be informative.

- **Local storage**: Physical investigations often involve a look through physical storage like file cabinets, and digital forensics should perform the digital equivalent by browsing local filesystems or removable media. Perhaps a criminal maintained some log of their activity that supports the investigation, or metadata exists that can prove certain actions like deletion of key files.

■ **Cloud storage**: Because of the lack of physical control over cloud systems, artifacts may require the investigator to follow legal procedures like getting warrants issued. The wide variety of cloud services means forensic investigation may be against a VM that is similar to investigating a physical computer or may target entirely novel tools like microservices where standard forensic artifacts aren't even available.

Network

Data in transit is an ephemeral state; that is to say, data moves across communication networks but does not get stored there. However, metadata about these communications is essential to investigating incidents, and in many cases, stored data or actors in an incident can be identified or tracked using the communication metadata. The following are some sources for network artifacts:

■ **NetFlow** analysis provides a picture of the Internet Protocol (IP) traffic flow and volume across a network device, typically a switch. It can be used to identify details of the communication such as ports, protocols, and addresses being used for communication.

■ **Packet analysis** (often known as pcap) is useful as it captures both details about communications and the data itself. Packet sniffer tools can capture packets in transit across a network and reconstruct data being sent or received, which can be further analyzed.

■ **Known bad traffic** can be used to identify suspicious or unwanted activity, such as a server sending data to known spam domains or communicating with known malware servers like command and control (C2) or botnets.

■ **Network device log files** can contain a wealth of useful information if they have been configured to store it. Devices like switches and routers contain details of traffic passing the network, and security-focused tools like proxies or Virtual Private Network (VPN) concentrators are a useful source of artifacts relevant to a security incident.

Mobile Devices

Forensic investigation of smartphones running Apple's iOS and Google's Android have been in the news frequently after major criminal cases due to encryption making forensics difficult or impossible. Strong encryption is often implemented by default on these devices due to their highly portable nature and wealth of sensitive private information. This makes it difficult or impossible to conduct forensics if investigators do not have the information needed to unlock the device and decrypt its data. The fact that software designed for these devices often assumes internet connectivity is also a potential issue — smartphone apps may not store data locally, instead accessing data from the cloud. In this case, forensics will require identifying all the sources of data and executing appropriate search techniques like gathering physical device evidence and issuing warrants for cloud-hosted data.

Gathering artifacts from mobile devices will follow many of the same procedures previous discussed. iOS is a variant of the macOS, and Android is a Linux-based system, so the process of gathering artifacts may be similar but utilize special tools. The largely consumer-focused nature of these devices may also prove a boon to investigators, as poorly coded apps or those with limited functionality may prevent users from thoroughly removing data. The always-on connectivity in these devices usually includes cellular, WiFi, Bluetooth, and near-field communication (NFC) standards, so network forensics will be similar to other devices, just with more network interfaces and tools for the specific protocols.

One unique situation posed by mobile devices' constant connectivity is the ability for data to be lost or destroyed. Services like Apple's Find My and Google's Find My Device allow a lost or stolen phone to be remotely locked or wiped, which destroys vital evidence. Mobile device management (MDM) can be useful if the organization can prevent these actions from being carried out on a device that might contain evidence. In these cases, special handling is required for the physical devices, including placing them inside a Faraday bag and analyzing them in a properly shielded room, to prevent cellular, WiFi, etc., signals from reaching the devices.

CONDUCT LOGGING AND MONITORING ACTIVITIES

Logging and monitoring can be somewhat confusing because logging involves proactive safeguarding measures as well as reactive countermeasures. Defining a logging strategy is proactive, including what events to capture, where to store the data, and mandatory review or monitoring activities. The occurrence of events and their recording in a log is, obviously, a reactive activity, and performing analysis or review of logs to determine what happened is inherently an after-the-fact activity. Defining a log strategy, choosing effective tools to implement it, and performing active monitoring or reviews based on the data logged are essential elements of security risk management.

Intrusion Detection and Prevention

Intrusion detection systems (IDSs) and intrusion prevention systems (IPSs) are narrowly defined categories of security tools, though in practice, they often have overlapping capabilities. Both are designed to detect signs of intrusion, but IDS stops at the point of detection and generating an alert, while IPS goes a step further to mitigate the intrusion activity. Once an intrusion is detected, IPS can take a variety of actions like implementing a firewall rule to block malicious traffic, restoring files to a pre-compromised state, or even shutting down an application, service, or server to prevent further intrusion.

IDS and IPS can be deployed in either network-based (NIDS and NIPS) or host-based (HIDS and HIPS) variants. Network-based systems are often dedicated appliances that scan all network traffic to look for signs of attack. They should be placed at crucial chokepoints of a network to monitor vital traffic flows, such as the connection between the demilitarized zone (DMZ) and internal networks or between a VPN terminator and an internal network. NIDS and NIPS can be integrated with other security devices such as firewalls and proxies, which are also deployed at the same network points, and IPS especially benefits from this integration because it allows the monitoring and response action to be integrated into a single device; for example, a proxy that can terminate a NIPS-identified malicious connection.

Host-based systems are designed to be deployed on a specific network endpoint like a server or a workstation, typically in the form of a software agent. HIDS and HIPS monitor host-specific network traffic, leverage signals from other tools such as anti-malware to detect attacks, or hash critical system or application files to detect unexpected changes. The emerging field of EDR combines functions like anti-malware, configuration management, and HIDS/HIPS into a single software agent.

✔ False Positives—More Is Not Always Better!

IPS sounds like an obviously better choice than IDS, since it does not rely on the intervention of a human to protect a system. However, an IPS may not be able to determine if unexpected traffic is legitimate or malicious. IDS and IPS can make deviation-based detections, where observed traffic deviates from an expected baseline, or utilize signature-based detection, which scans for known attack patterns in network traffic or host activity.

What is the expected system response, for example, if traffic normally comes from India during normal business hours, but one day traffic suddenly comes from the United States during nonbusiness hours? If your organization is under cyberattack, a swift response is merited! What, though, if one of your sysadmins is traveling to visit family and logging in remotely to work? An IPS may not understand this situation and could disrupt the remote work for no reason—which is a denial of service (DoS).

All IDS and IPS will require some tuning to calibrate them to a specific organization's baseline activity. In addition, most modern systems are a combination of both IDS and IPS; the difference is configuring the proactive prevention options, which should be done only with sufficient tuning to prevent an accidental DoS attack. As with many areas of computer security, there is a NIST special publication devoted to the topic of IDPSs: csrc.nist.gov/publications/detail/sp/800-94/final.

Security Information and Event Management

The volume of log data in even a small IT environment may quickly become over-whelming—a single user workstation can generate hundreds or thousands of log entries per day. SIEM is a composite of several tools and capabilities like log centralization, log data integrity protection, and analysis to generate actionable intelligence from the data stored in logs.

SIEM is a loosely defined term for a broad category of tools that different vendors may implement differently. However, most SIEM tools provide a specific set of services related to centralizing and managing log data, as well as extracting useful information from log entries to identify potential incidents. These include the following:

- **Centralization**: Individual systems generate their own log files, and without pulling them together into a central repository, the task of searching logs would be immense. Performing analysis across such a large environment is prohibitive, so centralizing log files is crucial. SIEM tools can use standard abilities on endpoints, often referred to as forwarding, to send a copy of their log file data to a central location. Endpoints that do not support log forwarding can be equipped with software agents to harvest and forward the logs. Data should be captured from devices including servers, user workstations, network equipment, cloud services, applications, and security tools like firewalls. Centralizing can also enforce a key access control for log data: users with credentials to monitored systems may be able to delete or change logs on those systems, but can be easily denied permission to the SIEM tool.

- **Normalization**: Log files generated by a Windows system will have data that is similar to but not exactly the same as files generated by a Linux system. Examples include numeric user IDs versus usernames, or timestamps in different formats like YYYY-MM-DD versus DD-MM-YY, and these differences can make it difficult to search and correlate traffic across systems. Normalization happens when logs are forwarded to the SIEM—data is converted into a standardized format or standard labels are applied for consistency.

- **Correlation and detection**: Once centralized and normalized, data can be processed to correlate activity across systems and detect potentially suspicious actions. A user may log in to their workstation and interact with company applications around the same time each day, generating log events on a workstation, a directory server, and applications. The same user logging in remotely, at a different time of day, and downloading large volumes of data from applications can easily be detected as an anomaly.
  - *Correlation* refers to discovering relationships between data; in the previous example, the logins from a unique location at a different time deviate from the

norm. This deviation is a correlation of the users' normal or expected behavior and allows for detection of potentially suspicious events, like a user's account being compromised and used to exfiltrate data.

- More advanced SIEM tools offer integrations to perform fine-grained detection. For example, an integration with a travel system could be used to determine if the employee has a documented work trip scheduled, which lowers the probability that the logins during odd hours or from a new location are malicious. Other sources of external information can also be correlated, such as data from external threat intelligence feeds or status information from a CSP to associate application downtime with known cloud service outages. Adding context to data via such external sources is known as *enrichment*.

- **Alerting**: Once data has been centralized, normalized, and analyzed, the SIEM's final value comes in the form of alerts being generated. The speed and continuous monitoring ability of a SIEM tool frees human resources, such as security operations center (SOC) analysts, from the tedious tasks of combing through data. Instead, tickets or other tasks can be generated by the SIEM for analysts to investigate, which is a better use of critical thinking and analysis skills. The tickets or work tracking should capture details of these investigations including assigned analyst, steps taken, and any artifacts that lead to the ticket or were captured during investigation.

Continuous Monitoring

Security control assessments were heavily focused on formal, point-in-time processes like audits or certification and accreditation well into the early 2000s. Popular frameworks like ISO 27001 and the U.S. government's Federal Information Security Management Act (FISMA) were on three-year audit cycles; as a result, many security programs performed monitoring activities only once every three years as the organization prepared for or underwent audit. The rapidly evolving threat landscape drove the need for more frequent assurance, and thus the practice of continuous monitoring was created.

Continuous monitoring, as the name implies, requires a more frequent set of checks to determine if security controls are in place and operating effectively to mitigate risk. The goal is more timely information should a control fail or be rendered ineffective by changing technology or threats, which allows the organization to respond more quickly. Continuous monitoring requires the use of automation and focuses heavily on metrics to provide data about controls and indicate needed changes.

When designing a continuous monitoring strategy, it is important to address several key concerns. This begins with policy and executive support and should enable the organization to document a strategy for designing and operating the continuous monitoring program. Aspects to consider in this strategy include the following:

- **Defined reference point**: Effective monitoring requires a baseline set of measures for ongoing comparison. This may be a compliance framework like PCI-DSS, ISO 27001, or NIST SP 800-53. System baselines may also be useful for the purpose of monitoring information system components like servers and applications and may be organization-specific baselines or public references like the CIS Benchmarks. Many frameworks and baselines will also contain prioritization information to guide the implementation of continuous monitoring. Higher-priority controls are selected first for implementation and targeted with more frequent or intense monitoring. Lower-priority controls may be assessed less frequently.

- **Automation**: Auditing an information system of even moderate complexity is a significant undertaking, and performing even a subset of those activities on a regular basis is no small task. Automated checks are critical and begin with identifying data sources necessary to enable this automation. Log files or system information that can be read and analyzed programmatically is a common starting point, and information in a SIEM tool is also useful to enable near real-time analysis of events to detect unexpected behavior. Tools designed to support automated security monitoring are becoming prevalent, such as EDR and user entity behavior analytics (UEBA) agents, both of which automatically scan a network endpoint for suspicious activity that violates policy or threats that have evaded detection mechanisms.

- **Frequency**: Continuous monitoring should ideally move from static audits to more frequent checking, but that does not mean controls will be assessed all the time. Determining a control evaluation cadence should be driven by the priority of the control as well as the cost of evaluating, both in terms of financial costs associated with the monitoring solution and any operational impacts like reduced system capacity.

- **Appropriate metrics**: There are any number of interesting numbers to monitor in an IT environment, but the metrics defined for a continuous monitoring program should provide actionable intelligence about the effectiveness of the controls. In addition, interpreting metrics must be done carefully. The number of bugs found per year in a given system can be useful to track, but it is to be expected that software will contain bugs, and that number does not provide meaningful insight into the effectiveness of vulnerability management. Tracking the patch deployment window is a more meaningful measure of how effectively the organization is handling risk presented by software flaws. Metrics should support clear decision-making when variances are detected.

- **Defined action plans**: Metrics are useless without context and action plans. A car's dashboard shows important information like fuel level, which a driver (hopefully) understands—a full tank means keep driving, and a tank nearing empty means it's time to stop and refuel. Metrics from the continuous monitoring program should provide similar calls to action, so it is critical to define acceptable ranges and action plans to address variances. If a configuration management tool indicates a patch deployment level below 75 percent two weeks after a patch is available, forced restarts to patch may be an appropriate next step.

- **Balance cost and value**: Monitoring control effectiveness can actually increase the value of the controls—if a risk mitigation becomes ineffective but the organization keeps paying for it, that money is wasted. If the change is detected and remedial action taken, the control continues to deliver value. Balancing the cost of the continuous monitoring program with the value received is less a technical activity than a business activity, but it is important for security practitioners to understand and communicate this value effectively.

Guidance for continuous monitoring systems can be found in NIST SP 800-37, with a special emphasis on implementing the practices within the NIST Risk Management Framework (RMF) and utilizing the SP 800-53 control framework and SP 800-53A assessment methods (`csrc.nist.gov/publications/detail/sp/800-137/final`). Another U.S. government initiative that is freely available is the U.S. Cybersecurity & Infrastructure Agency (CISA) Continuous Diagnostics and Mitigation (CDM) program (`us-cert.cisa.gov/cdm/home`). ISO 27004, "Security techniques – Information security management – Monitoring, measurement, analysis and evaluation," also provides a framework for designing and executing oversight and monitoring of security control effectiveness.

Egress Monitoring

When attackers gain access to a network, it is often with the goal of stealing sensitive information stored or processed on that network. This is known as *exfiltration*, and it relies on sending information using standard ports, protocols, and services like email, FTP, or HTTP. In many cases, this is done without an attempt at hiding the activity, but instead disguising it inside a high-volume data source like HTTP traffic. Because of the amount of web and other traffic using port 80, it may be difficult for organizations to monitor the traffic closely.

An exit point is known as an *egress*; in network terms, these can be web, FTP, or email servers, while in physical form, an egress point could be a door, loading dock, or garbage container where hardware like laptops, removable media, or even hard-copy material can be removed. Egress monitoring, therefore, comprises monitoring and restricting what data and storage devices can leave controlled environments.

Data loss or data leakage prevention (DLP) is one tool for managing electronic data leaving a network, and these tools can recognize information using common patterns or signatures like four groups of four numbers—1111 1111 1111 1111—which is commonly a Visa or Mastercard credit card number. DLP tools can be trained to recognize sensitive information specific to an organization. If your organization uses account numbers or other unique identifiers, the DLP tool can be configured to scan for and identify those in data sets using *regular expressions*, which are structured search parameters such as CUSTIDnnnnaaa. In this example, CUSTID is always present, while the *n* represents a number and *a* represents letters. Any string of data matching this configuration can be recognized by the DLP.

DLP solutions can perform a number of important functions once they have identified data. Discovery is the process of scanning a network to identify data based on pattern matching, signatures, or data labels, and DLP can be used to find unknown stores of sensitive data stored on a network. It can also be used to identify sensitive data moving around a network, like when files are copied from a fileshare to a workstation or attached to an email. Depending on the DLP's configuration, these actions may simply generate an alert, temporarily block the action and ask the user to confirm they intended to send the file, or block the action altogether. The choice of DLP action will depend on the sensitivity of the data in question.

In addition to monitoring data leaving the organization's control, some organizations may implement *ingress* monitoring to identify what data is entering the network. Data that should not be handled or stored may be rejected; for example, an email with a spreadsheet containing credit card information may be rejected by an email server. This prevents the organization from being forced to carry out cleanup and remediation tasks to contain a data breach. Physical ingress and egress monitoring may also be appropriate, such as screening physical media entering or exiting the facility to ensure data is not being transmitted on removable media or the like in contravention of organization policies.

Log Management

Logs are a vital source of information for a number of security operations activities, chiefly continuous monitoring and IR. Multiple frameworks including ISO 27001 and NIST SP 800-53 define key elements to consider when creating a logging strategy. In addition, NIST SP 800-92 provides a set of critical requirements for securely managing log data, as well as processes for standardizing and analyzing the information collected (csrc.nist.gov/publications/detail/sp/800-92/final).

Define Auditable Events and Thresholds

Defining auditable events and thresholds for logging is a proactive security decision. Determining which events are written into log files and which are not is done before activities occur, and there is a careful balance required. Log too much and the data can become overwhelming, both in terms of storage space and review effort required. Log too little and the organization won't be able to effectively reconstruct details of what happened should an incident occur.

Most platforms offer the ability to set auditable event thresholds based on some event information, while custom-built applications should have documented requirements to support logging. For example, standard informational events like a system status check with no issues noted can be ignored, while changes to vital system configuration files should definitely be logged. Threat intelligence and risks facing the organization should be used to define auditable events—if the organization is facing increased phishing attempts, then increased logging of unusual account activity is justified. Other auditable events to consider include the following:

- Successful and unsuccessful access attempts like system logins, file or data access, and application access

- Changes to user permissions, especially escalation like using sudo or other admin privileges

- Changes to or disabling of security tools like DLP

- Copy or export of sensitive files

- Sensitive data transactions performed in applications

Logs must contain sufficient detail to reconstruct the actions that occurred on an information system, including who, what, and when. This entails capturing sufficient details about the subjects (users or processes), objects (files, applications, etc.), and action (read, write, execute, delete, etc.). Data points that should be captured to support these requirements typically include the following:

- User or process IDs

- Timestamps, ideally in a standardized format like UTC or in a standardize time zone used by the whole organization

- Device identifier, hostname, IP address, or similar

- Name of object(s) accessed, like filename or function

- Policy identifier that triggered the log event, such as a failed login, admin privilege use, or file deletion

Protect Log Data

NIST SP 800-92 lays out requirements for securely managing and protecting log data, with particular emphasis on preserving the confidentiality and integrity of the data. It includes references to various compliance frameworks that mandate protection of log data, including Payment Card Industry Data Security Standard (PCI DSS), and highlights the critical role of integrity for log data. Information that is logged could become evidence in a future security incident, so the log collection and protection strategy must be designed to provide a defensible basis for authentic data and an unbroken chain of custody. Data contained in the logs may be highly sensitive due to internal confidential information (in the case of system information like IP addresses), or even possible protected information like Personally Identifiable Information (PII) in application logs.

Logs that need to be relied upon in forensics must have an intact chain of custody, so log files are often written to high integrity storage media like write once, read many (WORM) disks, which physically prevent log data from being changed after being written. Storing log files on segregated systems with different access permissions also supports integrity, and SIEM tools can implement this separation of duties. System administrators can tamper with log files on the systems they administer, but if the logs are forwarded to a SIEM tool where they have no access, tampering becomes much more difficult. As log files are written, copied, or forwarded, integrity checks should be performed by hashing the original and storing the hash for later comparison.

Sensitive information may be captured in logs by design, such as system event information, or incidentally, as is often the case with application logs. An application error may contain unexpected data, such as a user's form input that caused the error. An internal data breach is possible if unauthorized users are able to see that information, so protecting logs often requires restricting access to only authorized security personnel. Once again, SIEM or other tools used by SOC personnel can be provisioned separately from systems where logs are generated, thereby avoiding unauthorized access to the data.

Although integrity and confidentiality are crucial for log data, availability is also of concern. Log data increases over time as more events are recorded, so adequate capacity planning is required. This includes ensuring the storage space is sufficient and may also involve determining the length of time audit logs are held before they are overwritten. For local storage on servers, a short period like two weeks may be implemented to conserve space, while on a SIEM tool, the log data may be retained for months, years, or indefinitely. Log data may be archived using offline, cheaper storage methods, which offer slower access at a reduced cost.

Threat Intelligence

Risk-based security requires a holistic understanding of risk, comprising vulnerabilities that can be exploited by threats. Security practices like patch management focus on identifying and addressing vulnerabilities reactively. Threat intelligence is a proactive activity that allows security practitioners to identify threats and threat actors targeting their organization. For example, threat intelligence may aid in identifying a system compromised by latent malware, which threat actors have access to but have not yet used. In this case, a larger, potentially more serious breach can be prevented by isolating the infected endpoint and removing the malware.

Threat Feeds

Sources of information that can be used for threat intelligence vary based on your organization's industry, region, and level of technical sophistication. Organizations with high technical skills and a large staff of security practitioners may have the skills and resources to do their own threat hunting and generate relevant information. However, there are threat intel vendors that create data feeds of relevant information by performing threat hunting and research and that provide the data in an easily consumable feed. These feeds range from routine emails or other alerts to a data feed accessible via an application programming interface (API), which can be integrated with SIEM and SOAR tools. A SIEM integration may generate alerts, while a SOAR can proactively respond with actions such as deploying patches, instituting new firewall rules, or even isolating affected systems.

In addition to threat intel vendors, there are freely available sources. In many countries, government agencies tasked with cybersecurity roles will send notifications, such as CISA in the United States and the Canadian Centre for Cyber Security. Industry-specific groups known as information sharing and analysis centers (ISACs) also offer threat information to their members. Due to their focus on a particular industry, ISACs can offer more targeted information, and membership typically requires an organization to be either directly in or in some way related to the particular industry. ISACs exist for a variety of industries including retail and hospitality, financial services, municipal governments, and healthcare.

Threat Hunting

Threat hunters, as the name implies, are the human analysts or software agents looking for threat data. This data, when combined with useful information on how to counter the threat, comprise threat intel that can be used to take specific action. Threat hunters can look for threats at a variety of levels in the organization:

- **Strategic** threats to an organization are high-level issues like the need for a chief information security officer (CISO) to guide an organization's security program, or a requirement for better phishing training in an industry that is particularly hard hit by such attacks.

- **Tactical** details generated by threat hunters are commonly known as indicators of compromise (IoCs), which are gathered during forensic analysis of a security incident. These details can be used for detecting the particular threat targeting other systems, much the same way malware signatures are used to update anti-malware tools to spot known virus files.

- **Operational** threat hunting seeks to understand the tools, techniques, and procedures (TTPs) of attackers, which in some cases can be quite technical and in other cases may be as simple as "financial services firms are facing increased denial-of-service attacks from a particular country."

Threat hunting is often done as part of security research outside of any particular organization, and the community of researchers generally share their work and findings in the spirit of making everyone more secure. As a result, threat details are often shared in social forums like blogs, in conference talks, and on Twitter, while relevant information like IoCs is integrated with security tools including SOAR, SIEM, and penetration testing toolkits. Industry-specific feeds of threat intelligence generated by threat hunting activities can be found in respective industry-specific ISACs.

Some work done by threat hunters relies on searching the deep web or dark web, both of which require a specific set of technical knowledge and skill to access. The *deep web* comprises content that is accessible over the internet but not publicly exposed, such as online banking information, private social media feeds, and even content behind paywalls like news sites. The *dark web*, by contrast, exists on nonpublicly accessible networks that require the use of special access methods like the Tor network. The skills and complexity of access are what make threat intel feeds a valuable tool, as the cost to acquire talent with this knowledge is prohibitive for many organizations.

User and Entity Behavior Analytics

Although it has a complicated name, UEBA is a relatively straightforward security function. Entities are nonhuman actors on a network including hardware like routers and servers and software processes, threads, or daemons. Users are human users who log into and interact with information systems. UEBA combines machine learning and statistical analysis models to analyze and define a baseline of normal or expected behavior by users and entities interacting with information systems. Any activity that deviates from this anticipated baseline is flagged as suspicious and can be used as an input to other security tools.

Consider Alice, who logs into her workstation each day around 10 a.m. and typically downloads between 10–100 MB of data each day from the internal finance system. Next Monday, Alice's workstation begins downloading hundreds of gigabytes of data from highly sensitive systems that belong to the legal department and the research and development department, and it sends gigabytes of data to an external IP address. This is obviously a suspicious situation, but one that traditional security tools might miss due to a lack of targeted monitoring focused on Alice and her workstation.

UEBA allows for targeted and individualized security baselines to be developed based on individual users or entities. Alice's previous activity indicates that uploading large amounts of data to external sources is unusual—this could indicate her job function has changed, that her workstation has been infected with malware, or that she has begun selling company information to a competitor. If Bob works in the manufacturing department, he may routinely exchange large design files with manufacturing partners outside the company, so a security tool that blocks all large data transfers will be obviously problematic. UEBA provides more granular enforcement and the ability to adapt to unique user and organization requirements.

The output of UEBA monitoring can be a useful input to other security tools like a SOAR or IPS. An alert of suspicious activity on a server could trigger a network quarantine of the affected machine by placing it on an isolated virtual LAN (VLAN), or a user's access credentials could be temporarily suspended if suspicious activity is detected on their workstation. Alert of suspicious activity can trigger a manual investigation; if the trigger activity was unexpected but legitimate, the blocks can be removed. If the alert is related to malicious activity, the response limits the damage caused.

This targeted approach allows security tools to achieve a better cost-benefit trade-off by providing adaptability for unique circumstances in each organization. Some users need to download large amounts of data to their workstations in one organization, while a different organization doing similar work may implement all virtualized desktops with no local storage. UEBA provides the flexibility to identify a unique organizational baseline and generate alerts for behavior that deviates from that baseline.

PERFORM CONFIGURATION MANAGEMENT

Configuration management is a formal process of identifying key assets whose state—also known as *configuration*—should be controlled, and implementing practices designed to achieve that. It is desirable to keep information systems in a known good or secure state to ensure security controls like security agents, operating system configurations like full disk encryption (FDE), or placing systems in access-controlled networks continue to function. Making changes to these configurations can alter the security posture of the system, so assets under configuration management must go through formal change approval processes to control unwanted configuration changes.

CM requires several foundational elements. *Configuration items* (CIs) are the items under configuration management and can include entire systems, individual endpoints, and source code. The secure configuration of a CI is known as a *baseline*, and any changes from the baseline require the use of a formal change request and approval process known as change management. All systems over time will naturally undergo changes like patching, upgrades, and expansion of capabilities.

> ✔ **The Two Meanings of CM**
>
> CM can be used for both configuration management and change management, which often leads to confusion as the two processes are inextricably linked but subtly different. Configuration management deals with identifying and maintaining the known good state of CIs, while change management deals with the request, approval, and implementation of changes to CIs from one secure baseline to the next.
>
> Changes typically require the review of a change management board (CMB) or similar body, whose duty is to formally register a request for a change, assess the impact of the change, and grant approval if the proposed change does not negatively impact the security of the CI. Security practitioners should be one of the stakeholders in the CMB tasked with reviewing changes for security impact, and other stakeholders like finance and IT will also evaluate the change for cost or technology impacts.

The organization's guidance for implementing configuration management for hardware and software assets, including roles, responsibilities, and resources needed, should be documented in the configuration management plan. The CMB is often the organizational body responsible for implementing and maintaining change management practices, though the processes require participation across the organization. IT personnel responsible for systems maintenance will play a part in maintaining system configuration, while some nonobvious roles in change management include functions like purchasing and physical security and maintain controls like purchase order management and delivery verification controls that can prevent unwanted changes.

Provisioning

Provisioning is synonymous with setting up and deploying a system or application, and the connection to the practice of CM is obvious—if a standard exists for a system's configuration, it makes sense to follow the standard when provisioning. Deploying an information system can be as simple as installing an application on an existing operating system, or it may involve designing the entire system and developing custom application code or components.

Traditional provisioning requirements for CM might include purchasing only approved hardware/software and then installing and configuring it in accordance with defined baselines (which are described in the "Baselining" section). This can require a great deal of manual work, so tools like scripts and preconfigured system installation images exist to speed up and reduce the chances for error in the process. The advent of virtualization made this task simpler, as VMs can be automatically created from images with all necessary configurations applied.

Provisioning, built on the benefits of virtualization, has evolved in the world of cloud computing into extensively automated system and resource deployment. Virtualized cloud services allow provisioning at scale across globally distributed data centers, which relies on definition files for system deployment and configuration. *Infrastructure as code* (IaC) is the use of text-based definition files to specify virtual system parameters, such as amount of memory and processing capacity, and configurations like which system services should be enabled or disabled. Because the definition file is relatively small and easy to read, it is simple to perform thorough reviews and ensure the system configuration conforms to the expected baseline. The automated nature of deploying in an IaC environment also means there is less chance for human error.

✔ Hardening

The process of hardening reduces a system's vulnerability by configuring it into a known, secure state. Like all security activities, it requires a trade-off between functionality and risk—a totally secure system would have no network connectivity at all, but if you need to interact with customers, users, or business partners outside your organization, that system is impossible to use.

Hardening checklists are often used when provisioning as a way to verify the proper boxes are checked and settings are configured. The U.S. Defense Information Systems Agency Security Technical Implementation Guides (DISA STIGs) and the CIS Benchmarks are well-known examples covering secure configuration of applications, systems, and devices. They are freely available to the public and cover a broad range of technologies and platforms including network equipment, operating systems, and applications.

IaC implements hardening within the documented system definition, and all systems built using that definition file will use the same security configuration. CM benefits greatly from IaC as all systems built from the same definition always have the same configuration.

Asset Inventory

At the time of provisioning, entering an asset into the asset inventory is an essential element of a CM process. The organization cannot maintain configuration over assets it doesn't know about, so recording new hardware, software, cloud services, and other information system assets is essential. Due to its foundational role, the asset inventory may be worth implementing with a defense-in-depth strategy of both proactive and reactive inventory controls.

Proactive asset inventory controls include integration with purchase ordering and finance systems for hardware, software, and services purchases. When the organization acquires a new asset, it is entered into the inventory along with details such as manufacturer, hostname, version/model/serial number, etc. Deployment of new hardware/software can also be integrated with inventory update services, and automated deployment makes the process much easier by allowing for automated update of inventory data whenever new services are deployed using IaC. When systems are decommissioned, the inventory can also be proactively updated by removing or marking these assets as decommissioned, using the same manual or automated methods.

Reactive inventory controls primarily consist of discovering assets that were previously unknown and going through the process of adding them to the inventory. Many CM tools, network vulnerability scanners, and cloud management consoles offer the ability to enumerate or discover assets, and this list can be compared against the existing inventory to identify discrepancies. This type of detective control is less secure as previously unknown assets may be unwanted or misconfigured, but with increased automation, a nearly continuous asset detection scan can be an acceptable method of updating the inventory.

Baselining

A *baseline* is a set of agreed attributes for a system — in the context of CM and security, it is the set of configurations that are known to implement the desired security state. A baseline provides a reference point for determining the amount of risk mitigation the organization has achieved, as well as a way to identify if the organization's controls are not operating as intended. Maintaining the baseline's known good state is the ultimate goal of configuration management, while the closely related practice of change management is concerned with moving from one known good state to another in a controlled manner.

Each organization can develop its own security baseline to meet unique needs, though there are standard baselines available that can be used by any organization as written or as a starting point. These include the following:

- **DISA STIGs:** Since they are designed for the U.S. Department of Defense, which has strict security standards, these baselines are unlikely to be broadly useful as many common functionalities must be disabled to comply with a STIG. However, organizations may use these as a high-security starting point and then scope and tailor to enable needed functionality. STIGs exist for a wide variety of platforms.

- **CIS Benchmarks**: CIS publishes free security benchmark documents covering a wide variety of desktop and mobile devices from Apple, Google, Microsoft, and versions of Linux, networking devices including firewalls and routers, as well as cloud and server operating systems from Amazon, Microsoft, Apache, and Oracle just to name a few. These are based on global best practices and are usually less restrictive than DISA STIGs.

- **Vendor-provided guidance**: Large technology vendors including Microsoft, Amazon, and Apple publish security best practices and suggestions for their products, which include hardening and baseline configurations. These include documentation about how to enable specific features that enhance security like turning on encryption for data at rest. They also include documentation about configurations or features that may provide useful functionality but with increased security risk, such as basic username/password authentication support for older applications that do not support multifactor authentication (MFA).

Configuration management and compliance tools often incorporate the benchmarks mentioned earlier as part of automated capabilities for configuration management auditing. Baselines provide a consistent reference point, so these tools perform scans to identify any systems not configured according to the expected baseline, and the freely available nature of STIGs and CIS Benchmarks make them popular choices. A configuration management audit typically involves the comparison of a set of systems against the expected baseline to identify *configuration drift*, or systems that have been modified in such a way that they are no longer configured according to the expected, secure baseline.

Automation

Security misconfigurations are still one of the biggest causes of security incidents, and configuration management auditing is a key method to check for these misconfigurations. Even a moderately complex IT environment can be challenging to audit frequently. Continuous monitoring strategies require more frequent data collection; combined with increased expectations for frequent application and system delivery, supported by the move to DevOps and Agile methodologies, automated solutions for configuration management are required.

A proactive configuration management strategy enabled by DevOps and the use of dynamic cloud services involves the use of *immutable infrastructure*, which is infrastructure that is not designed to be changed. Immutable infrastructure is torn down each time a system is deployed and then rebuilt using IaC definition files. Changes to the infrastructure require this teardown and rebuild process, which is automated and less error-prone and labor-intensive than legacy system-by-system upgrades. Virtualized cloud environments make this process easy, and tools exist specifically for this purpose. These include vendor-agnostic tools and tools from the major CSPs like Amazon Web Services (AWS) CloudFormation and Microsoft Azure Resource Manager.

Automation supports not only the deployment of resources but can also be used to implement continuous audits. Dedicated configuration management tools exist to verify system and application configurations by querying system configuration files like the Windows Registry. This function is also available in other tools like vulnerability scanners and automated compliance checking tools, and file integrity monitoring (FIM) is a technique that uses hashes of key files, such as system and application source code or configuration files, to detect unwanted changes. Standalone FIM tools exist, and this capability is built into many HIDS and EDR solutions as well.

APPLY FOUNDATIONAL SECURITY OPERATIONS CONCEPTS

There are several concepts underpinning good security practices in SecOps, including need-to-know, job rotation, and Service Level Agreements (SLAs). These controls include both foundational elements of security programs and overarching concepts that may be implemented across multiple controls or parts of the organization. For example, restricting access based on least privilege requires a combination of personnel security as well as physical and logical access controls. These concepts should be implemented not just as individual controls, but also strategies used to guide the selection, implementation, and operation of other controls across the organization's people, process, and technology.

Need-to-Know/Least Privilege

Need-to-know and least privilege are often used interchangeably, but there is a subtle difference between them. *Need-to-know* is a concept describing a user's organization-defined requirement to access specific information, such as a project or data contained in a system. Users with a role in the finance department do not have a requirement to access sensitive data in a technical research project if it is not finance-related, and members of the research project likely do not have a need to access the company's general ledger. Need-to-know is often used in designing access control systems where compartmentalization is desired, where even users performing the same job or function but working on different projects across the organization are isolated from accessing data belonging to other projects. Isolating information in this manner is often known as *compartmentalization*.

Least privilege describes access controls designed to give users the absolute least amount of access needed to perform their job function, sometimes also known as *minimum necessary access*. This access should be sufficient to perform assigned job functions and not in excess of that requirement; for example, a data entry specialist likely does not need administrative privileges to achieve their job function.

Both least privilege and need-to-know underpin access management and are foundational to implement the controls discussed in Chapter 5 "Identity and Access Management (IAM)." From the perspective of the entire organization, these concepts may be applied when structuring business operations and architecting information systems, which is why they are SecOps concerns. If users with different need-to-know requirements will use the same system, that system must implement the ability to restrict access on a granular level. If not, multiple instances of the system may be required to properly isolate data; with the advent of virtualization and cloud services, this has become significantly easier.

These concepts can also be applied when looking at individual user access required at different times. For example, system administrators do not need elevated permission at all times to perform their jobs. When making a system configuration change, the elevated administrative privilege is obviously required, but checking email or writing a report can be done with normal user permission. An architecture of separate user and admin accounts, or providing a method of escalating privileges like sudo, implements access controls in line with these principles. An emerging concept in access management is just-in-time access, where users are granted access to privileged credentials when needed, and the privileges are revoked once the task requiring the credentials is complete.

Separation of Duties and Responsibilities

Separating duties or responsibilities can achieve multiple benefits. It can frustrate insider threats by making fraudulent activities much more difficult to pull off, and it also supports integrity of data and processes by requiring multiple parties to participate. This raises the chance of detecting errors and can protect the authenticity of data by preventing a single user from corrupting it.

Separation of duties (SoD) limits the potential for misuse of resources or malicious activities by separating process steps among multiple personnel. Typical examples include expense report submissions, where an employee submits an expense report that must be approved by a finance admin before being paid out, or retail stores where a cashier and manager are both required to count and validate cash at the close of each day. In both cases, the process is made less efficient, but the intention is to make it harder for any one individual to commit fraud, make a mistake, or commit an act alone which carries serious consequences. To do these things, two individuals must either act in collusion or be forced to commit fraud, which is more difficult than one individual acting alone or being coerced.

The cashier and manager close scenario cited is an example of *dual control*, which is a process requiring two or more individuals to perform the same action to achieve an objective. *Two-person integrity* is another related concept, whereby no single person can access an asset like a file or piece of equipment without another authorized individual present. Other systems where this is implemented include encryption key escrow recovery, where multiple users must sign in to the escrow system to recover a key.

> ✔ **Key Signing Ceremonies During a Global Pandemic**
>
> The Internet Corporation for Assigned Names and Numbers (ICANN) performs a critical key signing ceremony four times a year to digitally sign information that secures the Domain Name System (DNS). The ceremony is typically conducted in person, and multiple individuals are required to be physically present along with knowledge and keying material they possess. However, in light of travel restrictions put in place due to the COVID-19 pandemic, gathering these individuals in person was simply impossible for much of 2020, which highlights a key SoD issue: the additional overhead required can be problematic and frustrate critical operations. Due to pandemic travel restrictions, the signing ceremony was altered to allow remote key signing, which balanced the need for information systems security with the life, health, and safety of participants, which always takes priority. ICANN published documentation of their decision: icann.org/news/blog/conducting-a-key-signing-ceremony-in-the-face-of-covid-19.

Privileged Account Management

Privileges, often called permissions, are the abilities a user is granted on a system. Privileged accounts are those with elevated levels of access, oftentimes administrators or superusers; this increased level of access also means the risks associated with these accounts are higher—since an administrator can perform more functions, there is inherently more risk if they make a mistake, act maliciously, or have their credentials stolen.

Managing privileged accounts adds additional requirements to the user management lifecycle. Before privileged users are even provisioned, it is desirable to identify the positions and privileged functions required for the functioning of information systems and organizational processes. These roles, such as database administrators (DBAs) and access control administrators, should be designed with principles like least privilege and SoD in mind, and system architectural choices may be driven by these requirements. For example, DBAs may not require access to the actual data in databases they administer, so an application-level encryption choice is appropriate to allow DBAs access to the database but block access to plaintext data. Furthermore, privileged accounts may be dedicated to administrative functions, and users should be issued other nonadmin credentials for routine tasks like web browsing or checking email.

Privileged accounts typically require additional levels of rigor during the access management lifecycle, such as more frequent reviews. Additional controls at different phases include the following:

- **Provisioning**: Users who request or need privileged access should be subject to additional request and review procedures. This may require more documentation and multiple levels of review or approval prior to granting access. These reviews may utilize other security processes such as personnel screening, with privileged users subject to a more thorough background investigation.

- **Use**: If possible, credentials for elevated access should be time-bound and automatically expire. Just-in-time privileged access management allows users to gain temporary access to privileged credentials for a limited time and by following auditable procedures. Unix and Linux systems can implement this via sudo, which is usable for a set period of time before reauthentication is required. Dedicated privileged access management systems also exist and can be used to implement what is known as a "break the glass" process, where administrative credentials can be accessed for a limited period of time in the event of an emergency. After the time period passes, the credentials are automatically reset. The use of administrative privileges should be logged, and wherever possible, separate accounts for privileged and nonprivileged activities should be used. Where privileged accounts are necessary, additional authentication mechanisms are also appropriate, such as mandatory MFA.

- **Review**: Monitoring strategies should include a focus on privileged account usage, and monitoring tasks like automated or manual log reviews should be performed more frequently for privileged accounts. Reviews should identify either accidental or malicious credential usage. Accidental misuse might be a user forgetting to sign out from a privileged account before performing nonprivileged work, while malicious use might be a privileged account being used remotely from a different country.

- **Deprovisioning**: Compliance frameworks or obligations may require that privileged account activity be retained for a longer period of time, especially if the privileged access is to sensitive data like healthcare or financial information. Archiving logs associated with privileged users or unique deprovisioning actions like suspending accounts rather than deleting them are common practices for privileged accounts, as they support investigation of the elevated actions taken by these users.

Job Rotation

Rotating jobs among employees has two primary benefits. It provides cross-training opportunities, which offer employees the opportunity to enhance skills, and it provides more resilience to the organization. If one person is on vacation or unavailable, others can fill in for those job duties. This availability aspect is one reason a CISSP should consider implementing job rotation within an organization, as it supports business continuity (BC), disaster recovery (DR), and resilience capabilities.

The second function of job rotation is to mitigate insider threats like fraud. A single employee performing the same function repeatedly has the opportunity to commit fraud and cover their tracks, but if the job is done by another employee next month, the possibility of discovery increases. This is used in complement with separation of roles or duties, which forces collusion among multiple employees if fraud is to be committed. When an unknown employee will rotate into a job in the future, collusion becomes more difficult.

A new user taking over a process during job rotation also has the opportunity to spot and correct errors that are not malicious, which supports integrity. Forced vacations or leave, where employees are required to step away from their job, can also be effective at spotting either fraudulent or innocent errors, and provide cross-training opportunities that support availability.

Job rotation can be also used as a long-term strategy to disrupt potentially malicious outsiders from attacking employees. Open-source intelligence (OSINT) is often used to gather information like job function, department, or role, which is useful when crafting spear phishing or other social engineering scenarios. If employees do not stay in the same role for extended periods, this intelligence becomes much less valuable.

Service-Level Agreements

Organizations are increasingly acquiring technology in the form of services provided by outside parties. CSPs and managed security services providers (MSSPs) are two common examples. Due to the costs associated with building cloud IT infrastructure or security functions like a SOC, it might make sense for a business to instead pay a specialized provider for these services. In this case, the organization becomes an acquirer of services, and the CSP or MSSP is a provider.

Managing service providers can be a challenge since the provider is outside the direct control of the acquirer. If an organization wants IT systems that provide high availability and 99.9 percent uptime, they can specify those as requirements for internal system developers and operations personnel to meet. When a provider is used, those same requirements become service-level requirements (SLRs), which must be documented and agreed upon between the parties. SLRs should be recurring or continual needs that must be met, rather than infrequent events like meeting a disaster recovery time objective. A mutual agreement of SLRs is an SLA, which codifies the shared understanding of SLRs.

SLA objectives should be discrete and measurable, such as an application uptime of 99 percent over the course of a year. This can be measured by calculating $365 \times 0.99 = 361.35$. To meet the SLA, the application must be reachable and perform the desired function for at least 361 days out of the year. Put another way, the application should not be down for more than four days. These agreed-upon metrics must be documented and carefully reviewed to ensure mutual agreement. If the service provider excludes maintenance windows from uptime and the acquirer does not, then the parties may have different calculations of uptime, leading to disagreement about whether the service met requirements.

SLA monitoring is a form of third-party risk management and should be a critical part of continuous monitoring. Different strategies exist for different types of SLAs; for monitoring uptime, there are tools like synthetic transactions, which verify transaction results in the expected outcome, or heartbeat technologies, which check to see if a web page loads. SLA reports can also be calculated for services like response times, where a provider must respond to support tickets within a certain timeframe.

An SLA is a signed and legally binding document between the service provider and acquirer and may include payment discriminators when services do not meet the objectives. If the SLA is not met, then the provider must offer a discount or credit proportional to the duration the service was unavailable or degraded. These terms and conditions may not be the direct responsibility of a security practitioner, but it is important to ensure that alternative controls exist if needed to compensate for a service failure.

APPLY RESOURCE PROTECTION

Almost the entire contents of this book deals with protecting resources, including processes, procedures, and tools to preserve confidentiality, integrity, and availability of an organization's valuable assets. Media is any material that can hold data, so techniques are warranted to ensure the data is adequately protected from unauthorized disclosure, tampering, or destruction.

Many organizations publish their media, information, and records handling policies as a transparency measure, so customers or users are informed of how data they submit will be handled and stored. There are a number of resources that can be used to craft media handling policies including the A.8.3 "Media Handling" requirements in ISO 27001, or the Media Protection (MP) family of controls in NIST Special Publication 800-53. For specific guidance on secure media destruction procedures, NIST SP 800-88 revision 1, "Guidelines for Media Sanitization," is a freely available resource that covers specific methods and tools to securely destroy media and data.

While ISO and NIST documents provide a high-level standard for securing media, many organizations will also be required to follow specific guidance based on the industry regulations. A CISSP should be aware of these requirements and ensure any resource protection policies and procedures account for them. For example, securely shredding removable USB drives is a valid protection against data exposure, but some industry regulations ban the use of such devices altogether. In this case, policies and technical controls must be in place to prevent data from being written to USB drives, rather than focusing on their secure destruction.

Media Management

Media can be anything from paper records to traditional hard disk or solid state drives (HDD or SSD) and increasingly include storage in cloud environments. Data should be classified in accordance with the organization's classification policy, and the identified classification level should be used to select appropriate controls.

Labeling and Marking

All media should be labeled in some way to indicate the classification of the data it contains, and wherever feasible, data should also include an identifier of its classification level. In traditional hard copy, this might be a watermark or document header/footer with the classification level, while digital documents can have watermarks, header/footers, or even metadata like file tags, filenames, or other embedded attributes indicating the classification level.

Marking digital media can be more difficult for a variety of reasons. If an information system contains multiple files or datasets, what is the correct classification level? In that case, the policy should provide an answer—typically the media is classified to the highest level of data it contains. Similarly, if an information system contains multiple storage devices, the policy and media procedures should dictate if each storage device must be individually labelled. The ever-shrinking size of storage devices can make labeling data difficult, as there is not enough room for all vital information, while other technologies like VMs present additional challenges. In the case of the VM, the cluster or data center it is created in may be the method of "marking" it at a certain classification level, and restrictions must be in place to prevent the VM from moving to a cluster of a lower classification level.

Handling

The purpose of a label should be to communicate the classification level of the data, which in turn drives user behavior when it comes to handling the media and data. Users must be trained on classification levels and media handling procedures. For example, if data is on a drive marked "Internal Use Only," then users might be trained to never remove that drive or its data from an organization-controlled facility. Handling procedures also include destruction or disposal requirements, which may be indicated on the label and are discussed in the following section.

Media Protection Techniques

Protecting media involves applying the security controls indicated by the data's classification. Processes and procedures to apply the necessary controls must be documented, users must be trained, and of course, the users must actually implement the required controls.

NOTE Physical protection will be one of the most important concerns for media protection because media is a physical object, which means it is vulnerable to risks that information systems might not be. For example, it is relatively difficult to steal an entire server rack full of equipment in a data center due to the weight and typically strict access controls. A portable hard drive or user laptop is much easier to lose or steal, and modern devices can store large amounts of sensitive data. In situations like this, a CISSP must identify compensating controls like disk encryption, which can protect the confidentiality of data even if the device it resides on is stolen.

Organizations should restrict access to media using principles of least privilege and also provide physical security measures to be implemented by authorized staff. These may include locked bags or cases, security cables, or other physical security means, as well as training on the proper use of such tools. Media should also be subject to inventory and inspection from time to time to ensure it is accounted for and being handled properly.

Transporting Media

Although data-in-transit controls are typically discussed in the context of protecting network communications, data can also be transported on physical media. Controls for securing media in transit include the following:

- **Encrypt** data prior to storage on the media or use self-encrypting media that requires a user to enter credentials to access the data.
- **Hash** data written to the removable media and compare the data's current hash to the original to ensure data was not altered during transit.
- **Physically secure** the media with locked cases, nonobvious labeling, and strict procedures for the courier or other individual transporting the media to maintain awareness of the media's location and safeguard it from damage or theft.

Sanitization and Disposal

Media may be sanitized if the data contained is no longer needed, after which the media may be reused, sold, or disposed of. Various methods of sanitization and disposal exist, and are discussed in Chapter 2, "Asset Security," as part of the data lifecycle.. Choosing a destruction method must take into account several factors, including the speed of destruction and any desired reuse of the media. Obviously, media that is physically destroyed cannot be reused, but the time needed to sanitize media by overwriting may be so excessive that simply buying new media is a more cost-effective action.

In the case of FDE, it is possible to utilize an existing security control for data sanitization or destruction. The confidentiality of data on a disk with FDE can be preserved if the key needed for decryption is destroyed. Sanitizing the disk simply requires secure destruction of the key, which is a process known as *cryptoshredding* or *cryptographic erasure*. For SSDs where overwriting or degaussing is not an option, this may be a viable alternative to physical destruction, and in cloud storage solutions where the organization has no physical control over storage media, it is often the only way of ensuring secure data disposal.

Media destruction can often involve expensive equipment and require the use of an authorized destruction provider. In this case, proper management of the destruction vendor will be a key contract and SLA activity. The organization and provider should agree to specific physical security standards for the destruction task, and contracts should include language requiring insurance against any data breaches as a result of recovery from destroyed media.

NOTE   Due to the shared nature of media destruction equipment, many providers perform the service from mobile units like a van or truck to avoid assuming the risk of transporting another organization's data. The destruction provider's vehicle can be driven up to the customer's premises, and all media is destroyed under the supervision of a customer representative.

CONDUCT INCIDENT MANAGEMENT

There is a subtle but important difference between *events* and *incidents*; both are important for continuous monitoring and the practice of incident management.

- *Events* are any observable item like routine user or system actions, such as a user successfully logging into a system or a file being accessed. Many routine events will be logged but do not require additional action.

- *Incidents* are events that are both unplanned and have an adverse impact on the organization. They typically require investigation and remediation by some combination of IT, operations, and security personnel. Examples of incidents include unexpected restart of a system, ransomware preventing users from accessing a system, or a planned system outage that goes beyond the allotted time.

All incidents should be investigated and remediated to restore the organization's normal operations as quickly as possible and to minimize impacts like lost productivity or revenue. Resuming normal service is the primary goal of incident management. While legacy incident management processes focused on manual detection, investigation, and response to incidents, SOAR platforms are designed to reduce the time required to manage incidents. They do so by gathering and analyzing data to detect incidents and then automating response actions needed to defend and protect systems.

Not all incidents will require participation by the security team. For example, increased system utilization due to a new product launch is expected and simply requires operations resources to add additional capacity. A coordinated DoS attack by a foreign nation state, however, would require participation by both IT and security personnel to successfully remediate.

Incident Management Plan

Many security frameworks refer to incident handing as *incident response*, while operational frameworks such as ITIL use *incident management*. The goal of both is largely the same—dealing with the incident and restoring the organization to normal operations. The foundation of this IR capability is a documented IR plan, which is a proactive control designed to help the organization respond more effectively when an incident occurs.

The IR plan should document the tools, resources, and processes needed to identify, categorize, and remediate the impact of incidents. The IR plan typically contains the following:

- Definitions of incident types, such as internal operational incidents, security incidents, or emergency situations that require first responders.

- The incident response team (IR team) personnel. The team members and skills needed will depend on the type of incident, but an incident response coordinator should always be appointed to assess the situation and identify the skills and actions needed.

- Roles and responsibilities for the IR team personnel in each incident type. This includes roles internal to the organization, as well as responsibilities of external stakeholders like law enforcement or business partners.

- Resources required, such as operations or security management tools to facilitate detection and response like the SIEM or IDS. Checklists and procedure documentation is useful during an emergency to ensure team members perform the correct functions during a stressful event.

- Incident management processes must be laid out according to the lifecycle phases presented in this section, including processes for personnel to follow when an incident is first detected, under triage, and once a remediation plan is determined. Incidents must be detected to begin the process, and then the IRT will execute appropriate steps to investigate, respond, and remediate.

All incident response frameworks emphasize the importance of planning ahead for incidents by identifying likely scenarios and developing appropriate response strategies for each before they occur. Incidents can be a high-stress situation, and *ad hoc* responses are less preferable than preplanned, rehearsed responses. A variety of standards exist to support organizations developing an incident response capability, as highlighted by the following list:

- ITIL framework incident management processes

- NIST Special Publication 800-61, "Computer Security Incident Handling Guide"

- ISO 27035, "Security incident management"

- European Network and Information Security Agency (ENISA), "CSIRT Setting Up Guide"

- ISACA, "Incident Management and Response"

Another important aspect of the organization's incident management capability is the proper categorization and prioritization of incidents based on their impact and criticality. This is similar to risk assessments where risks are analyzed according to their potential impact and likelihood. Incidents have already occurred, so they are often measured by:

- **Criticality/impact**: The effect the incident has on operations

- **Urgency**: The timeframe in which the incident must be resolved to avoid unacceptable impacts

Many organizations utilize a priority score from zero to five (P0–P5) to categorize incidents. P0 is the most critical, and P5 is the least critical, and members of the IRT use this score to prioritize the work they must perform. In many organizations, an incident at or above a certain priority rating may also be a trigger for other organizational capabilities, such as invoking BC or DR plans.

Incident Response Testing and Exercise

IR planning is a proactive control, so the IR plan must be documented before an incident occurs. Conducting tests and exercises of the IR plan serves two vital functions.

First, testing the plan in a nonemergency situation can help to identify gaps, oversights, or issues that could prevent the successful execution of the plan during a real incident. Second, the exercise can be used to train members of the IR team on their duties, which reduces confusion or wasted effort during a real incident because team members are able to respond from memory.

IR testing can be conducted to exercise a particular scenario, with the goal of identifying how effective the plan is in dealing with that type of incident. For example, widespread outbreak of ransomware could be used as a scenario to gauge how effectively backup procedures or systems are at taking over operations. IR exercises can be integrated with the testing or exercise of other plans like BC and DR, as security incidents often create situations that necessitate the activation of these other processes.

Third-Party Considerations

Most organizations will have some dependencies on external entities including suppliers or vendors, especially for services like utilities and cloud computing. Activities like IR and business continuity and disaster recovery (BCDR) may need to include these vendors to ensure proper coordination with external service providers to allow the organization to continue functioning. The IR plan should identify any key external service providers or third parties like digital forensics and incident response (DFIR) providers, cyber insurance carriers, legal or communications experts, and data breach specialists who might need to be involved with an incident response. The IR plan should also contain contact information for these third parties to ensure the organization can engage any services needed during an incident.

Third parties whose services need to be utilized in emergencies should be included in the IR plan. Each provider's contact information should be documented for easy reference, as well as the circumstances that require the provider to be involved. Roles and responsibilities of the third party should also be documented, so it is clear to the team which tasks must be performed internally and which tasks will be handled by the third party.

Detection

An incident must be detected before the organization can take appropriate response measures. The tools and processes that are monitoring operations and risks detect the incident and then generate alerts or signals to security analysts. Automated platforms like SIEM tools, security tools like anti-malware, and even humans can be the detectives who notice something and report it, whether by generating an automated alert or by raising an incident report.

The organization's logging and monitoring strategy should be centered on identifying and alerting on potential incidents as quickly as possible. When an incident is detected, documentation should be automatically created to begin tracking work and decisions related to the incident—tools like SIEM tools will create a work ticket where the subsequent steps can be recorded. The process may initially generate false positive results, but with a process of continuous improvement and tuning of the detection capabilities, automated tools and alerts should become more accurate over time.

The detection of an incident can automatically trigger the incident response process by generating an incident report and initiating resources like a service ticket or checklist to begin investigation. Alternatively, the detection may go through a review process during which an analyst reviews the incident and conducts some basic research to determine if the incident is legitimate or a false positive. If the analyst deems the incident valid, response procedures are initiated.

Response

Triage is an early-stage response process for confirmed incidents and is designed to identify the criticality and categorization of the incident type. For technical incidents, a SOAR tool automates some or all of the response. If the incident is completely contained by the SOAR, no additional triage is needed. If the incident cannot be fully contained by the SOAR, identifying impacts of the incident such as data breached and users or systems impacted is essential.

These factors guide the creation of an IR team with appropriate resources to handle the specific incident at hand. For example, a ransomware incident affecting Windows-based systems is unlikely to require Linux administrator skills, while a data breach on a Linux system will definitely require Linux administrators as well as breach response personnel such as legal counsel.

The most obvious aspect of the IR phase is to begin responding to the incident at hand, which includes both gathering evidence and making decisions about how to restore normal operations. The IR plan should contain scenario-based guidance for likely incidents to guide the team's actions, such as responding to a widespread malware outbreak or breach of sensitive data. Following documented procedures and utilizing checklists is essential to ensure a coordinated response, though it is unlikely all possible circumstances will be accounted for in the IR plan. In uncertain circumstances, the IR coordinator or IR team lead must make executive decisions with the information available and coordinate the team's response accordingly.

The IR team must begin to collect and preserve evidence as soon as the incident is declared. As mentioned earlier about evidence collection and handling, it is not always possible to determine at the outset whether an incident will require law enforcement or the presentation of evidence in a court of law. Evidence gathered must preserve the chain of custody if the incident necessitates these actions, so the IR team's activities should follow strict standards to ensure any information gathered can be used later.

During response, the initial elements of reporting will also be performed. The primary goal of reporting is to accurately document what happens before, during, and after the incident, so the IR team should be generating documentation including the following:

- A summary of the incident detection
- Detailed steps taken to investigate and respond to the incident, including the team member name, time, and purpose of any activities conducted by the IR team
- Any information system events, IoC, and evidence related to the incident collected during investigation
- Origins of the attack and any evidence of the TTPs gathered during the investigation if applicable
- Evidence of interviews or other information gathering activities

The process of investigating and responding to an incident generates a large volume of data, and without structure, the data can be difficult or impossible to use. The communications and security company Verizon has produced a framework for categorizing, capturing, and managing data related to incident response called the VERIS framework. This provides a structured way of capturing and managing IR data, which is useful for directing activities of the IR team. Details of the project can be found here: `veriscommunity.net`.

Mitigation

Mitigation is the phase where the organization begins to implement actions necessary to fix the incident. This requires an understanding of the incident cause, as well as both people and technology resources to address it. Mitigation focuses on containing the incident quickly and stopping the impact from spreading, and may involve short-term fixes to address immediate problems but long-term fixes for root causes.

Isolating or containing an incident often involves isolating, quarantining, or otherwise disabling problematic systems or components like user accounts, servers, or workstations. These steps will be highly dependent on the type of incident—for example, a malware infection may involve logical isolation of affected servers or physically disconnecting network connections to prevent the malware from spreading, while a widespread phishing attack might necessitate a reset of all user passwords in the organization and disabling email to prevent additional users from being affected. Given the wide variety of potential incident circumstances, mitigation should follow playbooks, checklists, or other prepared reaction guides that reduce the amount of decision-making required—people in a crisis situation do not always make the best decisions, so planning ahead is crucial.

During mitigation, details of the response effort will need to be reported, as the actions taken can be used to estimate the impact of the incident and drive continued decision-making. For example, if a system infected by malware can be easily isolated and restored from a backup, the impact to the organization is minimal. However, if the same malware infection has spread widely among the network, isolation and recovery may not be an effective mitigation. Reporting these results will help executive decision-making about activating other plans like BCDR. The potential for rapidly evolving intelligence about the incident may necessitate the use of routine check in meetings, such as an hourly status briefing to ensure all stakeholders are apprised of the situation and can act accordingly.

Reporting

Although reporting is a single IR phase, the reality is that reporting is done continuously throughout the IR process. Various stakeholders will require information updates throughout the process, both for situational awareness and to provide resources needed for the IR team to carry out its duties. However, there will be formal reporting required at various points and to various stakeholders, and a single IR coordinator should be appointed to handle formal communications to stakeholders like executive management or the public.

Internal Reporting

Incident reports will be required by different internal stakeholders for a variety of purposes. Members of the IR team will require status reports to keep team activities aligned to the goal of restoring normal operations, and they will need details like systems or data impacted, investigation steps performed, and any findings. These reports may be informal and be generated as part of the investigation process, such as completion of checklists or logging of incident investigation and mitigation activities by IR team members.

More formal reporting to management and decision-makers will also be required. Depending on the incident and steps needed, the reporting may be informal, such as a metric on a dashboard showing the number of successfully resolved incidents, or a highly formal report for particularly serious incidents. In the latter case, this report may be presented to senior executives to drive strategic decision-making needed for long-term responses, like making a shift from on-premises to cloud hosting for vital services to decrease downtime. Formal reports or notifications to key decision-makers are also usually required to activate other organizational plans like BCDR.

External Reporting

Members of the IR team may need to prepare reports for external stakeholders in some circumstances. The contents of the report, format of the data, and timelines required for reporting will vary based on the external stakeholder's requirement, so the IR team will often need to coordinate with a communications or legal expert to ensure compliance. Note that none of this section deals with reporting a data breach incident, which is detailed in a later section. Non-breach-related external reporting may be required in a variety of circumstances, including the following:

- **Government organizations** (including private-sector entities like government contractors and critical infrastructure providers) may be required to report certain cybersecurity incidents like intrusions or data breaches to governmental agencies like a Computer Emergency Readiness Team (CERT). These bodies typically require specific methods and timeframes for reporting or submitting information.

- **Industry regulators** like the Payment Card Industry (PCI) may require that security incidents be reported if they meet certain thresholds such as number of affected users or number of records breached. In some cases, the industry regulator will have its own IR team and abilities that can be activated to assist with the investigation.

- **Law enforcement** agencies will require reporting and sharing of details in the event an incident is caused by criminal activity.

- **Business partners, vendors, and service providers** may require reporting of any incidents that could affect their business or data they share with the impacted organization. Requirements for these reports will be in contracts and should be accounted for when planning IR team capabilities related to communications. These external stakeholders may also need to be notified in the event that they were the cause of an incident or breach that impacted the investigating organization.

- **Users, customers, and the general public** may need to be informed of a security incident that impacts the usability or availability of services. Organizations that provide services to external parties may need to notify those parties of a potential suspension or degradation of the services during the incident. Note that this excludes data breaches, which are covered next.

Breach Reporting

The definition of a data breach varies subtly across different laws, regulations, and security frameworks, but it is essentially any unauthorized access to data. This definition can include both internal and external users, but different regulations carry different requirements for reporting. As a security practitioner, it is important to know what type of data your organization handles, to understand what regulations or jurisdictions you operate in, and to get proper legal guidance on your organization's requirements for reporting breaches.

In most privacy legislation, there is a requirement to report breaches affecting private information to a regulator within a certain period of time. This time period is typically a certain number of hours after an organization discovers a breach, which allows time for basic incident triage and response to occur—but it is worth noting that the initial report usually must be made before the full IR process is complete. Investigation and triage may be ongoing when the initial breach report is submitted, and it is likely the regulator will require updates as IR progresses. Privacy laws with breach reporting include various state-level laws in the United States, federal and provincial laws in Canada, federal laws in many South American and Asian countries, as well as the EU General Data Protection Regulation (GDPR) and data protection laws for each member nation in the EU.

Many of these laws also require direct notification to any impacted individuals and may require additional post-breach obligations as well. These can include ongoing monitoring for potential identity theft, and the costs of such obligations should be a key consideration in the organization's governance and compliance strategies.

Recovery

The primary goal of recovery is to restore normal operations. Not all incidents will involve a recovery, such as a violation of a security policy that only results in an employee being disciplined. That mitigation step is the end of the IR process, since normal operations were not disrupted; if the employee had utilized a software vulnerability to steal sensitive data, then recovery activities including system patching and breach response would be appropriate.

Recovery may begin as soon as detection occurs and continue until the incident is completely over. Action like changing a password after a user responded to a phishing email can be a recovery step, and the recovery phase ends when the organization returns to normal levels of service operations. If a BCDR event is declared due to the incident, the recovery phase may last until that declaration is also resolved.

Remediation

Remediation is a long-term strategic activity designed to eradicate any root causes identified for the incident. Underlying vulnerabilities identified as the root cause of an incident must be addressed during remediation, such as insufficient monitoring of patch deployment that allowed a software vulnerability to be exploited. If a user clicked a phishing link and entered their credentials, remediation might include more robust user anti-phishing training for all staff, blocking known malicious email senders or the domains used in the phishing attack, and implementing email security tools designed to block phishing.

Damages resulting from incidents are also addressed during remediation. This can include payment of monetary fees/settlements to stakeholders such as regulators, customers, or users impacted by the incident. Long-term organizational steps to address root causes, such as increasing security staff or resources, can also be remediation steps if the organization deems these additional resources necessary given the threats faced.

✔ The Cost of a Breach

In 2017, the credit monitoring firm Equifax suffered a data breach that exposed the personal information of up to 147 million people, primarily in the United States and the United Kingdom. It is difficult to estimate the total cost of the breach due to indirect costs like loss of reputation, but one direct cost is certain: U.S. $31 million, which is how much Equifax was required to set aside for direct payment to affected individuals. That amount of money could have paid for a large number of proactive security controls designed to prevent such a breach!

Lessons Learned

After an incident is remediated, it is important to document any lessons learned during the IR process. This serves two goals: first to identify any IR process improvements to be made, and second to address any underlying or root causes with the goal of preventing the incident from recurring. Metrics from the incident response process should be gathered and analyzed to support this decision-making, and the intent is to highlight both the positive and negative aspects of the incident response to facilitate improvement.

Lesson learned should be gathered in a formal process, documented, and assigned as action items with accountability for completion. These lessons should identify what went well and what could be improved for future incidents, and the process is often called a *postmortem* or *after-action* report. The process should be facilitated by a neutral party who can help participants separate relevant facts from personal feelings related to the incident. Incidents can be stressful and challenging, so the facilitator's role is crucial to ensure facts and metrics are properly documented to support improvement efforts.

OPERATE AND MAINTAIN DETECTIVE AND PREVENTATIVE MEASURES

Security controls can mitigate risks by preventing them from occurring and reducing the likelihood, or they can detect a risk that has occurred to trigger corrective actions designed to reduce the impact. A CISSP should design a security program using the defense-in-depth paradigm where controls are layered to serve both preventative and detective functions. This arrangement provides both proactive and reactive risk mitigation, and the types and number of controls implemented must be balanced against the value of the asset and associated costs to implement.

To be truly effective, security controls like those discussed next, including firewalls, intrusion detection, and next-generation tools incorporating machine learning and artificial intelligence, must not be treated as purely technology solutions. People and process must be considered to make these tools truly valuable and achieve the goal of mitigating risk. Security incidents that could have been stopped sooner or entirely prevented have occurred due to security tools that were improperly tuned or, even worse, ignored. Processes for investigating and responding to alerts and properly configuring platforms like SIEM are more important than having the latest technology, since the technology ultimately must support the human analysts who are tasked with addressing complex risks.

Security practitioners will be involved at multiple phases in the selection, implementation, ongoing management, and monitoring of these controls. For instance, the security team may be a key stakeholder in choosing network security tools like firewalls and should be consulted when gathering requirements. IT or network operations personnel will likely be in charge of installing and maintaining the firewall, but log data generated by the firewall about potential network attacks is a key input to continuous monitoring processes owned by the security team.

Operating and maintaining these tools requires security practitioners to collaborate with other departments or teams in the organization, so effective communication and partnership skills need to be a priority for a CISSP. Ensuring that IT and operations teams understand the requirements for and importance of the security measures they maintain is crucial, and being an effective partner requires offering reciprocal support when those teams encounter problems. Simply telling a network administrator "no" when they request to open a port on the firewall does not support the CISSP's mission of aligning security with the organization's mission, especially if the requested port is required for a legitimate business purpose.

Firewalls

Firewalls access control devices designed to isolate and control the flow of information between different segments of a network. They do this by analyzing traffic and applying rules to determine if the traffic is forwarded (allowed) or dropped (denied). Depending on the type of firewall, they can be used to prevent outside access to resources in a network segment, prevent malicious requests from reaching an application, or even control the flow of information into and out of a specific host.

There are several types of firewalls, and it is important for security practitioners to understand the specific uses cases where each can be deployed most effectively. They include the following:

- **Static packet inspection (stateless)**: These are the original firewall type, designed to inspect network packets and compare them against a ruleset. For example, the firewall might see TCP destination port 23 (Telnet) in a packet header and drop the packet since Telnet is an insecure protocol. Static firewalls operate very quickly but struggle with complex situations like videoconferencing where the ports used are less easily determined, which makes defining rules difficult.

- **Stateful**: These are an evolution of static firewalls and offer the ability for the firewall to understand context regarding communication (known as a state). A stateful firewall might normally block traffic on high-number ports but allow it for a specific endpoint if that endpoint has previously established a connection using port 20/21 (FTP). Since FTP clients often negotiate a custom port for transferring a file, allowing the higher port makes sense in the context of previous traffic. Stateful firewalls have more intelligence and flexibility, but come with higher processing overhead and cost.

- **Web application firewall (WAF) and API gateway**: These are a highly specialized form of network access control devices designed to handle specific types of traffic, unlike a generic firewall that handles all network traffic. WAFs and API gateways analyze traffic destined specifically for a web application or an application's API and can be useful for mitigating complex attacks such as SQL injection. These devices apply a set of rules to HTTP conversations and look for anomalous interactions with the application and can identify attacks that would not be immediately apparent in raw network traffic.

- **Host-based firewalls**: These are installed on a specific endpoint and use a ruleset specific to that endpoint. They can be a useful defense-in-depth measure that offers protection if a network-based firewall fails, but also introduce processing overhead on the endpoint. They can be particularly useful in virtualized environments and enable *microsegmentation*, whereby individual endpoints exist in their own network segment with customized access rules.

- **Next-generation firewalls (NGFW)**: These are more of a marketing term than a unique type of firewall, but NGFWs combine multiple security functions into a single device. This may include a stateful firewall and API gateway, and many include advanced analytics based on artificial intelligence or external threat data. NGFWs combine other network security protections like intrusion detection or VPN services as well. Centralizing these functions can offer lower overhead in configuring network security devices, with the downside of a potential single point of failure.

- **Security groups:** These exist in SDNs and cloud environments and serve many of the same functions as a firewall. A globally load-balanced application may exist in several data centers all over the world, and it would be difficult to place firewalls to control highly dynamic virtualized resources. Security groups (also called network security groups [NSGs]) are an abstraction layer that define protections required, and the virtualized infrastructure is created and deployed according to definition files in a process similar to IaC. This dynamic creation allows for consistent yet flexible deployments and supports microsegmentation.

Firewalls, security groups, and microsegmentation are useful access control devices in a zero-trust network architecture, where no part of the network is implicitly trusted. Individual endpoints and subnetworks that are within the organization's control are still viewed as potentially malicious and therefore require strict access controls. This assumes that an attack might be carried out by a trusted insider or an attacker who has gained an insider's credentials.

Intrusion Detection Systems and Intrusion Prevention Systems

IDS can detect system intrusion attempts, while IPS can both detect and react to system intrusion attempts. An IDS is a passive device that analyzes traffic or activity and generates an alert when activity is detected that matches a known malicious pattern, deviates from normal or expected system operations, or both. For example, a large volume of half-completed TCP handshakes — where a synchronize (SYN) packet is received but never acknowledged — is unusual and is a known signature of a TCP SYN flood attack. A more complex IDS might monitor key system files and system usage patterns and generate an alert when the activity on the system deviates from the established baseline.

An IPS goes one step further. Rather than just generating an alert and requiring a human to take action, the IPS can automatically take preventative action in response. In the TCP SYN flood example, the IPS might implement a new firewall rule to block traffic from the IP addresses creating the half-open connections. While there are obvious benefits such as faster response, which reduces the impact of an intrusion, there is also the potential for an IPS to take unwanted action. In the case of suspicious system behavior, the system in question could be shut down, which renders it useless. If the unexpected behavior is legitimate, the IPS has inadvertently caused a loss of availability.

Both IDS and IPS can be deployed in two ways, and the deployment model as well as location are critical to ensure the devices can see all traffic they require to be effective. Network-based IDS/IPS (NIDS/NIPS) sit on a network and should be placed to observe all traffic, such as at a network's perimeter, for optimum visibility. Similar to firewalls, however, NIDS/NIPS may struggle with a virtualized environment where network traffic between VMs never crosses a switch. Host-based IDS/IPS (HIDS/HIPS) are deployed on a specific host to monitor traffic, which helps overcome traffic visibility issues but introduces additional costs for licenses, processing overhead, and issues of compatibility with endpoints.

Whitelisting/Blacklisting

The terms *whitelisting* and *blacklisting* are being replaced with other terms like *allow list* and *deny list*; regardless of the terminology, these refer to a list of explicitly allowed or explicitly denied entities such as applications, IP addresses, network endpoints, or even network traffic originating from specific countries.

Explicitly allowing or denying entities will have different implementation methods depending on the type of entity. Allowing network traffic from only known, organization-controlled IP addresses to a cloud service is a common tactic for preventing unwanted access by outsiders and forces legitimate users to connect through organization-controlled networks where monitoring is enforced. Blocking all traffic from countries that are known to host criminal activity and that your organization does not interact with can reduce the likelihood of attacks. Both of these could be implemented using network technologies like firewalls or VPNs.

Allow lists or deny lists can also be used within other tools such as operating systems, app stores, and email clients. A list of explicitly approved and denied apps can be created and enforced through app store purchasing policies, configuration management tools, or even internal training material like "For accessing corporate email, only the approved smartphone email app is to be used." Many email security tools offer the ability to filter traffic from known-malicious domains or email servers, which effectively denies potentially malicious messages from ever reaching users' inboxes and is a form of deny listing.

Third-Party-Provided Security Services

One crucial decision a CISSP must make is whether to build security processes and services inside the organization or to acquire these services from external sources. Most organizations have core competencies in a field other than security, and limited resources must be shared across the organization for a variety of security and operational goals. Acquiring security services from a third party offers access to two primary benefits: less expensive security capabilities, and specialized knowledge. These benefits must be balanced against loss of control inherent in using a third party, the potential for the third party to be a target of attack, and the additional overhead of managing the third party.

Pooling and sharing resources is a fundamental business concept and in fact is a main driver for the use of cloud computing services. MSSPs perform common security functions like SOC or DFIR, where building the function, hiring the right staff, and running the service internally is typically a costly endeavor. MSSPs frequently have advanced tools, resources, and knowledge and can share these resources among all customers. Customers of the MSSP gain a more robust security capability at a lower cost, which supports the CISSP's objective to align security with organizational goals.

MSSPs also present drawbacks, so the organization must make an informed decision about the use of these external security services. As with any third party, the management of the resources is more complicated due to the indirect relationship, so strong contract language and SLA management will be required. The MSSP typically has access to sensitive data about the organization, so data security concerns must be addressed—the risk of sharing data like the organization's network architecture must not exceed the benefit of enhanced security capabilities offered by the MSSP.

Finally, it is not uncommon for MSSPs to be a target of attackers looking to compromise multiple organizations via the supply chain. Many security tools, like vulnerability scanners, require privileged access to perform security functions, and MSSPs may be authorized to perform administrative functions on infrastructure they monitor. Compromising an MSSP with 1,000 clients is a good way to gain privileged access to 1,000 organizations, so choosing an MSSP with a robust internal security program is an important consideration.

Security services that are commonly acquired from third parties include the following:

- **SOC**: Both full or partial SOC outsourcing can be useful to deal with the cost and complexity of building and running a 24x7 SOC operation. The organization's own SOC may be supplemented by a third party during nonbusiness hours, or entirely outsourced.

- **DFIR**: As a natural extension of continuous monitoring, investigating incidents and collecting evidence may be included in an MSSP's service offerings. It may also be included as part of another tool like managed detection and response (MDR), which enhances traditional anti-malware software with analysis and remediation services. Digital forensics requires a high degree of specialized knowledge that is not needed every day, and a third-party DFIR firm provides access only when needed.

- **Threat intelligence**: Threat intelligence services provide useful information about threats that could target the organization and are often industry- or technology-specific. These may be integrated into procedures like continuous monitoring and risk assessments, as well as technology like SOAR that can automate responses to known threats.

Sandboxing

Sandboxing may be a somewhat confusing term, as it applies to a broad concept as well as specific technologies. At the most basic level, a sandbox is an isolated environment with a restricted ability to connect to resources outside the sandbox. Examples of the term include a VM with no connectivity to other systems where researchers can execute malware without fear of infecting other systems (sometimes known as detonation). A proof-of-concept software environment can also be a sandbox, where users may experiment without violating data integrity in a live system.

In addition to conceptual sandboxes, there are software-enforced sandboxes, which implement a restrictive set of rules to govern the behavior of an application during execution. One example is Apple's iOS, which sandboxes apps to restrict the data and functions they can access. Some rules are absolute, while others are configurable—apps cannot run persistently in the background, while apps can access data in other apps only with explicit user permission.

MDM can be added as an additional layer of security on smartphones, which extends the concept of sandboxing to containers—not to be confused with the concept of application containerization, which is covered in Chapter 8, "Software Development Security." MDM containers install a specific set of apps on user smartphones to allow access to organization data but restrict data access from anything outside the secure container. These restrictions may be implemented as rules preventing file-level access to data, as well as user restrictions like preventing copy and paste or screenshot functions inside the sandboxed apps.

Honeypots/Honeynets

A honeypot or honeynet can be useful if deployed appropriately, to detect or gather information about unauthorized attempts to gain access to data and information systems. A honeypot appears to outsiders as a valuable resource such as a database or server but, in reality, does not contain valuable data. However, attackers attempting to access them may be distracted or deflected from high-value targets and, by accessing the honeypot, also give up information about themselves like their IP address.

In most jurisdictions, there are significant legal issues concerning the use of honeypots or honeynets, particularly regarding the concept of entrapment. Entrapment describes an agent inducing a person to commit a crime, which gives the perpetrator a legal defense against responsibility for the crime. Honeypots or honeynets should never be set up with an explicit purpose of being attractive targets or be designed to "catch the bad guys," but instead should be passive observation tools. Third-party honeypot services exist and provide a simple way to deploy and monitor honeypot devices. These services handle the legal challenge of dealing with honeypots and avoiding entrapment, and alerts they generate can be integrated into SIEM or SOAR tools.

Anti-malware

Anti-malware was one of the first widespread information or cybersecurity concerns, with antivirus (A/V) software dating back to the rise of the internet and personal computing. A/V was gradually replaced by the term *anti-malware* as the threat evolved from simple computer viruses to include more complex threats like Trojan horses, adware, and hoaxes or scams that combine malicious software with social engineering.

A/M software should be deployed using the defense-in-depth model to ensure traffic and activity can be scanned thoroughly to detect malicious activity. This software can be deployed on critical resources like email servers or file shares, as well as in network monitoring tools designed to look for specific attack patterns in network traffic, such as sudden increased traffic to UDP port 1434 associated with the SQL Slammer worm.

The most recent evolution of A/M is driven by the recognition that any endpoint that is a device connected to a network can be targeted by malware. This includes user workstations, routers, servers, mobile devices like tablets, and even Internet of Things (IoT) devices like home appliances. EDR solutions are the next generation and combine A/M features with other tools like host-based firewalls, file integrity monitoring, and UEBA. Some providers also offer services for responding to alerts or incidents detected by EDR, which is commonly sold as MDR and combines detective capabilities and third-party security service to address endpoint security risks.

Anti-malware, A/V, and EDR utilize a variety of methods to identify and respond to malicious software and activity on computer systems. *Signature-based* tools look for signatures associated with known malware, such as specific files or patterns of activity. More complex detection may rely on statistical analysis of activity patterns, known as *heuristics*, to detect potentially malicious actions. Once detected, the tool can perform actions like quarantining an affected file or system and generating an alert to the user or a centralized dashboard. These alerts can be integrated with tools like SIEM for centralized monitoring and response, or even SOAR for the automation of incident responses.

Machine Learning and Artificial Intelligence Based Tools

Machine learning (ML) and artificial intelligence (AI) are emerging areas of data science. ML is concerned with improving computer algorithms by experience; for example, asking a computer to identify photos of dogs and then having a human verify which photos actually contain dogs and which contain other animals. The algorithm learns and refines future identification; these algorithms can be used across a wide variety of applications, such as filtering out unwanted emails by observing which messages users mark as junk, and are widely implemented in security tools designed to learn and adapt to an organization's unique environment.

AI is a field of computer science that seeks to design computer systems capable of displaying intelligent thought or problem solving, though the term is often used to describe systems that simply mimic human tasks like playing strategy-based board games or operating autonomous vehicles. Both AI and ML require large sets of data to learn, and there are myriad security as well as privacy concerns inherent in providing your organization's data to an outside party for the purpose of training an AI or ML model.

The benefits of AI and ML in security tools include faster detection of and response to incidents, as these tools work 24x7 without needing time to sleep or take vacations. They can also, if configured correctly, remove the element of human error from decision-making—though it is arguable whether it is even possible to configure such systems for highly complex and poorly understood security issues like handling zero-day flaws. Applications like EDR and IDS are common implementation points for AI to enhance speed of detection and decision-making when dealing with novel threats like emerging malware.

Another potential drawback of AI and ML is their black-box nature of decision-making, which can make spotting errors or understanding their output difficult. The situation is similar to a complex math problem being solved without showing work—it's impossible to identify potential errors in the solution or learn how the solution was reached. Due to proprietary ML and AI algorithms, it may not be possible to access underlying data to analyze decisions from these tools, so taking action based on an alert may be difficult. As with any new technology, caution is warranted.

IMPLEMENT AND SUPPORT PATCH AND VULNERABILITY MANAGEMENT

Software that contains more than a few lines of code will likely contain unforeseen bugs, and even simple software runs on top of other complex system components that will contain vulnerabilities. Similar to other operational concerns, a CISSP or security practitioner may not be directly involved in the installation of patches, but security input is needed to design the process and technology systems that ensure timely patch deployment to address software vulnerabilities. Asset inventory and configuration management processes are closely linked to vulnerability and patch management. The asset inventory identifies the systems that must be kept secure, which means monitoring for vulnerabilities and installing available patches, while configuration management requires updates to baselines as new software versions or patch levels are deployed.

Patch Management

A patch is a software update designed to address a particular software vulnerability or issue. Not all patches fix security issues—some are designed to address functional limitations or bugs. Smartphone apps and major computer operating systems now support automated installation of patches, so the term *software update* is also becoming common—this can be somewhat confusing, as software updates are a broad category that may include adding new functionality. However, the automated nature of software updates can be beneficial, and the use of this feature is becoming a best practice as it ensures critical security updates are automatically installed.

Inputs to a patch management process include vendors publicly notifying users of patch availability, like Microsoft's monthly Patch Tuesday and Oracle's quarterly Critical Patch Update. Notice of these patches are typically widely published on the vendor's support website and are also broadcast to users via software tools like Windows Server Update Services (WSUS). Internally developed systems will also require patches to address functional or security issues identified during audits or scans, in which case the organization's release or deployment process should include notice to relevant teams that patches are available.

Patch management is a process with multiple stakeholders, including researchers or testers who find a vulnerability, developers who write a patch, and the support personnel who install the patch. A generic security patch process incorporating all stakeholders must include the following:

- **Vulnerability detection** by a scanning tool, security researcher, user reporting a bug, etc.

- **Publication of patch** by the vendor or development team, once the vulnerability is verified and relevant code is written to address it.

- **Evaluation of patch applicability** by each organization's administrative personnel to determine if the patch is needed in a given environment.

- **Testing** of the patch to ensure it will not introduce unwanted or problematic changes.

- **Application and tracking** of the patch to ensure it does not have a negative impact on functionality and is deployed to all relevant systems. In many organizations there will be an SLA for patch deployment related to the criticality of the vulnerability the patch addresses; for example, critical patches must be deployed within seven days of release.

- **Rollback** if issues are encountered.

- **Documentation** of the system including the patch, which becomes the new baseline used for configuration management.

Patch management, like many operational concerns, may involve a mix of both internal processes and third parties. CSPs or managed service providers (MSPs) may be responsible for some or all of patch management, and SLAs should be in place with appropriate monitoring to ensure the patches are applied in a timely manner.

Software composition analysis (SCA), discussed in more detail in Chapter 8, is another third-party element in vulnerability and patch management. Part of software deployment should be analyzing any third-party dependencies and ensuring the latest versions of those dependencies are always in use. Otherwise, outdated, vulnerable software will be incorporated into information systems, which then become vulnerable.

Vulnerability Management

Vulnerabilities are one-half of risk, so the practice of vulnerability management is a significant part of a security practitioner's responsibilities. A vulnerability management program can be as simple as a yearly vulnerability identification for threats facing a small organization's cloud-based IT infrastructure or as complex as a multinational organization with dedicated threat hunting teams working year-round to identify and test the organization's vulnerabilities. The level of effort and investment should, like all security decisions, be aligned to the organization's needs and may include the following:

- **Threat hunting** is the practice of looking for threats that evade the organization's existing security solutions and may exploit unknown vulnerabilities. It is typically broad in scope and can be performed continuously.

- **Vulnerability scanning** is usually an automated activity designed to detect known vulnerabilities like insecure configurations or unpatched software and is often a key detective control to identify patch management failures. Vulnerability scanners have one significant defect compared to other methods — they are only able to detect known vulnerabilities for which a signature has been created. However, they can be run nearly continuously to identify known vulnerabilities quickly.

- **Red teaming** involves a targeted form of testing for vulnerabilities, usually against a particular asset. Human testers, assisted by automated tools, can find previously unknown vulnerabilities and try to evade the organization's defenses, which are operated by the blue team. The adversarial relationship between the two is part of the testing, with the red team's success defined by acquisition of a target by exploiting vulnerabilities discovered, and the blue team's success defined by defense of the same.

- **Penetration testing and bug bounties** are human-run tests designed to detect vulnerabilities and may be broadly or narrowly scoped. Penetration (pen) testers are paid for the engagement of their services, while bug bounty hunters are paid individual bounties for each verified vulnerability they discover. Unlike a red team exercise, the scope of a pen test or bug bounty is usually broader, and the rules of the engagement may require that the tester only document, but not exploit, any vulnerabilities they find.

Many processes and workflows in vulnerability management are well-suited to automation using SOAR tools, such as vulnerability scanning and corresponding patch deployment to fix identified vulnerabilities.

UNDERSTAND AND PARTICIPATE IN CHANGE MANAGEMENT PROCESSES

Change management is concerned with keeping the organization operating effectively and moving from one secure state to another. It is closely related to configuration management, but configuration management is concerned with maintaining the organization's systems in a known good state, while change management deals with reviewing, approving, and managing the implementation of changes to move from one known good state to another. Security practitioners are stakeholders in both disciplines and should have input to process and procedure requirements.

Changes can range from minor modifications to existing applications or systems to adding/retiring entire information systems. To do this without negatively impacting security, organizations must proactively perform a set of formal activities and processes to request, review, implement, and document all changes. Many organizations utilize a ticketing system to document the steps required in change management. Creating a change request is the first step, and the request should capture important details like the purpose of the change, justification for the change, owner, resources required, and any anticipated impacts.

Once requested, the change goes through review by a change control or change advisory board (CCB or CAB). This review must verify if the proposed change offers business benefits/value appropriate to its associated costs, formally reviews the impacts of the change, and ensures any potential impacts or risks have been documented along with mitigation plans. This review may involve testing, may include additional processes such as decision analysis, and can be iterated if the change board needs additional information from the requestor.

Once a change has been approved, it can be executed by the owner according to the documented plan. Since many changes will result in the acquisition of new hardware, software, or IT services, several security concerns will operate concurrently with the change, including acquisition security management, security testing, and the use of the organization's certification and accreditation process if the change is large enough Although a CISSP may not be directly involved in processes like purchasing and deploying new hardware, coordinating with the relevant teams to ensure processes are followed is critical.

Delay is inherent in the change management process, as is any process that requires seeking approval. This delay is intentional and allows time to gather information needed to evaluate the impact of changes. In some cases, this delay is undesirable, so the organization's change management may be flexible. Organizations may utilize custom categories for changes. The ITIL-defined categories provide a useful reference point and are detailed here:

- **Standard changes**: These changes are low risk and are considered unlikely to have a negative impact, so they are preapproved to reduce operational overhead. Examples include applying standard patches, adding standard assets to address capacity (i.e., deploying a standard server build to provide additional processing capacity), or installing software from an approved list.

- **Normal changes**: These changes require the full change management process of request and review before implementing. They typically follow a schedule based on the routine meeting cadence of the change board.

- **Emergency changes**: In emergency situations like a security incident, the process of responding to the incident should not be hindered by the need to convene a change management meeting and get approval, or perform copious testing to rule out potential negative impacts of an emergency patch. In these scenarios, change management reviews may be performed retroactively—the change is made as needed to deal with the incident or emergency, and all details are documented for later review. Some organizations use a modified change process in these situations, where streamlined decision-making or less-cumbersome processes are utilized to balance security and speed.

IMPLEMENT RECOVERY STRATEGIES

Recovery is mainly associated with the availability security objective and incorporates strategies to ensure adequate capabilities exist to recover the organization's critical data, processes, and systems. Those critical assets are identified by performing a business impact analysis (BIA), which enumerates critical assets and capabilities, and the recovery strategies designed should balance the organization's availability needs with the costs associated.

The BIA establishes a management-approved acceptable level of operation for critical processes or functions and also establishes key parameters used to design recovery strategies. In the event of an incident that disrupts normal operations, the recovery capability is charged with restoring this minimum acceptable level of service. Recovery is measured by a number of key metrics, such as the following:

- **Recovery time objective (RTO)**: The amount of time after an incident or disaster that passes before the system or process is recovered using contingency procedures (not full restoration to normal).

- **Recovery point objective (RPO)**: The amount of data loss tolerable when a disaster occurs, usually expressed as a number of transactions or data points. RPO can also be expressed using time, like an RPO of no more than one day of data.

- **Maximum tolerable or allowable downtime (MTD or MAD)**: The amount of time the organization can survive without an asset or process, after which the organization may no longer be viable. RTO should always be less than the MTD; otherwise, recovery is a moot point as the organization will cease to function before it occurs.

All recovery metrics should be driven by business decisions of criticality and cost. At first, all systems and processes will be deemed critical and given very tight RTOs; once business leaders see the cost of high availability or redundant systems, these designations are likely to change. As with all operations tasks, this process involves multiple skills and teams, including business analysts, technology administrators, and the security team.

Backup Storage Strategies

Data backups are crucial to prevent loss of data that can occur for a variety of reasons including user error, equipment failure, malware corruption, ransomware attacks, or natural disasters. Designing the backup strategy will require understanding requirements like the RPO and RTO, as different technology and schedule choices will need to be made. For example, an RPO of 24 hours of data lost will not be met if backups are performed only once a week—in this scenario, it is possible to lose up to six days of data.

There are a variety of backup methods, each with different costs and benefits. *Full backups* take the longest to run and use the most space since they back up all data. *Differential backups* capture all data changed since the last full backup, meaning they run faster and require less storage. *Incremental backups* capture all data that has changed since the last full or incremental backup, meaning they capture the smallest amount of data and run the fastest. When restoring, incremental backups will typically take the longest to restore from, as they require the last full backup and all incremental backups made since, while differential backups require only the last full and differential backup. Versions, snapshots, and archives can also be used as backups of critical data, so long as these alternate copies are able to withstand loss, corruption, or failure of the main information system store.

Designing a backup schedule requires balancing the cost and speed desired for both backup and recovery. The length of retention required will determine the amount of storage capacity, and more storage will obviously cost more money. The process of a full backup also requires more processing capacity and system time, which can be an overhead cost to normal system operations. A system with a very high RTO or RPO is unlikely to require weekly full and twice-daily incremental backups, so the costs associated with that backup are not justified.

> ### ✔ The 3-2-1 Backup Strategy
>
> A common rule for a robust backup strategy is the 3-2-1 rule. This states that at least three copies of data should be kept: two stored locally or onsite, including the main copy of the data, and one copy stored offsite. In this way, simple data issues or hardware failures can be easily solved with the local backup, and more drastic issues like the destruction of a facility can be addressed by restoring from the offsite backup.

Integrity and Confidentiality of Backups

Although backups are strongly associated with the availability principle, the integrity of the data backed up is also of crucial concern. Some dedicated backup systems offer the capability to perform integrity checks of data after it is written to backup media like hard disks or tape drives. Even with systematic integrity checks, performing test restorations to verify the data is also a best practice to both double-check the integrity and ensure the correct data has been backed up.

Since backups contain all the data from a live production environment, it is important to treat backup media with at least the same level of security controls. In many cases, alternative or additional controls will be required; for instance, if backup media is sent to an off-site storage facility. Access requirements for data on backup media may also differ, so unique access controls like more robust encryption of the data at rest could be utilized to counteract the threat of the media being intercepted in transit to an offsite storage facility. Live systems rotate encryptions keys used for safeguarding live data at rest, but the old keys must be preserved, so data on backup drives encrypted with that key can still be read. Backup media and the data it contains should be tracked in the asset inventory, with full consideration during risk assessment and mitigation.

RAID

RAID can stand for either redundant array of inexpensive disks or individual disks. The concept behind RAID is pooling multiple disks, which may be cheaper than a single disk of equivalent size, to provide benefits of increased space, increased read/write speeds, data fault tolerance, or some combination of all three.

A RAID controller is used as an interface to the disks, which are presented as a logical storage point. The controller handles data operations like splitting up and recombining files when requested. Pooling multiple disks creates a single larger disk for users to access, while *striping* breaks incoming data into smaller pieces that are written across multiple drives to increase read/write speed. *Mirroring* makes copies of data and writes them across multiple drives, while *parity calculations* use a mathematical model to allow striped data to be reconstructed even if some stripes are lost. Both mirroring and parity increase tolerance against physical drive failures.

Common RAID configurations are identified by numbers—some are not commonly used or even viable, but the most common include the following:

- **RAID 0** is a striped disk array with no fault tolerance; the primary benefit is increased read/write performance.
- **RAID 1** is a mirrored array that provides fault tolerance, but no read/write performance benefit.
- **RAID 5** is striping with a parity array, which increases read/write performance and provides fault tolerance.
- **RAID 0+1 and 1+0** are nested RAIDs that implement both functions of RAID 0 and 1 in different orders. 0+1 is a striped array of mirrors, while 1+0 is a mirrored array of stripes. Both combine fault tolerance with increased performance.

Cloud

Cloud computing has changed backup strategies just as it has all aspects of computing. Cloud services like software as a service (SaaS) are often configured for high availability, automatic data replication, and *data durability*, which is the proactive management of data to preserve integrity and availability. In this case, the backup strategy may be simply using the cloud computing service. For a high-criticality application, a noncloud backup or alternative might be justified.

The cloud can also be used solely for backup purposes, due to its availability and relatively low costs compared to older solutions like offsite tape backup storage. In this case, storage solutions like infrastructure as a service (IaaS) or platform as a service (PaaS) may be appropriate to acquire storage capacity where backup data can be placed. PaaS may be utilized to create an environment similar to the organization's production environment, like a database, that can be easily switched over in the event of a disruption. As with all cloud services, the loss of physical control over data needs to be evaluated against cost savings. Encrypting data before storing it in a cloud environment may be a useful safeguard, if the encryption process does not cause unacceptable delays for restoration.

Recovery Site Strategies

The choice of a recovery site configuration and location should be driven by the cost-benefit analysis of the speed of recovery it can support and its proximity to the primary location. Many frameworks provide specific guidance for selecting the location of a recovery site to ensure it is geographically isolated from any large-scale event that impacts the primary site. However, the further away a recovery site is, the longer it will take key personnel to reach it in the event that operations must be moved. In organizations with very short RTO and MTD windows, dividing staff, resources, and processes permanently between multiple sites is an acceptable, but costly, solution known as a *mirror site*.

Physical recovery sites are categorized using a temperature scale, which indicates their status of usability in the event of a disaster. A *cold site* is an empty facility that must be provisioned with equipment and utilities before being useful, which takes time and does not support a short RTO, but it also does not incur the high costs of duplicate infra-structure before an incident. *Warm sites* have some equipment but also require some buildout, while a *hot site* has the same infrastructure and data as the primary site, which is costly but useful for meeting a short RTO or RPO.

Third-party vendors exist for warm and hot site recovery, helping to share some of the costs associated with building and maintaining these capabilities. Another recovery option is a *mobile site*, which is a data processing facility that can be deployed quickly wherever needed. These are often server racks deployed in a readily mobile structure like a shipping container, which can be loaded onto a truck, train, or boat and easily deliv-ered wherever needed. Many government disaster response agencies use mobile data cen-ters like these to provide mobile computing services after a natural disaster.

Cloud bursting is a relatively new recovery strategy that utilizes cloud services tempo-rarily in the event of a disaster. The use of infrastructure as code and similar technologies like containerization make it technologically feasible to deploy new virtual infrastruc-ture in the cloud quickly, though systems that require data may still require time to per-form data restoration in the cloud. Cloud bursting can be the temporary use of a cloud environment if an organization's own on-premises environment is not available and can also be used for adding temporary capacity if the on-premises systems come under increased demand.

Multiple Processing Sites

Organizations may be able to safeguard against impacts of a disaster by proactively designing processes or functions that span multiple processing sites, which should be geographically distributed to prevent multiple sites being impacted by the same disaster. For example, a data processor with incoming mail could have mail routed based on its origin postcode to facilities in eastern and western regions of the country. Both facilities perform the same processes, and in the event of a disaster in the west region, the mail is rerouted to the east region, and additional personnel are added to handle the data processing.

The obvious benefit to multiple processing sites is the redundancy built in. The same redundancy has the drawback of higher costs for rent, personnel, and equipment. For organizations processing data, there will also be technical challenges of replicating and synchronizing data among multiple processing sites, for which solutions like disk or database mirroring may be useful. Many cloud services are inherently designed to support this use case, and instantly replicated data storage is a standard feature in many cloud databases and SaaS tools. This can address risks related to data syncing and replication between sites, but as with any migration to a cloud or outsourced service provider, there are increased risks related to losing control over data.

System Resilience, High Availability, Quality of Service, and Fault Tolerance

Resilience describes the ability of a system or process to resist failure and typically relies on robust design that accounts for failure and builds in corrective actions. Examples include systems that can detect stuck or hung processes and automatically restart them by terminating and retrying the process. CSPs typically design their services with a high degree of resilience to not only meet customer SLA obligations, but also to automate the monitoring and maintenance of the massive infrastructure they control.

Systems can be designed to meet stringent levels of availability, and the requirements should be documented as part of the system development. High availability (HA) configurations are one option—through the use of technologies like load balancers or clusters, a system provides redundancy and dynamic rerouting of requests if one component fails. Quality of service (QoS) is frequently implemented for networking technologies, to allow for prioritization of highly important traffic in the face of limited bandwidth. This could be mission-critical data that should be prioritized over nonessential data like user web browsing, or it could be data that is time sensitive, like a remote conference stream that must be delivered on time to keep the audio and video synchronized.

Fault tolerance has specific meaning in the context of data center design. As defined by the Uptime Institute tier levels, Tier IV is "the ability to experience any unplanned failure in the site infrastructure without impacting IT." This requires a data center to maintain sufficient redundant components and distribution for utilities like power and network connectivity, which is costly. For applications or systems that can withstand outages, Tiers I, II, and III exist and provide less guaranteed uptime, usually at a lower cost. Tier specifications and resources can be found at the Uptime Institute's site: uptimeinstitute.com/tiers.

Fault-tolerant systems more generally can, as the name implies, tolerate a fault of hardware, software, or data handling and continue to function. A RAID might be able to tolerate the loss of one disk if it has been configured to allow reconstruction of the lost data, or a database system may tolerate faults by backing out and retrying transactions that fail if proper middleware applications support this capability.

IMPLEMENT DISASTER RECOVERY PROCESSES

With a completed BIA, the organization can begin the task of proactively planning what to do when an incident disrupts normal functions, processes, and service delivery. DR is focused on recovering and restoring normal IT, information, and telecommunication service. DR supports overall goals of BC, which is primarily concerned with continuing the business in the event of an incident. Both BC and DR, often referred to jointly as BCDR, require RTOs and RPOs for various systems. Based on these metrics, the organization can choose technology solutions that support these recovery objectives and can design the processes needed to activate or switch over to alternate systems and procedures in response to a disaster. Since recovering cross-functional organization processes requires the participation of a cross-functional team, security practitioners are not only key stakeholders, but will also be required to work in close coordination with other functions.

A disaster or contingency is *declared* when an official determination is made by an authorized individual, who assesses the situation and determines the organization cannot continue to execute normal functions under the circumstances. Declaration can happen before a disaster occurs, such as forecasted extreme weather, as the result of an unforeseen disaster like a major fire, or as an escalation of an incident which is initially handled by IR processes. After the incident is declared, the DR processes are activated to shift operations to alternatives identified in the DR plan.

DR is a subset of BC and is focused on restoring IT services and functions when a disaster occurs. By contrast, BC is focused on the continuity of the organization's business operations, which rely on systems and data that are handled in the DR plan. Once a disaster has been contained or otherwise dealt with, the DR plan is used to identify and execute steps needed to restore operations to either the original site or a chosen new primary site. The combined process areas and associated plan documents are sometimes referred to as BCDR.

Response

Security practitioners are often the personnel tasked with initial response to a disaster situation; often, the most senior security official is one of the limited group of personnel who are authorized to declare a disaster. Declaring involves significant financial costs and suspends normal processes and operations, so it is not a decision made lightly and should not be made by an untrained staff member.

Actions needed in response to a disaster will vary based on the type of disaster. Under stressful conditions, people do not make the best decisions, so it is best to have pre-approved responses and action plans documented in the DR and BC plans as guides. These action plans, combined with training and exercise of the plans, speed responses and help guide decision-making during a disaster. Some tasks to address in the plans include the following:

- **Life, health, and safety** of personnel, which is always the primary concern. Disasters that can physically destroy data or systems, like extreme weather or civil unrest, also place personnel in jeopardy, and the preservation of data and systems is of secondary concern.

- **Coordinated response** actions with direction and oversight of a designated disaster or crisis coordinator are crucial to provide focus.

- **Clear and consistent communications** must be made to various stakeholders including employees, executive management, and possibly members of the public or law enforcement.

- **Document** everything done to support post-disaster reviews, as well as to support any evidence needed for insurance or legal action.

NOTE   Keeping accurate and complete notes is vital. Many disasters will qualify for some type of insurance compensation, and the insurance carrier will require documentation regarding the cause of the disaster, what steps were taken to mitigate it, and what costs were involved. If criminal actions caused the disaster, the same details will be relevant and must be properly documented for law enforcement. A scribe or recorder is an essential role, and the BCDR plans should assign and document the responsibilities of this role.

Personnel

In all situations, the life, health, and safety of human beings is the most important goal of security. During a disaster or contingency operations, there may be novel risks to personnel, possibly from the same disaster that disrupted operations or due to response actions like new personnel performing equipment installation in an unfamiliar environment. A security practitioner must account for these when planning and ensure BC or DR plans include measures to minimize the risks.

In addition to personnel safety considerations, BCDR plans must also document roles and responsibilities for personnel needed to continue the organization's critical processes. These personnel are likely to have specific knowledge or skills related to the organization's processes, systems, and how to run, operate, or maintain them. Named personnel and contact details should be documented in the plan for vital functions, like disaster declaration or crisis communications, to ensure clear assignment of duties. Personnel practices like job rotation and cross-training can support contingency operations, as personnel capable of performing multiple roles can be critical in an emergency.

Major disasters or incidents may require coordination of personnel's family members outside of normal benefits or morale operations. During normal operations, concerns like arranging for housing or childcare are normally left up to members of staff, but in the event of a disaster, the relocation of operations and personnel may be necessary. In such cases, especially if the relocation is for a long period of time, plans should include arrangements for dealing with basic needs like housing and food for not only personnel but family members as well. Transportation to the alternate site should be considered, as disasters with physical implications like weather or civil unrest can render conventional transportation unusable.

✔ Food and Other Needs

Life, health, and safety aren't only concerned with preventing injury or death. Disaster operations can sometimes involve long hours spent in close proximity, which leads to a variety of problems. Tempers may be short, hygiene supplies may be limited, and people do need to eat. Make sure to consider and plan for these needs—some organizations may stock go-bags with vital rations and toiletries that staff will need, and break time diversions like video games or a nap room can be vital for employees under stress. In fact, costs like catering or entertainment associated with disaster operations may even be covered by cyber insurance as part of recovery costs!

Communications

Keeping stakeholders informed of relevant information is vital during an incident. Crisis communications are difficult due to limited or rapidly evolving information and the need to provide timely notifications to a wide variety of internal and external stakeholders. Incomplete or partial information may be complicated by rumors and fear, so a crisis communications plan that accounts for the dynamic environment and provides clear information is essential.

The "one voice" principle is essential to crisis communications and dictates that the organization should have a unified voice when communicating, especially with outside stakeholders like press or the public. Multiple accounts from different personnel, even if given with the best of intentions, can be confusing or possibly dangerous. This principle should be documented and included as part of training—any personnel who receive requests from media or other outsiders must refrain from making a statement and instead refer to the appropriate communications contact.

The different stakeholders in crisis communications will require different information and delivery methods. The purpose of each communication should also be assessed based on the stakeholders involved and requirements such as method and response requirements, which include the following:

- **Internal stakeholders** include employees and management, who need not only information about the incident but also instructions on how to participate in the response. Employees may be directed to an alternate work site or ordered to evacuate, and instructions should include security-relevant information.

  Methods and paths for communicating with internal stakeholders can include active methods like a phone tree, which requires a response from each person called, or passive, like a message posted on a website that employees can access. The method chosen should account for the criticality of the personnel receiving it and the information being conveyed.

- **External stakeholders** can include customers or users, members of the public, and business partners or vendors who are likely to be impacted by the organization's contingency operations. Some service providers may be included in this category, while others like contractor staff may be treated as internal stakeholders. Law enforcement and response providers like DFIR firms are also key external stakeholders who will need information and access to perform their jobs related to the response operations.

  Methods and paths of communication to external stakeholders may be determined by legal or contractual obligations, such as privacy notifications in the event of a breach. Active and passive methods should be used depending on the situation, such as actively mailing or calling customers to notify them or issuing a press releases for general consumption.

Assessment

Assessment of a disaster is similar to risk assessment—the primary goal is to ascertain the impact and prioritize steps needed to address it. This involves identifying the nature and source of the disaster, such as man-made or natural, and determining the priority of recovery actions such as evacuating personnel to an alternate site or powering down equipment gracefully and migrating operations to an alternative facility. This process may be ongoing as incidents are dynamic, and the response team must identify both the current and likely future impacts of an incident or disaster.

The results of a disaster assessment must be conveyed to management and decision-makers for determination of the correct course of action. If a well-written BCDR plan exists, then the response should follow an existing set of procedures or steps, with appropriate tailoring to adjust to the specifics of the particular disaster. These steps will of course need to prioritize life, health, and safety, and should also take into account any impacts to customers, regulatory obligations, and both direct and indirect costs like loss of revenue and reputation.

An assessment will also occur post-recovery to determine the total impact of the disaster or incident. This assessment should include the total financial cost to the organization, including costs to recover and any lost business or productivity, as well as information on how to improve disaster and continuity operations in the future. Documenting and using lessons learned is discussed in more detail in a later section.

Restoration

The organization may operate under disaster or contingency processes for a relatively long time, and restoration activities will begin simultaneously while these processes are in place. Contingency operations are often less than the organization's desired or ideal service level, but support the continuity of core functions and processes. Once this minimum level is reached, the focus of the DR team shifts to restoring the original site or facilities impacted by the disaster. In some cases, original facilities may be totally destroyed and new facilities are required, so the term *primary site* may be used to avoid confusion between the old and new facilities. The goal of *recovery* is a resumption of critical business functions—often at a reduced capacity—while the goal of *restoration* is the return to normal service levels at the primary site.

The shift of services and operations to the restored or new primary site can be just as disruptive as the move to the alternate site and includes the same logistical tasks such as relocating personnel and equipment. However, restoration usually happens under more ideal, nonemergency conditions. The decision to move back to the primary site will be driven by the safety and feasibility of the site itself. For example, if a building is damaged by a natural disaster, it must be repaired and possibly certified for occupancy before it can be used. This requires ongoing assessment by the DR team and reports to management responsible for making the restoration decision.

There are many variables in restoration that are outside the purview of the security team, but security practitioners are still critical stakeholders. The security function may have critical roles assigned in the DR plan and may need to be consulted regarding decisions like safeguarding data during relocation to the primary site.

NOTE The global COVID-19 pandemic forced many organizations to activate BCDR plans. Organizations in the financial sector, where influenza pandemic planning is commonly required by regulators, may have been more prepared than other industries that never considered the scenario of a pandemic in BCDR plans. The extended quarantine periods also forced many organizations into technology migrations that favored remote work, like cloud solutions, so the new primary site was no longer the organization's on-premises servers.

Training and Awareness

BC and DR plans must be written and tested, and key personnel must be trained on the details of the plans and their assigned responsibilities. All personnel should be trained on basic life, health, and safety plans, including how to spot and respond to emergencies like a fire or extreme weather preparedness specific to the region the organization operates in. The purpose of these trainings is twofold: personnel acquire a trained response that speeds up reaction times during an emergency, and the exercise provides an opportunity to identify incorrect weaknesses in the plan.

More advanced training is required for personnel with specific duties identified in the BC and DR plans. These include personnel with declaration powers and key personnel with assigned roles and responsibilities. IT and security have obvious roles to play in restoring IT services and ensuring security controls remain in place during contingency operations. Other functions like HR, finance, and legal teams may play crucial roles depending on the type of disaster. Personnel may need additional benefits like medical or relocation assistance, while costs incurred responding to the disaster may require special approval. If the disaster impacts legal or contractual obligations, legal counsel will be required to identify any requirements that must be met.

Training and awareness opportunities should be provided on a routine basis to ensure the knowledge remains current. Periodic fire or evacuation drills are one method, and routine tests and exercises of BC or DR plans can be useful for cross-training and refreshing knowledge for key personnel.

Lessons Learned

Continuous improvement is a useful model for many organizational processes including BC and DR. At a minimum, a formal review should be conducted after restoration is complete, and as time allows, additional opportunities may be used to identify:

- Actions or processes that went well.
- Actions or process that did not go well.

- Staff and personnel actions that either contributed to or hindered recovery and restoration. Note that this should *not* be designed to place blame or point fingers, but to identify opportunities to improve. As such, a facilitator can be useful to avoid issues like individuals feeling persecuted.

These types of reviews may be called a postmortem, after-action report, retrospective, or lessons learned. The goal is to identify parts of the plan or response that worked well, as well as things that did not go as planned and specific improvement opportunities in the case of future disaster.

Root-cause analysis of the disaster may also be valuable to identify proactive measures that reduce the likelihood or impact of a future incident. For example, a widespread malware outbreak that necessitated disaster recovery to alternate facilities might be used to justify the cost of more robust EDR tools. No matter what information is gathered after the incident, it is vital that it is used to drive improvements to the BCDR planning and processes.

TEST DISASTER RECOVERY PLANS

Designing and documenting a DR plan is one way to mitigate the impact of a disaster, though risks that could lead to a disaster may require other mitigations designed to reduce their likelihood, such as fire suppression systems to contain the damage of a fire and prevent it from destroying an entire facility. Testing the DRP is an essential, proactive risk mitigation and serves two main purposes.

First, testing can identify incorrect assumptions or out-of-date information in the plan that, if not corrected, limits the plan's effectiveness. Second, the process of testing or exercising the plan provides vital training opportunities for staff. A rehearsed response, like a fire drill, creates a trained response capability for staff and increases the effectiveness of actions during a real disaster or emergency, as personnel will execute familiar procedures. Finally, visible BCDR planning, testing, and exercises provide assurance to employees, customers, and other stakeholders that the organization is taking security seriously.

The best approach to testing starts simply, due to the cost and potential disruption inherent in a test and the need to build the testing capability. Staff who are unfamiliar with procedures should be given the opportunity to build knowledge over time, rather than be engaged in a complex test that, if incorrectly handled, can result in a real incident. The types of DR plan testing described next are presented in order from simple to complex; in addition to starting simple, the less burdensome types of tests like a read-through may also be conducted more frequently. Even with a full interruption test once a year, performing a read-through each quarter can be useful to identify changes in the organization that have not been reflected in the plan.

The output of DR plan testing should be lessons learned and plan updates, which the CISSP may be responsible for incorporating into the plan. Once necessary changes are completed, the plan should be distributed to key DR and BC personnel and should be in a format that is resistant to disaster. For example, paper copies of the plan may be distributed, and employees instructed to store them at home, in case a disruption renders information systems or organization facilities unusable.

Read-through/Tabletop

The simplest type of BCDR testing is a read-through of the plan, usually performed with a small group including managers or representatives from all stakeholder groups. This will typically involve any dedicated BCDR personnel in the organization, the security and IT functions, and representatives from other business units.

In a read-through, the key information each BCDR team member is responsible or accountable for is reviewed. This includes verifying information and procedures needed for communications during a disaster, and the goal is to spot missing or outdated details, as well as any assumptions that are incorrect.

A tabletop exercise gathers the key stakeholders, and the plan is placed in front of them—on the tabletop—for role-playing the response. Each participant talks through not only the information presented in the plan, but also talks through the steps they would perform to execute the procedures, information they require in the scenario, and issues they foresee. A moderator can be helpful to capture the details, keep the scenario moving, and document any needs, problems, or plan updates identified.

Read-through and tabletop are the least expensive method of testing, both in terms of time and cost, as well as the potential for disrupting normal operations. Even with a more robust form of testing, like an annual simulation, a read-through is a recommended as a more frequent supplement to identify and correct outdated information.

Walkthrough

A walkthrough extends the tabletop exercise but simulates responding in the actual locations described in the DRP. The response team not only talks through the elements of the plan, but physically walks or moves through the appropriate plan steps, as dictated by an exercise scenario such as a fire rendering a data center unusable. As an example, in this scenario, the network engineering team would not just say "Felicia and Joe drive to the alternate facility," but those personnel actually drive to the facility. Physically walking through response steps builds some familiarity for the key participants and helps uncover details like missing or relocated equipment needed in the response.

The goal of physically exercising the response is twofold. It can challenge assumptions made, such as "staff relocate to the alternate facility within one hour of a disaster declaration." If the facility is too far away to reach in an hour, the RTO will obviously not be met. Second, it offers the opportunity for staff to familiarize themselves with the procedures or facilities, enabling them to respond more quickly in the event of an actual disaster.

Simulation

Most people are familiar with a fire drill or fire alarm test, which is a form of disaster response simulation. In the event of a fire, personnel are expected to evacuate in an orderly manner to a defined gathering point. Some personnel will be assigned special duties to ensure all personnel have cleared the facility, while others may be responsible for ensuring disabled personnel have been assisted with evacuation. This simulation has an obvious effect on operations in terms of lost productivity, but the benefit of preserving life and safety in the event of a fire justifies that cost.

A fire drill is a type of simulation, but other scenarios can be used to simulate response capabilities. For example, the DR team can be called together and given a scenario that requires activating an alternate facility, recalling data from offsite storage, and loading it. This can be done to validate that the system can be restored according to defined RTO and RPO metrics and that the backup data integrity is intact.

Parallel

In a parallel test, the systems impacted by a disaster scenario are tested side by side with their alternates to ensure the alternate systems are capable of handling a realistic operational load. If the organization has a mirrored hot site, then all incoming data and system tasks may be duplicated between both the primary and mirrored sites. This is a form of continuous parallel processing; for organizations with a warm site, a parallel test would require getting the warm site operational and then directing traffic to both facilities to ensure the warm site can successfully handle the volume of processing.

Parallel tests reduce the impact on primary systems while providing relatively full coverage for testing recovery capabilities. They do incur significant costs and may have operational impacts like slightly delaying processing or reducing staff productivity as resources are split between daily operational tasks and the parallel test tasks. Due to the breadth of testing, a parallel exercise can find issues that other testing might miss, such as incorrectly configured alternate sites or incomplete data backups.

Full Interruption

In a full interruption test, the organization's DR capability is tested as if a real disaster had occurred, which involves high costs and the potential for disrupting normal operations if the test is not successful. A full interruption, as the name implies, interrupts normal processing and switches the organization to contingency procedures and alternate sites, with the goal of identifying all possible issues with BCDR plans and procedures.

Full interruption tests may be performed on a subset of systems to minimize the impact or costs involved. For example, a data center may perform a full interruption by cutting off commercial power. Backup systems like uninterruptable power supply (UPS) and generators are being tested to ensure they function as intended during a loss of commercial power. However, the organization's overall response to a natural disaster is not being tested even though such a disaster could lead to a loss of commercial power.

✔ **Monkey Business**

Online streaming company Netflix created the Simian Army, which was a set of automated services or "monkeys." Although many are now retired, these services performed crucial infrastructure testing tasks independently. One service, called Chaos Monkey, was designed to randomly "unplug" virtual resources throughout the infrastructure to ensure the system's resilient architecture was able to handle the loss. This continuous testing verified the system could withstand interruptions that might otherwise lead to a disaster declaration, but aimed to minimize the potential of unintended outages during testing.

PARTICIPATE IN BUSINESS CONTINUITY PLANNING AND EXERCISES

Security practitioners and CISSPs are key stakeholders in planning and executing critical continuity tasks, but they are often not the owners of the BC process. Key tasks include providing input on how security requirements change during contingency operations and implementing or managing the responses needed to meet these new requirements. For instance, electronic access control systems may normally prevent unwanted access to sensitive information, but a natural disaster that causes power loss requires alternate physical controls like padlocks to compensate.

Another critical role security practitioners can play during BC planning and exercise includes guiding the process of identifying changes that need to be reflected in the BC or DR plans. For example, changes to staff, processes, or lessons learned from prior incidents or contingencies may require plan updates. Once updates are completed, the integrity and availability of the plan document must be considered. New copy of the plan should be made available for all relevant stakeholders, including offline copies in case information systems are not accessible. Old copies must also be recovered and destroyed to ensure no outdated or incorrect information is utilized during an actual emergency.

Because security incidents can lead to declaration of a disaster, the security function may be critical in designing the scenarios used to test and exercise BC plans. For example, a ransomware attack would normally be handled by IR procedures, but if it is sufficiently widespread, it may require declaration of a disaster and activation of alternate facilities and procedures. A security practitioner is ideally suited to not only craft this exercise scenario, but also to act as a moderator as they likely have knowledge needed to answer questions during the simulation.

IMPLEMENT AND MANAGE PHYSICAL SECURITY

Physical security is often a function that falls outside the CISSP's responsibilities in information system security, but preventing unwanted physical access to systems and data is a vitally important part of risk mitigation. Even if physical security is not directly part of a security practitioner's background, it is easy to find examples in everyday life, as most of us use or interact with physical security systems in both professional and personal settings.

Implementing or changing physical controls is usually done less frequently than logical controls, since physical facilities typically change less frequently. Renovations offer the chance to build new physical structures required to implement or modify physical security controls, and many physical access control mechanisms rely on information system components that will be upgraded more frequently. Physical security requires management tasks that are shared with staff like facilities maintenance, groundskeepers or landscapers, and security guards, so as with many security disciplines, it requires active collaboration across internal teams and third parties.

It is difficult to safeguard data or system components if an attacker has gained physical access, so it is imperative that the security program utilize appropriate methods of physical access control. This is part of a sound defense-in-depth strategy that should consider multiple points of controlling access. There are effectively multiple perimeters surrounding the organization's key assets and resources, and the boundary between each perimeter offers a point to implement controls, much the way a firewall is used to subdivide segments of a network. Figure 7.1 shows these perimeters.

This extends the concepts of logical access control presented in Chapter 5, "Identity and Access Management," outside of the information system and into the real world. Users must be authorized and authenticated before gaining system access, and physical access controls should similarly restrict unauthorized users from gaining physical access to facilities or system interfaces like workstations.

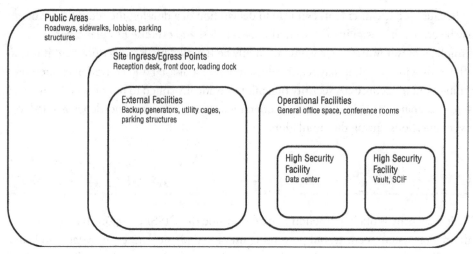

FIGURE 7.1 **Security perimeters**

Physical controls can and should be chosen from multiple control categories like preventive, deterrent, detective, compensating, recovery, directive, and corrective. They should also be implemented with a combination of physical (barriers, fences), technical (badge readers), and administrative controls (policies and procedures). The most effective physical access control program should consider facilities using a layered model, with multiple layers and chokepoints between the outside world and rooms or offices where high-value assets are stored or handled. As with all controls, the selection of physical access controls at each layer should be guided by the cost of the control and the value of the assets protected.

One methodology for designing a comprehensive physical security strategy is *crime prevention through environmental design* (CPTED), which informs the physical and environmental design of a facility based on its risk needs. For example, a facility with restricted or critical areas should be built so that those are isolated from both the public and routine employee traffic—a server room or other important facility should not be placed adjacent to an employee break room that is routinely occupied. Other principles of CPTED include the following:

- Landscape design can be used to provide physical security without designing the facility like a fortress. Water features, shrubs, and trees can all be used to restrict access without building walls or other barriers.

- Lighting plays a major role in deterring unwanted behavior. Well-lit spaces are less attractive to criminals due to the increased likelihood of getting caught.

- Decisions about placement of and materials used for windows should be made with respect to the security needs of the facility. For example, placing a window right next to a door could allow the window to be broken and the door opened from the inside, and windows may require additional reinforcement like metal screens or meshwork for high security applications.

Perimeter Security Controls

Perimeter security controls are designed to implement access restrictions between areas outside the organization's control, like public roadways or the lobby of a shared office building, and secured offices, workspaces, or equipment rooms. No two organizations will have the same facilities setup. Public areas may be outside a secure perimeter like a fence, if the organization maintains its own campus, or there may be public lobby spaces in shared buildings. Since these areas are outside the organization's direct control, there are fewer options available to control risk.

Public Areas

For public approaches to a facility, such as roads or sidewalks, barriers designed to slow, direct, or impede traffic may be deployed and typically require coordination with authorities like landlords or zoning/planning commissions. Shared public areas like parking structures may require coordination with the facility managers to implement controls like badge readers for employee access.

Monitoring public areas is typically easy to achieve, as there are few restrictions on the use of monitoring tools in public areas. Clear line of sight and adequate lighting are necessary, and cameras capable of covering large areas might be needed, such as wide-angle or pan-tilt-zoom (PTZ).

Personnel safety controls like storm shelters may need to be considered in public areas such as a parking structure, and public areas may also be part of workplace violence prevention procedures. In addition to monitoring for the safety of organization assets, cameras observing public areas may also need to be monitored for evidence of other criminal activity. Additionally, the presence of utilities like power, water, and sewer connections in public areas may require monitoring or hardening to prevent tampering, such as locked utility cages or dedicated camera coverage on utility hookups.

Site Ingress and Egress Points

Ingress and egress points are where traffic including personnel, vehicles, and assets enter and exit the facility. These include loading docks, mail facilities, and building entrances like lobbies. These are crucial implementation points for physical access controls, including the following:

- **Reception or guard staff**: These people will implement access controls like ID verification, visitor registration, and inspections of material entering or exiting the facility. This flow of personnel and assets should additionally be logged for traceability of who and what entered or left the facility, when, and why.

- **Physical access controls**: These include turnstiles, gates, doors, and mantraps for personnel, and bollards, delta barriers, and speed bumps for vehicular traffic. Administrative controls may also be used, like procedures for visitor inspection and escort or verification of deliveries against purchase orders for new IT assets entering the facility.

- **Sensors**: These can detect temperature or infrared light, motion, or pressure to identify the presence or movement of people. These will typically be connected to an alarm or monitoring console, and function to detect unwanted activity that triggers a response like a guard investigating or summoning law enforcement. Sensors deployed to detect intrusions are a form of physical IDS.

- **Cameras**: Due to their wide variety of uses, cameras deserve special discussion. The presence of cameras can be a deterrent to malicious activity, and they can be a key detective control if the camera feed is monitored. Guards are often used to monitor camera feeds, but many cameras include AI-powered object detection that can recognize people, vehicles, and even animals.

- **Guards**: These are similar to cameras in the range of control category functions they are able to perform. Human guards can deter, prevent, detect, correct, and assist with recovery from malicious action.

External Facilities

External facilities may be under the organization's direct control, but often require sharing control due to the presence of equipment that does not belong to the organization. For example, backup generators may be securely enclosed with a fence and gates, but third-party personnel must have access to perform maintenance. Similar situations will exist for utilities like commercial electric power, water, sewer, and telecommunications hookups to the facility, where the organization controls access and physical security but third parties are required to have access.

Controls in place for these external facilities will focus primarily on controlling physical access to prevent tampering. Life, health, and safety controls will also need to be considered due to dangerous elements like highly charged electrical equipment and dangerous chemicals like fuel. Safety equipment including gloves, fire suppression, and emergency shutoff tools are a good idea and may be required per local laws.

Landscaping can be part of the organization's physical security plan, as well as a way to add to the aesthetics of a facility. Landscape features like terraced gardens or trees can act as a barrier to human or vehicular traffic, and landscaping maintenance like clearing dead leaves or branches from the perimeter of the facility is a vital fire prevention control. Ensuring that landscaping does not impede monitoring capabilities is also an important concern, such as trimming trees or bushes that block camera views.

Internal Security Controls

The defining feature of internal security controls is the extent of control the organization can exert, because the area in question is under the direct control of the organization. Controls in these areas are designed to specifically safeguard the data and systems in use, but it is important to remember that most facilities will need to be designed with human life and safety in mind.

Operational Facilities

Operational facilities include those typically occupied by people on a regular basis, and they represent the bulk of an organization's physical security controls. Due to the presence of people in the facility life, health, and safety controls such as fire suppression are of paramount importance, and environmental controls like maintaining temperature or humidity are critical for both human life and equipment protection. Depending on the type of work and value or sensitivity of information being used, additional controls might be called for like secure building materials and intrusion detection sensors. Controls to consider in these areas include the following:

- **Fire detection and suppression**: Although primarily designed for human safety, fires can also damage valuable equipment. Fire and smoke detectors and corresponding suppression methods like sprinklers, gas-based suppression, and portable extinguishers can help minimize the impact of a fire.

- **Access controls**: Within a facility, there are likely to be shared or common areas like break and conference rooms, as well as areas where more sensitive work occurs like individual or team offices. Physical access controls should be implemented to segregate areas in the facility based on user authorization, with physical devices like badge readers or locks controlling access.

- **Policies and procedures**: Personnel working in operational facilities should be trained on and expected to follow policies and security procedures like clean desk and clear screen. This includes procedures for evacuation and shelter-in-place, which may be coordinated with groups outside security including HR or facilities management.

- **Lighting and surveillance**: Lighting should be sufficient to support safe human occupancy for facilities where personnel regularly work, and sufficient to enable monitoring by cameras in unoccupied areas. Camera coverage or routine inspection, such as a guard walkaround of the facility, should be implemented to ensure timely detection of issues or potential incidents.

- **Building materials**: Although often outside the scope of a CISSP's background, building materials sufficient to support security requirements are critical. For example, true floor-to-ceiling walls may be required to implement adequate physical access control for high-sensitivity information processing—many office buildings have drop ceilings, and walls between offices do not extend above the drop ceiling. Appropriate materials for doors and windows should also be considered, both for security and human comfort—bunker-like facilities where users do not see sunlight are not conducive to human happiness, but may be required for certain types of work.

Within operational facilities, there are special-purpose rooms such as closets or cages for uses like media storage and vital wiring, telecommunications, or utility hookups. These require additional security controls, typically in the form of increased access control due to the sensitivity of the assets they contain and visitor procedures if third-party maintenance is required. If the room contains potentially dangerous equipment like high-voltage wiring, special protective equipment like gloves or additional fire suppression may also be required.

High-Security Facilities

Within the operational facility, there may be specific areas designated as high-security due to the value or sensitivity of assets they contain. These include evidence storage rooms, secure compartmentalized information facilities (SCIFs), and server rooms or data centers. SCIF is a term most commonly associated with the highly sensitive U.S. government functions like military or national security, though the concepts described cover any highly secured data handling facility.

These high-security facilities require additional types of security controls, some of which may be quite burdensome to users, such as invasive searches of bags entering or leaving the facility, multiple layers of physical access controls with multifactor authentication, or restrictions against personal devices like smartphones. These controls will also drive increased costs such as special construction of walls designed to block electromagnetic fields (EMF), known as a Faraday cage, which are appropriate given the high value or sensitivity of assets store and handled in these areas.

Data centers are a special category of high-security facility with unique security considerations. The design and maintenance of data centers requires a specialized set of skills, and it is common to find security practitioners with specific expertise in this field. These facilities require a high level of security and typically involve much larger security budgets than normal office facilities. They also typically require fewer personnel to access the facility, so implementing physical access controls may be easier.

Design standards exist for environmental controls needed to maintain equipment and ensure availability in a data center, such as the ASHRAE thermal guidelines for data centers (`tc0909.ashraetcs.org/documents/ASHRAE_TC0909_Power_White_Paper_22_June_2016_REVISED.pdf`), and the Uptime Institute's tier ratings for data center equipment availability (`uptimeinstitute.com/tiers`).

ADDRESS PERSONNEL SAFETY AND SECURITY CONCERNS

Human health and safety are always the most important considerations for any security program—choosing security controls should be done with respect to the life, health, and safety of personnel who use the organization's systems and data. A number of personnel activities include requirements for security of both personnel as well as organizational assets like systems and data.

Travel

Personnel may be required to travel for work or may take assets containing organization data like smartphones and tablets with them on non-work-related travel. When traveling for work, personnel may require unique organization-provided services such as additional insurance, medical coverage, and organization-defined emergency procedures. In areas with civil unrest, additional physical or personal security services may be warranted, such as guards or secured transport, and additional services like translators or local guides may also be required.

Personnel who are traveling should have additional security and training on device security practices for devices containing organization data. This includes organization-owned as well as personal devices if a bring-your-own-device (BYOD) program exists. Securing this data might include encryption of all data at rest, provisioning secure network connectivity like a VPN, and additional controls like issuing dedicated devices for use while traveling, which are then wiped and reimaged before being issued to another traveling user. Personnel should also be trained on physical security measures like securing laptops in use outside the office before they depart.

Security Training and Awareness

Effective security requires knowledge and skills that require personnel to be trained, both on fundamental security skills as well as on organization-specific policies and procedures. Although training and awareness are often used together, they are subtly different. Personnel should receive knowledge appropriate to the skills needed to perform their job function, using one or more of the methods described here:

- **Awareness** is informal, broadly targeted, and optional. The goal is to provide or reinforce basic information to a general audience, often through devices like posters, notes on a company intranet site, or email notices. The level of detail is basic, targeted for all users to easily understand, and is designed to influence behavior.

- **Training** is focused on building proficiency in a specific set of skills, and training content will be different based on each user's job function or role. It is designed to convey specific knowledge needed for performing the job function, such as system administrators only using privileged accounts for certain tasks to minimize phishing risks. Training is delivered by an authoritative source and takes many forms including computer-based and instructor-led training. Completion is usually tracked to ensure key personnel have completed required sessions and acquired the necessary knowledge.

- **Education** is the most formal and is focused on explaining theories and their application. It often takes the form of academic classes, continuing education, or certifications like the CISSP. It demonstrates a deep level of knowledge for an individual and is suitable for specific roles in the organization like leading and managing the information security program.

Awareness, training, and education can be delivered in a variety of formats, but regardless of format, the effectiveness should always be measured. This may be difficult for general awareness but is relatively easy for training and education where tests or graded assignments can be used as metrics. The content of awareness, training, and education materials must also be kept current to ensure that staff are prepared to face rapidly evolving security threats.

Emergency Management

Emergency management and crisis management are terms often used to describe aspects of managing personnel security, communications, and organizational processes like

BCDR in the event of an emergency. Security practitioners may not directly own the process of managing the emergency response, but it is crucial to ensure critical security control requirements are understood, planned for, and conveyed in emergency management procedures. These include the following:

- **Coordination with responders**: First responders like medical, fire, or law enforcement can support the organization's response to some emergencies. Some organizations, like airports or large data center campuses, may coordinate emergency exercises or drills with these responders to ensure all relevant stakeholders are trained and able to identify weaknesses or issues with coordination among the different organizations involved.

- **Communications**: During a crisis, normal communications channels like email or company intranets may be unavailable, so emergency communications plans need to account for alternate means of getting critical information to required stakeholders. This includes details of BC or DR plans like alternate work arrangements and critical health and safety notices like shelter-in-place orders.

- **BCDR plan execution**: Emergencies often necessitate the activation of BCDR plans and contingency procedures. Crisis communications must include simple, easy-to-follow instructions designed to eliminate confusion and ambiguity. Security practitioners may not be directly involved in creating or delivering these messages, but as key stakeholders in the process, they must ensure vital security information is communicated effectively.

Duress

Duress describes a condition where a person is forced to do something against their will. Blackmail and being held hostage are extreme examples. Although certain personnel like senior executives are more likely to be targeted, any member of an organization could be placed under duress and forced to act against their own will or the organization's policies at risk of their personal safety.

Security controls to detect duress should focus on preserving the health and safety of the individual—if an attacker knows that their victim has summoned help, they may take actions to harm the individual. Subtle means of indicating duress, such as entering a special code on an electronic lock or using a code word or phrase with a co-worker, can allow for detection of duress without increasing the danger faced by the individual.

Duress code words or phrases should not be immediately recognizable by an outsider. The phrase might sound ordinary, but not something an individual is likely to say in normal conversation with a colleague, like, "By the way, my aunt Sylvia says hi!" It may be appropriate to rotate these codes on a regular basis and include training on the use of duress codes and procedures for particularly vulnerable employees, such as senior executives or employees traveling to high-risk areas.

SUMMARY

Security practitioners have myriad responsibilities when it comes to security operations. Running the SOC is just one function, where data from various tools like SIEM, IDS, and EDR are monitored, and incident response is initiated. Other functions require coordination and collaboration across different organization stakeholders and external parties, such as supporting digital forensic investigations, handling evidence chain-of-custody, or coordinating job rotations and mandatory vacation schedules with the HR department. As with all aspects of security, these SecOps functions must be designed to balance the costs of security controls against the benefits they offer, to ensure the organization's security programs and strategy align with the organization objectives. Physical security as well as the life, health, and safety of personnel must also be considered when designing facilities and security controls, and require close coordination with appropriate teams.

DOMAIN 8

Software Development Security

DISCUSSIONS OF INFORMATION SECURITY must include the security of the software powering those information systems. The scope of securing software extends to the environment in which it is developed, encompassing both technology and processes, fundamental software components such as operating systems, and the applications we use to handle data, whether custom-built, purchased off the shelf, or chosen from open-source repositories. Cloud computing has also introduced new ways of using and consuming software, especially software as a service (SaaS), which shifts many of the responsibilities for securing software from the consumer to a cloud provider.

Software can be both a target and a vector for attacks, and the complexity of the software environment makes it particularly challenging to secure. Computing systems require many types of software delivered by multiple providers, from firmware powering the hardware to an operating system or container software to the actual application code itself. Multiple developers are involved in the creation of these components, and each entity must practice software development security. Users or organizations may be responsible for securely configuring and using the software once it has been deployed, though *mobile code* — code that is delivered dynamically each time an application is run, typically via a web browser — presents unique challenges as the code cannot be verified ahead of time.

This chapter provides a broad overview of how software is developed, beginning with methodologies used to manage the process of software development, as well security controls that can be implemented across various technologies used in the development process phases. Methods for assessing the security of different software types are also discussed, as security practitioners play a key role in risk-based decisions to either allow or deny the use of software in a given environment.

UNDERSTAND AND INTEGRATE SECURITY IN THE SOFTWARE DEVELOPMENT LIFE CYCLE (SDLC)

Software is created in response to the needs of a user group that seeks to achieve a particular information handling goal, such as a desire to efficiently search for data contained in various records rather than reading each record one by one. This creation process, known as *development*, often follows an iterative lifecycle; as user needs change, so too must the software be updated to meet these new requirements. The repeated or iterative quality means the process is often referred to as the *software development life-cycle* (SDLC).

Like all lifecycles, the SDLC is broken down into phases that are logically ordered based on the inputs they require and the outputs they produce. Some of these are obvious; for example, developers must understand what users need in the requirements phase before they progress to the development phase where software is created to meet those needs. Others are less obvious, such as the need to perform design phase activities like interface mockups before beginning development. This gives rise to different methodologies such as Waterfall, which is rigid and mandates completion of all activities in a phase before progressing to the next. Other methodologies are more flexible, such as prototyping; reviews and input on a finished prototype are used to create a new, improved design.

Regardless of the SDLC methodology in use, security activities must be integrated throughout each phase to effectively implement software security. A Certified Information Systems Security Professional (CISSP) may not be directly in charge of the software development organization, but providing clear input and guidance on these requirements to developers is crucial. This means identifying security requirements for the system before development begins and providing adequate resources to support the design, development, and testing of security features or controls implemented to meet those requirements. It is also important to note that the system lifecycle (SLC) covers additional phases of the information system after its development (SDLC) is completed. This includes operations and maintenance as well as decommissioning and disposal, during which key security controls such as vulnerability management and media sanitization must be addressed.

Development Methodologies

An organization's choice of development methodology will be guided by a number of factors such as the time available, tolerance for errors or bugs in the software, and complexity of the project. There may also be multiple methodologies in use at the same organization, as different groups will have different requirements. In general, all methodologies contain similar fundamental phases, though they differ in the actual execution of each phase.

Software Development Lifecycle Phases

The model of SDLC activities as an isolated process is increasingly expanded by more holistic views of an organization's engineering processes, such as those defined by ISO/IEC/IEEE 15288, "Systems and software engineering — System life cycle processes." The National Institute of Standards and Technology Special Publication (NIST SP) that described security in the SDLC, SP 800-64, "Security Considerations in the System Development Life Cycle," has been withdrawn and replaced by SP 800-160, "Systems Security Engineering," which aligns security considerations to the SLC processes identified in ISO 15288.

This is not to say that SDLC models or phases are unimportant; rather, this reflects the need to address security not as a standalone function, but from an organization-wide, holistic perspective. It also provides more flexibility for an organization to implement processes (including security) in a way that best fits the evolving nature of software development. For example, testing and verification of security controls in a platform as a service (PaaS) environment may not be part of an individual system development effort, but part of an organization's larger cloud security efforts. This is a shared control that all development teams can utilize, and the responsibility for performing the testing rests with a cloud architecture team.

There are many SDLC models available with different names for each phase, though they execute roughly the same steps in logical order. These include the following:

- **Initiation:** The business need and case for a system is expressed, requirements are documented, and resources are allocated.

- **Development:** Activities are conducted to design the system and underlying architecture needed to meet requirements; then the system is created by developing custom code, purchasing or integrating external code, or otherwise constructing the system.

- **Deployment and delivery:** The system is placed into the operating environment and made ready for use, which will include testing to ensure the system is fit for purpose and meets requirements.

- **Operations and maintenance:** Most operations and maintenance activities are outside the scope of development work, but the SDLC can be iterated as user needs evolve, so crucial processes like change management may kick off another round of development activities.

- **Disposal:** Activities in this phase are almost entirely the purview of the SLC, but some development may be required to perform activities such as archiving or transitioning data to a replacement system.

Waterfall

The Waterfall methodology is one of the oldest and has fallen out of favor in many organizations due to its inflexibility and difficulty in meeting the complex requirements of modern information systems. The phases of a typical Waterfall development project include requirements, design, implementation, testing, deployment, and maintenance, as displayed in Figure 8.1.

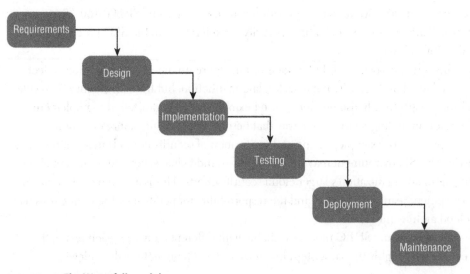

FIGURE 8.1 **The Waterfall model**

Like a waterfall in nature, this methodology follows a sequential series of phases, which require that all tasks be completed before the project progresses to the next phase. The Waterfall methodology is not designed to be iterative, which presents difficulties when requirements change. To progress to the design phase, all requirements must be gathered, documented, and agreed upon; once the project moves on to the design phase, new requirements cannot be incorporated. This rigor can be a security benefit, as the Waterfall method enforces strict control processes such as requirements gathering and testing. If security is properly integrated in the development project, this will result in well-documented and understood security requirements and robust testing of the final system. However, security benefits are inconsequential if the system is not fit for user needs.

The rigidity of the Waterfall model makes it useful for projects where it is possible to know all requirements up front and where no changes will be required once development has started. In the era of mainframe computing with limited capabilities and expensive hardware, it made sense. However, the malleable nature of software and virtualized hardware mean a more adaptable approach is possible to allow for fast and flexible software deployment. Rapidly evolving security requirements, which may necessitate major changes to system functionality, are particularly underserved by this model.

Agile

Recognizing that rigid development models like Waterfall do not adapt well to modern software development needs, a new high-level model emerged in early 2001 from a group of developers called the Agile Alliance. The group comprised members with diverse development backgrounds from methodologies such as Extreme Programming, Scrum, and Feature-Driven Development, many of which contained evolutions designed to address shortcomings of legacy methodologies like Waterfall. The Agile Alliance documented 12 principles to form the Agile Manifesto, which can be found at `agilemanifesto.org/principles.html`. The manifesto principles are designed to better structure development teams and allocate resources with the goal of increasing flexibility of development activities. For example, two of the principles state the following:

- **Our highest priority is to satisfy the customer through early and continuous delivery of valuable software.** Rather than striving for a complete set of requirements before a project begins, Agile development can identify the highest priority items and work to deliver them first and then repeatedly iterate to elicit deliver on the remaining requirements. The focus of development is to meet needs, rather than blindly follow processes.

- **Welcome changing requirements, even late in development. Agile processes harness change for the customer's competitive advantage.** By focusing on customer (user) value, Agile development strives to deliver systems that meet user needs. This obviously supports the security goal of availability, but it also means complex software systems can be better designed to meet changing confidentiality and integrity needs, such as more robust encryption or data validation controls that were not initially identified as requirements. As needs change over time, such as new security requirements, so too can the software project evolve.

The 12 Agile principles are not themselves a development methodology that can be followed to develop software but are instead guiding ideals for managing software development projects. When implemented correctly, they strive to achieve value by delivering functional software faster and with increased ability to respond to changes. Software is released quickly with basic functionality; then the development process iterates to include additional functionality, avoiding large all-at-once releases in favor of smaller, more frequent releases.

Each iteration will also take into account lessons learned from customers (e.g., changed requirements) as well as lessons learned by the development team. The team should ideally comprise cross-functional members from both development and business backgrounds and should emphasize clear and frequent communication among stakeholders. This development meta-methodology requires organizations to identify all relevant stakeholders, which must include the security team. All stakeholders should be involved at a minimum during requirements gathering and testing to ensure the system needs are documented and tests are conducted to verify they are met. Changes to requirements, including evolving security needs, are well-supported by Agile methodologies, since they are designed to reassess requirements frequently and incorporate those in the iterative development.

Agile Testing Approaches

Agile places a high value on speed and efficient use of resources, which gives rise to the use of integrated testing to support the delivery of functional software. Unlike the Waterfall methodology where testing is a separate phase conducted after development activities are completed, Agile methodologies integrate testing activities closer to the actual development activities. The goal is twofold. First, testing is on a smaller, more manageable target, so fixes are generally easier. Second, the need to be responsive to changing requirements necessitates robust testing to ensure newly delivered functionality does not introduce bugs, flaws, or vulnerabilities. The use of automated testing tools allows for security tests to be conducted closer to the time of development and against smaller targets. These support a goal of preventing defects from reaching production environments, as well as making test results easier to manage due to their smaller size.

Maintaining the speed of software delivery under Agile methodologies leads to a strong focus on automation. This is particularly true for repeated processes such as functional testing, which benefits from increased reliability since automated processes are less subject to human error. Security testing benefits from automation as well, as critical controls like software code reviews and vulnerability scanning can be conducted automatically and more frequently. Automated testing is an essential enabler of continuous integration/continuous delivery (CI/CD), which is discussed later in this chapter.

Agile Development Methodologies

As mentioned, Agile is a high-level set of principles and is implemented to some degree across a variety of development methodologies. Three examples of development methodologies implementing Agile principles include Extreme Programming, Test-Driven Development, and Scrum.

- **Extreme Programming:** Sometimes written as XP, this methodology introduces the use of integrated teams including developers, customers, and managers to drive the delivery of high-value software features. User stories are documented to capture what users are trying to achieve as well as the acceptance criteria of software that implements those features, and the stories are prioritized based on value. For example, in a system with 500 users who need to log in and save data to a database but 10 users who need to print records from the database, the ability to log in and save data will be prioritized. Full details of XP methods and implementation are at www.extremeprogramming.org.

  - XP utilizes a concept known as *pair programming*, which pairs developers. The developers take turns writing code and offering advice/input, with the goal of achieving higher quality code by providing extra oversight and knowledge to draw upon.

  - *Refactoring* code can mean many things, but it is essentially a way of removing obsolete, redundant, or unneeded code to improve software's functionality. Developers may have made decisions in the past that were sound but are no longer relevant as the system and requirements evolved. Refactoring can be used to ensure systems do not contain unnecessary junk code or functions known as *cruft*.

- **Test-Driven Development (TDD):** In education, there is an idea known as "teaching to the test"; classroom instruction is geared to ensure students are able to successfully pass an exam like a driver training course designed to prepare students for a driving test. TDD, as the name implies, is driven by the use of test cases: first a test is written, then it is run. If it fails, code is written or refactored as needed to make the test succeed; the ultimate goal is to ensure that all tests pass. Having the end goal in mind can be useful for developers to better understand the desired functionality they are trying to build. TDD is especially effective for existing systems where modifications or updates must be implemented with a minimum of complexity, such as implementing code-level security controls like fixing a buffer overflow or injection vulnerability.

- **Scrum:** The foundation of a Scrum project is a lightweight set of team members continuously iterating development work to achieve the overall product goal. Scrum has introduced many words that are associated with Agile development projects, such as *sprints* and *backlogs*. It focuses on a cross-functional team comprising three key members, a timeframe known as a sprint around which key activities are performed, and several important artifacts. Scrum roles and artifacts include the following:
    - **Scrum master:** The Scrum master is in some ways akin to a facilitator, whose role is to remove impediments to the team's success. These include tasks such as coaching team members on self-organizing work, gathering input from key stakeholders, and facilitating team events.

    - **Product owner:** As the voice of the customer, the product owner is responsible for ensuring developers understand the goals their software is being designed to meet. The product owner also owns the product backlog, where all work to be done is broken down into work units and prioritized, such as new features and bug fixes.

    - **Development team:** This is a broad team that includes traditional developers who write code, architects who design system infrastructure, data scientists or analysts, and, crucially to security, testers and Quality Assurance (QA) staff. Security testing should be done for all development work, so many code- and application-level security controls will be delegated to members of the development team.

    - **Backlogs:** One key artifact maintained in Scrum is the backlog. The overall product backlog contains all requirements the product owner has identified, along with prioritization based on value to the customer. Requirements may include a measure of effort or complexity to build, and a cross-functional effort is often needed to determine these numbers. The sprint backlog is a smaller list of requirements drawn from the product backlog that, in the team's estimation, can be delivered in the time allotted. Higher priority items are obviously delivered sooner, though low-complexity/effort/priority items might be added if there are free resources in a sprint, but not enough to address a higher priority or more complex item.

- **Key Scrum** activities and key inputs from the artifacts are depicted in Figure 8.2 and are described in the following points.

    - **Sprint:** A sprint is simply a time-boxed set of work to be done on the project; for example, all development work to be completed in two weeks is considered a sprint. While Scrum, as an Agile methodology, embraces change, changes are avoided if at all possible once work is committed to a sprint. Changed requirements can be addressed in a future sprint.

- **Sprint planning:** Prior to beginning a development sprint, the team meets to perform sprint planning. Based on priorities set by the product owner, certain backlog requirements will be selected for the sprint, and the team agrees upon the work they feel can be achieved in the given time period. Once this plan is set, changes are to be avoided, so this scoping and planning is a critical activity.

- **Daily Scrum:** The development team should meet daily to discuss progress, blocking issues, and the plan for the day's activities. According to the Agile Manifesto, these meetings are best conducted face to face and are often known as *standup meetings*.

- **Sprint review and retrospective:** Two key events happen at the end of a sprint. The sprint review identifies work completed and includes a demo to the customer, supporting the goal of integrating users and developers. A sprint retrospective is an opportunity for the development team to perform continuous improvement by reflecting on successes, failures, and opportunities based on the recent sprint.

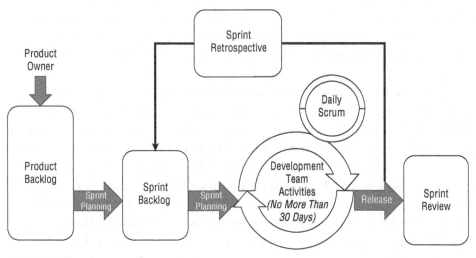

FIGURE 8.2 **Scrum process flow**

DevOps

DevOps is an integration of the traditionally disparate functional areas of development and operations, with the goal of better supporting the organization's information system resources. Developers and operational personnel traditionally worked in silos, and inefficient handoff procedures between the two meant critical information was lost when systems moved from development into production. DevOps teams implement practices advocated in Agile, such as combined cross-functional teams with an emphasis on frequent communication to overcome these challenges.

DevOps practices include the use of automation, frequent testing, and an emphasis on frequent software integration and deployment. Software delivery is sped up by following an assembly line approach, known as a *pipeline*, with a focus on building quality in. Developers are given a manageable unit of work to complete within a specific period of time (the requirements included in a sprint), and automated testing aims to identify and remediate flaws before the code is delivered to production.

QA is the third member of the DevOps team in addition to development and operations and is responsible for implementing many aspects of the cross-functional communication. Members of a QA team will typically participate in up-front activities related to testing, such as defining criteria for success, and then provide crucial feedback to developers when a test fails. These testing activities are included in the scope of work for a sprint, so the development team must ensure adequate time and resources are allocated to develop, test, and remediate any issues in the code being delivered during that sprint.

This QA focus can be a crucial point of enforcing security in the SDLC, if security requirements have been properly documented and QA is required to verify the system meets those requirements. Automated security testing and faster delivery reduce the number of vulnerabilities introduced when new software is deployed, and provide the benefit of quicker patch creation and deployment when a vulnerability is discovered in a system.

While there are benefits to speedier software delivery, developing and deploying secure software should not be sacrificed in favor of simply adding new functionality more quickly. There is a crucial governance task to consider for organizations using DevOps: the privileged role and permissions held by the DevOps team. Lengthy processes like change management reviews may frustrate the goal of fast software delivery, but they do provide useful checkpoints for security activities such as vulnerability scans and manual reviews. These must be replaced by automated tests where necessary, and defined procedures should also exist for software changes that cannot be fully tested via automated tools.

Members of the DevOps team are likely to have privileged access, such as being able to make changes in production environments, create new users and permissions, and access log data. Like all privileged access, additional monitoring is likely justified, as are controls like multifactor authentication (MFA) and additional training for these staff members. While cross-functional teams are useful, principles of least privilege and separation of duties must still be implemented. Members of DevOps require permissions specific only to their primary role, rather than having access to all abilities granted to the DevOps team; for example, developers may be able to mark their code complete and ready for deployment, but another user is required to verify that all required testing has been performed before the code is deployed. Here again, automation plays a crucial role, such as the use of an automated code deployment tool that systematically validates that all testing and other requirements have been met before pushing code to production.

DevSecOps

Although QA can perform critical security-related functions in DevOps if security is properly implemented in the SDLC, you will notice that security is not specifically addressed. The Agile transition of legacy software development has been mirrored in the security community as well with the creation of DevSecOps, right down to a manifesto and guiding principles documented at www.devsecops.org. The goal of DevSecOps is to favor iteration over perfection, where a workable security solution delivered today and improved tomorrow is preferred over a perfect solution delivered years from now — by which time the system may have suffered attacks or exploits!

The DevSecOps principles provide guidance for better integrating security and compliance activities and data into development processes. These principles demonstrate a focus on better communicating security in addition to the traditional DevOps and include data and security science over fear, uncertainty, and doubt, as well as red and blue teams exploiting testing over relying on scans and theoretical vulnerabilities, both of which help security practitioners deliver actionable knowledge. Rather than saying a theoretical vulnerability may lead to the complete loss of an organization's data, a DevSecOps practitioner, such as a CISSP, performs red team testing to determine the exact nature of a vulnerability. This, combined with real-world risk data, gives the organization's leaders and developers a justified and actionable path to mitigate risk.

The ultimate goal of DevSecOps, as the name suggests, is to ensure security is built into the process an organization uses to develop and operate its information systems. Traditional information security practices are often an add-on to the SDLC, and they suffer from the same challenges identified in legacy development methodologies. This evolution is also reflected in the evolution of standards documents, such as the migration in NIST documentation from SDLC security to security engineering processes, though it is helpful to note that there is not standard approach to implementing DevSecOps. Much like security risk mitigation controls, each organization may create or adapt processes to fit their unique environments.

Other Methodologies

There are other software development methodologies in addition to the Waterfall and the family of Agile methodologies previously discussed. While a CISSP is not expected to be familiar with all possible methodologies, it is a good idea to have a basic familiarity with popular methodologies and their associated security benefits and drawbacks.

For projects that need a small increase in flexibility over the traditional Waterfall, the *modified Waterfall* may be appropriate. This methodology provides two minor options to address projects that are not served by the rigorous approach demanded by the traditional Waterfall method. First, it may be possible to proceed to the next phase before all current phase activities are finished; for example, testing may begin on completed code while some code is still under development. Second, it is possible to step back a phase and iterate work if necessary. If the developers realize that architectural assumptions made during design are off in some way, the project can step back one phase, update the system design to address the deficiencies, then progress to implementation once again.

Another evolution of the traditional Waterfall approach is the *Spiral* methodology. The Spiral methodology is iterative; that is, it is designed to be executed in a repetitive series, and it places a heavy focus on risk assessment, analysis, and evaluation. Large, complex, and costly projects are a common use for this model, as it emphasizes risk control over time via repeated evaluation of project risks, costs, and benefits. The process iterates through four phases:

1. Determine objectives, alternatives, and risks
2. Evaluate alternatives and resolve risks
3. Development and testing
4. Plan next phase

Other SDLC methodologies may be used within each phase to perform activities such as gathering requirements or scheduling and performing development, and the iterative nature means changing or evolving requirements can be easily addressed. This model is expensive and introduces a great deal of overhead in the form of the repeated risk assessments at each phase; this overhead may be justified for projects where requirements are difficult to determine or long-term projects with requirements that are likely to change.

Some development methodologies were designed with iteration in mind and assume the project will be repeated. The *Prototype* model is one example, where a simplified version of a system or app is built and released for feedback and review. A subsequent round of development is done based on the feedback and then released for additional review, and so on, until the stakeholder's needs have been met. This methodology is useful for new categories or types of systems where clear needs may be impossible to elicit or when novel approaches will be tried.

Unlike iterative models, the *Cleanroom* methodology assumes that flaws cannot be fixed once development is complete. It focuses exclusively on defect prevention. The concept follows models used for delicate tasks like chip fabrication where the introduction of a flaw can render hardware completely unusable; this low-risk tolerance demands expensive preventative controls such as garments designed to trap hair or dust, as well as special air handling systems. In software development, similar controls can be deployed at the expense of development agility. The ultimate goal is to produce software that meets a defined level of reliability, sometimes known as *zero-defect*, with a focus on robust design and implementation rather than testing and remediation. The Cleanroom methodology is usually implemented with another development model such as Waterfall and demands a focus on gathering statistical data regarding flaws and control measures. These metrics are used to justify decisions like the release of software meeting the defined level of reliable, nondefective functionality.

Maturity Models

Maturity models provide a way of measuring an organization's progress on continuous improvement in a discipline, such as security management or software development. Much the same way music is graded based on the musician's level of practice, maturity model levels detail the skills and abilities that are expected in an organization performing certain tasks with a goal of improvement. Business maturity models are often known as *capability maturity models* and are usually specific to a particular organizational discipline like software development.

These models provide a baseline to measure the organization's current state of ability, define a desired goal state, and provide systemic recommendations for improving the capability. This is known as *process improvement*, and in general, an organization is more mature when its processes are more formal, repeatable, and well-managed rather than chaotic. Although discussed in the context of software development, process improvement and maturity models can be applied to organizations that acquire their key IT functions as services, as well as other disciplines such as managing the improvement of security capabilities.

✔ Process Maturity Is No Guarantee of Success!

Process improvements are often undertaken as a proactive way of managing risk, as well-managed, mature projects are typically more likely to succeed. Maturity does not guarantee success, however. Small technology startups with almost entirely ad hoc processes routinely succeed in delivering functional software and systems when they obviously lack the rigor to be highly optimized, process-driven organizations. Meanwhile, large, mature organizations have suffered embarrassing failures, such as the government contractor in charge of the U.S. Healthcare.gov project.

The website infamously buckled under the pressure of too many users trying to sign up simultaneously, despite that the firm was one of only 10 in the United States at that time to have achieved CMMI Level 5, which is the most mature state according to the Capability Maturity Model Integration (CMMI). The overall project encountered delays at every phase due to a mix of complexity and unclear requirements, which in turn led to an unstable system at launch. The organization's underlying processes weren't necessarily to blame as the project requirements changed unexpectedly close to the delivery date, but the high CMMI rating also failed to correlate to guaranteed success.

Common Maturity Model Components

Maturity models are usually structured with similar concepts, with the key difference being the process areas the model is designed for, such as software development or systems integration. Components that are similar across maturity models include the following:

- **Domains:** The domains are the processes or business aspects that the model is designed to help measure and are usually common activities such as measurement and analysis. The domains include descriptions of practices related to that domain, such as defining the source and frequency of metrics gathering.

- **Levels:** Maturity models organize sets of practices in each domain into a series of increasing levels, typically ranging from 1 to 5. Levels are arranged in a scale showing the organization's increasing capabilities and may describe individual process areas or the overall collection of processes described by the maturity model. Each level also includes audit or evaluation criteria, which are used by the organization or an outside auditor to determine the organization's current maturity level.

- **Criteria:** To achieve a specific level of maturity, an organization must meet the criteria for that level. In some models, specific domains are associated with each level, such as basic process definition being a low-level criteria while metrics-driven process analysis is a higher-lever criteria. Logically, an organization cannot measure an ad hoc or undefined process, so that practice is not introduced until the organization matures fundamental practices. In other models, each domain has a series of increasing requirements within each domain that correspond to increasing domain maturity, such as ad hoc documentation at lower maturity or template-driven documentation at higher maturity.

- **Targets:** A target describes the organization's desired maturity level. Just as security controls entail a cost-benefit analysis of risk reduction, so too must the choice to improve processes lead to a defined organizational benefit. While increased process maturity reduces the risk of failed or mismanaged projects, it also introduces cost and complexity; different organizations will choose different levels of desired maturity. The target can be used to perform a gap analysis and prioritize activities needed to close identified gaps. In some cases, like contracting organizations, a specific maturity level may be a requirement of doing business with certain entities like government agencies, while in other cases, demonstrating maturity to customers or business partners offers a competitive advantage.

The choice of a maturity model, specific domains or practice areas, and a target will be primarily guided by the organization's objectives. Some models are well-adopted in specific industries or are most applicable to organizations engaged in specific undertakings like software development. In other cases, maturity models have been established around common security practices like secure data handling and are quickly being adopted as a requirement for service providers handling data on behalf of clients and customers.

Capability Maturity Model

One of the earliest maturity models to be widely adopted, the Capability Maturity Model (CMM), was developed jointly by the U.S. Department of Defense and the Software Engineering Institute (SEI) at Carnegie Mellon University. It arose from the need to measure and improve the burgeoning field of software development in the 1980s, as increasing processing power and decreasing costs led to widespread adoption of computer systems. Development projects were often poorly estimated, controlled, and managed due to computer science being a nascent field at the time, so SEI formalized a set of best practices common across successful projects. The initial purpose of the model was to evaluate the capabilities of government contractors to deliver projects on time and on budget, but other development and business processes began to adopt the maturity model mindset.

Capability Maturity Model Integration

Recognizing that the CMM was being adapted to new business processes, the SEI designed the Capability Maturity Model Integration (CMMI). It was originally designed with specialized applications in development (CMMI-DEV), services (CMMI-SVC), and product and service acquisition (CMMI-ACQ), and the most recent version 2.0 of the framework was released in 2018. The model is now under the control of the CMMI Institute run by ISACA (cmmiinstitute.com/cmmi) and has been adapted to address Agile development as well as new areas of business concern including development, services, supplier management, and people (workforce management and professional development), as well as an emerging Cybermaturity program designed to apply maturity model concepts to governance and reporting of cybersecurity.

CMMI models are broken down into domains called *process areas* and five levels of maturity. Some process areas include increasing requirements at higher maturity, while others apply only at or above certain levels. The levels are as follows:

1. **Initial:** Processes are unpredictable and largely reactive. This is typical of an organization largely performing only ad hoc processes.

2. **Managed:** Processes are characterized or documented for projects and are often reactive. Certain projects may be well-managed and repeatable, but that success is not leveraged across the entire organization.

3. **Defined:** Processes are characterized for the organization and are proactive. An organization at level 3 has documented processes shared across various projects/efforts and takes proactive steps to ensure projects are successful, such as project risk management.

4. **Quantitatively managed:** Processes are measured and controlled by the measurements. This is an organization collecting and responding to metrics.

5. **Optimizing:** The organization focuses on process improvement. An organization at level 5 has documented processes, proactively controls them using lessons learned, and has a robust oversight function to gather metrics and manage activities.

Software Assurance Maturity Model

The Software Assurance Maturity Model (SAMM) is maintained by the Open Web Application Security Project (OWASP), located at owaspsamm.org. SAMM is a prescriptive framework for implementing a software security program and focuses on integrating security activities into an existing SDLC. It provides an action plan for assessing the current state, identifying a target state, and implementing necessary improvements across the SDLC including updates to processes, people, knowledge, and tools.

As with other models, there are domains, subdivided into security practices, as shown in Figure 8.3.

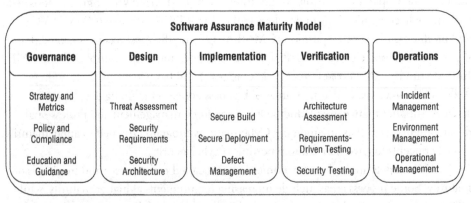

FIGURE 8.3 **SAMM domains and practices**

Within each set of practices, there are streams of activity, which often represent different responsibilities. In Security Testing Stream A, for example, automated security testing tools, which can be managed by a QA function, are required, while in Stream B, manual security testing of high-risk components is required. This testing is a specialized function that requires application security or penetration testing experience. Each security practice is also represented in three levels of maturity. For example, the Security Testing maturity levels are as follows:

1. Perform security testing (both manual and tool based) to discover security defects.

2. Make security testing during development more complete and efficient through automation complemented with regular manual security penetration tests.

3. Embed security testing as part of the development and deployment processes.

Building Security-In Maturity Model

The Building Security-In Maturity Model (BSIMM), as its name implies, is a maturity model focused on determining the current state of secure software creation capabilities, identifying improvement opportunities, and prioritizing efforts to improve secure software development. More information and the BSIMM documentation can be found at www.bsimm.com. It is an attempt to bring rigor to the practice of software security by determining which practices are actually effective, as determined through interviews with practicing software security professionals. These software security initiatives (SSIs) are ordered based on their observed frequency in the interviews. SSIs that are observed more frequently are considered to be widely adopted practices, while less-frequently observed practices may be either new concepts or performed only by organizations with a very high maturity.

Successful implementation of BSIMM relies upon an internal function dedicated to software security known as the *software security group* (SSG). The BSIMM sets out 121 activities across four domains of practice: Governance, Intelligence, Software Security Development Lifecycle (SSDL), and Deployment. The SSG is responsible or accountable for implementing and maturing the organization's chosen SSIs. As with all maturity models, not every organization must be at the same level, but BSIMM is a useful source of empirically based guidance for organizations to measure and improve the software security.

CMMC

A recently developed maturity model important to the field of cybersecurity is the Cybersecurity Maturity Model Certification (CMMC), which is published by the U.S. Department of Defense. Although broadly related to cybersecurity including but not limited to software development security, CMMC is designed for contractors who are handling sensitive information, known as *controlled unclassified information* (CUI), on behalf of government clients. It is freely available and contains broadly applicable guidance on assessing and maturing cybersecurity and information security capabilities. CMMC can be implemented and assessed at an organizational level or on specific projects or units as appropriate. The model and supporting documentation can be found at www.acq.osd.mil/cmmc/draft.html.

The maturity levels in CMMC are similar to CMMI, ranging from level 1, Performed (the activities associated with basic cyber hygiene are in place and functioning at the organization), up to level 5, Optimizing (an advanced, continuously optimized, and proactive cybersecurity program is in place). These maturity levels assess the organization's implementation of processes, capabilities, and practices, and are organized into domains that will look familiar to practitioners experienced in the NIST SP 800-53 control families:

- Access Control (AC)
- Asset Management (AM)
- Audit and Accountability (AU)
- Awareness and Training (AT)
- Configuration Management (CM)
- Identification and Authentication (IA)
- Incident Response (IR)
- Maintenance (MA)
- Media Protection (MP)
- Personnel Security (PS)
- Physical Protection (PE)
- Recover (RE)
- Risk Management (RM)
- Security Assessment (CA)
- Situational Awareness (SA)
- Systems and Communication Protection (SC)
- System and Information Integrity (SI)

Maturity Model Summary

Maturity models are useful in determining the level of competency and effectiveness that an organization's practices have achieved, as well charting a course to improvement. They are useful for complex activities such as software development and security where consistent, repeatable practices are desired, and where incremental improvements can be measured to justify the costs associated with management, operational, or security overhead.

Each of the models discussed comes with some form of assessment, whether informal internal assessment guides like BSIMM or formal external guides like CMMC, which requires an independent third-party assessment and certification. While useful for measurement, maturity models are not a guarantee of success in any particular endeavor, as they do not address all possible risks a software development project might face.

Operation and Maintenance

Operation and maintenance, often written O&M, is the phase when systems are in live use and running in what is known as a *production environment*, meaning they are actively being used by end users. Testing, verification, and validation activities mark the end of development, and the transition to O&M is often known as *promotion* or *deployment*. To keep software both running and secure, there are a number of critical tasks that must be performed during this phase. Not all tasks during O&M are the responsibility of a security practitioner since system operations is usually outside the purview of the security team. Some, like ongoing security testing or vulnerability assessments, are directly assigned to the security team; all operations and security tasks do support the goals of system security and particularly the goal of availability. These concerns include the following:

- **Continuity:** Resilience of systems in the face of adverse conditions, as well as the ability to recover when an interruption does occur, are critical. Activities for business continuity, disaster recovery, and cyber resilience all occur during the O&M phase, such as generating system backups.

- **Monitoring and incident response:** Live production systems are where a majority of security incidents occur, so a significant portion of the organization's monitoring capability will be focused on this environment. When an incident is detected, the process of investigation and recovery typically focuses on remediating the issue and restoring production to normal. Processes such as help-desk response and digital forensics will be critical to ensure security incidents are investigated properly.

- **Vulnerability and patch management:** Scanning systems for flaws and remediating them is a significant, ongoing security task. Some flaws may cause an iteration of the SDLC, especially for custom software, though routine patch deployment for third-party software is the bulk of this work.

- **Access control:** While controlling access to development and test environments is important, most systems typically have far more users than developers, and sensitive data is not usually used in testing or development. Procedures to provision, review, and deprovision access will primarily focus on operational systems.

- **Change and configuration management:** System-level change and configuration management is discussed in Chapter 7, "Security Operations," while the specifics of manging changes to source code are discussed separately in this chapter. It is worth noting that operational systems are likely to be placed under configuration management with defined processes for requesting, reviewing, and implementing changes to maintain a secure baseline.

During a system's life, a variety of maintenance tasks will also be performed to keep it operational and preserve security. These include identifying upgrades or updates necessary to keep the system running, such as end-of-life operating systems that require system upgrades or replacement of failing hardware. Maintenance can have a negative impact on system availability, and proactive scheduling is essential to preserve uptime. Maintenance windows are announced well in advance, and users are notified that the system will be unavailable; unannounced emergency maintenance typically requires an urgent situation as justification. Testing must be included in maintenance tasks, particularly regression testing designed to identify unintended consequences or loss of existing functionality due to a system change.

✔ Bug Fixes and SDLC Iteration

It is likely that, at some point in their life, custom-built systems will require an iteration of development or system integration activities to address bugs, flaws, or security vulnerabilities. Take, for example, a custom-built application designed to coordinate a company's logistics for ordering, inventorying, shipping, and re-ordering goods. Addressing a discovered security vulnerability will require some amount of development work, which introduces the risk of breaking existing functions or adding new code that must be tested.

The approach for addressing this system iteration will vary depending on the development methodology used. An organization with Agile methodologies will capture the new or changed requirements in a backlog, schedule them based on the priority, and address them during normal iteration of the SDLC. An organization using a Waterfall methodology may need to create an entirely new development project to address the changed requirements. In any case, the requirement for the SDLC in this example is an updated version of the application without the identified vulnerability. Testing criteria are obvious: The new code must close the identified flaw without impacting existing functionality or introducing new vulnerabilities.

Change Management

One key aspect of managing security for many systems is to maintain them in a known, secure state, which is the function of configuration management. However, change is necessary, and so processes by which changes can be requested, reviewed, implemented, and tested are also necessary, which is the goal of change management. These structured processes enable flexibility for systems to adapt to changing requirements or circumstances, while also sufficiently addressing security concerns to prevent changes that adversely affecting the security posture of the system.

It is important to remember that change management is typically not under the purview of the security department, but security practitioners do need to actively participate in the process. Changes must be reviewed for potential security impacts, testing plans must be documented to ensure security is not adversely affected, and security processes may be triggered in the event a change goes poorly. For example, a failed change could invoke business continuity processes until the change can be reversed.

Change management processes may be implemented on a number of different levels, with corresponding levels of rigor and sets of processes. At the organization level, changes such as operating system (OS) replacements would require significant budget and resource planning. At a source-code level, developers may follow secure coding standards like commenting code and performing peer reviews before code is checked into a repository, which acts as the configuration and change management system for the organization's source code. The code is maintained in a known good state, and approved methods of changing it such as pull requests and commits must follow rules to ensure the integrity of the source code is not lost by unapproved developer changes. At some point, code may also reach a state of completion after which no changes are permitted, in a process known as a *freeze*. This is useful for performing testing, verification, and validation exercises, as testing code that is undergoing changes may result in false positives or nonsensical findings.

Change Management Phases and Security Practices

Most organizations implement a formal change management body, and common names include some variation on change "something" board, like change management, change control, or change advisory (CMB, CCB, or CAB). The composition of a CMB typically includes permanent essential members from IT and security teams, as well as ad hoc members like finance or HR for changes with impacts on or input required from those departments. For example, a major OS shift will require significant investments, so finance and accounting will be involved, while HR will be able to contribute details regarding training and productivity impacts of the change.

The CMB is responsible for shepherding the change management process, which, much like the name of the group, will be unique across different organizations. A high-level change management process is outlined here, along with corresponding security practices recommended at each phase:

- **Request:** Many change processes involve the submission of a ticket or other formal request for a change; the advantage of a ticketing system is the ability to capture all details related to the change in a single location. The request must capture full details of the change as well as anticipated resource requirements and impacts.

- **Analysis and approval:** Once documented, the change is reviewed by the CMB to identify all anticipated requirements and impacts of the change. This follows a set of documented criteria, which should include reviewing any security impacts like introducing new risks or adverse effects on existing security controls. As an example, a change to transition all users from on-premises to remote access will have repercussions on virtually all the security controls an organization has implemented. Understanding these impacts and ensuring adequate resources are available to address them are crucial before the CMB can approve the change.

- **Change development:** Once a change is approved, the responsible parties must develop a plan to actually execute the change, such as scheduling time to perform needed IT tasks, gathering necessary resources, and purchasing or developing the changed system components. These actions must follow the documented and approved change request.

- **Implementation:** With a plan developed, the change can be implemented. As with the development phase, all approved change procedures must be followed. In the event a change is not successful, back-out or rollback procedures are required, and the creation of such plans and procedures is typically a requirement for change approval.

- **Testing:** The newly changed system must be tested to ensure the changes are working as expected, existing functions were not broken, and the security controls are still operating as intended. Depending on the organization and the magnitude of the change, this testing may include highly formal activities like certification and accreditation.

- **Postmortem:** There are a number of post-change activities typically required. Documentation of the changes performed must be completed, as the changed system is the new known state, which will be maintained by configuration management. Newly implemented features may require user training, and any lessons learned should be documented for continuous process improvement. This phase may also be called an *after-action* report, *lessons learned*, or *retrospective*, but the goal of identifying improvement opportunities is the same.

Emergency Change Management

Delay is an implicit part of change management processes, mainly because time is required to gather information and resources needed. There will be situations when this delay is unacceptable, such as a change needed to address a major outage or newly discovered critical vulnerability. In these cases, the risk of waiting for a change to be documented and reviewed at a weekly CMB meeting outweighs the risk of taking immediate action, so an emergency change management process is required. Details of standard processes and specific emergency change processes are discussed in Chapter 7, "Security Operations."

Emergency changes, unlike normal changes, are implemented either without approval or with very limited approval. Rather than requiring review by the entire CMB, a single member may grant approval, or IT personnel may be authorized to implement the change without any prior approval. Testing and verification processes are similarly streamlined. A patch to close a critical system vulnerability may be deployed to a single system and limited or ad hoc testing conducted before it is rolled out to all systems. In this case, the risk of operational downtime due to a flawed patch is acceptable compared to the risk of the vulnerability being exploited.

Emergency changes do not imply a total lack of process or procedures, but rather a modification designed for speed. Documentation is still required, and many organizations perform retroactive change review and approval after the change has been deployed to ensure any unintended consequences or unforeseen impacts are understood, documented, and appropriately handled. After-the-fact documentation is required to support this review, and testing should include regression tests or security assessments like vulnerability scanning and pen testing, depending on the change. When addressing a critical vulnerability, the priority is obviously to mitigate the risk as soon as possible rather than write complete documentation, but the documentation is still expected once the vulnerability has been addressed.

Integrated Product Team

Integrated product teams (IPTs) are collections of multidisciplinary individuals with a collective responsibility for delivering a product or process, similar to the combinations seen in DevOps, DevSecOps, and Agile software development. The guiding concept is that groups with diverse viewpoints—including users, customers, developers, and contractors, who are all stakeholders in the final product or process—can achieve success and enhance speed of delivery for complex projects such as software development.

The goal of IPT is to either assemble or make readily available all resources with a role, skills, or knowledge relevant to a project, and by assembling these resources, traditional delays or impediments can be removed. This includes security practitioners who understand the security and compliance requirements that a system needs to meet and who should be included as early as possible in the development or acquisition of a system. IPT is a concept that originated in the U.S. Department of Defense to integrate key stakeholders in complex projects.

The goal of integrated product and process development (IPPD) is to combine both product and process design to ensure a product, often an information system, has a holistic set of requirements used to design both systems and business processes. This holistic set of requirements should include security needs such as data encryption and access control, and a CISSP may be a key member of the IPT tasked with system development using IPPD practices.

IPPD relies on extensive modeling and testing of both system and process prototypes and on the use of IPTs. These teams combine stakeholders from the user community and developers with the goal of deepening the understanding of what users need from the system and any technical constraints that need to be overcome. This prevents decisions from being made with incomplete information and provides timelier feedback, with the goal of meeting cost and performance objectives for systems while reducing wasteful development efforts. These concepts are related to DevOps and Agile development methodologies, both of which foster closer collaboration between stakeholder groups to enable quicker development and closer integration between teams.

IDENTIFY AND APPLY SECURITY CONTROLS IN SOFTWARE DEVELOPMENT ECOSYSTEMS

Security practitioners need to understand the criticality of software security in an organization, as well as the foundational role filled by the software and tools used by developers when creating information systems. A CISSP does not necessarily need to be an expert in all aspects of programming and software development, but an overview of programming is important to understand the various risks and associated security controls that must be addressed in software development. Particularly important to understand are the concepts underpinning modern programming languages, the tools and environments in which they run, and the processes utilized by developers to write, test, and deploy code needed for modern information systems. A number of security tools are also designed to be integrated with and provide data to these developers, including a host of application security testing tools that are increasingly automated and provide near-continuous feedback to improve the security of software.

Programming Languages

Since code is the foundation of software and information systems, it is also a primary focus of security efforts. These efforts include ensuring code does not violate the integrity of systems by adding unwanted functions and testing systems to identify unintended flaws that could negatively impact the confidentiality or integrity of data, or the availability of the overall system. To perform these functions, it is important to understand several basic concepts.

Programming languages represent a set of instructions used to build programs that are executed by a computer, typically with a goal of processing information. These languages consist of instructions and a particular way of writing these instructions (known as *syntax*), as well as methods to manipulate data. These are combined to create algorithms, or specific sets of instructions, to achieve a data processing goal. Just as we use sentences, paragraphs, and punctuation to convey meaning in human languages, programming languages also have logical structures designed to allow computers to understand them, execute the instructions, and control the flow of data.

Language Types

There are two types of software language, and their main difference is the sequence of steps required to turn human-readable instructions like `print('Hello, world!')` into instructions a particular hardware system can execute. *Compiled languages* are translated into machine-readable form before being run in a process known as *compiling*. The developer uses a program called a *complier* to perform this task, which takes the written program as input and produces machine-executable code, often called a *binary*, as an output. Compiled programs can be run only by the system type for which they were compiled and are often optimized for that specific system type; for example, a program compiled to run on the Windows OS will not function if you try to run it on macOS or Linux. The optimization means the program can take advantage of specific system features at the cost of portability. In addition, compiled programs do not expose their source code to the end user, so if code is a valuable intellectual property asset, a compiled language is the best way to distribute it while preserving confidentiality. C# and Swift are examples of compiled languages.

Interpreted languages are translated into machine-readable format when they are run, also known as *on the fly*. This makes interpreted code more portable across system types, as users on various platforms can install an interpreter specific to their system so the developer does not need to compile system-specific versions. There are downsides to interpreted languages, and security can be particularly troublesome. Code is distributed as written or in an intermediate form, which is in human-readable form, so interpreted languages may expose sensitive intellectual property. Due to the interpretation process, there is additional operational overhead that makes interpreted programs slower than a compiled program, though the speed of modern computing systems makes this a negligible concern in many cases. JavaScript and Python are examples of interpreted languages. Security concerns with mobile code include its dynamic nature — since it is loaded at runtime, there is the possibility an attacker could modify the code that is requested when a user runs the application. This means previously tested code may not be loaded, but instead an attacker's malicious code is loaded and executed.

Database systems also have languages used to define their data structures, interact with stored data, and manage the database itself. Structured query language (SQL) is one example, which includes sublanguages for interacting with a database management system (DBMS). This includes the data definition language (DDL) for creating databases and tables, as well as data manipulation language (DML) for performing actions such as querying or inserting new records. The data control language (DCL) is primarily concerned with access control for data stored in the database, which makes it critical for implementing security.

Security testing is also impacted by the choice of language type. A compiled program installed on a particular computing system can be thoroughly tested, but many interpreted programs are delivered remotely in the form of mobile code in web applications. Integrity of program code may be a concern for some organizations, as interpreted program code is loaded anew each time the user requests a webpage. Variations among interpreters may also introduce security issues that are difficult to test for, as the number of testing targets is increased, and resources may not be available to perform thorough testing across all possible system and interpreter combinations.

Type Checking and Type Safe Languages

One important aspect of programming that often impacts security is the data a program is handling. In programming languages, data is usually categorized into different types like strings of text, numeric integers, or Boolean values like true/false. Data types have associated memory structures in code, which are often used as placeholders to represent data that does not exist when a program is created — variables that the program accepts as input. If a user enters data that does not conform to the expected structure (e.g., a user types their name into a field designed to hold numeric information about their birthday), the program is likely to encounter an error.

Static type checking is performed by a compiler to verify if the program's functionality matches type constraints for data inputs. For example, the expression `price + tax` can be successfully evaluated if both input variables are integer types storing values that represent currency. However, if the program has declared an integer and a text value of "yes" or "no" to define if sales tax applies to the item, attempting to add those two pieces of data isn't possible. Type checking can identify such programming flaws. *Dynamic type checking* checks the values stored in a program's variables as it is running to ensure data matches the expected type. Languages that implement these features are known as *type-safe*, and they support important security goals related to integrity of data.

Strongly typed languages require all variable type declarations to be checked at compile time, while a loosely or weakly typed language allows for dynamic type checking when an application is run. The use of a strong or weak typed language may can be a key architectural concern to be decided when a system is being developed. The requirements used to determine the use of a strong or weak language may be tied to data integrity or system availability goals, since applications written a strongly typed language should not perform functions with invalid data, resulting in errors. However, code written in a strongly typed language may be less reusable for different functions, leading to additional development work required.

Programming Paradigms

There are certain features of programming languages based on how they achieve the desired process of manipulating or handling data. *Declarative* programming expresses the logic of a task without describing how it should be executed; in these languages, a system must interpret the logic and execute appropriate tasks. SQL is an example of a declarative paradigm, where users issue commands and the DBMS is responsible for executing the commands following its own internal constraints. This abstraction is an important security capability, as it presents opportunities to control what users can and cannot do; for example, a DBMS may implement additional authentication requirements for sensitive SQL functions based on the user's identity.

The *imperative* paradigm of programming uses statements or commands that change a program's state, similar to issuing imperative commands in human languages like "stand up" or "study for the CISSP." Although this kind of direct control could be a security challenge, modern imperative programming often focuses on the use of procedures, sometimes known as *subroutines* or *functions*, which provide for greater control over how the program operates. A standardized subroutine for accessing data in a filesystem can be tested for access control flaws; each time that subroutine is reused, there is assurance that it will implement access controls in a consistent manner. *Procedural programming* is related to the imperative paradigm and is based on the concept of a program calling procedures, which are similar to routines or subroutines. Procedures are a set of steps to be executed and allow these steps to be logically grouped and called dynamically when needed.

Apart from procedures, languages may implement other structures for grouping elements of a program and the logical flow of a program's code. This offers the benefits of increased readability and clarity of the code's function, as well as increased maintainability over time since the code is more easily understood. This practice is called *structured programming*, because the code is structured using constructs like if/then statements that make it obvious what steps a program will execute at a given time. *Block-structured* programming languages utilize bocks as an organizational unit; the scope of program elements like variables and functions is restricted to the block to prevent conflicts with other elements elsewhere in the code.

Object-oriented programming (OOP) is a paradigm that focuses on objects rather than actions in programming. Instead of writing specific commands to gather input data and perform procedures on it, OOP treats both data and functions as objects, known as *classes*, which can be linked together through defined interactions. An object is anything that has a state that can be tracked, like data pending a mathematical transformation to render it unreadable (the process of encryption). Code objects are self-contained modules of functions that are "called" to perform their designated function. Many modern smartphone apps offer image transformations like sharpening a photo; in this case, the photo is a data object, and standard image transformations are code objects in the app. The photo is passed to the image transformation function, and the processed photo is passed back to the user interface once completed.

There are a number of security concepts related to OOP that are important, many of which relate to the abstraction inherent in viewing data and functions as objects that communicate in predefined ways. These concepts include the following:

- **Encapsulation:** This is also known as *data hiding* and is effectively a way of isolating data from being accidentally mishandled. Direct access to a class can be denied to external objects, thereby restricting access to only approved functions known as *methods*.

- **Inheritance:** Classes of data objects can have subclasses that inherit some or all of the main class's characteristics, such as access restrictions. For example, the `Employee` data class might have a `Salary` subclass, which implements the same methods for manipulating the data but additional role-based access control restrictions. This subclass can be reused as a building block, which speeds development.

- **Polymorphism:** This term refers to the multiple (poly) forms (morphs) an object may take when being created or instantiated. Instantiating a new object from an existing object typically duplicates the attributes and methods of the existing object, but data of a different type may cause security concerns because the new data type requires different methods. For example, a function that prints data to the screen is useful for a word processing program but could present security concerns if called to print sensitive data like a password.

- **Polyinstantiation:** This term means making multiple (poly) copies (instances) of an object, typically with the goal of supporting different levels of confidentiality and integrity for that object. Operating systems may create multiple instances of a shared resource space, like virtual memory, to prevent different processes from reading or writing over each other, or databases may create a copy of records for each classification level, omitting information above that classification level. This prevents users at a lower level from even knowing that more-sensitive information exists, reducing the likelihood of inference attacks.

Markup and Scripting Languages

When many people think of computer programming languages, they imagine complex languages like C, which require specialized knowledge and skills. However, languages that provide structure to data or automate basics sets of tasks also meet the definition, as these languages provide instructions as input to computer systems for handling data.

The security of these languages is often overlooked as they are simple enough for even relatively unskilled users to write. However, their use in mobile code environments like web pages delivered via the internet requires that the security be considered, with controls governing where such code may be loaded from or blocking remote code like JavaScript altogether due to its untrusted nature. These languages include the following:

- **Hypertext Markup Language (HTML):** Specifies layout or display elements of text delivered to a web browser.

- **Cascading Style Sheets (CSS):** Allows definition for how a web document should be styled for display, including fonts, color, and layout/spacing of elements on the page.

- **JavaScript:** Provides interactive applications inside a web browser on a client system, often for displaying and manipulating data on the user's screen. JavaScript may require access to privileged functions on user machines such as local file access, which is a major security concern since the code comes from an untrusted party across the internet.

- **Python:** A high-level language that can be used for a variety of uses ranging from small personal programs to large web applications. As an interpreted language, it can run on a variety of platforms and interact with data in other applications, such as a local script written by a single user to automate repetitive tasks like cleaning up data in a spreadsheet, or a distributed web app that communicates with other systems and user browsers via Application Programming Interface (API) calls.

Libraries

Software libraries are prewritten repositories of common functions, code, classes, scripts, procedures, or other software elements. They allow developers to more quickly and easily integrate functionality into programs without the need to write code from scratch, as relevant modules from the library can be called where needed. Many platforms like operating systems, social media networks, and cloud computing services include them in what is known as a *software development kit* (SDK), which speeds the task of developers building programs that integrate these platform's capabilities. In addition to the code or functions, many libraries also include other supporting elements such as help documentation and prewritten code templates.

The features of a library are shared among all programs written using the language or platform of the library, and their value comes from the easy reuse of elements. Not only does this reuse speed development, but it also offers increased dependability of software since these shared functions are likely to be extensively tested and improved by the community of developers and systems implementing the library. Many libraries also offer compliance-focused features, such as user interface components that are designed to meet accessibility requirements, or regulated functions such as credit card processing that can be implemented without the need to address Payment Card Industry Data Security Standard (PCI DSS) compliance.

Libraries typically implement a number of standard features, including subroutines, global variables, and class definitions. Depending on the library, additional capabilities may also be offered, such as prebuilt algorithms for common tasks like encryption, as well as data structures like lists, tables, and arrays. Libraries for specific platforms like operating systems also offer interaction with various functions of the OS, including filesystem access, handling data input/output, and accessing and controlling device through drivers. Programmers using libraries can easily implement these features like building blocks in their programs without going through the full task of writing software for each task.

The use of libraries in the organization should be governed by a number of requirements, including the need for validated libraries that meet proven security requirements. Organizations may use trusted vendor's libraries, develop libraries internally that can be shared across projects, or even use open-source project if the risks are considered acceptable. A library containing vulnerable or malicious code poses a risk to the entire application relying on it.

Toolsets

There are a wide variety of tools to assist programmers, engineers, testers, and others to develop software and systems. They perform various functions including creating and debugging code, maintaining consistency of code when multiple people are working on it, and enabling testing. Many of these tools are combined into toolsets that serve a number of developer needs, such as the following:

- Source code editors, which provide developers the ability to both write and check their code. These are similar to text editors, but include development-specific features like syntax checkers to identify incorrectly written code, library integrations that can automatically suggest appropriate functions, and even prebuilt templates of common functionality that developers can leverage to speed up their work. Functions like comment and documentation generation may also be part of the editor, allowing developers to write explanatory comments that help other developers understand the purpose of a given piece of code or that can be used to automatically generate user documentation about the particular features of a program.

- Code repositories and revision control tools provide centralized storage and integrity protection for code. Centralized storage supports multiple developers working simultaneously, while version control ensures that developers are not able to interfere with one another's work by locking code that is already open for edits and maintaining revision history with timestamps and details of the user who made changes.

- Debuggers and bug databases help developers find and fix issues with their code. Some work by highlighting known issues or identifiable flaws, such as function calls with incorrect inputs, while others can provide line-by-line execution of a program to identify where a particular error is occurring.

- Compilers are designed to create platform-specific application binaries that consist of machine language that can be run on a specific architecture. Many programming languages can be compiled to run on a variety of platforms, allowing developers to write a single program and then use an appropriate compiler for systems they want to support.

- Testing tools typically include static code analysis and unit testing tools. Static code analysis reviews the underlying code of a program without actually running the program itself; the goal is to identify problems like improper coding that could lead to buffer overflow conditions. Data flow analysis may also be performed by these tools, where possible values that a function could generate are reviewed to ensure they meet expected parameters.

Toolsets in use at the organization should be governed by security practices like configuration management, patch management, and audits. Proper versions of approved tools and controlled changes to those tools should be implemented, and the developers using these tools should be trained on their proper use and procedures for maintaining security. This includes only installing approved modules or functions, seeking approval for new modules, and making use of the existing tools to enforce security controls as defined by the organization's secure SDLC procedures.

Integrated Development Environment

An integrated development environment (IDE) is a combination of tools in a single environment, like a desktop program or web application, which supports the work of developers. The goal of combining and integrating tools is to enhance productivity as well as to ensure consistency by reducing the overhead of managing multiple tools. Capabilities frequently incorporated in an IDE include a source code editor, debugging tools, build automation tools like compilers, testing tools, and deployment automation like integrations with container orchestration and deployment platforms including Docker and Kubernetes.

IDEs for OOP languages typically include support features specific to the language, such as a browser for objects available in the language or classes that have been created for the specific program under development, similar to the formula editor in Microsoft Excel. Features of the source code editor may be specific to the language, such as visual programming for languages where classes or objects can be arranged and linked in visual layouts that model the flow of data or execution of a program.

As with toolsets, the security of the IDE should be a focus of the security program as well. The fundamental security of any application under development is impacted by the tools used to build it, so ensuring components of the IDE are approved and maintained is critical.

Runtime

Quite simply, a *runtime* is the collection of all hardware and software required to actually run an application. For many systems, this will be quite complex, as hardware may contain its own software (known as *firmware*) for proper operation, device drivers may be required to allow apps to communicate with the hardware, and an OS will need to coordinate actions and mediate access to the hardware. The various layers of hardware and software required to deliver these information system services are discussed as part of system architecture in Chapter 3, "Security Architecture and Engineering."

The combination of compiled program code, OS, device drivers, and firmware may be all the elements required for a compiled language program to function, though many will access functions or data needed to operate via APIs, remote procedure calls (RPCs), or other service calls. Interpreted languages will also require an interpreter as part of the runtime, which performs the translation of the code to a machine-executable format and may also be responsible for enforcing security controls like sandboxing. As with all information systems, security opportunities and vulnerabilities exist in all elements of a runtime and must be considered and addressed.

For high-security applications, secure hardware such as a trusted computing base (TCB) may be required. A TCB comprises all hardware, software, and firmware responsible for enforcing security and serves the function of a reference monitor to control access and enforce security policies within the system. Properly design, testing, and isolation of the TCB elements is required to achieve the TCB, which then supports trusted secure access to the system and its resources. The TCB is a primary candidate for configuration and change management, as are all OSs and information system components since they are obvious implementation points for both technical security controls like encryption and process security controls like patch management.

The traditional model of a runtime many people visualize consists of a desktop computer (or laptop) running a standard OS like macOS or Windows. Trends like Internet of Things (IoT) and edge computing now mean that the collection of hardware and software needed to perform computing functions is much broader. Smart washing machines, thermostats, and sensor-enabled devices are part of the runtime environment and may include some basic data acquisition and processing capabilities. Many of these devices rely on networking technologies like WiFi or Bluetooth to synchronize data, meaning these are part of the overall IoT runtime environment and must be considered as part of the organization's security plan.

Continuous Integration and Continuous Delivery

Development methodologies like Agile dramatically reduce the time it takes to deliver functional software, often cutting development time from years to months or even weeks. The driving factor is to support users by releasing functional software more rapidly to meet business and functional needs. *Continuous integration* (CI) is the practice of continuously merging developer's code to a shared main location, often known as a *repository*. Integrating code more frequently reduces the cost and time required to do large-scale reconciliation and integration activities like debugging any issues caused by the newly written or modified code. This in turn supports the Agile goal of delivering a progressive set of features with each iteration, rather than a monolithic deployment.

A code repository is an implementation of configuration management that enforces rules on how items enter and leave the controlled state. As an example, in the GitHub repository model, a developer creates a pull request that highlights the changes being introduced with the new code. The pull request must undergo inspection like manual review by other developers or automated testing before it is merged back into the base code branch. Automated security testing can also be combined with these integration activities. Although automated scanning can't find everything, performing it more frequently and on smaller units of code can increase its overall effectiveness.

Continuous delivery (CD) is a process that delivers code automatically to an environment other than live production or requires some manual steps to deploy to a production environment. This is often used in software development where a testing environment with manual testing processes is required, such as systems processing regulated or sensitive data, or complex systems where automation may not be possible. In these cases manual verification must be performed before new code goes live. The completion of testing can be an automated trigger to deploy the new code, or deployment may be manual after the testing is completed.

A closely-related and somewhat confusing term is continuous deployment (also referred to with the acronym CD), which extends the concept of CI by taking the integrated code and deploying it to the production environment automatically with no manual intervention needed — unless an automated step fails. Achieving continuous deployment demands a high degree of maturity in an organization's automated QA and testing processes, to ensure that code is thoroughly tested and passes before being deployed. Automated functional, integration, and regression testing are often required to ensure the newly developed code does not break the system or introduces bugs.

The combination of tools and processes to implement CI/CD is often known as a *pipeline*, and this pipeline includes all the steps and requirements to deliver functional software to the production environment. This will include manual steps like writing code and addressing any errors that arise, as well as automated steps like running tests and scans. Packaging the code, such as building containers, and deploying it are the final stages of the pipeline. CI/CD pipelines will span multiple systems from an IDE to a code repository to a cloud hosting environment, and each system and step in the pipeline is a chance to implement security controls like integrity verification, encryption to protect confidentiality, and manual or automated testing and reviews.

Emphasis on Testing in CI/CD Pipelines

CI/CD relies heavily on automation to achieve speed. Rather than manually building the computer hardware, OSs, and enabling applications like web servers, a CI/CD pipeline will likely take advantage of virtualized or cloud computing where these activities can be automated and orchestrated using definition files. These definition files specify the required computing resources that need to be provisioned when an application is deployed, and this practice is called *infrastructure as code* (IaC). Configuration management, testing, and auditing are much easier since definition files exist to specify exactly what the software and virtual hardware configuration should be; a CISSP can achieve a great deal of security impact by implementing small, automated, and repeatable security checks into this automated pipeline.

Application security (AppSec) is another important automated testing function supporting CI/CD pipelines. Although automated testing is not a total replacement for manual testing activities, it does offer several advantages. It can be performed more frequently than manual testing, often with each deployment or change, and it can test a larger portion of the application due to the speed of computerized testing. Unit, functional, and regression testing should all be included in automated testing activities, as well as security-specific testing like vulnerability scanning. DevOps and security practitioners can identify ways to design an AppSec program using Agile principles, with the goal of integrating security within a CI/CD pipeline to ensure security requirements are met without impeding the agility of the organization. Practices like continuous security codify many of these principles, and more details can be found at `devops.com/9-pillars-of-continuous-security-best-practices`.

Automated testing tools can shift the balance of work away from the security team and break down an important barrier that often leads to issues. Security testing is typically done by security personnel, and then results must be communicated to the developers. This transfer can cause information to be lost or miscommunicated, leaving security vulnerabilities unaddressed. Automated tools can be integrated into the IDE, allowing the testing results to be communicated directly to developers. For example, an application security vulnerability scanner may run automatically as code progresses to the testing environment, where it finds a SQL injection flaw on a particular page of a web app. Using an API, this finding — including the specific test case, address of the page, and other details — can be put immediately into a ticket and assigned to the developer responsible for that web app feature. The developer still has the code fresh in their mind and can easily use the data supplied to fix the flaw.

Security Orchestration, Automation, and Response

Security orchestration, automation, and response (SOAR) is a recently introduced term that combines multiple processes and domains, typically offered as a software platform or set of integrated tools. Its primary goal is to speed the time to detect and respond to security incidents, and it achieves this by integrating disparate data sources and systems to coordinate automated actions. SOAR is often confused with security information and event management (SIEM), but SIEM tools simply ingest data to support response activities by correlating data and generating alerts for human responders. The difference is similar to intrusion detection versus intrusion prevention: intrusion detection systems (IDSs) generate an alert, while intrusion prevention systems (IPSs) take action automatically to stop the intrusion.

Orchestration

This is where SIEM and SOAR have some overlap, in that they both integrate data from disparate systems into a single data set. However, SOAR goes beyond logs and includes data from security tools like user and entity behavior analytics (UEBA), IDS/IPS, external threat intelligence services, and domain-specific solutions like email anti-phishing tools, anti-malware, application security scanners, etc. In many cases, alerts on suspicious activity from a SIEM will be an input to a SOAR platform, relying on the SIEM's ability to correlate data across networks or systems. The use of APIs is critical for data ingestion as well as exposing functionality on the target systems to enable automation of responses. For example, a user receiving a phishing email that includes a malicious file will trigger alerts from an anti-malware tool and a UEBA agent, which the SOAR can identify as being related to a specific user, email, and set of actions. Orchestrating data from these disparate systems into coherent, actionable intelligence is the first step of value in a SOAR solution.

Automation

In the previous example, the malicious file download might trigger anti-malware action on the affected user's machine, such as quarantining the file, deleting malicious data, and alerting an administrator to the infection. However, that alert in isolation might miss the fact that other users received the same email or that the attachment exploited a flaw that could execute a worm that spread itself to other endpoints, where detection may or may not occur. Such a holistic overview of the problem requires an incident responder to investigate not only the cause of the malware but also its impact across the network, and this is a complex, time-consuming, and error-prone task. Orchestrated intelligence flowing to the SOAR enables automated response much faster than the speed of a human investigation.

Automation follows a set of machine-executable rules, often collected in a playbook or other set of instructions designed to respond to specific triggers like malware detection. The advantage of SOAR over legacy methods is the speed with which it executes. Speed is critical since this is a countermeasure activated after a risk event has occurred, and the goal is to reduce the duration and impact of the incident. Automating actions like forcing a password change after a user's workstation has been impacted by malware, isolating the affected machine from the network, quarantining or deleting the email from other users' inboxes, and opening an incident response case with relevant details prepopulated saves time and reduces the window of opportunity for the attack to do damage.

Response

SOAR evolves incident response from the legacy model of detecting and manually responding to a coordinated, automated response in which human expertise, knowledge, and talent are utilized in the most efficient manner possible. Information systems can receive and act on data faster than human analysts; even a fully staffed, 24/7 security operations center (SOC) will exhibit slower response times compared to an automated system with visibility into and automation abilities across the infrastructure. Repetitive or easily automated tasks can be handled by the SOAR platform, like identifying a malicious email received by one user and deleting it from the inboxes of other users before they click on links or open malicious attachments. This frees up human time and attention to focus on novel threats; the SOAR can also augment human capabilities by pulling together meaningful information to speed decision-making and reduce the time needed to respond to incidents, which again reduces their impact on the organization.

By way of example, consider the previously detailed malicious email incident. The original user who opened a phishing email likely triggered alerts due to the presence of malware on the network. The SOAR can take in relevant information as part of orchestration and then execute automated responses triggered by incoming data. In addition to the isolation steps mentioned already, the SOAR could also initiate malware scans to detect lateral movement throughout the network and institute firewall blocks to prevent traffic to any malicious sites or IP addresses associated with the phishing email and malware. These actions can be performed in mere seconds, while a human might take minutes just reading the initial alerts.

SOAR doesn't seek to completely remove human intervention in incident response. Many of the platforms include incident response case-management tools, with the aim of consolidating information needed for decision-making and providing automated chains of actions that can initiated by the responder. To continue the malicious email example, once the automated response is carried out, an incident case file may be created and assigned to a human responder. The case will include all relevant data including the impacted users, automated actions like password resets, and recommended manual next steps in the process. Presenting all information relevant to the incident in a single location allows the responder to make better informed and quicker decisions and can also provide a consistent source of information to all members of the response team.

Any system that implements automated responses, such as a SOAR or IPS, can suffer the problem of false positives leading to unwanted action. A SOAR might suspend a user's account if suspicious login activity is detected, but if the user is legitimately traveling or working outside normal hours on a critical time-sensitive task, the SOAR has created a denial-of-service (DOS) condition. Adjusting these tools to reduce the chances of false positives is achieved by *tuning*, which effectively trains them on the specifics of an organization's environment. This process is discussed in more detail in Domain 7, especially in the context of tools implementing artificial intelligence (AI).

Software Configuration Management

Software configuration management (SCM) is the implementation of configuration and change management practices to support secure software development. Its main purpose is to provide integrity for key software resources like source code and program resources like requirements documentation. These items placed under configuration management are known as configuration items (CIs). Each CI must be uniquely identified, and changes to CIs must follow a rigorous change process to ensure the changes are coordinated and do not introduce flaws or break functionality.

Common CIs include source code, software libraries, and individual configuration settings such as patch levels or software settings; together, a group of CIs represents a baseline, which is a known good configuration of a system. When choosing a set of CIs, it is important to balance the number of items being managed with their criticality. Controlling every script file or line of help documentation may be desired, but the extra time and overhead of managing so many items under configuration control can introduce unwanted operational delays.

Baselines represent a stable set of immutable configuration items that collectively provide a functional system — note that this term is also used in the context of security controls, where a baseline represents the minimum set of required controls. SCM baselines are often associated with desired system characteristics such as security settings and configurations or functionality requirements, such as the known good settings to enforce encryption requirements or versions of COTS products required for system functionality. Because the CIs comprising a baseline are under configuration management, changes to baselines must follow the change management process. This is often done by creating a branch, which is a set of versioned CIs undergoing development or change separate from the known baseline. Testing, quality assurance, and acceptance criteria must all be satisfied before the branch is merged back and the changes are incorporated into the baseline.

SCM's chief goal is to promote visibility and control over the state of and changes to all the elements in a software system. Changes can introduce bugs or flaws that negatively impact fundamental security concepts of confidentiality, integrity, availability, nonrepudiation, and authenticity (CIANA), and it is imperative to preserve the integrity of system elements like source code, requirements documentation, and settings. Uncontrolled changes can introduce vulnerabilities or have other unintended consequences. In the field of SCM, version control is often used as a way to identify software elements, based on a version number, and control changes to them by enforcing rules about how and when new versions are created. Tools that implement this management are known as source code version control or revision control systems.

Code Repositories

Repositories, or *repos* as they are commonly known, are a cornerstone of modern software development and provide key features needed to support multi-user teams developing software. They provide a centralized storage location and support collaborative work by allowing multiple users to access and make changes, as well as implementing restrictions such as branching, which allow a user to pull code and make nondestructive changes isolated from the main code. When complete, the changes can be tested and merged back into the main code.

Protecting Source Code

Source code is a valuable asset that faces risks just like any other data in the organization. A repository provides many points of control over the source code in support of the security fundamentals of CIANA, and the repository itself is a valuable asset due to its control capabilities and valuable contents. Implementing controls on the repository can be used to achieve security objectives including the following:

- **Confidentiality:** Repos provide access controls in the form of authorization. Some are more granular than others and allow for developers to be granted separate read and write permissions to specific projects, code modules, or branches, while others simply restrict the repo to access only by authorized users. Additional features to protect confidentiality may also include restrictions such as preventing copying of data to local computers or portable media devices, which allows for greater control over the dissemination of source code.

- **Integrity:** Most code repositories implement some form of configuration management and version control for software. Open-source collaborative projects may configure the repo to allow any authorized user to make changes, while a tightly controlled project may require a developer be specifically authorized to work on a particular software element. Some repos integrate with project management or ticketing systems to allow for dynamic access controls; for example, a developer is assigned a task to update a specific module, which grants them temporary write access that module's code. Version control systems that allow rollback to a previous version can also be used as a countermeasure to unintended or undesirable changes.

- **Availability:** The centralized nature of a repo can be a single point of failure. Having a single system hosting all data also makes it easier to back up and restore the system, as a robust backup schedule for that system guarantees that all the required data is available when needed.

- **Nonrepudiation:** Access control mechanisms implemented in repositories — such as unique user IDs, audit trails, and version history — can be used to identify and hold users accountable for changes they made to source code.

- **Authenticity:** Data is authentic if it can be proven that no corruption or unwanted alteration has occurred, and source code repositories can implement this using version control to roll back unwanted changes and using backups to support integrity.

Protecting the Repository

Apart from offering security benefits for managing code, software repos are themselves valuable assets in need of protection. They are valuable targets for a number of reasons, including the fact that they host sensitive data and can be used to introduce unwanted software or functionality. For this reason, the repo itself needs to be treated like all other valuable assets, with a risk assessment and corresponding security mitigations such as the following:

- **Data:** Tools like data loss prevention (DLP) and intrusion detection should be deployed to monitor data and activity on repository systems and hosts.

- **Communication and network:** Proper security measures to control and monitor access to the repository must be in place. Due to the remotely accessible nature and increased trend of distributed systems, it is particularly important to secure remote network access by implementing protocols like HTTPS and Transport Layer Security (TLS), or secure access solutions like a VPN or proxy service.

- **Access control:** Principles of minimum necessary and least privilege must be considered, and access control procedures such as request approvals and routine reviews should also be implemented.

- **Backup and availability:** Since software is the foundation of most modern business processes, the source code and resources needed to deploy it, such as IaC definitions or build instructions, are fundamentally important assets for preserving availability. Cloud-hosted software repositories offer high availability and resilient configurations, though organizations with stricter requirements may be forced to host and maintain their own repos. In all cases, the configurations should support the organization's availability goals by ensuring software code is accessible when needed.

Application Security Testing

Application security starts with the security of the code comprising the program. In an ideal world, this would require only a preventative approach — with unlimited time and resources, all possible bugs could be prevented. Sadly, that is not how most software development projects work, and there are a number of factors, such as legacy code and the evolution of software exploits, which mean application security must incorporate active hunting for vulnerabilities. This full lifecycle approach encompasses application design and SDLC management practices as discussed throughout this chapter, as well as ongoing assessment and hunting for flaws or vulnerabilities in existing code.

There are a number of application testing paradigms, outlined next. The best approach to application security testing will combine multiple approaches based on what components make up the system, as well as the organization's tools, knowledge, and maturity at performing software testing.

- **Static application security testing (SAST):** SAST evaluates source code and other nonrunning application elements like compiled binaries. It can be easily incorporated in an IDE and the developer workflow, with automated testing performed when developers check code in and immediate feedback to developers in a format that is easy for them to understand. Testing is performed in development or testing environments, which means there is no impact to live production environments.

- **SAST disadvantages:** SAST tools can typically understand only one programming language, so different tools will be required if multiple languages are in use. They may also be difficult for nondevelopers to access due to their IDE integration, meaning security practitioners who aren't developers are excluded. Since they do not test running applications, complex vulnerabilities due to interfaces between code and underlying system elements like OS exploits cannot be detected.

- **Dynamic application security testing (DAST):** The word *dynamic* is part of DAST and describes how these testing tools execute the application to look for flaws. They can typically run against any application with an interface or API regardless of underlying language and are not as tightly integrated with an IDE, which means access is easier for nondevelopers. Some include integrations with IDE or CI/CD pipeline tools; for example, an automated DAST scan is initiated when new code is pushed to a testing environment, and any findings are automatically pushed into developer tickets or task assignments.

  - **DAST disadvantages:** Due to their possible existence outside the developer's toolset, there may be organizational challenges related to getting information to the correct developer. Some DAST tools are designed for continuous monitoring of production environments as a detective measure; this may cause performance issues and, more importantly, allows software with flaws to enter production environments where it could be exploited until discovered.

- **Interactive application security testing (IAST):** This emerging set of tools and abilities combines elements of SAST, DAST, and penetration testing, often using complex algorithms and machine learning to analyze source code and correlate vulnerabilities discovered during dynamic testing. It has largely emerged since the rise of CI/CD practices, so most tools offer integrations with both developer tools and security platforms, ensuring better visibility into the testing efforts and results.

  - **IAST disadvantages:** Like any emerging technology, there will be growing pains like higher costs for in-demand new features and a lack of expertise in the marketplace. Since IAST incorporates source-code analysis like SAST, it is also language-dependent, meaning some languages may not be supported and the dynamic elements of IAST may cause performance issues if run in a production environment.

- **Runtime application self-protection (RASP):** As the name *runtime* implies, RASP executes alongside the application as it is run; RASP is also less of a testing tool but is often incorporated into overall application security to complement SAST and DAST. A RASP security tool integrates with an application and analyzes the program's execution to spot unusual or unexpected behavior, and then it takes corrective action. This can include blocking specific requests or functions to shut down an active attack and also implementing preventative measures like virtually patching an application to prevent the same attack vector from being used in the future.

  - **RASP disadvantages:** Like any automated reactive technology, false positive RASP hits can lead to DOS, much like an IPS shutting down unexpected but legitimate traffic. Similar to IAST, as a relatively recent technology, RASP will suffer from compatibility and a gap in skills to configure and manage the tools.

ASSESS THE EFFECTIVENESS OF SOFTWARE SECURITY

Software security must be measured to gauge its effectiveness and drive improvement over time, similar to concepts of measuring and auditing the effectiveness of security programs, like SOC 2 auditing, which was discussed in Chapter 6, "Security Assessment and Testing." Logging and auditing changes to software environments, not just production but also development environments, provides critical data needed to verify the integrity of software powering critical information systems. Risk analysis and mitigation, while a common practice across all domains of information security, requires specific practices for software security to ensure adequate treatment of software's unique risks. These include risks to applications and information systems, as well as to software development tools and the source code itself, both of which are valuable assets.

Auditing and Logging of Changes

Events can happen several thousand times a day in information systems of even moderate complexity. Users log in and out, applications and services start and stop, users enter incorrect passwords, servers and processes are restarted, and so on, all of which are non-malicious and expected actions. For example, a standard Windows 10 workstation used during a regular workday can easily generate tens of thousands of logged events; reviewing each of these manually is a virtually impossible task.

Most events change the state of the system in some way; for example, a server restarting means the system is not available for a period of time. This could be caused by an unexpected power failure or by a new deployment of code that adds user-demanded functionality. Keeping track of these changes and providing visibility into which are normal and which are not is crucial for diagnosing issues and for remediating events that rise to the level of security incidents.

Auditing and logging are different, though often confused, terms. They are often used interchangeably, such as in audit logs, even though each term actually has its own definition. These crucial terms, along with other related concepts, are defined here:

- Auditing is an official or systematic inspection of something such as an account, documents, or practices. In software environments, audits focus on the implementation and effectiveness of software security controls, and they often rely on an official standard of comparison such as the ISO, NIST, or OWASP security frameworks. Auditing processes like change management and QA often rely on data captured during normal process execution, which is where log data becomes important. Logs themselves may be subject to audit to identify instances of behavior that go against organization requirements, such as users attempting to access unauthorized resources.

- Logging is merely the recording of events. In a software system, logs are generated by all system events, like users signing into an application, and the logs should capture sufficient detail to definitely identify critical information about the event. This includes what the event was, who/what initiated the action, when it occurred (often called a *timestamp*), and other metadata about the event like a criticality level. Some events will be categorized as incidents if they violate security controls or cause a degradation of the system.

- Accountability is the ability to identify who or what is responsible for events that occur and is a key element of identity and access management. Sufficient data is obviously required; if log files do not record usernames or timestamps, it will be impossible to identify which user took a particular action at any given time.

- Nonrepudiation is an indisputable proof of a unique individual having performed a specific action. This concept is often confusing because it is a negative — repudiating an action means refusing to accept responsibility. Nonrepudiation, therefore, means having sufficient proof to prevent a user from denying that they took the action. Not all log data will support nonrepudiation; for example, physical access logs collected at a main door are not sufficient to prove a particular employee was in a specific location within the building, unless access controls create log data as the employee moves about the facility.

Applications of Logging and Auditing

Log generation and routine audits are both reactive and detective controls. Logs are generated after an action has occurred, so they do not work to prevent a risk being realized, though they support monitoring activities that detect when something has gone wrong. Logs are only made useful when audit and monitoring processes make use of them; much like policies, they are useless if documented but never read or used. SIEM tools ingest log data as a primary input and then perform monitoring activities on the collected data to look for suspicious or unwanted behavior. SIEMs typically perform this monitoring on a continuous and near real-time basis, and alerts generated are key inputs to the detection phase of incident response procedures.

Audits are a more formal and structured process of reviewing activity against an expected baseline, often as a way to demonstrate compliance with a legal, regulatory, or other compliance burden. Assessments are a more informal process of review and are often conducted to satisfy internal oversight goals rather than external compliance requirements. Log data is crucial for audits, as it presents a record of system activity over a period of time, which confirms if an organization is functioning in accordance with documented governance. For example, if all software changes must follow change management procedures, then version history in the software repository should align with documented change requests.

Source code management (SCM) is a particularly important application of logging and auditing for software security. SCM provides capabilities to track code changes being stored in a repository, sometimes down to the level of individual lines of code. These logs can be useful for operational troubleshooting if a particular piece of code is causing errors and can also be used to audit compliance by identifying code changes that might diverge from identified requirements. Code integrity is also maintained, as unintended or unwanted changes can be rolled back to known good versions.

Logging in operational environments provides insight into the activities being performed by users and processes while a system is in active use. These logs are often used for access reviews or audits, as well as investigations of both operational and security incidents. Examples of events that are typically logged include users signing in and out of systems or applications, application errors encountered during processing, and even environmental control issues like power fluctuations and hardware disruptions. Events like user sign-ins may be useful only for audit and forensic analysis, but operations teams may monitor log data for hardware and environmental controls, as these may be precursors to a failure that negatively impacts system availability.

Log data can be used for a variety of monitoring purposes by multiple teams in an organization, including the following:

- **Change management:** Logs of system changes like new app installations or changes to access permissions can be used to verify whether changes made correspond to approved change requests.

- **Security incidents:** Live production environments, especially those with public- or external-facing elements like web servers, will see a variety of suspicious and malicious activity. Logging and monitoring these actions are crucial tasks for security practitioners and often form a key pillar of security analysts' and incident responders' job functions.

- **Performance management:** Although not an obvious security task, availability is a component of security. Ensuring systems are running, reachable, and able to support the required user load can be achieved by monitoring various metrics from log files, such as CPU utilization, memory consumption, and network band-width usage.

- **Cloud environment changes:** When consuming cloud services, most organi-zations will lose physical and some logical visibility over parts of their IT infra-structure. Rather than deploying network sensors to detect problems, web pages or APIs with status information will provide vital logs and monitoring data, such as when a service began to experience degradation or an outage and when it is restored. As with other control modifications to accommodate cloud computing, logging and monitoring must take into account what types of data are made avail-able for monitoring and how to make effective use of the data.

There are definitive resources for logging and monitoring practices as well as audit standards. NIST SP 800-92, "Guide to Computer Security Log Management," and the OWASP Logging Cheat Sheet cover basics like policy requirements and best practices for implementing logging functions. Many compliance frameworks mandate certain types of logs or require that logs generally contain sufficient data to support account-ability. These compliance frameworks, such as PCI DSS, also provide auditing stan-dards for assessing the implementation and operating effectiveness of security controls including logging.

Software Development Auditing

Audits are an important compliance tool for verifying conformance with established gov-ernance and are discussed in more detail in Domain 6. Software development projects should be audited to ensure desired security controls are followed when creating secure software, as well as to ensure software under development is implementing the required functions to meet security requirements. Audits are useful across multiple aspects of the business outside of security as well, such as schedule, budget, and resource management, to ensure projects are running smoothly and meeting deadlines, which enables business objectives like launching new products or staying ahead of competitors.

Auditing activities differ at various phases of the SDLC, and the audit program needs to be adaptable to fit various SDLC methodologies. An annual audit schedule may catch large Waterfall projects in the same phase each year, so evidence collection should be an ongoing activity throughout the year to ensure auditors have a complete picture when they perform reviews. Considerations at each phase of the SDLC include the following:

- **Requirements phase:** Audit artifacts from this phase will mostly be documentation such as requirements analysis documents and the documented requirements themselves. Key activities to audit include reviews like privacy impact assessment (PIA) and data classification or system categorization. Ensuring complete requirements and documented understanding is critical to designing and building a system with adequate protection mechanisms for data.

- **Design phase:** During design, alternatives will be evaluated against requirements, such as cloud versus on-premises hosting for a system. Key activities to be audited include the formal risk assessment and decision processes utilized to determine which of the proposed solution alternatives adequately meet the stated requirements, and formal acceptance of the residual risk.

- **Implementation phase:** Hands-on activities like writing code, testing system functionality, and security tests like code reviews or penetration tests should all be in scope for the audit program. Auditors may perform documentation reviews to verify testing activities were conducted and the results properly acted upon, and they may conduct interviews with developer personnel to test the level of knowledge regarding key processes and procedures. Testing is also an important audit method used to demonstrate that processes and technical controls respond as expected, like trying actions known to violate separation of duties policies and ideally observing the actions being blocked. For example, an auditor might write and attempt to deploy code using the same user account to verify that system controls are in place to block the deployment.

- **Verification phase:** Audits of testing activity are important to verify oversight functions are implemented and effective. These should include checks for adequately designed test cases or data, coverage of testing, execution of all required testing, and successfully passing required tests before system deployment.

- **Operation and maintenance phase:** Since systems will spend most of their life in this phase, the bulk of auditing occurs here. Systems in this phase may also be subject to more external audits, as many laws and regulations require auditing on live production systems. Many audit frameworks now incorporate live system audits as well as SDLC auditing, due to the key role that secure software development plays in overall system security.

✔ **Auditing CI/CD Environments**

Auditing has evolved over time from a static, point-in-time activity to a continuous monitoring model that recognizes the continually evolving nature of risk. Continuous monitoring relies heavily on automation of audit activities, such as configuration management checks performed by a security tool every 24 hours rather than an annual review by a human. Audits validate the implementation and operating effectiveness of risk mitigation controls, so waiting years between these checks is simply ineffective! CI/CD environments also implement more frequent, faster performance, though for software delivery rather than auditing.

Audit programs must adapt to ensure this sped-up delivery doesn't sacrifice security. In some cases, this will involve both automation as well as near real-time execution of the automated checks for compliance. Some organizations will perform audits against their live production environment, while others may perform automated system configuration automated scanning in a staging or preproduction environment. If any errors are found, the deployment is halted, but if all checks pass, the process can continue. This ensures the CI/CD goal of more frequent, functional software deployments is met without sacrificing the security of the system.

Automation can also reduce human error in the scanning and audit process. Repeatedly building a system by hand introduces risk, while automation ensures the system is configured the same every time. Shifting the focus of audits is one method of adaptation — rather than auditing all production system configurations, it may be more effective to focus audit and QA efforts on the infrastructure definitions used to create those production servers. Of course, spot checks of the live production environment should also be performed to verify whether configuration drift is occurring.

Risk Analysis and Mitigation

Risk assessment, analysis, and treatment are covered in depth in Chapter 1, "Security and Risk Management," so concepts including risk tolerance and methods for assessing and mitigating risk are not covered here. Software development and security requires ongoing assessment and mitigation of risks, so these concepts must be applied across all SDLC phases and software environments including development and end user or live production. The goals are still the same, chiefly identifying assets to protect, likelihood and impact of various vulnerabilities and related threats, and the most cost-effective ways to manage the risks.

Software risks require unique analysis approaches, and the first step is determining targets for analysis. Aspects of software development environments and practices that should be considered when performing this risk assessment include the following:

- **Data risks:** Information systems store, transmit, and process information that requires protection, so the systems themselves are often at risk due to their role in handling data. The complex assortment of software, hardware, and technology services like network connections and data centers make it difficult to find a starting point for the analysis, and the sheer number of information systems in many organizations multiplies the challenge. Security practitioners should prioritize based on classification levels; systems handling the most sensitive or highly regulated data are likely to cause the most impact in case of a breach. That doesn't mean lower-sensitivity systems can be ignored, however, and the possibility of an adversary compromising a lower-classified system and pivoting to a higher one must also be considered.

- **New technology risk:** Information systems running standardized commercial software with well-known configuration and support needs (and with proper support and maintenance) are usually less risky than emerging technologies. A lack of knowledge and expertise increases the likelihood of a misconfiguration when deploying systems based on new or emerging technology, and their novelty can mean security options are not yet available. Smartphones are a recent example — although workstation operating systems had advanced full disk encryption (FDE) when smartphones were originally popularized, hardware and software limitations meant FDE support on smartphones was limited. This restricted the risk mitigation options available to organizations using these devices.

- **System changes:** There are a variety of reasons a system might change over time. Organizational needs evolve, new technologies become available, and old technologies cease to be supported. System changes can introduce new risks and significantly alter existing risks, though in some cases, changes may reduce or eliminate risks as well. Migrating a legacy application from on-premises hosting to a cloud-based microservices architecture can reduce the likelihood of system outages due to high availability cloud services, but the loss of physical control over data center hardware adds physical security risk while simultaneously changing the mitigation options available. Rather than physical locks and access controls, organizations might use insurance to transfer risk of data theft at a cloud provider, as well as additional encryption to reduce the impact of data theft. These risks should be identified as part of change management, and requirements must be documented and carried through all SDLC phases to address these risks appropriately and test the mitigations in place.

- **Code risks:** Software is code, and unintended or malicious changes introduce serious risk to all elements of security. Improperly handled changes can introduce bugs or flaws rendering a system unavailable, while the integrity and authenticity of data processed by a system can be compromised by unapproved code changes. SDLC activities like code reviews, change management, testing, and vulnerability management should all be designed to detect and correct these risks. Code is also a source of confidentiality risk, as improperly programmed and configured systems will not implement the desired levels of data confidentiality.

Risk Assessment and Treatment

Risk assessment methodologies are covered in Domain 1 and include a variety of approaches for understanding the likelihood and impact of various risks on the organization's operations. There are best practice–based standards for performing risk assessments across entire organizations or individual information systems, including ISO and NIST. Frameworks for risk assessments in technology and information security include Operationally Critical Threat, Asset, and Vulnerability Evaluation (OCTAVE) and Failure Modes and Effect Analysis (FMEA).

Risk analysis is one component of risk assessment and involves a systematic review of the identified risks for the impact or likelihood. Specifically, to software development security, a CISSP should be able to assist various teams responsible for software development and delivery with tasks like identifying system- or software-specific risks. Once identified, these risks require mitigation plans to reduce either the likelihood or impact to a level below the organization's defined risk threshold.

Sources of risk in software development or points where risks can be detected in the SDLC include the following:

- **Planning:** The organization's approach to system development can introduce operational risks like schedule or budget concerns. If security is broadly planned as one day of testing before a system launches, it is unlikely the security effort will be effective, or findings will be adequately remediated.

- **Requirements:** New system features, like exposing systems to access from the internet or adding new features like credit card processing, introduce risks such as new attack vectors or regulatory compliance burdens.

- **Design:** The chosen design for a system may increase or decrease various risks like remote access, lack of features to support needed security controls, or cloud vendor lock-in. For example, a choice of one cloud vendor and DBMS may introduce limits to the granularity of access controls or available encryption options. The cost of an alternative DBMS or cloud provider may be too high, which drives the need for compensating security controls.

- **Development:** While being developed, all the security controls discussed in this chapter must be addressed to mitigate software development risks. This includes appropriate use of developer toolsets, proper use of secure coding guidelines and standards, and testing to ensure the software being developed meets both functional and security requirements.

- **Operations and maintenance:** The vast majority of risks against a system impact it during live use by end users. The routine assessment of risk and a continuous monitoring program will be crucial to measuring these risks and the effectiveness of chosen mitigations. Key sources for identifying new risks will include the routine risk assessment as well incident response processes.

  Ongoing processes like patch and vulnerability management, monitoring threat intelligence and continuous monitoring via the SOC all take place during the operations phase. Addressing maintenance issues like applying patches, system upgrades, or preventative maintenance are also crucial risk mitigation activities performed during this phase.

Mitigation Strategies

As with risk assessment, mitigation strategies including cost-benefit analysis, risk mitigation versus risk transfer, and residual risk acceptance are covered in Chapter 1, "Security and Risk Management." When discussing security control selection for software development, it is important to note that implementation of these controls must be integrated into existing SDLC processes for the systems they are designed to protect.

Some costs to be measured when performing the analysis include direct costs like software or product purchases, professional services support, and operating costs like support contracts. Indirect costs may be more difficult to define or measure discretely due to the commingling of many factors in a development project. For example, it might be difficult to definitely state how much additional testing time is attributable to implementation of a new security control when a development sprint also included other features. Indirect impacts like staff productivity can also be difficult to discretely measure. A drop in productivity after the launch of a new security control process might be attributable to the control's overhead, but other factors like seasonal productivity loss during summer and winter vacations or a large number of untrained new hires could also be the cause. Costs must be measured to guide selection of a mitigation strategy, but uncertainty and accounting for other factors should also be considered, and in very complex situations, a qualitative measurement may be the best course of action to prevent becoming bogged down by the measurement process.

Measuring the benefits of security controls can be similarly difficult, especially if the benefits are a negative or hypothetical. Measuring the cost of a user abandoning a signup process, which leads to lost business, can be done by looking at the average revenue generated by a customer. Deciding whether to add additional authentication requirements that lead to some users abandoning the signup process can utilize this data. The cost of, for example, not being sued due to inadequate authentication security measures or negligence is difficult to quantify, while the price of a lawsuit against the organization is obviously easier to measure but difficult to hypothesize before it occurs.

Qualitative impact measurement can help in these situations; for example, a "minor" incident is unlikely to result in a business-ending fine, while a "catastrophic" incident could cause the business to become insolvent. Partial quantitative measurements can also be made by looking at publicly available data on similar events that impacted peer organizations or publicly available studies like the annual Verizon Data Breach Investigation Report (DBIR), available at `enterprise.verizon.com/resources/reports/dbir`. Security practitioners will often find that they need to justify security controls based on nonsecurity benefits as well, such as enhanced usability of a cloud-based system for a mobile or remote workforce. In many cases, the end result of the cost-benefit analysis will be a presentation to management of various alternatives to mitigate, transfer, and ultimately accept residual risk, so the costs as well as any benefits resulting from controls must be clearly documented and communicated.

ASSESS SECURITY IMPACT OF ACQUIRED SOFTWARE

With regard to security, acquired software is more complicated to assess and control than custom-built software. The situation is similar to the added complexity of managing third-party service providers that are not directly bound by your organization's policies and procedures. When software is developed by an organization, it is possible to implement and gain direct evidence of security controls in place throughout the SDLC. The ability to proactively control software development processes or make software fixes to address vulnerabilities typically does not exist when the organization does not control the development processes. This loss of control may seem like an unacceptable security risk, but it is balanced against the similarly steep costs of trying to develop skills and resources needed to build complex information systems. Acquiring software from the appropriate source can speed the achievement of critical business objectives, and compensating security controls should be chosen to mitigate risk to an acceptable level.

Commercial Off-the-Shelf

As the name implies, commercial off-the-shelf (COTS) software is readily available for sale to the public and may be purchased, licensed, or leased. COTS can be expensive, but the expense is offset by the availability of support, a more robust feature set available from a dedicated vendor, or the speed at which the software can be deployed due to its design for specific use cases. The most immediate security drawback of COTS software is the lack of visibility into the source code and development practices, and organizations using it have no ability to make direct changes — they may be able to request changes, but the vendor is not obliged to make them. Most software vendors do not provide any visibility, though some share audit and assurance reports like code scanning or a certification like ISO 27001, which provides assurance over the vendor's security program, or ISO 27034, which provides assurance over the vendor's application security controls.

The US Cybersecurity & Infrastructure Security Agency (CISA) maintains a best practices guide for managing COTS software security: (`www.us-cert.cisa.gov/bsi/ articles/best-practices/legacy-systems/security-considerations-in-managing- cots-software`). Although cloud hosting and novel IT services like serverless and microservices architectures are increasingly adopted for modern information systems, the guidance provided in the COTS Security Considerations document is relevant to many organizations with legacy or on-prem hosted systems. This includes the following:

- **Identifying why COTS is risky:** Well-known and widely used software such as Microsoft Windows and Internet Information Services are also well known by threat actors. Wide adoption of these systems increases the profitability of exploiting them since the pool of potential targets is bigger, and the software developer typically has limited liability in the event a flaw in their software leads to a security incident. A CISSP should be aware of the cost-benefit trade-offs of using COTS, which should be factored into organizational risk-based decisions such as build versus buy.

- **Common methods of attack:** COTS software is often subject to malicious modification or interference like remote code execution (RCE) flaws or DOS attacks. The black-box nature of the source code also means the COTS software may contain unwanted malware or functionality, which the organization is unable to identify through conventional means like SAST.

- **Standard risk assessment and mitigation strategies:** Organizations using COTS software must have adequate risk management practices adapted to their use cases. This includes compiling an accurate inventory of COTS software and components and identifying sources of information for vulnerabilities, such as vendor disclosures, penetration testing, and routine security reviews. Defect prevention strategies during the SDLC are not an option, so mitigation must focus on corrective and compensating controls such as intrusion detection systems and network access controls.

Open Source

Open-source software (OSS) is a category of software that, as the name implies, makes its source code freely available. OSS is typically developed by a community for the benefit of all, allowing organizations to share and collaborate to improve the software while offering the benefit of source-code visibility. Unlike COTS, all organizations using OSS can perform code testing to verify security, bugs, or unwanted functionality, and they can share fixes made to address security flaws back to the software project for the benefit of the community.

The community-driven approach of OSS has arguable security implications. On the one hand, the open nature means that bugs or flaws should eventually be caught, and the software is generally freely available for use. On the other hand, the complexity of OSS projects, the technical skills required to use the software, and the lack of dedicated support can make them less attractive than COTS alternatives. When evaluating OSS, there are a number of key concerns:

- **Performing sufficient evaluation:** There is an assumption that with sufficient eye-balls on software code, all flaws will become apparent. This is true but leaves out one crucial element: time. The Heartbleed bug existed in the OpenSSL for nearly five years before it was discovered, and the software is one of the most widely used on the internet. Relying on testing and evaluation performed by untrusted outside parties can also lead to testing with insufficient coverage, differing objectives, or even results that are outdated or inaccurate if not performed by qualified testers. Similarly, it may be possible for a system administrator to pull open-source software from a project repository and build a functional system from it without sufficient knowledge to review the code and find potential bugs. Simply relying on the wisdom of the community or an administrator is insufficient.

- **Validate source code integrity:** OSS repositories are typically configured for public visibility and contributions, meaning anybody can add, modify, or delete source code. There have been multiple instances where OSS projects had malicious code inserted, as well as instances of prepackaged OSS being made available from inauthentic sources. In both cases, unsuspecting users who down-loaded and deployed the software got unwanted malware in addition to the legiti-mate software. Always ensure you review the changes made to OSS to ensure they are expected and properly documented, and only download OSS from the legiti-mate, official repositories.

- **Look for commercial support:** OSS is typically licensed for free use and distri-bution, which means organizations are also left to find their own support. Com-panies such as Red Hat have sprung up by offering support for popular OSS like Linux, and the dedicated resources of such an arrangement have beneficial impacts on the overall quality and security of the OSS. These firms may be able to attract dedicated talent to projects and also offer the benefit of contributing lessons learned from support back to the community in the form of documentation and code updates.

Third-Party

Third-party software is developed under contract by a firm outside your organization's direct control, and the resulting software is typically for your organization's exclusive use. The outside organization usually specializes in software development and has skills, resources, and knowledge that make them more proficient at software development. This reduces project risks to the contracting organization from unfamiliar technology or lack of software development process maturity; lack of familiarity or maturity in development processes can also lead to less secure software development as developers are prone to make simple mistakes because they lack knowledge. The more experienced, shared resources of the third-party development organization are less likely to make such mistakes, so the added cost of contracting is offset by decreased project and security risks.

As with all acquired software, there are risks inherent in giving up control of the software development process, and specialized mitigation strategies are required to enforce contracts, service-level agreements (SLAs), and additional acceptance testing to ensure the delivered software meets the organization's requirements. The use of a third party to develop software is a decision that should be made after a deliberate consideration of the costs and benefits. Increased costs for high-quality development and project management oversight required may be justified by the quality or speed of delivery that a specialized third-party development firm can provide.

The availability of the source code itself is another important aspect of third-party software security to consider. If the development organization goes out of business, the contracting organization may find itself without support for critical systems; *code escrow* is a contractual arrangement often used to prevent this eventuality. The developing organization deposits a copy of the source code with a trusted third party, called an *escrow agent*. The contracting organization can get access to the code under limited circumstances, such as the developer going out of business or breaching the contract, which enables continued support and development of the system.

Managed Services (SaaS, IaaS, PaaS)

A combination of financial drivers and the availability of innovative services has driven organizations across all industries to adopt cloud computing. Direct financial incentives like reducing costs for unneeded hardware or software capacity, as well as indirect incentives like secure remote accessibility to enable distributed teams, have combined to push many organizations to consume information systems as managed services. These services are billed via metered consumption, which is often a pay-as-you-use model. Choosing the correct services will depend on an organization's needs and technical abilities.

Widely agreed upon definitions of the various cloud service models are found in NIST SP 800-145, "The NIST Definition of Cloud Computing," and are also covered in Chapter 3. Emerging cloud services must be considered with respect to software security, including serverless and microservices architectures, which combine elements of managed software, infrastructure, and platform to enable faster deployment of code. The choice of cloud services impacts the consumer's software security assessment abilities and responsibilities.

Assessing Shared Responsibilities

The shared responsibility model defines a demarcation line between the cloud service provider (CSP) and cloud consumer with respect to handling various security tasks. For example, in all service models, the CSP is responsible for physical security of the data center, while in all service models, the consumer retains legal liability and responsibility for safeguarding data placed in a cloud environment.

Other responsibilities vary depending on the service model chosen. For example, in Infrastructure as a Service (IaaS) the consumer is responsible for applying software patches to any software they deploy, while in SaaS, that responsibility falls to the CSP. Software assessment responsibilities follow a similar split based on the service model:

- In all service models, it is the responsibility of the consumer to verify the CSP's suitability for particular uses, like processing highly sensitive data. The choice of a particular CSP or cloud deployment model will be informed by the level of control available when performing software assessment; for example, a private or community cloud will offer greater direct control over assessment than a large public CSP whose policies do not allow consumers to directly audit the service.

- In IaaS, the consumer will have the most flexibility to deploy software and therefore the most ability to perform software assessments. IaaS offers building blocks of information system functionality, so assessment software security assessment will incorporate COTS, OSS, and third-party software as appropriate to the type of software the consumer deploys in the IaaS environment.

- In PaaS, some options are removed from the consumer's control, so compensating processes like reviewing audit reports and SLAs for software assurance are needed.

- SaaS offers consumers the fewest options for directly assessing the security of software. However, given the shared nature of SaaS providers, there are often audit reports and robust control documentation available regarding the CSP's software development, testing, and hosting security practices.

Audits and Assurance

As with all third-party and supply-chain security concerns, *assurance* is a key concept for managed software services. Direct observation and control are not available, because the organization is not responsible for software development, so a trusted third party is often involved to perform an impartial review in the form of an audit. This prevents the CSP from being subjected to constant review by consumers, while providing consumers with a trusted source of information on the design, implementation, and effectiveness of security controls.

There are multiple security and compliance frameworks related to cloud computing, and these are covered in detail in Chapter 6. Frameworks like the Service Organization Controls (SOC), Cloud Security Alliance Security Trust Assurance and Risk (CSA STAR), and the ISO 27000 family (including ISO 27001, 27017, 27018, and 27034) all provide some assurance related to cloud services and applications. Maturity or compliance with other frameworks like CMMI or BSIMM may also be reported by CSPs as a way of providing consumers with assurance that the software development and hosting practices of the CSP are robust and do not present unacceptable risks. The benefit of so many organizations sharing the CSP's resources is obvious: the CSP has a vested interest in providing the most robust security to ensure it retains these customers, and the pooled resources of so many consumers make robust security control and oversight programs financially feasible. The downside, obviously, is that the consumers give up some measure of direct control over their risks.

DEFINE AND APPLY SECURE CODING GUIDELINES AND STANDARDS

Domain 1 introduces the hierarchy of documentation that organizations can use to manage risks. Policies provide strategic high-level guidance regarding objectives and expectations, while standards and guidelines provide direction for specific tasks and activities. Standards are generally mandatory, while guidelines are recommendations designed to provide guidance on how to achieve a specific goal or task.

Software developers should be provided with guidelines and standards to enable them to write code that achieves the organization's strategic objectives, particularly the requirement to safeguard confidentiality, integrity, and availability of systems and data. There is significant commonality for secure coding practices across industries and organizations, which has led groups like OWASP to design coding guidelines and standards for a variety of languages, software libraries, and application environments like web and mobile.

These are freely available and can be used by any organization or team, with contributions from the community for continual improvement and knowledge sharing.

Documented guidelines and standards can be used to implement multiple control actions. They can prevent bad programmer behaviors like developing code according to preference or familiarity rather than organizational standards. Programming practices related to security have evolved over time, so developers who use outdated development practices present additional risk. Standards can also be used for detection of vulnerabilities, by serving as a baseline for comparison when auditing or running automated scans on code. Guidelines and standards may be implemented as administrative controls in the form of documentation and training, as well as technical controls if they are implemented in tools like the IDE or testing platforms.

Security Weaknesses and Vulnerabilities at the Source-Code Level

Weaknesses and vulnerabilities are closely related, but there is a nuanced difference between the two terms. Vulnerabilities exist due to the presence of a software weakness such as a bug or flaw in the system's source code, which may result from errors or incorrect design choices made when architecting, developing, and implementing the system. Weaknesses can exist in a system with no practicable method of exploiting them, in which case they are not vulnerabilities; weaknesses can also impact nonsecurity aspects of a system, such as a poor database design that causes slow search performance. As a CISSP, the distinction is important to recognize, as nonsecurity weaknesses may be addressed by other teams in the organization, while vulnerabilities are directly related to the security risk a CISSP is responsible for.

A vulnerability, by contrast, is the way in which a weakness could be exploited in a software system. Nonsecurity weaknesses obviously are not exploitable, and some insecure source-code-level weaknesses may be compensated for by other parts of the overall system, such as an OS memory manager that prevents buffer overflow conditions otherwise allowed by poorly written source code. This is one of the challenges presented in software security testing: if a source code weakness is not exploitable, the cost-benefit analysis of fixing the weakness may not support the effort and resources needed to fix it. Definitively asserting a weakness is not exploitable can be difficult, so subjective measurements are used that are open to debate.

Vulnerabilities are typically tracked by the software in which they exist, and more specifically by the affected version, allowing organizations to determine if a vulnerability affects their systems. Weaknesses and vulnerabilities are cataloged and scored using common systems to aid in identifying, communicating, and testing for them.

This tracking and scoring are useful for prioritizing fixes like patches or the deployment of compensating controls.

Common Weakness Enumeration

The Common Weakness Enumeration (CWE) is maintained by the Mitre Corporation in partnership with various U.S. government agencies including the Department of Homeland Security. It is freely available and is integrated with security products such as scanning tools as a common way of identifying and reporting on potential weaknesses in information systems. CWE is best defined on the Mitre website, `cwe.mitre.org`:

> CWE™ *is a community-developed list of software and hardware weakness types. It serves as a common language, a measuring stick for security tools, and as a baseline for weakness identification, mitigation, and prevention efforts.*

This community-developed list identifies common weaknesses in hardware, software source code, and implementations of software features that can lead to exploitable vulnerabilities. Each CWE is given a unique identifier such as CWE-561: Dead Code, as well as the following:

- **Description, Extended Description:** Details of the weakness and its effects. The description for CWE-561 is: "The software contains dead code, which can never be executed." This is code that, when executed, skips over certain portions or never calls those functions, thereby preventing it from ever being run.

- **Relationships:** Other types of related weaknesses, such as the high-level category of Bad Coding Practices.

- **Modes of Introduction, Applicable Platforms:** This identifies when this weakness may be introduced to software by SDLC phase, which is useful when designing security controls to deploy in the SDLC. Applicable Platforms identifies what languages or systems are susceptible. CWE-561 arises during the implementation phase and impacts all programming languages.

- **Common Consequences, Demonstrative Examples:** These sections are self-explanatory. Consequences of dead code include the likelihood of unintended program behavior, since the function expected of the dead code will never be performed. Demonstrative examples help software developers by showing example code demonstrating the weakness.

- **Observed Examples:** If the weakness has led to an actual exploit, the relevant Common Vulnerabilities and Exposures (CVE) reference is included. CVEs are discussed in detail in the following section.

- **Potential Mitigations, Detection Methods:** These categories are most useful for security practitioners, as they provide actionable guidance to detect and mitigate the weaknesses, such as static code analysis to detect dead code, and mitigation tactics. In the case of CWE-561, the mitigation is deceptively simple: remove the dead code. However, if the dead code had an intended purpose, new code that does not exhibit the same weakness is required.

- **Miscellaneous metadata:** CWEs contain additional metadata like ordinality, taxonomy, references, and version history of the weakness.

Common Weakness Scoring System

The Common Weakness Scoring System (CWSS) is an attempt to score weaknesses and determine a priority for addressing them based on the score. This can help identify high-risk weaknesses that should be addressed first given limited time and may also be used to identify low-risk weaknesses that will not be addressed due to the costs required and small benefit achieved.

The CWSS score comprises an evaluation of several factors, which are organized into three groups: Base Finding, Attack Surface, and Environmental. Each factor has values to account for uncertainty inherent in complex software projects, as well as the evolution over time of how much information is available about a weakness. The factors are as follows:

- **Base Finding:** This helps quantify results of a weakness being exploited. Metrics include the following: Technical Impact (TI), Acquired Privilege (AP), Acquired Privilege Layer (AL), Internal Control Effectiveness (IC), and Finding Confidence (FC).

- **Attack Surface:** This provides an explanation of the factors needed to exploit the weakness. Metrics include Required Privilege (RP), Required Privilege Layer (RL), Access Vector (AV), Authentication Strength (AS), Level of Interaction (IN), and Deployment Scope (SC).

- **Environmental:** This describes the impact and likelihood of exploiting the weakness. Metrics include Business Impact (BI), Likelihood of Discovery (DI), Likelihood of Exploit (EX), External Control Effectiveness (EC), and Prevalence (P).

Universal scores rarely provide enough context for an organization to use without modification, so the CWSS score may be a useful starting point to categorize weaknesses and then perform further analysis within your own organization to determine prioritization of fixes. Full details of the CWSS are at `cwe.mitre.org/cwss`.

Common Vulnerabilities and Exposures

Similar to CWE, the Common Vulnerabilities and Exposures provides a consistent way to not only identify but also describe common cybersecurity vulnerabilities. CVEs are often tied back to CWEs. For example, the "goto" fail vulnerability in Apple's macOS and iOS (CVE-2014-1266) resulted from poor coding practices that lead to code never being executed, which is an example of the previously discussed CWE-561, Dead Code.

The CVE ID consists of two key pieces of information: the year in which the vulnerability was registered on the CVE list and a numeric ID. Given the number of vulnerabilities disclosed each year, this prevents the ID from being too long to be useful. Note that the year indicates only when a formal entry on the CVE list was created, not when the vulnerability was discovered or reported.

CVE records include a description of the vulnerability with details like impacted software and versions, any versions that are not impacted, risks related to the vulnerability, and workarounds or fixes. References are also provided, and they often consist of vendor-issued material like knowledge base articles or patching information, and links to relevant material about the discovery of the vulnerability. Security researchers often publish the details of their research in blog posts, proof-of-concept code, and presentations, and the references typically contain these links as well.

The full list of all CVEs reported, which goes back to 1999, is available at `cve.mitre` `.org/index.html`.

Common Vulnerability Scoring System

CVEs are merely identifiers of a vulnerability and do not provide any useful way to identify high-priority vulnerabilities. The Common Vulnerability Scoring System (CVSS) provides that information, similar to CWSS. Currently in version 3.1, CVSS provides context related to the impact and severity of each CVE. They are accessible in the National Vulnerability Database (NVD) maintained by NIST at `nvd.nist.gov/vuln-metrics/cvss`.

CVSS scores measure three categories of information related to each vulnerability, which are used to calculate three subscores that together comprise the overall CVSS score. A CVSS vector is also created, which provides a text-based reference to the underlying vulnerability measurements, such as CVSS:3.1/AV:A/AC:L/PR:N/UI:N/S:U/C:H/I:N/A:N. This is made up of the scores on each metric, as detailed here:

- **Base Score** metrics are related to the exploitability and impact of a particular vulnerability and, once established, do not typically change. Exploitability metrics include the Attack Vector (AV), Attack Complexity (AC), Privileges Required (PR), User Interaction (UI), and Scope (S). Impact metrics cover the standard security triad of Confidentiality (C), Integrity (I), and Availability (A).

- **Temporal Score** metrics capture how the risk of a particular vulnerability changes over time, which means this number also changes over time. When a vulnerability is first discovered, it may be a highly manual process to exploit it, which is technically difficult and reduces risk, though organizations are unlikely to have patches in place to remediate, which increases the risk. Over time, vulnerability exploitation is automated and included in tools like Metasploit, which increases the risk, but organizations also respond by patching, which decreases risk. Metrics comprising the temporal score include Exploit Code Maturity (E), Remediation Level (RL), and Report Confidence (RC).

- **Environmental Score** metrics capture how a particular vulnerability impacts an individual organization. A highly exploitable, high-impact vulnerability sounds drastic, but if an organization's only system with that vulnerability is in a secure physical location and not connected to a network, the patching process is not an emergency that should interrupt all other work. Environmental score metrics modify metrics from the other categories and are subdivided into three groups:

    - **Exploitability** includes Attack Vector (MAV), Attack Complexity (MAC), Privileges Required (MPR), User Interaction (MUI), and Scope (MS).

    - **Impact** measures the specific effect of the vulnerability against the organization's CIA triad, including Confidentiality Impact (MC), Integrity Impact (MI), and Availability Impact (MA).

    - **Impact Subscore Modification** modifies the Base Score impact metrics to tailor them to the organization's specific CIA requirements, including Confidentiality Requirement (CR), Integrity Requirement (IR), and Availability Requirement (AR).

CVSS scores range from 0 to 10, with higher numbers denoting a more critical vulnerability that should be prioritized for fixing. A score of 0 is categorized None and is mainly informational. A score between 0.1 and 3.9 is Low severity, between 4.0 and 6.9 is Medium severity, between 7.0 and 8.9 is High severity, and a score between 9.0 and 10 is Critical. Security practitioners can monitor the NVD and use the CVSS calculators to determine the environmental scores of specific vulnerabilities to prioritize remediation activities. As an example, the previously discussed Apple "goto" fail vulnerability, CVE-201401266, had a score of 5.8 resulting from the high impact of a loss of confidentiality due to no encryption, while also considering the limited likelihood as the software flaw did not always cause a loss of encryption.

OWASP Top 10

The Open Web Application Security Project (OWASP) is a community-driven effort that originally started to share knowledge and develop best practices around web application development. It has since expanded in scope to include other application types, such as mobile apps, driven mainly by the increased prevalence of applications that rely on system components or services accessed over the internet and the wide variety of languages that are used for both web and traditional desktop apps.

One of OWASP's most visible projects is the Top Ten, which is a compilation of the 10 most commonly seen vulnerabilities in web applications (`owasp.org/www-project-top-ten/`). Note the Top Ten list is not a collection of discrete vulnerability identifiers like CVE, nor is it a scoring/prioritization system like the CVSS. Instead, it provides guidance to developers, QA and testing practitioners, and security practitioners to help them identify common vulnerabilities and attempt to avoid them when programming or catch them with testing and security monitoring.

The vulnerabilities on the list are identified by a numeric identifier and the year they appeared on the list, which was last updated in 2017. Each vulnerability is also broken down into the threat agents and/or attack vectors likely to exploit it, the security weakness posed by the vulnerability, and the impact an exploitation of the vulnerability is likely to cause. The current list includes the following:

- **A1:2017-Injection:** Injection is the unwanted insertion of code through channels not intended for code, like data form fields on a web page. If an attacker enters a SQL code statement rather than an account number in a data field, this value may be passed to an application that executes the SQL.

- **A2:2017-Broken Authentication:** Authentication is a key pillar of access control, so if users are able to bypass or break the authentication, they are likely to gain unauthorized access. This vulnerability can include credential stuffing attacks against applications as well as session hijacking attacks.

- **A3:2017-Sensitive Data Exposure:** This vulnerability is quite simple. Application flaws may expose sensitive data to unauthorized users, such as by including it in error messages. This can also be a secondary effect of an application with broken authentication.

- **A4:2017-XML External Entities (XXE):** This is a highly technical vulnerability related to improper handling of user-supplied XML. Rather than just expected data, the XML may include references to external entities like files or storage locations, which causes the application to execute unwanted remote code or load malicious data from the external storage location. This is due to the vulnerable functioning of the XML processor, which must accept and process untrusted data.

- **A5:2017-Broken Access Control:** This one is also self-explanatory, though it can be easily confused with A2. Vulnerabilities that fall into this category include bypassing access controls by modifying a URL to gain access to unauthorized resources, replay attacks like sending the same session credentials, or improper granularity of access control within an application.

- **A6:2017-Security Misconfiguration:** Misconfigurations are often the biggest category due to the complexity of modern software environments. Ensuring the correct parameters are set, boxes are checked, and services are configured is error prone. A web server with unwanted support for outdated Secure Sockets Layer (SSL) or TLS versions is an example of a misconfiguration.

- **A7:2017-Cross-Site Scripting (XSS):** XSS exploits the dynamic and remote nature of web applications, which are designed to accept and execute remote code like JavaScript. An application vulnerable to XSS may load untrusted or unsanitized data from a remote source and execute any code it contains, allowing a remote attacker to perform unwanted actions in the user's browser like redirecting them to malicious sites, reading data, or even hijacking a user's session with a secure site.

- **A8:2017-Insecure Deserialization:** This is another complex technical vulnerability. Data is serialized by transforming it into a common format to be embedded into a communications stream, like data being structured using JSON and sent over the internet. The receiving system then deserializes the data and translates it into a format that the recipient software can understand. Insecure deserialization, like executing code embedded in the deserialized data, may lead to unwanted or unauthorized application behavior.

- **A9:2017-Using Components with Known Vulnerabilities:** Modern programs are rarely created entirely by a single entity. Developers rely on libraries and open-source modules, which make software delivery faster, more efficient, and more secure. However, components like web servers, code libraries, and other dependencies can introduce vulnerabilities. An otherwise secure application could be compromised if an external library used to format data has a flaw, similar to building an entirely secure house but putting a lock that can be easily bypassed on the front door.

- **A10:2017-Insufficient Logging & Monitoring:** This is another human factor in software security and is similar to misconfigurations. Applications without sufficient monitoring or logging capabilities in place simply do not support incident detection and response. If an incident occurs on a system but no alert is generated, no security countermeasures will be deployed. Similarly, an incident without any data to support investigation and recovery is unlikely to be dealt with effectively due to the lack of intelligence available to the security responders.

Each of the vulnerabilities on the Top Ten list are presented with tips and guidance on how to prevent them, such as using code frameworks that automatically implement anti-XSS or implementing repeatable and audited hardening procedures to avoid and correct security misconfigurations. These should be incorporated into security and awareness materials in the organization, specifically for developers working on applications and security practitioners with responsibility for access controls, configuration management, and application security.

Software Composition Analysis

One emerging area of security concern is the increasing use of open-source components, libraries, and modules in modern programs. These show up even in custom-developed applications, and their use is directly related to Top 10 item A9:2017-Using Components with Known Vulnerabilities. These components are often known as free and open-source software (FOSS) *dependencies* and bring obvious benefits such as faster development and increased reliability if well-known components are used. FOSS means that these software components can be used at no charge, and the code is open for inspection or modification. There is a security drawback, however: if a dependency has a flaw or bug, the resulting application will also be vulnerable. This mirrors the complexity of systems reliant on underlying architecture, such as a web application that is also subject to vulnerabilities in its underlying web server and OS software.

An OWASP presentation given in 2019 found that the percentage of FOSS components in applications increased from around 10 percent in 1998 to 90 percent in 2019, but many organizations struggled to reckon with the security implications of these FOSS components (`wiki.owasp.org/images/b/bd/Software_Composition_Analysis_OWASP_ Stammtisch_-_Stanislav_Sivak.pdf`). Asset inventories should capture all elements of a system, such as underlying OSs and hardware, and this inventory is a key input to the vulnerability and patch management process. However, the practice of inventorying and analyzing dependencies for flaws had not kept pace to address their rising usage.

Software composition analysis (SCA) is a security practice specifically designed to address FOSS component vulnerabilities and their impact on software. There are a number of tool vendors and approaches, but most include basic functionality to create an inventory of all dependencies and identify vulnerabilities they contain. Open-source projects often publish security notices or include release notes or documentation addressing remediated vulnerabilities with updates, which an SCA tool can use to continuously identify vulnerabilities in an application using that component. This process is similar to OS vendors publishing notes about vulnerabilities and updates.

Once a vulnerability has been identified in a dependency, the remediation step is usually to apply an update. In some cases, the FOSS flaw does not translate to a vulnerability in a given system dependent on that component, so no action is required. Alternatively, the organization may need to iterate the SDLC in response to changes in the component's functionality as a result of the flaw. DevOps and DevSecOps practices can also be utilized to address these flaws, such as CI/CD pipelines that incorporate automatic checks and incorporate the latest update dependencies when building an application. This is the equivalent of automatic patch deployment and can automate vulnerability remediation, though sometimes at the expense of availability if a patch breaks functionality.

Security of Application Programming Interfaces

An API provides standardized access to the features of a system without the need to understand its inner workings. Features that are accessible through an API are often referred to as being exposed via API, meaning they can be called using standardized methods such as HTTP requests. Representation state transfer or REST APIs expose functions using URLs similar to web applications and accept commands using common HTTP verbs like GET and POST for retrieving or sending data to the API. Rather than creating a custom communication scheme for each application, the use of a REST API allows other programs to interact using these commonly understood protocols.

APIs are a form of modular software development, and modern application architectures often rely on APIs to send data between functions, modules, or tiers of complex systems. There are other forms of APIs as well, including internal software APIs in modern OSs for access to generic system functions like creating interactive windows in a user interface, simple object access protocol (SOAP) APIs designed for exchanging messages between system components, and RPC APIs that are used for executing functions across nodes in distributed systems. Most cloud services are built on an API foundation, with tasks such as cloud environment administrative, data handling, and services like data storage buckets and machine learning models exposed to users via URLs, commonly known as API *endpoints*.

APIs function much the same as web applications, and the security requirements are often similar for both. The first and most obvious step is to understand the risks facing a particular system and its API. Is it a publicly accessible API that grants access to read or update sensitive information? Such an API would obviously face high risks against confidentiality and integrity and should implement appropriate security controls to ensure information is not read or altered by unauthorized users or programs via the API. Is the API read-only access to public information like weather data? In this case, confidentiality and access controls are unlikely to be a high priority.

API Security Best Practices

API security guidelines and standards are similar to secure coding guidelines and standards, though they are slightly less mature since APIs are a newer concept. OWASP publishes a number of freely available resources on API security, including a cheat sheet for REST APIs (`cheatsheetseries.owasp.org/cheatsheets/REST_Security_Cheat_Sheet.html`) and an API Security Top 10 list detailing common vulnerabilities and issues facing API security (`owasp.org/www-project-api-security`). In addition to OWASP's guidance, there are a number of key practices to keep in mind when building and security systems with APIs to handle data. Although similar to security requirements for web applications, the extensive use of APIs for system-to-system interactions rather than human interfaces does present unique challenges.

Authentication and Access Control

APIs typically do not utilize the same combination of username and password that a web application uses, but the goals of authenticating the user of an API, called a *consumer*, are still the same. The consumer must prove their identity and should only be granted access to appropriate resources based on that identity. Authentication can be done in a number of ways, each with various advantages:

- **Basic authentication** utilizes a simple authentication scheme that is part of the HTTP protocol and sends a username:password string encoded in base64. Since this is not a form of encryption, this form of authentication method should never be used alone. Stronger authentication methods are preferred, but if basic authentication must be used, the communication channel requires protection, such as TLS encryption.

- **Key-based authentication** serves dual purposes. A secret, shared symmetric key is used to encrypt data being passed. If the recipient can decrypt the data with a secret key associated with a unique identity, then the sender's identity can be authenticated, and the data is also protected in transit. Many applications with APIs allow users to log into a secure web application to retrieve the API key needed for encryption and authentication, providing an out-of-bound channel for key distribution.

- **Certificate-based authentication**, as the name implies, relies on authenticating an identity using digital certificates. This can be one-way, in which only one party provides a certificate asserting an identity, or mutual authentication where both parties exchange certificates and validate them. This obviously requires a Public Key Infrastructure (PKI) in place, meaning this may not be a valid choice for all situations.

- **Federated and single sign-on** authentication relies on another organization's identity and access management (IDAM) tools to control access. Technologies like security assertion markup language (SAML) and Oauth can be used to federate, or combine, IDAM capabilities across organizations. API security can rely on these federations to delegate access control decisions; rather than the API provider enforcing access controls, consumers grant permissions to their users and then pass relevant authentication and access control information via SAML statements or Oauth assertions.

Access control must be implemented for authenticated consumers. There are a variety of methods for implementing this, similar to controlling access for users in an application, such as role-based access control, access control lists, and the like. When designing systems with APIs, care must be taken to ensure adequately granular access controls are available to restrict access to data and functions, whether access is requested by an individual user of a web app or a consuming system via an API.

Input Validation and Sanitization

Whenever data is supplied by an outside system or user, it should be considered untrusted and treated appropriately. This can avoid unwanted application behavior like code injection attacks and may also be implemented as a control for data integrity. The API layer of an application is a key control point as it accepts and processes untrusted data supplied by external users or systems.

Escaping content places characters around it to explicitly denote it as data and not code; this is a form of input sanitization, where the supplied data is rendered harmless, and is a safeguard against injection attacks. The configurations, characters, and methods used for escaping content vary between languages and technologies, so input validation must be documented as a requirement and appropriate design decisions made to enable it. The OWASP SQL Injection Cheat Sheet provides examples of various escaping strategies: `cheatsheetseries.owasp` `.org/cheatsheets/SQL_Injection_Prevention_Cheat_Sheet.html`.

Input validation checks should be implemented at the API layer to validate the incoming data matches expectations. *Syntactic* validation enforces correct syntax of data, for example, a U.S.-formatted phone number should consist of 10 digits grouped `nnn-nnn-nnnn`, and *semantic validation*, which enforces correct values; for example, "555" is not a valid area code in the U.S. calling system and should be rejected as an invalid phone number. A phone number in Zimbabwe, by contrast, should consist of a proper area code, prefixing number, and subscriber number such as (027) 2317555, which requires different application logic to perform semantic validation.

Performing syntactic and semantic validation can help avoid data integrity issues and unwanted system behavior due to unexpected values, while semantic validation can also help identify unwanted content like SQL statements in a field such as `Last_Name` where a simple text string is expected.

Unfortunately, semantic validation is extremely difficult, as the various combinations of human language make it tough to write the rules needed to check. For example, the `'` character has special meaning in SQL and could be an unwanted character in a name field, but rejecting it would cause common names like O'Brian to be rejected. As a result, escaping content is considered a better safeguard against injection attacks, while semantic validation is generally more useful for data integrity. The OWASP Input Validation Cheat Sheet provides a comprehensive resource on validation strategies: `cheatsheetseries.owasp.org/cheatsheets/Input_Validation_Cheat_Sheet.html`.

Protection of Resources

APIs must be designed with the same level of rigor applied to user access management to ensure the functionality exposed cannot be exploited to attack the system's confidentiality, integrity, or availability. This is a broad category of security concern but one that is often overlooked since APIs are typically designed for system-to-system communication or for privileged access, and the possibility of their use in an attack is not considered during threat modeling.

Take, for example, the Facebook developer API, which offered a "View As" feature designed to let developers see a Facebook profile as if they were a particular user. Rather than just showing the profile, the API also delivered a user authentication token, which allowed hackers to access Facebook with that user's credentials. Since developers are considered trusted users, the level of rigor applied to testing this functionality was obviously not sufficient, or it was assumed that nondevelopers would not be able to access the feature for malicious uses. Facebook has since changed the behavior of this API to prevent this unintended behavior.

Protecting Communications

Web applications and other communications implement protections like TLS for encrypting data in transit, and API access should be no different. Luckily, encryption serves multiple purposes — symmetric key-based authentication not only can verify a user's identity but also provide security of data in transit, as can certificate-based authentication where a public key can be used either for encryption of data or for a session key. The use of standard web protocols is a benefit of REST APIs, as they utilize HTTPS with little developer effort. The level of communications security required should of course be driven by the sensitivity level of the data — public data may need only integrity validation, while highly sensitive information should implement strong encryption for confidentiality and hashing for integrity.

Cryptography

Cryptography is covered in detail in Domain 3 and can be used for a number of security functions. As a general best practice, cryptographic modules that are trusted, tested, or validated are preferred custom-built cryptography. When applied to APIs, cryptography can provide the following:

- **Confidentiality:** As discussed previously, both symmetric and asymmetric keys can be used, depending on the system requirements. A key design choice that must be made is when to encrypt data, as it can be encrypted prior to transport or utilize secure communications channels.

- **Integrity:** Hash functions should be applied whenever the integrity of data being accepted through an API needs to be validated.

- **Authenticity:** Proving the authenticity of data often relies on proving that the parties in communication are the legitimate sender and recipient. Strategies such as Hashed Message Authentication Code (HMAC) can be used to verify that the communications partners are still the intended parties.

- **Nonrepudiation:** Proving the source of data or the identity of a system actor rests on identifying the holder of keying material. For example, if Alice can decrypt data using a secret key shared only with Bob or with Bob's public asymmetric key, she can reliably assume Bob sent the data in question.

- **Access control:** Access to encrypted data relies on decrypting it, so by extension, controlling access to the key controls access to the data. In the case of symmetric keys, this involves implementing secure distribution and management mechanisms for the encryption keys. For asymmetric encryption, it involves the choice of which key is used to encrypt data. Using a sender's private key will allow anybody to decrypt the data with the corresponding public key, which proves authenticity but provides no confidentiality. Using a recipient's public key to encrypt data provides confidentiality because only the recipient's private key can decrypt it, but without proof of the sender's identity since the public key is widely available.

Security Logging, Monitoring, and Alerting

System actions performed via API must be part of a logging and monitoring strategy to verify that system usage via the API meets security requirements. Actions to be logged might include successful or unsuccessful authentication of an API consumer, results of input validation against supplied data, and details of API connections including the sender's IP address and timestamp. The events to be logged should be determined by the system's requirements for both operational and security monitoring. Major cloud service providers offer API gateways that provide functions to secure and monitor custom-developed APIs hosted on the CSP's infrastructure, including logging access and forwarding logs to a customer's SIEM.

Logs are made meaningful by reviewing them, so they must be either reviewed by a person or ingested into a log monitoring tool like a SIEM that automates the process, depending on the organizaiton's monitoring strategy and resources. Events that violate security constraints or indicate operational issues should generate alerts to invoke processes like incident response to investigate. Where possible, log data from multiple sources should be correlated to provide investigators with a holistic view of the incident, like network device logs showing traffic, application logs showing API access and use, and even, possibly, external data such as known malicious IP addresses that can be used to determine whether a security incident is a malicious attack.

Security Testing APIs

As with all system functionality, APIs must be tested to verify they meet security, performance, and user requirements. All the testing methods and considerations presented in Domain 6 apply to APIs, such as designing a testing strategy with appropriate depth and coverage as indicated by the API's risk profile. An internal API used to exchange financial data between departments without any public access should not be scheduled for a pentest before undergoing functional testing to ensure proper data integrity, since the risk to integrity is greater than the risk of breaching confidentiality.

There are a number of API security tools available to design and test APIs. The choice of a tool and associated testing strategy should be driven by the technologies in use, such as SOAP or REST, the sensitivity level of data being handled by the API, and the features exposed by the API. OWASP also has a dedicated API security project, which contains resources such as a Security Top 10 and planned cheat sheet for API security, available at `owasp.org/www-project-api-security`.

Secure Coding Practices

Secure coding practices comprise the entirety of actions taken during software and systems development processes. Nonexistent, disorganized, or poorly understood organizational practices tend to produce software and systems with flaws or bugs, which in turn become weaknesses and vulnerabilities. Standardized secure coding practices that are well-documented, disseminated to all stakeholders, and applied effectively throughout the organization can increase the quality of development projects. This leads to software and system development processes that seek to minimize flaws and bugs, as well as testing and monitoring processes designed to catch and fix vulnerabilities as soon as possible. Although a CISSP may not be directly involved with the daily use of secure coding standards, they play a crucial role in defining requirements for such practices and validating organizational practices designed to meet these requirements.

Standards for Secure Software Development

As with many practices in software security, there are well-regarded standards available that bring together common knowledge and conventions related to secure coding and development. Remember that no standard is a guaranteed match for every organization, so these should be used as starting points from which organizations can develop and implement their own practices, in a process known as *tailoring*.

The OWASP project contains a multitude of resources for secure coding practices. The Cheat Sheet Series (`owasp.org/www-project-cheat-sheets`) is an entirely library of guidance on secure practices, such as the following:

- Implementing authentication and access controls
- Preventing common vulnerabilities and attacks like XSS and injection
- Architectural security for technologies like microservices, REST APIs, and SAML
- Technology-specific security guidance including XML, HTML5, Docker, and Kubernetes

A technology-neutral OWASP Secure Coding Practices Quick Reference Guide (`owasp.org/www-pdf-archive/OWASP_SCP_Quick_Reference_Guide_v2.pdf`) is also available and provides recommendations and best practices across a set of common development activities. Although primarily written for web and mobile apps, the guidance is broadly applicable to almost any application and system architecture.

Each category contains key focus areas for secure coding practices, and these practices can be used to guide the development and implementation of organization-specific practices tailored to your unique technology stack, programming languages, and security requirements. There are 13 categories, each of which contain a checklist of common practices, covering the following:

- Input validation
- Output encoding
- Authentication and password management
- Session management
- Access control
- Cryptographic practices
- Error handling and logging
- Communication security
- System configuration
- Database security
- File management
- Memory management
- General coding practices

The Carnegie Mellon University Software Engineering Institute (CMU SEI) publishes guides covering both secure coding practices as well as secure coding standards. The Top 10 Secure Coding Practices, which actually contains two bonus practices, is a very high-level set of principles for implementing secure coding like using input validation and following the "keep it simple" rule. The Coding Standards are a set of publications designed to provide standards for secure software development in specific languages including C/C++, Android, and Perl. While not entirely focused on security, they do cover best practices for each language and include some security-specific guidance. These documents and others related to secure coding can be found at the CMU SEI CERT Secure Coding wiki at `wiki.sei.cmu.edu/confluence/display/seccode/SEI+CERT+Coding+Standards`.

Education and Culture

Documentation alone is not enough to solve security problems; the daily activities of all members in the organization must follow the guidance laid out in policies, standards, and procedures. This is the essence of building a security culture, in which all stakeholders understand, support, and actively carry out security efforts, and it is essential that this is widely adopted across the organization, since cybersecurity is a broad discipline underpinning any process that relies on data and information systems. Building security culture obviously encompasses more than just software and system development, but these activities are especially important given their pivotal role in designing secure systems.

Security culture begins with clear and effective policies and other documentation that provides clear guidance to members of the organization on their security roles and responsibilities. Reading policy documents alone is not sufficient, as many security policies will deal with or include concepts that are not familiar to all. While the documentation should be clear enough for broad consumption, additional documentation like procedures, guidelines, standards, and checklists must be created to provide specific guidance to different stakeholders. For example, a policy describing the desired levels of entropy in password construction is no doubt thorough, but the majority of users in the organization are unlikely to know what entropy is. A password section of the acceptable use policy written in plain language, supplemented with training, education, and awareness materials on secure password practices, is a much more suitable way to communicate this requirement. Incorporating security objectives into organizational goals and priorities and promoting engagement with security are also essential.

One crucial element of a security culture is the set of principles it is built on, and the foundational role played by software development means a number of key principles must be considered in order to create a successful security culture. These principles include the following:

- **Secure by design:** This principle largely stems from a paradigm shift as the field of software engineering matured and decisions that led to insecure technologies like DNS and SNMP were examined in light of modern information security risks. Rather than attempting to retrofit security after deployment, this principle espouses practices that require the inclusion of security at the outset of a system: in the design phase. Anticipating that the system will come under attack drives design and implementation decisions that provide inherent security abilities, rather than relying on more expensive and error-prone compensating controls.

- **Secure by default:** This principle is a collection of best practices for delivering more secure software, such as the inclusion of layered security controls and conservative default settings designed for security. Many data breaches share the underlying root cause of improperly secured cloud storage services exposing data to the public. In a secure by default configuration, those services should be private by default and require extra steps be taken to turn on public access.

- **DevSecOps:** Although not strictly a security principle, one of the foundational ideas of DevSecOps is to shift security "to the left" — in other words, to push security activities earlier in the software development lifecycle rather than developing security strategies only after a system is built and deployed. Implementing DevSecOps in an organization is, fundamentally, an opportunity to build a culture of security and deliver higher quality software.

- **Build security in:** SAMM and BSIMM were discussed earlier in this chapter and represent a set of practices and principles that can be used to drive enterprise change to a culture of security. The maturity model supports this by providing a convenient measure of the organization's current state, metrics to track progress toward a desired future state, and a set of practices to implement to mature the secure software development capability.

Software-Defined Security

The world of technology is rapidly evolving to software-defined replacements for systems that previously required a combination of physical hardware and software. For example, software-defined networking (SDN) abstracts physical networking gear and software configurations into purely software-configurable virtual networks that can be reconfigured with far less effort than their hardware-based equivalents. Cloud services also make use of software-defined infrastructure in the form of virtualization, with common infrastructure elements such as server and networking hardware replaced by more flexible software-only equivalents.

Software-defined security, sometimes abbreviated SDS or SDSec, mirrors this trend to create virtualized, software-controlled security infrastructure. It extends concepts like virtualized infrastructure configuration via definition files, as well as leveraging SDN to provide easy reconfiguration of network functions, routes, and protection mechanisms. Provisioning, monitoring, and management of security functions can be extensively automated and controlled via software configuration, which replaces previously manual, human-driven processes. Deploying SDS represents an evolution of security architecture to support more targeted and flexible controls. It also accounts for new application and system architectures that do away with traditional designs due to novel services available in cloud computing.

Consider, for example, a legacy application that comprises three tiers: a web server, a business logic server, and a database server. Each has traditional security tools installed like anti-malware, file integrity monitoring, IDS/IPS, etc., and is hosted in a data center with traditional perimeter controls like a firewall. A modern application, by contrast, may comprise a web server delivering a browser-based application to users, whose actions create API calls to a set of microservices for specific tasks like processing data, which in turn involves API calls to a cloud-hosted database. All of these system elements are also geographically disbursed and configured for high availability, so user requests may be processed in data centers all over the world with different hardware and software configurations. There is no traditional perimeter, and the business logic and database cannot be monitored with traditional tools. The microservices don't exist on a traditional server, and the cloud-hosted database server is not under the purview of the organization's security program.

In this new paradigm, SDS can achieve a number of security goals and offers several important advantages:

- **Enhanced availability:** Implementing security controls requires an element of determinism; for example, deploying a firewall requires the practitioner to know data will be flowing between two points, and the firewall is placed in the middle. If a different communications channel is used, the firewall's protection is rendered moot. Dynamic and geographically distributed cloud applications make this task difficult with traditional security, but an SDS paradigm can be used to ensure security controls follow the data. Software definition files are easily portable, so it is possible to ensure a new virtual server will have the same configuration and protections regardless of its location. Increased security tool flexibility allows organizations to take advantage of high availability in cloud environments.

- **Infrastructure neutrality:** Security controls often require administrators with system-specific configuration and administrative knowledge. SDS allows for a generic definition to be interpreted as appropriate for underlying system and for the process to be automated. For example, an encryption setting of "AES with minimum 256-bit key length" can be interpreted by a virtualization server and appropriately applied to all new servers regardless of the host OS being deployed. This is similar to the interpreted code paradigm, which allows for write-once, run-anywhere portability. SDS definitions also support increased configuration reliability and consistent application of security policy, similar to using standard configuration files rather than relying on manual build processes.

- **Micro-targeting:** Security tools are often blunt and lack adequate granularity for enforcing controls, which requires trade-offs or compensating controls. This is especially apparent in network segmentation, which is covered in Domain 4, "Communication and Network Security," and it is a problem solved by the micro-segmentation that SDNs enable. Rather than requiring a balance between protection of individual hosts and network administration overhead, individual hosts automatically receive appropriate firewall rules applied based on purpose-driven templates. Other security tool deployment and configurations can be similarly automated, such as IDS with rules appropriate for the server's function, or encryption configuration based on the classification label applied to the system. This granularity avoids trade-offs between management overhead and insufficient granularity of controls.

- **Centralized management:** Many security tools are platform- or technology-specific, and they tend to be siloed along these lines. SDS enables centralized management and oversight by abstracting security control details away from the infrastructure and associated management tools. SDS enables security practitioners to see a consolidated view of access control policies and control implementations, while system administrators are still able to perform their tasks in system-specific tools like Active Directory or an LDAP server.

- **Standardization, integrations, and automation:** Standardization and integrations are key to enabling the features of SDS discussed here. Definition files are written in standard formats such as YAML, which alternatively stands for Yet Another Markup Language or the recursive YAML Ain't Markup Language. These can be interpreted by various cloud providers, systems, or platforms to enforce the desired security configurations appropriate to the infrastructure. This standardization, coupled with integrations between infrastructure and security components like cloud services and SOAR tools, enables automated security control deployment, enforcement, and reconfiguration.

- **Dynamic response:** Security controls can proactively reduce the likelihood of a risk or reactively reduce the impact of a risk after it is realized. SDS incorporates and extends automated capabilities from SOAR to enable faster response times. Restricting the time an attacker has to move laterally from a compromised server to other hosts reduces their chances of successful malicious activity. Dynamic response leverages the ease of reconfiguring virtualized software infrastructure to speed up the response, and the use of orchestration and automation capabilities means intelligence from an incident can be used to automatically deploy proactive mitigations to other hosts and systems. Tools with these capabilities are often described as self-healing, though it is important to note that security practitioners must still maintain vigilance and perform some actions manually.

Just as cloud service providers have made enterprise-grade infrastructure available to a broader audience, SDS can deliver greater security capabilities to organizations with limited resources. Integrations with common systems and platforms coupled with automation require fewer time and security practitioner resources and can free up existing personnel to focus on other concerns. SDS may be the only option in some cases where legacy security tools are not compatible with novel architectures and technologies like microservices, where software agents cannot be deployed for monitoring. Microsoft published a document outlining its shift away from traditional perimeter-based security and legacy tools to SDS. The change is driven in part by the move to a cloud-first IT infrastructure, and the document lays out the strategy behind the change; it can be read here: `microsoft.com/en-us/itshowcase/designing-a-software-defined-strategy-for-securing-the-microsoft-network`.

SUMMARY

Software development security is a foundational pillar of modern information security, because information systems rely so heavily on software. It is also, unfortunately, somewhat challenged by the late realization of its importance compared to the field of software engineering, as well as by the all-too-common prioritization of shipping features or addressing operational concerns rather than security.

Developing software is a complex activity, and the addition of requirements is not always welcome. However, failing to address security when developing information systems does not lead to positive outcomes, so as with all security concerns, practitioners must strike a careful balance between costs and benefits associated with secure development practices, testing and assessment, and the integration of security tools into developer practices and environments.

Proactive risk mitigations available in the software development domain include documenting secure coding standards and guidelines, implementing maturity models to increase the organization's secure development capabilities, and implementing practices like DevSecOps and SOAR to provide automation and efficiency gains. Reactive risk mitigations to consider include designing and enforcing appropriate logging and monitoring strategies, as well as assessment and testing programs designed to detect and correct vulnerabilities.

Security practitioners are not expected to be software developers. However, given the crucial role played by software in modern information systems, it is essential to understand the process by which software is engineered and developed, and appropriate controls needed to mitigate the risks posed by insecure software.

Index

Type 2 authentication factors, 392–394
Type 3 authentication factors, 394–395
authentication, authorization, and accounting (AAA), 417
authentication header (AH), 312
Authentication Server (AS) (in Kerberos), 416–417
authentication systems
    common access control errors, 395
    implementation of, 414–417
authenticity, 6, 8
Authority to Operate (ATO) status, 441, 445
authorization, in IAM systems, 388
authorization mechanisms, implementing and managing of, 404–408
automated capture, 469
automatic repeat request (ARQ), 288
automation, 493–494
autonomous system (AS), 290
autonomous system number (ASN), 290
availability
    as concept of Parkerian Hexad, 8
    as principle of CIA Triad, 6–7
AWS Lamda, 215
Azure. *See* Microsoft

B

background investigations, 64
backup storage strategies, 524–527
backup verification data, 450
Bandler, John, 464
baseband cables, 347
"Baseline Security Recommendations for IoT" (EU), 114
baselines, 57, 490, 492
baselining, 492–493
basic authentication, 614
basic service set identifier (BSSID), 329
bastion host, 339–340
beacon frame, 329
behavior analytics, of users and entities, 488–489
Bellare, Mihir, 255
Bell–LaPadula (BLP) model, 169, 170–172, 406
beyond a reasonable doubt, 49
BeyondCorp (Google), 164
Biba integrity model, 169, 172, 406
binary, 573
bind variables, 192
Bitcoin, 253
black-box testing, 429, 435
blacklisting, 515
block ciphers, 231, 232–233
blockchain, 252–253
Bluetooth, 287, 331
Border Gateway Protocol (BGP), 289, 290, 291, 343

botnet, 307
bottom-up approach, 15–16
branch history buffer (BHB), 182
breach reporting, 509–510
break attack simulations (BAS) (also known as breach and attack simulations), 440–441
Brewer–Nash (BN) model (formerly Chinese Wall model), 173–175
bridges, 342
bring your own device (BYOD) policy, 356, 385, 545
broadband cables, 347
broadcast domain, 284, 336
browsers, 475
brute-force attack, 258–260
BS 6266:2011, 278
BS EN 15713, 124, 126
bug bounties, 521
Building Security-In Maturity Model (BSIMM), 565, 604
burden of proof, 49
bus topology, 350, 351
business continuity and disaster recover (BCDR), 451–452, 505, 510, 529, 530–531
business continuity (BC), identifying, analyzing, and prioritizing of requirements for, 58–63
business continuity plan (BCP), 58, 61–63, 538–539
business impact analysis (BIA), 59, 523
business impact assessment (BIA), 424, 451
Business Software Alliance (BSA), 36
business strategy, 9–10

C

cables, 347–349
cache-timing attack, 262
Canadian Centre for Cyber Security, 487
candidate screening and hiring, 63–64
Canetti, Ran, 255
Capability Maturity Model (CMM), 561, 563
capability maturity model integration (CMMI), 561, 563–564, 604
captive portals, 330
Carbon Black, 167
Carnegie Mellon University, Software Engineering Institute (SEI), 88, 619–620
Cascading Style Sheets (CSS), 577
Cavoukian, Ann, 165
CCleaner, 89
CCTV surveillance, 384
cell-level encryption (CLE), 193
cellular networks, 333–334
Center for Internet Security (CIS), 21, 493
centralized general security services, 150, 156–157
centralized IAM administration, 381
centralized parameter validation, 150, 156

certificate authorities (CAs), 186, 244, 245, 246, 252

certificate revolution list (CRL), 245

certificate-based authentication, 614

certificate-signing request (CSR), 243

certification, defined, 445

Certified Public Accountant (CPA), 460

chain of custody, 466

Challenge Handshake Authentication Protocol (CHAP), 368, 371

change advisory board (CAB), 522, 569

change control board (CCB), 522, 569

change management board (CMB), 490, 569–570

change management (CM), 114–115, 490, 492, 522–523, 568–571

Chaos Monkey (Netflix), 538

Cheat Sheet Series (OWASP), 619

Check Point, Phillips Hue smart lightbulb hack, 209

Chef, 112

chief information security officer (CISO), 14, 15, 487

chief security officer (CSO), 14

Child Pornography Prevention Act (CPPA) (US), 29, 32

Children's Online Privacy Protection Act (COPPA) of 1998 (US), 42, 43–44

China

    Cybersecurity Law, 121

    data localization laws in, 41

    and information technology, 40

    unlicensed software use of, 36

Chinese Wall model. See Brewer–Nash (BN) model (formerly Chinese Wall model)

chosen ciphertext, as cryptanalytic attack, 261

chosen plaintext attack, 260

CIA Triad, 3, 4–8, 199, 200, 224, 253, 265, 609

CI/CD environments, auditing of, 595

Cipher Block Chaining (CBC) mode, 228, 229, 236, 237

Cipher Feedback (CFB) mode, 228, 229, 236, 237

ciphertext, 225, 230

ciphertext only, as cryptanalytic attack, 260

circuit level firewalls, 338, 339

CIS Benchmarks, 482

CIS Critical Security Controls (CIS Controls), 17, 21–22

civil investigations, 52–53

Clark, David, 173

Clark–Wilson model, 173

Cleanroom methodology, 560

cleartext, 225

client-related vulnerabilities, 187–189

cloud access security broker (CASB), 143–144

cloud bursting, 527

cloud computing, 203–204, 526–527

Cloud Forensics Capability Maturity Model, 475

Cloud Security Alliance (CSA), 176, 216, 475

Cloud Security Alliance Security Trust Assurance and Risk (CSA STAR), 460, 461, 604

cloud service models, 204–205

cloud service provider (CSP), 88, 166–167, 385, 474, 603

cloud-based system, vulnerabilities of, 203–207

cloud-first, 403

CloudFlare, 334

CloudFormation (AWS), 494

cloud-native, 403

coaxial cable (also known as coax), 346–347

code analysis tools, 472

code repository, 581, 586–588

code review and testing, 436–437

coding guidelines and standards, defining and applying secure coding guidelines and standards, 604–624

coding practices, 618–621

cold site, 527

collision, 255

collision domain, 284, 336

command control (C&C) server, 208

command-line interface (CLI), 439, 475

commercial off-the-shelf (COTS) software, 89, 189, 599–600

Committee on National Security Systems (CNSS) (U.S.), 98

common controls, 136–137

Common Vulnerabilities and Exposures (CVE), 425, 608

Common Vulnerability Scoring System (CVSS), 425, 427, 435, 453, 608–609

Common Weakness Enumeration (CWE), 435, 606–607

Common Weakness Scoring System (CWSS), 607

communication

    assessing and implementing secure design principles in network architectures, 283–334

    in disaster recovery (DR), 531–532

    implementing secure communication channels according to design, 357–374

    securing network components, 335–357

community cloud, 207

compartmentalization, 494

compensating control, 76

compensating security controls, 137

compiled languages, 573

compiling, 573

complexity, as enemy of security, 162

compliance

    defined, 23

    industry standards and other compliance requirements, 25–27

    legislative and regulatory requirements, 23–25

    management reviews for, 445–446

cryptology protocols, 196
cryptoprocessors, 182–186
crystal-box testing, 428
"CSIRT Setting Up Guide" (ENISA), 504
Cybercrime Act 2001 (Australia), 29
Cybercrime Investigations: A Comprehensive Resource for Everyone (Bandler and Merzon), 464
cybercrimes, 28
Cybersecurity & Infrastructure Security Agency (CISA) (US), 483, 487, 600
Cybersecurity Law (China), 41, 121, 358
Cybersecurity Maturity Model Certification (CMMC), 565
cyclic redundancy check (CRC), 323

D

data at rest, 133, 134
Data Breach Investigation Report (DBIR), 599
data breaches, 29, 511
data capture, as investigative technique, 469
data categorization, 100–101
Data Center Design and Implementation Best Practices (ANSI/BICSI 002-2014), 267
Data Center design certification (Uptime Institute), 275
data centers, security controls for, 267–268
data circuit-terminating equipment (DCE), 372
data classification, 99–100, 120
data collection, 120
data collision, 336
data communications, 371–373
data control language (DCL), 575
data controller, 46, 118, 119
data custodians, 118
data de-identification, 107
data destruction, 123
data dictionary protection, 192
data durability, 526
data encryption key (DEK), 247
Data Encryption Standard (DES), 196, 228, 233, 235, 238
data hiding, 577
data in motion, 133, 134–135
data in transit, 133, 134–135
data in use, 133, 135
data leak, 158
data leakage prevention, 141–143
data lifecycle, management of, 115–127
data link layer (of OSI reference model), 286, 287, 288
data localization laws, 40–41
data location, 120–121
data loss prevention (DLP) systems (also known as data leakage preventions), 105, 111, 141–143, 484

data maintenance, 121–122
data manipulation language (DML), 575
data owner, 116–117
data processing agreements, 118
data processors, 118–119
Data Protection Act 1998 (U.K.), 42, 45
Data Protection Directive (EU), 42, 44–45
data protection methods, 141–144
data recovery tools, 472
data remanence, 123
data retention, 122–123, 127–129
data roles, 116–120
data security, determining controls and compliance requirements for, 131–144
data states, 133–135
data subjects, 46, 120
data tampering, 85
data terminal equipment (DTE), 372
data users, 120
database administrators (DBAs), 496
database management system (DBMS), 575, 576
database system vulnerabilities, 191–193
datagram, 295
decentralized IAM administration, 381
declarative programming, 576
decryption, 225
defense in depth (or layered security), 167, 213, 270, 355
delicts, defined, 28
demilitarized zone (DMZ), 285, 433–434, 479
Deming cycle, 178
denial-of-service (DDoS) attack, 86, 158, 306–307, 600
deny list, 515
dependencies (FOSS), 612
deployment, 567
deployment models, 207
deprovisioning, 377, 388–389, 411–412
design principles, 150, 155–157
detect (DE), as core function of NIST CSF, 20
detection, 505
detective and preventative measures, in SecOps, 511–519
development, defined, 550
developmental methodologies, in SDLC, 551–561
device identification, in access control systems, 383
devices, in access control systems, 381–382
DevOps, 557–559
DevSecOps, 559
Diameter, 368
differential backups, 524
Diffie, Whitfield, 241
Diffie–Hellman–Merkle, 240, 241
DigiNotar, trusted CA is compromised, 246
digital certificates, 243, 250–252

N

National Centre for the Protection of National Infrastructure (CPNI) (U.K.), 200
National Checklist Program (NCP), 114
National Counterterrorism Center (NCTC), 35
National Cyber Security Centre (NCSC) (U.K.), 92
National Institute of Standards and Technology (NIST). *See also specific NIST publications*
    Computer Forensics Tool Testing Program (CFTT), 473
    Computer Security Resource Center (CSRC), 467
    defined, 18
    described, 81–83
    National Vulnerability Database (NVD), 608
    as responsible for researching and recommending suitable cryptographic algorithms, 255
National Security Agency, 40
National Vulnerability Database (NVD), 608
near field communication (NFC), 478
need-to-know, 494
Neighbor Discovery Protocol (NDP), 354
Netflix, Chaos Monkey, 538
NetFlow, 477
Network Access Control (NAC), 323
network access control (NAC), 352–354, 382
network address translation (NAT), 303–305, 344, 428
network architectures, assessing and implementing secure design principles in, 283–334
network attacks, 306–311
network cabling, 346
network device log files, 477
network hardware, operation of, 335–341
network interface cards (NICs), 300
network layer (of OSI reference model), 286, 287, 289–293
network security
    assessing and implementing secure design principles in network architectures, 283–334
    implementing secure communication channels according to design, 357–374
    securing network components, 335–357
network topologies, 349–352
network traffic analysis tools, 471
network-attached storage (NAS), 315
network-based intrusion detection systems (NIDS or NIPS), 479, 514
next-gen firewall (NGFW), 339, 513
NFPA 75, 278
NFPA 76, 278
NIST 800-94, 479
NIST 800-154, 87
NIST Cybersecurity Framework (CSF), 17, 19–21, 83, 138, 176, 177, 459

NIST SP 800-33, 7
NIST SP 800-37, 138, 176, 177, 178, 483
NIST SP 800-53, 17, 18, 20, 122, 135, 177, 482, 483, 484, 499
NIST SP 800-53 Rev 5, 139
NIST SP 800-53A, 459, 483
NIST SP 800-53A Rev 4, 139
NIST SP 800-55, 448
NIST SP 800-61, 504
NIST SP 800-63, 391
NIST SP 800-64, 551
NIST SP 800-70, 114
NIST SP 800-82, 200
NIST SP 800-86, 467
NIST SP 800-88, 499–500
NIST SP 800-92, 129, 484, 486, 593
NIST SP 800-124, 356
NIST SP 800-133, 199
NIST SP 800-145, 204, 603
NIST SP 800-160, 551
NIST SP 800-192, 404
no read down, 172
noncompete agreement, 65
nondisclosure, 457
nondisclosure agreement (NDA), 65
noninterference model, 169–170
nonrepudiation, 6, 252–253
North American Electric Reliability Corporation (NERC), 200
n-tier architecture, 152

O

objectives, 9–10
object-oriented programming (OOP), 577
objects, in access control systems, 378
Office 365 (Microsoft), 212, 362
Official Secrets Act (OSA) (U.K.), 98
OIDC provider (OP), 415
on premises (on-prem), 402–403
on the fly, 573
onboarding, 65–66
one-time pad, 232
one-time passwords (OTPs), 393
Online Certificate Status Protocol (OCSP), 245
Open Authorization (OAuth), 402, 414, 614
Open ID Connect (OIDC), 415
Open Shortest Path First (OSPF), 289, 290, 292, 343
open source intelligence (OSINT), 432
open system authentication (OSA), 321, 322
Open Systems Interconnection (OSI) model, 284, 285
Open Web Application Security Project (OWASP), 58, 397, 564, 604, 609–612, 613, 619
openBmap, 331

privilege flag, in containers, 215
procedural programming, 576
procedures
    defined, 57
    relationship between policies, procedures, standards, and guidelines, 56
Process for Attack Simulation and Threat Analysis (PASTA), 86–87, 159–160
processes, in business continuity plan (BCP), 62
production environment, 567
professional ethics, (ISC)² code of, 2–3
program manager (or manager), 15
programming languages, 572–577
promiscuous mode, 311
promotion, 567
property list (PLIST) files, 475
Proprietary, as classification scheme, 100
protect (PR), as core function of NIST CSF, 20
protected computer, 30
Protected Extensible Authentication Protocol (PEAP), 324, 368
protected health information (PHI), 16, 43
protocol translators, 343
protocols, weaknesses of, 194
Prototype model, 560
provisioning, 377, 388, 408, 411–412, 490–492
proxies, 343–344
pseudorandom number generators, 247
PTSN, 366
Public, as classification scheme, 100
public cloud, as deployment model, 207
Public Company Accounting Oversight Board (PCAOB), 25
public key cryptography, 239
Public Key Cryptography Standard (PKCS), 364
public key infrastructure (PKI), 243–246, 399
Puppet, 112
Python, 577

Q

quality assurance (QA), 558
quality of service (QoS), 528
quantitative risk calculation, 71–72
quantum computing, as threat to sustainability of encryption, 196
quantum cryptography, 242
quantum key distribution (QKD), 242
quarantine processing, 354

R

radio frequency identification (RFID), 112, 216, 383
random number generators (RNGs), 247

ransomware, as cryptanalytic attack, 264
RC2, 239
RC4, 195, 228, 239, 260, 322, 325
RC5, 239
RC6, 239
read-through, 536
Reagan, Ronald, 162
real user monitoring (RUM), 435
real-time location system (RTLS), 216
records retention, 129–131
recover (RC), as core function of NIST CSF, 20
recovery, in incident management, 510
recovery point objective (RPO), 60, 524
recovery site strategies, 527
recovery time objective (RTO), 60, 524, 527
Recycle Bin (Windows), 475
red teaming, 521
redundancy, as architectural principle, 150, 153–154
redundant array of individual disks (RAID), 525–526
redundant array of inexpensive disks (RAID), 525–526
refactoring code, 555
registration, proofing, and establishment of identity, 397–398
registration authorities (RAs), 399
regular expressions, 484
regulations, defined, 54
regulatory investigations, 53–54
regulatory issues, understanding of as pertaining to information security in a holistic context, 28–48
relying party (RP), 415
remediation
    in identifying deficiencies with security controls, 454–455
    in incident management, 510–511
remote access, 365–371
Remote Authentication Dial-In User Service (RADIUS), 368, 417
remote code execution (RCE), 600
Remote Desktop Protocol (RDP), 366
remote meeting, 359
remote procedure calls (RPCs), 296, 439, 613
remote terminal units (RTUs), 315
repeaters, 341
reporting
    breach reporting, 509–510
    in incident management, 508–510
    in investigations, 467–469
    mandatory reporting, 457
    on security controls, 77–78
repository (repo), 581, 586–588
Representational State Transfer (REST), 439, 613, 616, 618, 619
repudiation, 85–86, 158
residual risk, 68